P9-CMT-106

MICHAEL JACKSON

ALL THE SONGS

An Hachette UK Company
www.hachette.co.uk

Original title: *Michael Jackson, La Totale*
Texts: Richard Lecocq and François Allard
Published by Editions du Chêne / EPA – Hachette Livre 2018

This edition first published in Great Britain in 2018 by Cassell,
an imprint of Octopus Publishing Group Ltd
Carmelite House
50 Victoria Embankment
London EC4Y 0DZ
www.octopusbooks.co.uk

Distributed in the US by
Hachette Book Group
1290 Avenue of the Americas
4th and 5th Floors
New York, NY 10104

Distributed in Canada by
Canadian Manda Group
664 Annette St.
Toronto, Ontario, Canada M6S 2C8

ISBN 9781788400572

A CIP catalogue record for this book is available from the British Library.

Printed and bound in China

10 9 8 7 6 5 4 3 2 1

For this edition:
Commissioning Editor: Joe Cottington
Senior Editor: Pollyanna Poulter
Translators: Simon Jones, Andrea Reece, Elettra Pauletto
Copy Editor: Lisa Dyer
Proofreader: Helena Caldon
Senior Production Manager: Katherine Hockley

MICHAEL JACKSON

ALL THE SONGS

THE STORY BEHIND EVERY TRACK

RICHARD LECOCQ & FRANÇOIS ALLARD

CONTENTS

6 Foreword
8 From The Jackson Five to The Jacksons: The Childhood of the King of Pop

54

66

78

94

140

174

198

258

290

364

436

492
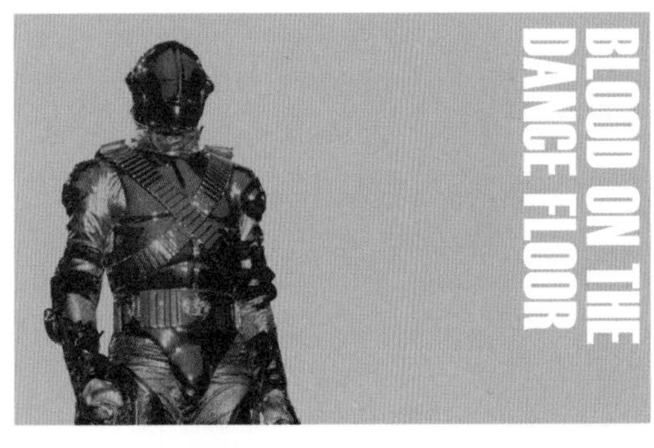

520

550

600 Index
606 Bibliography

FOREWORD

Michael Jackson was born on 29 August 1958. He was only five years old when he made his first appearance onstage with his family's musical group, alongside his four brothers. The Jackson Five soon became a musical phenomenon, largely thanks to Motown Records, the famous soul label created by Berry Gordy Jr. Although the youngest member of the group, Michael soon became the leader. He established himself as a fully-formed star and within a blink of an eye he was tasting the fruits of success as a solo artist.

Just after turning 21 years old, Michael broke from the group and set out on his own, building a solo career, hit song by hit song. He created his own universe: his music, dancing, and fashion fascinated a growing number of the public. He had only just turned 25 when *Thriller* became the bestselling album of all time and established the music video as an artistic medium that would be available to the public at large via MTV.

Despite all this, few books are dedicated entirely to Michael Jackson's music, or his art more generally. Throughout his lifetime, Michael managed his career by showcasing the end results of his labor, which he painstakingly curated while hiding the work he did behind the scenes. It wasn't until after his death that the artistic heritage of the man known as the King of Pop was finally reassessed.

This book establishes itself alongside other volumes of his grand total collection by endeavoring—for the first time ever—to delve into Michael Jackson's musical career, song by song. The oeuvre of the creator of *Billie Jean* is more complex than it seems and unfolds here in four parts:

- Michael Jackson began with The Jackson Five (Motown) and The Jacksons (Epic). For the purposes of this book we sorted through the discographies of these two groups and selected the pieces that best represent Michael's contributions.
- At thirteen years old, Michael Jackson recorded his first solo albums with Motown. His adult solo career, which was entirely under his control, launched with the 1979 release of *Off the Wall*. We delved into these two eras, illustrating how some of Michael's Motown colleagues would remain by his side throughout his career.
- In addition to the albums and singles Michael released in a group or as a solo artist, we made sure to include the numerous collaborations that allowed him to rub shoulders with certain artists, who would often join him on his personal adventures in music.
- Lastly, Michael hid a treasure trove of songs that have never been released. We discussed all the ones we were able to document as completely as possible, even though some of them remain unavailable through official channels.

While Michael Jackson is known across the world for a long list of hits, most of which he composed himself, he is also known for his decisive contribution to the evolution of music videos, known in the Jackson universe as "short films." As such, and for the first time in a collection of his work, we analyze in detail the videography of this artist.

We searched for the names of all the musicians and contributors involved in Michael Jackson's artistic projects. When we didn't have all of the information, or the information could not be verified, we marked it with the word "unknown," opening the door to further research and findings.

Now as we launch into this extraordinary journey and history, we begin with the early 1960s in the very humble city of Gary, Indiana, and five young siblings tirelessly practicing songs and dances under the watchful eye of their father, Joe Jackson. The story of The Jackson Five has begun. Little Michael can scarcely imagine that he will one day become the King of Pop.

The Jackson family pose for *Life* magazine in their house in Encino, in 1971. From top: Michael, Marlon, Tito, Jermaine, Jackie, Joe, and Katherine Jackson.

FROM THE JACKSON FIVE TO THE JACKSONS: THE CHILDHOOD OF THE KING OF POP

Gary, Indiana

In 1950, in northern United States, a region still dominated by the steel industry, Joseph (known as Joe) and Katherine Jackson set up home in the city of Gary, Indiana, not far from Chicago. The little house at 2300 Jackson Street had just three rooms, and soon got too small for the young couple and their growing number of children: Rebbie (born 1950), Jackie (1951), Tito (1953), Jermaine (1954), La Toya (1956), Marlon (1957) and his twin, Brandon, who died prematurely, Michael (1958), Randy (1961), and Janet (1966).

Joseph was employed in a steelworks; his job was hard and dreary. With wages of just over $60 a week, meals were often frugal. To earn some extra money, Joseph turned to music, specifically, rhythm and blues. He played guitar in a band called The Falcons, who performed in clubs in Indiana. Sadly, success was not forthcoming, and the group split up.

As for Katherine, she was a young, loving, and caring stay-at-home mom, whose prime concern was her children's well-being. She had contracted polio in her youth and still suffered some of its aftereffects, which caused her difficulties in accomplishing her daily household chores. However, she could count on the unswerving support of her eldest daughter, La Toya, who helped bring up her siblings.

One day in 1955, the family TV set broke down. To kill time, Katherine, who was a great country music lover, gathered her children together in the living room, and they had fun singing together. She accompanied them on the guitar that Joseph had stored away in the cupboard after the breakup of his band; he had forbidden his children to go near his pride and joy.

The Jackson Five are born

It wasn't long before Tito began to accompany these musical get-togethers using his father's guitar. His mother thought he was talented. Needless to say, the young boy ended up breaking a string—something that happens often enough. The whole family was dreading Joseph's anger on making this unwelcome discovery, but Joe nevertheless agreed to listen to his son explain himself. His wife flew to her kid's defense: "You should listen to him play," she told her husband. "He's pretty good, you know..." Tito had no choice but to perform. As his eyes filled with tears, he strummed a few chords and sketched out a tune. Joseph Jackson saw that his son had potential, embryonic, for sure, but it cried out for encouragement. Accordingly, he agreed to motivate his sons and to share his passion for music. Jackie, Tito, and Jermaine initially made up a trio of singers; Marlon and Michael joined them a little later. The Jackson brothers began to perform on stage, chiefly in shopping malls. It was at this time that a neighbor, Evelyn Leahy, suggested to Katherine that she name the group The Jackson Five.

Joseph's hopes grew alongside the increasing workload he assigned to his offspring. An extremely harsh taskmaster, his sometimes brutal methods left a permanent scar on the Jackson family. According to his mother, Michael was not a child like the rest: faced with his father's harshness, he was one of the few who stood up to him. Nevertheless, his father's punishments left him traumatized. It wasn't until he reached adulthood that he felt able to speak in public about these physical and psychological wounds.

In the face of this assertion of authority, Katherine tried to maintain a calm, spiritual atmosphere. Ever since her earliest

JACKSON 5 BLVD.
JACKSON 5 BLVD.

A steelworks in the industrial north of the United States in the late 1960s. Like Joe Jackson, many musicians in Chicago were also manual workers.

youth, she had belonged to the Jehovah's Witnesses community. Kindly by nature, she was now even more concerned about her children's future. In the early 1960s the streets of Gary had the reputation of being unsafe, so the Jackson children were confined to the house, and rehearsals became more onerous, lasting up to three hours every day after school.

Michael becomes the leader

In 1965, during a performance at Garnett Elementary School, Michael revealed his talent as a singer. Just six years old, he performed the song *Climb Every Mountain* (from the movie *The Sound of Music*), unaccompanied, before an audience consisting of his teacher, schoolmates, and his parents, who were moved to tears. His gift for singing, already so well developed for someone of his age, earned him the position of leader of the family group, much to the annoyance of Jermaine.

The young musical group won first prize for singing at Roosevelt High School in Gary. This success inaugurated a series of performances in various auditoriums in the city and as far afield as Chicago. The Jackson family's life thus reached a turning point, despite questions—and sometimes mockery—from the neighborhood. Weekends were no longer a time of rest, but were instead devoted to appearances all over the state. The children tirelessly traveled the region's roads, while at the same time complying as far as possible with the school calendar.

Joe increasingly nursed the hope that his sons might sign a a record label contract. He tried his luck with local companies, first One-derful! Records, then Steeltown Records. The latter took them on to record their first single: *Big Boy* (see page 16).

Motown in their sights

The 1950s and 1960s saw the emergence of labels whose mission it was to promote African-American music. Atlantic, Stax, and Buddah Records brought together the greatest artists of the time. These functioned as a voice for the black community, at a moment in history when young Americans were acquiring a social and political awareness that was prepared to break free of an outmoded system.

In Detroit, Michigan, one record label pulled off the feat of promoting African-American artists by releasing recordings that were listened to by both black and white people. Founded by Berry Gordy Jr. in 1958, first under the name Tamla Records, the Motown Record Corporation attempted to act as an interracial bridge, describing itself as "the sound of young America." Its young boss aimed to promote his vision of "crossover" by breaking through the social and racial barriers that were still very much in place. He sought out and signed up a large number of talented artists, who would go on to write the finest chapters in the history of black American music. Very soon Motown (the name comes from Motor Town, the nickname for Detroit, center of the US automobile industry) was running at full speed, like a brand-new racing car. The label became a star factory, running singing, dancing, and deportment classes, and laying down an official line to follow during media interviews. Motown was the public face of a black America that was proud of its success, open to the world, and bent on achieving the goal of reaching a wide audience.

The record label was like one big family. From the late 1950s, its success stories were brought to the attention of an ever wider public. Diana Ross delivered glamour, the young Stevie Wonder was an innovator, with his musical genius and creativity, while Marvin Gaye wrote and recorded music that was as sensual as it was climactic.

Joe Jackson secretly hoped to sign up his five sons to the Motown family. As a result of their performances all over the state, the reputation of the group from Gary became established. They surprised and charmed their audiences, and also Motown artists such as Gladys Knight, on whom they made an impression.

One of the first official photographs of The Jackson Five. From left: Tito, Jackie, and Jermaine. Center: Marlon. In front: Michael.

But the decisive meeting was with musician and producer Bobby Taylor, who set up an audition for the group at Motown headquarters on 23 July 1968. The audition was filmed and revealed a Michael Jackson fired up with an animal agility worthy of James Brown, channeled through the body of a ten-year-old boy. Behind him his four brothers, acting as his solid backers and teammates, sang the choruses.

Berry Gordy was reluctant at first to sign up a group of children; he had an unhappy memory of taking on the young Stevie Wonder. Also, he no longer wanted to put minors to work, with all the constraints involving working conditions. However, his assistant, Suzanne de Passe, managed to persuade him, and The Jackson Five signed their contract on 25 July 1968. Gordy decided that he would crown the golden decade of the 1960s with one last super-group, the culmination of his record label's expertise. The Jackson Five were to be the last stars Motown created according to the precise instructions of its founder. During the 1970s, the business strategy was to abandon the recording studio in favor of promoting Motown in the movies.

Like a preacher, Gordy promised the five kids that their first singles would reach the top of the prestigious *Billboard* charts. His prophecy came true and for the first time in the history of recorded music, a group's first four singles all got to No.1.

History's first boy band

Hits and albums came thick and fast. Motown moved its headquarters permanently to Los Angeles and, under the Californian sun, the Jackson brothers learned their craft. Although they had cut their teeth on the famous "chitlin' circuit," the network of performance venues and clubs that were frequented and run by African-Americans, it was in Hollywood that they came of age. With studio sessions, TV appearances, concerts, and endless tours, The Jackson Five machine was going full pedal to the metal, and gave birth to a hitherto unseen phenomenon: the boy band.

When the group was playing live, the shrieks of the audience would drown their music. The Beatles had gone through the same experience and The Jackson Five were soon dubbed the

The Jackson Five in April 1973, before leaving for their first tour of Japan. From left: Tito, Katherine, Michael, Jermaine, Marlon, Jackie, Randy, and Joe Jackson.

black counterpart of the Fab Four—with the difference being that they did not write their own songs. At the time, they embodied a vision of the American Dream that appealed to the public at large: with their carefree pop music, devoid of any political message, they set an example for American youth. In a way, they were the ideal representatives of the now famous "sound of young America."

On stage, on television, and in photographs, one star dominated and eclipsed his brothers: Michael, the new leader, whose high-pitched voice and dance steps mesmerized audiences. Berry Gordy and Motown fully understood the young man's potential and decided to get him to record solo albums.

The early 1970s saw The Jackson Five turn out albums at a relentless rate, and the sales of these records financed the group's incessant touring. After the tidal wave of popularity generated by the release of the singles *I Want You Back*, *ABC*, *The Love You Save*, and *I'll Be There*, the group experienced its first minor crisis in 1971, when the song *Maybe Tomorrow* struggled to reach 20th place in the *Billboard* charts.

But it was only normal that five boys on the threshold of adolescence should hit a rough patch. The group's innocent, childlike image was threatened, as each brother began to follow his own path. Subsequently, Michael's elder brothers married, and Randy, the youngest, was brought in to try to rejuvenate the group's image. But Michael Jackson realized that the charmed life of those early years was now coming to an end.

One step back to take a great leap forward

A potential musical and family crisis received a temporary reprieve thanks to the song *Dancing Machine*, on the album *Get It Together* (1973). The lightweight pop of *I Want You Back* gave way to a classy, psychedelic funk, thanks to the masterly hands of producer Hal Davis.

Dancing Machine nailed it, and reached No. 2 on the *Billboard* charts. Euphoric at this unexpected success, Motown decided to repeat the formula for the next album: in 1975 the album *Moving Violation* explored other moods and ranges that flirted openly with the disco genre. But the concerns of The Jackson Five lay elsewhere: by now young adults, they felt they had served their apprenticeship, and they sought greater artistic freedom. Their father supported them in this endeavor. Unbeknown to Berry Gordy, Joe secured a short residency for the group in Las Vegas. Slowly but surely, the Jackson clan was shaking off the Gordy yoke.

The unavoidable parting of the ways came on 28 May 1975: The Jackson Five left Motown for CBS. Although only 17, Michael Jackson helped his father in negotiations with the new label. He also managed the crisis, facing up to Berry Gordy and telling him about the group's grievances. All the group's

The Jackson Five, with their younger brother Randy, rehearse for one of their TV performances in 1972.

members accepted the contract with CBS except Jermaine; now married to Hazel, Gordy's daughter, he remained loyal to his father-in-law.

This musical divorce went to court. Motown accused The Jackson Five of breach of contract. In the battle, Joe and his sons lost their magic name. The contract drawn up by Berry Gordy's team in 1968 stipulated that the group's name should remain the exclusive property of Motown, and so Jackie, Tito, Marlon, Michael, and Randy arrived at CBS with a new name: simply The Jacksons.

The Jacksons

On 5 November 1976, the group's first, eponymous album produced a reasonably successful single, *Enjoy Yourself*, and two songs: *Blues Away*, which Michael wrote himself, and *Style of Life*, cowritten with Tito. CBS allowed them this relative artistic freedom while at the same time assigning two chaperones to them: the famous duo Gamble and Huff.

In 1971, Kenny Gamble and Leon Huff had founded the Philadelphia International label as an alternative to Motown. They championed a more committed, sensual brand of soul music, territory into which Berry Gordy preferred not to venture. Initially, they contacted Atlantic Records with a request that it distribute their first records, which included names such as Billy Paul and The O'Jays, who were beginning to be talked about. Atlantic turned them down. At the same time, talks were under way with CBS, and came to fruition thanks to its CEO, Clive Davis.

And so, in 1976, Gamble and Huff were given the job of chaperoning The Jacksons on their arrival at CBS. Although their names shone on paper, the duo struggled to achieve lasting chemistry with the group. The second album recorded with the two producers, *Goin' Places*, was a commercial and critical failure, and plunged The Jacksons into a new artistic crisis. The group broke up, accepting a juicy contract with the CBS network, which offered a weekly TV show. This televisual overexposure blurred the group's image so much that record sales plummeted and deprived them of any respectable rating in the charts.

The collaboration with Gamble and Huff ended on a somewhat bitter note, and The Jacksons were on the point of being forgotten by the public altogether. Talks began with CBS's new boss, Walter Yetnikoff, who was impressed by Michael Jackson's determination. The young man gave a realistic assessment of the failure of *Goin' Places*, and was candid about the family's grievances. Michael had already faced up to Berry Gordy, to inform him of The Jackson Five's unhappiness at Motown. Supported by his father, who was well aware of his son's charisma, Michael attempted to reinvent himself in the eyes of his new boss.

The Jacksons on tour in Europe to promote their album *Destiny* in London, 1979. From left: Marlon, Jackie, Randy, and Tito. Michael is in front.

The Jacksons, 1977. From left: Marlon, Randy, Michael, Jackie, and Tito.

Destiny

In truth, Yetnikoff was already thinking of ridding himself of The Jacksons. But a guardian angel, in the shape of Bobby Colomby, head of A&R at Epic Records, appeared to save them. He supported Michael and Joe Jackson's request, and managed to persuade CBS to give the group one last chance. Yetnikoff allowed himself to be convinced, but made a demand of his own: The Jacksons had carte blanche, but Colomby was to remain in the background, ready to take over and bring work to an end if things got out of control in the studio.

Destiny was a double or nothing album. The Jacksons could not afford to make mistakes. They recorded seven of their own compositions, three of them performed by the duo of Michael and Randy: *Shake Your Body (Down to the Ground), All Night Dancin'*, and *That's What You Get (For Being Polite).*

Shake Your Body (Down to the Ground) is a timeless dancefloor hymn, a benchmark in the funk canon. The song reached No. 7 in the US *Billboard* charts and earned The Jacksons a Platinum single (more than two million copies sold). The approach was to woo both hardcore fans and a new generation who didn't necessarily know The Jackson Five's early hits. It worked.

With *All Night Dancin'*, lasting eight minutes, The Jacksons were back in the groove, and *Dancing Machine* came back into play. On stage, they tried out timid routines and dreamed of improvising, quite a feat for young performers brought up on the precise, psychologically rigid, "made in Motown" techniques.

That's What You Get (For Being Polite) brought the album to a close, endowing it with both contrast and depth, As a conclusion, and as if to foreshadow his future solo years, Michael sang of loneliness, lack of love, and eternal dissatisfaction.

To bring their songs to life, the brothers treated themselves to the luxury of bringing together some Californian tenors: Michael Sembello, Greg Phillinganes, Nathan Watts, and Paul Jackson Jr. These old studio hands, accustomed to recording alongside artists such as Stevie Wonder and Steely Dan's Donald Fagen, enabled *Destiny* to find its musical identity, which was well rounded and solid.

Thanks to the album, which was a real critical and commercial success, The Jacksons once again became America's beloved group. On 21 June 1979, Tom Bradley, mayor of Los Angeles, inaugurated "Jackson Day": The Jacksons and 300 guests gathered in the basement of the City National Bank in Beverly Hills to celebrate the family group's ten-year career, and its latest achievements in the recording studio (*Destiny* had become a Platinum album) and on stage.

From 1967, the year of their first recording session for their modest single *Big Boy*, to the life-saving success of *Shake Your Body* in 1979, Michael Jackson had known the highs and lows of fame, which was as dazzling as it was precocious. And to think that those 12 years were just the prelude to the story and the career of Michael Jackson!

The first version of *Big Boy*, released as a single and CD in 2014 by Secret Stash Records (www.secretstashrecords.com).

[THE JACKSON 5]

BIG BOY

Eddie Silvers / 2'55

Original title: *I'm a Big Boy Now*

Musicians
Version recorded 13 July 1967:
Michael Jackson: lead vocals
Jermaine, Tito, Jackie, and Marlon Jackson: backing vocals
Jermaine Jackson: bass guitar
Tito Jackson: guitar
Larry Blasingaine: guitar
Version recorded November 1967:
Michael Jackson: lead vocals
Jermaine Jackson: bass guitar
Tito Jackson: guitar
Johnny Jackson: drums
Richard Brown: backing rhythm guitar
Freddie Young: backing lead guitar
Ray Grimes: backing bass guitar
Lamont King: bongos
Recording
George and Ernie Leaner Studio, Chicago: version recorded 13 July 1967
Sunny Sawyer Studio, Chicago: version recorded November 1967
Technical team
Producer: Gordon Keith
Version recorded Thursday 13 July 1967:
Recording engineer: Steve Puntolillo (mixed 2014)
Version recorded November 1967:
Recording engineers: Vaughn Morrison and Gordon Keith (mixing)

Single

A-side: *Big Boy* / 2'30
B-side: *You've Changed* / 2'30
Released by Steeltown Records: USA, 31 January 1968 (ref. 681)

Various accounts of the beginnings of The Jackson Five have circulated over the years, sowing ever more confusion in the minds of fans. Versions sometimes even differ as to where the group's first songs were recorded. There are many who claim to have made "discoveries." However, thanks to work by the journalist Jake Austen in 2009, the story of The Jackson Five's first recording has finally been documented with great precision.

Genesis

For a long time the only known version was the one that dates from late 1967, when the song was recorded for the Steeltown label, however, Jake Austen has demonstrated that, as early as the summer of 1967, *Big Boy* may have been released by the One-derful! Records label. The journalist began digging when he noticed a vital piece of information in an interview Larry Blasingaine gave to Bob Abrahamian of the WHPK radio station (Chicago). In the mid-1960s, the guitarist and his band, The Four Dukes, were working as young session musicians at the recording studio of George and Ernie Leaner, of One-derful! Records, in Chicago. Larry spoke with conviction about a recording session with The Jackson Five during the summer of 1967. The songwriter, Eddie Silvers, assisted by the producer Otis Hayes, had apparently asked him, as he happened to be passing by, to show Jermaine Jackson how to prevent his bass guitar rumbling. He also asked him to play a guitar riff in the intro that was far too difficult for Tito. So the theory took shape that the group visited the George and Ernie Leaner Studio, 1827 South Michigan Avenue, and with it the idea that perhaps there existed an earlier version of the song than the one recorded at the Sunny Sawyer Studio.

The singer Billy McGregor also remembered that in 1966 Joseph Jackson had visited the Leaner studio with Michael, who passed an audition on his own. "He was a little boy, he sang a cappella *Tobacco Road* for George Leaner, who said he had talent but it would take a lot to put him out there because of his age, he'd have to have someone with him all the time."[1] Perhaps this is why George Leaner stepped back from the idea of bringing out a record with The Jackson Five on the One-derful! label. However, that assertion did not back up the theory that a recording session had taken place in July 1967.

Jake Austen then contacted the Leaners' heirs. He learned that after One-derful! Records closed down in 1969, and until

The George and Ernie Leaner Studio in Chicago, home to One-derful! Records. The studio was the first where the singer made a professional recording.

the death of George Leaner in 1983, the tapes had not been stored properly. An attempt was made at sorting through them starting in 1990, the year Ernie Leaner died. Finally, in August 2009, Austen was informed that a tape dated 13 July 1967 had been unearthed, and that it seemed to be in excellent condition. It was labeled "Jackson Five—*I'm a Big Boy Now.*"

In 2014, five years after the discovery of this mysterious tape, a call for subscriptions was launched on the website www.secretstashrecords.com to fund the release of the One-derful! catalog on vinyl and on CD. Starting 28 October 2014, 12 LPs and six CDs were released, one by one, to a rapturous reception from the global Jackson community. The project's web page featured audio of *Big Boy* and its instrumental version, as recorded in the summer of 1967 in Chicago. That tape sure contained a fabulous treasure! For the first 500 orders, each double LP came with an exclusive single featuring, of course, the coveted *Big Boy*. For subscribers who preferred the CD format, a compilation of exclusive tracks was sent out after the release of the last volume. Thanks to this work by dedicated enthusiasts, we can now state with certainty that Michael Jackson was not yet nine years old when he recorded his very first song.

Production

The song was written by Eddie Silvers. A native of St. Louis, he had worked for a long time with Fats Domino and Ike and Tina Turner. He moved to Chicago in 1965 and joined One-derful! Records as a songwriter and arranger, later becoming musical director.

The song is simple but energetic. The bass line, well rounded and insistent, is repetitive and underpins the piece. The guitar overlays it skillfully, enriching the listening experience and creating a warm, soothing, groovy ambiance. The chorus repeats the long notes. These elements admirably support Michael Jackson's young voice, whose sound develops with ease and confidence. The underlying talent of this astonishing child is clearly audible in this very first song. The relentless, strict rehearsals imposed by Joseph Jackson make themselves heard here, too, and Michael demonstrates a still-fragile but burgeoning maturity.

Big Boy suits Michael's vocal range to perfection. It is tempting to think that he is imitating the greatest black stars of the time when he drops down to the lowest notes to suggest a certain sadness. This sung version of the track is full of charm and almost spellbinding. *Big Boy* is the solid bedrock and the undeniable model for the group's future Motown output.

In his autobiography, *Moonwalk*, Michael recalls: "It was a nice song about a kid who wanted to fall in love with some girl. Of course, in order to get the full picture, you have to imagine a skinny nine-year-old singing this song. The words said I didn't want to hear fairy tales any more, but in truth I was far too young to grasp the real meanings of most of the words in these songs. I just sang what they gave me. When that record with its killer bass line began to get radio play in Gary, we became a big deal in our neighborhood. No one could believe we had our own record. We had a hard time believing it."[2]

The Steeltown Records version

Four months after this long-forgotten session at One-derful! Records, the group recorded *Big Boy* once again for the Steeltown label, with a view to releasing it as a single.

In 1988, Michael Jackson briefly revisited this time of his career. He remembers arriving at a studio that he says belonged to Gordon Keith, producer of *Big Boy* and cofounder of Steeltown Records. He entered a cubicle and they put some

Big Boy, the group's first single to have been released and put on sale in 1967 by the Steeltown Records label.

headphones over his ears. He also remembers singing with a group of singers and a chorus. It was a Sunday morning, just before he would watch his favorite cartoon, *The Road Runner Show.* According to Gordon Keith, there is confusion over the recollection Michael gives in his autobiography: it was in fact for post-production of their songs that the boys would have gone to Bud Pressner's studio in Gary that Sunday morning. On the insistence of the producer, the recording itself would have been made in the influential city of Chicago rather than in small-town Gary. So it was indeed, if we believe Gordon Keith's account, in the Sunny Sawyer Studio in Chicago that *Big Boy* and three other tracks were recorded in November 1967.

The recording

Musician Jerry Mundo talked of the studio as if it were a room that was alive, with a rounded ceiling specially designed to diffuse sound and fitted with extremely high-quality equipment: Austrian microphones and a four-track Ampex MR-70 tape recorder—though only three of the tracks worked properly, which meant more mixing was needed.

As well as the five brothers and their friend Johnny Jackson on drums, a whole team had been assembled. Gordon Keith had hired session musicians to support the performance of the young Jermaine on bass guitar and Tito on guitar: Ray Grimes (bass guitar), Richard Brown (rhythm guitar), Freddie Young (lead guitar), and Lamont King (bongos). Keith and Ludie Washington, as well as Delroy Bridgeman, supplied the backing vocals.

The large number of takes tired out the brothers, who also recorded three other songs: *You've Changed,* on the B-side of the single and later rerecorded with Motown, *You Don't Have to Be Over 21 (To Fall in Love),* and *Some Girls Want Me for Their Lover.*

Gordon Keith sent the master tape to Summit at Willow Springs, Illinois, for the record pressing. *Big Boy* was officially released as a single on 31 January 1968 and, according to Keith, sold more than 60,000 copies. The Atlantic Records label, attracted by the record's success, contacted Steeltown to sign a contract for wider distribution through its subsidiary ATCO. On 5 March 1968 a new edition of *Big Boy* was pressed.

Betrayal, response, and claim

Gordon Keith spoke of the double betrayal of Joseph Jackson and Berry Gordy, who signed The Jackson Five to Motown. The famous record label claimed it had discovered the group and tried to ensure that the early recordings would be forgotten. Atlantic Records, which was then the group's record distributor, took legal action against Berry Gordy. The drawn-out lawsuit did not involve Keith, who was not invited to the negotiating table. The legal dispute was resolved without the previous arrangements fully being known, and The Jackson Five's first album on the Motown label was finally released only in the fall of 1969.

The response to The Jackson Five's huge success at Motown came in several phases, sometimes supported by Gordon Keith himself.

In December 1970 a second Jackson Five single was released by Steeltown: *We Don't Have to Be Over 21 (To Fall in Love) / Jam Session* (this appeared to be an improvisation, and the sound was rather poor).

In March 1971, Steeltown brought out another single on the New York label Dynamo Records: *We Don't Have to Be Over 21 (To Fall in Love)* but renamed *You Don't Have to Be Over Twenty One to Fall in Love / Some Girls Want Me for Their Lover.*

Finally, in 1972, both songs, *You Don't Have to Be Over Twenty One to Fall in Love* and *Some Girls Want Me for Their Lover,* were issued once more as part of the Musico Records compilation *Getting Together with the Jackson 5.*

Big Boy in the 1990s

In 1989, the Steeltown songs appeared on the CD *The Jackson 5 and Johnny—Beginning Years 1967–1968.* In order to make the compilations more substantial, some rather dubious tracks, with poor sound quality, were added. They had probably been recorded on a private or home tape recorder. These arrangements aimed to be faithful to the sound of the late 1980s, but they rendered the group almost inaudible. In 1993 a CD was released, initially in Japan and then worldwide, containing 24 tracks, including some equally dubious original recording sessions. In 1995, as the album *HIStory* was about to hit the shelves, Ben Brown (cofounder and CEO of Steeltown

The group's first promotional photograph. From left: Marlon, Tito, Jackie, Jermaine, and Michael. At the drums: Johnny Jackson (no relation), the group's drummer in their early years.

Records) released the single *Big Boy / You've Changed* on CD for the first time; it was distributed internationally. In 1996, at the same time as the album *HIStory* was being promoted, the compilation *Pre-History—The Lost Steeltown Recordings* revisited some hideously overdubbed tracks. The lack of a contractual framework and poor management of rights led to the proliferation of releases containing the early recordings of The Jackson Five. The public lost interest in the band at this period almost completely, even though certain releases featured some interesting variants. The internet finally made available to the most devoted fans the Steeltown versions, without added musical gimmicks and in their purest form, though these were still of mediocre quality.

PORTRAIT

BOBBY TAYLOR
THE JACKSON FIVE'S GUARDIAN ANGEL

Born 18 February 1934 in Washington DC, Bobby Taylor was one of those brave artists who, in the 1960s, frequented the "chitlin' circuit." After starting out as a doo-wop singer in the New York area, he joined the group The Four Pharaohs, which enjoyed critical acclaim in and around Columbus, Ohio. In San Francisco, Bobby met the members of the group Little Daddy and The Bachelors: Tommie Melton (vocals), Tommy Chong (guitar), Wes Henderson (bass guitar), Bernie Sneed (piano), and Floyd Sneed (drums).

Bobby Taylor in New York, circa 1968. Berry Gordy Jr. gave the famous leader of the Motown group Bobby Taylor and the Vancouvers the mission of putting The Jackson Five on track for success by producing their first songs.

Bobby arrives at Motown

In 1965, at the instigation of Mary Wilson and Florence Ballard of The Supremes, the group caught the eye of Berry Gordy, and performed many concerts featuring numbers from the Motown catalog. Bobby Taylor and The Vancouvers (as they were known from 1963) thus landed a contract with the Gordy label, a subsidiary of Motown. Their lineup changed: from now on the group comprised Bobby Taylor, Wes Henderson, and Tommy Chong, plus Eddie Patterson (guitar), Robbie King (keyboards), and Duris Maxwell (drums). Bobby Taylor and The Vancouvers recorded the song *Does Your Mama Know About Me?*, which tells the story of a mixed-race couple, still a taboo subject in racially divided America. This mini-hit reached a very respectable No. 29 in the *Billboard* charts.

Meeting with The Jackson Five

In 1967, Gladys Knight, who with her group The Pips also belonged to the Motown stable, noticed The Jackson Five during a concert and told Berry Gordy about them. Her enthusiasm failed to arouse his interest. The week of 12 July 1968, the five brothers were the warm-up act for Bobby Taylor and The Vancouvers at Chicago's Regal Theater. During a concert a few days earlier at the High Chaparral club, also in Chicago, Weldon McDougal, whose job it was to promote Motown to disc jockeys, noticed the young group's ability and mentioned it to Bobby Taylor. According to some accounts, it was McDougal who bent Taylor's ear. But the latter, for his part, asserted that he had focused attention on the group after advice from Marshall Thompson, one of the Regal Theater managers, who apparently took him aside and quietly told him that The Jackson Five were a talent to watch. Impressed by the group's performance, Bobby Taylor promised to secure them an audition at Motown. This took place on 23 July 1968 at the record label's offices, in the absence of Berry Gordy. The brothers' performance was filmed. After viewing it, Gordy, who

Bobby Taylor and the Vancouvers in New York, circa 1968. Top: Bobby Taylor. Bottom left: Tommy Chong. Bottom right: Wes Henderson.

had initially been reluctant to sign a children's group, decided to take them on.

A dose of the blues

The arrival of The Jackson Five at Motown marked the start of a new era in the label's history: Berry Gordy moved all its activities to California, determined to make his mark in the movies, which were still an unattainable Eldorado for the African-American community. Bobby Taylor remained in the Hitsville offices to supervise the young group and The Jackson Five began to record the tracks for their first album under his direction. He endowed the five brothers with a soul sound tinged with blues, though this gave way in subsequent years to arrangements that were more pop in character.

As so often in the world of Motown, the autocratic Berry Gordy consigned Bobby Taylor to oblivion, crushed by a flawless marketing strategy: in order to highlight the group's arrival in the record industry, Gordy decided to appoint Diana Ross as the Jackson boys' official godmother. He used this anointing of Ross as a springboard to announce The Supremes' leader's solo career, while at the same time co-opting The Jackson Five into the public eye. Gordy assured Taylor, who was still attached to his protégés, that the brothers wouldn't remember him on their climb to fame. But history has shown many times that The Jackson Five never forgot the person who first introduced them to the legendary Motown offices. Years later, both in interviews and on television, the Jackson family made numerous references that bore witness to the importance of this obscure footsoldier.

PORTRAIT

BERRY GORDY JR.
THE MENTOR

Berry Gordy was born on 28 November 1929 in the industrial city of Detroit, Michigan, into a close-knit family that had fled the oppression of the American South. His upbringing extolled hard work and family values, noble codes of conduct that progressively shaped his character. He was passionate about boxing and music. His role model, the great champion Joe Louis, inspired his whole generation, however, it was not his destiny to join the exalted line of black boxers. Instead, it was as a composer, and later as the founder of the Tamla Motown record label, that he would promote America's greatest black stars, starting in the 1960s.

A beginning out of step with the times

In 1953, Berry Gordy gained his first experience in the music industry, selling jazz records. But he soon realized that the public was chiefly interested in R&B and, before long, the rock 'n' roll of Elvis Presley. These styles were much closer to the tastes and expectations of the working classes and, consequently, of the general public. He shut up shop, got a job in an automobile factory, and devoted himself to composition in his spare time, without ever losing hope of having his music recorded.

A decisive meeting with Jackie Wilson

The summer of 1957 marked a real turning point in Berry Gordy's life. He met Jackie Wilson, who agreed to record *Reet Petite*, a song Gordy had cowritten, mostly with his family. It was Wilson's first solo recording—he had just left his band, Billy Ward and The Dominoes—and *Reet Petite* is still his best-known song today.

Encouraged by this initial success, which reached a respectable place in the *Billboard* Pop 100 chart at the time, Berry Gordy continued working with the singer, and in 1958 recorded *To Be Loved*, followed by *We Have Love* and the famous *Lonely Teardrops,* which reached No. 1 in the *Billboard* R&B chart. This song would come to symbolize the completion of a stage in Gordy's early career, and he made sure to get Michael Jackson to record it a few years later. In 1959, Berry Gordy cowrote two songs for Wilson, *That's Why (I Love You So)* and *I'll Be Satisfied,* which further strengthened this wonderful partnership.

Berry Gordy Jr. and The Supremes in 1965. Clockwise from top: Berry Gordy, Diana Ross, Mary Wilson, and Florence Ballard.

Berry Gordy in his office in 1965, ready to conquer the world with the Motown sound.

Berry Gordy forges his destiny

On a quest for recognition in the music industry, Berry Gordy applied the logical, well-founded principles of a factory to realizing his ambitions—"Create, make, sell"[3] —and applied himself to learning the ropes. After divorcing Thelma Coleman, whom he had married in 1953, he found help, advice, and musical assistance in the shape of Raynoma Singleton, with whom he would lay the foundations for the Motown label.

At the end of 1957, Gordy met Smokey Robinson, leader of The Miracles, and the two became firm friends. At the same time, the talents of the composer Eddie Holland began to make waves, and he and his brother Brian joined Motown as soon as the label was founded.

In January 1959, Smokey Robinson persuaded Gordy to stop passing on his songs to Fortune Records or Rayber, and encouraged him instead to start up his own record label. Very soon the Tamla label and the music publishing company Jobete were founded. History had begun to be made.

Tamla needed to appeal to the widest possible public, both black and white. The label's first record was *Come to Me* by Marv Johnson, which made a big impact locally and landed Johnson a gig at the Apollo Theater, a famous venue in Harlem, New York, and one of the symbols of African-American music. Local radio stations welcomed the next record, *Merry-Go-Round* by Eddie Holland. Gordy wanted to release only music by solo artists on the Tamla label. So he founded Motown (the name is a contraction of Motor Town, the nickname for Detroit) and released *Bad Girl* by The Miracles. Smokey Robinson and his band thus ushered in the meteoric rise of the new label.

Hitsville USA in 1965, headquarters of Motown Records, at 2648 West Grand Boulevard, Detroit, Michigan. Since 1985 the premises have been home to the Motown Museum.

Hitsville, USA

In July 1959, Raynoma found an old photographer's studio at 2648 West Grand Boulevard, which would become the premises of both Tamla and Motown. The wooden house bore on its façade the evocative name "Hitsville, USA." Gordy, who wanted total control, occupied the first (ground) floor. The studio, which was a welcoming space, was set up in the former darkroom. Raynoma was responsible for organizing the configuration of the premises. Until 1968, Berry Gordy had the label's greatest artists record there: The Contours, Mary Wells, The Miracles, The Marvelettes, Martha and The Vandellas, Stevie Wonder, The Isley Brothers, The Four Tops, Diana Ross and The Supremes, The Temptations, Marvin Gaye, Gladys Knight and The Pips, and many more.

Gordy owed the high quality of the songs to producers and composers who have since become legendary: the Holland brothers, Lamont Dozier, Norman Whitfield, and Smokey Robinson.

The Jackson Five, symbols of the new Motown

In summer 1968, the singer Bobby Taylor met Suzanne de Passe, Gordy's new assistant, with the aim of setting up an audition for The Jackson Five. The group was asked to come to Motown's new building on Woodward Avenue on 23 July. Berry Gordy recalled how Suzanne called out to him:

> "There's a kid booked you've got to see—they're auditioning in the next room," she said. "And we just love him, and you're going to love him." And I said, "I don't have time. In fact, I don't like a kids' group. I don't want a kids' group."
> I've got Stevie Wonder [18 years old at the time] who had a major entourage...So she dragged me into this audition room, and I saw this kid who was doing all this stuff, this James Brown thing and he did a twirl and a split. Then she asked me, "So, you still don't like this kids' group?," and I answered "No I don't," but I immediately asked someone to bring me the movie camera.
> I noticed...on stage he was one kind of person, like a master of what he was doing...and then when he got through he was very quiet, almost shy...I was concerned because here was a kid who was about seven or eight years old singing a Smokey song like he had been living it for 30 years. It was like he was an old man in a kid's body because he sung *Who's Loving You* better than Smokey!
> Then we thought about a song for this kid that a kid would sing...and then came the hits *The Love You Save* and *I'll Be There* that made history, because no group had ever seen its first four records go straight to No. 1 [the others were *I Want You Back* and *ABC*]. And they became a major thing.
> Michael would complain to me about his childhood, and I would say: "You don't have such a bad childhood, Michael, I mean, you're doing what you want to do. If people could have that passion at the age of eight or nine and do it for the rest of their life—my goodness."[4]

Smokey Robinson in Detroit in 1967, in the office of Esther Gordy Edwards, vice-president of the Motown label.

Bobby Taylor worked on, directed, and recorded The Jackson Five's early songs in the Hitsville, USA, studio. They were soon snatched from his grasp and taken, at Berry Gordy's request, to Hollywood, where Motown's activities were progressively being moved. There, in his mansion on Boston Boulevard, Gordy asked them to perform in front of a hundred people, including the label's artists. That was when Diana Ross met them.

On 11 March 1969, the group's final contract was signed. The Jackson family stayed at Gordy's home, with the exception of Michael, who mostly stayed with Diana Ross, who lived close by. She became the confidante and role model for the talented youngster. Work began, with rehearsals, recording sessions, choreography sessions, one after the other and organized to perfection by Suzanne de Passe. It all went very quickly. On 11 August 1969 the group was presented to the media. Five days later, The Jackson Five were the warm-up act at a concert by Diana Ross and The Supremes in Los Angeles. On 7 October, *I Want You Back* was in the stores.

The Motown "school" and the flight to pastures new

Berry Gordy admitted: "It would seem that the Motown machine was only waiting for the arrival of The Jackson Five."[1] During this apprenticeship, Michael wandered around the studios and corridors. He observed, analyzed, and dissected the whole process of making and producing music. In 1971, *Got to Be There*, his first solo recording, was released, and new horizons opened up for him. One hit followed another, even though there was sometimes a lack of coherence between one album and the next, whether group or solo. Jackie, and especially Jermaine, were also granted the privilege of solo recordings. Jermaine married Berry Gordy's daughter Hazel. But Joseph Jackson, who was becoming jealous of the influence of Gordy and Diana Ross over his children, especially Michael, started to cause trouble. With the arrival of disco, The Jackson Five wanted to innovate. At the instigation of their father, they left the label (with the exception of Jermaine) and formed The Jacksons, under the direction of the Epic group (see page 13).

A still unbreakable tie

In May 1983, Berry Gordy asked Michael to take part in the Motown 25 show. Michael hesitated, but eventually accepted. He was the only artist permitted to sing a song not in the Motown catalog. What happened next is well known: his performance of *Billie Jean* left a permanent mark on the character and history of television, music, and dance. Gordy had given Michael the springboard that was to catapult him to the position of the greatest entertainer of his generation.

Berry Gordy was never far away. He accompanied his former protégé, whom he spoke about, nonchalantly, as being like one of his sons. Throughout Michael's career, the two would meet spontaneously, or out of need, as if they were family, beyond the world of contracts and business.

[THE JACKSON 5]

I Want You Back

The Corporation / 2'59

Taken from the album: *Diana Ross Presents The Jackson 5*
Released by Motown Records: USA, 18 December 1969 (ref. MS700) / UK, March 1970 (ref. STML 11142)
Chart position: USA R&B No. 1, Pop No. 5 / UK No. 16

Musicians
Michael, Jermaine, and Jackie Jackson: vocals and backing vocals
Marlon Jackson: backing vocals
Keith and Ludie Washington, Delroy Bridgeman: backing vocals
David T. Walker: rhythm guitar
Don Peake: lead guitar 2
Louie Shelton: lead guitar 1
Clarence McDonald: keyboards
Gene Pello: drums
Joe Sample: piano
Wilton Felder: bass guitar
Sandra Crouch: percussion
Freddie Perren: piano
Recording
Sound Factory Studio, Los Angeles: July to September 1969
Technical team
Producer: The Corporation
Arrangements: The Corporation
String Arrangements: Freddie Perren

1969

Single

A-side: *I Want You Back (mono single version)* / 2'59
B-side: *Who's Lovin' You (mono single version)* / 4'20
Released by Motown Records: USA, 7 October 1969 (ref. M 1157) / UK, January 1970 (ref. TMG 724)
Chart position: USA R&B No. 1, Pop No. 1 / UK No. 2

Genesis

I Want You Back was written at a key point in the history of Motown. The record label was in the process of making a pivotal move, leaving the industrial north of Detroit for the sunny West Coast and the palm trees of Los Angeles. Berry Gordy gave one of his best artists, the guitarist Deke Richards, the task of supervising the teams in the new premises. His role consisted, above all, in seeking out new composers. Richards quickly understood that it would be a masterstroke if he combined these new talents with the youth and freshness of The Jackson Five, whose arrival at the label had been announced as a major event. He came across two young keyboard players: Freddie Perren and Fonce Mizell. Richards, one of the few white individuals in the Motown stable, recruited these two young black musicians who had recently graduated from Howard University, and in doing so set yet another example of Motown's "crossover" approach to create the "sound of young America."

In the early 1960s, Gordy and Richards had created a collective of composers, known as The Clan, which was responsible for, among other things, The Supremes' hit *Love Child*. This system made it possible to get around any ego issues that might arise between the label's various teams. Indeed, Gordy believed in healthy competition between his staff and would not hesitate to have the same song recorded by different artists to see which version came up to his expectations. Over the years, however, this approach reached its limits, and many musicians and composers condemned the often autocratic way in which Motown's founder managed his artists. Motown created a new team of super-composers, in the mold of The Clan and the Holland-Dozier-Holland trio, known simply as The Corporation. Its four members were Berry Gordy, Deke Richards, Freddie Perren, and Fonce Mizell; from 1969 they set about writing hits tailored for The Jackson Five.

Perren, Mizell, and Richards got together and worked on a song entitled *I Want to Be Free*. Richards reserved it for Gladys Knight and The Pips, to whom he had allocated his first compositions when he arrived at Motown. His aim was to relaunch the career of this group, which had gone off the boil somewhat since its last famous hit, *I Heard It Through the Grapevine*, which had reached No. 2 in the *Billboard* chart in November 1967. Richards recalled: "The chord structure was complete

Promotional photo of The Jackson Five, 1970. From left: Marlon, Tito, Jackie, Jermaine, and Michael

and so was the melody. The lyrics were still sketchy, and I didn't have a middle or a breakdown, but I decided to go ahead and cut the track anyway."[5] Gordy listened to a demo of this syrupy soul piece and declared that it needed a "Frankie Lymon-style" treatment. With his high voice, Lymon had been the child star of the second half of the 1950s, notably with the hit *Why Do Fools Fall in Love*. Motown's boss thought that *I Want to Be Free* gave off a childlike innocence that did not fit with Gladys Knight's suave voice. On 11 August 1969 he invited Richards to a concert that The Jackson Five were giving at the Daisy in Los Angeles, and suggested he adapt the song for the group. Richards agreed. Gordy then got involved in reworking the title, and gave his ideas, which resulted in the finished song *I Want You Back*. The Motown boss, with his critical eye, had made sure that the song found its musical identity. The combination of the talents of the Richards-Perren-Mizell trio and Gordy enabled the polishing of the showcase song, like a bowling ball being readied for an infallible strike, that would reveal The Jackson Five to the general public.

And so *I Want You Back* and The Corporation came into being at the same time. It was at Motown's new headquarters in Los Angeles that The Jackson Five's first hit—and, in a sense, the whole philosophy behind Michael's musical career (an incredible fusion of commercial ambition and a desire to create songs that stood the test of time)—materialized for the first time.

The keyboard player Freddie Perren in his mixing studio in 1979.

FOR JACKSON ADDICTS

Motown reissued *I Want You Back* several times to get it into the charts in the 1980s and 1990s. The best-known remixes were released in 1988 by the PWL Studio (ruled by British producers Stock, Aitken, and Waterman) and in 1998 by producer Puff Daddy. During the 2000s, Motown approved new remixes by artists such as Dimitri from Paris, in compilations.

Production

"We were particularly impressed with the *I Want You Back* session then because that one song took more time (and tape) than all the other songs on the record combined," recalls Michael Jackson in his autobiography, *Moonwalk*.[2] For this song, recorded in Motown's studios in California, Michael, Jackie, Marlon, and Jermaine shared the solos, whereas Tito was content to stay in the background, singing the backing vocals. He was forbidden to play the guitar, just as Jermaine was not allowed to plug in his bass guitar. Berry Gordy preferred to use his faithful session musicians, which incidentally meant he avoided having to pay the Jackson brothers extra royalties as instrumentalists. The musicians he brought together were among the best that frequented the recording studios of the day. There was the now much-missed Wilton Felder of The Crusaders on bass guitar, and Sandra Crouch on percussion. She was the sister of Andraé Crouch, who was to work with Michael Jackson later on several occasions while he was developing his solo career in the 1980s and 1990s. In July 1998, when Motown celebrated its 40th anniversary, Felder related: "The bass part, which essentially mirrors and counters the melody, was mostly written out. I added just a bit of myself to it. As a sax player, I related to the line's hip chromatic movement, but being self-taught, I found the fingerings a bit intimidating."[6]

Although the instrumental track was recorded in a few days by Deke Richards and his team, with the almost military approach that was peculiar to Motown, it was a different story for the vocal takes. Richards was aware of the group's vocal maturity, especially Michael's. Once they were at the microphone, the Jackson brothers sang in a spontaneous fashion, giving an effect that was unpolished compared to Motown's other output. On hearing the early mixes of the song, Berry Gordy listed all the points that needed improving, notably the punctuation and stress of certain words. The Motown boss was, as ever, a visionary who knew how to make a song resound to the point that it became a hit that was played endlessly on the radio.

It took a fortnight to finalize the recording of the lead and backing vocals. The guitarist Louie Shelton recalled of these sessions:

> He blew me away. For the Motown sessions the artists generally weren't there, it was just the writers and the producers. So we'd put the tracks together without even hearing how the song went. But I was fortunate because they had called me down to do a guitar overdub and Michael was there doing the vocal on *I Want You Back*. So, other than the producer, I was probably one of the only people who got to see him sing that live in the studio.
>
> And I was absolutely blown away by what I was seeing. He was out there on the mic and I think he was 11 years old at the time, and he was singing so great, with such energy, conviction, feel, pitch—everything, and doing it with every ounce of his little body.[7]

Pleased with and proud of the results of the first day's recording, Michael quickly became disillusioned when Berry Gordy briefed the whole team to correct details that he alone could see, and which he said would make all the difference. Take followed take, relentlessly. The Jackson Five's young leader described this first big session on the BBC in 1972: "God, we spent so much time on that song. He was really patient with me, all of us. Over and over and over, I think I must have recorded that thing two dozen times. That was hard work. I remember falling asleep at the mike. I wondered if it would ever be finished. Just when I thought we were through, we'd have to go back and do it again."[8]

But with hard work and perseverance, the definitive version of *I Want You Back* was finally mixed and ready for pressing on 2 October 1969. A few days later Deke Richards played one of the single's test pressings to Stevie Wonder: "...this was a guy I really respected. We were friends. Everyone else was too influenced by Berry to give me an objective opinion. He listened to it carefully, and he said, 'Naw, man. I don't like the drums.' I had to laugh."[8] On the song's right-hand channel

Promotional photo of The Jackson Five, 1969. Rear, from left: Tito, Jackie, and Jermaine. Front: Marlon (left) and Michael.

(that was how stereo was highlighted in the late 1960s), the famous drumming sounded like the beating of a heart so young and ardent that it verged on syncopation. Katherine Jackson, the Jacksons' mother, did not have a pleasant memory of her first hearing either: "I thought that the tracks were too crowded, and that the producers hadn't brought out the boys' best vocal qualities."[9] For their first Motown recording, the Jackson brothers' backing vocals were mixed on the right-hand channel, the same one used for the drums. In the final version, Michael's voice and the rhythm guitars were in the foreground.

Despite the reservations of two individuals who were influential in the group's life, the firm stance of Berry Gordy, who wanted a mix as robust, energetic, and invigorating as it could be, was a resounding success: *I Want You Back* brought a new sound and a breath of fresh air to Motown. With this song, and the album on which it appeared (*Diana Ross Presents The Jackson 5*), the five Jackson brothers marvelously embodied that courageous transition that Motown underwent at the end of the 1960s. Out went the blues of Bobby Taylor's recordings, made on the label's home patch, Detroit, and in came the pop avant-garde dreamed up by The Corporation, engraved forever in the somewhat acid grooves of *I Want You Back*.

Berry Gordy, introducing this young group with a song that had been fine-tuned to a hair's breadth, was inaugurating a new style: bubble-gum soul. This musical genre, which was light but produced thanks to ultra-sophisticated production secrets, served as a template for the countless teen groups that sprang up from the early 1970s. This first attempt by Motown hit the nail on the head: *I Want You Back* sold more than six million copies in the United States alone, thus becoming a Platinum record. In 1999, the song entered the prestigious Grammy Hall of Fame.

PORTRAIT

DIANA ROSS
GODMOTHER AND MUSE

As rags-to-riches stories go, that of Diana Ross has no equal: despite her humble beginnings, she was destined to become a global star. Born Diane Ernestine Earle Ross on 26 March 1944 (her birth certificate erroneously gave her first name as Diana), she grew up in a family of modest means, living in one of the tallest housing projects in Detroit. As a little girl she dreamed of fashion and glamour. Diana experienced a difficult period early in her life when her mother contracted tuberculosis. In order to help her recovery, Diana's father decided to move the family to Alabama. When the mother's health improved, the Ross family returned to the gray skies of Detroit. As a young teenager Diana did a series of odd jobs. At that time, all the city's young kids dreamed of becoming singers. Hits began to pour out of the Motown factory founded by Berry Gordy, and the Hitsville building became a kingdom to be conquered.

In 1960, Florence Ballard formed a group with Mary Wilson, Betty McGlown, and Diana Ross: The Primettes. Diana, one of whose neighbors was Smokey Robinson, leader of The Miracles, managed to land an audition with Motown. Decked out like veritable up-and-coming starlets, the Primettes began their performance. Diana ended the set with an unaccompanied rendition of *There Goes My Baby* by The Drifters. At that point, Berry Gordy pricked up his ears and saw a possible future for the group. Diana Ross sang with a high, nasal voice, very different from the deep, soul timbre of Florence Ballard. Despite this handicap, she succeeded in asserting herself as the group's leader. Berry Gordy saw in her the potential to become a goddess of black music, an icon that could bring to Motown that touch of glamour and crossover that would enable the company to appeal to a wide audience. However, when he discovered the girls' ages, he advised them to come back a year later.

Queen of Motown

At this point, Diana showed her will of iron and smashed Gordy's summary refusal to pieces. She persuaded her colleagues to go to the Hitsville Studio every day until something would happen. By hanging around there, Diana, Florence, and Mary (Betty had left the group to get married) managed to sing some backing vocals for Mabel John. The session enabled the trio to prove that theirs was a talent not to be ignored. Young Diana set about charming Berry Gordy. A person of vision, he understood that he was dealing with a solid group that included a rough diamond who, as well as being their leader, had the potential to acquit herself well as a soloist.

The Primettes, now renamed The Supremes, signed their contract with Motown in 1960. Their first single, *I Want a Guy*, came out in March 1961. After a number of their songs failed to make it into the US Top 40, their first success came in July 1964, when *Where Did Our Love Go* went to No. 1 in the *Billboard* charts. The Supremes followed this with more No. 1 hits, becoming the first group to have five songs in a row in the top spot. Berry Gordy had succeeded in bringing three young black women into the record collections of America's households. Acting as true ambassadors for the Motown label, The Supremes appeared multiple times on the top-rated television shows of the time: Ed Sullivan regularly had them as guests on his Sunday evening show.

A true working girl who managed to stay in control of her activities in what was still a very male-dominated industry, Diana Ross also crossed swords with other women who entered her sphere and might have constituted a threat. The first major fight was the one she started with Florence Ballard, a founder member of The Supremes. These two-strong characters were constantly in conflict; disagreements and jealousy erupted very soon after signing. Diana remained in favor with Berry Gordy, whereas Florence, who was struggling with problems relating to alcohol dependence, felt pushed to one side. In 1967, Gordy decided to rename his biggest groups by adding the name of each group's leader in front. Thus The Supremes became Diana Ross and The Supremes. Eventually Florence Ballard's behavior led to her being excluded altogether, and from April 1967 Cindy Birdsong replaced her. This enabled the group to hang on to a certain amount of success, despite the departure of the Holland-Dozier-Holland trio of composers—notably with the singles *Reflections* and *Love Child*, which remained at No. 1 in the *Billboard* charts for two weeks in a row.

The Jackson Five pose alongside their famous godmother, Diana Ross, in 1970.

Diana Ross Presents The Jackson 5

By the close of the 1960s the popularity of Motown's supergroups was waning. Times were changing, and solo artists such as Stevie Wonder and Marvin Gaye embodied the label's renewal. The end of the groups' reign nevertheless proved to be fertile territory, where Berry Gordy planted five last green shoots, which were to burst into bloom like fireworks—a masterly product of the expertise Motown had deployed since its foundation. When The Jackson Five signed their contract with Motown in 1968, Berry Gordy was already looking to California as the next place to conquer. He planned to take Diana Ross with him and develop her solo career, both as a singer and as an actress. To perfect this coup, which would ensure the death of The Supremes, he decided to promote his favorite to the position of godmother of The Jackson Five. Thus Ross, the label's latest star and the queen of Motown, passed the baton to these five young black boys from Gary, Indiana. There was a wonderful rapport between Diana and young Michael. Although his idols included James Brown and Jackie Wilson, whose every dance step he had learned from watching them on television or on stage, he experienced a veritable emotional earthquake when he came into contact with the goddess of soul.

The young artist had only just arrived in Los Angeles to finish off The Jackson Five's first album when he went to stay with Diana Ross. He was to remain there for 18 months. Ross acted as chaperone, and took charge of his education while waiting for his mother, Katherine, to move to LA as well. The Motown star took an active role in the artistic awakening of her protégé, introducing him to old masters and encouraging him to draw. Judging by Michael Jackson's own account in his autobiography, *Moonwalk*, their meeting had something of the fairy tale about it. "You wouldn't think a big star like Diana Ross would take the time to teach a kid to paint, to give him an education in art, but she did it and I loved her for it. I still do,"[2] he comments, recalling his early months in Los Angeles.

Their relationship became one of mutual admiration. Michael found in Diana Ross not just a godmother, but a muse and a model whom he would love and admire throughout his life. The back of the cover of The Jackson Five's first album, entitled *Diana Ross Presents The Jackson 5* (1969), reflected Berry Gordy's desire to seal, in vinyl, this unique godmother role. Diana Ross's name appeared at the bottom of a note that followed the laws of marketing, obliging her to state that she was responsible for having discovered the group. The note ended with Diana Ross's signature, with an "R" sporting a loop that appeared a few years later in Michael Jackson's own signature (he used the "L" of Michael to produce the same motif).

Diana Ross, the incarnation of glamor, Motown style (1977).

Diana the solo artist

In the 1970s Diana Ross embarked on her solo career; her second single, *Ain't No Mountain High Enough*, topped the *Billboard* 200 chart. While Florence Ballard had been her rival in The Supremes, Cher was now the woman to beat. The two women traded blows by way of killer singles, which very often became Gold or Platinum records. When she made her debut on the big screen in 1972 with *Lady Sings the Blues*, a movie loosely based on the life of Billie Holiday, Diana dreamed of outshining the hottest actress of the time, Barbra Streisand. When Motown moved permanently to Los Angeles, Gordy and Ross enjoyed Hollywood life to the full, giving free rein to their fantasies and desire to conquer this new world of showbiz. This paid off in the recording studio, and Diana Ross chalked up hit after hit, until she ran out of steam with the arrival of disco.

Probably because she was too thinly spread performing in rather forgettable movie projects, Diana Ross struggled to cope with new trends. In 1977, Motown started up *The Wiz*, a project that was an African-American adaptation of *The Wizard of Oz*. Ross co-opted Michael Jackson, who landed the role of the scarecrow. The young man and his family were by now involved in a legal battle with Motown over a breach of contract (the Jackson brothers left Motown in 1975 and were signed up by Epic Records). However, thanks to Diana Ross, hard feelings were quickly put aside. Michael fitted in with the casting, and met the producer who was going to change his destiny: Quincy Jones.

In 1979 the release of the album *The Boss* heralded a renaissance, gradually asserting Diana Ross's position as an icon of the dance floor and of the gay community. She cut her last album for Motown, *Diana*, produced by the Chic team, which yielded the hit *Upside Down*, a Platinum single that topped the *Billboard* chart for four consecutive weeks. The 1979 to 1980 season saw both Ross and Jackson reach a crossroads in their lives. Tired of lacking total control over her work, and reassured by the success of the album *Diana* (which she successfully remixed with Russ Terrana, Motown's official mixer, unbeknown to the project's original producers, Nile Rodgers and Bernard Edwards of Chic), Ross negotiated a historic contract with RCA, which offered her $20 million to join its stable.

Friends for life

Meanwhile, Michael Jackson was enjoying success as a solo artist with *Off The Wall*, his first album as an adult, made with

Diana Ross and Michael Jackson, closer than ever, at the American Music Awards in Los Angeles, 30 January 1981.

Quincy Jones. The two friends and Motown survivors celebrated their new departure on CBS's TV special, *Diana,* produced by Ross in February 1981 to celebrate the success of the eponymous album. On it, she recalled tenderly how, ten years earlier, she had had the opportunity of supporting her friend when he was starting out, and how he had since become the best-selling black American artist. This was the moment when Diana in effect handed the baton to Michael: from then on, he embodied the future toward which she had worked for many long years. Two years later, with the album *Thriller*, Michael Jackson fulfilled the vision Gordy had for Diana Ross—he became a global artist and an icon for a generation. As Quincy Jones explains in the bonus audio interview on the reissued *Thriller* that came out in 2001: "For the first time, all kids the world over had a young black man as their idol. That had never happened before."

Michael Jackson's undisputed success did nothing to damage the admiration he felt for his godmother and longtime friend. In 1982 he composed and produced *Muscles*, the star track of her album *Silk Electric*, which went proudly to No. 10 in the Top 40. During the *Thriller* years, Diana had been a reassuring presence on whom Michael could rely, especially in his rare public appearances. In 1985, when he cowrote the song *We Are the World* with Lionel Richie for the super-group USA for Africa, Diana was by his side and they sang the first refrain together. The same year, Michael cowrote for her, with the brothers Gibb, *Eaten Alive*, whose modest success nevertheless offered the advantage that it drew him out of a planned (and much-needed) period of retirement to create the successor to *Thriller*. This idyllic relationship hit a rough patch in 1986, when Diana married Arne Næss, a wealthy Norwegian businessman. At that point, the two Motown soulmates grew apart. Michael found refuge in Neverland, an extravagant private kingdom that he had built for himself. Nevertheless, they continued to meet on tour and also at the inauguration of Bill Clinton in 1993.

Michael Jackson's life took a different turn in the 1990s. His entourage was constantly changing, and he ended up navigating the world of showbiz alone, a world where the rules were always being rewritten. On 8 May 1996, by which time he had been elevated to the status of royalty, especially in Europe and Asia, he again met his eternal godmother, on the occasion of the World Music Awards in Monte Carlo. The scene was revealing, and their sincere affection was mesmerizing to behold. Diana Ross began a medley of her greatest hits. Michael Jackson, like a real Motowner, could not take his eyes off her, and giggled when she sat on his knee while singing *Ain't No Mountain High Enough*. The pupil and the teacher, the godson and the godmother, were now on equal terms: Diana showing her pride at seeing her showbiz protégé become a superstar, while his candid gaze clearly showed fascination, love, and humility.

Although Michael Jackson also formed a strong and unique friendship with Elizabeth Taylor, Diana Ross remained a faithful friend to the end. On 24 April 2002, at his final live performance at a gala organized by Bill Clinton for the Democratic Party, Michael Jackson performed several songs from his album *Dangerous*. He concluded his performance with *Heal the World*, sharing the stage with Diana Ross. They had come full circle, and reached a conclusion: the two Motown stars appearing on stage together for the last time, singing the notes of a humanitarian hymn that chimed perfectly with the generosity that had held them together, and which they had shared with the public, for all these years.

Who's Lovin' You

William "Smokey" Robinson / 3'57

From the album: *Diana Ross Presents The Jackson 5*
Released by Motown Records: USA, 18 December 1969 (ref. MS 700) / UK, March 1970 (ref. STML 11142)
Chart position: USA R&B No. 1, Pop No. 1 / UK No. 2

Musicians
Michael Jackson: lead vocals
Michael, Jermaine, Tito, Jackie, and Marlon Jackson: backing vocals
The Funk Brothers:
James Jamerson: bass guitar
Earl Van Dyke: piano
Joe Messina: guitar
William "Benny" Benjamin: drums
Recording
Motown's Hitsville Studio, Detroit:
instrumental tracks: 19 July 1969;
backing vocals and demo: 20 July 1969;
lead vocals: 25 and 29 July 1969
Technical team
Producer: Bobby Taylor
Arrangements: David Van De Pitte

Genesis

In early 1960, Smokey Robinson wrote *Who's Lovin' You* and recorded it with his group The Miracles. The song was the first track on their first album, *Hi...We're The Miracles,* and also on the B-side of *Shop Around,* their first real hit. By coincidence the same song, recorded almost a decade later by The Jackson Five, was also chosen to be on the B-side of their first hit single, *I Want You Back*.

The Motown philosophy was based on an overriding principle: the label's songs were recorded by several artists, in different arrangements, until they became hits. Once this goal had been attained, the songs were given to new artists to prolong their life even further and promote the Motown sound. Smokey Robinson saw his hit snatched away by Michael Jackson, the top star at the time. This song, which he would transform and elevate to another dimension, was to be the catalyst for a breathtaking start to the group's career.

Who's Lovin' You was one of the first songs Michael sang for Berry Gordy. His adaptation was so captivating, heartfelt, and personal, that it totally demolished the Motown founder's position that he would not sign up children's groups (see page 11). However, even in the face of the obvious talent the auditions revealed, and impressed by so much potential, Gordy admitted that he hesitated for a long time before signing The Jackson Five. Michael was barely ten years old when Gordy heard him perform this song for the very first time, though Gordy shaved a few years off Michael's age in his telling of the story. Berry Gordy would often describe his first meeting with Michael, and how he sensed in him a thirst for learning and a natural curiosity that would enable him to become the best, especially as he was prepared to work as hard and long as necessary.

At first Smokey Robinson was doubtful that someone so young could breathe so much feeling and soul into a performance. However, when he recalled the day when Berry Gordy asked him to come and hear the group, he admitted he experienced an emotion he had never felt before. Even today, he always praises Michael Jackson's version of the song and reaffirms that the young prodigy made his dream as a songwriter become reality.

Who's Lovin' You brought young Michael's immense talent to the ears of the widest possible audience when it featured on the *Ed Sullivan Show*. That evening he gave a performance that, even today, is considered the finest ever given for that song.

Michael Jackson greets the famous TV host Ed Sullivan on the occasion of the first appearance of The Jackson Five on *The Ed Sullivan Show,* broadcast 14 December 1969 on CBS.

FOR JACKSON ADDICTS

The mono single version (4'21) is 20 seconds longer than the album version. It is included in the compilation *Michael Jackson—Love Songs* (2002) and the box set *The Complete Motown Singles, Vol. 9: 1969* (2007). The live version released in 1992 features as a bonus on the reissue *Two Classic Albums on One CD—Goin' Back to Indiana / Lookin' through the Windows* (2001).

The presenter, Ed Sullivan, played a major role in establishing a television presence for Motown's artists. He quickly agreed with Berry Gordy to welcome The Jackson Five on his show on 14 December 1969, just two months after a discreet appearance on the show *Motown at Hollywood Palace.* As he introduced them, Sullivan promised his audience they were about to see a sensational group. Michael, a little guy in a pink broad-brimmed hat and blue frock coat, began his performance with *Stand!* by Sly and The Family Stone: a clear, fresh rendition that was both dynamic and precise. It was a well-executed introduction, with perfect choreography that enabled the audience to easily focus on each of the group's five members. Already, Michael was captivating the camera, darting around, lighting up the stage, surprising considering his young age and apparent fragility.

Next, with blues-like notes and in an astonishingly deep tone, Michael continued with a spoken introduction that created an intimate atmosphere, totally at odds with his previous rendition. This kid, barely ten years old, completely devoid of any constraint, shyness, or reserve, dared almost shamelessly to tackle the highly mature blues idiom. He let himself go wholeheartedly before millions of TV viewers:

I met a girl at school one day
During sandbox
Older Brothers: Sandbox?!
We toasted our love during milk break
Older Brothers: Aw man
I gave her my cookies!
Marlon: Come on Mike!
We fell out during finger paints
So one day, I stepped up to her and I said...Wheeeeeeennnn
I had you...

His strong self-belief and precise interpretation combined to produce an incredibly convincing performance. This was the exact moment when Michael Jackson embarked on his immense and talented career.

As Weldon McDougal said: that evening the career of The Jackson Five was truly launched. Requests for their records from radio stations and disc jockeys skyrocketed.

Production

Berry Gordy soon entrusted The Jackson Five's musical direction to Bobby Taylor, giving him carte blanche (see page 20). He expected rapid results, and the young musicians' talents showcased to the full, but soon criticized his employee for having them record songs that were out of fashion. Taylor argued that these classics would gradually nourish Michael Jackson's soul and personality.

The Jackson Five's first album was recorded at a point when the label was going through a change, gradually transferring its operations to the West Coast. At the same time as Bobby

The Jackson Five perform *Sing a Simple Song, Can You Remember,* and *I Want You Back* on the set of the special TV show *Motown at the Hollywood Palace,* broadcast on the ABC network in October 1969. It was their first large audience.

Taylor was working with the group, the hit factory known as The Corporation got going and the era of "bubble-gum soul" was quietly starting its revolution.

Bobby Taylor retained essential control of the first album, *Diana Ross Presents The Jackson 5,* which he chose to record at Motown's Hitsville Studio in Detroit. The instrumental tracks were entrusted to The Funk Brothers, much to the regret of Tito and Jermaine who had yet to master their instruments. The Funk Brothers had created the sound of Motown's biggest hits. Their main members included James Jamerson (bass guitar), Earl Van Dyke (piano), Joe Messina (guitar), and William Benny Benjamin (drums). Their interaction and musicality were vital to the label's output but, oddly, were not highlighted very much. It wasn't until the extraordinary success of *What's Going On* and Marvin Gaye's *I Heard It Through the Grapevine* that anyone showed interest in session musicians and their work, which had been in the shadows since the early 1960s.

Taylor chose soul classics of the 1960s, and was keen to include them on the album. As a result, *Can You Remember* by The Delfonics, *Standing in the Shadows of Love* by The Four Tops, *You've Changed* (from the Steeltown period), *My Cherie Amour* by Stevie Wonder, *Chained* by Paul Petersen, *(I Know) I'm Losing You* and *Born to Love You* by The Temptations, and finally *Stand!* by Sly and The Family Stone all joined *Who's Lovin' You* and the new songs written by The Corporation, as well as the Disney song *Zip-a-Dee-Doo-Dah*.

Although the instrumental sections of *Who's Lovin' You* were recorded separately from the vocal takes, this had the advantage of giving completely free rein to the masterly, warm, melancholy, and almost suave interpretations of the young Michael Jackson. His uplifting of the soul and his vocal variations, doubtless inspired by David Ruffin's version on the album *The Temptations Sing Smokey* (1965), came through like in no other song on the album.

The single *I Want You Back / Who's Lovin' You* was released Tuesday 7 October 1969, and sold more than two million copies in six weeks. It was a Gold disc, but not certified by the Recording Industry Association of America (RIAA) because Motown was not a member.

In 1992, *Who's Lovin' You* was reissued as a single worldwide to coincide with the promotion of the television series *The Jacksons: An American Dream*. It was a hitherto unseen live recording of a concert on 29 May 1971 in Gary, Indiana. This version, which was even more impressive than the studio one, had the advantage that the instrumentals were recorded at the same time as the vocals, which added to the interpretation by Michael Jackson, who was galvanized more than ever. A short video clip accompanied the promotional single; it showed Jason Weaver, the actor who played Michael Jackson as a child in the series.

DICK CLARK
FATHER OF THE AMERICAN MUSIC AWARDS

Dick Clark, the iconic presenter of the show *American Bandstand,* around 1957.

Dick Clark (1929–2012) is the embodiment of the evergreen American pop presenter and TV host. With his finger forever on the pulse of America's youth, he won fame as the charismatic, iconic presenter of the show *American Bandstand*. From 1956 to 1989 he welcomed on his show those who made headlines in American and international music. An interviewer whose jokes were unoriginal but nonetheless effective, he also produced a series of radio shows for local stations, entitled *Dick Clark's Rock, Roll & Remember.*

Dick Clark and Michael Jackson forged a showbiz friendship that defied the passage of time. From The Jackson Five's earliest days at Motown, Michael and his brothers appeared regularly on *American Bandstand*. Michael made his solo debut on it with *Rockin' Robin* and *I Wanna Be Where You Are,* songs from his first album, *Got to Be There*. Clark interviewed the group several times from the 1970s to the beginning of the *Thriller* period. When the presenter launched his own awards ceremony, the American Music Awards (AMAs), in 1973, Michael Jackson was among the first stars invited to present prizes to the winners. Unlike the Grammy Awards, where professionals receive prizes from their peers, the AMAs are based on votes by the public. And there lies the crucial difference: throughout his career, Clark placed the stars and the public at the center of the debate. The voice of the people prevailed. And this inescapable truth was regularly proved when he and Michael Jackson came together. During the *American Bandstand* show on 10 February 1979, Dick Clark welcomed the Jackson brothers as they were starting the promotion of their new album, *Destiny*. They sang three songs: *Shake Your Body (Down to the Ground)*, *Things I Do for You*, and *Push Me Away*.

Rock-solid loyalty

Michael Jackson turned to the legendary presenter at various key moments in his career: he reserved the first TV screening of the short film *The Triumph—Can You Feel It* for *American Bandstand*, where it was shown on 19 September 1981. On 16 January 1984, to celebrate the global success of the album *Thriller*, Clark regaled Jackson with a dream panel of personalities to present him with the 11 awards that the public had bestowed on him; Diana Ross and Lionel Richie, but also Paul McCartney via a video message, paid tribute to his talent and success.

On 25 January 1993, when the album *Dangerous* received a series of well-deserved awards, Clark suggested to Jackson that he open the 20th edition of the American Music Awards with an exclusive performance of the eponymous song. Michael Jackson took advantage of this to add new elements to his performance—a maneuver that has since been widely adopted by pop artists. During this ceremony, Dick Clark retitled the International Artist Award the Michael Jackson International Artist Award. It was given to artists whose achievements go beyond simply hit albums or songs—in other words, major artists.

On 20 April 2002 Dick Clark and Michael Jackson met for the last time on a television set. Clark was celebrating the 50th anniversary of *American Bandstand* and Michael Jackson gave his last performance specifically for television, again, from *Dangerous*. The two men represented, in their respective fields, a modern, people-based, and unifying vision of the world of entertainment. The work of Dick Clark has lived on since his death in 2012: the American Music Awards have continued to be a flagship ceremony of the music industry. And some of this event's finest moments came about courtesy of Michael Jackson.

[THE JACKSON 5]

ABC

The Corporation / 2'55

From the album: *ABC*
Released by Motown Records: USA and UK, 8 May 1970 (ref. MS 709 and ref. STML 11156)
Chart position: USA R&B No. 1, Pop No. 4 / UK No. 22

Musicians
Michael, Jermaine, Tito, and Jackie Jackson: vocals and backing vocals
Marlon Jackson: backing vocals
Wilton Felder: bass guitar
Gene Pello: drums
David T Walker, Louie Shelton, and Don Peake: guitar
Freddie Perren: keyboards
Recording
Sound Factory Studio, Los Angeles: December 1969
Technical team
Producer: The Corporation
Arrangements: The Corporation

1970

A-side: *ABC (mono single version)* / 2'56
B-side: *The Young Folks (mono single version)* / 3'10
Released by Motown Records: USA, 24 February 1970 (ref. M 1163) / UK, May 1970 (ref. TMG 738)
Chart position: USA R&B No. 1, Pop No. 1 / UK No. 8

Genesis

With *I Want You Back*, Berry Gordy had perfected a devastatingly effective formula: a team of inspired composers writing for young, enthusiastic, talented individuals. Like the first song the Jackson brothers recorded for Motown, *ABC* and *The Love You Save* were also written by The Corporation. The aim was to repeat the winning formula but tweak it so it would continue to appeal to the general public and establish The Jackson Five sound, a carefree blend of soul and pop. *ABC* uses many chords that feature in *I Want You Back*, such as C major, D major, and G major. *The Love You Save* also uses some of the same chords as *ABC*, with a few variations. *ABC* was put together by Deke Richards, who reused the melody and chords of *I Want You Back*, simplifying the rhythm and giving a childlike feeling by repeating the first three letters of the alphabet.

Production

Recording of *ABC* began immediately after the sessions for the first album, *Diana Ross Presents The Jackson 5*, had wrapped up. Berry Gordy decided to put his faith in the group without waiting to see how the first single would fare. The sessions took place in Motown's California studios. Various versions of *ABC* were recorded. Two are officially known today: the one that appears on the album, which was also released as a single, and an alternative version, lasting 3'24, which was revealed for the first time in the compilation *I Want You Back—Unreleased Masters*, released by Motown in 2009. This mix contains a slower melody and progression to the refrain. The result, which was also more mature, enabled Tito to perform one of the phrases of the first couplet. These variants give the song a more conventional feel that is maybe too close to *I Want You Back*. Gordy decided to polish the shorter version, which was tighter and with a decidedly more pop-like feel.

The Jackson Five and their parents, Joe and Katherine, in front of the swimming pool at the family home in Encino, in 1971.

The Jackson Five during the promotion of the album *ABC* in 1970.

[THE JACKSON 5]

THE LOVE YOU SAVE

The Corporation / 2'59

From the album: *ABC*
Released by Motown Records: USA and UK, 8 May 1970 (ref. MS 709 and ref. STML 11156)
Chart position: USA No. 4 / UK No. 22

Musicians
Michael and Jermaine Jackson: vocals and backing vocals
Marlon Jackson: backing vocals
Jermaine, Tito, and Marlon Jackson: additional vocals
Marlon, Tito, and Jackie Jackson: additional backing vocals
Wilton Felder: bass guitar
Gene Pello: drums
David T. Walker, Louie Shelton, and Don Peake: guitars
Freddie Perren: keyboards
Recording
Sound Factory Studio, Los Angeles: March 1970
Technical team
Producer: The Corporation
Arrangements: The Corporation

Genesis

For *The Love You Save*, Deke Richards was aware that the song's structure needed to be innovative and differ from the group's first two singles. "The only difference was we just had to come up with a new punch and groove for the beginning, and a new, different structure for the verse."[13] He kept the same chord progression as can be heard in *ABC*.

The Corporation took advantage of these two songs to strengthen the teamwork between the brothers at the microphone—an important element for appearing on stage when on tour in the future. So it was that the first exchanges between Jermaine and Michael on *I Want You Back* became routine and regularly featured in other songs on later albums.

Production

In *The Love You Save*, the formula created by Berry Gordy and The Corporation was established, but had undergone some modifications. The recording produced a template that was to be reused in other hits, such as *Sugar Daddy* and *Mama's Pearl*.

ABC and *The Love You Save* were included in the Jackson brothers' second album, *ABC*. It was released on 8 May 1970, preceded by the title track's release as a single in February 1970. *The Love You Save* was released as a single in May 1970.

1970

In less than six months, The Jackson Five had three singles at No. 1 in the US Top 40, beating The Beatles twice: *ABC* and *The Love You Save* knocked *Let It Be* and *The Long and Winding Road* respectively off the top spot.

Single

A-side: *The Love You Save (mono single version)* / 3'02
B-side: *I Found That Girl (mono single version)* / 3'09
Released by Motown Records: USA, 13 May 1970 (ref. M 1166) / UK, July 1970 (ref. TMG 746)
Chart position: USA R&B No. 1, Pop No. 1 / UK No. 7

PORTRAIT

SUZANNE DE PASSE
AN ESSENTIAL SUPPORT

Suzanne de Passe was born in 1946 in Harlem, New York City. She was barely 20 years old when Berry Gordy noticed her initiative and dedication in her job as program coordinator at the Cheetah Disco Club in New York. She became his personal assistant and very soon the Motown label's trusted lieutenant.

It was Suzanne de Passe who interceded with her boss to persuade him to listen to The Jackson Five's audition. Fate saw to it that he granted her wish. Apart from her high degree of competence as a manager, she was the female presence and surrogate mother for the group when they were on the road in America. She acted as choreographer, dresser, and prop-woman, but was also responsible for making sure the children received an education. She liked to relate how the choreography of *I Want You Back* had been developed and rehearsed at her house in Los Angeles. She also recalled with emotion and amusement the first time The Jackson Five appeared on the *Ed Sullivan Show* in 1969. That day, Suzanne had scoured the shops of Greenwich Village in search of costumes for the program. She brought Michael a brown shirt, complemented by a blue tunic and a pink, broad-brimmed hat. An outfit he would never wear again, but which was to become iconic. According to Jermaine Jackson, when Michael saw himself in the mirror dressed in those strange garments, he exclaimed: "I love it!"

Once they had become famous, the brothers avoided contact with the public, and spent hours playing in hotel rooms. Suzanne nicknamed Michael "Casper, the little ghost," because he was a mischievous prankster and enjoyed eavesdropping.

Suzanne de Passe was an enthusiastic, committed, and especially creative woman. In 1973 she became the first African-American to receive an Academy Award nomination for cowriting the screenplay of the movie *Lady Sings the Blues*, starring Diana Ross as Billie Holiday. She also helped to get Motown artists exposure on TV. One of the things she was most proud of as president of Motown Productions (from 1972) was the show *Motown 25: Yesterday, Today, Forever*, which was broadcast on 25 March 1983. It left an indelible mark on the history of American television, bringing The Jackson Five back together for an evening and showcasing the first ever appearance of the moonwalk on *Billie Jean*. Suzanne de Passe could take pride in having been the instigator of this event: once again, she had managed to persuade Berry Gordy to organize it. Later she took on the challenge of putting together a project highlighting the extraordinary rise of the Jackson brothers. In 1992 she produced the TV series *The Jacksons: An American Dream*, for which she won an Emmy award. She continued this line of work as co-president of De Passe Jones Entertainment, the successor to Motown Productions, which Berry Gordy passed to her in the early 1990s.

Berry Gordy and his faithful right-hand woman, Suzanne De Passe, who supervised The Jackson Five from the time of their arrival at Motown.

She was a veritable point of reference in Michael Jackson's career. In 2005, when he was interviewed by Jesse Jackson, the singer recalled his years with her: "Remember Suzanne de Passe, she was so wonderful, you know. She was pretty much our manager...She was very helpful and instrumental in the early days of our careers that she remains a friend. And I do, I do…I miss her."[10]

WELDON ARTHUR MCDOUGAL III
AN OFTEN-FORGOTTEN LINK

Weldon Arthur McDougal was born on 28 October 1936 in Philadelphia, Pennsylvania. He cofounded the Harthon label during the 1960s and was one of the pioneers of "Philly soul." From 1969 to 1980 he was the East Coast head of record promotion for Motown. This discreet man's involvement in The Jackson Five's route to Motown was recognized only late. It appears that he was the link between Joseph Jackson and Bobby Taylor. While he was preparing a VIP suite for the arrival of Bobby Taylor and The Vancouvers at the High Chaparral club in Chicago in 1968, McDougal heard some shouting. The Jackson Five appeared on stage, he saw them, and was impressed. In the documentary *Michael Jackson: The Life of an Icon*, he related how Joseph Jackson, who was introduced to him that evening by the venue's manager, told him: "Hey man, we wanna be on Motown."[11] Weldon McDougal explained to him that he had no way of signing up anyone to the label. Joseph insisted: "Could you introduce me to someone at Motown?"[12] That same day, Weldon did indeed tell Bobby Taylor about the conversation.

McDougal would tell anyone who would listen that Bobby Taylor worked very hard to gain recognition for The Jackson Five—even harder than for his own group. One day, when he was rehearsing at the Apollo Theater in Harlem, New York, Bobby Taylor asked Weldon McDougal to come because he had a surprise for him. When McDougal arrived outside the venue, he saw, to his delight, that the Jackson brothers were on the bill. He admitted that he had never known this happen so quickly for a group without an album to its name and thus unknown to the general public. But people were constantly crying out: "Jackson Five!"

In 2010, in an interview with Adam Worthy, McDougal returned to the subject of his background in promoting Motown artists to radio stations and disc jockeys. He explained that it was just after the *Ed Sullivan Show* was broadcast that the group's popularity skyrocketed and radio stations called him asking for a copy of *I Want You Back*. From that moment on, everyone was waiting for the next single from the group.

Weldon McDougal was given the task of promoting Motown's products, and played an active role in getting the music of The Jackson Five known throughout the US.

The Michael Jackson Scrapbook

In February 1985, Weldon McDougal published *The Michael Jackson Scrapbook*, which contained many photographs of Michael and his brothers. Michael and Tito possessed a camera, and regularly asked McDougal to immortalize them. On 26 September 1970, during the World Series in Cincinnati, the young singers performed *The Star-Spangled Banner*, and Weldon took photographs that made the next day's headlines. From that day on, he took many shots using his own camera, and brought them together in the book. It was apparently greatly appreciated by Michael Jackson, who reportedly consulted it in the presence of his childhood friend David Gest, producer of the documentary *Michael Jackson: The Life of an Icon* in 2011; Michael never let David touch it for fear of it being damaged.

[THE JACKSON 5]

I'll Be There

Berry Gordy, Hal Davis, Willie Hutch, Bob West / 3'57

From the album: *Third Album*
Released by Motown Records: USA, 8 September 1970 (ref. MS 718) / UK, February 1971 (ref. STML 11174)
Chart positions: USA R&B No. 1, Pop No. 4 / UK No. 4

Musicians
Michael and Jermaine Jackson: lead vocals
Michael, Jermaine, Tito, Jackie, and Marlon Jackson: backing vocals
Arthur Wright, David T. Walker, and Louie Shelton: guitars
Bob West: bass guitar
Joe Sample: keyboard (harpsichord)
Gene Pello: drums
Jackie Jackson: tambourine
Recording
Sound Factory Studio, Los Angeles: instrumental tracks
Record Plant Studio, Los Angeles: vocals and backing vocals
April to September 1970
Technical team
Producer: Hal Davis
Arrangements: Bob West

1970

A-side: *I'll Be There* (*mono single version*) / 3'42
B-side: *One More Chance* (*mono single version*) / 2'59
Released by Motown Records: USA, 28 August 1970 (ref. M 1171) / UK, November 1970 (ref. TMG 758)
Chart position: USA R&B No. 1, Pop No. 1 / UK No. 4

Genesis

In the space of a few months The Jackson Five had already released two albums and had their first three hits at the No. 1 spot in the pop and R&B charts. Between them, the singles *I Want You Back*, *ABC*, and *The Love You Save* had already sold almost ten million. Before the first anniversary of the group's official launch, it was planned that a third album—entitled, appropriately enough, *Third Album*—would go on sale. The privilege of such a title was normally reserved for established, widely influential artists; the title therefore promised much and presented even more in the way of a challenge. *I'll Be There* was the first ballad by the brothers to have been released as a single; its tone was deliberately more peaceful, serene, and calm. It was therefore a risky enterprise for Motown, which here was shattering the convention for wild songs that had marked the work of The Corporation up until then. Michael Jackson's performance of *Who's Lovin' You* on the *Ed Sullivan Show* (see page 35) had doubtless made an impression on Berry Gordy, who had decided to adopt a new strategy to reinforce his protégés' stature and position on the market.

This gentle ballad is a romantic lament, in which the voices of Michael and Jermaine are almost completely without instrumental accompaniment. In *I'll Be There,* Michael asserts himself: no longer does he dream only of love, but he now also undertakes to become a strong, kindly support, with this promise to "be there." Moreover, and this is a marked change, he is for the first time the true protagonist in his desire for love. *I'll Be There* ushered in a mature phase that the young artist was preparing to champion before his audience.

Special care was taken in the writing of this song. Berry Gordy played his best card in asking Hal Davis, a loyal, talented composer in the Motown stable, to outshine the work produced by The Corporation. It was a challenge he took up with ambition and commitment.

Some accounts of the writing of this song are confused, but all seem to agree that there was a mysterious instrumental track hit upon by Hal Davis and worked on originally by the bassist and arranger Bob West. Davis sensed it had great musical potential and soon came up with the title *I'll Be There.* He immediately contacted Willie Hutch, another talented composer and a lyricist who was highly respected within Motown. The two composers then recorded the basics of the song in the

The Jackson Five pose in 1971 with their first Gold records, awarded to Motown. At the time, the label did not declare its sales figures to the RIAA.

space of one night and played them to Berry Gordy, who liked both the tone and the title. Willie Hutch had taken it upon himself to write two variants. The first dealt with a love that was rather brotherly in character, whereas the other was more romantic. Berry Gordy chose the romantic theme, but the brotherly aspect was not, for all that, neglected: "You and I must make a pact / We must bring salvation back."

The Motown boss later added the famous interjection: "Just look over your shoulder, honey!" which admirably vitalizes and punctuates the song. According to Hal Davis, Berry Gordy was a true creative force when he got involved in the production of songs. However, Gordy admitted that, on hearing the first version of the song, he was not especially impressed. Nevertheless, as work progressed, he became more and more convinced that a ballad was the right way to go. *I'll Be There* was to give the group a credibility they had never had before and prove that *Who's Lovin' You* had not been a one-off success. Hitherto associated with bubble-gum soul, The Jackson Five were on the point of becoming a pop phenomenon that was as high profile as it was credible.

Production

Graham Betts states in his encyclopedia, *Motown*, that the various instrumental tracks were recorded at the Sound Studio Factory under the impeccable direction of Hal Davis himself, and with the involvement of the very best musicians on the West Coast. Although the intro begins with the sound of a harpsichord, that is simply because the composer himself judged it appropriate to use an instrument which he personally associated with love themes in movies.

Michael Jackson performs *I'll Be There* on the set of the special TV show *Diana!*, broadcast 18 April 1971 on ABC.

I'll Be There was performed on all of Michael Jackson's tours. Unlike The Jackson Five's earlier hits, which were brought together in the form of a medley, he sang it in full every time, using marvelous vocal variations, along with an homage to his brothers and their collective rise to stardom.

Willie Hutch, cowriter and lyricist of *I'll Be There.*

FOR JACKSON ADDICTS

In 2002 the compilation *Michael Jackson—Love Songs* included an alternative bonus version. Worth hearing is *I'll Be There—Minus Mix* (*Michael Jackson—The Stripped Mixes* 2009).

The vocals were recorded at Record Plant Studio. Jermaine was earmarked as the song's lead singer. However, the instrumental tracks were so high that only Michael's voice, pushed to the limit, could hope to record the most complex passages.

Berry Gordy related an amusing story: "At the end of *I'll Be There*, when he shouted out, 'Look over your shoulders, honey,' everyone said: 'Shoulders should be singular, not plural. He said it wrong.' But I love spontaneity, so I said, 'He said it right. Let's leave it.'"[14] The words had been borrowed from the song *Reach Out I'll Be There* by The Four Tops, a complete version of which Michael would record, and in which he would repeat exactly the same mistake (this can be heard on the bonus record that came with the 1995 compilation *Soulsation!*). Berry Gordy admits that, when he heard the final master of *I'll Be There*, he thought Hal Davis's work was, as he had betted, superior to that of The Corporation. Mission accomplished and challenge met.

Michael Jackson recalled:

> *I'll Be There* was our real breakthrough song; it was the one that said, "We're here to stay." It was No. 1 for five weeks, which is very unusual. That's a long time for a song and the song was one of my favorites of all the songs we've ever done...But that song grabbed me from the moment I heard the demo. I didn't even know what a harpsichord was until that record's opening notes were played for us. The song was produced thanks to the genius of Hal Davis, assisted by Suzy Ikeda, my other half who stood next to me song after song, making sure I put the right emotion and feeling and heart into the composition. It was a serious song, but we threw in a fun part...[2]

Before the TV show *Diana!* was aired in April 1971, the original soundtrack was released on 29 March 1971. It revealed the lineup of artists who would appear. The medley *I'll Be There / Feelin' Alright* had been studio recorded the previous year, on Saturday 5 December 1970. It became, in a certain sense, the first Ross / Jackson duo to be released (also as a single). The comfort of the studio did not, sadly, enable Michael Jackson to radiate the spontaneity and charisma that he conveyed live on the evening of the TV show. It was aired on Thursday 18 April 1971 at 8 p.m. on the ABC channel. As he had done when performing *Who's Lovin' You* on the *Ed Sullivan Show*, Michael really got into his groove, and his vocal variations were astonishing.

I'll Be There was the single that would really establish the group, becoming their fourth song in a row to reach No. 1 in the charts. This was an unheard-of record—and what's more, it had been achieved in less than a year. The song was from then on considered one of Motown's greatest, with four million sold. However, according to J. Randy Taraborrelli, in his 1991 book, this figure was heavily rounded up for the purposes of PR and marketing, and in fact sales amounted to exactly 3,178,523. Nevertheless, the song was the biggest success in The Jackson Five's history, and the most in demand by the public.

PORTRAIT

STEVIE WONDER
A TRAVELING COMPANION

Were it not for the genius of Stevie Wonder, the world of pop music would never have become what it is today. He was an artist of such vision that his career is one of the few that bear comparison with that of the legend that is Michael Jackson. His music brought innovation, character, modernity, and timelessness, and his songs displayed an unmatched sensitivity and musicality. The sounds of his synthesizers, like his vocoder breaks, resonate in the collective unconscious like nothing else, and are immediately recognizable. Stevie Wonder's enthusiasm, charisma, warmth, and generosity had the power to move people to tears. He is a giant who, like Michael Jackson (videos and dance steps aside), is one of the cornerstones of pop, rock, soul, and R&B music. Who in the world could have understood and guided the development of the young Michael Jackson better than this other child star? He was a logical and natural link in Michael's musical education and the motivating force that drove him throughout his career. Theirs was an indestructible friendship. Michael Jackson saw in Stevie Wonder a mentor, a model, and a point of reference that stayed with him in his development as an artist. The two stars had their hits, both together and individually, but there was never any rivalry between them. These two giants were to leave an eternal mark on the history of late 20th-century African-American music.

Stevland Hardaway Judkins

Later rechristened Stevland Morris, Stevland Hardaway Judkins was born on 13 May 1950 in Saginaw, Michigan. He was born prematurely and developed a retinopathy at birth that rendered him blind. In 1954 he moved in with relatives in Detroit. He grew up in a poor but loving family, and he adored sport and music. He played the harmonica, drums, and piano, and his musical talents were the joy of the parishioners of his local church. He was discovered by Ronnie White, the songwriter and vocalist of the group The Miracles, who introduced him to Berry Gordy. Gordy offered him a contract with Tamla when he was just 11 years old.

Little Stevie Wonder

The earliest efforts of Little Stevie Wonder, as Clarence Paul, his first producer and music teacher, named him, were uncertain and did not really allow his talent to emerge. *The Jazz Soul of Stevie Wonder* and then *Tribute to Uncle Ray* in 1962 received good reviews. But it was with *Fingertips* (1963), which appeared on the live album *Recorded Live: The 12-Year-Old Genius*, that the sensation took off like a rocket, reaching No. 1 in the charts. However, there followed a second period during which hits were not forthcoming. It was not until the years 1966 to 1967 that he enjoyed success with more hits: *Up-Tight (Everything's Alright)* and then *I Was Made to Love Her*, which opened the door to European exposure.

Meeting Michael Jackson and The Jackson Five

Stevie was soon to meet another child star. He told *Time* magazine: "I first met Michael when I was in Detroit. He came to Motown, and they were talking about this boy from Gary, Indiana, and The Jackson Five, and everyone was excited. He was a little boy then. He would always come into the studio curious about how I worked and what I did. 'How do you do that?' 'Why do you do that?' I think he understood clearly from seeing various people do the music scene that it definitely took work. He must have been around nine or ten then, and I definitely felt he was going to be someone. You heard the voice, and all he could do was grow. And that's what he did."[15]

The Jackson Five worked indirectly with Stevie Wonder from their first album at Motown. They performed the hit *My Cherie Amour,* as the label's policy at the time dictated. It was released as a single by Stevie Wonder in January 1969, reaching No. 4 in the *Billboard* pop and R&B charts.

A model of artistic freedom

The success of Stevie Wonder's early hits produced considerable revenue for Motown. But the young artist soon wanted to have more control over his work and see the money transferred to his personal account. He had just turned 21 when he

Michael Jackson and Stevie Wonder, close friends, backstage at the 28th Grammy Awards ceremony, 27 February 1986.

began protracted negotiations with Berry Gordy. Little by little he gained his artistic freedom and succeeded in producing his very first album—the aptly named *Signed, Sealed, and Delivered*—himself. In 1970 new versions of his songs *I Don't Know Why I Love You* and *Never Had a Dream Come True* featured on the tracklist of The Jackson Five's album *ABC*. On the album *Ben* (1972), Michael performed, solo this time, *Shoo-Be-Doo-Be-Doo-Da-Day*, another Stevie Wonder hit. Around this time, the older artist began a change of musical direction with *Music of My Mind*, an album that blended soul with jazz and rock.

His album *Innervisions* (1973) heralded a host of masterpieces including *Higher Ground*, *Don't You Worry 'Bout a Thing*, and *Living for the City*. Stevie Wonder scooped up six Grammy Awards. That same year, he was involved in a car accident that left him in a coma for several weeks, before returning to the stage in Cannes on the invitation of his friend Elton John, where he performed *Confusion* for the first time.

Also in 1973, during their tour of Japan, The Jackson Five humbly performed his song *Superstition*, which can be heard on the album *Live in Japan*. A few months earlier, Stevie Wonder had gone to No. 1 in the US charts with that song. It featured on the exceptional *Talking Book*, in which he confirmed his electronic aspirations. The second single from the album, *You Are the Sunshine of My Life*, was also a great success.

Early collaboration

The year 1974 saw concrete collaboration with The Jackson Five. They provided the backing vocals on the song *You Haven't Done Nothin'*, which featured on an album that was very intimate and more personal than ever: *Fulfillingness' First Finale*. Among the first shots taken by the photographer Todd Gray is an incredible one of Michael Jackson watching his mentor during the session at Record Plant Studio, Hollywood. His gaze is brimming with humility and respect. He is standing back, whereas Stevie Wonder is busy at the console. Of course, this picture of a shared moment did the rounds of the music media, which announced that maybe an album was forthcoming. Fans dreamed of this and talked endlessly about it. Although the song *Buttercup* (written and produced by Stevie Wonder) was indeed recorded at this time, it was not released until 2009, on the compilation *I Want You Back! Unreleased Masters*, which celebrated the 40th anniversary of The Jackson Five's hit single.

After a period of inactivity, in September 1976 Stevie Wonder finally released the long-awaited *Songs in the Key of Life*, a double album featuring contrasts that were as astonishing as they were wonderful. *I Wish*, *Sir Duke*, and *Isn't She Lovely* were hits that made the album into a major event and a resounding success. Then, little by little, Stevie Wonder began to reduce his work rate and embark on his "commercial" period.

Stevie Wonder and Quincy Jones in the studio in 1987—two emblematic figures in the Jackson world.

The 1980s

Stevie Wonder wrote a song specifically for Michael Jackson for the first time in 1979, for the album *Off the Wall*. The enchanting and deeply humble *I Can't Help It* adds to the fresh, dance-like quality of the album. At the same time, Motown assembled a compilation of unreleased songs by The Jackson Five, and released *I Was Made to Love Her* on the album *Boogie*. It was a song cowritten by Stevie Wonder and his mother in 1967.

He was back in action in the fall of 1980 with *Hotter Than July*, an album containing melodies that some found unoriginal, but nevertheless intoxicating and no less brilliant. The song *Masterblaster* was performed at Madison Square Garden, New York, by Michael Jackson and Stevie Wonder in November 1980. It was a rare moment. The tour that promoted the album was organized with the aim of establishing a national holiday in memory of Martin Luther King Jr., a goal that was attained in November 1983 during the presidency of Ronald Reagan. The famous song *Happy Birthday* is a touching homage to the minister and civil rights activist who was murdered in 1968. *Hotter Than July* also contains the song *All I Do,* in which Michael Jackson makes a discreet but noticeable appearance in the backing vocals.

The early 1980s saw Stevie Wonder undertake numerous collaborations, notably on the evergreen *Ebony and Ivory*, a duet with the great Paul McCartney. The single was a big sensation; *The Girl Is Mine*, later that year, less so. The early 1980s, for Stevie Wonder as for Michael Jackson, were a time of duets and guest appearances. There were further collaborations with Elton John and Dionne Warwick. For Donna Summer, under the direction of Quincy Jones, Stevie Wonder provided backing vocals for the song *State of Independence*, together with several other artists, including his faithful friend Michael Jackson. In 1984, with *I Just Called to Say I Love You,* he attempted to declare his love for a certain woman in a red dress, who featured in the movie *The Woman in Red*. A year later, he also took part in the USA for Africa project, on the single *We Are the World.*

Michael Jackson: "I learned so much from him!"

Michael Jackson piled on the superlatives to pay homage to this genius. In 1983 he said: "I learned so much from him, just by sitting in on his sessions and talking to him and listening. He is phenomenal. I had an interview with George Harrison in England. We did it together. And we were speaking of Stevie and he said that Stevie Wonder makes him want to retire. He said he can't even explain what Stevie does. He said that Paul [McCartney] feels the same way. He said he's just incredible. I feel the same about Stevie. I'll come in the door and he'll sing: 'Michael's here, Michael's here!'; and he'll come up with a song just by singing that. I love Stevie. I learn so much from him!"

Michael Jackson added: "He's a master. I'm not joking. I would put him in the same range as Beethoven or another of the other greats. For now, for today, he is way ahead of us musically, of the world really. His vocals are phenomenal [about *Send One Your Love*]—so close to perfection."[16]

Stevie Wonder in concert at the Rainbow Theatre, London (January 1974).

Just Good Friends

The year 1987 saw the two friends once more join forces on album projects. *Just Good Friends* was recorded as a duet and included on *Bad.* Spike Lee's documentary *Bad 25* gives a sensitive sneak peek behind the scenes of this recording. The song did not figure on the long list of singles drawn from the album, probably to make way for the single *Get It*, another duet released the same year on Stevie Wonder's album *Characters*.

On 28 November 1987, during the *Bad* tour in Brisbane, the audience was thrilled at the announcement that Stevie Wonder would appear on stage. He came on to accompany the final passage of the song *Bad*, making sure he added his fair share of improvisation. To this day, fans fantasize about getting their hands on a video of this moment of togetherness.

During the 1990s Stevie Wonder made himself scarce; only the album *Conversation Peace,* featuring *For Your Love,* served as a reminder that the genius was still in action. The two friends quietly collaborated in the minor song *Yeah* on Eddie Murphy's album *Love's Alright* (1992), thus adding themselves to the long list of artists on the piece. The success of the duet of Steve Wonder and the singer Babyface on *How Come, How Long* made an impact in 1996; his harmonica resounded, bringing to mind the roots of his music. On 4 August 1998, Michael Jackson and Stevie Wonder visited the Motown Museum in Detroit—a return to roots and a public display of their close bond. It was, in all probability, the last public appearance by the two men side by side.

A Time 2 Love

Fans had to wait until 2005 to hear *A Time 2 Love* and Stevie Wonder's collaboration with Prince on *So What the Fuss.* Since then, Stevie Wonder has not released an album, confining himself to live appearances, alone or as part of a duo, when he electrifies his devoted fan base. The musician who produced 23 albums and 98 singles can afford to rest on his laurels with passion.

He attended the memorial service for his friend at the Staples Center in Los Angeles in 2009, performing his 1971 hit *Never Dreamed You'd Leave in Summer,* which since then has taken on new meaning. Stevie revealed that he had told Michael he loved him many times and was at peace with that. He strongly urged the media to stop their squalid hunt for sordid news and instead to concentrate on the musical work and humanitarian activities of an exceptional artist. For the most part his message was heard and heeded. More than ever, Stevie was keeping watch over and protecting his illustrious friend's heritage and message.

At the series of concerts celebrating the 25th anniversary of the Rock and Roll Hall of Fame in 2009, Stevie Wonder and John Legend proudly paid homage to Jackson. The wound was too recent for Stevie to reach the end of his performance. He was overwhelmed by emotion, sobbing, and had difficulty resuming his tribute. More recently, a private recording of the song *I Can't Help It* was made public. In it, fans could hear the message of a strong, sincere love for an exceptional person and lifelong friend; the finest gift he could have offered to Jackson.

At the 2014 Grammy Awards, Stevie appeared alongside Nile Rodgers and the new musical generation of Pharrell Williams and Daft Punk—proof of his relevance for future generations.

PORTRAIT

RUSS TERRANA
MOTOWN'S RECORDING ENGINEER

Born on 6 July 1942 in Detroit, Russ Terrana and his twin brother devoted themselves to music when they were barely ten years old. The group they set up together eventually developed into the band Rare Earth, which was signed up by Motown, and made up entirely of white musicians—an exception for Motown but duly granted to the person who was to be, for 18 years, the chief recording engineer on the label's greatest hits. At the age of 23, armed with his electronic engineering diploma, he was quickly hired by Berry Gordy.

Russ Terrana's humility and discretion were apparent whenever he spoke:

> When I first started working at Motown I got to know Berry Gordy. He saw that I had certain talents that would benefit him, so he encouraged me to really open up and follow my strengths. For me, that was mixing. I loved to mix. His whole philosophy was to surround himself with strong people. He could recognize good talent, from singers to producers, writers, engineers, salespeople, and promotion people. Once you got his blessing, you could do whatever you wanted; he encouraged that freedom, especially on the creative side.
>
> After I moved to LA...I had a great group of some of the best people in the industry, but it was because of him. [He] trusted my abilities, the producer's abilities, and the songwriters.[17]

The Motown genius

From 1966 to the mid-1980s, Russ Terrana mixed the greatest hits by The Supremes, Marvin Gaye, The Four Tops, The Temptations, Stevie Wonder, Jimmy Ruffin, The Miracles, and of course Michael Jackson and The Jackson Five, with whom he rubbed shoulders in the studio when they were starting out. During his career, from eight track to 48 track and right up to the arrival of digital, he witnessed the various developments in recording technology close up. He was helped in his work by Motown's head of engineering, Mike McLean, whom he respected enormously: "He was a super genius of audio—he would buy a piece of gear, take it apart, and re-do it into what he wanted it to be. They even had this thing called the Motown EQ, which was this eight-band EQ with the faders. The guy had a mind on him that was unbelievable; he was so good at his job."[17]

As a highly respected member of Berry Gordy's entourage, Russ Terrana made an invaluable contribution. This is the recipe he used to produce the Motown sound: "I'd usually start off with the rhythm tracks, then some overdubs, then some vocals, then some backgrounds."[17]

A man adaptable to any situation, he was called upon by Diana Ross to remix her album *Diana* (1980), as she felt that the group Chic, who had produced it, had placed her voice too much in the background. Russ Terrana made a new master of the album, which remains one of the great highlights of the Motown catalog.

With Michael and The Jackson Five

When Motown moved to the West Coast, Russ Terrana remained in Detroit for a time. After The Jackson Five had finished recording their first album, he was summoned by Berry Gordy: "We signed these kids. We finished the album and listened to all the mixes, and I don't like any of the mixes. I'll send you the multitracks, and I want you to remix the whole album."[17]

Alone in his studio, the recording engineer heard the voice of the young Michael Jackson for the first time:

> His pitch was great and he had good emotion. He was like an adult in a kid body. He really impressed me. He wasn't just singing words—he came from the heart. Once I moved up to LA, I was with him a lot. Michael was a good kid; I really liked Michael. He would sit next to me in the control room and would ask, "What does this do? What does that do? Why does that happen?" He was very into the behind-the-scenes thing, too. He was always fascinated by the equipment...He was very soft-spoken and very polite, until he got behind a microphone, and all of a sudden, bang—"Who is that guy?" I liked him a lot. He was a very nice person. He was genuine.[17]

In 1969, Rare Earth, Russ Terrana's group, released its album *Get Ready* on a label that bore the group's name and belonged to Motown.

For the recording sessions with Michael Jackson, Russ Terrana used a Neumann U87 microphone to which he added slight compression with a Urei LA-3A. This enabled peaks in the singing to be avoided and the recording to be kept even. For Terrana, the near-absence of a compressor allowed a certain purity to be retained in the final mix, and thus to go from a quiet note to a sudden, harsh one. Russ Terrana had 89 No. 1 *Billboard* hits to his name. No other recording engineer has ever achieved such a feat. His humility was as legendary as the songs that he masterminded in the 1970s and 1980s.

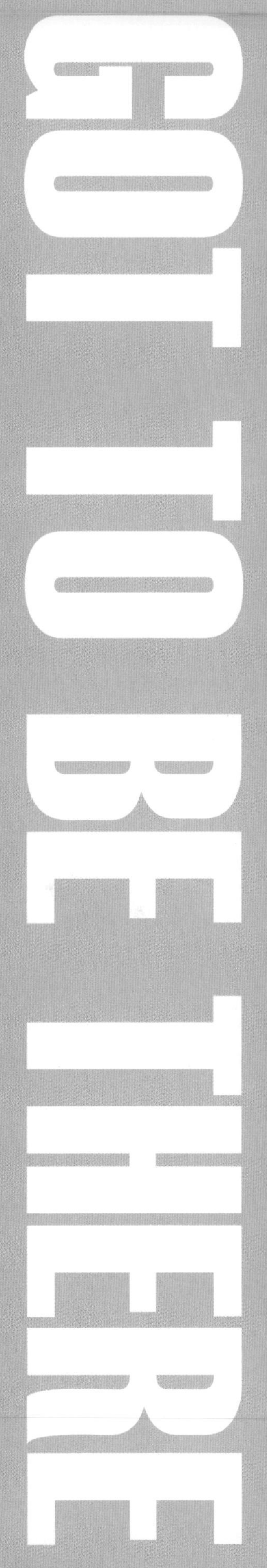

1. AIN'T NO SUNSHINE
2. I WANNA BE WHERE YOU ARE
3. GIRL DON'T TAKE YOUR LOVE AWAY FROM ME
4. IN OUR SMALL WAY
5. GOT TO BE THERE
6. ROCKIN' ROBIN
7. WINGS OF MY LOVE
8. MARIA (YOU WERE THE ONLY ONE)
9. LOVE IS HERE AND NOW YOU'RE GONE
10. YOU'VE GOT A FRIEND

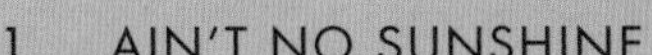

Got to Be There **ALBUM**

Released by Motown Records: USA, 24 January 1972 (ref. M 747 L) / UK, May 1972 (ref. STML 11205)
Chart position: USA R&B No. 3, Pop No. 14 / UK No. 37
RIAA: certified Gold 2 August 2013

GOT TO BE THERE, THE LITTLE PRINCE OF MOTOWN GOES SOLO

1972

Right from The Jackson Five's first arrival at Motown, all eyes were instinctively turned to young Michael. On 18 October 1969, Diana Ross introduced the five boys as Michael Jackson and The Jackson Five on the television show *Hollywood Palace*. Joe, their overprotective father, was furious, reminding Berry Gordy that this was a family group and Michael should not be introduced as the lead singer.

This attempt to protect the brothers, and force people to see the group as an inseparable whole, crumbled in the face of Michael's talent and instant popularity. Right from his very first television appearances on the *Ed Sullivan Show* and *The Dick Clark Show*, he was the charismatic lead singer, way ahead of his four brothers. He stood out from the rest for the sheer agility and speed of his dance steps. His inspired style revealed his talent as a singer who was at ease with a range of registers and themes that would not usually concern a twelve-year-old boy.

A made-to-measure album

As well as being a superb stage performer who could sway his hips like James Brown and Jackie Wilson, Michael proved with this first Jackson Five album that he could put emotion into melancholic ballads like *Who's Lovin' You* or *Can You Remember.* As an experienced manager and record label executive, Berry Gordy was well aware of the young boy's huge potential, and decided right from the start to use the same formula that he had applied ten years previously to promote Diana Ross and The Supremes. At the same time as The Jackson Five became the heroes of a Saturday morning cartoon on ABC, first aired on 11 September 1971, Motown released Michael Jackson's first solo 45 rpm, *Got to Be There,* on 7 October that same year. This ballad composed by Elliot Willenski gave the young prodigy the opportunity to let his voice soar as the notes reached higher and higher. It was as if he had been set free: this first single gave the impression that the singer was already happy to strike out on his own, away from his family.

As executive producer for the record, Berry Gordy had his very young and very talented singer record some cover songs that would have unnerved artists twice his age. But whether it was with Bill Withers' *Ain't No Sunshine,* Carole King's *You've Got a Friend*, or *Love Is Here and Now You're Gone* by the legendary Holland-Dozier-Holland trio, Michael, driven by sheer energy and a certain candor that overcame any feelings of intimidation, delivered his own first-class renditions.

Got to Be There is Michael Jackson's most balanced solo album at Motown. The songs follow a logical order. Hal Davis, who produced the record, managed to assemble a patchwork of songs that defined R&B trends at the time, moving the young prodigy away from the bouncy pop numbers that he'd been doing with The Corporation. Hal Davis had already used Clifton Davis' ballad *Never Can Say Goodbye* for The Jackson Five where Michael's voice reached new levels of maturity and confidence.

Michael Jackson visits the gardens of the Kiyomizu Kannon-do temple in Tokyo, May 1973.

The little prince of soul

On *Got to Be There*, Michael became the little prince of soul, or rather the captain. Jim Britt's photos on the album cover show him proudly posing with a peaked cap, looking quite the leader. On the back cover, he adopts a more melancholic attitude, but still with the same self-confidence. The record was enthusiastically received by the public, and Motown decided to produce three singles from it: the title song, *Rockin' Robin*, and *I Wanna Be Where You Are*. The first reached the Top 5 in the US charts, while *I Wanna Be Where You Are* achieved a very respectable 16th spot.

The overall results were promising. Michael's first solo project set sparks flying: the album *Got to Be There* sold almost 1.6 million copies whereas The Jackson Five album *Maybe Tomorrow*, released several months earlier, sold only half that number. Berry Gordy realized that he could capitalize on the group by involving its strongest personalities in solo projects. He produced solo albums first with Jermaine, then with Jackie. However, these were less successful than their younger brother's albums.

Got to Be There was the start of a solo career that would take almost seven years to reach maturity. But the ten songs in this album already included all the ingredients that would define Michael Jackson's style: dance rhythms and melancholic melodies wrapped in a dreamy romanticism.

Michael Jackson during rehearsal for the Royal Variety Performance at the London Palladium in October 1972.

Ain't No Sunshine

Bill Withers / 4'09

Musicians
Michael Jackson: lead vocals
Backing vocals: (unknown)
Musicians: (unknown)
Recording
Motown Recording Studios, Los Angeles: July 1971 to January 1972
Technical team
Producer: The Corporation
Arrangements: The Corporation and Eddy Manson

For Jackson Addicts

On 27 August 1972, Michael performed this at the San Diego International Sports Center, California, before an emotional audience who were blown away by his poignant, intoxicating performance. The live audio recording appears on the double CD *Jackson Five Live at the Forum*, released in 2010 (Hip-O Select B0014405-02).

1972

Genesis

The original version of the song was composed and sung by Bill Withers, one of the most respected tenors in 1970s soul music. Like many artists of his time, he was still working in a factory when he recorded the song. *Ain't No Sunshine* was one of the tracks on his very first album, *Just as I Am* (Sussex Records, 1971). It was released as a single in September 1971. The song was well received by both the music industry and the public and did extremely well in both the R&B Top 10 (No. 6) and the pop charts (No. 3). Paradoxically, it had little impact in Europe, failing to crack the UK Top 40. The song was nominated for a Grammy Award in 1971 in the best male vocal performance category. It won the extremely prestigious and coveted best R&B song of the year.

Ain't No Sunshine is a song about a lover who has gone away, and who might or might not come back. The lyrics are strung out like a plaintive lament and fueled by a forlorn hope. The heavy pounding bass provides a great accompaniment to Bill Withers' vocals, and brings out all the pain in the song. The guitar and violin accompaniments resonate like touches of optimism and render the sense of waiting even more palpable.

Knowing that they had missed out in Europe with the Bill Withers' version, Motown had Michael Jackson record the number as part of the plan to pack his first solo album with hit songs.

Production

Michael Jackson's version is more pop in style, with an electric guitar bringing greater depth. This time around, the violins are more pronounced and, rather than accompanying a fatalistic lament, the song is a desperate call for the lost love to return. The percussion (tambourine and drums) is like a heartbeat that fades away to leave room for an explosive cry from the heart. The Corporation was responsible for the orchestration, which made Michael Jackson's version a hit in its own right without betraying the original work. The young prodigy's rendition is mellow but fragile at the same time, and this song marked a turning point in his solo career. The single went to No. 8 in the UK charts, thus doing credit to Bill Wither's creation. Meanwhile in the US, the singer achieved his first ever No. 1 with the song *Ben*.

Single

A-side: *Ain't No Sunshine (stereo single version)* / 4'10
B-side: *I Wanna Be Where You Are (stereo single version)* / 2'57
Released by Motown Records: UK, July 1972 (ref. TMG 826)
Chart position: UK No. 8

I Wanna Be Where You Are

Arthur Ross, Leon Ware / 3'00

Musicians
Michael Jackson: lead vocals
Musicians: (unknown)
Recording
Motown Recording Studios, Los Angeles: fall 1971
Technical team
Producer: Hal Davis
Arrangements: James Carmichael

I Wanna Be Where You Are spawned many cover versions over the years, from Thelma Houston to Jennifer Holliday, and of course Beyoncé. Michael Jackson's version was released as a single in the US where it reached No. 16 in the general charts (and No. 2 in the R&B charts). Unlike *Ain't No Sunshine*, this song has never been released as a single in the UK.

Like a harbinger of the music video revolution of the 1980s, the song was used as a soundtrack for an episode of *The Jackson 5ive* cartoon series called "Michael White" that was televised on 16 September 1972.

1972

Single

A-side: *I Wanna Be Where You Are (stereo single version)* / 2'57
B-side: *We've Got a Good Thing Going (stereo single version)* / 3'00
Released by Motown Records: USA, May 1972 (ref. M 1202F)
Chart position: USA R&B No. 2, Pop No. 16 / UK No. 37

Genesis

The album *Got to Be There* was the first collaboration between two composers who provided Motown with some of the great songs of the 1970s: Arthur Ross, Diana's younger brother, and Leon Ware. This duo was a great example of how knowledge is passed down through the generations. Ware joined Motown in 1967 as a staff composer. He also worked for the Isley Brothers and Tina Turner. Arthur Ross joined the label as a songwriter with the help of his sister Diana who, once her solo career was officially launched, managed to impose certain conditions on Berry Gordy. This string-pulling by Diana gave young Arthur the opportunity to develop his talent. The Ross-Ware duo achieved huge acclaim in 1974 with *I Want You*, written for Marvin Gaye, a towering work of incredible sensuality that has never been equaled. Ware was also one of the links in the chain that brought Michael Jackson and Quincy Jones together. In 1974, he helped compose the songs *If I Ever Lose This Heaven*, *One Track Mind*, and *Body Heat* for the Quincy Jones album *Body Heat*.

Production

The *Got to Be There* sessions took place in the fall of 1971. The title track was released as a single in October. The concert given the same year by The Jackson Five in their hometown, Gary, Indiana, was broadcast as a special show that was also produced as an album under the Motown label. The group had reached the peak of their commercial success, which encouraged Berry Gordy to further develop the talents of young Michael, on whom media and public attention was focused. The young man therefore found himself back in the studio to get on tape his first solo recordings. His brothers were replaced by Motown's regular backing singers. The album only included one song composed by The Corporation: *Wings of My Love*. *I Wanna Be Where You Are* was produced by Hal Davis, who on a number of occasions in the Jackson brothers' career at Motown suggested new elements that could be added to their music. This song was the first joint composition by Arthur Ross and Leon Ware to be made into a record. It starts with a harpsichord introduction, an instrument that had already appeared on *I'll Be There*. But here it sounds like a theme introducing someone who is dreaming about being back with the person they love. *I Wanna Be Where You Are* was one of the original compositions that enabled Michael Jackson to develop his own musical style.

On 30 September 1972, The Jackson Five perform *I Want You Back*, *ABC*, and *I Wanna Be Where You Are* during one of the Black PUSH Expo concerts held in the International Amphitheatre, Chicago.

Girl Don't Take Your Love Away from Me

Willie Hutch / 3'46

Musicians: (unknown) / **Michael Jackson:** lead vocals / **Backing vocals:** (unknown) / **Recording: Motown Recording Studios, Los Angeles:** July 1971 to January 1972
Technical team: Executive Producer: Berry Gordy / **Producer:** Gene Page / **Arrangements:** Gene Page / **Recording engineer:** Russ Terrana

The intro sets the scene: a winter backdrop for a Christmas tale, as if Bing Crosby or Perry Como were about to launch into one of those songs that people listen to around the fireside, cradling a mug of hot chocolate. Michael Jackson's voice slides in wonderfully over the melody composed by Willie Hutch. Once again, it is a story of unrequited love. The 13-year-old singer plays the part of a lover who is doing all he can to win back his sweetheart. The chorus rises to a crescendo that peaks on the words "Don't take your love from me." At 2'12, Michael launches into a spoken, almost rapped, verse before his voice rises again in a chorus that takes flight on the last note, with the word "love."

In Our Small Way

Beatrice Verdi, Christine Yarian / 3'34

Musicians: (unknown) / **Michael Jackson:** lead vocals / **Backing vocals:** (unknown)
Recording: Motown Recording Studios, Los Angeles: July 1971 to January 1972
Technical team: Executive Producer: Berry Gordy / **Producers:** The Corporation / **Arrangements:** The Corporation and Eddy Manson / **Recording engineer:** Russ Terrana

Composed by Beatrice Verdi (who made her name with the many great songs she wrote for Dusty Springfield) and Christine Yarian, *In Our Small Way* is a ballad that brings a unique feminine sensitivity to young Michael's repertoire. The lyrics are particularly striking for their spiritual feel. This time, the young boy is not singing about the sadness of love, but lyrics like those on *I'll Be There* that contain a promise: "We will be there to share each lonely road / Because we love, I know / We care enough." *In Our Small Way* was a more polished version of a style that had already been tested on several Jackson Five songs, such as *I'll Be There* or *Never Can Say Goodbye*. The ballad was so effective that several months later Motown decided to add it to the tracklist of the album *Ben*.

Got to Be There

Elliot Willensky / 3'23

Musicians
Michael Jackson: lead vocals
Backing vocals: (unknown)
Musicians: (unknown)
Recording
Motown Recording Studios, Los Angeles: June 1971
Technical team
Producer: Hal Davis
Arrangements: Dave Blumberg
Vocal arrangements: Willie Hutch

1972

A-side: *Got to Be There (mono single version)* / 3'22
B-side: *Maria (You Were the Only One) (mono single version)* / 3'40
Released by Motown Records: USA, 7 October 1971 (ref. M 1191F) / UK, January 1972 (ref. TMG 797)
Chart position: USA R&B No. 4, Pop No. 4 / UK No. 5

Genesis

Got to Be There is the title of Michael Jackson's very first album and his first solo single. According to Graham Betts, the young artist's solo career was launched as the result of an artistic rivalry. At the same time as The Jackson Five, another family group called The Osmonds reached the top of the charts in 1970 with the smash hit *One Bad Apple*. Up until that point, it had been a healthy rivalry that fueled a sense of competition and promoted record sales for both groups. The five brothers from Gary, Indiana, had very little to worry about as one hit followed another. The rules of the game changed, however, in summer 1971 when MGM Records decided to propel Donny Osmond, the youngest member of the family, into a solo career. His single *Go Away Little Girl* immediately shot to the top of the *Billboard* charts, which Motown executives, Berry Gordy in particular, were not too happy about. Up until then there had been absolutely no plans and no thought at all of a possible solo career for the young Michael Jackson. However, it was glaringly obvious that the Motown prodigy had far greater potential than Donny Osmond. Berry Gordy was not too keen on pushing his young protégé forward and, equally, Joe Jackson made it clear that this was a united, inseparable family group. In the end, though, Gordy gave his approval. He put Hal Davis in charge of the project, and the album was put together very quickly with the usual selection of cover versions and some new numbers, including the wonderful *Got to Be There* written by Elliot Willensky. It is a song about a fervent desire to love and be loved. Michael gives a sensational performance under the impeccable vocal direction of Willie Hutch. There is a short harpsichord introduction, and Michael Jackson immediately starts hitting the high notes, as if he wanted to demonstrate his vocal capacities. Donny Osmond had better watch out!

Production

Got to Be There was recorded in June 1971 in the Motown Studios in Los Angeles. Berry did not like the initial mix nor the fact it was yet another ballad, because the group had just released and promoted four sentimental love songs, one of which had just missed out on a Top 10 spot in the US charts. The track was reworked and eventually came out as a single, although Motown did not have high hopes for it. *Got to Be*

This photo, shot by the photographer Jim Britt, appeared on the back of the album *Got to Be There* (1971).

There never made it to the No. 1 slot, which was occupied by Donny Osmond's *Go Away Little Girl,* but it did manage a respectable and comfortable No. 4 spot in the *Billboard* charts. The album met with an encouraging critical reception, and Michael Jackson's solo efforts were favorably received. *Rolling Stone*'s Vince Aletti wrote: "On *Got to Be There,* Michael's voice echoes and swirls, whispers and cries out, with this unbelievable purity: 'Oo-oh what a feeling there'll be / the moment she says she loves me.' It's a weird combination of innocence and utter professionalism, real feeling and careful calculation, that's fascinating and finally irresistible."[17]

Michael Jackson performed the song on television but very rarely live, as was the case on the *Hellzapoppin'* variety show on 1 March 1972.

The same year, Smokey Robinson recorded the song with The Miracles for the *Flying High Together* album, then in 1973, Diana Ross recorded the track for the *Touch Me in the Morning* project, although in the end the song was not included in the final selection. It reappeared in 2009 on the expanded edition of the album published by Hip-O Select.

Michael Jackson has fun at the piano during a concert rehearsal at the Modern Musical, Los Angeles, 1971.

FOR JACKSON ADDICTS

Rockin' Robin was released in the US in February 1972 (M 1197F). It reached no. 2 in the R&B and Pop charts. It was released in the UK in May 1972 (TMG 816), reaching no. 3. A-side: Stereo Single / 2'30; B-side: Mono Single / 2'51

Rockin' Robin (Single)

Jimmie Thomas / 2'30

Musicians: (unknown) / **Michael Jackson:** lead vocals / **Backing vocals:** John and Thomas Bähler
Recording: Motown Recording Studios, Los Angeles: July 1971 to January 1972
Technical team: Executive Producer: Berry Gordy / **Producers:** Mel Larson and Jerry Marcellino / **Arrangements:** James Carmichael / **Recording engineer:** Russ Terrana

Leon René used the pseudonym Jimmie Thomas to compose *Rockin' Robin*, a song originally recorded by Bobby Day in 1958. Thirteen years later, this rock 'n' roll number was reborn in the studios of Motown in an electrifying version where country chords accompany each chorus. Michael Jackson met the Bähler brothers, John and Thomas, at these recording sessions. Working as arrangers for Motown at the time, they performed the backing vocals for this number. Michael became friendly with Tom, with whom he would work on many occasions in subsequent years. *Rockin' Robin* became one of the songs the young singer regularly performed on TV shows and on tour with The Jackson Five.

1972

Wings of My Love

The Corporation / 3'32

Musicians: (unknown) / **Michael Jackson:** lead vocals / **Backing vocals:** (unknown)
Recording: Motown Recording Studios, Los Angeles: July 1971 to January 1972
Technical team: Executive Producer: Berry Gordy / **Producers:** The Corporation / **Arrangements:** The Corporation and Gene Page / **Recording engineer:** Russ Terrana

The Corporation had great fun writing and producing *Wings of My Love*, a laid-back ballad in which Michael sings of a reassuring love. His melancholic delivery gives the number a Northern Soul feel, mixed with the kind of country tones that featured in Elvis Presley songs in the 1970s. Gene Page, a specialist in string arrangements who had also made his name in the world of film soundtracks, made the composition sublime by inserting notes that sprinkled a pinch of fairy dust here and there.

Maria (You Were the Only One)

George "Horgay" Gordy, Lawrence Brown, Allen Story, Linda Glover / 3'41

Musicians: (unknown) / **Michael Jackson:** lead vocals / **Backing vocals:** (unknown)
Recording: Motown Recording Studios, Los Angeles: July 1971 to January 1972
Technical team: Executive Producer: Berry Gordy / **Producer:** Hal Davis / **Arrangements:** James Carmichael / **Recording engineer:** Russ Terrana

Hal Davis produced *Maria* with the sense of theatricality in which he exceled. This little-known number tucked away in the grooves of the *Got to Be There* album is nevertheless a special track. The intro resonates like a clap of thunder, smashing open the love story, and echoing the subject's feelings about a sweetheart who has gone away. The bass drum produces rounded mute notes reminiscent of the raw soul sound of Detroit Motown. This heavy rhythm, although pleasant, seems to carry on forever, before giving way to the beat of a snare drum in pure Motown style. This two-beat pattern later appeared on *I Am Love*, an ambitious soul-rock number that opens The Jackson Five album, *Dancing Machine* (1974).

Love Is Here and Now You're Gone

Brian Holland, Lamont Dozier, Edward Holland Jr. / 2'51

Musicians: (unknown) / **Michael Jackson:** lead vocals / **Backing vocals:** (unknown)
Recording: **Motown Recording Studios, Los Angeles:** July 1971 to January 1972
Technical team: **Executive Producer:** Berry Gordy / **Producer:** Hal Davis / **Arrangements:** James Carmichael / **Recording engineer:** Russ Terrana

This song is another Hal Davis production, in which the spoken passages are clearly the forerunners of later songs like *P.Y.T.* or *The Girl Is Mine*. James Carmichael composed a second melody line for the chorus that responds to the main theme. The Supremes had recorded the song in 1967, which was released as a single and became the group's ninth No. 1 in the US pop and R&B charts. The cover version of this jazz standard written by the Holland-Dozier-Holland trio was a passing of the baton from Diana Ross to young Michael. Berry Gordy gave his protégé a first-class song on which to cut his teeth as a solo artist.

You've Got a Friend

Carole King / 4'45

Musicians: (unknown) / **Michael Jackson:** lead vocals / **Backing vocals:** (unknown)
Recording: **Motown Recording Studios, Los Angeles:** July 1971 to January 1972
Technical team: **Executive Producer:** Berry Gordy / **Producer:** The Corporation / **Arrangements:** The Corporation and Gene Page / **Recording engineer:** Russ Terrana

The album finishes as it started, with a cover version. Just like *Ain't No Sunshine* by Bill Withers, Michael did a version of a song that had recently been written and released by another artist, Carole King, who wrote the song in January 1971 for her album *Tapestry*. While *Got to Be There* opens with a bluesy feel and the story of a lost love, *You've Got a Friend* is an anthem to brotherhood and universal love. The young singer follows the melody right to the end, where his vocal exploits are a reminder that he had a gospel heritage and knew how to use it. There have been many cover versions of *You've Got a Friend*, from artists as diverse as Bing Crosby, Shania Twain, Dusty Springfield, and The Brand New Heavies. It is one of the greats in American music, and won two Grammy Awards: best pop performance for James Taylor, who recorded his version at the same time as King's, and song of the year for the songwriter.

1. BEN
2. GREATEST SHOW ON EARTH
3 PEOPLE MAKE THE WORLD GO 'ROUND
4. WE'VE GOT A GOOD THING GOING
5. EVERYBODY'S SOMEBODY'S FOOL
6. MY GIRL
7. WHAT GOES AROUND COMES AROUND
8. IN OUR SMALL WAY
9. SHOO-BE-DOO-BE-DOO-DA-DAY
10. YOU CAN CRY ON MY SHOULDER

Ben **ALBUM**

Released by Motown Records: USA, 4 October 1972 (ref. M 755L) / UK, December 1972 (ref. STML 11220)
Chart position: USA R&B No. 4, Pop No. 5 / UK No. 17

Poster for the movie *Ben*, directed by Phil Karlson and first screened on 23 June 1972.

BEN, A HASTY RELEASE

1972

Barely six months after his first solo project was released, Michael Jackson's second album for Motown, *Ben*, was launched. A string of productions, adding to those of The Jackson Five, considerably increased the young star's recording commitments, but Berry Gordy wanted this record out quickly because his label was repositioning itself on the market. Two economic and strategic factors also led to him prioritizing the album.

While producing *Lady Sings the Blues,* Berry Gordy had made some new contacts in the movie world. This led to him being asked to produce the theme song for the soundtrack to *Ben*, the sequel to *Willard* by Daniel Mann, and 1971's blockbuster movie. He chose the young Michael Jackson to lead his label's incursion into Hollywood, which he was determined to conquer.

Motown executives were keeping a close eye on the charts, worried by a particular phenomenon, a family group that were racing up the listings. The Osmonds were an MGM creation, a lineup of young white singers based on The Jackson Five model. They were stealing the limelight from Berry Gordy's protégés, already had a number of hits to their name, and were looking like they might make inroads into The Jackson Five's popularity. This would mean significant financial loss for Motown. Propelling Michael Jackson even further into his solo career seemed the obvious counterattack to fend off the smart maneuver by MGM Records, who were pushing the young Donny Osmond onto center stage.

Production

Ben's success was entirely down to the title track. Berry Gordy was executive producer on what was a very hastily conceived project that included the usual batch of cover versions: *People Make the World Go 'Round* by The Stylistics, *My Girl* by The Temptations, and *Shoo-Be-Doo-Be-Doo-Da-Day* by Stevie Wonder. Hal Davis and Bobby Taylor produced the album in close collaboration with the Mel Larsen / Jerry Marcellino duo. Several teams of writers were kept busy writing and composing the album's other tracks, which further contributed to the overall product's lack of musical coherence. There were a few little gems like *Greatest Show on Earth*, *In Our Small Way* (which had already appeared on the album *Got to Be There*), and *You Can Cry on My Shoulder*, composed by Berry Gordy.

The Jackson Five caught in a trap

More than ever, the Jackson brothers' careers were held captive to Motown's new, overriding ambitions. Any semblance of a rational approach had vanished in the face of Berry Gordy's insatiable desire to distribute more records. Their father, Joe Jackson, sounded the alarm and argued that his sons should be more involved instead of just singing the same cover versions that impoverished their albums. As 1972 came to a close, *Ben* was one issue that contributed to an oppressive atmosphere.

The first No. 1

The single was left to fend for itself in the charts while Motown's attention was completely focused on the movie

January 1973: Michael Jackson arrives at a party held to celebrate the success of his hit *Ben*, which had become a Gold record. He is carrying four pet rats on his shoulders. Randy is to his right. In the background: Jackie and Marlon.

Lady Sings the Blues. The track took everyone by surprise and gave Michael Jackson the very first No. 1 of his career. No other single was released to promote the album. A single of *Everybody's Somebody's Fool* was planned but in the end the project was canceled.

Motown dreams of the Oscars

As Berry Gordy's label strengthened its position, year on year, as leader in the promotion and distribution of great talent in African-American music, paradoxically it was a struggle to establish black actors in the movies and very hard for them to get a foot in the door at the Oscars. In 1940, Hattie McDaniel made history by becoming the first black woman to win an Academy Award, for her role as supporting actress in *Gone with the Wind*. But it was Sidney Poitier who really paved the way for change in 1964 when he received the Oscar statuette for best actor in a leading role in *Lilies of the Field*. The comedy actor from *Guess Who's Coming to Dinner?* became an icon for an entire generation. Mental attitudes were finally changing. Motivation and hope always spur artists into action, and Motown, which had every intention of being part of this sea change, set itself the goal of winning the award for best actress in a leading role for Diana Ross. Suzanne de Passe worked tirelessly writing a screenplay that would give the singer the opportunity to demonstrate her talents in the role of Billie Holiday, while Berry Gordy was busy managing the movie launch, leaving him very little time to devote to the careers of The Jackson Five.

The movie

The schedule was tight, as the movie *Ben* was planned for release in cinemas on 23 June 1972. A promotional 45 rpm was hastily pressed by the distribution company Cinerama and sent to radio stations on 17 June. It included two commercials for the movie and an exclusive presentation of the piece sung by Michael Jackson. The single was released on 12 July 1972, a couple of weeks after the movie came out.

Ben was the sequel to the hit movie *Willard*, the story of a rat trained to kill that gangs up with his fellow rats and turns against his owner. However, the sequel is the story of a slightly weird friendship between a sick child and a rat called Ben, who recruits other rats to attack humans. The motion picture is a paradox in itself. The day after it was released, critics were merciless. Vincent Canby slated it in the *New York Times*: "Trick photography, dreadful acting by a dreadful cast, the decline and fall of Phil Karlson (*The Phenix City Story*) as a director and a screenplay that never has the courage to acknowledge its comic impulses."[19]

Michael Jackson recalls seeing the movie many times. He liked the story, although the public found the friendship between a child and a rat very strange. He loved waiting for the credits to come up, and seeing his name on them. Michael bred rodents himself, to his mother Katherine's despair. Some family photos show him smiling proudly with no less than four rats on his shoulders.

BEN

Walter Scharf, Don Black / 2'42

From the film: *Ben* (Cinerama®)

Musicians
Michael Jackson: lead vocals
Backing vocals: (unknown)
Musicians: (unknown)
Recording
Motown Recording Studios, Los Angeles: November 1971 to February 1972
Technical team
Producers: The Corporation
Recording engineer: Russ Terrana
Arrangements: The Corporation

FOR JACKSON ADDICTS

With the success of the single *Ben* behind him, Michael Jackson recorded *Happy*, the love theme from the soundtrack of the movie *Lady Sings the Blues*. This went on to become one of the tracks on *Music and Me* (1973) his third solo album for Motown. To date, the movie version of the song *Ben* has never been produced as a separate recording (only available on DVD and Blu-ray).

1972

A-side: *Ben (stereo single version)* / 2'43
B-side: *You Can Cry on My Shoulder (stereo single version)* / 2'28
Released by Motown Records: USA, 12 July 1972 (ref. M 1207F) / UK, November 1972 (ref. TMG 834)
Chart position: USA R&B No. 5, Pop No. 1 / UK No. 7

Genesis

The title track for *Ben* was written by the English lyricist Don Black (Gerald Blackstone) and the American musician, conductor, and film score composer, Walter Scharf. *Ben* was originally planned to be sung by the teenage singer from The Osmonds, Donny Osmond, who appeared to have been booked for a tour. In January 2015, the artist recalled in *The Huffington Post*: "*Ben* was written for me...Michael and I would talk about this all the time. It's funny, because we eventually ended up laughing at this one. I will never forget, we stayed up to like two in the morning, laughing about the fact that I had a hit about a puppy (*Puppy Love*, 1972) and he had a hit about a rat."[20]

The song is a ballad about a touching and sentimental friendship between a child and a rat. The radio stations were largely unaware of the context and initially reluctant to give the song airtime. Some of Michael Jackson's close collaborators were amazed that the star once sung a love song to a rodent. Many years later, Thomas Bahler, author and composer of the famous track *She's Out of My Life,* admitted that, despite pressure from Quincy Jones, he had thought long and hard about giving his composition to Michael Jackson because he had once sung *Ben*.

Accomplishment

Ben was Michael Jackson's biggest hit at Motown, with worldwide sales of almost five million albums, but unfortunately very little is known about the production and recording of the song.

Ben increasingly broke away from the movie, becoming a global success in its own right. The single reached the No. 1 spot in the US charts on 14 October 1972 and remained in the *Billboard* Pop charts for 16 weeks. It was Michael Jackson's first No. 1 of his solo career and the only one at Motown. He had only just turned 14 years old. Over 1.7 million copies were sold in the US and more than 2.8 million worldwide.

From July to November 1972, Michael Jackson performed the song on TV shows such as *American Bandstand* and *The Sonny and Cher Comedy Hour.* CBS even broadcast a whole program on The Jackson Five.

The gap between the success of the song and that of the movie grew ever wider. However, the original album sleeve and some of the images on the single sleeves around the world clearly showed the connection between the two. In the magni-

Michael Jackson during a concert by The Jackson Five at the Inglewood Forum, Los Angeles, 26 August 1972.

ficent photo by Jim Britt, the creator of some legendary album sleeves on the African-American music scene, a horde of rats is shown in the foreground, led by Ben. But the rodents scared young audiences and stopped them from buying the album. So the label promptly removed them from the sleeves of new editions.

Ben definitively broke free of the movie when the song won the Golden Globe Award for best original song in 1973, while the movie did not make it into any category. Katherine Jackson remembers what Michael said when the songwriter went up to receive his prize without mentioning the young singer: "Mother, did you notice that in his acceptance speech the writer of *Ben* didn't thank me for singing the song and helping to make it a success? That he even didn't mention my name?"[9]

The track was nominated for best original song at the Oscars in 1973. However, neither Michael Jackson's rendition of the song nor Charlton Heston's introduction of the young prodigy was enough to land the precious trophy. Diana Ross also remained seated in the audience that night, missing out on an Oscar for best actress for her role in *Lady Sings the Blues*, with the award going to Liza Minnelli for *Cabaret*. Paradoxically, while there had been great expectations for Diana Ross, only Michael Jackson actually went up on stage at the Academy Awards, to perform the song.

Ben was one of the tracks that The Jackson Five and The Jacksons performed in all their tours up until 1981. At the *Victory Tour* concerts in 1984, Michael would begin the intro and then suddenly stop, saying that he wanted to sing another of his favorite tracks instead. It was all carefully staged, and audiences were in raptures. *Ben* was then sidelined and replaced by *Human Nature*, and would never be performed again. The hits from the album *Thriller* would progressively replace the hits of the past.

Today *Ben* still sounds fresh and charismatic, and there are now many remixes, some better than others.

Greatest Show on Earth

Mel Larson, Jerry Marcellino / 2'47

Musicians: (unknown) / **Michael Jackson:** lead vocals
Recording: **Motown Recording Studios, Los Angeles:** 1972
Technical team: **Producers:** Jerry Marcellino and Mel Larson / **Recording engineer:** Russ Terrana / **Arrangements:** James Carmichael

This original creation by the Larson / Marcellino duo, based on a circus theme, gave Michael Jackson the opportunity to sing a love song. The trapeze artists and sparkling carnival costumes that feature in the lyrics are all part of the song's imagery. The track is built around a rhythmic variation, starting off slowly then becoming faster and faster. Michael delivers his vocals with great agility and pushes his voice to go higher, although on the eve of his 14th birthday, there was a limit to how high he could go. "Get your ticket right away / Love, love, love / Is the greatest show on earth."

1972

People Make the World Go 'Round

Thom Bell, Linda Creed / 3'15

Musicians: (unknown) / **Michael Jackson:** lead vocals
Recording: **Motown Recording Studios, Los Angeles:** 1972
Technical team: **Producer:** Hal Davis / **Recording engineer:** Russ Terrana / **Arrangements:** Gene Page and John Bahler

In July 1972, The Stylistics achieved a respectable 20th place in the *Billboard* Pop 100 with this song, at the same time as Michael Jackson was already recording a cover version, confidently produced by Hal Davis.

The song builds thematic layers from issues such as the environment, money, strikes, and poverty, before coming to the conclusion: "But that's what makes the world go 'round." Its aim was to encourage change in an unequal and closed society. "Go underground young men / People make the world go 'round."

The same year, The Ramsey Lewis Trio also recorded a cover version in support of the activists' position at the 1972 PUSH Expo in Chicago. One of the organizers was the Reverend Jesse Jackson. The event brought together a large number of black artists who wanted to make their voices heard in protest at the ongoing segregation of African-Americans in society, businesses, and government. The song was one of the tracks on the live album, *Save the Children*. At the event, The Jackson Five, seen as symbols of hope, sung with greats such as Marvin Gaye, The Temptations, and Bill Withers. Michael also gave a solo performance of *I Wanna Be Where You Are*.

We've Got a Good Thing Going

The Corporation / 3'01

Musicians: (unknown) / **Michael Jackson:** lead vocals
Recording: **Motown Recording Studios, Los Angeles:** 1972
Technical team: **Producer:** The Corporation / **Recording engineer:** Russ Terrana / **Arrangements:** The Corporation

We've Got a Good Thing Going is a song about lasting love. In a confident serene tone, Michael sings: "My life I dedicate to lovin' her." The arrangements by The Corporation are precise and harmonious with some beautiful, warm, and dynamic backing vocals.

Repeated chords on the harpsichord open the piece. Michael whispers then continues with vocal variations in range. The teenager's declarations of love were becoming increasingly believable.

The song appeared for the first time on the B-side of *I Wanna Be Where You Are*.

Michael Jackson during the recording of the TV show *The Sonny and Cher Comedy Hour* for CBS in Los Angeles, 28 July 1972.

Everybody's Somebody's Fool

Gladys Hampton, Regina Adams, Ace Adams / 2'58

Musicians: (unknown) / **Michael Jackson:** lead vocals
Recording: Motown Recording Studios, Los Angeles: 1972
Technical team: Producers: Jerry Marcellino, Mel Larson, and Bobby Taylor / **Recording engineer:** Russ Terrana / **Arrangements:** Gene Page and John Bahler

As he frequently did, Bobby Taylor here harks back to the great blues and jazz classics with a new version of the hit *Everybody's Somebody's Fool* by Dinah Washington (1961). The weak instrumentation makes the track sound lifeless, and it fails to render all the melancholy of the subject: when it comes to love, *Everybody's Somebody's Fool*. Vocally, Michael cranks it up a notch in the second half of the piece, where the violins soar alongside another demonstration of his voice hitting the high notes. This track was originally planned as the second single in the album but the project ended up being canceled in December 1972 (ref. M 1218).

Michael Jackson on stage in 1972. Alongside his brothers, he performed some hits that were recorded as solo performances for Motown.

My Girl

William "Smokey" Robinson, Ronald White / 3'05

Musicians
Michael Jackson: lead vocals
Backing vocals: (unknown)
Musicians: (unknown)
Recording
Motown Recording Studios, Los Angeles: 1971 to 1972
Technical team
Producers: Jerry Marcellino and Mel Larson
Arrangements: James Carmichael and John Bahler

This song has often been forgotten in the various compilations of Jackson's Motown years, which is why it is generally unknown to the public. It could well have been produced by Bobby Taylor, but Jerry Marcellino's and Mel Larson's names appear in the credits. Berry Gordy asked the duo to work alongside the dedicated army of talented producers committed to developing the young singer's talents.

1972

The producers Mel Larson and Jerry Marcellino.

Genesis

In the mid-1960s, for a Miracles concert at the Apollo Theater in New York, Smokey Robinson and his friend Ronald White got together to write and compose the fabulous *My Girl*. The song was then taken up by The Temptations and it quickly became their biggest hit, topping many charts in 1964. It peaked internationally with the masterful version by the great Otis Redding, and would continue to be part of the collective unconscious with numerous cover versions by artists from Stevie Wonder to The Rolling Stones, and of course the young Michael Jackson.

In spring 1966, the Jackson brothers won their very first young talent show, held at Theodore Roosevelt High School in Gary, Indiana, with their version of *My Girl*. The song really set the ball rolling for the group, and played a very special role in Michael Jackson's solo career. "We won the citywide talent show when I was eight with our version of The Temptations' song *My Girl*. The contest was held just a few blocks away at Roosevelt High. From Jermaine's opening bass notes and Tito's first guitar licks to all five of us singing the chorus, we had people on their feet for the whole song. Jermaine and I traded verses while Marlon and Jackie spun like tops. It was a wonderful feeling for all of us to pass that trophy, our biggest yet, back and forth between us..."[2]

Production

The Jackson Five performed the song on many occasions and it became one of their mainstays, evolving with every performance. *My Girl* also appeared in various recordings from the Steeltown era (1968), but unfortunately was never really developed as a single. The solo version of the song was used on the album *Ben* in 1972. Michael Jackson's performance is remarkable for its passion, maturity, and sheer energy. Like *Who's Lovin' You,* also composed by Smokey Robinson and performed so well by the young star that his version is widely considered to be the best (see page 34), this latest cover version consolidated the success and fame of the young singer. He once again proved his vocal capabilities as he dared to measure himself against the versions of this song performed by the greatest black singers of the time. Only a few Irish and British 45 rpm versions gave the single a life independently from the album when they appeared as the B-side of the single *Morning Glow* in 1973.

Stevie Wonder, cowriter of *Shoo-be-doo-be-doo-da-day*.

What Goes Around Comes Around

Allen Levinsky, Arthur Stokes, Dana Meyers, Floyd Weatherspoon / 3'35

Musicians: (unknown) / **Michael Jackson:** lead vocals
Recording: Motown Recording Studios, Los Angeles: 1972
Technical team: Producer: Hal Davis / **Recording engineer:** Russ Terrana / **Arrangements:** Gene Page and John Bahler

Fresh and joyful, with simple harpsichord, flute, and tambourine variations, *What Goes Around Comes Around* addresses the trials and tribulations in Michael Jackson's love life. The tone is mocking. He taunts a girl who left him, only to be dumped herself: "Yeah baby, he put you down, now you're the clown / And you want me to come back home." Hal Davis' brilliant and lively resonances are a perfect match for Michael Jackson's vocals.

1972

In Our Small Way

Beatrice Verdi, Christine Yarian / 3'39

Musicians: (unknown) / **Michael Jackson:** lead vocals
Recording: Motown Recording Studios, Los Angeles: 1972
Technical team: Producer: The Corporation / **Recording engineer:** Russ Terrana / **Arrangements:** The Corporation and Eddy Manson

In Our Small Way had already appeared on the album *Got to Be There* and was given a second chance on *Ben*. Reusing this song was further evidence that *Ben* had to be produced quickly so that it could be released at the same time as the movie.

Shoo-Be-Doo-Be-Doo-Da-Day

Sylvia Moy, Henry Cosby, Stevie Wonder / 3'19

Musicians: (unknown) / **Michael Jackson:** lead vocals
Recording: Motown Recording Studios, Los Angeles: 1972
Technical team: Producer: Hal Davis / **Recording engineer:** Russ Terrana / **Arrangements:** James Carmichael

Hal Davis produced an up-tempo version with funk overtones of this Stevie Wonder tune from his 1968 album *For Once in My Life*. Michael gets into the groove and his vibratos can be heard throughout the three-minute piece. Listening to *Shoo-Be-Doo-Be-Doo-Da-Day*, it seems a shame that this was not done as a duet with Stevie Wonder, his Motown friend. But Michael's polished performance is a perfect tribute. It is another song about the trials and tribulations of love. The instrumentation is lavish and sparkling: bass guitar, trumpets, and drums are a divine combination, and make this track the best musical piece on the album. The song was not released as planned on the B-side of *Everybody's Somebody's Fool* (ref. M 1218).

The finest photographs of Michael Jackson at this time were shot by the official Motown photographer, Jim Britt. This photograph was on the back of the sleeve of the album *Ben* (1972).

You Can Cry on My Shoulder

Berry Gordy / 2′32

Musicians: (unknown) / **Michael Jackson:** lead vocals
Recording: Motown Recording Studios, Los Angeles: 1972
Technical team: Producer: Hal Davis / **Recording engineer:** Russ Terrana / **Arrangements:** Gene Page

In 1964, the single *You Can Cry on My Shoulder,* performed by Brenda Holloway, had made it no further than 116 on the *Billboard* charts. To complete the tracklist for *Ben*, the boss of Motown asked Hal Davis to rerecord the tune with Michael Jackson. With a more hard-hitting tempo than the original, Hal Davis achieves a real musical feat by giving the artist unusually free rein to express himself. The album finishes on a friendly note when Michael offers his shoulder to cry on to a young girl who has been unlucky in love.

1. WITH A CHILD'S HEART
2. UP AGAIN
3 ALL THE THINGS YOU ARE
4. HAPPY (LOVE THEME FROM "THE LADY SINGS THE BLUES")
5. TOO YOUNG
6. DOGGIN' AROUND
7. JOHNNY RAVEN
8. EUPHORIA
9. MORNING GLOW
10. MUSIC AND ME

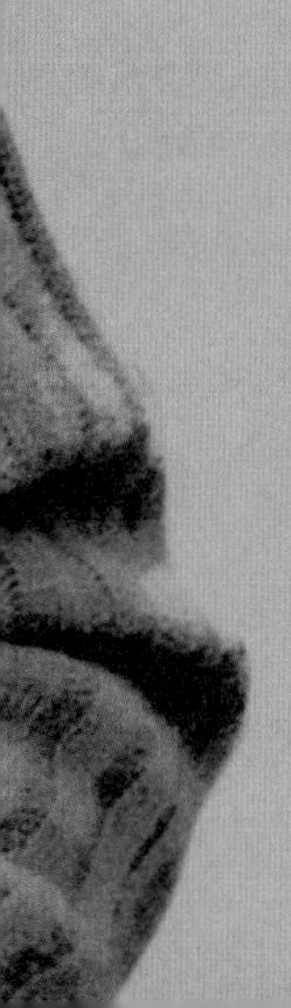

Music and Me **ALBUM**

Released by Motown Records: USA, 13 April 1973 (ref. M 767L) / UK, July 1973 (ref. STML 11235)
Chart position: USA R&B No. 24, Pop No. 92 / UK: no position

Michael Jackson during the photo shoot for the image used on the album *Music and Me* (1973).

MUSIC AND ME, A BREATH OF FRESH AIR

1973

Several weeks after the 45th Academy Awards ceremony, at which Michael Jackson performed the theme tune to the film *Ben*, Motown released the young artist's third solo album. At the same time, Motown also continued promoting *Skywriter* by The Jackson Five and the single *Hallelujah Day*.

Music and Me included two major tracks: *With a Child's Heart*, the opening track, and *Music and Me*, the closing track. Hal Davis was mostly in charge of the production of this album. As a result, it was much more cohesive musically than *Ben*, which had been hastily composed and distributed.

From the movies to Broadway

Many of the tracks on *Music and Me* are about film and musical comedies, choices that tell us much about the mood of the Motown executives at the time. The love theme from the movie *Lady Sings the Blues*, composed by Michel Legrand, inspired the song *Happy*. With lyrics by Smokey Robinson, the song revived the dashed hopes of the record label, or at least helped them recover from the disappointment of the movie losing out at the Oscars. In *Johnny Raven*, Michael steps into the boots of a wandering cowboy, and in *Morning Glow*, he imagines that he is Prince Charming in the musical *Pippin*.

Production

The main tracks have listeners drifting between daydreams and the exhilaration of love (*Euphoria*), while cover versions of the great anthems by the legends of black American music complete the tracklist with their solid reassuring presence. Michael gives an admirable rendition of *All the Things You Are*, another number from a Broadway musical (*Very Warm for May*), originally performed almost ten years earlier by the great Ella Fitzgerald. His rendition of Nat King Cole's hit *Too Young* can be seen as a gentle rejoinder to Donny Osmond's version that had been released as a single several weeks previously.

Music and Me was mostly about showcasing Michael Jackson's inspired vocals. His voice was still producing juvenile timbres as his voice was yet to break as adolescence approached.

Commercialization

In 1973, *With a Child's Heart* was the only solo single to be released virtually worldwide. Some of the album's other tracks were released as singles in certain regions, such as *Morning Glow* in the UK, but had little impact on the young artist's career. Re-pressed versions of *Music and Me* are rare both in vinyl and CD form; versions on different media, all abridged for some strange reason, reappeared intact on the CD box set *Michael Jackson—Hello World: The Motown Solo Collection* (ref. USA Motown / Hip-O Select B0012421-02) (2009). In 1982, somewhat surprisingly, the compilation *Michael Jackson—Motown Legends* (ref. DE TL 72308) reused nearly all the tracks from the album, and it feels almost like a rerelease.

A Motown Christmas

The year 1973 finished on a modest note for young Michael, who was asked to record *Little Christmas Tree* for the compilation *A Motown Christmas*, featuring carols by the big Motown stars.

WITH A CHILD'S HEART

Sylvia Moy, Henry Cosby, Vicki Basemore / 3'31

Musicians
Michael Jackson: lead singer
Musicians: (unknown)
Recording
Motown Recording Studios, Los Angeles: late 1972 to early 1973
Technical team
Producers: Freddie Perren and Fonce Mizell
Recording engineer: Russ Terrana
Arrangements: Freddie Perren

1973

HEADPHONES AT THE READY

The first version of the song began with a few notes on the xylophone that disappeared in subsequent rereleases of the album. From 1984 onwards, a few random compilations featured these three introductory seconds before they were definitively restored on the CD box set *Michael Jackson—Hello World: The Motown Solo Collection* (ref. USA Motown / Hip-O Select B0012421-02) (2009).

Single

A-side: *With a Child's Heart* (*stereo single version*) / 3'25
B-side: *Morning Glow* (*album version*) / 3'36
Released by Motown Records: USA, April 1973 (ref. M 1218)
Chart position: USA R&B No. 14, Pop No. 50

Genesis

When Stevie Wonder recorded this song for his album *Up-Tight* in 1966, the tone was more lighthearted. In Michael Jackson's version, the style and tempo were rearranged by Freddie Perrin and Fonce Mizell, two of the members of The Corporation, who had produced The Jackson Five's first successful hits. As a result, this song, the first track on the album, is quite different from the others. Melancholic and inward-looking, Michael takes a phlegmatic look at his life. The tone is serene, sometimes even meditative and perceptive.

Production

The pure, simple chords on the piano skillfully underline the singer's fragile aspirations. The backing vocals carry and reinforce this feeling of melancholy before being speedily dispatched by a series of undulations that oscillate then rise in rapid crescendo from a whisper to some outstanding vocal flights. With no filter to hold them back, the emotions shine out.

The single was distributed in North America, Europe (except Great Britain), and Japan. A limited number of records were pressed for small markets. They are among the rarest in Michael Jackson's career and are highly sought-after collectors' pieces, as this track is one of the favorites of fans of his solo period at Motown.

With a Child's Heart made a respectable showing in the charts, reaching No. 14 on the *Billboard* Top R&B, although it failed to surpass *Hallelujah Day*, which raced to No. 10 in almost the same amount of time.

FOR JACKSON ADDICTS

The song was used on the soundtrack for the Motown video *The Legend Continues* with images of Michael with children of all nations.

Michael and his brothers play with a boomerang while on a trip to Australia to perform a concert in July 1973.

Up Again

Freddie Perren, Christine Yarian / 2'47

Musicians: (unknown) / **Michael Jackson:** lead vocals
Recording: Motown Recording Studios, Los Angeles: 1973
Technical team: Producers: Freddie Perren and Fonce Mizell / **Recording engineer:** Russ Terrana / **Arrangements:** Freddie Perren and Fonce Mizell

Freddie Perrin (The Corporation) cowrote this piece and, like *With a Child's Heart*, it is full of contemplation and feelgood moments. Michael declares his love for a woman who stayed loyal to him during a painful moment in his life: "Girl when my life got stormy / You stayed for the ride / You stayed by my side / You make the sun shine." A sprinkle of magic is added to the ritornello with the appearance of the nursery rhyme character Humpty Dumpty as a metaphor for daydreaming. The backing vocals and the music calmly and discreetly accompany Michael's voice. With its fresh and positive feel, the track would have been ideal as part of a cartoon soundtrack.

All the Things You Are

Oscar Hammerstein II, Jerome Kern / 2'55

Musicians: (unknown) / **Michael Jackson:** lead vocals
Recording: Motown Recording Studios, Los Angeles: 1973
Technical team: Producers: Mel Larson and Jerry Marcellino / **Recording engineer:** Russ Terrana / **Arrangements:** James Carmichael

Michael Jackson injects empathy and energy into this song from the Broadway musical *Very Warm for May* (1939). The orchestra pushes his vocal range while the funky passages give him some rich variations. Several years earlier, in 1961, Ella Fitzgerald sung a jazz version of this tune (*Ella Fitzgerald Sings the Jerome Kern Songbook*). Michael Jackson's rendition is halfway between a feverish pre-funk and a brilliant orchestral version. The duo of producers, Mel Larson and Jerry Marcelino, accomplish a real feat of musical production with this track.

Michael Jackson and Donny Osmond at the first American Music Awards in Hollywood, 19 February 1974.

FOR JACKSON ADDICTS

Happy (Love Theme from Lady Sings the Blues) was released as a single in July 1983 and became globally known during the promotion of the Motown compilation *Michael Jackson plus The Jackson 5—18 Greatest Hits* (ref. UK CD, WD 72629). Multiple pressings of the single emerged around the world, including a magnificent picture disc that still delights collectors today.

Too Young is the title of an EP distributed in Mexico. It consists of four tracks from the album *Music and Me* (ref. MEX MOT-10692).

1973

Happy (Love Theme from Lady Sings the Blues)

Michel Legrand, William "Smokey" Robinson / 3'19

Musicians: (unknown) / **Michael Jackson:** lead vocals
Recording: Motown Recording Studios, Los Angeles: 1973
Technical team: Producer: Hal Davis / **Recording engineer:** Russ Terrana / **Arrangements:** Gene Page

Michael Jackson's cherubic voice was perfect for the melody of the love theme from Berry Gordy's beloved movie, *Lady Sings the Blues*. Two big names partnered up to write *Happy*: Michel Legrand, the French musician, composer, singer, and arranger (a friend of Quincy Jones since the mid-1960s), and the Motown tenor Smokey Robinson. It was a true meeting of minds and together they produced a joyful blues number especially written for young Michael's voice: "Sadness had been close as my next of kin / Then happy came one day, chased my blues away." Hal Davis' harpsichords play the music of love. The violins and backing vocals soar, reinforcing the theme.

Too Young

Sidney Lippman, Sylvia Dee / 3'37

Musicians: (unknown) / **Michael Jackson:** lead vocals
Recording: Motown Recording Studios, Los Angeles: 1973
Technical team: Producer: Hal Davis / **Recording engineer:** Russ Terrana / **Arrangements:** Gene Page

Too Young was recorded by the great Nat King Cole in 1951 before it became the hit we know today. On 10 June 1972, Donny Osmond, Michael Jackson's then rival, released the song as a single at MGM Records. Berry Gordy responded instantly by having his own protégé record it for the album *Music and Me*, produced by the highly experienced Hal Davis. Let battle commence! The rich instrumentation along with Michael Jackson's crystal-clear and well-balanced tonalities make his version indisputably the best. However, the song was never made into a single, to the great irritation of MGM executives. The young protégé ends the piece with a vocal demonstration that speaks volumes about his need to annihilate the competition. In this cockfight, it is interesting to note that *Too Young* is nevertheless a song about love that ends with a moral that the record label executives may well have reflected upon: "And then someday they may recall / We're not too young at all."

Leon Ware, a discreet but influential composer on the soul scene (2009).

Doggin' Around

Lena Agree / 2'52

Musicians: (unknown) / **Michael Jackson:** lead vocals
Recording: Motown Recording Studios, Los Angeles: 1973
Technical team: Producer: Hal Davis / **Recording engineer:** Russ Terrana / **Arrangements:** Gene Page

Originally recorded in 1960 by the legendary Jackie Wilson, *Doggin' Around* is a blues number in which the young Michael sings a beautiful homage to one of his great idols. The backing vocals fire up in the second half of the song like transcendent gospel, as Michael serenely delivers his flawless cover version. Michael warns: "You better stop / Your doggin' around… / I'm gonna have to put you down." The song was planned for release as a single in January 1974 (ref. USA M 1270) but the project was canceled. It did, however, come out as a single in the Netherlands, with *Up Again* as the B-side (ref. 5 C 006 94-738).

Johnny Raven

Billy Page / 3'31

Musicians: (unknown) / **Michael Jackson:** lead vocals / **Backing vocals:** (unknown)
Recording: Motown Recording Studios, Los Angeles: 1973
Technical team: Producer: Hal Davis / **Recording engineer:** Russ Terrana / **Arrangements:** Gene Page

The tone is set by the backing vocals in the intro: "He's born to be wild." Michael plays a wanderer or cowboy whose words are accompanied by tambourines, creating a rhythm like the sound of spurs as someone walks. In the song Michael wanders wild and free, breaking hearts wherever he goes. Forever the rebel, he sings: "I'm going to leave your nest girl / Another nest to try." The guitar and violins take turns to echo one another, creating a soundtrack straight out of a Western. The backing vocals complete the myth with their gospel-style call and response.

The introduction to Johnny Raven, longer on the original LP than on later editions and the first CD versions, was restored on the CD box set *Michael Jackson—Hello World: The Motown Solo Collection* (ref. USA Motown / Hip-O Select B0012421-02) (2009).

Euphoria

Leon Ware, Jacqueline D. Hilliard / 2'48

Musicians: (unknown) / **Michael Jackson:** lead vocals
Recording: Motown Recording Studios, Los Angeles: 1973
Technical team: Producer: Hal Davis / **Recording engineer:** Russ Terrana / **Arrangements:** Gene Page

Like a transfixed lover, Michael Jackson sings of an exhilarating love, his words illuminated by rainbows and flowers. This tune was composed by the great Leon Ware specifically to showcase the young singer's vocal talents. The music is restrained, the drums come in to accompany the voice as it soars. The bass guitar brings warmth and resonance, and the violins give a brilliant, sparkling touch to the overall composition.

Morning Glow

Stephen Schwartz / 3'36

Musicians
Michael Jackson: lead vocals
Musicians: (unknown)
Recording
Motown Recording Studios, Los Angeles: late 1972 to early 1973
Technical team
Producer: Bob Gaudio
Recording engineer: Russ Terrana
Arrangements: Dave Blumberg

1973

Logo of the musical *Pippin* (New York, 1976).

Single

A-side: *Morning Glow (album version)* / 3'36
B-side: *My Girl (album version)* / 3'08
Released by Motown Records: UK, 27 July 1973 (ref. TMG 863)

Genesis

Alongside the movie *Lady Sings the Blues*, Motown was co-funding the production of Stephen Schwartz' Broadway musical, *Pippin*. The story of the hazardous voyage undertaken by Charlemagne's son, Pippin, as he searches for meaning in his life, is gradually revealed in different songs performed against sumptuous medieval scenery. The script disregards historical facts in favour of the prince's noble quest. The show premiered on 23 October 1972 at the Imperial Theatre, New York.

Motown used brothers' fame to attract young audiences. They recorded *Corner of the Sky* with a theme taken from the musical's soundtrack. Their version appears on the *Skywriter* album; the single was released worldwide, except in Europe.

In 1973, when the musical first played in London, *Morning Glow* was released in the UK, recorded by Michael Jackson alone. It contains an extract from the show's soundtrack. The song is a poetic, schmaltzy ode to the diurnal cycle and to morning light, which Disney would have been happy to call their own: "Morning glow fill the earth / Come and shine for all you're worth."

Production

The arrangements by Dave Blumberg, originally written for the musical, worked well on the Michael Jackson version. You can hear Michael's voice gradually but noticeably acquiring an adult tonality. The low notes are deeper and the soaring high notes reach his limits, which the young singer must have found frustrating. The electric guitar resonates, providing a musical cycle that perfectly echoes the song's theme. The undulating and unique timbre of the instrument seems to mimic the plucking of a zither.

The single went unnoticed in the UK. The promotional 45 rpm version included a leaflet about the Broadway show: "Follow-up to *Ben*, which turned into Michael's biggest hit world-wide, is a tune from the current Broadway smash show, *Pippin*. The show has already given The Jackson Five a US million-seller with *Corner of the Sky*, and this tune has much the same potential. Michael's delivery, as always, is amazingly perceptive—he really is developing a vocal style all of his own. He handles this Stephen Schwartz song with the kind of zest that would steal any show. On the B-side is Michael's much requested version of *My Girl*."

Music and Me

Jerry Marcellino, Mel Larson, Don Fenceton, Mike Cannon / 2'35

Musicians
Michael Jackson: lead vocals
Musicians: (unknown)
Recording
Motown Recording Studios, Los Angeles: late 1972 to early 1973
Technical team
Producers: Mel Larson and Jerry Marcellino
Recording engineer: Russ Terrana
Arrangements: James Carmichael

Michael Jackson poses for the magazine *Right On!* in the family home in Encino, 28 November 1972.

Genesis

Music and Me feels introspective in the same way as *With a Child's Heart*. The song seems to express Michael Jackson's love and passion for music. The simple lyrics are sung calmly, without haste or overly demonstrative vocal variations. The tune was recorded just as the young boy was losing the reedy texture to his voice, and his new timbre brought a tender softness that listeners may find moving. His adult voice was still struggling to assert itself over the child's high-pitched tonalities, but his natural development pushed him to produce a new warm and gentle tone. Like a faithful friend, music accompanies him wherever he goes as the metaphors stack up during the short 2'35 track. The song finishes on a high note, as if to mark his eternal connection with music.

Production

In the intro, the melancholic tone is set by an acoustic guitar solo, quickly joined by a violin ensemble that intensifies the song's solemn feel. The album cover shows Michael Jackson posing with a guitar, although he did not play one. The superb image by photographer Jim Brett is therefore ambiguous, but mainly intended to convey the message that strings provide most of the instrumentation on the album. A light and discreet drumbeat punctuates the music like heartbeats. Trumpets put in a few rare appearances to extol this passionate love of music. Michael had to do several takes to find the right vocal range and pitch for his new timbre. Many fans hope that one day these extra takes will be added as a bonus to a rerelease or a Motown compilation.

Single

A-side: *Music and Me* (album version) / 2'35
B-side: *Johnny Raven* (album version) / 3'31
Released by Motown Records: UK, May 1974 (ref. TMG 900)

[**BONUS TRACK**]

LITTLE CHRISTMAS TREE

George Clinton, Artie Wayne / 3'37

From the compilation: *A Motown Christmas*
Released by Motown Records: USA, September 1973 (ref. M 795V2) / UK, November 1976 (ref. STML 12037)
Chart position: USA *Billboard* Christmas No. 1

Musicians
Michael Jackson: lead vocals
Michael, Jermaine, Tito, Jackie, and Marlon Jackson: backing vocals
Musicians: (unknown)
Recording
Motown Recording Studios, Los Angeles: summer 1973
Technical team
Producers: Mel Larson and Jerry Marcellino

1973

George Clinton, inventor of P-Funk, circa 1970.

Single

A-side: *Little Christmas Tree (single version)* / 3'33
B-side: The Jackson 5: *Have Yourself a Merry Little Christmas (stereo single version)* / 5'10
Released by Motown Records: The Netherlands, September 1974 (ref. 5C 006-96 007)

Genesis

Many artists produce a Christmas album at some point in their careers. Every year, Christmas carols and other original productions are released in this musical tradition, which of course included recordings from Motown artists. The Jackson Five were no exception. In the second year of their meteoric rise to fame, they delivered a Christmas album that reached the top of the special *Billboard* Christmas charts. Although this kind of production often only has limited artistic impact, the way that the record business worked at the time meant that labels could capitalize on their protégés' popularity and generate substantial income.

In 2009, Artie Wayne, the co-author of *Little Christmas Tree*, wrote a blog post about how he got the idea of pitching a Christmas tune to Motown as a natural follow-up to the success of the single *Ben*.

In 1973, Wayne was responsible for pitching music written by authors at Warner Brothers Music to other record companies. He realized that only a cover version by The Jackson Five or young Michael would be good enough for his boss. So he approached Jerry Marcellino and Mel Larson, as he knew they loved the work of the great George Clinton, Warner Brothers' staff writer. Artie Wayne discovered that Berry Gordy had just asked his producers to come up with new recordings for Michael Jackson. So he suggested a Christmas song, a track that would sell as well as *Ben*. Jerry Marcellino and Mel Larson were interested in the proposal. Wayne claimed, untruthfully, that he and George Clinton had already begun writing a Christmas tune for Michael and he promised to return the following Monday so they could listen to it. To substantiate his claim, he said that the song was based on the true story of how his girlfriend left him outside in the cold, like the last unsold tree in a Christmas tree lot. Artie Wayne then put in an urgent call to Clinton, who was obviously completely unaware of the commitment made on his behalf. On the Saturday morning, the two men met up for an initial session where first a verse and then a chorus gradually took shape. By Monday morning, George had already recorded a piano-voice demo, which Wayne rushed over to Marcellino and Larson as promised. They loved what they heard and chose the tune for their album without hesitation.

Michael Jackson in a three-piece suit, 1973. *Little Christmas Tree* was the only solo Christmas song he recorded in his career.

Production

Michael Jackson then recorded the song, which it was hoped would match the success of *Ben*. But what followed was somewhat disappointing. Berry Gordy decided not to use *Little Christmas Tree* because *Ben* had just been nominated for an Oscar, and he did not want to release anything before the awards ceremony in case it affected the chances of winning.

Several days later, Artie Wayne pitched a compilation of Christmas songs by Motown artists including his own creation *Little Christmas Tree*. *A Motown Christmas* was completed and released in late 1973, topping the *Billboard* Christmas charts. Wayne was delighted to see his tune published as one of the tracks, but it went largely unnoticed. The Netherlands was the only territory to release the tune as a single—the 45 rpm is now one of the rarest objects from Michael Jackson's solo career. In 1999, the double LP *A Motown Christmas* was rereleased as a CD, thus making the tune available to many more fans. In 2003, *Little Christmas Tree* ended up as a bonus track on the anniversary rerelease of *Christmas Album* by The Jackson Five. It went on to appear on the many subsequent releases.

The Jackson Five perform *Dancing Machine* during the *Bob Hope Special* TV show in Los Angeles, 26 September 1973.

[THE JACKSON 5]

Dancing Machine

Hal Davis, Don Fletcher, Weldon Dean Parks / 3'12

From the album: *Get It Together*
Released by Motown Records: USA, 12 September 1973 (ref. M 783VI) / UK, November 1973 (ref. STML 11243)
Chart position: USA R&B No. 4, Pop No. 100

Musicians
Michael and Jermaine Jackson: lead vocals
Michael, Jermaine, Tito, Jackie, and Marlon Jackson: backing vocals
Arthur Wright and Dean Parks: guitar
James Gadson: drums
Recording
Sound Factory Studio, Los Angeles: instrumental tracks
Record Plant Studio, Los Angeles: vocals and backing vocals
1973
Technical team
Producer: Hal Davis
Arrangements: Arthur Wright
Vocal arrangements: James Carmichael

1973

Genesis

The Jackson Five had not been in the American Top Ten since December 1971 and, after their success with *Sugar Daddy*, they experienced a major crisis throughout 1972 and 1973. It was as if bubble-gum soul had run out of steam. Record sales fell, and the public became more interested in a new kind of music that was all the rage on the dance floors: disco. The five brothers had grown, and Michael's voice had begun to break. All this meant that the group could not continue relying on a musical style that, however successful, was no longer commercially viable in the mid-1970s. Berry Gordy took stock of the situation and decided to break the mold that had ended up imprisoning The Jackson Five. The *Skywriter* album had mostly been arranged by The Corporation team so the Motown boss decided to shuffle his cards and entrust the new Jackson album to Hal Davis. Like Norman Whitfield, who had given The Temptations a new musical style in the early 1970s, Davis reinvented The Jackson Five's sound, slotting them in somewhere between funk and disco.

Get It Together, the album that emerged from these sessions, included mostly cover versions of songs by artists such as The Temptations and Gladys Knight and The Pips. *Dancing Machine* was the work of the trio Davis, Fletcher, and Parks, who in a different time and place could have taken over from The Corporation. The song was fine-tuned for the dance floor, and a break was written in to give young Michael an opportunity to display his dancing skills on stage.

In the early 1970s, *Soul Train* hired young dancers who showcased new dance steps, originating from street dancing.

Dancing Machine took The Jackson Five back into the US Top 10. The song reached No. 1 in the Top R&B and No. 2 in the pop charts. It was so successful that Motown, always with a keen business eye, marketed an extended album version of *Get It Together*, called *Dancing Machine*, which failed to match the success of the original. The title track appears as a shorter 2'41 version—a good excuse to have *Get It Together* in your collection.

Single

A-side: *Dancing Machine (single version)* / 2'35
B-side: *It's Too Late to Change the Time (single version)* / 3'53
Released by Motown Records: USA, 19 February 1974 (ref. M 1286F) / UK, June 1974 (ref. TMG 904)
Chart position: USA R&B No. 1, Pop No. 2

FOR JACKSON ADDICTS

Patricia Davies and Gary Keys, two *Soul Train* dancers, spent hours at the Jacksons' house teaching young Michael the robot walk. On 13 October 1973, while the brothers were recording *Dancing Machine* for *Soul Train*, the producer Don Cornelius gave Michael permission to direct the cameraman. The young singer had been disappointed by his first performance to the track on the *Bob Hope Show* a month earlier, and asked the cameraman to film him close up during the break in the song. This was how the robot walk in *Dancing Machine* became a step that was imitated the following day by many teenagers at school as well as in the discos.

The Jackson family, who frequently appeared on the program, approached some of the dancers. Michael had noticed the robot walk, which he then choreographed into the Jacksons' live performances of *Papa Was a Rolling Stone*.

This was the golden age of *Soul Train* and groundbreaking dance steps, and *Dancing Machine* served as an homage to the *Soul Train* girls and their sensual hip movements.

Production

When James Gadson sat down at the drums at the Motown studio in Los Angeles to record *Dancing Machine*, he played a totally improvised break. The song's producer, Hal Davis, and his arranger, Arthur Wright, looked at each other in surprise. After a short consultation, they asked Gadson to play the break again. The drummer thought they did not approve and was worried he was going to lose his job. In fact, the exact opposite happened, and that is why there is an audible kick drum during the break.

The *Dancing Machine* sessions allowed the group to break away from the oppressive 2'30 format; the published version on the *Get It Together* album lasts 3'24. *Dancing Machine* was edited and cut for the album, which has many of the features of a concept album, and the song itself resembles a long and wonderful jam session. The final version was 4'25 long, and Berry Gordy briefly considered using it for the promising new maxi single market. *Dancing Machine* was the first sign of the group's growing preference for long tunes crammed with breaks and repeats, however, they were only able to fully indulge this preference after leaving Motown in 1975. The long version ended up appearing on a wonderful compilation of previously unpublished tunes called *I Want You Back—Unreleased Masters*, released by Motown in 2009.

PORTRAIT

DON CORNELIUS
SOUL BROTHER

That voice. Don Cornelius (1936–2012) had a way of making his every utterance seem like a solemn declaration of utmost importance. Every time he introduced or interviewed artists on his TV show *Soul Train,* his choice of words, intonation, and pronunciation were instantly engraved on viewers' memories. Cornelius, an ardent supporter of the Civil Rights movement, began his career as a journalist before launching *Soul Train*, which he presented from its very beginnings in 1971 up until 1993. The program was initially broadcast only in the Chicago area, but in 1972 shifted its home base to Los Angeles, where it became a point of convergence for all the top R&B and soul artists. This meteoric success encouraged Dick Clark to launch a copycat program called *Soul Unlimited*. With the support of the Reverend Jesse Jackson, Cornelius claimed that this was unfair competition, and forced ABC to stop broadcasting their program.

Don Cornelius in 1973 on the set of *Soul Train,* the show he presented until the early 1990s.

Save the Children

In the early 1970s, singers such as Marvin Gaye, James Brown, and Stevie Wonder gave soul music a social conscience. As well as getting kids to dance, Cornelius used *Soul Train* to broadcast Martin Luther King Jr.'s message to an America suffering from a social and moral crisis. He wanted to remind people that they should be proud to be black in a world where segregation and discrimination still existed. The Jackson Five was a fine role model: a black family from humble origins who had achieved success in an industry that was too often restricted to whites. On 27 September 1972, at the Save the Children charity concert during the Black Expo Festival, organized in association with Jesse Jackson's Operation PUSH (People United to Save Humanity), Don Cornelius welcomed the Jackson brothers on stage by making the claim that they were children who had been saved and who were going to help save others. Although The Jackson Five had already participated in some charity events in previous years, the Save the Children episode made their involvement in humanitarian work official. Michael Jackson would continue to show the same kind of generosity throughout his life.

Dancing Machine

As the careers of The Jackson Five enjoyed a second wind thanks to the album *Get It Together*, and in particular the track *Dancing Machine*, Don Cornelius invited the group to appear on *Soul Train* on 3 November 1973. Michael executed some robotic dance steps that marked a milestone in the maturity of his style. It was as if the raw passion of James Brown had merged with the crazy grace of Fred Astaire.

Michael's affiliation with *Soul Train* did not stop there. The young singer spent a lot of time watching the dancers inventing and polishing dance steps that he absorbed and integrated into his own performances. He hired the best dancers from the Electric Boogaloos, including Jeffrey Daniel, who was encouraged by Cornelius to join the group Shalamar and who also helped Michael Jackson perfect his street-dancing style and technique.

When We Grow Up

Stephen J. Lawrence, Shelley Miller / 2'21

From the TV show: *Free to Be...You and Me*
Broadcast: USA, 11 March 1974 (ABC)

Musicians
Michael Jackson: lead vocals
Roberta Flack: lead vocals
Musicians: (unknown)
Recording
Motown Recording Studios, Los Angeles: 1974
Technical team
Producers: Stephen J. Lawrence and Bruce Hart
Arrangements: James Carmichael

Marlo Thomas, founder of the children's educational project *Free to Be... You and Me*.

For Jackson Addicts

The TV show that had *When We Grow Up* sung by Michael Jackson and Roberta Flack, was rereleased as a DVD in the 2000s (Hen's Tooth Label). On 19 October 2010, Marlo Thomas rereleased the video. The duet was not released as a record, the only song with different singers on the album and TV show.

Genesis

In the early 1970s, the actress, producer, and activist Marlo Thomas had the idea of creating a collection of children's stories with no gender stereotypes. It was called *Free to Be...You and Me.* The aim was to avoid infantilizing children by telling them stereotypical stories. It was about giving them the means to find and understand their place in the world.

Marlo Thomas wanted the project to raise money for charity, so she decided to donate the proceeds to the Ms Foundation for Women. The president of the charity, Gloria Steinem, introduced Thomas to the journalist and feminist, Letty Cottin Pogrebin. Thomas and Pogrebin were looking for a producer for the album that would accompany the book. They chose Carole Hart, known for her work on *Sesame Street*.

Free to Be...You and Me would be accompanied by an audio album and a TV show with a dream cast that saw Marlo Thomas starring alongside Harry Belafonte, Mel Brooks, and Diana Ross.

Production

The first version of *When We Grow Up* was recorded for the album that accompanied the book (published in November 1972). Diana Ross accepted Marlo Thomas's invitation to perform this gentle ballad about the dreams every child can have. In early 1974, the author signed an agreement with ABC to make a televised version of the book. The program was broadcast for the first time on 11 March 1974, and was then made into a VHS video.

Although Diana Ross had made time in her schedule for the album, her busy life as a solo singer, actress, and mother meant that she was unable to join the cast of the show. That was how Michael Jackson, Diana's "godson" in the music profession, was invited to perform the song as a duet for the TV version. Marlo Thomas and the producers approached the singer Roberta Flack, who was riding a wave of popular success at the time, notably with her rendition of *Killing Me Softly*. The two recorded their vocals on a track that had already been cut for the 1972 album version. This new rendition was used as the soundtrack for a sequence featuring Michael Jackson and Roberta Flack on the ABC program.

Over the years, the *Free to Be* franchise created by Thomas became part of the wider public consciousness and spawned other projects. A follow-up, *Free to Be...A Family,* appeared in 1987.

FOREVER, MICHAEL

1. WE'RE ALMOST THERE
2. TAKE ME BACK
3 ONE DAY IN YOUR LIFE
4. CINDERELLA STAY AWHILE
5. WE'VE GOT FOREVER
6. JUST A LITTLE BIT OF YOU
7. YOU ARE THERE
8. DAPPER-DAN
9. DEAR MICHAEL
10. I'LL COME HOME TO YOU

Forever, Michael **ALBUM**

Released by Motown Records: USA, 16 January 1975 (ref. M 6-825S1) / UK, March 1975 (ref. STMA 8022)
Chart position: USA R&B No. 10, Pop No. 101

1975

FOREVER, MICHAEL, FAREWELL TO MOTOWN

The 1974 season saw The Jackson Five back on center stage, once again to public acclaim, this time with *Dancing Machine*. Motown decided to capitalize on this song taken from *Get It Together* (1973) and even produced an album called *Dancing Machine*, mostly composed of previously recorded songs that had not been used on the group's other albums (see page 90).

These projects delayed the launch of Michael's fourth solo album, originally due to be released in 1974. By then, Berry Gordy was totally absorbed in his movie projects. He was convinced that Motown should be spelt out in huge letters on the Hollywood Hills, and some felt that he was increasingly neglecting the management of his record label. It was in this environment that the executive producers who had helped build the company's reputation took charge of operations and ensured that *Forever, Michael* saw the light of day.

A changing voice

In 1973, Michael Jackson's voice began to break and he was forced to confront the painful reality of puberty. His voice became harsher and lower, enabling him to produce some great vocals to funky rhythms like those on *Dancing Machine*. But on the whole, this natural change caused problems for the songwriters who had been asked to create new songs for him. The young artist could now no longer sing the cheeky pop songs that had been characteristic of the Jackson sound for several years, and it was still too early to challenge him with more adult tracks.

Berry Gordy put Brian and Edward Holland Jr. in charge of the repertoire of The Jackson Five's lead vocalist. At the time, the two brothers were suing Gordy for unpaid royalties, but the parties came to an arrangement. Lamont Dozier, the third brain in this magic trio, had left the team in 1973. The Holland brothers worked well together without Dozier, however, and they composed and produced three songs for *Forever, Michael*: *We're Almost There*, *Take Me Back*, and *Just a Little Bit of You*. On these mid-tempo numbers, Michael's voice sought out new notes, but the young star struggled to work his magic. He had potential and a great deal of promise, but on this occasion he hit a glass ceiling.

Hal Davis once again stepped in and produced four classic tracks that were occasionally permeated by the melancholy that would feature in some of Michael Jackson's subsequent melodies. The album took shape with a contribution from Sam Brown, *One Day in Your Life*, a ballad that quietly but forcefully attempted to present a new Michael Jackson. Brown was the one who came closest to understanding the young man's musical ambitions. But he was in no position to compete with staff writers and producers such as Davis and the Holland brothers, and the album was built around some songs that lacked the necessary touch of genius.

From Motown to CBS

The album came out in early 1975 in the midst of a rather tense situation at Motown. Joe Jackson had repeatedly made it clear to Berry Gordy that he was dissatisfied with the way his sons were being treated at the label. In April 1974, the Jackson clan had taken a step back by performing a series of concerts

Michael, assisted by his little sister, Janet, presents the award for best soul group of the year 1975 to Gladys Knight & The Pips, at the American Music Awards (Santa Monica, 18 February 1975).

at the MGM in Las Vegas, which gave all nine children the opportunity to strut their stuff on stage.

Michael Jackson ended up siding with his father and confronting Berry Gordy, telling him that he too felt that his style was being cramped at the label. Deprived of any artistic freedom, it became his duty to support his family and represent his brothers' interests. For a 16-year-old boy, this was a lot of pressure. But as the true professional that he had become, he continued promoting the album on TV shows. His friend Dick Clark was always delighted to host him on *American Bandstand*.

Forever, Michael was completely snubbed by the American and British pop charts, achieving a No. 10 spot in the Top R&B as the consolation prize. Only the hard-core fans stood by Motown's beloved child star. The creative split between the Jackson family and the record label was now obvious, and the family decided to take charge of its own destiny. On 28 May 1975, The Jackson Five signed a contract with CBS and Epic Records. In the months prior to this relaunch of their careers, morale within the family, and in particular in Michael's case, had been extremely low. One of the consequences of the family's battle with Motown had been Jermaine's decision to remain at the label, as by then he was married to Berry Gordy's daughter. Michael would therefore no longer have his brother by his side in the studio or on stage. Given the atmosphere, it was hard to put body and soul into producing and promoting an album whose title was both ironic and a prediction. Michael Jackson's career certainly turned out to be long lasting, a rare occurrence in the pop world, but the best artistic chapters of that career would be written at a rival label.

We're Almost There

Brian Holland, Edward Holland Jr. / 3'41

Musicians
Michael Jackson: lead vocals
Backing vocals: (unknown)
Musicians: (unknown)
Recording
Motown Recording Studios, Los Angeles: June to November 1974
Technical team
Producer: Brian Holland
Arrangements: James Carmichael
Mixing and recording: L.T. Horn

1975

We're Almost There was a much underestimated song for many years but was reevaluated in 2001 when DJ Spinna remixed the track for the compilation *Soul Source Jackson 5 Remixes 2*, published in Japan.

USA, 1975
A-side: *We're Almost There* (*single version*) / 3'33
B-side: *Take Me Back* (*alternate version*) / 3'29
UK, 1981
A-side: *We're Almost There* (*single version*) / 3'38
B-side: *We've Got a Good Thing Going* (*album version*) / 2'59
Released by Motown Records: USA, February 1975 (ref. M 1341F) / UK, July 1981 (ref. TMG 977)
Chart position: USA R&B No. 7, Pop No. 54 in 1975 / USA R&B No. 4, Pop No. 23 in 1981 / UK No. 46 in 1981

Genesis

The Holland brothers, who had been called in to breathe new life into Michael Jackson's solo career, were doing their best for Motown but were struggling to build a solid and convincing narrative to suit the young singer. *We're Almost There* makes a good attempt to distill some good, infectious vibes. In the lyrics, Michael sings about believing in, and wanting to reach, that distant point on the horizon where happiness becomes reality: "Look at the lonely lovers / That didn't make it." The Holland brothers guide the young man by showing him what he needs to avoid. *We're Almost There* provides a life lesson on attaining happiness that the adolescent is doing his best to assimilate. Will he succeed? The other tracks on the album are an often rather clumsy attempt to answer this question.

Production

The breadth of the rhythm in *We're Almost There*, with its double snare drum track, was ambitious in scope and very probably ahead of its time. In 1975, funk and disco rhythms were still binary, while in this track a drum resonates, filling time and space. The intro comes in, driven by bass drum rolls and soaring brass, giving the impression that young Michael is enticing us aboard a cruise ship where all of life's promises will be fulfilled. The polished production is a clear indication that Motown was counting on this track to help the album do well in the charts. Vocally, the singer tackles the lyrics head on, giving the song a funky touch reminiscent of his performances with The Jackson Five. James Carmichael adjusted the balance between strings and brass to emphasize the different sections in the tune. At the time, only R&B fans would have been aware of the track's sheer inventiveness. In 1981, a maxi single identical to the single version was released as a 3'33 disco mix.

Michael Jackson in Beverly Hills Gardens Park, Los Angeles,1973.

Take Me Back

Brian Holland, Edward Holland Jr. / 3'29

Musicians: (unknown) / **Michael Jackson:** lead vocals / **Backing vocals:** (unknown) / **Recording: Motown Recording Studios, Los Angeles:** June to November 1974 / **Technical team: Producer:** Brian Holland / **Recording engineer:** Russ Terrana / **Arrangements:** James Carmichael / **Mixing and recording:** L T Horn

Take Me Back is a mid-tempo song in which Michael begs his lover to have him back again. It follows a linear beat that creates an unexpectedly soft disco ambience. This collaboration between the young artist and the remaining members of the Holland-Dozier-Holland trio sounds a little like a missed opportunity. The melody, wrapped up in the arrangements written by James Carmichael, brings little relief. It is an attempt to echo the theatrical effects of the great jazz standards created by the Holland brothers in the past, but instead gives the impression that no one involved in the production was willing to take any risks. The song merely continues its sedate rhythm, and even a change in the chord structure is too weak to make any difference.

An alternative version of *Take Me Back* appears on the B-side of the US 45 rpm of *We're Almost There* with a few short ad-libs that make it slightly different.

ONE DAY IN YOUR LIFE

Sam Brown III, Renee Armand / 4'15

Musicians
Michael Jackson: lead vocals
Backing vocals: (unknown)
Musicians: (unknown)
Recording
Motown Recording Studios, Los Angeles: October to November 1974
Technical team
Producer and arranger: Sam Brown III
Recording engineer: Russ Terrana
Mixing and recording: L T Horn

1975

FOR JACKSON ADDICTS

In fall 1975, Johnny Mathis recorded his own version of *One Day in Your Life* on his album *Feelings*. Produced by Jack Gold and arranged by Gene Page, it came out as a single but failed to reach the popular US Top 40.

UK, 1975 and 1981
A-side: *One Day in Your Life (album version)* / 4'15
B-side: *With a Child's Heart (album version)* / 3'00
USA, 1981
A-side: *One Day in Your Life (single version)* / 4'08
B-side: *Take Me Back (album version)* / 3'23
UK, 1981
A-side: *One Day in Your Life (album version)* / 4'15
B-side: *Take Me Back (album version)* / 3'23
Released by Motown Records: USA, March 1981 (ref. M 1512 F) / UK, April 1975 (ref. TMG 946), May 1981 (ref. TMG 976)
Chart position: USA R&B No. 42, Pop No. 55 in 1981 / UK No. 1 in 1981

Genesis

Sam Brown III, a promising songwriter who created *One Day in Your Life* with the help of Renee Armand, who was also working at the time with the Ohio Players, Dusty Springfield, and The Carpenters, with whom she recorded the song *Lost* in 1971. Brown came up with a romantic ballad, a genre of which Michael Jackson was particularly fond. In a far cry from the friendship with the rat that he once sung about in *Ben*, here Michael recalls a wonderful past love. The songwriters took the singer's talent seriously by having him sing lyrics that describe memories and thoughts normally more appropriate for an older person. The composition relies on long crescendo notes, adapted to the young man's deeper tone of voice. The chorus takes flight just like the one in *Got to Be There* several years earlier.

Production

One Day in Your Life was recorded at the end of the *Forever, Michael* sessions, and showcases a Michael Jackson with a slightly deeper, more self-assured voice. Sam Brown's production, which uses guitar arpeggios like waves on the surface of a lake, creates a nostalgic feel. It was a classic production, which helped to ensure that the song would not date and was suitable for all the charts. It was only released in the UK in 1975, but British audiences snubbed the 45 rpm and it did not enter the UK charts. The song rose from the ashes in 1981, at the time when the *Off The Wall* album was enjoying international success. Motown decided to capitalize on the catalog of its former child prodigy, and reissued the song as a single in the US and the UK. American audiences continued to give it a lukewarm reception but in Europe the song was successful and the record was regularly played in nightclubs, at a time when slow dances were still popular on dance floors at the end of the night.

Michael Jackson during a trip to Jamaica with his family, 28 February 1975.

Cinderella Stay Awhile

Mack David, Michael Burnett Sutton / 3'11

Musicians: (unknown) / **Michael Jackson:** lead vocals / **Backing vocals:** (unknown)
Recording: Motown Recording Studios, Los Angeles: June to November 1974
Technical team: Producer: Hal Davis / **Recording engineer:** Russ Terrana / **Arrangements:** David Blumberg / **Mixing and recording:** L T Horn

Cinderella Stay Awhile was co-written by Mack David, who notably wrote the lyrics to *Bibbidi-Bobbidi-Boo* for the Disney film Cinderella (1950). The young Michael Burnett Sutton composed the music to accompany the lyrics and pitched the song to Hal Davis. Davis brought his funk expertise to the piece, using sound effects that portrayed to perfection the magical world described in the lyrics. For Michael, the song was a playground where he could have fun with what was essentially an extension of the disco and psychedelic feel of the ambitious tracks that The Jackson Five had recorded for the album *Get It Together*.

We've Got Forever

Mack David, Elliot Wilenski / 3'12

Musicians: (unknown) / **Michael Jackson:** lead vocals / **Backing vocals:** (unknown)
Recording: Motown Recording Studios, Los Angeles: June to November 1974
Technical team: Producer: Hal Davis / **Recording engineer:** Russ Terrana / **Arrangements:** James Carmichael / **Mixing and recording:** L T Horn

We've Got Forever reunited a prestigious duo of writers: Mack David, who wrote numerous musical scores for American TV as well as for the English adaptation of Edith Piaf's *La Vie en Rose*, and Elliott Wilenski, who features in the Jacksonian story as the man who wrote young Michael's first solo track, *Got to Be There*. These two artists, who had also built their reputations on Broadway, reunited to compose a song that directly alludes to the name of the album. Like an attempt to come full circle, the title shouts out loud and clear a message about the rarity of friendship. In the long melancholic notes of this ballad, young Michael seems to be searching for a stable and close fraternal connection. This number brings the first side of the album to an intense close.

Michael Jackson in Jamaica, 1 March 1975. The Jackson Five were the opening act for Bob Marley on 15 February 1975 at the National Heroes Stadium, Kingston.

Just a Little Bit of You

Brian Holland, Edward Holland Jr. / 3'14

Musicians
Michael Jackson: lead vocals
Backing vocals: (unknown)
Musicians: (unknown)
Recording
Motown Recording Studios, Los Angeles: June to November 1974
Technical team
Producer: Brian Holland
Recording engineer: Russ Terrana
Arrangements: James Carmichael
Mixing and recording: L T Horn

1975

Genesis

Brian and Edward Holland adapted their taste for dominant chords to a youthful mid-tempo funk that chiefly relies on the joyful theme that can be heard right from the intro. This cartoon-style opening gives way to a groove that is hammered out to a buoyant disco beat. The song suggests that love keeps you healthy. This idea of endorphins as a miracle drug would be explored seven years later by Marvin Gaye in the last hit of his lifetime, *Sexual Healing*. But in 1975, the Holland brothers merely had Michael acting out an unlikely doctor scenario.

Production

Just a Little Bit of You features insistent electric keyboards overdubbed by a simple piano line, with the whole composition framed by rhythmic guitars. Brian Holland included an instrumental bridge with a small brass section that repeats the notes from the chorus. The final album mix is simply a reading of the score with no real risks taken. The calm rhythm is no contest for the disco production that was played on the airwaves and in clubs at the time, and dampens the rhythmic flights that appear on the paper version. Between February and May 1975, Michael Jackson performed this song on a few television shows, but his stiff one-dimensional performance of a series of endlessly repeated dance steps shows that he struggled to work with this half-hearted track that was too weak for his ambitions as a dancer and entertainer.

Single

A-side: *Just a Little Bit of You (single version)* / 3'08
B-side: *Dear Michael (album version)* / 2'37
Released by Motown records: USA, April 1975 (ref. M 1349F) / UK, October 1975 (ref. TMG 1006)
Chart position: USA R&B No. 4, Pop No. 23

1975

You Are There

Sam Brown III, Christine Yarian, Rand Meitzenheimer / 3'23

Musicians: (unknown) / **Michael Jackson:** lead vocals / **Backing vocals:** (unknown)
Recording: Motown Recording Studios, Los Angeles: June to November 1974 / **Technical team: Producer:** Sam Brown III / **Recording engineer:** Russ Terrana / **Arrangements:** Sam Brown III / **Mixing and recording:** L T Horn

Sam Brown continued to weave romance into the album when he cowrote *You Are There* with Christine Yarian and Rand Meitzenheimer. During the recording session, Michael Jackson asked Brown to let him do his own rendition. He reassured him by saying that he was not obliged to keep Jackson's version if he felt it was unsuitable. Brown understood that he needed to express himself. The take was directed by Michael, then recorded and mixed by Russ Terrana. Brown listened to the playback and realized that The Jackson Five lead vocalist had got it just right. That session version made it to the final album mix.

Dapper-Dan

Hal Davis, Royce Esters, Don Fletcher / 3'08

Musicians: (unknown) / **Michael Jackson:** lead vocals / **Backing vocals:** (unknown)
Recording: Motown Recording Studios, Los Angeles: June to November 1974
Technical team: Producer: Hal Davis / **Recording engineer:** Russ Terrana / **Arrangements:** Arthur Wright / **Mixing and recording:** L T Horn

More than five years before New York stylist Dapper Dan, dresser to the emerging American hip-hop stars, exploded onto the scene, Michael Jackson sang about another *Dapper-Dan*. This imaginary character, inspired by the famous 1920s gangster of the same name, wanted to be the king of disco ("I'm gonna be king of the Disco tech"), and dominate the dance floor, where all the girls would have eyes only for him. Hal Davis and Don Fletcher brought to life this male alter ego of the heroine of *Dancing Machine*, a hit that they had composed for The Jackson Five in 1973 (see page 90). The overtly risqué and rather sexual character of this song came perhaps a little too soon in young Michael's recording career, and it would be four years before he definitively got down on the dance floor and delivered some uncompromising adult grooves (*Get on the Floor* and *Burn This Disco Out*).

Dear Michael

Hal Davis, Elliot Wilenski / 2'37

Musicians: (unknown) / **Michael Jackson:** lead vocals / **Backing vocals:** (unknown)
Recording: Motown Recording Studios, Los Angeles: June to November 1974
Technical team: Producer: Hal Davis / **Recording engineer:** Russ Terrana / **Arrangements:** James Carmichael / **Mixing and recording:** L T Horn

Michael barely had the time to create a party atmosphere with *Dapper-Dan* than he was assailed by a deep melancholy, the kind felt by superstars condemned to terrible loneliness. Ever since he had started working at Motown, the singer's life had been different to that of other boys of his age. *Dear Michael* lays down on vinyl a young boy's fantasies about an imaginary correspondence with one of his female admirers. Throughout the track, the repetition of the word "Michael" sounds like a cry for help, to which no reply is forthcoming. Directed by Hal Davis, the tune has all the elements of an ambitious soul ballad in which we discover Michael Jackson the crooner, supremely self-confident at the age of just 16.

Michael Jackson on the show *The Music Thing*, presented by Dick Clark at KTLA studios, Los Angeles, on 7 September 1975.

I'll Come Home to You

Freddie Perren, Christine Yarian / 3'05

Musicians: (unknown) / **Michael Jackson:** lead vocals / **Backing vocals:** (unknown)
Recording: Motown Recording Studios, Los Angeles: June to November 1974
Technical team: Producers: Freddie Perren and Fonce Mizell / **Recording engineer:** Russ Terrana / **Arrangements:** Freddie Perren and Eddy Manson / **Mixing and recording:** L T Horn

Reading between the lines of *I'll Come Home to You*, the lyrics tell the story of everything that would not happen between Michael Jackson and Motown. Although the lyrics of the song declare "whatever I do, I'll always come home," this ballad, which closes the record, is in fact a last postcard, a final love letter, a bittersweet announcement of an inevitable breakup. To end Michael's career at Motown, the ever-loyal Freddie Perren, who had been there since the start of The Jackson Five in the late 1960s, concocted a tearjerker of a production, full of carefully mixed chords reminiscent of the inspired flights of older Jackson Five tracks like *Maybe Tomorrow* or *You've Got a Friend* on the album *Got to Be There*.

PRESENT
JACK
LONDON : ODEON
TUESDAY 24TH MA
TICKETS: £3.00 £2.50
THEATRE BOX OFFICE TEL:-

M.D. ALYN AINSWORTH
MMERSMITH
9.00 P.M.
AVAILABLE FROM
4081 AND USUAL AGENTS

PORTRAIT

KENNETH GAMBLE & LEON HUFF (AND MFSB)

THE JACKSONS' PHILLY SOUND

Kenny Gamble and Leon Huff, inventors of the Philly sound, a sophisticated, sensual type of soul that dominated the 1970s R&B scene.

Kenneth Gamble and Leon Huff were both born in the city of Philadelphia, Pennsylvania. They first combined their creative talents in 1971 as producers on the Philadelphia International Records (PIR) label. In the 1970s, the pair profoundly transformed the way African-American music was produced, as it evolved toward the disco era. They wrote or cowrote over 3,000 songs, and propelled many artists to center stage both in the United States and worldwide. These artists included The Intruders, The O'Jays, The Three Degrees, The Blue Notes, Teddy Pendergrass, and Billy Paul.

The Sound of Philadelphia

Gamble and Huff worked with Joe Tarsia's Sigma Sound Studios in Philadelphia. It became so famous in the 1970s that David Bowie used it to record his album *Young Americans* in August 1974. Like the Funk Brothers at Motown, Sigma Sound's studio musicians, which were collectively known as MFSB (Mother Father Sister Brother), added perfectly polished and glossy sounds to all the Philly productions, which were recognizable for their dynamic string and brilliant brass sections. They used instruments like the vibraphone and marimba, filtered through an echo chamber. This became their hallmark sound. The recording techniques developed by the Philly teams made their tunes both popular and timeless. The pool of 30 MFSB musicians understood very early on that a record's success was in the hands of the disc jockeys, who gave it airtime, thus popularizing it with large audiences.

The two producers developed an alchemy of sounds varying from enthusiastic ballads to funky tunes, a clever combination better known to the world as Philly Sound. Their songs of peace, love, and social conscience sold millions of records and won them numerous Gold and Platinum awards throughout their career. In black music history, Gamble and Huff's names will go down most notably for the essential *TSOP (The Sound of Philadelphia)*, the theme tune for the variety show *Soul Train*. Reaching the top of the *Billboard* Pop 100 in 1974, the song became an anthem for an entire generation and culture. The same year, along with Thom Bell, their long-standing partner, the duo were named producers of the year by *Billboard* magazine.

With The Jacksons

From then on, the PIR label was seen as the worthy heir to Tamla Motown, which was mostly focused on the movie business at the time. With this undisputed success and its growing reputation, the label was approached by Joseph Jackson, who was looking to extract his sons from Motown. All of them, except Jermaine, finally signed a contract with Epic / CBS on 28 May 1975.

Sophisticated string arrangements were one of the hallmarks of soul music from Philadelphia.

The Jackson brothers had to wait for almost a year before they started working at the Sigma Sound Studios, because the recording contract with Motown did not officially expire until 10 March 1976. The break was much too long and the group was on the verge of being forgotten. The music industry and the public started to believe that the young musicians had lost their motivation or creative spark.

The albums *The Jacksons* (1976) and *Goin' Places* (1977) were expert productions by Kenneth Gamble and Leon Huff, who approached these initial projects as a personal challenge. Eight tracks were cut with additional contributions by Dexter Wansel and the Gene McFadden and John Whitehead duo.

In 2014, Kenneth Gamble talked on WBLS Radio about working with Michael Jackson:

> The Jacksons were signing with Epic Records, we were working with Epic and Colombia at the same time. So they were like our competition…So when we finally worked with them...they were going through some changes, because Jermaine wasn't with them. He had stayed with Motown when the rest of them left and went with CBS. We wrote some good songs for the group...'cos we were really busy at that time, we had The O'Jays, Teddy Prendergrass...we had so many projects on then…with songs like *Show You the Way to Go*, *(Think about the) Good Times,* and *Find Me a Girl.*
>
> *Find Me a Girl,* that was a good one. One day Michael told me that he gotta get some "sneaks," so we walked up to Chestnut Street. It was only a couple of blocks away from us…and I saw the crowd just growing outside the store. First there was three girls, then there was ten, twenty, there must have been about thirty or forty people outside the door. Michael said: "What should I do with these girls?" So I said make out and snatch one of them girls, you gotta find yourself a girl. That's where that title came from. Michael was a beautiful person, very very talented. *Man of War*, you ever heard that one? *Man of War*? That was the direction that we wanted to take him into. Michael really loved that song; it was really like a message song.[21]

However, The Jacksons' Philly period did not really bring out the creative potential of the new group and its lead singer. All Gamble and Huff really did was produce new tunes with the same established formulas. Kenneth Gamble would later regret not having had enough time to nurture a real partnership between the team and The Jacksons.

So the Philadelphia adventure stopped there. It had produced mixed results and was something of a missed opportunity, but as a consequence, the brothers were now in a position to compose and produce their own albums. The Jacksons were preparing to take charge of their own destiny, as the title of their next album (*Destiny*) suggested.

[THE JACKSONS]

ENJOY YOURSELF

Leon Huff, Kenneth Gamble / 3'24

From the album: *The Jacksons*
Released by Epic Records/CBS: USA, 27 November 1976 (ref. 34229) / UK, 27 November 1976 (ref. EPC 86009)
Chart position: USA R&B No. 6, Pop No. 36 / UK No. 54
RIAA: certified Gold 5 August 1977

1976

Musicians
Michael Jackson: lead vocals
Michael, Tito, Jackie, Marlon, and Randy Jackson: backing vocals
MFSB (Mother Father Sister Brother): other musicians
Recording
Sigma Sound Studios, Philadelphia: June 1976
Technical team
Producers: Kenneth Gamble and Leon Huff
Recording engineer: Joe Tarsia
Assistant recording engineers: Jeff Stewart and Pete Humphreys
Arrangements: Bobby Martin
Mixing: Jay Marks

Genesis

Enjoy Yourself benefited from the good vibes surrounding Philly Sound. In June 1976 it was the first-ever track that The Jacksons worked on at Sigma Sound Studios. According to Kenneth Gamble, The Jacksons were already consummate professionals. They had just left Motown and were increasingly keen to produce their own album. Michael was the one who put in the most effort in the studio. He worked on and perfected his knowledge of all the different production techniques, continuing what he had begun with Stevie Wonder several years earlier. Paradoxically, Gamble says that he too learned a lot from Michael Jackson, such as how to overdub his voice on certain tunes to make the sound more intense, or test new harmonies.

Looking back now, it is obvious that CBS pushed Gamble and Huff to work fast to release this first album. The two producers were dealing with a flood of requests from all quarters, and were also still managing their own label, PIR. Gamble quietly made it known that he would like to have involved the brothers in a real creative partnership.

The Jacksons were beginning to discover Philly Sound, and the syncopated structure of *Enjoy Yourself* is very unusual. T.J. Tindall, an MFSB guitarist, provided inspiration for the song. One day, he was playing a riff on the guitar and Kenneth Gamble thought the melody was so amazing that he decided to turn it into a song.

The first song on the album, *Enjoy Yourself,* opens with a simple piece of advice to do just that. It uses the imperative, like most of the tracks on the record. It is immediately clear what the song is aiming to achieve: the brothers wanted to produce dance-floor music.

The melody line of the tune is linear, and the arrangements are repetitive and formal, leaving space for Michael's adult timbre, which he was managing much better than at the end of the Motown era. He delivers variations and a vibe that were astonishingly new, expressing himself with a newfound energy that he tests, relentlessly pushing himself to go further. It is obvious that he really enjoyed singing the simple lyrics, and a natural sparkling joy shines through. This same joy can be heard on all his songs right up to the period in which he filmed *The Wiz.*

Single

A-side: *Enjoy Yourself* (*single version*) / 3'24
B-side: *Style of Life* (*album version*) / 3'21
Released by Epic Records/CBS: USA, November 1976 (ref. 8-50289) / UK 7-inch, 22 October 1976 (ref. S EPC 4708) / UK 12-inch (*extended version*), 18 March 1977 (ref. S EPC 5063)
Chart position: USA R&B No. 2, Pop No. 6 / UK No. 42
RIAA: certified Gold 10 February 1977 / certified Platinum 14 February 1989

One of the first promotional photos of The Jacksons taken for Epic/CBS, 1976.

Production

Two weeks before The Jacksons started work in Philadelphia, with relations between Motown and the group at an all-time low, their former label released the last official Jackson Five album, *Moving Violation*.

Meanwhile, to bring the new group back into the public eye, and to give Gamble and Huff the time they needed to write the first album, a TV series was broadcast on CBS TV. The old songs from the Motown era were used on the first four episodes in summer 1976, along with covers of well-known American tunes and sketches featuring the entire family. On Sunday 10 October 1976, to announce the recent release of the single, *Enjoy Yourself,* was presented exclusively on the *Sonny and Cher Show* (CBS). Michael did his usual spins and dance moves, captivating the camera as always; Jackie officially replaced Jermaine as second vocalist. The stage glowed red, the costumes sparkled, Michael's performance was flawless. There was just one big drawback: CBS rules meant that the boys had to mime, which came across as irritating and unnatural. This meant that young Michael was denied the freedom to express himself, and he felt that the shows did nothing for the group's career: "They were totally wrong. We had to dress in ridiculous outfits and perform stupid comedy routines to canned laughter. It was all so fake."[2] Another similar program was scheduled in early 1977. The new songs finally got the opportunity to be heard, and *Enjoy Yourself* opened the show on Friday 19 January 1977.

The single was targeted for dance-floor play and became part of the disco wave, although there was nothing particularly innovative about it. The Jackson family was still in litigation with Motown, and their former label somewhat ruined the launch of the single and the album by issuing a compilation of unpublished tracks by The Jackson Five under one of its sub-labels, Natural Resources, on 26 October 1976, entitled *Joyful Jukebox Music*. From then on, Motown would regularly release this kind of compilation as it provided them with a good income stream, thanks to the fame and artistic impact of the young star.

After selling 500,000 copies, the single was certified Gold, a first for the group as CBS, unlike Motown, was a member of the Recording Industry Association of America (RIAA).

The music and discotheque market was gradually becoming more open to extended versions, and *Enjoy Yourself* was extended to 5'48 and issued as a maxi 45 rpm for the European market in March 1977. This new version made up for the relatively short playing time of the songs on the album, most of which did not exceed 5'. The tune did well in the American charts, reaching No. 2 in the Top R&B, but failed miserably in Europe, possibly because it came out too late in the booming disco era and was buried in an avalanche of other mouthwatering musical morsels.

1976

[THE JACKSONS]

Show You the Way to Go

Leon Huff, Kenneth Gamble / 5'28

From the album: *The Jacksons*
Released by Epic Records/CBS: USA, 27 November 1976 (ref. 34229) / UK, 27 November 1976 (ref. EPC 86009)
Chart position: USA R&B No. 6, Pop No. 36 / UK No. 53
RIAA: certified Gold 5 April 1977

Musicians
Michael Jackson: lead vocals
Michael, Tito, Jackie, Marlon, and Randy Jackson: backing vocals
MFSB (Mother Father Sister Brother): other musicians
Recording
Sigma Sound Studios, Philadelphia: October 1976
Technical team
Producers: Kenneth Gamble and Leon Huff
Recording engineer: Joe Tarsia
Assistant recording engineers: Jeff Stewart and Pete Humphreys
Arrangements: Bobby Martin
Mixing: Jay Marks

Single

A-side: *Show You the Way to Go (stereo single version)* / 3'24
B-side: *Blues Away (album version)* / 3'14
Released by Epic Records/CBS: USA, April 1977 (ref. 8-50350) / UK, May 1977 (ref. S EPC 5266)
Chart position: USA R&B No. 6, Pop No. 28 / UK No. 1

Genesis

Show You the Way to Go is one of the songs that Gamble and Huff presented to the Jacksons at a meeting in their hotel to select the tracks for their first album at Epic / CBS. This song is the one that best represents the Philly Sound, both for its social and universal message and for its sumptuous orchestration.

In it, Michael sings:

"I don't know everything / But there's something I do know / ...That we can come together / And think like one / ...The job is hard to do / But only we can work this out / Cause we can help each other to overcome."

This track positions Michael as a role model. He embodies the social conscience of the real world, far from the lovey-dovey and sometimes surreal utopias of the Motown era. The moral values that he expresses here had never before appeared in the group's repertoire.

Production

The young singer spent many hours in the studio analyzing the way the two producers worked. Watching Huff on the piano and Gamble singing, he learned how a song fits together and he understood the importance of melody. Michael was particularly fond of *Show You the Way to Go*, which he felt expressed CBS's desire to bring the group's vocals to the fore.

The harmonies are extremely rich, initially in the orchestration and then in the brothers' backing vocals. They accompany Michael Jackson's voice perfectly and do much more than just echo his words, really carrying his message and maximizing its impact. The repetitive bass is incredibly dynamic, and the guitar adds some colorful tones. Foreground and background come together, but also exist and express themselves independently. The guitar and the marimba breaks provide ornamental pauses in the song before it starts up again with Michael's explosive groove, where his joy and elation are apparent.

The Jacksons were performing at Queen Elizabeth II's Silver Jubilee at the King's Hall in Glasgow when the single first went on sale in the United Kingdom in May 1977. *Show You the Way to Go* was their first European No. 1. It stayed in the British charts for ten weeks, reaching No. 1 on 25 June 1977. Like *Style of Life* by Tito Jackson (which appeared on the B-side of the single *Enjoy Yourself*), *Blues*

The Jacksons near Hyde Park Corner, London, 19 May 1977. They met Britain's Queen Elizabeth II during her Silver Jubilee celebrations.

Away, a Michael Jackson composition, became the B-side of this second single. For some time, the group had wanted to produce their own records, and this showed that CBS was prepared to allow them to do so.

Teddy Riley produced a cover of *Show You the Way to Go* in 1996 for the group Men of Vizion.

FOR JACKSON ADDICTS

The group Men of Vizion covered the track in 1996, produced by Teddy Riley, bringing it a new dynamic. Their album *Personal* was issued under Michael's MJJ Music label.

[THE JACKSONS]

BLUES AWAY

Michael Jackson / 3'01

From the album: *The Jacksons*
Released by Epic Records/CBS: USA, 27 November 1976 (ref. 34229) / UK, 27 November 1976 (ref. EPC 86009)
Chart position: USA R&B No. 6, Pop No. 36 / UK No. 53
RIAA: certified Gold 5 April 1977

1976

Musicians
Michael Jackson: lead vocals
Michael Jackson: background vocals
MFSB (Mother Father Sister Brother): other musicians
Recording
Sigma Sound Studios, Philadelphia: music
Paragon Studios, Chicago: vocals
June to October 1976
Technical team
Producers: Kenneth Gamble, Leon Huff, Gene McFadden, John Whitehead, Dexter Wansel, and The Jacksons
Recording engineer: Joe Tarsia
Assistant recording engineers: Jeff Stewart and Pete Humphreys
Arrangements: Dexter Wansel
Mixing: Jay Marks

Genesis

The Jacksons album reproduced Gamble and Huff's previously successful formulas. The two men liked to alternate songs about love, social problems, and solidarity. This profound humanism is evident in all their work and went hand in hand with the raising of social awareness in the African-American community in the 1970s. Many artists at the time were questioning the state of the world around them and the racial barriers that continued to exist.

That said, two of the ten tracks on the Jackson brothers' first album at Epic feel somewhat out of place. The first one, entitled *Blues Away*, was composed by Michael Jackson. The mid-tempo is remarkably gentle, and the lyrics are surprising. At just 18, the singer tackles a rather unexpected theme for a young man of his age: depression. A disconcertingly real sense of despondency simply oozes out of the three short minutes of this song with its repetitive theme.

Whereas the songs delivered by Gamble and Huff sound like a series of cheerful commandments that celebrate the Jacksons' liberation from Motown, *Blues Away* exudes a feeling of melancholy that seems to come from the depths of young Michael's soul. The separation with Motown caused the first prominent division in the Jackson family, with the departure of Jermaine, who preferred to stay with Motown as a solo artist. Joe Jackson, the patriarch of the clan, insisted that Michael accompanied him to meet the record label executives and negotiate the contract in CBS headquarters. This was a period when the young artist was living out his adolescence subject to merciless public scrutiny. The "little Michael" years were now firmly behind him. Ever since he had first arrived at Motown, he had been living in an overprotected bubble that distanced him from "normal" altruistic human relationships. These unusual circumstances meant that the transition to adulthood would be tricky for him. All the pressure and changes he was encountering seemed to echo in his work.

In his autobiography, *Moonwalk*, Michael Jackson has an emotional recollection of the first of his own compositions that he presented to the public: "*Blues Away* was one of my first songs, and although I don't sing it anymore, I'm not embarrassed to hear it...It's a light song about overcoming deep depression."[2] Like a door into the world of his life as a songwriter, Michael Jackson tackles a dark subject with a catchy

The producers Gene McFadden and John Whitehead in London in 1979.

melody and harmonies—a pattern he would regularly repeat throughout his career.

Production

The instrumental tracks were recorded at Sigma Sound, in the best Gamble and Huff tradition. For this last track on the first side of the album, the two chief producers worked with the McFadden and Whitehead duo, who went on to produce the classic *Ain't No Stoppin' Us Now* in 1979; Dexter Wansel completed the team. All of them provided guidance to Michael during recording sessions that featured one of Michael's very own compositions. The Jackson brothers as a group were credited as coproducers, but it was the youngest member who came up with all the ideas about how to immortalize his composition on vinyl.

Musically, *Blues Away* laid the foundations for what became Michael Jackson's style as a songwriter. The tune reveals a thinly disguised fascination for Stevie Wonder's work (*Blues Away* sounds like the distant cousin of *Summer Soft* or *Knocks Me off My Feet*, published the same year on the album *Songs in the Key of Life*), combined with a passion for carefully constructed layers of backing vocals.

The production and balance of *Blues Away* stands in sharp contrast to the rest of the album. Gamble and Huff came up with some dynamic rhythmic guitar and dominant brass on tracks like *Think Happy* and *Living Together*, but *Blues Away* prefers muted arrangements similar to those used by crooners such as Teddy Pendergrass. The listener can hear Michael Jackson stretching his voice over the long melodies, just as he used to do on the Motown tracks *Ben* and *One Day in Your Life*.

The vocals were recorded in Paragon Studios in Chicago. As if he were recognizing how far he had come, Michael Jackson chose a studio near his hometown to record the vocal tracks for his first composition. It is a studio that has been used by famous names such as Elvis Presley, Pink Floyd, and David Bowie, and it was in this setting that Michael Jackson took his first steps as a producer. He had fond memories of the recording session: "...it showed what good regard the Epic people had for our singing. We were all over that record and it was the best one we did. I loved the high hat and strings fluttering alongside us like birds' wings."[22]

On *Blues Away*, Michael Jackson sang both the lead and backing vocals. The production highlighted the keyboard riff, which looped throughout the whole song. The arrangement written for strings adds to the impression of lightness that seems to pull the singer out of his depression from time to time. It is a two-part tune. After a short break, the young man finishes by singing "la, la, la, la" alongside ad-libbed lyrics. This technique would also be used in future compositions. The end of the song is punctuated by the singer's handclaps, which accentuate the sound of each snare drum. Handclaps, like finger snapping, are Michael Jackson's signature sounds. They first appeared in *Blues Away* and would become a regular feature throughout his career.

The Jacksons in New York in 1977. Top, from left: Tito, Michael, and Marlon. Bottom: Randy and Jackie.

[THE JACKSONS]

Style of Life

Tito and Michael Jackson / 3'21

1976

From the album: *The Jacksons*
Released by Epic Records/CBS: USA and UK, 27 November 1976 (ref. 34229 and ref. EPC 86009)
Chart position: USA R&B No. 6, Pop No. 36 / UK No. 53
RIAA: certified Gold 5 April 1977

Musicians
Michael Jackson: lead vocals
The Jacksons: backing vocals
MFSB (Mother Father Sister Brother): other musicians
Recording
Sigma Sound Studios, Philadelphia: music
Paragon Studios, Chicago: vocals
June to October 1976
Technical team
Producers: Kenneth Gamble, Leon Huff, Gene McFadden, John Whitehead, Dexter Wansel, and The Jacksons
Recording engineer: Joe Tarsia
Assistant recording engineers: Jeff Stewart and Pete Humphreys
Arrangements: Dexter Wansel
Mixing: Jay Marks

Genesis

"*Style of Life* was a jam that Tito directed, and it was in keeping with the nightclub groove that *Dancing Machine* got us into, but we kept it a little leaner and meaner than Motown would have cut it."[2] The second track by the Jackson brothers for their first album at Epic was a joint effort between Tito and Michael. Michael wrote the lyrics and created the melody and arrangements with his brother.

Style of Life picks up on the theme of love betrayed, which regularly featured in the group's productions at Motown. This time, the tone is more vindictive, as if the brothers, now on the threshold of adulthood, were trying to share their experience and wisdom through the advice the hero of the song gives his sweetheart.

The track was one of the songs that the young musicians wrote while they were still under contract at Motown. It was initially cut as a demo, and the group were keen to present it to Gamble and Huff during their first joint work sessions.

Production

Like *Blues Away*, the instrumentals were recorded by musicians from the Philadelphia stable, MFSB. The brothers' opinions were taken into account and they had a say in the final production. In previous years, they had been preparing for this moment by producing demos in the family studio in Encino. For the first time in their ten-year career, they had some control, which although limited enabled them to gain a grounding for future projects.

The vocals were recorded in Chicago, as they had been for *Blues Away*, where Michael's solo performance featured soaring vocals set to floating strings. In contrast, *Style of Life* was about group harmonies, with the brothers' joyful backing vocals accompanying and threading their way through the lines sung by Michael.

Listening to this song, it is clear that the group had well and truly moved on to a new stage in their careers. Michael became the undisputed leader. Jermaine was no longer there to perform the lead vocals on certain tracks or to share any of the verses or bridges with his young brother.

CB

[THE JACKSONS]

1977

Different Kind of Lady

The Jacksons / 3'36

From the album: *Goin' Places*
Released by Epic Records/CBS: USA, 18 October 1977 (ref. JE 34835 and EPC 86035)
Chart position: USA R&B No. 11, Pop No. 63 / UK No. 45

Musicians
Michael Jackson: lead vocals
The Jacksons: backing vocals
Tito Jackson: guitar
Randy Jackson: congas
TSOP (The Sound of Philadelphia): other musicians
Recording
Sigma Sound Studios, Philadelphia: December 1976 to August 1977
Technical team
Producers: The Jacksons
Recording engineer: Joe Tarsia
Assistant recording engineers: Pete Humphreys and Jim Dougherty
Arrangements: Dexter Wansel
Mixing: Jay Marks

Genesis

Just as recording of the album *Goin' Places* was coming to an end, Michael Jackson proudly declared to journalists at *Valley News* on 18 August 1977: "In our new album I like *Different Kind of Lady*. It's smoking. You can dance to it."[23] Whereas *The Jacksons* album had been about trying to give the group a more adult image, *Goin' Places* showed all the signs of the brothers wanting to get their music back on the dance floors as soon as possible.

Finally released from the contract they had signed with CBS TV for a weekly show, which was significantly damaging their record sales, The Jacksons were working on the production of their second album at Epic. Gamble and Huff were once again looking after the five young men. The aim was to build on the respectable first attempt to create an album that would be at least as successful as *Dancing Machine*.

The five boys started rehearsing in the family studio, creating songs that suited their style. Gamble and Huff had done a good job developing a concept album based on the theme of peace and eternity for *Goin' Places*, in which the central track, *Man of War*, and its antiwar discourse sounded naive, although it was certainly sincere, when sung by young Michael, but the group now—finally—wanted to find its own musical identity.

Different Kind of Lady is a declaration of love to a girl who is described as "different." The uniqueness and originality that the group was seeking when producing this track were expressed through the story of a budding love affair. The word "different" was telling: Michael Jackson frequently used this word in interviews to describe his work and his desire to stand out. In 1983, the journalist Diane Collins ended up asking him: "Ok. So basically that's the key word, 'different,' for Michael Jackson?" The singer's response was an unambiguous "yeah."

FOR JACKSONS ADDICTS

Different Kind of Lady and *Do What You Wanna* were released respectively on the B-sides of *Find Me a Girl* and *Blame it on the Boogie*, indicating that Epic were reluctant to release and promote a single written by the Jacksons.

Production

The lyrics of *Different Kind of Lady* reused all the groovy ingredients of *Dancing Machine*. A melody line at the end of the chorus performed via a talkbox plugged into an electric guitar was something that even Peter Frampton would have been proud of.

Even though Dexter Wansel was always nearby to supervise the sessions, this time The Jacksons were responsible for the

The Jacksons pose on a Ford Model T while promoting their latest album, *Goin' Places,* in Los Angeles, July 1977.

track and produced it themselves. Tito provided the guitar chords and gave substance to the song's central groove.

Young Randy provided the rhythm on the congas, his favorite instrument, which he had used on stage ever since he had unofficially joined the group during the Motown years.

The production was fairly solid and very similar to some of the more effective songs from the 1973 to 1974 season when The Jackson Five had successfully negotiated a daring shift to disco and psychedelic sounds with *Get It Together* and *Dancing Machine*.

An initial mix with brass in the foreground was issued on the vinyl and cassette versions of the album. The picture disc version features an alternative mix without the brass, which makes the track sound harder, leaner, and much less disco. The second mix ended up on a series of cassettes that were produced in the 1980s and on some CD compilations, notably in Australia.

Despite its oomph and an enthusiastic reception from DJs, who proved more than happy to play the track, the single *Different Kind of Lady* did not make it into any of the charts. But this commercial failure nevertheless enabled the group to show Gamble and Huff's team that the time was ripe for them to be producing their own music. In 1980, Michael Jackson said to *Billboard*: "I think what really convinced people was when we wrote a song on the *Goin' Places* album, *Different Kind of Lady*, which was a hit in the clubs. Even Kenny Gamble came to us and told us, 'You are all good enough to do your own stuff.'"[23]

[THE JACKSONS]

1977

Do What You Wanna

The Jacksons / 3'32

From the album: *Goin' Places*
Released by Epic Records/CBS: USA, 18 October 1977 (ref. JE 34835 and EPC 86035)
Chart position: USA R&B No.11, Pop No. 60 / UK No. 45

Musicians
Michael Jackson: lead vocals
The Jacksons: backing vocals
Tito Jackson: guitar
Randy Jackson: congas
TSOP (The Sound of Philadelphia): other musicians
Recording
Sigma Sound Studios, Philadelphia: December 1976 to August 1977
Technical team
Producers: The Jacksons
Recording engineer: Joe Tarsia
Assistant recording engineers: Pete Humphreys and Jim Dougherty
Arrangements: Dexter Wansel
Mixing: Jay Marks

Genesis

Titles do not lie, and if anyone had any remaining doubts about what motivated Michael Jackson, *Do What You Wanna* provided an unequivocal answer: do what you want. Here, the five brothers sing a simple song that fluctuates between disco party and the fraternal soul style typical of the group.

The theme that opens the song and returns as a break in the middle of the track sounds like one of the tap-dancing or musical sequences that the brothers performed on their TV variety show on CBS from 1976 to 1977.

The Jacksons managed to survive their difficult teenage years and grow with their talents by relying on what was available at the time, namely disco and its sometimes labored arrangements on the one hand, and on the other, the polished, slightly outdated sound of Broadway musicals (at best) and Las Vegas musicals (at worst).

The lyrics of *Do What You Wanna* are quite a contrast to the declaration of love made in *Different Kind of Lady*. The brothers had finally shaken off the childish image that they had got stuck with at Motown, and were now very different from the cartoon characters on the Saturday morning TV show, which was broadcast throughout most of the 1970s. They exuded a dash of hope and self-denial with some lines that resembled gospel: "...and when you reach the top, happily you will live," they sang in *Do What You Wanna*. In what became a healthy obsession, the Jacksons were demanding total control of their lives, careers, and public image.

Production

Do What You Wanna was the latest sign that The Jacksons were gradually taking over the production of their music. Dexter Wansel continued as arranger, but the harmonies of the choruses developed by the brothers sounded self-assured and gave a glimpse into the highly developed sound that would be apparent on their next album, *Destiny*.

A few rare videos filmed at Sigma Studios during the recording sessions for the track *Jump for Joy*, which also features on *Goin' Places*, show the brothers gathered around the microphone recording their backing vocals. This technique probably improved the cohesion and authenticity of their harmonies.

All the sessions for this album, including the ones for the two songs that were written and produced by The Jacksons,

The Jacksons in Amsterdam in 1977, during a promotional trip.

took place at Sigma Sound Studios. By deliberately choosing not to lay down their vocals in Paragon Studios, in Chicago, the five brothers definitively stepped into Gamble and Huff territory.

Do What You Wanna wasn't as successful as *Different Kind of Lady*, but, like all tracks written and produced by The Jacksons on the two albums that they did with the Philadelphia label, it appeared on the B-side of one of the singles.

[THE JACKSONS]

Blame It on the Boogie

Mick Jackson, Dave Jackson, Elmar Krohn / 3'34

From the album: *Destiny*
Released by Epic Records/CBS: USA and UK, 16 December 1978 (ref. 35552 and ref. EPC 83200)
Chart position: USA R&B No. 3, Pop No. 11 / UK No. 33
RIAA: certified Gold 13 March 1979 / certified Platinum 8 May 1979

Musicians
Michael Jackson: lead vocals
Michael, Tito, Jackie, Marlon, and Randy Jackson: backing vocals
Nathan Watts and Gary King: bass guitar
Tito Jackson, Mike Sembello, Roland Bautista: guitar
Greg Phillinganes: keyboards
Laudir de Oliveira and Claudio Slon: congas
Rick Marotta: drum and percussion
Recording
Cherokee Recording Studios, Total Experience, Record Plant and Dawnbreaker, Los Angeles
Heiders/Filmways, San Francisco: summer 1978
Technical team
Producers: The Jacksons
Executive Producers: Bobby Colomby and Mike Atkinson
Recording engineers: Peter Granet and Don Murray
Rhythmic arrangements: Greg Phillinganes and Jerry Hey
Mixing: (unknown)

Promotional video: end 1978
Production: Image West Studio (Scanimate Technique)
Length: 3'44

Single

A-side: *Blame It on the Boogie (single version)* / 3'32
B-side: *Do What You Wanna (album version)* / 3'31
Released by Epic Records/CBS: USA, November 1978 (ref. 8-50595) / UK, September 1978 (ref. S EPC 6683)
Chart position: USA R&B No. 3, Pop No. 54 / UK No. 8

Genesis

Blame It on the Boogie is the only song on the album that was not composed by The Jacksons but chosen by CBS. It was the advance single for the *Destiny* album and was released in late 1978. The tune was written by a talented British artist, coincidentally also called Michael Jackson (or "Mick" Jackson). He wrote the track with his brother Dave and Elmar Krohn. Apparently, the project was presented to Bobby Colomby by Mike Atkinson (an A&R man, and executive coproducer of the song).

As Michael Jackson (the singer) remembers, *Blame It on the Boogie* was a good example of what the group was trying to cultivate at the time, an up-tempo rhythm (above 180 bpm) with finger snapping. When the track was presented to him, he adored the chorus because he could sing it in one go, without taking a breath or closing his lips.

Blame It on the Boogie is like a musical electric shock. With simple but dynamic lyrics, Michael explodes into action like never before, totally surrendering himself to the music and the song: "I just can't control my feet..." The track is packed with rhythm and positive vibes, and accentuates the funky tones that in many ways recall the powerful energy of the glory days of black music, when the body moves of its own accord. The song and its message were thoroughly modern and in keeping with the music trends of the time.

The text is somewhat flimsy. After kissing his sweetheart goodbye at the end of a night spent clubbing in San Francisco, Michael blames the boogie for bewitching him and taking control of his body. The young star's vocal performance sparkles and exudes positivity, as if saving him from himself and providing him with an outlet for his energies. The music and lyrics come together as a celebration of rhythm and dance, which spin out of control. The riffs are clear and funky, and the brass simply explodes, sparkles, and propels the track into orbit right from the first chorus. The rhythms are enchanting and carry to perfection the theme of the song, especially conceived for the dance floor. It was the best possible introduction to the tidal wave of music that would give rise to *Shake Your Body (Down to the Ground)* in early 1979.

Production

The recording sessions began at Dawnbreaker Studio in San Fernando, California, in a fairly relaxed atmosphere, where

The Jacksons perform *Shake Your Body* for a TV show in Leysin, Switzerland, in February 1979.

Michael allowed his voice to fully express itself in the simple, fresh, and very danceable track. Bobby Colomby remembers that the singer really made his presence felt and put a huge amount of effort into the recording sessions for the *Destiny* album. One day, he was in the booth recording when he suddenly ripped off his headset and shot out of the studio. Colomby asked the recording engineer if the volume of his headphones was perhaps too high, but then he discovered Michael in the foyer dancing and spinning frenetically. By way of explanation, he said: "I'm sorry, I can't stand still and sing that section. I'm gonna get this out."[24]

Steve Knopper also has an interesting story to tell about the exclamations in the chorus: "Sunshine! Moonlight!" He says that Colomby decided to try a vocal technique that he learned from Roy Thomas Baker, the producer of the group Queen. Instead of laying down each vocal track separately, the idea was to stack the vocals on the same track to create a thick, layered effect that gave energy and dynamics to the record. The boys sang in unison, one syllable at a time: "Sun!-Shine! Moon!-Light!" Michael encouraged the use of this technique, which he would go on to use on many occasions throughout his career.

In the United States, the launch of the album *Destiny* and the single *Blame It on the Boogie* was scheduled for the same time as the release of the movie *The Wiz*, Sidney Lumet's latest motion picture project, a musical comedy produced by Motown starring Michael Jackson and Diana Ross (see page 128). The single from the musical, *Ease on down the Road,* was distributed by MCA Records from September 1978 and overshadowed *Blame It on the Boogie*. The latter struggled to reach 54th spot in the US Hot 100 and only stayed in these charts for six weeks (however, the tune made a brilliant showing in the R&B charts, reaching No. 3). At the end of the year, in an attempt to boost the promotion of the single, CBS brought out a video with psychedelic effects that were very modern for the time, created using Scanimate (a computer-assisted special-effects package). The video featured the five brothers appearing one by one in front of the camera shouting out the positive features in their new song.

In Europe, *Blame It on the Boogie* was planned as a standout single. Its author, the other Michael Jackson (Mick Jackson), decided to record and market it as a single himself. The same song, performed by the two Michael Jacksons and marketed at the same time, caused confusion among the public. The British press referred to it as the "Battle of the Boogie." The Jacksons' version did better, reaching No. 8 in the British charts, ahead of Mick Jackson.

Blame It on the Boogie enabled The Jacksons to reposition their image on the market by returning to the fundamentals of disco with noticeably more energy. As with the track *Enjoy Yourself*, a long version of *Blame It on the Boogie* was produced and directed by John Luongo (*John Luongo Disco Mix*), paving the way for the successful return of the group to dance floors in America and Europe.

FOR JACKSON ADDICTS

At the same time, The Jacksons recorded *Be a Pepper* for a commercial for the oldest American brand of soda, Dr Pepper™; it was about a minute long and used music from *Blame It on the Boogie* with specially arranged lyrics. It is a rare item available only on certain formats.

1978

[THE JACKSONS]

Shake Your Body (Down to the Ground)

Randy and Michael Jackson / 7'59

From the album: *Destiny*
Released by Epic Records/CBS: USA and UK, 16 December 1978 (ref. 35552 and ref. EPC 83200)
Chart position: USA R&B No. 3, Pop No. 11 / UK No. 33
RIAA: certified Gold 13 March 1979 / certified Platinum 8 May 1979

Musicians
Michael Jackson: lead vocals
The Jacksons: backing vocals
Tito Jackson: guitar
Greg Phillinganes: keyboards
Michael Boddicker and Greg Phillinganes: keyboards
Ed Greene: drums
Paulinho Da Costa: percussion
Recording
Cherokee Recording Studios, Total Experience, Record Plant and Dawnbreaker, Los Angeles Heiders/Filmways, San Francisco: summer 1978
Technical team
Producers: The Jacksons
Executive Producers: Bobby Colomby and Mike Atkinson
Recording engineers: Peter Granet and Don Murray
Vocal arrangements: The Jacksons
Rhythmic arrangements: Greg Phillinganes
Brass and string arrangements: Tom Tom 84
Mixing: (unknown)

Single

USA
A-side: *Shake Your Body (Down to the Ground) (stereo single version)* / 3'43
B-side: *That's What You Get (For Being Polite) (album version)* / 4'56
UK
A-side: *Shake Your Body (Down to the Ground) (stereo single version)* / 3'43
B-side: *All Night Dancin' (album version)* / 6'09
Released by Epic Records/CBS: USA, February 1979 (ref. 8-50656) / UK, March 1979 (ref. S EPC 7181)
Chart position: USA R&B No. 3, Pop No. 7 / UK No. 4

Genesis

At the same time as the Jackson brothers were taking control of the recording studio to create their own first album as adult artists, they were also composing songs that finally enabled them to define their style. Two young talents in the family formed a winning duo of composers that immortalized some of The Jacksons' greatest hits: Michael and Randy. They worked together on creating songs that were frequently based on piano / vocals. "I was at home," recalls Michael in a video, "and Randy was playing some notes on the piano [he hums the music to *Shake Your Body*]. I asked him what it was, he replied, 'Nothing.' I said to him, 'No, that's not nothing.' I started singing along to his music and that's how we got the song."[24]

The chemistry that developed between the two brothers was also owed to two famous singers who had a huge influence on the group. In 1977, Marvin Gaye fired a rocket onto the dance floors. It went by the name of *Got to Give It Up*. In the final lyrics of the song (ad lib), he sings, "Let's dance / Let's shout (shout) / Gettin' funky's what it's all about." Michael and Randy, consciously or subconsciously, picked up this exact same phrase and used it as the basis of the chorus for *Shake Your Body*. The rhythmic structure has its roots (or inspiration) in a track issued by the record label Philadelphia International, which the two brothers had just quit: the melody line in *Shake Your Body* is similar in many ways to that of *Get Up, Get Down, Get Funky, Get Loose,* sung by Teddy Pendergrass and released in spring 1978. The two influences of PIR and Motown show that The Jacksons simply could not turn their backs on their past. Even though they were writing and producing their own music, their first major hit contained a melodic nod to the two black princes of the prestigious Motown and PIR labels.

Production

The Jacksons put down a demo of *Shake Your Body* in the family recording studio in Encino (available on *The Ultimate Collection* box set, 2004). The intro begins with a very short jam session entitled *Things I Do for You*, an effective groove written by the five brothers. *Shake Your Body* follows quickly on to the sound of two rhythmic guitars, a piano looping the theme, and a haunting bass guitar that initially stresses every beat. This barebones version was submitted to Greg

The Jacksons perform *Shake Your Body* during a TV appearance in Germany in 1979.

Phillinganes, a keyboard specialist hired by Bobby Colomby to help the brothers develop their ideas. In *Vibrations Magazine* in 2010 Phillinganes talked about how the rhythmic part of the tune came into being: "The first time I heard the demo of *Shake Your Body* it was...Well, the melody was there of course. It was powerful. And you could hear the piano. But not a lot was happening with the rhythm."[25] So he wrote the rhythmic arrangement with the tom-tom drum and cymbals that gives an effect of chopping and changing around, which blends in well with the bass guitar line. The song moves away from the well-used disco and funk standards of the time and does not adopt the classic bass drum / snare drum rhythm. Because it was so unusual musically, it was almost dropped from the album. The record executives at Epic did not want the track because it did not fit into any of the standard pigeonholes. Only Paris Eley, who was in charge of R&B at the label, believed in *Shake Your Body* to the extent that he used it heavily to promote the album.

The brass section establishes a second theme in the song. Tom Tom 84, who was already working with Maurice White and his group Earth, Wind, and Fire, wrote a superb melody line that gave the tune greater depth.

All these ingredients created a recipe for a track that became a benchmark in the world of funk. Just as Kool and The Gang and Earth, Wind, and Fire, two formations with very strong jazz roots, decided to set out to conquer the dance floors, The Jacksons delivered a riposte that brought them renewed public and critical acclaim, but also marked them out as a group to be reckoned with in the new funk scene of the late 1970s. And they were quite open about their ambitions. At the very end of the recording of the demo version of *Shake Your Body*, Jackie, the oldest brother, shouts out, "I want the Bee Gees to hear this shit!" At the time, the Bee Gees were riding high thanks to the soundtrack of the movie *Saturday Night Fever*, until of course that album was surpassed by *Thriller* as the best-selling album in history.

Marlon and Michael Jackson on stage during the *Destiny Tour* in London, 1979.

1978

[THE JACKSONS]

DESTINY

Tito, Jackie, Marlon, Michael, and Randy Jackson / 4'53

From the album: *Destiny*
Released by Epic Records/CBS: USA and UK, 17 December 1978 (ref. JE 35552 and ref. EPC 83200)
Chart position: USA R&B No. 3, Pop No. 11 / UK No. 33
RIAA: certified Gold 13 March 1979 / certified Platinum 8 May 1979

Musicians
Michael Jackson: lead vocals
The Jacksons: backing vocals
Tito Jackson, Paul Jackson, and Mike Sembello: guitar
Nathan Watts: bass guitar
Greg Phillinganes: keyboards
Ed Greene: drums
Randy Jackson: congas
Recording
Cherokee Recording Studios, Total Experience, Record Plant, and Dawnbreaker, Los Angeles
Heiders/Filmways, San Francisco: summer 1978
Technical team
Producers: The Jacksons
Executive Producers: Bobby Colomby and Mike Atkinson
Recording engineers: Peter Granet and Don Murray
Vocal arrangements: The Jacksons
Rhythmic arrangements: Greg Phillinganes
Brass and string arrangements: Tom Tom 84
Mixing: (unknown)

Single

A-side: *Destiny* (single version) / 3'44
B-side: *That's What You Get (For Being Polite)* (album version) / 4'56
Released by Epic Records/CBS: UK, February 1979 (ref. S EPC 6983)
Chart position: UK No. 39

Genesis

Although the song *Destiny* was never heavily marketed as a single, The Jacksons promoted it on stage while on tour, as well as on a number of TV shows. The song after which their third album is named seems to be the perfect synthesis of two worlds that were important to them. On the one hand, an idyllic vision of life full of good intentions and humanism, which was directly inherited from the Gamble and Huff philosophy. Seen from this viewpoint, the lyrics of *Destiny* seem a logical follow-on to *Show You the Way to Go* (*The Jacksons*, 1976) and *Man of War* (*Goin' Places*, 1977). On the other hand, *Destiny* was a product of the spiritual influence that the Jackson brothers had felt since birth. They were Jehovah's Witnesses and had been brought up to reject idol worship and materialism. The song's lyrics are about seeking a simple lifestyle, far from the urban environment, which is seen as synonymous with the unrest that sows confusion in men's minds (very much in keeping with the vocabulary used in the scriptures of Jehovah's Witnesses).

In the song, the Jackson brothers imply that self-fulfillment is found elsewhere than in the city. The group produced a text that follows the great tradition of the two major genres in black American music: the gospel of salvation that originated in and spread across rural areas, and soul music, which had its origins in cities and their associated vices.

Production

Bobby Colomby recalls struggling when Michael Jackson sang the lyrics "What the city offers me ain't naturally." It should have read "natural" rather than "naturally." But the lead singer of The Jacksons could not help singing "naturally," which fitted better with the music. Colomby soon realized it was not worth fighting over; he understood the importance of giving the young singer room for maneuver and a certain amount of freedom. Michael put his foot down, and it was the "naturally" version that appeared on the album. Although by now The Jacksons controlled their music in the studio, it was Michael who was the undisputed leader and often had the last word on the final cut.

The guitarist Paul Jackson laid down the solo that appears toward the end of the tune. It was the first time that he had worked with the Jackson brothers. Over time, Michael developed a close relationship with him, and Paul ended up working with Michael right up until the release of *Invincible* in 2001.

Michael Jackson in New York, 17 November 1977.

THE WIZ
MICHAEL JACKSON IN THEATERS

On 28 September 1977, Michael Jackson, Diana Ross, Nipsey Russell, and Ted Ross arrived at Astoria Studios in Queens to announce the release of *The Wiz*. This African-American remake of Lyman Frank Baum's famous *Wizard of Oz* was an adaptation of the eponymous Broadway play, created in 1975 by Charlie Smalls and William F. Brown.

Barry Gordy, in his quest to conquer Hollywood, had bought the rights to the musical so he could bring it to the big screen. When he heard of the project, Michael Jackson wanted a role at all costs. He was on bad terms with Motown, but after the intervention of his friend and champion Diana Ross, he landed the role of the Scarecrow, a key character in this timeless story.

The Wiz flops

Sydney Lumet directed *The Wiz* at the height of his career, at a time when he held significant sway in the filmmaking world. Notably, he'd directed *Serpico,* with Al Pacino in the role of the title character. As for the soundtrack, Lumet enlisted the help of his friend Quincy Jones, whose track record of putting together top-notch musical arrangements had made him an impressive and versatile producer.

Jones likened the project to a great kitchen in which top ingredients were being wasted on a bad recipe. He accepted the job anyway in thanks to Lumet who, a few years before, had hired him to write the soundtrack to the *The Pawnbroker*, which made Jones the first black musician in history to write an original movie soundtrack.

Filming took place in New York between October and December 1977, during which time Michael began to discover life in New York, with his older sister La Toya as his only chaperone. At 19 years old, it was his first time living far from the family fold, and he often found himself frequenting the legendary Studio 54. This temple of the night was a maker and breaker of trends. Some of the most popular stars and beautiful people of the time would float across the dance floor and sink into one of the club's luxurious armchairs. Graceful yet high on drink and drugs of all kinds, they would weave in and out of relationships that were as superficial as they were ephemeral.

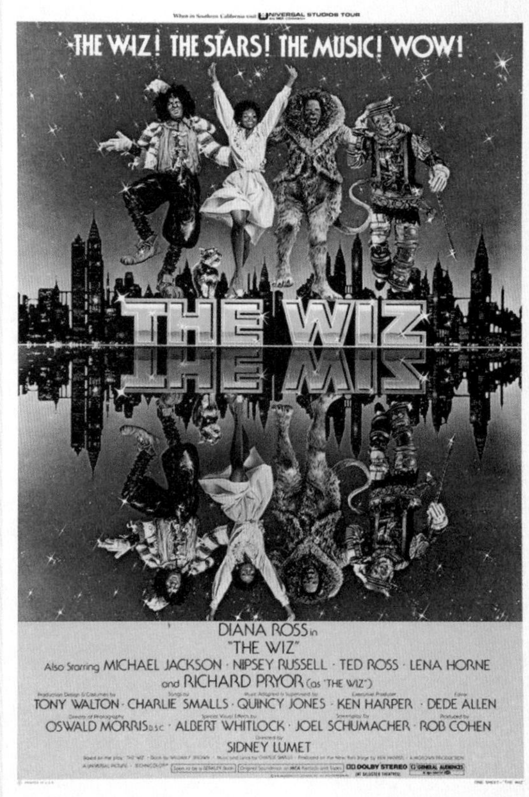

Although *The Wiz* was a failure, Michael Jackson's performance was hailed by both the critics and the public.

When *The Wiz* came out just before Christmas 1978, the public and critical responses were harsh: of the $24 million invested, only $21 million was recovered. Journalists blamed Diana Ross, saying that as a 34-year-old she wasn't capable of playing a convincing Dorothy. A critical and commercial flop, *The Wiz* was a disaster that Motown could have done without.

Ease on down the Road

Charlie Smalls / 3'19

From the album: *The Wiz: Original Motion Picture Soundtrack*
Released by MCA Records: USA, 21 September 1978 (ref. MCA2-14000) / UK, October 1978 (ref. MCSP 287)
Chart position: USA Black Albums No. 33, Pop No. 40
RIAA: certified Gold in the first half of 1979

Musicians
Michael Jackson and Diana Ross: lead vocals
Nipsey Russell and Ted Ross: backing vocals
Steve Gadd: drums
Eric Gale: guitar
Richard Tee: piano
Anthony Jackson: bass
Michael Brecker: saxophone
Recording
A&R Recording, New York City: November 1977 to January 1978
Technical team
Producers: Quincy Jones and Tom Bahler
Recording engineer: Bruce Swedien
Assistant sound engineer: Skip Taylor
Vocal arrangement: Quincy Jones
Mixing: Bruce Swedien

Single

A-side: *Ease on down the Road (single version)* / 3'19
B-side: *Poppy Girls (album version)* / 3'27
Released by MCA Records: USA, September 1978 (ref. MCA-40947) / UK, October 1978 (ref. MCA 396), July 1984 (ref. MCA-898)
Chart position: USA R&B No. 17, Pop No. 41 / UK No. 45

Genesis

Before it was the first film to feature a cast entirely made up of African-American actors and dancers, *The Wiz* was a musical comedy performed in Baltimore in 1974, and on Broadway the following year. The show's original title was *The Wiz: The Super Soul Musical—Wonderful Wizard of Oz.* Charlie Smalls composed the music to this new adaptation of L. Frank Baum's legendary novel. The project was ambitious: it needed to live up to the brilliant version filmed by Victor Fleming in 1939 starring Judy Garland as Dorothy.

Ease on down the Road was one of the first songs written for *The Wiz.* It accompanies the heroes as they journey to the kingdom of the wonderful Wizard of Oz. The song recurs each time a new central character (Dorothy, the Scarecrow, the Tin Man, and the Cowardly Lion) appears, as a theme representing the drive and courage they need to follow their path to Oz.

An early version of *Ease on down the Road* was released on vinyl in 1975 for the show's original Broadway soundtrack. It was performed by the main actors: Stephanie Mills (Dorothy), Hinton Battle (Scarecrow), Tiger Haynes (Tim Man), and Ted Ross (Cowardly Lion). It never came out as a single. A different instrumental piece, *Tornado*, was released instead, though it did not achieve the expected success.

Consumer Rapport, which arrived on the American disco scene in the mid-1970s, recorded its own version of the song and released it as a single in 1975. The group's lead singer, Frank Floyd, was also a member of the Broadway cast. This recording, released by A Wing and a Prayer, a subsidiary of Atlantic Records, saw some success on the club scene after a longer version of 6'27 was made, especially because of its catchy rhythmic section.

The version appearing in Sidney Lumet's film was performed by Diana Ross as Dorothy and Michael Jackson in the role of a barely passable Scarecrow. Just like on Broadway, the song recurred each time a new character appeared. Nipsey Russell played the Tin Man and Ted Ross, the only cast member brought in from the stage version, retained his role as the Cowardly Lion.

Nothing could escape Barry Gordy when it came to marketing. Michael Jackson was no longer associated with Motown, and the record label was in the midst of suing the Jackson

Michael Jackson, Nipsey Russell, Diana Ross, and Ted Ross on the set of *The Wiz* (1977).

FOR JACKSON ADDICTS

In January 1980, for the TV show *Kraft Salutes Disneyland's 25th Anniversary*, Michael Jackson sang *Ease on down the Road* without Diana Ross but alongside many Disney characters, including Mickey Mouse, Winnie the Pooh, Pinocchio, Goofy, Donald Duck, Minnie Mouse, and the Seven Dwarves. In 1981, the singer met with his fairy godmother again to sing for a special program on CBS simply called *Diana*.

family. But this ambitious project was close to Gordy's heart, and he saw it as his golden opportunity to unite—on the big screen and in record stores—two of his most treasured stars: Diana Ross and Michael Jackson.

In the end, this is the only version that remains, to the detriment of all those that were recorded before or after. This song earned Michael Jackson his very first Grammy nomination outside of The Jackson Five. He and Diana Ross were nominated in the category of best R&B vocal performance for duo in 1979.

Production

The Wiz allowed Quincy Jones and Michael Jackson to work together for the first time. *Ease on down the Road* was the first song they recorded together. They worked under the watchful eye of Diana Ross, who once again asserted her role as Michael's fairy godmother.

When the recording sessions started in 1977, Quincy Jones and his team were aware they would be starting from scratch. They had to create a new soundtrack from start to finish and package all of the background music for the scenes that would later be filmed outdoors in New York City.

Confined to the Big Apple's A&R Recording studios, Quincy's musicians recorded the songs that would appear in the film. Anthony Jackson obeyed the nuances of Charlie Smalls' bass line, which oscillated between precise notes punctuating the start of each bar and a melody that followed the piano played by Richard Tee, a studio musician who'd learned the ropes at Motown.

Behind the mixing console was an old man with a moustache that made him look as if he were constantly laughing: it was Quincy's favorite recording engineer, Bruce Swedien. Swedien was in charge of ensuring that all background music and songs were recorded under the best possible conditions in order to better serve the film and obtain the perfect sound for the movie theater.

For his first collaboration with Michael Jackson, Bruce Swedien produced several mixes, all of which were later released on disc. The main version, lasting 3'19, was the one that appeared on the album, while the one on the single lasted 3'02. Three other variations were recorded. The first, lasting 1'30, included Jackson, Ross, and Nipsey Russell (the Tin Man). In the second, lasting 1'24, Ted Ross joined in as the fourth character (the Cowardly Lion). The last version to see the light of day lasted 6'02. It can be found on the song's maxi single and is characterized by a generous drum interlude that works well as a dance remix. In this version, *The Wiz* definitively departs from Broadway in favor of the club scene.

Ease on down the Road became a true commercial success, to the point where it surpassed that of the film, which struggled to fill theaters ahead of Christmas 1978. Though the song never reached the Top 40 in America (it remained relegated to 41st place), it did place 17th in the disco charts. It is interesting to note that Motown and Epic, two rival record companies, joined forces in order to ensure the success of this song, which promoted their respective stars: Diana Ross and Michael Jackson.

With this song, Bruce Swedien and Michael Jackson also began a collaboration that would last until the 2000s. During his first sessions, Swedien prepared several mixes in order to highlight the same song for different venues (single, film, and so on). They continued to apply this method to all their common projects.

1978

You Can't Win (Part 1 & 2)

Charlie Smalls / 3'14

From the album: *The Wiz: Original Motion Picture Soundtrack*
Released by MCA Records: USA, 18 September 1978 (ref. MCA2-14000) / UK, October 1978 (ref. MCSP 287)
Chart position: USA Black Albums No. 33, Pop No. 40
RIAA: certified Gold in the first half of 1979

Musicians
Michael Jackson: lead vocals
Anthony Jackson: bass
Recording
A&R Recording, New York City: November 1977 to January 1978
Technical team
Producers: Quincy Jones and Tom Bahler
Recording engineer: Bruce Swedien
Vocal arrangement: Quincy Jones
Mixing: Bruce Swedien

COVERS In January 1979, when *You Can't Win* was released as a single, Motown commissioned Lee Holdridge (arranger and project coproducer alongside Diana Ross and Suzanne De Passe) to assemble an album of solos Diana Ross had sung in the film. The project was canceled and didn't reach fans until 2015 via legal music-sharing sites. *Ease on down the Road* and *You Can't Win* were among her solos.

Single

A-side: *You Can't Win (Part 1)* / 3'43
B-side: *You Can't Win (Part 2)* / 2'58
Released by Epic Records: USA, January 1979 (ref. 8-50654) / UK, 27 April 1979 (ref. S EPC 7135)
Chart position: USA R&B No. 4, Pop No. 81

You Can't Win was first written for the original soundtrack to *The Wiz* (1975), Charlie Smalls' musical comedy. It was later scrapped. It was meant to introduce the little characters from Oz known as the Winkies. *I Was Born on the Day Before Yesterday* was the song sung by the Scarecrow in the original show.

Genesis

Quincy Jones chose to resurrect *You Can't Win* for the role of the Scarecrow in the film version, which was performed by Michael Jackson. According to Quincy, Sidney Lumet insisted that the soundtrack include songs representative of the film's main characters, especially Dorothy, who was portrayed by Diana Ross.

When filming started, Michael Jackson was only singing *Ease on down the Road* and part of *A Brand New Day*. Although this was his first time meeting Quincy Jones professionally, he told him, out of the blue, that he was looking for a producer. "Michael, look, you don't even [have] a song in the picture yet," said Quincy. "I don't want to think about that. Let's get you a song!"[28] This seemingly trivial request allowed Quincy Jones to test the young star's abilities early on. *You Can't Win* thus became the very first real collaboration between Quincy and Michael on a solo song. Together, they would soon begin the greatest musical revolution of the end of the 20th century.

The song undeniably stands out from the other songs in the film. It sends the message: "You can't win / You can't break even / And you can't get out of the game!" *You Can't Win* carries a humiliating message and is structured around a disheartening chorus. In the film, as he recites his commandments to the crows, Michael Jackson seems to embody the fears of an entire African-American generation. In his autobiography, he recalls: "My character had plenty to say and to learn. I was propped up on my pole with a bunch of crows laughing at me, while I sang *You Can't Win*. The song was about humiliation and helplessness—something that so many people have felt at one time or another—and the feeling that there are people out there who don't actively hold you back as much as they work quietly on your insecurities so that you hold yourself back."[2] Freed from his stake, thanks to Dorothy's (Diana Ross's) encouragements, the Scarecrow displays great bravery and ambition—two quali-

FOR JACKSON ADDICTS

In the United Kingdom, a 7-inch picture disc of *You Can't Win* was included with *Off the Wall* in 1979. This allowed the public to rediscover the song after the single had failed in Europe a few months before. *Can't Get outta the Rain* was included in the *Thriller* Ringle CD single (2007) (USA, 88697 18009 2) and *Thriller 25: Limited Japanese Single Collection* (2008) (JAP, EICP 945-951).

Michael Jackson at the première of the movie *The Wiz* in New York, 24 October 1978.

ties Michael Jackson would adopt in real life as well. The icon of a new generation was about to be born.

Production

While New York's A&R studios hosted most of the sound-track's orchestral recordings, little is known of the locations of the solo, duet, or group recordings. Quincy Jones' comings and goings between the East and West Coasts were difficult to keep up with.

Under the musical direction of his new teacher and vocal coach Tom Bahler, Michael began to inject electrifying, hot, and dynamic idiosyncrasies into his singing style. He used his new position as a film star to heighten the energy and vitality that would come to characterize his voice for the rest of his career. The shouts, the breathless and groovy interjections, brightened the song until its strong, deep, and husky blues finale: "You can't get out of the game." After the film version wrapped, Quincy Jones called Michael into his studio to continue working on this amazing song. They recorded a second part known popularly as *Part 2*. There was no doubt that Jones wanted to further test Michael's talent. With the production of this second part, he announced almost officially his commitment to becoming Michael's producer.

The second part of *You Can't Win* marked a true reorientation toward funky and jazzy music. The song picks up where *Part 1* ends: "You can't get out of the game." Without distorting the original motif, this second part is nevertheless lighter: Michael shouts with glee, laughs, and claps his hands. It's a true jam session held together flawlessly by Anthony Jackson's bass line.

In January 1979, *You Can't Win* became the newest single after *Ease on down the Road*. *Part 1* and *Part 2* were released on each side of the disc. Unfortunately, this single had no success in the United States. From May 1979 on, Europe stopped playing the song altogether. DJs nevertheless delighted in the longer 7' version remixed by Bruce Swedien (who, for the occasion, adopted the pseudonym Solvang). This version brought together both parts and can be found on *Michael Jackson—The Ultimate Collection* (2004).

The story doesn't end there

The story of *You Can't Win* didn't end there: the piece popped up again at the end of 1982 in *Can't Get outta the Rain*, an overdubbed version of Part 2. It came out on the B-side of some singles, including *The Girl Is Mine*, *Billie Jean*, and *Thriller*. The humiliation message of the first part was now making way for rain. The song was brightened, even emptied of its negative connotations. The jam session remains intact, the bass still strikes a chord. Michael gets groovy, screams, pokes fun at the rain, which is the new focal point of the song. It is surprising that Quincy Jones and Michael Jackson are both credited as composers for the piece.

PORTRAIT

QUINCY JONES
A SPIRITUAL FATHER

Quincy Jones was the first African-American musician to have written a film soundtrack: *The Pawnbroker* (1968).

"The producer's main job is to find the right tunes,"[26] was how Quincy Jones, in just a few words, described the vision he had of his role. Meeting Michael Jackson was a decisive moment for him: in addition to helping Michael's solo career take off, Quincy Jones spearheaded a revolution that would introduce new norms to the world of music and entertainment.

Quincy and Ray

Quincy Delight Jones was born in Chicago on 14 March 1933 into a low-income family. He was separated from his mother early on, when she was diagnosed with schizophrenia and committed to a specialized institution. Quincy developed his passion for music by listening to his neighbor Lucy Jackson play the piano for hours. Music allowed him to escape the sadness of his daily life, in which he sometimes had nothing to eat but the rats that his grandmother captured and cooked.

In 1943, the Jones family moved to Washington and later settled in Seattle. In 1947, Quincy met a young musician from Florida: his name was Ray Charles, and he soon became Quincy's role model. Blind and determined to live by music, Ray took care of himself and lived alone in his own apartment despite being only 17 years old. Quincy decided that if Ray could succeed under those conditions, he'd do just fine. Thus began Quincy's long journey toward often unexpected horizons.

In 1952, Quincy, who was already making the rounds of the local jazz clubs as an itinerant trumpet player, seized the opportunity of a lifetime: he joined Lionel Hampton's prestigious orchestra, with whom he traveled to Europe. There, freed from the social divisions still prevalent in the United States, he became aware of a whole new world where cultural diversity only added to the pleasures of social interaction.

Quincy in France

In 1957, after a tour of the Middle East and South America with Dizzy Gillespie, the young artist settled in Paris. He studied composition with Nadia Boulanger—whose students included Maurice Ravel—and struck up friendships with such artists as Eddy Mitchell.

His strong love affair with France was what led him to Barclay Records. Eddie Barclay trusted Quincy implicitly, and the two men would remain friends for years. Notably, Quincy was invited to each of Barclay's many weddings. In 1963, Quincy Jones produced a version of *It's My Party* by Lesley Gore. Composed by John Gluck, Wally Gold, and Herb

Quincy Jones with some of his French friends: Henri Salvador, Johnny Hallyday, Eddie Barclay, and Eddy Mitchell.

Weiner, the song was first recorded by The Chiffons and later by Helene Shapiro. But Gore's version was the one that hit the jackpot, allowing Quincy to dominate America's Top 40 charts for two weeks in May 1963.

The 1960s also brought their share of misfortune: Quincy created his own orchestra, The Jones Boys, but it was too big, too costly, and it soon became unprofitable. Resulting financial difficulties caused Quincy to sink into depression.

Quincy and Sidney

He soon bounced back. When he was named vice president of Mercury Records in the United States, he became the first black man to occupy a post of that magnitude. When his friend, the director Sidney Lumet, asked him to compose the original soundtrack to *The Pawnbroker*, Quincy broke further racial barriers.

From then on, Quincy's career took off for good. He moved to Los Angeles in 1975 and founded Quincy Jones Productions. He continued to produce records, notably for his friend Frank Sinatra, whom he'd met in the 1960s. As for his own music, he became increasingly well known through a series of concept albums released by A&M, including *Body Heat* and *Sounds... and Stuff Like That!,* all of which were well received by the public and critics.

In 1977, to thank Sidney Lumet for allowing him to break into the exclusive world of film-score composers, Quincy Jones agreed to produce the soundtrack to *The Wiz*. Barry Gordy had hired Lumet to direct the film, which for the first time in history was made up of an entirely African-American cast of actors, singers, and dancers. The project ended up drowning in its own ambitions: the $24-million budget was never recovered through box office sales, which only reached $21 million. It was during the shooting of this enormous flop that Michael Jackson and Quincy Jones finally got to know each other.

Off the Wall, *Thriller*, and *Bad*

Not long after *The Wiz*, Quincy Jones started production on Michael Jackson's first solo album for Epic / CBS, *Off the Wall*. The album was an undisputed success, with global sales reaching ten million copies. It also proved to skeptical CBS managers that jazz wasn't the only thing Quincy knew how to do. Emboldened by this stroke of genius, Quincy created his own label, Qwest Records, in 1980. George Benson congratulated him by releasing *Give Me the Night*. Though widely successful, the song drew the wrath of jazz purists, who accused Benson of wasting his talent as a jazz musician to sell out to the masses of pop fans.

Two years later, Quincy Jones and Michael Jackson created *Thriller*, which became the bestselling album of all time, with more than 60 million copies sold. This album was also instrumental in the development of the music video industry. Throughout his career, Quincy Jones never stopped combining his musical ambitions with film. He nurtured a

Quincy Jones was 14 when he met Ray Charles, then aged 16. The two men remained friends for life.

relationship with Stephen Spielberg, who in 1986 asked him to write the score to *The Color Purple*, adapted from Alice Walker's novel of the same name.

Once the contract for Jackson's three albums was fulfilled in 1987 with the release of *Bad*, Quincy Jones focused on his new solo album, which he'd been planning since the start of the decade but which had been repeatedly delayed. *Back on the Block*, released in 1989, was emblematic of the 1980s as well as a large part of his career as a producer. Legends such as Ray Charles sang alongside young, yet-to-be-discovered talents such as Tevin Campbell, and jazz mingled with rap in an unprecedented way. With this album, Quincy Jones delivered his last notable creative effort in a studio.

The legacy of a genius

In the 1990s, Quincy Jones distanced himself from the music world, as if he were expecting it to implode at any moment. Encouraged by his children, he began to embrace hip-hop culture, especially thanks to his daughter Kidada, who was engaged to Tupac Shakur. During this time he launched *Vibe*, a monthly magazine dedicated to urban culture. The greatest artists of the 1990s appeared on its covers, making it a major hit, while its in-depth interviews allowed musicians to open up more than ever before.

Quincy Jones also joined Warner in developing a television series that would popularize another young man at the forefront of the scene: in September 1990 NBC aired the first episode of *Fresh Prince of Bel Air*, starring a young Will Smith. At the time, Smith and his friend Jeff Townes were rapping together under the name of DJ Jazzy Jeff and The Fresh Prince.

Since then, Quincy's body of work has continued to inspire new generations. His song *Soul Bossa Nova* was highlighted in the original soundtrack to *Austin Powers in Goldmember.*

Michael Jackson and Quincy Jones celebrate the success of *Thriller* at the Grammy Awards in Los Angeles, 28 February 1984.

Quincy used his connections to launch new artists, and AKG even developed a line of headphones in his name—a quiet response to the Beats by Dre headphones.

For Quincy Jones, the record industry died with the arrival of music streaming and its associated financial turmoil. The proliferation of home studios and the decrease in revenue from record sales led to many problems, not least of which was the closure of the big recording studios, which producers such as himself used to create songs that withstood the test of time.

Goodbye Michael

When Michael Jackson died on 26 June 2009, Quincy Jones wrote a touching open letter that spoke of the strong friendship he cultivated with Michael through the years, one that, despite its inevitable ups and downs, had been built on a solid foundation of respect. "I am absolutely devastated at this tragic and unexpected news," he wrote. "For Michael to be taken away from us so suddenly at this young age, I just don't have the words…He was the consummate entertainer and his contributions and legacy will be felt upon the world forever…I've lost my little brother today and part of my soul has gone with him."[27]

A few years later, Michael's estate broke the contract he'd made with Quincy in the 1980s regarding songs they'd worked on together. This resulted in a hefty accumulation of unregulated royalties. Quincy Jones asserted his rights and won the case before a judge. The lesson he'd learned in the 1960s, when his orchestra went bankrupt, finally bore fruit. He knew that two things existed in this world: music and business. A truly wise man, he was a breath of fresh air and an eternal ambassador to the spirit of jazz. The man widely known as The Dude remains a respected emperor of music.

PORTRAIT

BRUCE SWEDIEN
MUSIC FIRST

SOLD! Laurent Brancowitz, the guitarist for Phoenix, bought the Harrison 4032 used in *Thriller* on eBay for the pretty sum of $17,000 (instead of the original $32,000). Once it was delivered to Paris, Phoenix recorded the album *Bankrupt!* (the working title had been *Alternative Thriller*).

The musical history of the 20th century wouldn't be the same without Bruce Swedien. Since the 1950s, he helped some of the most prestigious artists, from B.B. King to Paul McCartney, Barbra Streisand to Donna Summer, and Duke Ellington to George Benson. But it was his four-decade-long collaboration with Michael Jackson that allowed him to write some of the most memorable lines in the history of pop music.

Early days in the studio

Bruce Swedien was born on 19 April 1934 in Minneapolis to parents of Swedish descent. They, too, were musicians, and the young Bruce found his calling during a rehearsal for the Minneapolis Symphony choir. With the encouragement of his mentor Bill Putnam—the inventor of modern recording techniques who had worked with Elvis Presley and Duke Ellington, among others—he became a recording engineer and joined the Schmitt Music Company, which he later bought. In 1959, he met Quincy Jones, who was then vice president of Mercury Records and was producing a record for Dina Washington called *What a Diff'rence a Day Makes!* After that, the two men never parted and went on to collaborate on an endless number of recordings. In 1962, Bruce Swedien received his first Grammy nomination for *Big Girls Don't Cry* by Frankie Valli and The Four Seasons. He received 13 nominations throughout his career, winning five of the precious trophies.

Sound according to Bruce

Bruce Swedien was an ardent defender of the natural stereo school of thought. He rejected more sophisticated concepts like the surround-sound method. For him, a simple stereo image in 2.0 was like a slate on which the listener could project his or her own idea of the music they were listening to. This concept, known as sonic landscape, perfectly reflects Swedien's philosophy: every piece of music or sound that we perceive allows us to project images and colors that are uniquely ours. Swedien perfected his methods based on this intimate relationship with music, which gave rise to an expression he'd been using since the days of *The Wiz* and which appeared in the credits of his records: "acusonic recording process," a method consisting in using multiple multitrack tape recorders to better capture recording nuances. This expression was the combination of the words "accurate" and "sonic." In short, sonic accuracy.

The birth of a trio

Bruce Swedien first met Michael Jackson in 1977 on the set of *The Wiz*. In addition to supervising the film's soundtrack (the original songs had been performed by the New York Symphony Orchestra), Swedien was in charge of producing the songs performed by the film's characters. During the making of *The Wiz*, Bruce Swedien showed that he understood how important it was for the background music and pop songs that characterized the film to complement each other.

Swedien, Jones, and Jackson worked together swimmingly in New York. The trio had found themselves on a sinking ship, but from this artistic and commercial chaos emerged a promise: all three of them ended up meeting again in California to put together Michael Jackson's first solo album as an adult.

Bruce and Michael

Swedien's collaborations with Michael Jackson were true testaments to the evolution of recording techniques taking place from the end of the 1970s to the dawn of the 2000s. While *Off the Wall* was recorded using standard techniques, *Thriller* was born thanks to the unique, precise sound of the mythical Harrison 4032 console (series 32C). This war machine has since fueled the dreams of many musicians, to the point where home studio models have been developed along with plug-ins that simulate the console's unique sound.

When Quincy Jones and Michael Jackson ended their collaboration at the end of the 1980s, Bruce Swedien remained the central pillar, or backbone, on which the King of Pop would lean to ensure the success of his albums, which became patchworks of rich and diverse influences. While his albums were, by then, being made by multiple producers, Bruce

The magic trio: Michael Jackson, paying tribute to his idol Charlie Chaplin, with Bruce Swedien and Quincy Jones in Los Angeles, 1979.

Swedien remained the lead recording engineer supervising and synthesizing Michael's growing repertoire.

He also became a producer. For *Dangerous,* he showed his mettle with *Keep the Faith* and maintaining the thread started by Quincy Jones in *Off the Wall.* He adopted new technological developments and would spend hours adjusting the sound of the synthetic snare drum, knowing full well how to return to more traditional recordings with a symphony orchestra, as with *Childhood* and *Smile* in *HIStory.*

Few recording engineers can embody the very sounds they create for their prestigious clients. Bruce Swedien was in this special category, in the manner of George Martin or Phil Spector. Likely underestimated, he remained a shadow figure without whom Michael Jackson's musical career wouldn't have been the same. More discreet than his colleagues, he kept himself apart from the public eye and cultivated, with his wife Bea, an intimacy and familial fold that fostered equilibrium. He embodied the quiet force, humility, and composure with which he tackled each project.

Michael Jackson was able to see him as a faithful right-hand man, infallible and loyal despite challenges. Despite unpaid bills for his last studio work with Michael, Bruce Swedien never betrayed the memory or trust of his friend. While Swedien's mantra was "music first," it could equally have been "high-fidelity friend."

OFF THE WALL

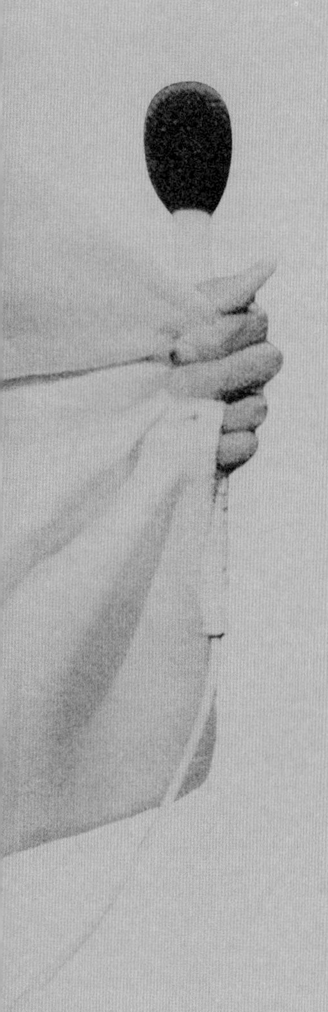

1. DON'T STOP 'TIL YOU GET ENOUGH
2. ROCK WITH YOU
3 WORKING DAY AND NIGHT
4. GET ON THE FLOOR
5. OFF THE WALL
6. GIRLFRIEND
7. SHE'S OUT OF MY LIFE
8. I CAN'T HELP IT
9. IT'S THE FALLING IN LOVE
10. BURN THIS DISCO OUT

Off the Wall **ALBUM**

Released by Epic Records: USA and UK, 10 August 1979 (ref. USA 35745 / UK EPC 83468)
Chart position: USA R&B No.1, Pop No. 3 / UK No. 3
RIAA: certified Gold and Platinum on 10 December 1979 / certified 8-time Multiplatinum on 21 August 2009

Michael Jackson and Quincy Jones just after having finished recording *Off the Wall* in Los Angeles, 1979.

OFF THE WALL, THE EMANCIPATION OF A PRINCE

The fiasco of *The Wiz* allowed Michael Jackson to take a step back and focus on his own activities. Critics spared him and commended his performance, which had the effect of giving him a bit more self-confidence.

Michael prepares his comeback as a soloist

Ever since The Jackson Five quit Motown in 1975, Michael had put aside his private ambitions to devote himself to ensuring his family's success. The songs in his last solo album for Motown, *Forever, Michael,* reflected his unconditional love for ballads. They were heavy on guitars and strings and weak on groove and dance rhythms.

In Michael's last solo, he reminds us of a dejected teenager, who has been robbed of his freedom and forced into the family business. *Dear Michael,* in which he reads the letter of an admirer, consolidated his status as a young idol surrounded by devoted fans.

The contract signed between CBS and The Jacksons contained a clause allowing Michael to publish solo albums. But between 1976 and 1978, he prioritized returning the family franchise to the top of the charts. Once his mission was accomplished with *Destiny*, which generated the hit *Shake Your Body* and became a Platinum disc in the United States, Michael was able to focus on his future.

The manifesto

As The Jacksons hit the road for the *Destiny* tour, Michael relegated himself to the back of the bus and wrote a note that would become the roadmap to his solo career. At 20 years old, he listed the things he should and shouldn't being doing to become the greatest artist of all time. Michael's estate released the handwritten note in September 2013:

> MJ will be my new name. No more Michael Jackson. I want a whole new character, a whole new look. I should be a totally different person. People should never think of me as the kid who sang *ABC*, [or] *I Want You Back*. I should be a new, incredible actor / singer / dancer that will shock the world. I will do no interviews. I will be magic. I will be a perfectionist, a researcher, a trainer, a masterer. I will be better than every great actor roped into one.[29]

Michael and Quincy

The two men first met in 1972 at Sammy Davis Jr.'s house in Los Angeles. They were at an informal gathering watching an episode of the *Ed Sullivan Show* starring The Jackson Five. But their real connection wasn't established until the shooting of *The Wiz*.

Michael was discovering the fascinating process of filmmaking while secretly dreaming of becoming an actor. What he gained instead from this missed cinematographic opportunity was a musical partner who would become essential to his career as a singer.

At the start of the project, Michael Jackson didn't have any solos in the film. Quincy Jones then rearranged Charlie Small's compositions so that he could sing *You Can't Win*. The young

On 3 September 1980 in Los Angeles, Michael Jackson received a special award for *Off the Wall* from the Hollywood Chamber of Commerce.

singer participated in his first recording sessions with Quincy at the A&R Recording studios in New York alongside Diana Ross, with whom he sang *Ease on down the Road*.

Quincy Jones saw commitment, talent, and perseverance in Michael. So when the young singer had to redo a scene in which he missed the pronunciation of Socrates, the producer took it in his stride. It would be the beginning of a wonderful partnership.

Quincy versus CBS

After *The Wiz* was released and soon forgotten, Michael dedicated himself to making his first solo album with Epic. He wanted to find a producer who could help him polish his ideas and create his own musical identity. When he asked Quincy Jones for advice, the conversation turned to a discussion on different potential producers.

Jones ended up putting himself out there by asking, "Michael, why don't we try and work on an album together?" This anecdote has been told time and again, and has become legendary. And just as with any legend, it holds an element of mystery: Was the young artist too shy to ask Quincy Jones directly?

When Michael Jackson told CBS that he wanted to record his first album with Quincy Jones, he was met with a firm denial. Jones was considered to be too jazzy, not poppy or commercial enough. Berry Gordy believed him to be out of touch with current musical trends and therefore incapable of propelling songs to the top of the charts. Marvin Gaye and Stevie Wonder had already tried to work with the renowned producer, but their hopes had been dashed by Motown executives. However, Michael Jackson stood up to his label and his managers, prompting CBS to reconsider the situation and take caution, after all, the young artist had just sold his songs to Warner Music. They also knew that Warner was in the midst of negotiating a contract with Quincy Jones to set up his label, Qwest, which was established in 1980. These events gave Michael leverage in his battle with Walter Yetnikoff, the CEO of CBS. In the end, Yetnikoff gave in and accepted Jackson's conditions.

Off the Wall: Michael as his own man

From Monday 4 December 1978 to Sunday 3 June 1979, Michael Jackson and Quincy Jones threw themselves into the making of *Off the Wall*. They settled into Allen Zentz studios and built the exceptional team responsible for the ten-song work of art. In addition to his faithful acolytes, such as recording engineer Bruce Swedien and trumpet player and composer Jerry Hey, Quincy Jones poached another talented composer: Rod Temperton, keyboarder and songwriter for Heatwave, an English group who had been dominating dance floors for some time. Temperton had written some of Heatwave's disco songs, such as *Boogie Nights*, which reached No. 2 in the August 1977 *Billboard*. Temperton wrote three songs for Quincy Jones and Michael Jackson, hoping that they'd choose at least one. All three were included in the final tracklist.

In 1975, Jones put The Brothers Johnson on the map with the album *Mellow Madness*. Four years later, Louis Johnson's bass was getting groovy in *Off the Wall*.

John Robinson was the only drummer who worked on the album. Percussionist Paulinho Da Costa used all the percus-

On 30 January 1981 in Los Angeles, Michael Jackson received two American Music Awards for *Off the Wall.*

sion instruments he could think of to bring to life the frenzied rhythms Michael Jackson came up with.

The album can be divided into three parts: the trilogy composed by Rod Temperton (*Rock with You*, *Off the Wall*, and *Burn This Disco Out*), Michael Jackson's three songs (*Don't Stop 'Til You Get Enough*, *Working Day and Night*, and *Get on the Floor*, which he cowrote with Louis Johnson), and four written by other renowned composers: Paul McCartney, Stevie Wonder, Tom Bahler, and Carole Bayer Sager with David Foster. Support from these talented peers is what lies at the heart of *Off the Wall's* success. Paul McCartney, a former Beatle, provided *Girlfriend*, sugar-pop that allowed Michael to sing something very different from the mournful tunes he did for Motown. Stevie Wonder, Michael's musical big brother and perennial influence, sent him *I Can't Help It*, a jazzy and timeless gem that was cowritten with Susaye Greene, the former Supreme and protégée of Ray Charles. *She's out of My Life,* written by Tom Bähler, had first been envisaged for Frank Sinatra. *It's the Falling in Love* could seem like a low-key song, but it's not: it combines the sharp pen of Carole Bayer Sager, ex-wife of the legendary Burt Bacharach, and David Foster, who worked alongside the greatest names in American music, from Whitney Houston to Earth, Wind, and Fire, not to mention Céline Dion.

An undisputed public success

When *Off the Wall* was released on 10 August 1979 it won public support. The album sold more than 10 million copies and generated four singles, all of which reached the Top 10 in the American charts. *Don't Stop 'Til You Get Enough* and *Rock with You* even reached the top of the French charts. In so doing, Michael Jackson broke records that had never been broken by a black male artist. In the United Kingdom, *Off the Wall* was the first album to generate five singles: *Girlfriend* was played on the radio and became available in 45 rpm singles.

This success provoked an artistic schism between Michael and his siblings. The figures spoke for themselves: *Destiny* attracted four million fans; *Triumph,* the album The Jacksons put out a year after *Off the Wall*, only attracted three million. But as it turned out, Quincy and Michael's gamble paid off: *Off the Wall* allowed Michael to assert his style as a solo artist. His look, which was completely reimagined by designer Mike Salisbury, was that of a character who was as elegant as he was urban, with a modern attitude and confidence that couldn't help but draw attention. By this point, his image was contrasting with that of his siblings. In the twilight of the 1970s, Michael was laying the foundation for a musical and financial empire that would further distance him from his family.

The dawn of the music video

To promote *Off the Wall*, CBS spent their tight but still significant budget on making videos of the album's best singles. Two young directors, Bruce Gowers and Nick Saxton, were put in charge of Michael Jackson's first three solo videos: *Don't Stop 'Til You Get Enough, Rock with You*, and *She's out of My Life*.

These videos were rudimentary and were not to Michael's satisfaction. Since by then the album had already yielded large commercial success, CBS didn't want to finance a video for the fourth single, *Off the Wall*. Michael kicked up a storm and took advantage of a family project to get into his first tussle with the record company. He convinced his siblings to adapt the funk-rock song *Can You Feel It*, from the album *Triumph*, to video. At the time, futuristic effects were gaining in popularity. The cultural tsunami created by the movie *Star Wars* had inspired science-fiction scenes where everyone dressed in silver suits and moved around in sleek spacecrafts. Michael reached out to Robert Abel, who made avant-garde commercials packed with then-revolutionary visual effects. Disney hadn't wasted any time in hiring his team to work on the sci-fi film, *Tron*.

Can You Feel It—The Triumph took shape from a simple idea, without any real planning or brainstorming approved by CBS. The shooting, which shouldn't have lasted longer than three weeks, took more than nine months to finish. CBS protested, estimating that the allocated budget had largely been surpassed. Negotiations between the recording house, the singer, and Robert Abel soured. Michael Jackson ended up investing his own money in the making of the nine-minute short.

Once the promotion of *Off the Wall* was over and that of *Triumph* concluded without incident, Michael focused on making a video of a song he'd recorded with his siblings. This was a risky play, since at the time MTV was in its early days (and in any case wasn't airing many videos made by black artists). *Can You Feel It—The Triumph* was ultimately used as the opening film for the famous American tour The Jacksons did between July and September 1981. It was like handing out Michael's business card, as if its purpose was to announce the young singer's artistic ambitions and his desire to make a significant contribution to filmmaking.

Michael abandons television

During their Motown days, the Jackson siblings used television to win over millions of American families. As guests on some of the most widely watched television shows, they dominated the silver screen and solidified their image as young idols for kids who were dying to go to their concerts. But Michael was learning that television could have negative consequences for an artist. During the 1976 to 1977 season, his father Joe had the brilliant idea (he thought) to create a variety show for CBS. The program consisted of sketches that turned out to be clumsy attempts to put the Jackson family in improbable situations surrounded by fake-looking set designs. Following this disaster, Michael became more selective of the television engagements he accepted. When *Destiny* came out, however, the success of *Shake Your Body* motivated the group to appear on all the greatest shows of the day. When *Off the Wall* hit the stands and saw immediate success, the public wanted to see Michael Jackson on television. The star agreed to sing *Rock with You* at a UNICEF gala on 29 January 1980, and he did so again when Disney asked him to record a few songs for a special that celebrated the 25th anniversary of its park in Anaheim, California. But what was meant to be a happy moment turned into artistic disappointment. Michael sang the theme song from *Pinocchio, When You Wish upon a Star,* on the famous rock in front of Sleeping Beauty's Castle. When Michael saw the cut made by director Dwight Hemion, he realized that close-ups on his face, which was expressing the emotion of the song, were edited in favor of a wide angle that showed him standing on the rock. It was a huge disappointment for him.

Michael Jackson and Diana Ross come together on the set of the TV show *Diana!*, and perform *Rock With You* in Los Angeles in 1981.

While *Off the Wall* became the most popular album of the early 1980s, Michael Jackson refused to make any more television appearances. He also refused to respond to the numerous interview requests that were received by his managers. Both decisions reflected his ambition to reinvent himself as a solo artist.

He made only one exception to his rule. In February 1981 he agreed to sing alongside Diana Ross on a show she was hosting for CBS to celebrate the success of her album *Diana*, produced by Chic.

Praised by the public, shunned by his peers

Off the Wall allowed Michael Jackson to become the most popular black artist of the 1979 to 1980 season. All the work he'd put into his songs, and his image as a young musician, paid off. In the second half of 1981, he signed a publicity contract with Suzuki to promote a line of scooters. During this three-ad campaign, he dusted off his tux and paired it with the rhinestone socks he wore on the cover of the *Off the Wall* album. His profile in Japan confirmed something that many already knew: in the Jackson family, Michael was the star, the one who sold the records.

Dick Clark, founder of the American Music Awards (see page 37), was thrilled when his friend won numerous distinctions in 1980 and 1981. Based on the public vote, this prize was a confirmation of the overnight success Michael had achieved with *Off the Wall*. But there was a dark cloud on the horizon. The Grammys, which took place on 27 February 1980 in Los Angeles, dealt a hard blow to young Michael. While all the signs pointed to *Off the Wall* taking home the loot, the record only received one, lesser nomination. Michael won best R&B vocal performance for *Don't Stop 'Til You Get Enough*. He decided not to pick up his award, especially since it was handed out during one of the live program's many commercial breaks. His frustration was significant. Sitting in his family home in Encino, and with his mother as his witness, he swore that no one in the world would be able to ignore his next album.

Don't Stop 'Til You Get Enough

Michael Jackson / 6'02

Musicians
Michael Jackson: lead and backing vocals
Louis Johnson: bass
John Robinson: drums
Greg Phillinganes: electric piano
David Williams and Marlo Henderson: guitars
Michael Jackson, Randy Jackson, Richard Heath, Paulinho Da Costa: percussion
The Seawind Horns: brass section
Jerry Hey: trumpet and flugelhorn
Larry Williams: tenor and alto saxophones, flute
Kim Hutchcroft: baritone and tenor saxophones, flute
William Reichenbach: trombone / **Gary Grant:** trumpet
Gerald Vinci: first violin
Jim Gilstrap, Augie Johnson, Mortonette Jenkins, Paulette McWilliams, and Zedric Williams: additional backing vocals
Recording
Cherokee Studios (studio 3), Los Angeles: strings
Allen Zentz Recording, Los Angeles: rhythm tracks and vocals
Westlake Recording Studios, Los Angeles: brass and mixing
4 December 1978 to 3 June 1979
Technical team
Producers: Quincy Jones and Michael Jackson
Recording engineer: Bruce Swedien
Horn arrangement: Jerry Hey
Rhythm arrangement: Greg Phillinganes and Michael Jackson
Vocal and percussion arrangements: Michael Jackson
String arrangement: Ben Wright

Single

A-side (USA): *Don't Stop 'Til You Get Enough (US single version aka long version with rap) / 5'45*
A-side (UK): *Don't Stop 'Til You Get Enough (European single version aka short version with rap) / 3'55*
B-side: *I Can't Help It (album version) / 4'29*
Released by Epic Records: USA, 28 July 1979 (ref. 9-50742) / UK, August 1979 (ref. S EPC 7763)
Chart position: USA R&B No. 1, Pop 100 No. 1 / UK No. 3
RIAA: certified Gold on 29 November 1979 / certified Platinum on 14 February 1989

SONG

Genesis

In the fall of 1978, shortly after *Destiny* gave him his first taste of artistic freedom, Michael started on his inaugural solo project with Epic Records. He wrote a few songs intending to show them to his new producer, Quincy Jones. His creativity and talent as a songwriter improved at breakneck speed during this time.

Don't Stop 'Til You Get Enough, Workin' Day and Night, and *Get on the Floor* bring to mind Quincy Jones' ear for music. In fact, not only did he coproduce these songs, but he also worked with the greatest musical artists of the day to polish them. This virtuous cycle was a daily blessing to Michael, who had only just turned 20. By then he had found his feet and traded in his sneakers for a pair of loafers. Having extricated himself from his tribe, at least for a while, he was now free to fully express himself. The production of this album is still considered today to be a true reference point in contemporary music history. The style is unique, the formula is perfect. It combined the best influences of pop, folk, jazz, funk, soul, and blues. The composition of *Off the Wall* is masterful: its tonalities are fresh, dynamic, and powerful, and the arrangements are top-notch.

Michael said he was at home in Encino and humming a few notes while dancing around the house when *Don't Stop 'Til You Get Enough* came to him. "It's about love and forces of love and the power of love," he said. "The main theme goes 'keep on with the force, don't stop, don't stop 'til you get enough…'" In order to get started on the demo, Michael called Randy to the piano in his family studio, which was equipped with professional systems, to record 24 tracks. It was a very relaxed atmosphere, and Janet even played percussion. The first notes are impossible to ignore: they're powerful, solid, and convincing. This demo, which was included in the 2001 reedition of the album, became the frame and backbone of the other tracks. Quincy loved it at first listen and recorded it in his studio. The words to *Don't Stop 'Til You Get Enough* could seem ambiguous: "You know, I was / I was wondering, you know, If you could keep on / Because the force, it's got a lot of power / And it make me feel like ah, It make me feel like...oooh!"

Michael Jackson performs *Don't Stop Til You Get Enough* during the *Triumph* tour in 1981. The number was directed by Doug Henning.

Even though the first *Star Wars* movie had been spreading a certain idea of the "force" since 1977, the force that Michael emitted seemed to come from something deep within him, ready to spring forth, uncontrollable as it bubbled up within. When Katherine Jackson heard the words to this song, she thought her religious beliefs were being challenged, to the point where Michael had to reassure her that there was absolutely nothing sexual about the words. However, anyone can hear, or interpret, what they want. The inspiration for this song almost certainly came from New York's Studio 54, a club that Michael had just started to frequent. Nights bursting with scandal and strong sexual overtones likely inspired and intensified Michael's creativity. Were his intentions as puritanical as he'd told his mother? By then, he'd already learned that shock, or at least the act of eliciting curiosity, was the way to attract attention and gain recognition.

Production

Benjamin Wright was responsible for the string arrangements in *Don't Stop 'Til You Get Enough*. In a 2014 interview with the Red Bull Music Academy, he said of his work:

> Quincy made me feel at home and gave me Michael Jackson's stuff...I was nervous about this Quincy Jones thing, because Quincy was so big. I had about a month, 30 days, to prepare the charts. And for 28 days I did no writing, because I didn't know what to do with it. Finally, the Lord talked to me. He says, 'You better put some notes on this paper.' I did. On session day I'm nervous all over again. This is not the norm for me, because everybody knows Benjamin is extremely confident. Not arrogant, but he's in charge. This time, I'm scared. I'm scared to death...I walk in the studio and somebody says, 'Hey Ben.' It was none other than the great Bruce Swedien. Then Bruce makes it worse. 'Hey Q, piece of cake. Ben is here.' I think I'm going to have a heart attack. I pass out the music. We began to play. I'm not frightened anymore. I'm in charge now. I'm watching Quincy on the other side of the glass and he's falling down on his knees and it's like, 'Oh my God, is this stuff that bad?' The first tune I did was *Don't Stop 'Til You Get Enough* and Quincy is going crazy. I don't know if it's good or bad. I'm still nervous at that point. So we do the take and I go in the control room...Is this good or bad? It was good. In fact it was so good that he gave me another song that day: *Rock with You*.

Quincy Jones put together a team of brilliant musicians for the making of *Off the Wall*. For *Don't Stop 'Til You Get Enough,* the incredible Louis Johnson (of The Brothers Johnson), used

Second session with the famous *Off the Wall* tuxedo. Taken in 1981, almost two years after the album was released.

Greg Phillinganes, who was credited as co-writer on some pressings of the single, excelled at rhythm arrangements.

FOR JACKSON ADDICTS

In his book *Michael Jackson—Off The Wall, For The Record* (2016), Chris Cadman recalls that during summer 1979, Michael gave several impromptu performances of *Don't Stop 'Til You Get Enough* in clubs across the USA – possibly even dancing on tables!

his bass to give the intro the most beautiful forward thrust ever given to a song. In the documentary *Michael Jackson's Journey from Motown to Off the Wall* (2016), producer Rodney Jerkins spoke of it with admiration, saying, "That's the phrase that pays, that's the hook right there, Michael ain't gotta say a word yet. They can play that bass line, and they can run it nonstop."[24] Paulinho Da Costa, a true silversmith, shaped and hammered the rhythm into an outstanding product. John Robinson's drums were the thread that tied the album together. David Williams, on the guitar, brought freshness and charisma to the ensemble. Greg Philliangnes, picking up from the work he'd put into *Destiny*, added his magic touch to the whole arrangement. Michael's voice came alive with new thrusts, cries, and sighs. It is no surprise that what came of all this was instrumental in launching the album. *Don't Stop 'Til You Get Enough* became its first single. The charts loved this brilliant creation and rewarded Michael with a new No. 1 hit, the first since *Ben*, with the major difference being that, this time, Michael had written the song. The cry of freedom from the song's introduction rang out in all the living rooms and all the dance floors of the world: a new Michael Jackson was born!

THE VIDEO

Nick Saxton: director
Length: 4'11
Don't Stop 'Til You Get Enough was Michael Jackson's first solo video. It wasn't yet a short, since it still only consisted of music superimposed on a dance scene. Director Nick Saxon nevertheless provided Michael with the perfect platform for his new character, his ardor, and his incessant energy. Michael is clearly overjoyed to perform his own piece. His pride shows through the radiant smile he wears throughout the length of the clip. Against the backdrop of a starry sky, a close-up of his face pans out until it progressively reveals the tuxedo he's wearing. The tone is confident, that of an adult taking over from a child or adolescent who'd grown out of his outlandish sequined suits. He is elegant, relaxed, cool, and almost brazenly taking possession of his new artistic maturity. He wants to break all ties to his past career with his siblings. His cry for freedom causes the screen to explode with new artistic possibilities. Michael sings at the center of a translucent set made from crystals and resplendent with transparent beads, as if to light up his new persona. During the bridge, he splits into three dancers about to challenge each other to a dance off. In perfect harmony with the time, this video marks the launch of the audiovisual revolution that would take over a few years later.

On Tuesday 29 January 1980, Michael sang *Rock with You* at UNICEF's *Because We Care* gala, which marked the start of his humanitarian engagement.

Rock with You

Rod Temperton / 3'38

Musicians
Michael Jackson: lead vocals
Bobby Watson: bass
John Robinson: drums
David Williams and Marlo Henderson: guitars
Greg Phillinganes and Michael Boddicker: synthesizers
David "Hawk" Wollinski: electric piano
The Seawind Horns: horns
Jerry Hey: trumpet and flugelhorn
Larry Williams: tenor and alto saxophone, flute
Kim Hutchcroft: baritone and tenor saxophone, flute
William Reichenbach: trombone
Gary Grant: trumpet
Gerald Vinci: first violin
Recording
Cherokee Studios (studio 3), Los Angeles: strings
Allen Zentz Recording, Los Angeles: rhythmic tracks and vocals
Westlake Recording Studios, Los Angeles: brass and mixing
4 December 1978 to 3 June 1979
Technical team
Producer: Quincy Jones
Recording engineer: Bruce Swedien
Horn arrangement: Jerry Hey
Rhythm and voice arrangement: Rod Temperton
String arrangement: Ben Wright

Single

USA
A-side: *Rock with You (single version)* / 3'20
B-side: *Working Day and Night (edited album version)* / 4'55
UK
A-side: *Rock with You (single version)* / 3'20
B-side: *Get on the Floor* / 4'44
Released by Epic Records: USA, 3 November 1979 (ref. 9-50797) / UK, 28 January 1980 (ref. S EPC 8206)
Chart position: USA R&B No. 1, Pop No. 1, UK No. 7
RIAA: certified Gold on 14 February 1980 / certified Platinum on 14 February 1989

SINGLE

Genesis

Work on *Off the Wall* was already underway when Quincy Jones reached out to Rod Temperton, the successful songwriter from Heatwave. The producer remembered the rich and jazzy tonalities of *Boogie Nights*, which appeared on Heatwave's album *Too Hot to Handle* (1976). Jones knew he had to build a team that could find the right sound to make the album stand out and reach its full potential. While Rod was working with Phil Ramone on a new album in New York, Quincy called him and asked if he would write for Michael Jackson's first solo album. That's when Temperton suggested three songs that all ended up on the album: *Rock with You, Off the Wall,* and *Burn This Disco. Rock with You,* like the other two, follows a simple but precise rule of composition: its notes, staccato and short, allow for suspension to occur between the lyrics and the music, which reinforces the rhythm and dynamism of the piece.

Rock with You is at once a declaration and an invitation to love and dance. The words that Michael sings are sensual, like whispered foreplay. Never before had he included so many suggestive hints in his repertoire. On the album, *Rock with You* comes after *Don't Stop 'Til You Get Enough,* confirming the birth of a new Michael Jackson. In the prime of his life, Michael was becoming a sex symbol of some credibility, someone sensual and sexual and very much unlike the model innocent image he had cultivated within The Jackson Five.

Production

When the album was rereleased in 2001, Rod Temperton thought back to the recording sessions:

> [Quincy and Michael] booked the studio in Los Angeles on the weekend when I wasn't working and I flew in over the weekend to cut the tracks...I remember the very first session for *Off the Wall.* This was on the Saturday that they flew me in from New York, on the Saturday afternoon. Quincy had said to me on the phone a couple of days before, asked me what kind of musicians I needed to record the tracks, so I said two guitar players and a keyboard player, drums, bass...

Michael Jackson performs *Rock With You* at the Nassau Veterans Memorial Coliseum in Uniondale (New York, 9 November 1979).

> I arrived that afternoon, came from the airport directly to the studio...where all the musicians were ready to play...This was my first session outside my own band...where I was walking in cold and meeting a whole bunch of people I never knew, and all very famous names in the business...I said to Quincy at the end of the session, "Well, which song do you want for the record?" and he said, "We want all three."[32]

Michael used the word "competition" when talking about working with Rod Temperton, but it was a friendly atmosphere, where each person constantly brought in new ideas that served to improve the quality of the work. Rod Temperton returned to Los Angeles, this time to record Michael's voice. "The following week I came back again to do the vocals with Michael," he explained. "We did all the backgrounds and all three tracks on the Saturday afternoon and then on the Sunday afternoon we did all the three lead vocal tracks. And Michael was amazing because he stayed up the whole of that Saturday night to learn the lyrics."[32]

The same dream team of musicians took the reins for the making of *Rock with You*. Louis Johnson's legendary bass nevertheless gave way to that of Bobby Watson of Rufus (the group to which he belonged along with drummer John Robinson). Quincy Jones had brought him in, and even though Louis Johnson had also recorded the bass track, Watson's was the one that captured Bruce Swedien's attention. "Man, we pulled up that *Rock with You* track and we had to keep your bass. You were pumpin' it!" he said.[6]

The single topped the charts, where it remained for four weeks in a row.

FOR JACKSON ADDICTS

The original *Rock with You* album mix was replaced by a new one when it first came out as a single, then again for the CD released at the start of the 1980s. The second mix was punchier, and contained guitar acoustics that stood out more, handclaps, and new sound elements in the chorus. The original version wasn't reedited until 2008 for the compilation *Michael Jackson—King of Pop (The French Fan's Selection)*, which replaced a unique and very rare Japanese CD that had contained it previously.

Michael Jackson during the shooting of *Rock With You* in 1980, which cost about $3,000.

THE VIDEO

Bruce Gowers: director
Studio: 800 Stage
Length: 3'21

The *Rock with You* music video is simple and full of grace. Michael commands the dance floor with aplomb. Every now and then he turns back to his footwork, and with a youthful but ambitious charm, he releases an energy that is positive and infectious. He lights up the screen with his sequin suit, made by Bill Whitten, which is perfectly fitted to his body and accentuates the movement of his hips as he dances. This extraordinary look earned him the status of king of the dance floor but also of a veritable Prince Charming. From that moment on, Michael dedicated himself to breaking the hearts of young women everywhere. He'd become the perfect man; the one who can kill it on the dance floor and cause other men to look up to him. He was on his way to conquering new audiences.

Production

Bruce Gowers, director of the video, had this to say about the *Rock with You* video:

> In those days they were done for peanuts. Absolute peanuts. I think about all we could afford was the laser. This one was probably about $3,000. If you look at it, there's nothing there but a laser and Michael Jackson. When we did this, this was the start of his solo career. He was very, very timid, very quiet, very unassuming. Really nice, he's an absolute professional, even in those days. It was filmed on a little stage in LA called the 800 Stage, a little stage that we got cheap because we were shooting quite a lot of music videos. There was minimal editing as well, because obviously in those days editing costs money. It was about $350 per machine per hour. If you were using two playbacks and one record, that was a lot of money. Everything was rented, trust me: the cameras, the stage, the Duvetyne drop, the smoke.[33]

PORTRAIT

ROD TEMPERTON
THE INVISIBLE MAN

Heatwave in February 1976. From left: guitarist Eric Johns, keyboard player Rod Temperton, vocalist Keith Wilder, bassist Mario Mantese, drummer Ernest 'Bilbo' Berger, and vocalist Johnnie Wilder.

Rod Temperton was born on 9 October 1949 in Cleethorpes, United Kingdom. In a 2008 interview on BBC radio he spoke of the origins of his passion for music. "My father wasn't the kind of person who would read you a story before you went off to sleep," he said. "He used to put a transistor radio in the crib and I would go to sleep listening to Radio Luxembourg, and I think somehow that had an influence."[34] In school, he joined a group as the drummer and tried to land a few local gigs.

Heatwave (1975 to 1984)

He joined the famous disco funk group Heatwave, for which he composed *Boogie Nights,* which appeared on the album *Too Hot to Handle*. In 1977, the single rose to No. 2 in the British and US charts. The song soon became a model for the perfect combination of jazz, funk, and boogie. The extravagant ballad *Always and Forever*, the second excerpt from the album, also saw instant success across the pond (taking No. 2 in the Top US R&B charts.)

Rock with Quincy

In 1978, Rod Temperton left Heatwave to devote himself to songwriting. Quincy Jones immediately recognized his talent and asked him to write a song for Michael Jackson's *Off the Wall* album. The three songs he wrote were *Rock with You, Off the Wall*, and *Burn This Disco Out,* all of which made it onto the album.

Thriller is his!

He hit the jackpot when, in 1982, he became the author and composer of the global hit *Thriller*. His influence radiated from the album with sensible and creative subtlety. Much like the songs he wrote for *Off the Wall*, those for *Thriller* maintained the alternating rhythms of mid-tempos and ballads, which allowed for some wonderful songs: *Baby Be Mine, The Lady in My Life,* and *Hot Street*. This was also the case with *Someone in the Dark,* written for *E.T. The Extra-Terrestrial Storybook*, which was recorded alongside *Thriller*. The music world fell in love with his creative genius. He worked with Rufus (which would have received songs not chosen for *Off the Wall*...had there been any), The Brothers Johnson (*Stomp!, Light Up the Night),* and Donna Summer *(Love Is in Control*), not to mention Herbie Hancock, Aretha Franklin, George Benson, James Ingram, and Patti Austin, and all the way up to Boyz II Men.

Rod Temperton hit the scene in the first half of the 1980s as a musical messiah. He brought to America an intelligent blend of the best music that black cultures had generated through the ages. He was a rare artist, and made a significant mark on Michael Jackson's career while participating in the evolution of pop and rock music.

Toward the end of the 1980s, Rod Temperton made himself scarce both professionally and publically. He chose a quiet life far from the limelight. The music world, which nicknamed him the Invisible Man, mourned his passing on 5 October 2016.

Working Day and Night

Michael Jackson / 5'12

Musicians
Michael Jackson: lead vocals
Louis Johnson: bass
John Robinson: drums
Greg Phillinganes: electric piano
David Williams and Phil Upchurch: guitars
Michael Jackson, Paulinho Da Costa, and John Robinson: percussion
The Seawind Horns: brass
Jerry Hey: trumpet and flugelhorn
Larry Williams: tenor and alto saxophone, flute
Kim Hutchcroft: baritone and tenor saxophone, flute
William Reichenbach: trombone
Gary Grant: trumpet
Recording
Cherokee Studios (studio 3), Los Angeles: strings
Allen Zentz Recording, Los Angeles: rhythmic tracks and vocals
Westlake Recording Studios, Los Angeles: brass and mixing
4 December 1978 to 3 June 1979
Technical team
Producers: Quincy Jones and Michael Jackson
Recording engineer: Bruce Swedien
Vocal and percussion arrangements: Michael Jackson
Rhythmic arrangement: Michael Jackson and Greg Phillinganes
Brass arrangements: Jerry Hey
Mixing: Bruce Swedien

Genesis

According to Quincy Jones, *Working Day and Night* was the last song Michael Jackson showed him. Jones also loved to point out the extent to which the young artist's songs were autobiographical. Who could Michael Jackson be talking about? Who was this lover for whom he was ready to work day and night in order to make her happy? This love story, about a challenging love conquest, was actually adapted from *Things I Do for You*, a song Michael had written with his siblings for *Destiny*.

In his early 20s the singer seemed to be obsessed with dark themes saturated with resentment: in these two songs, he sings of how ungrateful people can be for his intense devotion to them.

The writing is very lively and reflects Michael's fascination with complex rhythms. The bass line, simple and intoxicating, is repeated on a loop throughout the piece and accompanied by piano chords that accentuate the theme. Michael had composed a breathtaking piece with jolting couplets and refrains. Here, too, the influence of African sounds is undeniable.

The demo version of the song, which came out in the rerelease of *Off the Wall* in 2001 (and for some reason was removed for the rerelease of the same album in 2016), includes percussions from Michael's younger sister Janet and his brother Randy, and bears vivid testimony to the creative fervor that pervaded the family studio in Encino.

Michael Jackson took on the role of conductor for this song. Instruments as unusual as glass bottles were used in the intro. As soon as the piece's theme sets in, these very rudimentary instrumentals give way to an explosion of funky rhythm, rich in handclapping and a round bass line that recalls *I Heard Music in the Street* by Unlimited Touch.

Michael Jackson sings in falsetto, as in *Don't Stop 'Til You Get Enough*. Even if this demo—which was made by very young musicians—seems rudimentary, it already contained all the elements Quincy Jones needed, which he amplified and magnified for the final version.

Production

Michael, Randy, and Janet worked hard on the demo by using different props for the intro. The effort paid off, and Michael, as coproducer of the song, would use it to give Quincy Jones a clear picture of the sound he wanted to achieve. That's when Jones

Marlon and Michael Jackson on stage during the *Triumph* tour in Atlanta, 22 July 1981. The profits from this concert were donated to charitable causes.

called in percussionist Paulinho Da Costa, who chose bongos, congas, shekerees, and cabasas, among others, from the more than 200 instruments he mastered. He recorded all of them, one after the other, track after track, creating a complex percussion wall that was strong enough to support the song.

Greg Phillinganes played the main chords on the electric piano, and as with *Don't Stop 'Til You Get Enough*, he contributed to the arrangements. He suggested including a false ending in the middle of the piece, just before the song picks up again ahead of the final verses.

The song is linear and runs at breakneck speed. To allow for time to breathe, Quincy Jones asked Jerry Hey to write in a break. The effect was intoxicating: placed smack in the middle of the song, it breaks the main bass line and sets up another repetitive theme of obsession while William Reichenbach's trombone intervenes on the offbeat before the theme returns for the last measures of the song.

Michael Jackson's elegant funk, the sounds inspired by Da Costa's African roots, and the impeccable brass section led by Jerry Hey make *Working Day and Night* a brilliant blend of jazz and modern African-American music.

The simplicity of the song evokes an environment where musicians are playing happily. The song's length of 5'12 is somewhat frustrating, as it could easily have been turned into an endless jam session. Michael Jackson would fall in love with *Working Day and Night* and its unique rhythmic whimsy, to the point where he would perform the song on all of his tours until the early 1990s.

FOR JACKSON ADDICTS

Will Smith sampled this track in *Can You Feel Me*, on his album *Willennium* (1999).

Get on the Floor

Michael Jackson, Louis Johnson / 4'44

Musicians
Michael Jackson: lead and backing vocals
Jim Gilstrap, Augie Johnson, Mortonette Jenkins, Paulette McWilliams, Zedric Williams: additional backing vocals
Louis Johnson: bass
John Robinson: drums
Greg Phillinganes: clavinet
Paulinho Da Costa: percussion
Wah Wah Watson: guitar
Jerry Hey and The Seawind Horns: brass section
Jerry Hey: trumpet and flugelhorn
Larry Williams: tenor and alto saxophone, flute
Kim Hutchcroft: baritone and tenor saxophone, flute
William Reichenbach: trombone
Gary Grant: trumpet
Gerald Vinci: conductor
Recording
Cherokee Studios (studio 3), Los Angeles: strings
Allen Zentz Recording, Los Angeles: rhythmic tracks and vocals
Westlake Recording Studios, Los Angeles: brass and mixing
4 December 1978 to 3 June 1979
Technical team
Producer: Quincy Jones
Coproducer: Michael Jackson
Recording engineer: Bruce Swedien
Rhythmic arrangement: Louis Johnson and Quincy Jones
String arrangement: Benjamin Wright
Vocal arrangement: Michael Jackson
Mixing: Bruce Swedien

Genesis

According to Quincy Jones, *Get on the Floor* was one of the songs The Brothers Johnson (the musical duo consisting of brothers George and Louis Johnson, see page 160) had written for one of their albums, but which they had never finished.

Louis Johnson had already collaborated with Quincy in 1975 on his album *Mellow Madness*. He was among those California studio musicians who'd worked alongside the full gamut of stars and legends, as if collecting the greatest names in music: Aretha Franklin, George Benson, Stevie Wonder, Michael McDonald, James Ingram, Bill Withers, and Björk—they all entrusted their bass lines to Louis. He is widely credited with the popularization of "slapped" bass (see King of Slap on page 160).

When Quincy Jones and Michael Jackson chose the songs for *Off the Wall*, the draft written by The Brothers Johnson popped up unexpectedly. "I was in my car after a session, playing a tape I'd made at home of some song and bass ideas," said Louis Johnson in a 2010 article published on bassplayer.com. "Michael came out to say goodbye and he heard this particular part. He said, 'Man, that's bad—can I write a song around it?'"[6]

The future King of Pop loved Louis Johnson's bass line, and he arranged the melody and vocal arrangements for this song around its rhythmic structure.

The lyrics to *Get on the Floor* resemble those in earlier songs by The Jacksons. The song is an ode to joy and to dance in the purest Jacksonian tradition. It is also perhaps the most obvious reflection of the impressions a young Michael Jackson made while on the dance floor of Studio 54, the legendary New York club he frequented while shooting *The Wiz*. It is interesting to note that this song was completed with Michael's help, even though Quincy Jones, who was already working with the Johnson brothers by then, could have finalized it with Louis just as well.

This collaboration between Michael Jackson and Louis Johnson marked the first time Michael had composed a song with someone who wasn't a member of his family.

Get on the Floor remains widely underestimated and underexploited. It reveals Michael Jackson's love for bold rhythmic combinations and ethereal melodies, a blend of musical elements that he would use again and again.

The first photo session for images for *Off the Wall* (1979). These images were dropped in favor of the concept created by Mike Salisbury.

Production

The magic of *Get on the Floor* rests on its intoxicating bass line. Strong and elegant, it is enriched by funky slaps and notes that rise and fall to a hypnotizing groove. The bass in question is that of Louis Johnson, whose notes span two octaves to give greater depth to this funky theme. He recorded his performance with a 1978 Music Man StingRay 4.

Johnson has repeatedly spoken of his pride in the bass line, which revolved around a 125 bpm beat. "That's two bass patterns that I created," he said in a 1989 interview with MTV. "I paired them to create this line."[35]

One of the most enjoyable parts of the piece is the break, where Paulinho Da Costa and Michael Jackson engage in a dialogue punctuated by percussion instruments and onomatopoeias that evoke both the feverish rhythms of South America and the energy of African music.

Get on the Floor closes *Off the Wall*'s A-side. An early mix, which highlighted John Robinson's drums and the brass of The Seawind Horns led by Jerry Hey, was included in the 1979 release. Starting in 1980, a second mix emerged on the cassette tape version of *Off the Wall*. The balance calibrated for this mix saw the drums largely fall into the background, Wah Wah Watson's rhythmic guitar standing out and punctuating each refrain. This second mix was systematically used in all commercial releases of the album from the mid-1980s onward. Few can boast of owning the first mix of *Get on the Floor*, which is only available on CDs produced in Japan since 1983.

PORTRAIT

KING OF SLAP Louis Johnson strove to popularize "the slap" with his bass guitar, a technique invented by Larry Graham, which produced percussive sounds on a non-percussive instrument.

Louis Johnson, supreme bassist of the Jackson circle.

LOUIS JOHNSON
THUNDER THUMB

Louis Johnson was born in Los Angeles on 13 April 1955. An unparalleled musician and bassist, he and his brother George devoted themselves to music early on. In between classes or at church on Sundays, the Johnson brothers played tirelessly, accompanied by family members. At the end of the 1960s, they won a talent show in California and signed their first recording contract with Venture Records. Bobby Womack became the producer of their first song, *Testify*. As Louis Johnson told Funk-U.fr, a French site, shortly before his death in 2015, "The Jackson Five weren't around yet. We had about the same amount of popularity that they would later gain. When we played in schools, we made waves! Everywhere! It was great. We were bad! The other groups were afraid of us."[36] The brothers made their presence increasingly known throughout the 1970s, to the point where they were playing for the greatest stars of the day, including Bill Withers and The Supremes.

The Brothers Johnson

The brothers then founded The Brothers Johnson and began a successful career, releasing eight albums between 1976 and 1988. The success of their first album, *Look Out for Number One* (1976), was instant. Louis became the most in-demand studio musician of the second half of the 1970s. His rhythm and his dynamic notes enchanted funk music, then disco, and finally, in the first few years of the following decade, they became musical reference points.

The Quincy years

Quincy Jones discovered the group in 1975. Blown away by Louis' bass, he invited the brothers to join him on a tour of Japan. It was the start of a long and prosperous musical collaboration. Quincy Jones produced their first four albums, up to *Light Up the Night* (1980), including their last masterpiece, the legendary *Stomp!*, which topped the charts. After so much success, it became difficult for them to meet the increasing demands of their record label, A&M Records, which eventually decided to terminate their contract. The group dissolved in the second half of the 1980s. Conflict between the two brothers certainly didn't help.

This had to be...

While playing with The Brothers Johnson, Louis was also pursuing his own career on Quincy Jones' best projects. His first lines for Michael Jackson appeared in 1979 in *Off the Wall*. His bass rang out in, gave rhythm to, and accompanied almost every piece. *Get on the Floor* remains one of the best bass lines of all Michael Jackson's songs. In a September 2015 interview with bassplayer.com, George Johnson spoke of a precious moment in his friendship with Michael Jackson. "Michael was a big fan of The Brothers Johnson and *Look Out for Number One*," he said. "In '79, when *Stomp!* was out and he and Quincy were doing *The Wiz*, we played Carnegie Hall, and Michael surprised us by introducing us—'Ladies and gentlemen, The Brothers Johnson!' He stayed on the side of the stage for the whole show."[37]

For *Light Up the Night*, in 1980, Michael cowrote *This Had to Be* and provided backing vocals. The artists met again for many more projects, such as *The Dude* (Quincy Jones) and *State of Independence* (Donna Summer), in 1981 and 1982 respectively, under the renewed direction of their common teacher.

Mid-1980s

Louis was hired again to work on *Thriller*. *Wanna Be Startin' Somethin'*, *The Girl Is Mine*, *Billie Jean*, *P.Y.T.*, and *The Lady in My Life* all feature his bass line, which gives the album a playful sense of musical seduction. In 1985, he played bass for *We Are the World*. Testimony to that song's creative process and to the warm professional atmosphere that surrounded it can be seen in a short video of the studio jam session with Lionel Richie and Michael Jackson.

Back to the studio

During his last days collaborating with Michael Jackson, Louis worked on *Who Is It*, for which he provided the texture for its distinctive atmosphere, and on *Come Together*, on the album *HIStory*. In 2002, the two brothers regrouped for an American tour. Louis Johnson, who passed away too soon, made a strong and rhythmic mark on music history and the young singer.

THOMAS BÄHLER
THE BENEVOLENT LEADER

Thomas Lee, or Tom, Bähler was born on 1 June 1943 in Inglewood, California. Throughout his career, he worked independently as a composer, producer, artistic director, songwriter, singer, and arranger on many television programs, films, and albums. During his school days, he created groups by connecting musicians, advising them, and helping them make artistic choices. Naturally, music and writing soon became his main priorities in life. He radiated positivity, and never stopped sharing his passion and love for life.

Early career

He began his television career in the 1960s as a singer on CBS's *The Smothers Brothers Show*, then gradually moved to studio work, where he found his talent for composition and developed it.

When working at Motown with his brother John in 1972, he crossed paths with the young Michael Jackson. The Bähler brothers were tasked with helping The Jacksons consolidate their voices and work on their arrangements, notably on *Rockin' Robin*, *My Girl*, *People Make the World Go 'Round*, *Everybody's Somebody's Fool*, *What Goes Around Comes Around*, and *Ben*.

Thomas Bähler, the arranger who worked with Michael Jackson from the Motown years until the early 2000s.

Tom and Quincy

In 1973 Tom started working with Quincy Jones on *Body Heat* (1974), *Mellow Madness* (1975), *Sounds...and Stuff Like That* (1978), and *Q's Jooke Joint* (1995). Notably, he coproduced the original soundtrack to *The Wiz* (1978) and Michael Jackson's very first single with Epic / CBS, *You Can't Win*. At Quincy's suggestion, Tom gave Michael a magnificent piece for the album *Off the Wall* in 1979. *She's out of My Life* was a timeless ballad he'd originally planned on giving to Frank Sinatra (see page 166).

But the story doesn't stop there. The long working relationship and friendship between Quincy Jones and Tom Bähler reached its peak in 1985, when Tom was named associate producer and vocal arranger for *We Are the World*.

Crossing paths

Bähler never strayed far from Michael Jackson's professional trajectory and sometimes worked on lesser known or more isolated projects. He took charge of the musical programming for Siegfried and Roy, while Michael sang *Mind Is the Magic* for the show's theme song.

Not many people know that he also directed the backing vocals for *People of the World* (1999), a song Michael Jackson had written for the Japanese group J-Friends to raise money for the victims of the Kobe earthquake.

The vocals and anthems in the album *Invincible* (2001) resonated and excelled under Tom's direction, largely due to his work on *The Lost Children*.

FOR JACKSON ADDICTS

Just like *Don't Stop 'Til You Get Enough, Off the Wall* was used in an ad campaign for Suzuki scooters. Multiple commercials were shot, all of which used one of these two pieces as the soundtrack.

OFF THE WALL

Rod Temperton / 4'05

Musicians
Michael Jackson: lead and backing vocals
Louis Johnson: bass
John Robinson: drums
David Williams and Marlo Henderson: guitars
Greg Phillinganes: electric piano and synthesizers
George Duke: synthesizers
Paulinho Da Costa: percussion
The Seawind Horns: brass
Jerry Hey: trumpet and flugelhorn
Larry Williams: tenor and alto saxophone, flute
Kim Hutchcroft: baritone and tenor saxophone, flute
William Reichenbach: trombone
Gary Grant: trumpet
Recording
Cherokee Studios (studio 3), Los Angeles: strings
Allen Zentz Recording, Los Angeles: rhythmic tracks and vocals
Westlake Recording Studios, Los Angeles: brass section and mixing
4 December 1978 to 3 June 1979
Technical team
Producer: Quincy Jones
Recording engineer: Bruce Swedien
Horn arrangement: Jerry Hey
Rhythm and voice arrangements: Rod Temperton
Synthesizer programmers: Michael Boddicker and George Duke

Single

USA
A-side: *Off the Wall (US single version)* / 3'47
B-side: *Get on the Floor (album version No. 2)* / 4'37
UK
A-side: *Off the Wall (European single version)* / 3'59
B-side: *Working Day and Night (album version)* / 5'09
Released by Epic Records: USA, 18 February 1980 (ref. S EPC 8045) / UK, November 1979 (ref. 9-50838)
Chart position: USA R&B No. 5, Pop No. 10 / UK No. 7
RIAA: certified Gold on 14 February 1989

Genesis

An album's title song bears a big part of the responsibility for the success of that album. In this case, *Off the Wall* was initially going to be called *Girlfriend*, the song Paul McCartney had passed on to Michael in 1977. From a strategic standpoint, this was a good choice, because it valorized Michael's name by association. Fans were always scrutinizing pieces promoted on album covers, searching for clues to a musical identity, or for a strong and inspiring message. *Off the Wall* had to appeal to listeners in a way that ensured the song would be a hit. It's almost certain that the title song changed around the time Rod Temperton joined the project. In an interview about the album, he admitted that he was expecting Quincy to choose *Off the Wall* from the three songs he'd written. "I could tell from Michael [from] melodies he would sing on up-tempo songs, [that] he was very rhythmically driven," he explained. "And so I tried to write melodies that had a lot of short notes to give him some staccato rhythmic things he could do. I think the *Off the Wall* title song gives you the best example...The other thing I knew from his previous records is that he loved harmony work. That's really the side of me that I would have brought from Heatwave."[32]

Much like *Workin' Day and Night* or *Burn This Disco Out*, *Off the Wall* provides continuity and a pronounced up-tempo feel. However, tone and energy come across differently here. Michael sings the song as if he were acting a part in a film or on stage. From the start, the introduction raises questions. At once mocking and delirious, it transports the listener to a parallel and offbeat world to which only the singer has the keys. In the lyrics, Michael plays the role of a judge presiding over mournful daily drudgery. He then metes out advice so radical that we can't help but join him on an exciting journey of unexpected, wild situations: "Livin' crazy that's the only way." The song is also very visual: there are resounding explosions of color, scenes blend together. *Off the Wall* thus became the obvious choice for the title song, promising an experience that was both off the wall and powerful, new, and unusual, all the while accompanied by deliriously rich instrumentals.

Michael Jackson during the *Triumph* tour in 1981.

Production

Off the Wall is a pearl of a song, sewn with threads of golden instrumentals and set against a velvet backdrop. It was recorded over the course of two weekends: first the instrumentals, then the vocals. An army of musical prodigies used Rod Temperton's three pieces to create songs of rare artistic prowess. Greg Phillinganes and George Duke play their synthesizers in beautiful harmony with Louis Johnson's leading bass line. The rearguard of trumpets and saxophones takes off in musical flights that are both sweet and powerful, inundating the piece with magic. Michael's voice permeates the piece to the point where he sometimes seems to be forming his own chorus. All this transmits the energy of the song and the force of its message.

Because of the strength of this recording, The Jacksons included *Off the Wall* in all of their tours. Its reach and popularity remained intact throughout the years (and can be heard on The Jacksons' live album from 1981).

The single was a huge success, placing in the Top 10 of all the main charts, though it never took the No. 1 spot, maybe because its release was divided between two markets at two different times. It first came out in Europe in November 1979 as the second excerpt from the album, around the time that *Rock with You* was making the rounds in the United States. The single wasn't then released in the United States until February 1980.

Girlfriend

Paul McCartney / 3'04

Musicians
Michael Jackson: lead and backing vocals
Louis Johnson: bass
John Robinson: drums
Greg Phillinganes: electric piano
David Foster: synthesizer
Wah Wah Watson and Marlo Henderson: guitars
Jerry Hey and The Seawind Horns: brass section
Jerry Hey: trumpet and flugelhorn
Larry Williams: tenor and alto saxophone, flute
Kim Hutchcroft: baritone and tenor saxophone, flute
William Reichenbach: trombone
Gary Grant: trumpet
Larry Williams: alto saxophone solo
Recording
Cherokee Studios (studio 3), Los Angeles: strings
Allen Zentz Recording, Los Angeles: rhythmic tracks and vocals
Westlake Recording Studios, Los Angeles: brass and mixing
4 December 1978 to 3 June 1979
Technical team
Producer: Quincy Jones
Recording engineer: Bruce Swedien
Synthesizer programmers: Steve Porcaro and George Duke
Rhythmic arrangement: Quincy Jones, Tom Bahler, and Greg Phillinganes
Vocal arrangement: Michael Jackson and Quincy Jones
Mixing: Bruce Swedien

Single

A-Side: *Girlfriend* (*album version*) / 3'04
B-Side: *Bless His Soul* (*album version*) / 4'55
Released by Epic Records: UK, July 1980 (ref. S EPC 8782)
Chart position: UK No. 41

Genesis

When Paul McCartney composed *Girlfriend* in 1974, he thought The Jackson Five would be performing it. He gave it to Michael after an evening in Beverly Hills on 24 June 1976, and went so far as to sing the first few lines for him. This occasion marked the start of a great friendship between the leader of The Jacksons and the former Beatle. It is also interesting to note that when Michael left The Jacksons, his solo career took off and surpassed the ambitions of his family's group. For his part, Paul McCartney was also pursuing a career outside The Beatles with Wings, though he was never able to repeat the worldwide success of the Fab Four.

When Paul McCartney later realized that The Jacksons never recorded the song, he decided to revisit it. While he was staying in the Virgin Islands working on the album *London Town*, he recorded it using his most convincing falsetto, as a nod to Michael's Motown days.

In early 1979, Quincy Jones and Michael Jackson were working on the making of *Off the Wall*. During a very difficult song selection process, Quincy pulled out a song that had been sent to him a few months before: it was *Girlfriend*. The coincidence was disarming, and it ensured that *Girlfriend* would come to be part of Michael's permanent repertoire.

"Girlfriend, I'm gonna tell your boyfriend (yeah) / Tell him (woo hoo), exactly what we're doing (yeah)." These are the first lines of the chorus, an innocent tale of clandestine love that sounds just like the story of a first love between two teenagers.

Production

Girlfriend opens the second half of *Off the Wall* and sees Michael Jackson venturing into new territory: that of a mid-tempo ballad with pop accents. The musicians already working on the album's funk and soul pieces, like *Don't Stop 'Til You Get Enough* and *Working Day and Night*, mastered *Girlfriend's* lighter ambience with unsettling ease. This new interpretation was a far cry from what Paul McCartney had recorded a year earlier for *London Town*. Quincy Jones, Tom Bahler, and Greg Phillinganes wanted a rounder and warmer sound for this version, and diluted the somewhat acidic, even satirical, aspect of McCartney's recording.

The version in *Off the Wall* was a success. It made the song's love story seem credible and more mature. Quincy

Michael Jackson and his friend, the young actress Tatum O'Neal, at a party in Los Angeles, 1 July 1979.

FOR JACKSON ADDICTS

Girlfriend was supposed to be the album's title song, and Michael Jackson's managers issued a few cover sketches based on this title. In the end, however, it was Rod Temperton's _Off the Wall_ that managed to best encapsulate Michael's ambitions for his first solo album with Epic.

Jones' production lifted the piece from its English cradle and set it in a California college campus, the sort of place where the song's lovers might meet after class.

The Seawind Horns punctuate precisely the end of each verse. Louis Johnson's slapped bass bursts forth during the breaks, as if to highlight the piece's carefree and lighthearted feel. John Robinson's drums roll out a soft beat that evokes the style of The Doobie Brothers or Michael McDonald. David Foster, George Duke, and Steve Porcaro's synthesizers add instrumental warmth. The lead synthesizer, played by Foster, adds a theme that is absent in McCartney's version, and seems to embody the hide-and-seek nature of the song.

While Paul McCartney's version remained confined to *London Town*, Michael Jackson's take on it soon came out as a single, though only in the United Kingdom. With that release, *Off the Wall* became the first album in history to generate four singles.

She's Out of My Life

Tom Bähler / 3'38

Musicians
Michael Jackson: lead vocals
Louis Johnson: bass
Larry Carlton: guitar
Greg Phillinganes: electric piano
Gerald Vinci: first violin
Recording
Cherokee Studios (studio 3), Los Angeles: strings
Allen Zentz Recording, Los Angeles: rhythmic tracks and vocals
Westlake Recording Studios, Los Angeles: brass section and mixing
4 December 1978 to 3 June 1979
Technical team
Producer: Quincy Jones
Recording engineer: Bruce Swedien
String arrangement: Johnny Mandel
Mixing: Bruce Swedien

Single

USA
A-side: *She's out of My Life* (album version) / 3'36
B-side: *Get on the Floor* (album version No. 2) / 4'37
UK
A-side: *She's out of My Life* (album version) / 3'36
B-side: The Jacksons *Push Me Away* / 4'18
Released by Epic Records: USA and UK, 29 April 1980 (ref. 9-50871 and ref. S EPC 8384)
Chart position: USA R&B No. 43, Pop No. 10 / UK No. 3
RIAA: certified Gold on 14 February 1989

SONG

Genesis

At once arranger, producer, and brilliant choir director, Thomas Lee Bähler is among a handful of people familiar with each of Michael Jackson's artistic periods. He can boast of being part of the exclusive circle responsible for the success of the young artist's solo career with Epic / CBS. After his Motown days, Bähler got back in touch with Michael in 1978. The two of them worked on the soundtrack to *The Wiz*, and later, on *Off the Wall*, to which Bähler contributed *She's out of My Life*, a beautiful creation Michael Jackson nicknamed "The Single." In an interview with *Invincible Magazine*, Tom Bähler speaks passionately of how this song came about:

> I was talking to myself on the freeway. There was a woman I was very much in love with, she was in love with me, and we were going to get married. But I wasn't ready...And I didn't respond. And so I was really torn apart...I was driving home from another vacuous date, and it wasn't the women who were vacuous, it was me. Have you ever been so upset that you talk aloud to yourself? Well that's what I did. So I said to myself "She loved you, she wanted to marry you, you didn't take the step when you were required to, so deal with it, she's out of your life." As soon as those words left my lips... it started coming in and I had to keep repeating it because I was driving down the freeway...and I didn't have a recorder with me, and I kept saying it over and over and singing it over and over because the melody and lyrics came in at the same time...When I got home I sat down at the piano...it took me till 4 a.m. to get it under my fingers.[38]

In 1977, Bruce Swedien and his wife Bea were the first to hear the piece. Tom Bähler played it for them on the piano at the A&R studios in New York, where they were working on the original soundtrack to *The Wiz*. Quincy Jones learned of the song's existence after telling Tom that he would be working with Michael Jackson and that he was looking for a ballad for *Off the Wall*. At first, Tom thought his song should be sung by a more experienced singer like Frank Sinatra, who'd already agreed to record it with him. To that, Quincy Jones said "Sinatra will not sing it." Tom retorted that he loved Michael

During the shooting of the very low-key clip of *She's Out of My Life* (1980).

FOR JACKSON ADDICTS

The deluxe edition of *This Is It* includes the demo version of *She's out of My Life.* According to Tom Bähler, this wasn't actually a demo but a rehearsal that Michael had likely recorded at home. There is a slight change in that "I took it for granted," became "I took her for granted," which was Quincy Jones' suggestion.

Jackson, but his ballad was about a rat, and so he couldn't give Michael a song written with a woman in mind. Luckily, Quincy Jones had a talent for persuasion that only required a few words. "It gives him adult emotions," he said.[38] And that's exactly what happened with *She's out of My Life*.

The ballad, plaintive and introspective, tells the story of a lost love. Confronted for the first time with indecision and agony, Michael's performance is more credible than ever. He pairs his heartbreak with a new sensibility, he opens up his soul and frees his emotions without filtering them. His voice and intonation emanate new warmth and charisma.

Production

The strings create a very nice atmosphere at the beginning of the piece. Quincy Jones had hired ten of the greatest arrangers around, but without giving them any instructions, as was his habit. He simply asked for a defining atmosphere. Everyone did an excellent job, but Johnny Mandel stood out by highlighting the melancholy of the song's theme.

When the song comes out of the bridge the lyrics are: "Damned indecision and cursed pride / Kept my love for her locked deep inside," but then it was supposed to say "Instead of being my wife, she's out of my life," which is what Michael Jackson was working with. When it came time to record it, he asked for the words to be changed, because he had a problem with "Instead of being my wife." "...I'm 19, it's not on my radar screen," he said.[38] With the creator's blessing, the lyrics were finally revised. Michael also wanted to sing the song a semitone higher. Tom gave his seat at the piano over to Greg Phillinganes, who was only 22 at the time, in order to ensure the success of the new musical track. Although a dozen takes were made; Bähler chose the first one because it better expressed the song's sincerity. In it, one can hear Michael cry out at the end of the piece "Sorry fellas, could we do it again?" *She's out of My Life* was the fourth single generated by the album. The single was only successful in Europe, where it reached No. 3 in the British charts. Michael Jackson would perform the song on each tour. Under the gaze of millions of admirers, and with the help of Greg Phillinganes, he succeeded in creating a true moment of intimacy on set.

THE VIDEO

Bruce Gowers: director
Studio: 800 Stage
Length: 3'36

The lighting used in the *Rock with You* video failed during shooting at the 800 Stage, but Bruce Gowers continued to film Michael singing *She's out of My Life*.

The resulting video was plain and unconvincing: Michael simply sang the song while sitting on a stool. The expressions on his face struggled to convey the depth and emotion of the piece, which he had done in the studio. Discrepancies are unfortunately very noticeable. Michael himself barely tolerated the final product, which almost certainly made him realize just how hard it was to turn a ballad into a video. As per Michael's will, the video for *She's out of My Life* was forgotten until it finally found a home on the 2010 DVD compilation *Michael Jackson's Vision*.

I Can't Help It

Stevie Wonder, Susaye Greene Brown / 4'27

Musicians
Michael Jackson: lead vocals
Louis Johnson: bass
John Robinson: drums
Greg Phillinganes: electric piano and synthesizers
Paulinho Da Costa: percussion
The Seawind Horns: brass section
Jerry Hey: trumpet and flugelhorn
Larry Williams: tenor and alto saxophone, flute
Kim Hutchcroft: baritone and tenor saxophone, flute
William Reichenbach: trombone
Gary Grant: trumpet
Gerald Vinci: first violin
Recording
Cherokee Studios (studio 3), Los Angeles: strings
Allen Zentz Recording, Los Angeles: rhythmic tracks and vocals
Westlake Recording Studios, Los Angeles: brass and mixing
4 December 1978 to 3 June 1979
Technical team
Producer: Quincy Jones
Recording engineer: Bruce Swedien
Synthesizer programmer: Michael Boddicker
Horn arrangement: Jerry Hey
Rhythmic arrangement: Greg Phillinganes and Stevie Wonder
String arrangement: Johnny Mandel
Mixing: Bruce Swedien

Genesis

Stevie Wonder was a true mentor to Michael Jackson, a spiritual guide and role model throughout his career. Michael often spoke of those precious moments he spent in the studio watching his mentor work. When The Jackson Five were still with Motown, Stevie composed four songs for the group. *Buttercup* was included in the 2009 compilation *I Want You Back! Unreleased Masters*, while *You're Supposed to Keep Your Love for Me* and *Where Are You Now* appeared on Jermaine Jackson's 1980 album *Let's Get Serious*. There is no evidence these three songs were ever recorded by The Jackson Five, while the fate of the fourth piece remains a mystery. In 2016, in the documentary *Michael Jackson's Journey from Motown to Off the Wall,* Stevie Wonder says he wrote *I Can't Help It* while he was working on his 1976 album *Songs in the Key of Life*. Susaye Greene, a former Supreme, was Stevie's colleague and longtime friend, and as the main songwriter of the piece she was by his side throughout the making of the video. She was nevertheless surprised to hear this new piece of information.

In 2015, for the French magazine *Invincible*, Susaye Greene said of the creation of *I Can't Help It:*

> Stevie often sang in gibberish, without any real words, with the notes and melodies coming from his soul. And just listening to him I knew what he was talking about, that was the kind of friendship we had. And since we were recording it, I kept all the documents for *I Can't Help It*. Once we found the chorus, we knew what direction we wanted to go in. He told me to remember it and to let the song mature. If the rest doesn't just come, you have to let it sit until you say to yourself "There it is!" You have to give your emotions time to sort themselves out…I came to the studio the day Michael was there to tell Stevie he loved the song. And once Michael left, Stevie and I just jumped with joy! We thought it was incredible.[39]

As for the young singer, he had fond memories of his friend's song. In 1983, in a brief radio interview, he said "I was at home and he invited me to the studio. And he played me this song. I said 'I love it! What is it? When are you going to put it out?' 'I'm not putting it out,' he said. 'It's for you.' I said 'Woo!' I was so excited because he is so good and the melody is so good."[16]

The Supremes in 1976: Susaye Greene, with Scherrie Payne (left) and Mary Wilson (right).

The lyrics were innocent and melodious. Michael took on a certain softness: he appealed to love and expressed it with strong emotion. There is no doubt that this beautiful song echoes Stevie Wonder's warmth and genius.

Production

Little is known about the recording of *I Can't Help It*. It's clear that because of its jazzy outburst, Quincy Jones couldn't resist including it in *Off the Wall*. Stevie Wonder said he never expected the producer to be interested in such a piece.

Unlike the other songs in the album, aside the instrumental tracks, Michael's voice was warmer than ever, free for a time of his new vocal idiosyncrasies. He held the notes longer and paused on a bewitching chord, as if he wanted to thank his friend for his invaluable gift. Michael had watched Stevie Wonder and Susaye Green navigate the different stages of the making of *Songs in the Key of Life* and he remembered his mentor's musical spirit. Stevie supervised Greg Phillinganes' rhythmic arrangement for *Off the Wall*. Louis Johnson's bass was at the heart of the piece more than ever: the percussion and synthesizers blended into the background, creating a muted ambiance. *I Can't Help It* found its home on the B-side of the first single of the album *Don't Stop 'Til You Get Enough*. Rather than a sly marketing strategy, this was a nod to Michael's mentor.

It's the Falling in Love

Carole Bayer Sager, David Foster / 3'46

Musicians
Michael Jackson and Patti Austin: lead and backing vocals
Louis Johnson: bass
John Robinson: drums
Greg Phillinganes: electric piano
Wah Wah Watson and Marlo Henderson: guitar
David Foster: synthesizers
Jerry Hey and The Seawind Horns: brass section
Jerry Hey: trumpet and flugelhorn
Larry Williams: tenor and alto saxophones, flute
Kim Hutchcroft: baritone and tenor saxophones, flute
William Reichenbach: trombone
Gary Grant: trumpet
Recording
Cherokee Studios (studio 3), Los Angeles: strings
Allen Zentz Recording, Los Angeles: rhythmic tracks and vocals
Westlake Recording Studios, Los Angeles: brass and mixing
4 December 1978 to 3 June 1979
Technical team
Producer: Quincy Jones
Recording engineer: Bruce Swedien
Rhythmic arrangement: Quincy Jones and David Foster
Vocal arrangement: Quincy Jones and Tom Bahler
Synthesizer programmer: Steve Porcaro
Mixing: Bruce Swedien

Carole Bayer Sager, composer of more than 400 songs.

Genesis

Quincy Jones and Michael Jackson envisaged a new musical universe in which Michael could come into his own independently of his siblings and their shared adventures. *Off the Wall* gained recognition thanks to its intense funk songs, slight disco accents, and a mature tonality that appealed to the masses with songs that increasingly touched upon the world of pop, even middle of the road (MOR).

In the beginning, MOR applied to songs that borrowed from pop and classical music. Later, the expression was used to describe compositions aimed at pleasing the largest possible audience. These songs achieved their commercial ambitions by aiming for maximum airtime even if it meant being used and adapted for commercials.

To make his vision come true, Quincy Jones called in the best members of his team, starting with his protégé, the young Canadian composer David Foster, who was then in his early 30s. Foster had started his career with the group Skylark in the early 1970s. When the group broke up, he moved to Los Angeles, where he became a composer and arranger. His meeting with Quincy Jones was decisive. The illustrious producer gave him a piece of advice that would guide him for the rest of his career. "He said to me, 'If something isn't exactly the way you think it should be, don't put your name on it.'"[40] Foster's name has gone down in history for having formed the original soundtrack to *The Bodyguard,* which starred Whitney Houston and Kevin Costner.

In the days of *Off the Wall*, Foster worked on Carole Bayer Sager's 1978 album *...Too.* The young woman, who was then married to composer Burt Bacharach, released her second album with Elektra/Asylum Records. She and David Foster made a resourceful pair. They worked on two songs together: *I Don't Wanna Dance No More*, a slightly disco song whose brass section reveals Jerry Hey's touch, and *It's the Falling in Love.*

When Carole Bayer Sager recorded this song for *...Too*, she called upon Michael McDonald, who'd achieved great commercial success as part of the Doobie Brothers. He agreed to sing the backing vocals for this first version of *It's the Falling in Love.*

A year later, Michael Jackson redid this song with Patti Austin, a young singer from Harlem who had been discovered by Quincy Jones.

Patti Austin, one of Quincy Jones's protégées. The producer launched her onto the R&B and pop scene in the late 1970s.

Production

The softness of the synthesizers gives *It's the Falling in Love* a warm and cozy sound. Steve Porcaro, then a member of Toto, supervised the programming of the machines, while the core musicians for *Off the Wall* provided the foundation of the piece.

Patti Austin sang with Michael Jackson. She recalled meeting him and her first moments with him in the studio:

> He had a very silly sophomoric sense of humor...Whenever I would be heading for the studio and he knew I was coming he would always be behind the door and he'd jump out and say "Boo!"...When I knew Michael the relationship [with his family] was not great. He got along great with his sisters, but did not speak fondly of the guys in the family. He always felt kind of put upon. At the time that I met Michael it was right when he was doing *The Wiz*, and he wasn't even speaking at that time. Michael used to sit in the studio with a pad and pen and if he heard somebody say something remotely intelligent, he would write it down. He was always trying to learn and absorb anything that he thought was intelligent. He was very very quiet, very very shy, frighteningly shy. We didn't even start working together until Quincy Jones' album *The Dude*. That's when I started talking to him. A lot of our conversations were about his relationship with his family. He adored his mother, he adored his sisters, but at that particular time, he didn't have the greatest relationship with his brothers or with his dad. He was really trying to branch out on his own...so he kind of felt that they were holding him back... He loved the fact that he was able to become a great entertainer, but he hated the fact that he lost his childhood in the process. I started in the business when I was a kid so this was a conversation we used to have a lot.[41]

It's the Falling in Love was Michael Jackson's first famous duet after *Ease on down the Road*, which he'd recorded with Diana Ross the year before (and which was also a cover). This tradition, which would accompany his career and solo albums, started out as a secret. Despite its strong commercial potential, *It's the Falling in Love* was never made into a single and remained confined to the end of the album.

Burn This Disco Out

Rod Temperton / 3'38

Musicians
Michael Jackson: lead and backing vocals
Louis Johnson: bass
John Robinson: drums
Greg Phillinganes: electric piano
David Williams and Marlo Henderson: guitar
Paulinho Da Costa: percussion
Jerry Hey and The Seawind Horns: brass section
Jerry Hey: trumpet and flugelhorn
Larry Williams: tenor and alto saxophones, flute
Kim Hutchcroft: baritone and tenor saxophones, flute
William Reichenbach: trombone
Gary Grant: trumpet
Recording
Cherokee Studios (studio 3), Los Angeles: strings
Allen Zentz Recording, Los Angeles: rhythmic tracks and vocals
Westlake Recording Studios, Los Angeles: brass and mixing
4 December 1978 to 3 June 1979
Technical team
Producer: Quincy Jones
Recording engineer: Bruce Swedien
Vocal and rhythmic arrangements: Rod Temperton
Mixing: Bruce Swedien

In the late 1970s the Disco Sucks movement was in full swing, sounding the death-knell of disco music.

Genesis

Of the three songs composed by Rod Temperton, *Burn This Disco Out* came closest to the style of Heatwave, the English composer's original group.

The lyrics tell the story of a night on the dance floor, where the atmosphere has reached its peak and the remaining dancers have given themselves to the night, as the DJs mix music from the stands. There's a trance-like quality, a certain playfulness in the air, an attempt to relive those last sacred moments on the dance floor before leaving for the night.

Burn This Disco Out: the expression says it all. This song can also be interpreted in the figurative sense, as by 1979 disco music had already lived its finest hours. The emergence of punk and hip-hop movements had just presaged the end of this genre, which some believed to be corrupting the record industry.

A kind of discophobia set in at the end of the 1970s in the US. When even popular artists like Rod Stewart and The Rolling Stones yielded to the efficient and easy sound of disco with *Do Ya Think I'm Sexy* and *Miss You,* respectively, they angered hard-core fans in the rock community. On 12 July 1979 radio presenter Steve Dahl organized a spontaneous, momentous event at Chicago's Comiskey Park, where he was promoting the Chicago White Sox–Detroit Tigers game. He became the spokesman for a movement hailed by rock fans across the United States: Disco Sucks. He asked the listeners of WLUP-FM, which was sponsoring the game, to come to the stadium and burn their disco records. Game organizers hoped to fill the 20,000 seats in the stands, but in the end about 50,000 people showed up. The event spiraled out of control and the police intervened. After Dahl set the records on fire, fans invaded the field.

This event was groundbreaking because it consolidated the large-scale rejection of disco culture and, in a less obvious way, of the life it espoused: drugs, alcohol, and uninhibited sexual liberation. At the time, Disco Sucks was even accused of homophobia.

In this difficult context, *Burn This Disco Out* was released as the tenth and final track on *Off the Wall*. Whether it meant to or not, it sounded the death knell of the musical genre that had popularized the single maxi format, but which had also flooded the music industry with records, weakening it at a time when it was competing with other mediums such as film and video games.

Michael Jackson grooves on stage during the *Triumph* tour in 1981.

With that, Rod Temperton put his name to his last disc. The following year, George Benson's *Give Me the Night* was already leaning toward a funkier sound, one more permeated with soul.

Production

Rod Temperton got into Heatwave mode to write this song. Of the three songs he gave to Quincy Jones and Michael Jackson, *Burn This Disco Out* was the one that most followed the formulae that had made Heatwave's success: a defiant brass section, tangy guitars, and flamboyant rhythms.

Along with Michael Jackson, the stars of this song were the musicians in charge of Jerry Hey's brass section. Jerry Hey was used to R-121 microphones by Royer, but recording engineer Bruce Swedien convinced him to use RCA44 microphones on the trumpets in order to achieve a more dynamic sound. At that time, Hey was about to quit The Seawind Horns to pursue his own career as a studio musician and arranger. His contribution to *Off the Wall* decisively paved the way for his other ventures, both in music as well as in film and television.

David Williams' rhythmic guitar had supported The Jacksons on stage during their tour; here he was able to heat up the groove and maintain it at a high temperature throughout the song, making *Burn This Disco Out* a perfect blend of disco and funk.

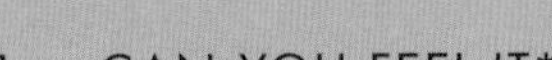

1. CAN YOU FEEL IT*
2. LOVELY ONE*
3 YOUR WAYS
4. EVERYBODY
5. THIS PLACE HOTEL*
6. TIME WAITS FOR NO ONE
7. WALK RIGHT NOW*
8. GIVE IT UP*
9. WONDERING WHO

* Only those songs with which Michael Jackson was significantly involved are covered in the following pages.

Triumph **ALBUM**

Released by Epic Records: USA (ref. FE 36424) and UK (ref. S EPC 86112), 26 September 1980
Chart position: USA R&B No.1, Pop No. 10 / UK No. 13
RIAA: certified Platinum on 10 December 1980

The Jacksons in 1981: Michael, Randy, Marlon, Jackie, and Tito.

TRIUMPH: MICHAEL AND THE JACKSONS, THE ADVENTURE CONTINUES

After the praise he received for *Off the Wall*, Michael joined his siblings to record *Triumph*. Back in the studio, one thing was hard to ignore: on his own, Michael aroused more interest than all the Jacksons put together. His career as a solo performer was taking off, and his talent shone bright, free from pretense or fancy packaging. No doubt aware of this, the other Jacksons put their hearts and souls into the making of this album. In his autobiography, Michael Jackson explains the situation, saying that his siblings "knew they were trying to keep up with the *Off the Wall* songwriters and they did a good job."[2]

Ably assisted by some of California's biggest names in music, *Destiny* had allowed The Jacksons to consolidate their status as young authors and producers. While *Triumph* ended up sounding like a direct response to *Off the Wall*, it nevertheless enjoyed its own strong musical identity: a sharp ethereal funk that wasn't afraid to use its edge on the dance floor. *Can You Feel It* is six minutes of funk-rock rhythm, and featured in *The Triumph*, a short film made in 1981. Cultish and completely unheard of in music videos today (where innocence has long since gone out the window), *Can You Feel It* was a foray into the increasingly overlapping spheres of video and film. It was the precursor to the music videos Michael would create in the 1980s.

Lovely One, the first single and latest song by Michael and Randy, rides the same groove as *Shake Your Body*. Michael hits the ground running in *Your Ways* before taking off with *Everybody* (which Michael thought of as a direct response to *Off the Wall*'s *Get on the Floor*). The B-side opens with the nightmarish *Heartbreak Hotel*, which was thankfully renamed *This Place Hotel* to avoid confusion with Elvis Presley's classic hit. It is a highly visual song full of great ideas, and it shows that Michael retained a thing or two from Quincy Jones and Stevie Wonder. By working with one and observing the other, Michael gained the necessary confidence and audacity to put his wildest ideas—the fruits of his limitless genius—on tape. *Time Waits for No One*, which comes right after the ghoulish cry in *This Place Hotel*, pays tribute to Quincy Jones' arrangement style. The end of the album shifts between a hot and heavy funk (*Walk Right Now* and its breakneck interludes; *Wondering Who* and its explosiveness) and an ultra-light mid-tempo (*Give It Up*).

The result was nine tracks that could hold their own against *Off the Wall* and the rest of the funk elite of the time. There was only one problem: the sound, which was too clean, was not as exciting as other, bolder, funk songs that had the advantage of being more easily applied to the dance floor, a critical factor for a song's desirability. This is not to insult The Jacksons. *Triumph* was more inspired and sophisticated than it appeared to be, and it allowed them to become the best version of themselves: a group that no longer had anything to prove, despite mediocre ratings and a somewhat feeble promo. The *Triumph* tour, The Jacksons' last real tour, became the ultimate coronation for these young millionaires and true stage artists. The public had spoken, and an infectious fever spread to all sides of the double album released in November 1981.

Nevertheless, Michael's family's grip remained too tight for the star. As if it had been fate, *This Place Hotel* was a real blow to the Jackson household. It opened a serious rift that kept widening.

[THE JACKSONS]

Can You Feel It

Michael and Jackie Jackson / 5'58

Musicians
Michael and Randy Jackson: lead vocals
Nathan Watts: bass
Ollie Brown: drums
Greg Phillinganes, Ronnie Foster, Bill Wolfer: keyboards
Tito Jackson, David Williams: guitars
Gary Coleman: vibraphone
Audra Tillman, Brian Stilwell, Brigette Bush, Gerry Gruberth, Lita Aubrey, Peter Wade, Rhonda Gentry, Roger Kenerly II, Soloman Daniels, Yolanda Kenerly: children's choir
Arnold McCuller, Bob Mack, Bunny Hull, Carmen Twillie, Carolyn Dennis, Gerry Garrett, Gregory Wright, Jim Gilstrap, Josie James, Lewis Price, Lisa Roberts, Paulette Brown, Paulette McWilliams, Phyllis St. James, Tyrell "Rock" Deadrick, Roger Kenerly-Saint, Ronald Vann, Roy Galloway, Venetta Fields: adult choir
Recording
Hollywood Sound Studios, Los Angeles: rhythmic tracks and vocals, postproduction and mixing
Sound City Studios, Los Angeles: strings and brass, additional recordings
January to June 1980
Technical team
Producers: The Jacksons
Associate Producer: Greg Phillinganes
Recording engineer: Tom Perry
Arrangements: Michael and Jackie Jackson
String arrangement: Tom Tom 84

Single

USA
A-side: *Can You Feel It (US single version or 7-inch edit)* / 3'50
B-side: *Everybody (album version)* / 5'04
UK
A-side: *Can You Feel It (European single version or 7-inch edit)* / 4'04
B-side: *Wondering Who (album version)* / 4'19
Released by Epic Records: USA, April 1981 (ref. 19-01032) / UK, February 1981 (ref. S EPC 9554)
Chart position: USA R&B No. 30, Pop No. 77 / UK No. 6

SONG

Genesis

The commercial success of *Off the Wall* changed the stakes and upset the dynamics of the Jackson family. *Destiny*'s success had given Michael's siblings the confidence to push their taste for writing a little further. The goal was that of recording a strong, solid album capable of providing a logical continuation to *Off the Wall*, as far as this was possible.

While *Destiny*'s songs had been written by everyone in the group, each song in *Triumph* was created by a small team: the siblings often broke up into pairs to write new songs.

Can You Feel It became an important song for The Jacksons. Its emphasis on rock reflected the musical maturity the siblings had developed over the years. One must go back to *I Am Love*, which opens The Jackson Five's album *Dancing Machine*, to hear the group flirt with rock sounds, which were a far cry from the strictly pop and soul sounds used by Motown musicians.

Can You Feel It, which assertively opens The Jackson's fourth album with Epic, was composed by a surprising team: Jackie and his little brother Michael had worked together to bridge funk with rock. This was the first time the eldest Jackson sibling had participated in writing a song. Quiet but efficient, he was able to bring in fresh ideas.

While the song didn't top the charts as a single, reaching only 77th place on *Billboard*, it did become a classic song for the group. They used it as the opening number for the 1981 *Triumph* tour, and they turned it into a music video that was ambitious for its time.

The Jacksons had been raised as Jehovah's Witnesses by their mother Katherine, and the lyrics to *Can You Feel It* encapsulated the principles and philosophy of their religion. Either because of the golden prison in which Motown had trapped them, or because they'd received the keys to their artistic freedom from CBS, the Jackson siblings were never ones to use their music to respond to societal issues. Unlike socially engaged record labels like Stax or Chess, The Jacksons stood by their plan to defend and share messages of love and peace. *Can You Feel It*, with its symbolic phrases and rock riffs bursting with hope, may come across as naive, but its message

The Jacksons perform *Can You Feel It* during the *Triumph* tour in 1981. Hits from the album *Off the Wall* made up much of the setlist for concerts.

faithfully reflects the artistic convictions of a group of siblings that had finally seized control of their own careers.

Production

In an interview with *Wax Poetics* magazine, lead recording engineer for *Triumph* Tom Perry talked about the album. He confirmed that *Can You Feel It* had been the hardest song to make. While the rhythmic foundation had been recorded at the Hollywood Sound Studios, the string instruments, along with all the other strings in the album, had been recorded in Sound City, whose infrastructure could accommodate a mini orchestra.

Ollie Brown played a steady drum beat, a nod to the Motown hits, like *Baby Love*, from the good old days. Tom Perry estimated that the snare drum was too heavy and weighed down the piece. But Michael, the project's true conductor, wanted this song to deliver a huge rock sound, bigger than anything The Jacksons had ever done before. The chorus to *Can You Feel It* was the work of two separate groups of children and adults. As if to signify the passing of the torch from one generation to the next, this cast of 30 singers gave the refrain an epic depth. Tom Perry used an API hybrid console and added a second table to it in order to mix 48 tracks in total, instead of the 24 that could be done on the base configuration. This allowed him to capture the nuances of each chorus. Tom Perry knew the Hollywood Sound studio well, and had to navigate between Michael's drive to record the arrangements he was hearing in his head and Perry's own ambition to create natural-sounding takes that didn't abuse the equalizers or other dynamic range compressions, which he believed would damage the quality of the sound.

Michael and Randy sang the lyrics and refrains together. Their contrasting voices, deep and full of suspense for Randy, sharp and liberating for Michael, evoked some of the duets Michael had sung with Jermaine in their Motown days, such as *Ask the Lonely*.

Though not credited, keyboardist Bill Wolfer was very much involved in this song. He recalled having been asked by Michael Jackson to play some overdubs. "Michael wanted an effect that fades in and builds to a crescendo, sounding almost as if it were played backwards. It makes its first appearance at 3'14 on the song. It was done on a Yamaha CS-80, a massive 220-pound beast of a synthesizer."[42]

Backstage at the *Triumph Tour* (summer 1981).

THE SHORT FILM

Directors: Michael Gibson and John Grower
Producers: Robert Abel and Michael Jackson
Year: 1981
Location: Zoetrope Studios, Hollywood
Length: 9'37

Genesis

In late 1980, Michael Jackson floated the idea of making a film about *Can You Feel It*. He got in touch with Robert Abel's studios, whose work he admired, believing its technological and visual innovations were as impressive as those of Walt Disney in his day. At the time, Robert Abel and Associates enjoyed worldwide popularity: they created the graphics for many American (ABC) and French (TF1) television channels and they produced musical documentaries such as *Elvis on Tour* and *Let the Good Times Roll*.

The short film was written in real time, as Michael Jackson and his creative team's ideas took shape. Michael Gibson, the artistic director, took inspiration from the graphic world he'd created in his 1978 commercial for the "Man and Woman" perfume by Jovan. Robert Abel gave him free rein with only a few directions that he could follow as he saw fit, as long as the result remained catchy. The film had to contain many visual effects and show the Jackson siblings' love for the world and all the races within it. Gibson designed the storyboard, which instead of telling a story expressed very strong visual ideas. Michael agreed to these directions. Filming, which was supposed to last a few months for a video of three minutes max, was ready to begin.

Production

Michael Gibson, John Grower (who was then a young technical director), and cameraman Pat Kenly, made up the creative and technical core of the project, which was finally titled *The Triumph—Can You Feel It*. The three colleagues, then 20 years old, worked seven days a week over the course of almost nine months. Michael Jackson visited them regularly to watch the filming and express his ideas.

The team had holed up at Zoetrope Studios in Hollywood, which then belonged to Francis Ford Coppola. By day, it was the site of a Levi's commercial called *Working Man*. By night, the same studio and equipment were used for *The Triumph*. Robert Abel directed the Levi's commercial and allowed his three young acolytes to direct The Jacksons. László Kovács,

Maynard Jackson, the mayor of Atlanta, presents a prize to the Jacksons after their concert at the Omni, 22 July 1981. The profit made by the concert was donated to the Atlanta Children's Foundation.

who was already well known for his work on the cult classic film *Easy Rider*, was in charge of photography. The team built a few set designs, but the majority of the scenes were made up of Gibson and Grower's visual elements and special effects.

Filming lasted for several months. A financial dispute arose when Michael confronted his record company: CBS wanted something commercial, while Michael argued for a more abstract and spiritual approach. As a result of this disagreement, the label refused to finance filming, and Michael had to dip into his savings to top off the budget. Months passed, and negotiations faltered.

During this time, the team filmed, added, and cut some scenes. One of them showed Tito plucking at a guitar from the ground. This part was cut. The final version lasted more than 9'30. *The Triumph* was born of pain, but Michael Jackson defended it tooth and nail and decided to sidestep his record company's reluctance.

The final scene was the one that changed the most. One Friday evening, as filming was about to wrap, Gibson and Gower found a note from Robert Abel saying that Michael Jackson wanted to change the finale. New storyboards were created on Monday. Exhausted from nine months of intense work, the two young men cracked: the artistic director quit, severing ties with Robert Abel for a long time. Despite these differences, his name was kept in the credits. As for Grower, he resigned after the completion of the project, which he stayed to see through.

Inspired by *The Outer Limits*, Michael wanted to include comedians in the finale, particularly Italian-American actor Iron Eyes Cody, who was then famous for an antipollution campaign in which he portrayed a Native American man shedding a tear for the ravages that man has wrought upon his environment.

When the final version finally came through, Michael Jackson decided to promote it. MTV was still in its infancy, and other television channels weren't used to airing this type of content. So he turned to his longtime friend Dick Clark and asked him to broadcast *The Triumph* on his ABC show, *American Bandstand*. The presenter was skeptical, but he allowed himself to be persuaded and agreed to air the full short on the 19 September 1981 show. At the time, The Jacksons were reaching the end of their American tour for *Triumph*, an ambitious show that opened with the broadcasting of this film on the big screen. After later appearing on MTV and other music channels, the video was finally released for sale in *Vision*, a DVD that was released posthumously in 2010.

[THE JACKSONS]

Lovely One

Michael and Randy Jackson / 4'51

Musicians
Michael Jackson: lead vocals
The Jacksons: backing vocals
Nathan Watts: bass
Ollie Brown: drums
Greg Phillinganes: keyboards
Tito Jackson, David Williams, Mike Sembello: guitars
Paulinho Da Costa: percussion
Recording
Hollywood Sound Studios, Los Angeles: rhythmic tracks and vocals, postproduction and mixing
Sound City Studios, Los Angeles: strings and brass, additional recordings
January to June 1980
Technical team
Producers: The Jacksons
Associate producer: Greg Phillinganes
Recording engineer: Tom Perry
Arrangements: Michael Jackson and Tom Tom 84
Intro arrangement: Jerry Hey
Mixing: Tom Perry

USA
A-side: *Lovely One (single version) / 3'45*
B-side: *Bless His Soul (album version) / 4'55*
UK
A-side: *Lovely One (single version) / 3'45*
B-side: *Things I Do for You (album version) / 4'05*
Released by Epic Records: USA, 12 September 1980 (ref. 9-50938) / UK, 16 October 1980 (ref. S EPC 9302)
Chart position: USA R&B No. 2, Pop No. 12 / UK No. 29

Genesis

Destiny was a testament to just how well Michael and Randy worked together. So well, in fact, that their song *Shake Your Body* sold more than two million singles in the United States and became a classic disco and funk hit. They knew that because of this fans would be eagerly awaiting a sequel, so they wrote *Lovely One*, which Michael described as a logical continuation to *Shake Your Body*.

This time the lyrics were gloomier. There is a hint of resentment. Michael sings to a playful and funky rhythm as he tells of his falling for someone who's toying with his feelings. This darkness stands in stark contrast to the motivating and carefree qualities of *Shake Your Body*, as if *Lovely One* was the negative to the first's positive.

To further confirm this, the two songs complement each other through the chords that make up the motifs: *Lovely One* seems to play *Shake Your Body* backward, rather like a mirror effect.

This piece, which was well crafted despite missing the improvisation and spontaneity that were so charming in *Shake Your Body*, was only partially conclusive: while *Lovely One* placed 12th in the *Billboard* chart, it didn't manage to earn Gold or Platinum status.

Production

Aside from Ed Greene on drums and Michael Boddicker on the keyboards, the original team from *Shake Your Body* reconvened at Hollywood Sound to create *Lovely One*. Ollie Brown, the dynamic drummer from *Triumph*, played a simple funk rhythm, free of those diabolical offbeats perfected by Greg Phillinganes in *Shake Your Body*.

Nathan Watts, who was already playing for Stevie Wonder on a regular basis, played a bass line full of slapped notes that added depth and variation to the straightforward and linear rhythm played by Ollie Brown.

Lovely One's groove primarily rests on its rhythmic arrangements. The guitars of Michael Sembello, Tito Jackson, and especially David Williams—who would have the difficult task of playing the song on stage during the group's tours—firmly set the tone. Greg Phillinganes' piano blended into the background and became a support, or a distant echo, to the harmonies and the rhythms of the guitars.

Randy Jackson wears ski goggles on stage during the *Destiny* tour in 1980.

Michael hired Paulinho Da Costa for the song, though his contribution remained somewhat under the radar. Rather than imposing on the main rhythm, Da Costa limited himself to enriching the background. This subtle detail in the mixing showed just how much Michael had learned from Quincy Jones: attention to detail was one of the key elements that allowed him to create such astonishing music time and time again over his career.

As with *Shake Your Body*, Tom Tom 84 was in charge of the brass section. Lively and dynamic, it matched the precise, warm sound developed by Tom Perry. Keen ears have noted with surprise that the album *Raise!* by Earth, Wind, and Fire used a similar sound. This made it hard for the media of the day to perpetuate the rumor that the two groups were in competition with each other, especially after it came out that they were part of the same record company and used the same arrangers.

[THE JACKSONS]

This Place Hotel
(aka Heartbreak Hotel)

Michael Jackson / 5'44

Musicians
Michael Jackson: lead vocals
Nathan Watts: bass
Ollie Brown: drums
Greg Phillinganes: keyboards
Tito Jackson, David Williams, Mike Sembello, Paul Jackson Jr.: guitars
Marlon Jackson: timpani
La Toya Jackson: scream (intro)
The Jacksons, Paulinho Da Costa: percussion
Stephanie Spruill, Maxine Willard Waters, Julia Tillman Waters: backing vocals
Recording
Hollywood Sound Studios, Los Angeles: rhythmic tracks and vocals, postproduction and mixing
Sound City Studios, Los Angeles: strings, brass, and additional recordings
January to June 1980
Technical team
Producer: Michael Jackson
Associate producer: Greg Phillinganes
Recording engineer: Tom Perry
Special effects: Gene Corso
Arrangements: Michael Jackson
Horn arrangement: Tom Tom 84
Intro arrangement: Jerry Hey
Mixing: Tom Perry

USA
A-side: *Heartbreak Hotel (single version)* / 4'49
B-side: *Things I Do for You (album version)* / 4'05
UK
A-side: *Heartbreak Hotel (single version)* / 4'47
B-side: *Different Kind of Lady (album version)* / 3'36
Released by Epic Records: USA, 24 November 1980 (ref. 19-50959) / UK: 5 December 1980 (ref. S EPC 9391)
Chart position: USA R&B No. 2, Pop No. 22 / UK No. 44

Genesis

The global success of *Off the Wall* allowed Michael Jackson to become a more confident composer and producer. He increasingly collaborated with other artists while continuing to work on his own compositions, including the famous "different" music he explained to Diane Collins in a 1983 interview aired globally around the time of *Thriller* (see page 200). Categorized as a horror, *Heartbreak Hotel* was an oddity among the *Triumph* songs. As if walking through a door to a parallel world that would only stay open for 5'44, Jackson lead the listener into a haunted mansion, where the lost souls of those who had been murdered by tragic love stories roamed.

Michael wrote *Heartbreak Hotel* partly by drawing on the slightly horrifying atmosphere in the intro to *Off the Wall*, which evokes dark scenes of festive spirits breaking free and giving themselves to the drunken revelry of the night. Above all, Jackson wanted this song to be futuristic and avant-garde, which he achieved with a three-part structure: intro, song, and outro. The opening sequence sets up a story in which listeners can lose themselves. The ending, a theme played on the piano and accompanied by string instruments, signifies the moment of awakening from the nightmare.

The lyrics describe a hotel run by wicked women who make their own laws, and they mark the first instance of a theme that the young star would repeat throughout the years: the female as synonymous with vice, a danger to men, someone willing to stop at nothing to get what she wants.

Production

Unlike other songs on *Triumph*, Michael led the making of *Heartbreak Hotel* singlehandedly. The casting choices were somewhat unusual: instead of providing backing vocals, the Jackson siblings played percussion alongside Paulinho Da Costa.

Accustomed to terrifying his family with fairly skillful tricks, Michael chose his older sister La Toya to deliver the terrifying scream that opens the song.

Heartbreak Hotel evokes a cinematographic universe, like the soundtrack of a horror movie unfolding in the listener's head. The many special effects in the song were created by Gene Corso (1932–1996), a recording engineer who was expert in special effects and who worked on *Roots* (1974) and

Heartbreak Hotel was one of the highlights of the *Triumph* tour in 1981.
From left: Marlon, Michael, and Jackie Jackson.

Star Wars (1977). Michael applied to the letter a philosophy he'd learned from Quincy Jones while at Motown: he surrounded himself with artists who were at the top of their respective fields. At the same time, he knew how to yield the floor to Tom Tom 84 and Jerry Hey's brass and intro arrangements.

Paul Jackson Jr. played the guitar solo to precise instructions. "With Michael Jackson's *Heartbreak Hotel*, I went to the studio and he wanted me to play a solo on the song," he said in an interview with Bridgid Rousseau. "He put a tape in that plays him singing the solo the exact way he wants me to play. I did it phrase by phrase. So, the solo on the song is exactly what Michael sang."[43]

Michael did the same with bassist Nathan Watts. "Bass-wise, for the most part, he would tell me to do my thing," he explained for an article for bassplayer.com. "On *Heartbreak Hotel* (aka *This Place Hotel*), however, he started dancing and singing rhythmically, to show me what he wanted."[6]

Whether it was because of the richness of sound or the clinical precision of the recording, *Heartbreak Hotel* was one of Michael's solos to be included in The Jacksons' album as a bonus track. The time it took for him to visit the creepy hotel for broken hearts was the time it took for Michael to isolate and distance himself from his family. He let his imagination run wild and laid the solid groundwork for a style he would never stop perfecting.

FOR JACKSON ADDICTS

The song was originally called *Heartbreak Hotel*, like Elvis Presley's 1956 piece. To avoid confusion, Epic and the group agreed to name it *This Place Hotel* for the album.

[THE JACKSONS]

Walk Right Now

Michael, Jackie, and Randy Jackson / 6'28

Musicians
Michael Jackson: lead vocals
Nathan Watts: bass
Ollie Brown: drums
Greg Phillinganes: keyboards
Tito Jackson, David Williams, Mike Sembello: guitars
Paulinho Da Costa: percussion
The Jacksons: backing vocals
Recording
Hollywood Sound Studios, Los Angeles: rhythmic tracks and vocals, postproduction and mixing
Sound City Studios, Los Angeles: strings, horns, and additional recordings
January to June 1980
Technical team
Producers: The Jacksons
Associate producer: Greg Phillinganes
Recording engineer: Tom Perry
Arrangements: Michael Jackson and Tom Tom 84
Mixing: Tom Perry

USA
A-side: *Walk Right Now* (*US single version*) / 4'25
B-side: *Your Ways* (*album version*) / 4'32
UK
A-side: *Walk Right Now* (*European single version*) / 4'39
B-side: *Your Ways* (*album version*) / 4'32
Released by Epic Records: USA, 15 June 1981 (ref. 19-02132) / UK, 18 June 1981 (ref. S EPC A1294)
Chart position: USA R&B No. 50, Pop No. 73 / UK No. 7

Genesis

Jackie, Michael, and Randy Jackson joined forces for *Walk Right Now*. Its incandescent funk resembles certain songs from *Destiny*, such as *All Night Dancing*.

The lyrics aren't particularly original. Once more, they tell the story of unrequited love: "I don't care, what you're sayin' / Walk right now, I ain't playin' / Love elsewhere, for you I'm prayin'." Michael does not beat around the bush.

This emotional hostility goes perfectly with the pounding rhythm. *Walk Right Now* is an almost perfect blend of The Jacksons' sense of rhythm and groove: a jumping bass line, a break riddled with percussions that reply to each other stereophonically, and also funky but perhaps slightly too abrupt handclapping. The three brothers drafted a song that was meant to echo the sound of *Destiny* as well as the energy Michael gave off in *Off the Wall*. In his autobiography *Moonwalk*, Michael claimed that "*Walk Right Now* and *Wondering Who* were closer to the *Destiny* sound, but for the most part they were suffering from too many cooks and not enough broth."[2] In music, as in love, the dose remains a key element.

Production

Walk Right Now reunited part of the team from *Destiny* and *Off the Wall*. This first-class team worked hard to give the song all the funky pep it needed.

The balance was perfect: the version that appeared on the album sounded clean, maybe too smooth for a funk song that was supposed to set fire to the dance floor.

Nathan Watts' bass and David William's rhythmic guitar kept the tune alive. The percussion instrumental played by Paulinho Da Costa tried to insert a breather. This rather ad-hoc sound sequence would undoubtedly have taken a different direction had the song been performed on stage. Unfortunately, *Walk Right Now* only enjoyed a modest reception as a single, and the Jackson siblings would never sing it live. At the time, they gave up television shows like *American Bandstand* and *Soul Train* in order to concentrate on preparing for their *Triumph* tour. The song was then revisited during rehearsals. The five siblings tried to perform it on stage, but Michael—who remained the head of operations both in studio and in public—finally scrapped the idea.

Walk Right Now was one of the songs rehearsed for the *Triumph* tour but eventually dropped from the final lineup.

Only the remixer John Luongo was able to eke out a long version and an instrumental and remaster them on tape, to the delight of DJs everywhere. As he said on his website, "Here is one such song which I am particularly proud of the instrumental version, since it had everything that the great records I admired growing up had and was a tribute to one of my musical heroes, Quincy Jones, since it was how I believed he might have approached this song! This song had a great pumping rhythm section, amazing orchestral elements, as well as strings and percussion that were unique for a song such as this, and lifted the song and the audience to new heights!"[44]

Luongo's enthusiasm shines forth from the two mixes, which have been widely distributed commercially since their initial release in 1981, to the point where they have become classics among Luongo's portfolio as a remixer and producer.

FOR JACKSON ADDICTS

Walk Right Now **didn't make an impression in the US charts, floundering at 73. But in the UK CBS marketed it as a picture disc, which remains prized among collectors.**

Andy Warhol with Michael and Randy Jackson backstage on the *Triumph* tour at Madison Square Garden, New York, 19 August 1981.

[**THE JACKSONS**]

Give It Up

Michael and Randy Jackson / 4'20

Musicians
Michael Jackson, Marlon Jackson: lead vocals
Clay Drayton: bass
Ollie Brown: drums
Greg Phillinganes: keyboard
Tito Jackson, David Williams, Mike Sembello: guitars
Gary Coleman: vibraphone
Paulinho Da Costa: percussion
The Jacksons: backing vocals
Recording
Hollywood Sound Studios, Los Angeles: Rhythmic tracks and vocals, postproduction and mixing
Sound City Studios, Los Angeles: strings and brass, additional recordings
January to June 1980
Technical team
Producers: The Jacksons
Associate producer: Greg Phillinganes
Recording engineer: Tom Perry
Arrangements: Michael and Jackie Jackson
String arrangement: Jerry Peters
Mixing: Tom Perry

Genesis

When Jermaine decided to continue his solo career with Motown, Michael lost his sounding board for song lyrics. The team that gained recognition with legendary songs like *I'll Be There* (1970), dissolved once The Jacksons signed on with CBS.

Michael and Randy gathered around the family piano in Encino to compose *Give It Up*. The song's structure and ethereal melody confirmed that the success of their ballad *That's What You Get (For Being Polite)*, two years before, hadn't been an accident.

The song shifts back and forth between ethereal verses where Michael's voice soars to a crystalline falsetto, and serene breaks where Marlon infuses gentle romance into the song. The pre-chorus allows Michael to raise the stakes by pushing his voice to ever higher levels.

Of all *Triumph's* songs, *Give It Up* was the only one that put a positive spin on romantic relationships. The two brothers sang of their hopes for a simple, unfettered love.

Production

Give It Up was among the songs that quickly reached record stores. Michael and recording engineer Tom Perry had hired a small orchestra that was just large enough to perform the piece without distorting it. They leaned heavily on a team of solid guitarists, namely David Williams, Mike Sembello, and Tito Jackson.

Clay Drayton played bass. He had worked with the Jackson siblings while at Motown in the mid-1970s, helping them write a number of songs that were quite psychedelic, such as *Life of the Party, She's a Rhythm Child, We're Gonna Change Our Style*, and *Window Shopping*. He also took credit for some of the arrangements in Diana Ross' legendary *Love Hangover*. By the end of the decade, he was working regularly with the Jackson family, of which he said "I also wrote and produced some things [with] Randy and Janet when they were young. Unfortunately, these things were not released."[45]

Gary Coleman (not the actor) added the crystalline notes of the vibraphone. At the time, he mostly created original soundtracks for television series produced by Mike Post, but he also occasionally worked on musical projects for artists such as Aretha Franklin and Barbra Streisand.

THE MUSIC INDUSTRY DISCOVERS A NEW TALENT

At the start of the 1980s, Michael Jackson was asked to work on a number of projects with the people responsible for the success of his first solo album with Epic, *Off the Wall*. Quincy Jones, Carole Bayer Sager, Stevie Wonder, and Louis Johnson asked him to sing with them, compose a song for them, or record backing vocals for their music. His appearances, often under the radar and modest, fulfilled his insatiable artistic curiosity and consolidated wonderful friendships. Bursting with creativity, these experiences allowed Michael to learn new skills that would enrich his style and studio experience. He also kept his family in the spotlight by composing songs for each brother or sister who wanted to release a solo album.

KENNY LOGGINS
WHO'S RIGHT, WHO'S WRONG

Kenny Loggins, Richard Page / 5'38

From the album: *Keep the Fire* / **Released by Columbia Records:** USA (ref. JC 36172) & UK (ref. CBS 83869), October 1979 / **Chart position:** USA Pop No. 16 / **RIAA:** certified Gold on 6 February 1980 / certified Platinum on 1 November 1985 / **Musicians: Michael Jackson and Richard Page:** vocal harmonies / **Recording: Filmways / Wally Heider Studios, San Francisco:** (unknown)

Michael Jackson used recording sessions in California as opportunities to weave a strong artistic, social, and professional network. He respected the work of Kenny Loggins and The Doobie Brothers, and working with them allowed him to learn, hear, and discover the rock fusion that would influence *Thriller* and the rest of his career.

In 2014 Kenny Loggins said of his collaboration with Michael:

> I was at a benefit that Michael was at, and I asked him if he would like to sing on the record. He said yeah—I think he had just finished *Off the Wall* and I just got lucky. He was available, he wanted to do it, he was a fan. Had I really thought it through, I should have probably recorded something up-tempo with him. I kick myself and think that was a waste of his talent. Great tune and everything, but just not the right tune for Michael Jackson to be singing on...He was a total sweetheart and was willing to go in any direction. I remember at one point I said, "Put more of your 'thing' on it; it feels a little too stiff." And he said,"You mean you want it *stinky?*""Yeah! I want it stinky." So he put more juice on it.[46]

Michael revealed to Chris Cadman, author of *Michael Jackson—Off the Wall, For the Record,* during a 1980 interview, that he helped select *Keep the Fire's* cover, refusing payment due to his friendship with Loggins. In 1985, Loggins appeared on *We Are the World.*

Louis and George Johnson made *Stomp!* part of the pop history of the 1980s.

THE BROTHERS JOHNSON
THIS HAD TO BE

Louis Johnson, George Johnson, Michael Jackson / 5'13

From the album: *Light Up the Night* / **Released by A&M Records:** USA (ref. SP-3716) & UK (ref. AMLK 63716), early 1980 / **Chart position:** USA R&B No. 1, Pop No. 5 / **RIAA:** certified Gold on 29 April 1980 / certified Platinum on 25 September 1980 / **Musicians: Michael Jackson:** backing vocals / **Recording: Kendun Recorders, Burbank; Allen Zentz Recording, Los Angeles; A&M Studios, Los Angeles:** (unknown)

Light Up the Night was the last work that Quincy Jones produced for The Brothers Johnson. The musicians who worked on *Off the Wall* were at the reins, imbuing each track with their charm and making the sounds explode. Rod Temperton worked with the brothers on *Stomp!*, the group's greatest hit and a major landmark in the establishment of funk. Michael Jackson also played his part: he helped to write the backing vocals for *This Had to Be*. His high-pitched voice was a wonderful addition to the musicality of the piece, though not much is known of the true reason for his participation. It may have been out of kindness, which was common for him, as a way to thank Louis for the superb bass lines that he'd played for *Off the Wall*.

COLLABORATIONS

DAVE MASON
SAVE ME

Jim Krueger / 3'38

From the album: *Old Crest on a New Wave* / **Released by Columbia Records:** USA, July 1980 (ref. JC 36144) / UK, June 1980 (ref. CBS 83828) / **Chart position:** USA Pop No. 74 / **Single: Released by Columbia Records:** USA, June 1980 (ref. 1-11289) / Europe, July 1980 (ref. CBS 8754) **Chart position:** USA R&B No. 70, Pop No. 71 / **Musicians: Michael Jackson:** backing vocals / **Recording: Hollywood Sound Studios, Los Angeles:** (unknown)

The story of Dave Mason and Michael Jackson's collaboration starts in 1971 on the set of the TV show *Diana!*. The child star and Diana Ross were singing *Feelin' Alright*, which Mason had written when he was only 19 years old. The studio recording of the piece can be found on the show's original soundtrack and on the Motown single. However, their first actual meeting wouldn't take place until 18 January 1980 at the American Music Awards, where Dave Mason presented Michael with the prestigious award for Favorite Male Artist in the soul/R&B category.

Michael Jackson's involvement in the making of *Save Me* was almost accidental. At the time, both musicians were working in the same studio. Mason was desperately looking for a high-pitched voice to back one of his songs, and no one in his team could do it. So he asked Michael, who readily accepted. What had originally been conceived as simple backing support became a quasi-duet between the two artists.

The song, which radiates freshness, was released as a single in June 1980. It only met with minimal success in the US and it wasn't even noticed in Europe, maybe because Michael Jackson's involvement hadn't been made clear.

MINNIE RIPERTON
I'M IN LOVE AGAIN

Minnie Riperton, Richard Rudolph / 4'05

From the album: *Love Lives Forever* / **Released by Capitol Records:** USA, August 1980 / **Chart position:** USA R&B No. 11, Pop No. 35 / **Musicians: Minnie Riperton and Michael Jackson:** lead vocals / **Recording: Hollywood Sound Studios, Los Angeles:** April to May 1980

Stevie Wonder had hired Minnie Riperton as a vocalist before producing her 1974 album *Perfect Angel*, which contains the wonderful *Lovin' You*. She passed away from cancer on 12 July 1979, at age 31.

The following year, her husband and producer Richard Rudolph decided to release a posthumous album by using her 1978 recording sessions. The project involved finalizing the songs using artists with whom who she had been friends, and with whom she had shared artistic sensibilities. It was like "keeping the bridge, but moving the water," according to Quincy Jones.[47]

Michael Jackson and Minnie Riperton had met several times. Here they sing a "virtual" duet called *I'm in Love Again*, a sweet ballad that highlights Minnie Riperton's incredible vocal talent, which spans more than four octaves. Michael, humbled by this impressive sound, sings a beautiful echo of her voice, like a responsive mirror.

Along with the other artists, such as Stevie Wonder, George Benson, and Roberta Flack, Michael wrote a dedication on the back of the album, which said "She was phenomenal...She did things with her voice that were incredible..." Stevie Wonder's words became the album's title, *Love Lives Forever*.

La Toya Jackson in the early 1980s.

La Toya Jackson

Night Time Lover

Michael and La Toya Jackson / 3'40

From the album: *La Toya Jackson* / **Released by Polydor Records:** USA (ref. PD-1-6291) & Europe (ref. 2391 475), September 1980 / **Chart position:** USA R&B No. 26, Pop No. 116 / **Single: Released by Polydor Records:** USA (ref. PD 2117) & Europe (ref. 2095 274) September 1980 / **Chart position:** USA, R&B No. 59 / **Musicians: Michael Jackson and La Toya Jackson:** lead vocals / **Recording: Daulin Studios / Hollywood Sound Studios, Los Angeles:** (unknown) **Technical team: Producer:** Michael Jackson / **Arrangements:** Michael Jackson and Larry Farrow

In the late 1970s, Joe Jackson asked his daughter La Toya if she wanted to go solo. With her consent, he negotiated a contract with Polydor and launched her self-titled debut album. Michael was asked to support the launch. Michael and La Toya had written a song together called *Fire Is the Feeling,* which they had planned on giving to Donna Summer but never had the chance. *Night Time Lover* was based on this song.

In her autobiography, *La Toya: Growing Up in the Jackson Family* (1991), La Toya expresses a certain frustration with the work that went into the album and the song. In particular, she felt that too many changes had been made to *Night Time Lover* and she regretted making the original mix in the family studio.

Following Michael's death, she explained the origins of the song in an interview with Chris Yandek:

> He was sitting on the floor and I was sitting on the bed and we just started writing *Night Time Lover.* He felt that this is a great song for me. We started writing for me actually and Michael produced it on me and he, at one point, told me, "I think I want to put that out again." This is much later on. He says, "I think I want to put that song out again and I sing on it and he'd sing it actually, but he never did it, he never did. That was just wonderful to know that.[48]

La Toya seemed to float the idea of the existence of a solo demo sung by Michael Jackson. Fans would give a lot to hear it.

The album and single were barely noticed, even though La Toya promoted the song on various television shows. *Night Time Lover* nevertheless remains a very lovely, dancy, and funky piece, rich in harmonies, fresh, and invigorating—it's the best song in the album, along with *If You Feel the Funk.*

Stevie Wonder at the keyboard in Abbey Road Studios, London, 1980.

STEVIE WONDER
ALL I DO

Stevie Wonder (music), Stevie Wonder, Clarence Paul, and Morris Broadnax (lyrics) / 5'06

From the album: *Hotter Than July* / **Released by Tamla Motown Records:** USA (ref. T8-373M1) & UK (ref. STMA 8035), 29 September 1980 / **Chart position:** USA R&B No. 1, Pop No. 3 / UK No. 2 / **RIAA:** certified Gold and Platinum on 3 February 1981 / **Michael Jackson:** backing vocals (in collaboration with Eddie Levert, Walter Williams, Jamil Raheem and Betty Wright) / **Recording: Wonderland Studios, Los Angeles / Record Plant Remote Truck:** (unknown)

After the wonderful *Songs in the Key of Life* (1976) and the musical *Journey through the Secret Life of Plants* (1979) were released, Stevie Wonder began work on *Hotter Than July* (1980), whose song *Master Blaster (Jammin')* launched his return to pop, funk, and reggae. Stevie was returning to his foundations and previous influences. He also wanted to address civil rights issues, and symbolically, he dedicated the album to Martin Luther King Jr. The single *Happy Birthday* was a strong career move. It popularized the demand for Martin Luther King Jr.'s birthday to be designated a national holiday in the United States, allowing the proposal to be brought to Congress. On 2 November 1983, Ronald Reagan signed into law the decree creating Martin Luther King Jr. Day, which has been celebrated on the third Monday of each January since 1986. Through his mentor, Michael Jackson learned the extent to which music can rouse crowds and make changes, a lesson that he soon applied with *We Are the World* (1985).

In *Hotter Than July*, Stevie also talks about love. He had started working on *All I Do* some 15 years before. The song, with its all-consuming rhythm, acts as an insistent declaration: "All I do is think about you..." After Stevie wrote *I Can't Help It* for *Off the Wall*, Michael agreed to sing backing vocals, which gave the piece a soul mood. Further collaborations between the two friends would soon follow. In 2007, for the magazine *Ebony*, the young star reiterated his admiration, saying, "Now Stevie Wonder, he's a musical prophet. He's another guy I have to credit. I wanted to experience it all. So Stevie Wonder used to literally let me sit like a fly on the wall. I got to see *Songs in the Key of Life* get made, some of the most golden things."[49]

Quincy Jones at the time of the release of *The Dude* (1981).

QUINCY JONES
THE DUDE

Quincy Jones, Rod Temperton, Patti Austin / 5'35

From the album: *The Dude* / **Released by A&M Records:** USA (ref. SP-3248) & UK (ref. AMLK 63721), 26 March 1981 / **Chart position:** USA R&B No. 3, Pop No.10 / UK No. 19 / **RIAA:** certified Gold on 16 June 1981 / certified Platinum on 24 February 1982 / **Single:** only published as a maxi single in the United Kingdom (AMSX 8207) and as a 12" promo in the United States (SP-17147) / **Michael Jackson:** backing vocals, in collaboration with Quincy Jones, Patti Austin, Syreeta Wright, James Ingram, Jim Gilstrap, and Lalomie Washburn / **Recording: Westlake Audio, Los Angeles:** (unknown)

All of the energy Quincy Jones put into *Off the Wall* and *Light Up the Night* (The Brothers Johnson) still animated him by the end of 1980. He made use of all the talent that gravitated toward him to create *The Dude*, an album named after himself and the last one for A&M Records before he created his own label, Qwest Records, with Warner Brothers. While he could have ended his collaboration with the record company with a simple production, free of grand musical innovations, he instead delivered a truly timeless landmark in African-American music. Quincy Jones had the ability to reinvent his music almost at will. Given the successes of his protégés—Michael Jackson, Rufus and Chaka Khan, George Benson, and Donna Summer—he reoriented his style toward a sound that was more poppy and firmly electric. The former trumpet player was gone, his instrument was now the studio, and he was working with some of the best artists of all time. Patti Austin, Stevie Wonder, Michael Jackson, Rod Temperton, Greg Phillinganes: they all came to support their teacher's brilliant project. For the piece called *The Dude*, Michael Jackson provided backing vocals. The song can be considered as a prelude to Donna Summer's *State of Independence* or *We Are the World*, by the super-group USA for Africa.

The Dude garnered 12 Grammy nominations, of which it won half, including for best instrumental arrangement and best R&B performance by a duo or group. The surprise came from the band's newcomer, James Ingram, who had never worked on an album before. He landed three prestigious individual awards: best artist of the year, best male vocal performance for the song *Just Once*, and best male R&B vocal performance for *One Hundred Ways*. *Ai No Corrida* was a worldwide success and conveyed just how impressive this project was. Quincy Jones barely had the time to enjoy these awards before he returned to the studio with Michael Jackson to start work on *Thriller*.

At the start of the 1980s, Kenny Rogers made it his mission to reach the top of the R&B scene, something he achieved with the single *Lady*.

Rogers, Richie, and Jackson would meet again in 1985 for *We Are the World*. Kenny Rogers would simultaneously continue his collaboration with Gladys Knight, with whom he released the duet *If I Knew Then What I Know Now* in 1989.

Kenny Rogers
Goin' Back to Alabama

Lionel Richie Jr. / 4'30

From the album: *Share Your Love* / **Released by Liberty Records:** USA (ref. LOO-1108) & UK (ref. LBG 30339), early 1981 / **Chart position:** USA, Top Country Albums No. 1, Pop No. 6 / **RIAA:** certified Gold and Platinum on 28 August 1981 / **Musicians: Michael Jackson and Lionel Richie:** backing vocals / **Recording: Lion Share Recording Studios, Los Angeles:** (unknown)

In 1980, Liberty Records released Kenny Rogers' first *Greatest Hits* album, to celebrate the five years he'd been working with United Artists Records. In order to improve the compilation's marketing, Liberty executives commissioned a few bonus tracks, including a new single. No one was expecting Kenny Rogers to write a song that would make it into the Top R&B charts. Executives were skeptical and even thought he'd lose some of his fans. Rogers enlisted the help of Lionel Richie, who was just starting his solo career after his success with The Commodores at Motown. The single *Lady*, a real international hit, would reach No. 1 in the US charts.

Strengthened by this success, Kenny Rogers entrusted Lionel Richie with his new masterpiece, *Share Your Love* (1981), which was dedicated to blues notes and R&B. In order to further legitimize the project, Rogers suggested calling some of his friends from Motown. This is how Gladys Knight and Michael Jackson were brought on board. They joined the team at the Lion Share Recording Studios and provided backing vocals for *Share Your Love with Me* (Gladys Knight) and *Goin' Back to Alabama* (Michael Jackson and Lionel Richie).

Goin' Back to Alabama is a sweet ballad about a man who only wants to start over after being down on his luck. Lionel and Michael sound warm and reassuring, and lift the chorus with beautiful notes of optimism.

Carole Bayer Sager shared Michael Jackson's love of beautiful tunes.

FOR JACKSON ADDICTS

Carole Bayer Sager cowrote *You Are My Life* with Michael for the album *Invincible*, and *We've Had Enough*, which appeared on *Michael Jackson—The Ultimate Collection* (2004).

As surprising as it may seem, *Sometimes Late at Night* was transferred to disc in mono. In 2006, a Japanese edition of the album used the K2 HD coding technique to rerelease the album in stereo (ref. Victor VICP-63253).

CAROLE BAYER SAGER
JUST FRIENDS

Carole Bayer Sager, Burt Bacharach / 3'16

From the album: *Sometimes Late at Night* / **Released by Boardwalk Records:** USA (ref. FW 37069) & UK (ref. EPC 85110) first half of 1981 / **Chart position:** Chart position: USA Pop No. 60 / **Michael Jackson:** backing vocals / **Recording: Record Plant, Los Angeles:** (unknown) / **Technical team: Producers:** Michael Jackson and Burt Bacharach.

Michael Jackson's collaboration with Carole Bayer Sager began on *Just Friends* when the two artists were in a Dominick's Steakhouse not long after finishing *Off the Wall*, for which Sager had cowritten *It's the Falling in Love.* She told Michael she was working on a record with Burt Bacharach, and he suggested he visit them at the Record Plant studio. In her autobiography, which came out in 2016, Sager recalled this moment and their subsequent collaboration:

> When he came by, I was recording a song called *Just Friends*. He listened for a while, then asked, "Do you mind if I play around with something?" We didn't mind at all, Burt admired him as much as I did, which was saying something. Michael took Paul Jackson, a wonderful guitarist who was playing guitar on the session, into the bathroom with him to work on another concept of the track and came back with a totally different arrangement with a whole new feel that even Burt said was better than what he had done. Somehow I got up the courage to ask him if he would sing with me on the record. "Sure," he said, "let's do it. Let's work it out. Let me hear you sing it." We started to trade lines, and he built some background parts where he was doubling his own voice to give it more thickness and texture in the musical track. I was thrilled. Michael Jackson and I were singing together. It was mind-blowing to me.[50]

1. WANNA BE STARTIN' SOMETHIN'
2. BABY BE MINE
3 THE GIRL IS MINE
4. THRILLER
5. BEAT IT
6. BILLIE JEAN
7. HUMAN NATURE
8. P.Y.T. (PRETTY YOUNG THING)
9. THE LADY IN MY LIFE

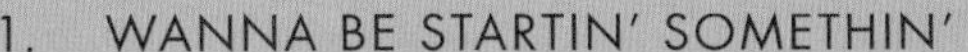

Thriller **ALBUM**

Released by Epic Records: USA (ref. QE 38112) and UK (ref. EPC 85930), 30 November 1982
Chart position: USA R&B No. 1, Pop No. 1 / UK No. 1
RIAA: certified Gold and Platinum 31 January 1983 / certified 33-time Multiplatinum 16 February 2017

An alternative image created by the photographer Dick Zimmerman, which was not retained for the sleeve of the album *Thriller*.

THRILLER, A GLOBAL IDOL

At the very start of the 1980s the fashion for disco and the emergence of video games were hurting the record market. Consumers were turning their backs on vinyl and cassettes in favor of ever more sophisticated consoles. The television set became the main place of entertainment, and the video market—still in its infancy—was gradually becoming established, affording the opportunity to watch the best films at home.

Quincy Jones and Michael Jackson realized that the golden age of the 1970s, which had allowed so many rock groups to take off, was no more. This critical situation drove them to produce a record that would tempt the general public back to recorded music.

The singer also told Quincy Jones in confidence that not only did he want *Thriller* to beat the sales of *Off the Wall*, but he wanted to make it the biggest-selling album of all time. The producer doubted this could be achieved, especially with the economy in such a depressed state. But the musician was convinced his goal was attainable. On 15 November 2006, at the World Music Awards in London, he would remember his dream of almost 24 years earlier: "It was my dream that *Thriller* would become the biggest-selling album ever…And God has answered my prayers. I thank God and you for this incredible success."[51]

1982

In 1982, the recording sessions for *Thriller* took place in an atmosphere of intense concentration. Michael Jackson put himself under extreme pressure and surpassed himself. The idea was to choose nine songs, each of which could do well as a single.

The young prodigy applied his boundless determination to attain his goal. *Thriller* was the result of tireless work, coupled with a desire to capitalize on every marketing opportunity to promote the album. The singer and those working around him managed to make the most of the record market and galvanize it back to life. By the end of its first run of sales, *Thriller* had sold almost 60 million copies. Thanks to the revenue it generated, CBS was able to launch a whole new generation of artists, including George Michael, Sade, Cyndi Lauper, and many others. This economic resurgence allowed the major record labels and audio equipment manufacturers to launch a product that, for a time, was to reign supreme in the world of music: the CD.

Three months to save the world

While *Off the Wall* had been recorded in a fairly relaxed atmosphere, with a compact, tightly knit team, the recording sessions for *Thriller* had something of a musical Who's Who about them. Michael Jackson's artistic ambitions drove him to widen his field of operations. He shared with Quincy Jones that taste for musical cross-fertilization, which produced unexpected collaborations between artists from sometimes very different backgrounds.

For *Off the Wall*, some famous songwriters had been called upon: Stevie Wonder for *I Can't Help It*, David Foster for *It's the Falling in Love*, and Paul McCartney for *Girlfriend*. Now the ex-Beatle found himself brought in again, this time at the microphone, to sing a duet in Michael Jackson's song *The Girl*

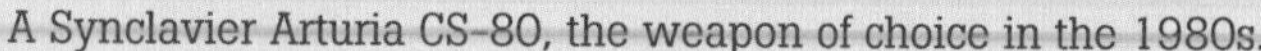

A Synclavier Arturia CS-80, the weapon of choice in the 1980s.

The Linn LM-1 Drum Computer, made by Linn Electronics.

Is Mine. This teamwork illustrates the spirit in which *Thriller* was recorded: discreet contributions from famous songwriters gave way to guest appearances by big names. As well as Paul McCartney, Michael Jackson and Quincy Jones invited Eddie Van Halen to play a supercharged guitar solo on *Beat It,* and the king of horror, Vincent Price, to record a gothic rap on *Thriller*. The intimate alchemy of *Off the Wall* stepped aside to make way for a Hollywood super-production.

The album is divided into three trilogies: *Wanna Be Startin' Somethin'*, *Baby Be Mine*, and *The Girl Is Mine*, which echo the blueprint of *Off the Wall*; *Thriller*, *Beat It*, and *Billie Jean*, which are the three cornerstones on which the album rests; and *Human Nature*, *P.Y.T.*, and *The Lady in My Life*, which provide gentle pop tones that complete the picture and reach out to a wide audience.

The team set up shop in the Westlake Recording Studios. Bruce Swedien connected multitrack machines together to obtain 48 useable tracks for each session. At the time, sequencers were very far from reigning supreme in the recording studio. Although the legendary Linn LM-1 drum machine was used for some songs, several dance numbers still made use of drum kits. Analysis of a piece using audio software proved that measures sometimes contained slight discrepancies, characteristic of sessions recorded using real musicians.

Thriller thus embodies the ultimate synthesis between a production made using traditional means and the progressive arrival of powerful machines such as the Synclavier. This formidable synthesizer made it possible to create and modulate sounds to the point that it created "sound signatures." Bruce Swedien, Quincy Jones, and Michael Jackson wanted to create songs that were unmistakable from the first note—like the digital gong at the start of *Beat It*, which was unique and recognizable, and made the song stand out from all others. The idea was extended to other songs such as *Billie Jean*, where the sound of the drums was precisely calibrated by the recording engineer, Bruce Swedien.

The cursed master

The team assembled around Michael Jackson and Quincy Jones plunged headlong into a three-month marathon to produce solid results with *Off the Wall*, but also to record another project, which the producer had accepted at the last minute: an audiobook and soundtrack album telling the story of Steven Spielberg's movie *E.T.* which, in 1982, had smashed all records at the box office (see pages 242–45).

Quincy Jones monopolized the Westlake studios. Deadlines were tight, and the pressure increased. Michael Jackson slept on the premises and worked against the clock to finish the two albums. His record label, CBS, watched the work in progress from a distance, hoping to release *Thriller* in time for the New Year celebrations.

In early October, when Larkin Arnold, artistic director at Epic, Michael Jackson, Quincy Jones, and key members of the team got together to hear the final master, their disappointment was palpable. The songs did not fit together well and some mixes were too long. The final result on the tape, hastily mastered by Bruce Swedien at Bernie Grundman's studios, revealed a technical limit: the duration of the album was too long for a vinyl disc pressed to a high standard. Anything beyond 20 minutes' music per side meant that the groove was too fine, which did not allow the bass frequencies to "breathe" when the record was played. Michael Jackson, with tears in his eyes, decided to stand up to his record label and refused to release the record in that condition. Larkin Arnold followed suit and informed CBS's CEO, Walter Yetnikoff. Despite his annoyance, the businessman understood that the economic stakes were high, and that the project needed to be given the best chance if it was to succeed.

In October 1983, Michael Jackson celebrated the success of the album *Thriller* with members of Epic Records management: Quincy Jones, Frank DiLeo, and Walter Yetnikoff, the label's CEO.

Quincy Jones suggested a timetable for remastering the album. After two days' rest, he, Michael Jackson, and Bruce Swedien prepared a new mix, at the rate of a song a day. With a heavy heart, they shortened some songs, such as *The Lady in My Life*, in order to keep the album to a reasonable length.

Thriller arrives without fanfare

At the end of that crucial week, *Thriller* was ready at last. *The Girl Is Mine*, a single released to test the waters on 25 October 1982, gave an indication of what to expect. The album hit the shops all over the world on 30 November. The public was presented with Michael Jackson sporting a new look: like a negative of the image on the sleeve of *Off the Wall*, he had abandoned the black tuxedo in favor of an elegant white Hugo Boss suit, borrowed on the day of the now legendary shoot with the photographer Dick Zimmerman.

By the beginning of 1983, the album was already a Platinum record, with more than two million sold in the United States. Slowly but surely, *Thriller* was starting a climb that would eventually go through the roof. The critics hailed its release, while noting that the album was opening up to other genres, such as rock and pop. The public reaction to *The Girl Is Mine* was lukewarm; its duet was pleasant but, coming after *Ebony and Ivory*, recorded a few months earlier by Paul McCartney and Stevie Wonder, it had a sense of *déjà vu* about it. This first single, with its star-studded lineup, was just a taster. Things took off in earnest when CBS launched the second single from the album, *Billie Jean*.

The golden age of video

Thriller contained nine songs which, in themselves, constituted the album's strength. Such was its musical quality that it was to become a recording used as a benchmark by many hi-fi buffs to adjust their systems.

But this musical success was soon linked to images that would forever leave their mark on the collective unconscious. *Thriller* certainly made its presence felt on radio stations, but it took on a whole new dimension thanks to the videos that were shot for three of the seven singles released.

Michael Jackson had retained a certain resentment about the way his previous videos had been produced. Those for *Off the Wall* had not allowed him to take his ambitious ideas to the limit. The short movie shot for *Can You Feel It* was able to come to fruition only thanks to supplementary funding that he was forced to provide from his own pocket, as his record label had told him it would advance no more money for the project.

For *Thriller*, Michael Jackson decided to create and to give to the public a different, and richer, offering in the way of musical videos. Most artists were content to perform their hits accompanied by simple video images, but Michael Jackson wanted to tell a story in the space of a song. To achieve this, he brought in novice but promising partners (the young British director Steve Barron for *Billie Jean*), top advertising filmmakers (Bob Giraldi for *Beat It*), and fashionable film directors (John Landis for *Thriller*).

Little by little, Michael Jackson took financial and artistic control of these musical videos, which he preferred to call

In 1983, Michael agreed to allow *Beat It* to be used for a campaign against drink-driving entitled *Drinking and Driving Can Kill a Friendship*, run by the National Highway Safety Commission. On 14 May 1984 the US president, Ronald Reagan, welcomed the singer to the White House to thank him for, among other things, his contribution to this campaign.

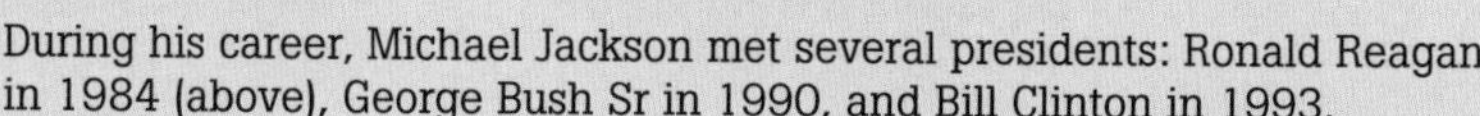

During his career, Michael Jackson met several presidents: Ronald Reagan in 1984 (above), George Bush Sr in 1990, and Bill Clinton in 1993.

"short films." This innovative approach found a ready audience, and the *Thriller* clips helped the album to sell. You didn't listen to *Thriller*—you watched it. The public demanded that TV networks show the videos. One station alone remained deaf to these appeals: the new musical channel MTV, founded in 1981 by Bob Pittman, showed few black artists at that time. Legend has it that Walter Yetnikoff offered the channel's bosses a deal that bore some resemblance to an ultimatum: either MTV showed *Billie Jean* and the other clips that were to come from Michael Jackson or he would order the immediate withdrawal of all CBS videos from the channel. Yetnikoff won: the clips for *Billie Jean* and *Beat It* were added to MTV's playlist. Ironically, it was thanks to the success of *Thriller* that the channel built its reputation.

The first moonwalk

Michael Jackson had had an aversion to TV studios ever since the 1980 *Disneyland 25* project (see page 146) and balked at appearing on shows to promote *Thriller*. At the same time Motown, whose popularity was falling because it lacked emblematic stars to fly the label's flag, hastily put together a TV show to celebrate its 25th anniversary. In fact, 1983 was the label's 24th anniversary, but no matter: the idea of a show bringing together all the artists that had contributed to the Motown legend was pitched to ABC, CBS, and NBC. The last of these secured the broadcasting rights.

Many artists had left Motown when this event was being organized. Michael Jackson and his brothers had left in 1975, while in the early 1980s Diana Ross had left the stable where she had started her career for a lucrative contract with RCA. However, with courage and persuasion, Berry Gordy and his team managed to bring together the artists who embodied the label's finest years. All agreed to appear, except Michael Jackson, who would not hear of Motown or any TV project. At the suggestion of Suzanne de Passe, who was in charge of the retrospective, Berry Gordy caught up with his former protégé in a recording studio to try to convince him. Eventually Michael Jackson agreed, but on one condition: that evening he would perform his latest song, *Billie Jean*. It would be the only non-Motown number on the program. An obliging Berry Gordy eventually agreed.

On 25 March 1983 the six Jackson brothers presented themselves at the Pasadena Civic Center in Los Angeles to rehearse and film their sequence for the *Motown 25* show, which NBC planned to broadcast 16 May on prime time. Everyone knew that Michael would perform a solo number, but no one knew which one. Even the show's scriptwriter, Buz Kohan, did not know. He had simply written the few lines that the young singer was to say on stage to pay tribute to his brothers at the end of their joint performance and to introduce his solo song.

That evening Michael Jackson gave a performance of *Billie Jean* that surpassed the power of the video made a few months earlier by Steve Barron. He performed, for the first time, the famous moonwalk, a dance move that gave the illusion that he was moving forward when in fact he was sliding backward on the stage. He had learned the basics of this years earlier by watching dancers on *Soul Train*, especially Jeffrey Daniel, a member of the group Shalamar, who appeared regularly on the show.

In the space of one song, the artist had cemented his iconic image: his sequined costume, the single glove worn on the left hand, and the official inauguration of the moonwalk. This image was magnified by the music arrangement he had supervised. He was not, however, happy with his pose on tiptoe, which he could not hold as long as he would have liked. Despite this bug, his performance of *Billie Jean* earned him an Emmy Awards nomination and, above all, recognition from Fred

Michael Jackson sings *Billie Jean* and performs his famous moonwalk for the first time on the show *Motown 25,* which aired on 25 March 1983.

Astaire, who called him to congratulate him and thank him for stepping into his shoes.

Michael Jackson's performance on *Motown 25* sparked a run on the record stores. The artist's image remained highly prominent in the media during the summer of 1983, even though the singles *Wanna Be Startin' Somethin'* and *Human Nature* were released without accompanying videos. Each song released as a single made the Top 10. *Thriller* went to No. 1 on the *Billboard* chart on 26 February 1983, remaining there for 37 weeks. Record stores soon realized that it was pointless to plan on returns for any unsold copies of *Thriller*; instead, they simply left them on the shelves, because sales did not drop off.

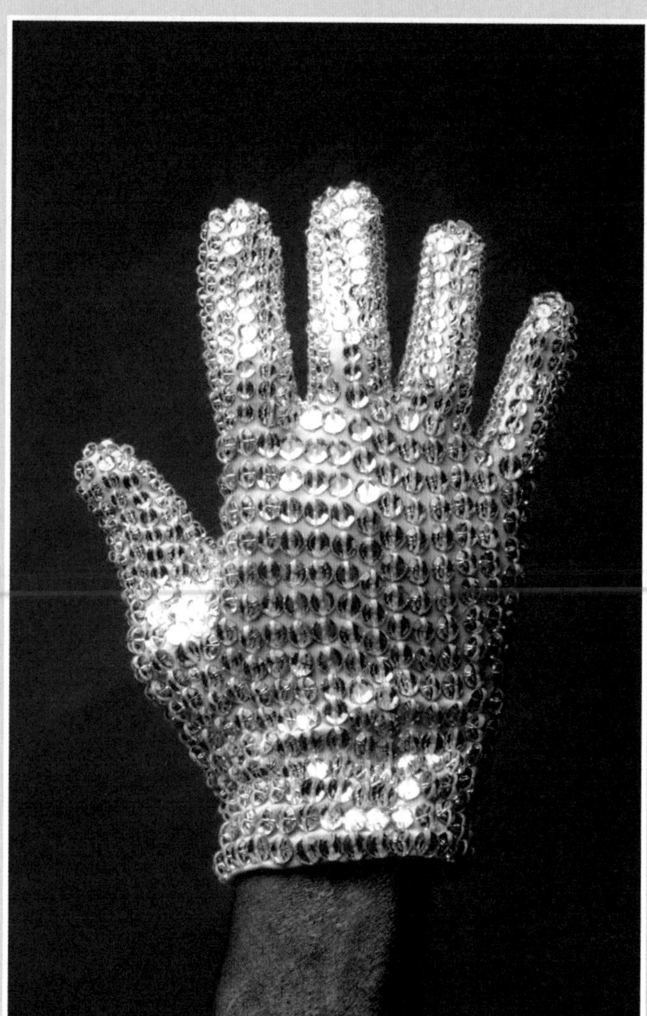

Michael Jackson was anointed by the music industry when he received eight awards—seven for *Thriller* and one for the *E.T. Storybook*—at the 26th Grammy Awards ceremony at the Shrine Auditorium in Los Angeles, 28 February 1984.

With the global success of *Thriller*, Michael Jackson's single glove, which first appeared during the *Off the Wall* years, became his trademark.

The cherry on the cake

By October 1983, promotion of the album seemed to have run its course. It had already sold 15 million copies. *Thriller* had overtaken the sales of *Off the Wall*, but it wasn't the best-selling album of all time. That record was still held by the Bee Gees: the original soundtrack of *Saturday Night Fever* had sold 22 million.

To drive the point home and create a final wave of interest that could revive the album's sales, Michael Jackson wanted to shoot a third video for the title track. Walter Yetnikoff refused to finance this project, given that the album had already proved a resounding success. No problem: the young artist and his team secured funding by persuading the MTV and Showtime channels to cofinance the project.

On 2 December 1983, just over a year after the album's release, MTV broadcast the *Thriller* clip for the first time. The 14-minute video, made by John Landis, showed Michael Jackson transforming himself first into a werewolf, then into a zombie, before embarking on a *danse macabre* through deserted streets. Half horror, half musical, the film completed the construction of the *Thriller* legend beyond a mere album.

In a circle that grew ever greater as clips were shown on TV and songs played on radio stations, *Thriller* became the must-have Christmas present. By early 1984 it had sold almost 25 million, overtaking the Bee Gees! During the 1983 to 1984 season, the whole world was plunged into Thrillermania.

On top of the world

Michael Jackson was the big winner of the awards ceremonies for the year's best records and artists. He got his revenge on the Grammy Awards jury, winning eight awards on 28 February 1984 at the Shrine Auditorium in Los Angeles. He also picked up eight crystal pyramids at the American Music Awards, produced by Dick Clark, on 16 January 1984, becoming the first artist to win so many prizes that evening. As the years passed, *Thriller* managed to retain its title of bestselling album of all time, and was added to the Library of Congress in Washington, a privilege reserved for exceptional works.

With an album, three clips, and a single TV appearance, Michael Jackson had climbed an Everest that he would try to surpass for the rest of his career. And he had also relaunched a record industry which, during those years, was counting on the arrival of the CD to secure its newfound financial strength.

Wanna Be Startin' Somethin'

Michael Jackson / 6'02

Musicians
Michael Jackson: lead vocals
Michael Jackson, Julia Waters, Maxine Waters, Oren Waters, James Ingram, Bunny Hull, and Becky Lopez: backing vocals
Greg Phillinganes: Rhodes piano and synthesizers
Michael Boddicker and Bill Wolfer: synthesizers
David Williams: guitar
Louis Johnson: bass guitar
Paulinho Da Costa: percussion
Jerry Hey and Gary Grant: trumpets and bugles
Larry Williams: saxophone and flute
William Reichenbach: trombone
Michael Jackson, Nelson Hayes, and Steven Ray: bathroom stomp board
Recording
Westlake Studio, Los Angeles: 14 April to 8 November 1982
Technical team
Producer: Quincy Jones
Coproducer: Michael Jackson
Recording engineer: Bruce Swedien
Vocal arrangements: Michael Jackson
Rhythmic arrangements: Michael Jackson and Quincy Jones
Brass arrangements: Michael Jackson and Jerry Hey

Single

USA
A-side: *Wanna Be Startin' Somethin'* (*single version*) / 4'15
B-side: *Wanna Be Startin' Somethin'* (*instrumental*) / 4'15
UK
A-side: *Wanna Be Startin' Somethin'* (*single version*) / 4'15
B-side: The Jacksons *Rock With You (live)* / 3'55
Released by Epic Records: USA, 28 May 1983 (ref. 34-03914) / UK, June 1983 (ref. EPC A 3427)
Chart position: USA R&B No. 5, Pop No. 5 / UK No. 8

Genesis

Michael Jackson wrote *Wanna Be Startin' Somethin'* at the end of the 1970s, with a view to recording it for the album *Off the Wall*. An initial demo was made in the family recording studio in Encino.

In the song, Michael Jackson describes the unhealthy relationships people can have with each other. Although it was rumored that the words referred to the strained relations between the sisters and wives of the Jackson brothers, it seems clear that these jaded, cynical observations on human nature reflect the young Michael's experiences since he entered the world of showbiz. Indeed, he had grown up in an environment where alliances based on self-interest often took the place of sincere friendships. In the realm of Hollywood, it became difficult for the star to meet people who were disinterested in him, and to have confidence in those with whom he came into contact.

The artist sings of his fears over a wild, festive rhythm. Allied with an obsessive bass line playing just three notes—D, E, and B—the singer launches into jerky couplets. These alternate with backing vocals that reply as if to support what he says.

When the young singer suggested the song to Quincy Jones, the producer was excited by the rhythm, which was inspired by African music. To complete the last couplet, which came at 4'28 and in which Michael frees himself from poisonous rumors, Quincy Jones suggested adding some words in Swahili that he wanted to borrow from a traditional song. The melody of this phrase, sung at the end of the song ("ma ma se ma ma sa ma ma coo sa"), is in fact a straight copy-and-paste of the theme *Soul Makossa* by the Cameroonian saxophonist and composer Manu Dibango. In 1972, this musician had proposed to the Cameroon minister for sport that he record a song to support the national soccer team. When it came to releasing the single, he did not know what to suggest for the B-side. So he hastily wrote a theme that referenced the Makossa movement, a type of Cameroonian music known for its arrangements rich in bass and brass notes. Thus *Soul Makossa*—and therefore the theme heard at the end of *Wanna Be Startin' Somethin'*—came to be written. When the album *Thriller* was released and achieved global success, the resemblance between his song and Michael Jackson's was not lost on Manu Dibango, who began legal proceedings in a Paris court. He won the case,

Michael Jackson during the shooting of a sequence advertising a special issue of *People* magazine (1984).

Extended and extended instrumental versions lasting 6'30 each, were released as maxi singles worldwide.

FOR JACKSON ADDICTS

Jennifer Batten, Michael's touring guitarist, recorded her own version of *Wanna Be Startin' Somethin'* for her first album, *Above and Beyond*, released in 1992.

and a financial agreement was reached whereby he was paid an undisclosed percentage of *Thriller*'s sales in France.

Production

The album begins with a triple kick on a snare drum, a brilliant start to the complex, spellbinding rhythm of *Wanna Be Startin' Somethin'*. To emphasize the difference with the traditional rhythms played by John Robinson on *Off the Wall*, *Wanna Be Startin' Somethin'* makes use of a Linn M-1 Drum Computer drum machine, the first that used samples of real drum sounds. Developed by Roger Linn, it earned the confidence of many artists during the 1980s, and the sound it produced became a distinguishing mark that stood out among all others.

The song's break lets David Williams' guitar explode into life, playing a theme as obsessive as the bass line and which discreetly heralds the arrival of the African song, performed by the backing vocalists, at the end of the piece. Williams was one of the few musicians taking part in these recording sessions who was to accompany Michael Jackson on his *Victory*, *Dangerous*, and *HIStory* tours, and to provide this solo that had been perfected over many long hours within the Westlake studios.

In *Wanna Be Startin' Somethin'*, Michael Jackson had in mind a singular, sharp-sounding snare drum. To produce this sound, he came up with a homemade solution: he got together a few planks of plywood used for bathroom flooring, which he struck, accompanied by his assistant Nelson Hayes and Quincy Jones' assistant, Steven Ray.

Although the song accomplished its mission as a record and in the charts, the artist admitted in 1999 that he was never fully satisfied with the end result. He said: "Songwriting is a very frustrating art form. You have to get on tape exactly what's playing in your head."[23]

Michael Jackson and Jane Fonda during a press conference at CBS headquarters in Los Angeles, 25 February 1983. He received a Platinum record for *Thriller*.

BABY BE MINE

Rod Temperton / 4'20

Musicians
Michael Jackson: lead and backing vocals
Greg Philliganes: keyboards and synthesizers
Michael Boddicker and David Paich: synthesizers
David Williams: guitar
Ndugu Chancler: drums (intro)
Jerry Hey and Gary Grant: trumpets and bugles
Larry Williams: saxophone and flute
William Reichenbach: trombone
Recording
Westlake Recording Studios, Los Angeles: 14 April to 8 November 1982
Technical team
Producer: Quincy Jones
Recording engineer: Bruce Swedien
Synthesizer programming: Steve Porcaro, Brian Banks, and Anthony Marinelli
Vocal arrangements: Rod Temperton
Voice, rhythm, and synthesizer arrangements: Michael Jackson and Quincy Jones
Brass arrangements: Jerry Hey

Genesis

Rod Temperton joined Quincy Jones and Michael Jackson to work on *Thriller*. He wrote *Baby Be Mine* as a logical sequel to *Rock with You*, but chose to offer different delights by dropping the groovy calm of the latter in favor of a quiet funk where the voice of Michael Jackson glided over the melody, rising and falling at leisure.

Unlike the young artist, Quincy Jones loved this song and was keen to include it on the album. He preferred it to *Hot Street*, another song cowritten by Rod Temperton and Michael Jackson, which is a more cheerful funk number. Following a legal action connected to plagiarism that was filed in Mexico on 10 November 1993, Michael Jackson declared he loved *Hot Street* and regretted not having released it on *Thriller*. The duel between *Baby Be Mine* and *Hot Street* was part of the musical jousting that took place between the two men at the mixing console.

The producer made his choice. He remained convinced that *Baby Be Mine* allowed Michael Jackson to show what he could do in a different register. He said: "If you break down *Baby Be Mine*, it's like John Coltrane, just disguised with pop lyrics and a pop arrangement."[52]

Production

The drummer Ndugu Chancler had the onerous task of playing the song's jazzy intro. The drum roll that shattered the silence following the end of *Wanna Be Startin' Somethin'* acted as a transition, before a soft funk rhythm programmed on the formidable Linn M-1 took over.

The challenge was to get the song to swing using arrangements driven by machines. Michael Boddicker and the members of Toto produced layers of synthesizer sounds that sparkled and succeeded in creating a warm atmosphere, to the point that they made *Baby Be Mine* into a romantic medium-tempo number, elegant and urbane.

The bass line, played on a synthesizer, sustained a clean groove that set it apart from the less complete and less meticulously produced electro-funk pieces that abounded in the record stores at the time.

With *Baby Be Mine*, Quincy Jones was both a producer and a wizard of sound: his brilliant demonstration proved that swing could survive even through machines, as long as these were used and configured with a respect for arrangements and with real care taken to convey a musical emotion.

FOR JACKSON ADDICTS

Michael Jackson never performed *Baby Be Mine* live. The only notable performance of this song was by Debbie Allen during a special concert given by the cast of *Fame*, entitled *Fame Looks at the Music of 1983*, broadcast on 24 January 1984 by NBC.

THE GIRL IS MINE

Michael Jackson / 3'42

Musicians
Michael Jackson and Paul McCartney: lead and backing vocals
Greg Phillinganes: Rhodes piano
David Paich: piano
David Foster: synthesizer
Dean Parks and Steve Lukather: guitar
Louis Johnson: bass guitar
Jeff Porcaro: percussion
Recording
Westlake Recording Studios, Los Angeles: 14 to 16 April 1982
Technical team
Producer: Quincy Jones
Recording engineer: Bruce Swedien
Synthesizer programming: Steve Porcaro
Vocal arrangements: Michael Jackson and Quincy Jones
Rhythm arrangements: Quincy Jones and David Paich
Synthesizer arrangements: David Foster
String arrangements and direction: Jerry Hey
First violin: Gerald Vinci

To announce Michael Jackson's comeback in record stores, Epic Records released *The Girl Is Mine* as a picture disc (UK) and yellow (Peru, Israel) and orange (Israel) vinyl records.

Single

A-side: *The Girl Is Mine (album version)* / 3'41
B-side: *Can't Get Outta the Rain (unreleased)* / 4'02
Released by Epic Records: USA, 25 October 1982 (ref. 34-03288) / UK, 29 October 1982 (ref. EPC A 2729)
Chart position: USA R&B No. 1, Pop No. 2 / UK No. 8
RIAA: certified Gold 13 January 1983

1982

Genesis

As work began on *Thriller*, Quincy Jones suggested to Michael Jackson that he might think about a song dealing with a dispute between two men who wanted the same woman and were bitterly jealous of each other. *The Girl Is Mine* made its own way through the singer's mind, as he recalled during a court hearing in December 1984, when musician Fred Sanford wrongly accused him of having plagiarized one of his songs: "I woke up from my sleep and I had this song, and I went over to the tape recorder and I sang it into the tape recorder and I sang exactly what I heard in my head, starting with the melody and the keyboard and the strings and everything. So, I just orally put it all on tape."[53] During the hearing, this recording was played in public. On it, Michael Jackson can be heard suggesting that the melody be left to develop quietly: "Let the song create itself—let it tell you where to go."[53] He also conceived the song as a duet to sing with Paul McCartney, who had written *Girlfriend* for *Off the Wall*, and put it together specially so that their two voices could blend in the best way.

Production

This ballad is rich in light, reassuring harmonies, offering a breathing space after the dynamic songs *Wanna Be Startin' Somethin'* and *Baby Be Mine*, which begin the album. The initial dispute that introduced the theme soon turns into friendly verbal sparring between the two protagonists. As Michael Jackson wanted, the duet fits with the music, the voices supported by sumptuous arrangements. Jerry Hey is on the strings, which are particularly soaring in this song. David Foster maintains a cheerful tone on the synthesizers, and David Paich contributes a teasing rhythm.

Recording sessions were held over three days at the Westlake Studio in Los Angeles, and the atmosphere was extremely relaxed, with laughter, jokes, and various games played during the sessions. Those in the studio were keen to announce this extraordinary collaboration. Lionel Richie, Katherine and La Toya Jackson, and Dick Clark came to give their regards to the two artists between takes.

Quincy Jones suggested that the song's dynamic be strengthened by a bridge in the form of a dialogue between the two singers. Michael Jackson and Paul McCartney readily agreed. A very rare version of *The Girl Is Mine*, known as the

Michael Jackson arrives at Westlake Recording Studios in Los Angeles to record *The Girl Is Mine* with Paul McCartney, 16 April 1982.

FOR JACKSON ADDICTS

In 2008, as part of the anniversary project *Thriller 25*, the demo of *The Girl Is Mine* was released on the third track of the eponymous CD maxi single, 2008 version, recorded at Allen Zentz Recording.

"New Edited Version" (3'32) and available as a US promotional single (Epic ref. 34-03288), omitted this dialogue in order to make the most of the instrumental bridge.

David Paich (from the group Toto), a keyboard player and arranger, reminisced in 2015 about the recording sessions for *The Girl Is Mine*: "That was a magic moment in the studio. To start off an album, where you look around, and there's Paul and Linda McCartney, and there's George Martin and Geoffrey Emerick, and then there's Quincy Jones and Bruce Swedien, it was like, 'I've died and gone to producer's heaven and artist's heaven, and I'm sitting in the room with these guys.' It was one of those 'pinch me' moments."[54]

Paul McCartney filmed the Westlake sessions. Some of those images were projected at certain concerts of his World Tour (1989 to 1990), but the complete footage remains unreleased today.

Quincy Jones and Michael Jackson agreed that the song should be the first single from the album to be promoted. Its release did indeed focus the interest of the media, for the press immediately started to speculate about this astonishing collaboration. However, the media had no inkling of the mighty *Thriller*, then in its tentative, preliminary stages. The single was a success in the United States and United Kingdom, but went completely unnoticed in most other countries.

FOR JACKSON ADDICTS

Two other versions of *Thriller* were suggested for the maxi single: a remixed short version (4'05) and an instrumental version (5'57).

THRILLER

Rod Temperton / 5'57

Musicians
Vincent Price: rap
Greg Philliganes, Rod Temperton, Michael Boddicker, and Brian Banks: synthesizers
David Williams: guitar
Jerry Hey and Gary Grant: trumpet and bugle
Larry Williams: saxophone and flute
William Reichenbach: trombone
Ndugu Chancler: additional drums
Recording
Westlake Recording Studios, Los Angeles: 14 April to 8 November 1982
Technical team
Producer: Quincy Jones
Recording engineer: Bruce Swedien
Synthesizer programming: Anthony Marinelli
Arrangements: Rod Temperton
Brass arrangements: Jerry Hey
Sound effects: Bruce Cannon and Bruce Swedien

Single

USA
A-side: *Thriller (US single version)* / 3'55
B-side: *Can't Get Outta the Rain* (unreleased) / 4'02
UK
A-side: *Thriller (special edit)* / 4'37
B-side: The Jacksons: *Things I Do For You (live)* / 3'31
Released by Epic Records: USA, February 1984 (ref. 34-04364) / UK, November 1983 (ref. EPC A 3643)
Charts : USA R&B No. 3, Pop No. 4 / UK No. 10
RIAA : certified Gold and Platinum on 4 December 1989

1982

SONG

Genesis

Among the songs he suggested to Michael Jackson and Quincy Jones, Rod Temperton had high hopes for one titled *Starlight*. The lyrics followed on logically from those of *Off the Wall*: they describe how oppressed people escape stress by celebrating together, in the sunshine, their love of life. The chorus repeats the words: "starlight, starlight sun" several times. Musically it is an ambitious song, and contains an effective bass line (*Starlight* was even the provisional title of the album *Thriller* for several weeks).

But when Michael Jackson recorded a fairly elaborate initial version of *Starlight*, the team realized it was missing that special something that would put it on a par with *Wanna Be Startin' Somethin'* or *Billie Jean*. Rod Temperton was given the task of rewriting the lyrics. He began by making a list of songs that he felt were striking and whose titles could be used as the title of both the song and the album. *Midnight Man* was seriously considered, but was not unanimously favored by the team. Temperton finally found inspiration in a surprising way. "I went home and wrote down 200 to 300 titles...and then went to bed. In the morning I woke up and said this word 'Thriller.' I thought this is the title. I could visualize it. I could see the merchandise. It was a strong title, and the sound of the song we had fitted perfectly."[55]

With this new title for *Starlight*, which also became that of the album, Rod Temperton had finally found a direction for finishing work on the words. Drawing inspiration from the fantastic universe of *This Place Hotel*, written by Michael Jackson for the Jacksons' album *Triumph* in 1980, he came up with a text in which monsters and the living dead emerge to terrorize anyone unfortunate enough to be out wandering alone at night. Temperton had in mind a terrifying epilogue in the form of a rap delivered by a voice from beyond the grave. As he was searching for the lucky person who would be given that task, Peggy Lipton Jones, wife of Quincy Jones, mentioned that she knew Vincent Price well. Price was well known for his roles in many horror films, such as *House of Wax*. The actor, then aged 71, accepted. He was no novice: in 1975 he had recorded the introductory words for Alice Cooper's song *The Black Widow*.

It was not until the *Bad* tour in 1987 that Michael Jackson performed *Thriller* onstage for the first time.

Production

The connection between *Thriller* and *This Place Hotel* is plain to see. Both songs are divided into three parts: an intro that sets the atmosphere, the main body of the song, and an outro which in *This Place Hotel* seems to herald the end of the nightmare, but continues to a climax in *Thriller*.

The intro is sustained by a minimalist rhythm that accompanies increasing tension until there is an explosion of chords played on the synthesizers, marking the start of the main body of the song. Ndugu Chancler plays what is heard in these opening measures, before giving way to the Linn M-1 drum machine.

For the very first few seconds of the song, Bruce Swedien deliberately limited the bandwidth and volume, so that the arrival of the synthesizers playing the main theme would sound even more spectacular.

In the intro a wolf can clearly be heard howling at an imaginary full moon. To capture a realistic sound, Bruce Swedien decided to make use of his own dog, Max. However, despite numerous attempts, the animal refused to cooperate, which left the team without an alternative candidate. In the end, Michael Jackson himself agreed to howl at the start of the final version of *Thriller*.

The song's structure allowed effects to be put in place that were worthy of a film soundtrack. Bruce Swedien worked with special-effects editor Bruce Cannon, who had been part of the team on Steven Spielberg's movie *E.T.*, drawing on his expertise in sound and images to give *Thriller* its highly theatrical quality. Cannon was to stick around, later working on the project *E.T. Storybook*, an album and book produced by Quincy Jones and Steven Spielberg (see pages 242–44).

The song, which is exactly six minutes long, is the last on the album's A-side. It is driven by a hypnotic rhythm, similar to that in the record's first track, *Wanna Be Startin' Somethin'*. Vincent Price declaims a gothic rap in the final measures. The day before the actor was to arrive at the studio, Rod Temperton was still far from having finalized the words: "I had one verse done. Then I started writing more in the back of the taxi to the studio. When we got there, I saw a limousine and out stepped Vincent Price, so I said to my driver, 'Go round the back.' I gave the words to the secretary to photocopy. Vincent Price sat down with it and got it in (only) two takes. Amazing."[56]

Rod Temperton had written three paragraphs for Vincent Price's rap, but only the first and last of these figure in the final version of *Thriller*. The second verse was revealed only in 2001 on the reissued album. The actor was offered two options for payment: a percentage of the sales, or a check for $20,000. At the time, no one believed in the record's potential as much as Michael Jackson. Price chose to be paid immediately, by check. It was a decision he would ceaselessly regret in the coming years, when the album became the biggest-selling in history.

Vincent Price, the spellbinding voice of *Thriller*, seen here in the movie *The Bat* (1959).

THE SHORT FILM

Director: John Landis
Producers: Michael Jackson, John Landis, and George Folsey Jr.
Leading actors: Michael Jackson and Ola Ray
Extras: Miko Brando, John Landis, Rick Baker
Shooting dates: 11 to 23 October 1983
Shoot locations:
• Griffith Park, Los Angeles, California (scene with the werewolf in the forest);
• Rialto Theatre, 1023 S. Fair Oaks Avenue, South Pasadena, California (scene in the movie theater);
• Downtown Palace Theatre, 630 S Broadway, Los Angeles, California (scene outside the movie theater);
• 3701 Union Pacific Avenue, Los Angeles, California (dance scene with zombies);
• 4300 Maywood Avenue, Vernon, California (studios and sets for transforming the werewolf, the scenes in the cemetery, and those inside the house);
• 1345 Carroll Avenue, Los Angeles, California (scene with the house at the end of the film).
Duration: 13'43

Genesis

At the end of the summer of 1983 it became clear that *Thriller* was the album of the year. When *P.Y.T.* was released as a single in October 1983, the album was still in the *Billboard* Top 5. But Michael Jackson believed the record had still more potential, and that the title track also deserved to be released as a single. Inspired by the song's horror theme, he dreamed of making a video in which he could turn into a monster.

Accordingly, he contacted the director John Landis, who in 1981 had made *An American Werewolf in London*, a horror movie whose hero, David Naughton, survives an attack by a monster but, as a consequence, gains the ability to turn himself into a ferocious beast.

Proud of his idea and convinced that the album warranted a video clip to revive sales, Michael Jackson called Walter Yetnikoff, CEO of CBS, and asked him to back the project financially. But Jackson was unable to secure funding from his label for a project promoting an album released almost a year earlier that had already met with great success.

The young man then turned to John Landis and his producer, George Folsey Jr. Both advised him to raise funds by finding partners who could also help him promote the film. The three approached the MTV and Showtime channels with a tempting offer: if they agreed to contribute $250,000 and $300,000 respectively, they would secure the broadcasting rights for the 14-minute clip for a period of some months, together with a 45-minute documentary on its shooting. The full TV program, running for 60 minutes in total, would allow them to attract advertising while it was being broadcast. Michael Jackson provided the necessary extra funds, and thus the $800,000 budget was secured.

Shortly afterwards the Vestron company, which released films in the VHS and Betamax formats on the market, signed a contract with Landis, Jackson, and Folsey to distribute *Thriller* and the documentary. Instead of selling the video cassette for $80 (the price of most films on the market at the time), the company decided to launch the product at the loss-leader price of $29.95.

The program, which was finally given the title *Making Michael Jackson's Thriller*, was launched on 14 December 1983. Although it was sold to TV channels via CBS, many viewers wanted the video so they could watch it whenever it suited them.

Michael Jackson and choreographer Michael Peters watch videos in search of new ideas.

Thus Michael Jackson, in the twilight of the promotion of the album *Thriller*, produced an artistic shock by offering a video, in a format never seen before, to illustrate a song. He also caused an economic revolution in the world of entertainment by creating an unprecedented synergy between music and image: after *Thriller*, nothing was the same—especially when *Making Michael Jackson's Thriller* became the best-selling music video in history, with 500,000 sold in the United States in the first month after its release.

Production

The team that would make the *Thriller* clip was drawn from Michael Jackson and John Landis's list of contacts. Michael Peters, who had already been in charge of choreography on *Beat It*, was brought on board once again, and Vincent Paterson rejoined as assistant choreographer. For his part, Landis called again on Robert Paynter, who had been his director of photography on the movie *Trading Places*. George Folsey Jr. was thrown in at the deep end as executive producer, and Deborah, Landis's wife, who had designed the clothing worn by Harrison Ford in *Indiana Jones*, created the red leather jacket worn by Michael Jackson in the second part of the short film. Makeup and special effects were entrusted to Rick Baker. Known as the master of makeup in Hollywood, Baker was responsible in 1981 for transforming the actor David Naughton into a monster in *An American Werewolf in London*.

While the short films of *Billie Jean* and *Beat It* showed Michael Jackson as a magician or peacemaker on the streets, *Thriller* gave him a more manly image with, for the first time on screen, a girlfriend playing opposite him. The lucky woman was Ola Ray. In 1980 she had appeared in the clip by George Benson entitled *Give Me the Night*, and had posed in *Playboy* magazine. John Landis picked her out from the hundreds of other women who applied for the part in the short film. When the singer discovered her Playmate past, he was initially reluctant to work with her. However, the director managed to convince him, and Ola Ray landed what is still her biggest screen role.

The team headed for Griffith Park, in the footsteps of James Dean, who had played some scenes of *Rebel without a Cause* there. The area around the park was a backdrop for the film's first scene. Michael Jackson and Ola Ray played two young lovers in the1950s. The young man, driving his Chevrolet, pulls the old trick of pretending to have run out of gas, and takes advantage of the situation to declare his love for his girlfriend.

Rick Baker conceived Michael Jackson's metamorphosis into a werewolf in several stages. Computerized special effects were still in their infancy at the time, so he designed a series of four masks, tracing the change in Michael Jackson's face and body. As when filming *The Wiz*—during which the singer had remained seated for many hours in order to become, under the direction of the makeup artist Stan Winston, the famous scarecrow—he patiently put up with long makeup and preparation sessions. In order to create the frightening yellow eyes of a feline, he agreed to wear contact lenses, despite the irritation they caused during and after filming.

The scene in which he is transformed into a werewolf was shot at the EFX studios in Los Angeles. The animal mask featured pockets connected to tubes, which were operated to bring to life certain parts of the face, such as the temples, in order to make the singer's terrifying transformation look realistic. One sequence in the documentary released with the clip shows one of these pockets bursting when a stagehand operates an air pump.

Rick Baker and his team created the zombies' makeup in record time. The living dead were divided into two categories:

Michael Jackson on the *Thriller* shoot in October 1983.

the actors and extras emerging from the cemetery, and the dancers who accompanied the singer in his macabre ballet. The master of special effects produced some flexible latex masks that clung to the skin and produced a highly realistic effect. Unfortunately the makeup sessions were painful for all the artists in this scene, including Michael Jackson himself.

The dance sequence was created by Michael Peters and Michael Jackson, with Vincent Paterson lending a hand as assistant choreographer. Rehearsals took place at the Debbie Reynolds Studio, which the actress had founded in 1979 to cater for dancers from the world of music and movies. The choreographers created the dance steps and linking sequences, then showed them to Michael Jackson, who would then contribute his own ideas and suggestions. In this way, they came up with an intuitive choreography, with jazzy influences, which paid tribute to Bob Fosse and to numbers from Hollywood's great musicals. The cast had only a week to rehearse. The two choreographers insisted that the dancers play their parts to the full, and put themselves inside the skin of the zombies—or what remained of it.

The dance sequence immortalized in the clip was shot at the intersection of Union Pacific Avenue and Calzona Street, Los Angeles. This industrial area, which lay outside the city and was deserted in the evenings, was the ideal setting for filming a number from beyond the grave. The dancers put their heart and soul into the task, especially as it was getting cold in the streets. The steam coming out of some of the dancers' mouths and the clouds of mist rising from the streets (which had been wetted by the stagehands) were not the result of additional special effects.

In the middle of this fateful intersection, Ola Ray is surrounded by the zombies, including Michael Jackson. She escapes and seeks refuge in a house at 1345 Carroll Avenue—a fairly unique street for LA, because all the houses there are built to the same Victorian design—a few yards from the Echo Park neighborhood. Alfred Hitchcock would have been right at home in this building, which resembles the house in his movie *Psycho*.

As well as background music composed by the great Elmer Bernstein, the short film's soundtrack features a completely reworked mixing of *Thriller*. John Landis and his team hurriedly finished work on the song's audio tracks, as the timetable was tight, but on the rap track recorded by Vincent Price there remained the sound of a synthesizer, which made it unusable for the video. The actor agreed to rerecord the two verses; his performance in the short film is therefore slightly different from the studio version.

Once shooting was complete, John Landis and George Folsey Jr. shut themselves away in the editing studio to put together a 14-minute short film. Michael Jackson, who joined

At the start of the short film, Michael Jackson sings and dances around Ola Ray in one of the legendary sequences of *Thriller*.

FOR JACKSON ADDICTS

In December 2009 the short film *Thriller* was added to the Library of Congress in Washington. It was the first video clip to receive this honor—in the company of other classics such as Sergio Leone's *Once upon a Time in the West* (1968), Jack Arnold's *The Incredible Shrinking Man* (1957), and Sidney Lumet's *Dog Day Afternoon* (1976).

them, followed these sessions closely. He influenced the proceedings, suggesting ideas that Folsey and Landis took into serious consideration. Shot in 35 mm, the movie benefited from skillful lighting and calibration in the masterly hands of Robert Paynter, who gave it rich colors, amplifying the effect of the main scenes, such as the one in which the singer changes into a werewolf.

The movie was converted for television broadcasting: MTV and Showtime were eagerly awaiting their copies in order to recoup their financial investment. The version calibrated for the cathode ray tubes of television delivered a much darker and less finely shaded image. Only the version on film showed the movie's real colors, as shot by Robert Paynter and approved by John Landis and Michael Jackson.

This famous footage narrowly escaped being destroyed, because a few days before the preview screening in Los Angeles, Michael Jackson was seized by panic: the elders of the Jehovah's Witnesses, on learning that he had been filmed with monsters and the living dead, threatened to excommunicate him if the movie was released. So he called his attorney John Branca and ordered him to destroy the film. The latter went to see Landis and Folsey at the editing studio. After some discussion, they decided unanimously not to follow this instruction. A few days later, the artist contacted the director to apologize, and acknowledged that he had given in to fear. To assuage the elders, the director suggested inserting a disclaimer at the start of the video stating that Michael Jackson did not believe in the occult. The movie theater version of *Thriller* was shown for only a week, as the short film screened before Walt Disney's movie *Fantasia* at the National Theater in Westwood, Los Angeles. On 2 December 1983, just over a year after the release of the album *Thriller*, the clip was shown for the first time on MTV. It had an immediate impact. Not only did viewers clamor for it to be shown again, but many fans descended on record stores to buy—or buy again—an album that CBS had considered to be moribund just a few weeks earlier.

With those 14 minutes of *Thriller*, Michael Jackson introduced the art of the video clip to the world of entertainment. He also provided MTV with a flagship product on which the channel was able to build its already growing popularity.

Beat It

Michael Jackson / 4'17

Musicians
Michael Jackson: vocals and drum case beater
Eddie Van Halen: guitar
Greg Phillinganes: keyboards (Rhodes piano, synthesizers)
Bill Wolfer: keyboards
Tom Bahler: Synclavier
Greg Smith: Synergy synthesizer
Steve Lukather: guitar, electric bass
Paul Jackson: guitar
Jeff Porcaro: drums
Recording
Westlake Recording Studios (studio A) and Ocean Way, Los Angeles: 14 April to 8 November 1982
Technical team
Producers: Quincy Jones and Michael Jackson
Recording engineer: Bruce Swedien
Assistant recording engineers: Matt Forger and Steve Bates
Synthesizer programming: Steve Porcaro
Vocal arrangements: Michael Jackson
Rhythmic arrangements: Michael Jackson and Quincy Jones

1982

Single

A-side: *Beat It (single version)* / 4'11
B-side: *Get on the Floor (album version)*/ 4'44
Released by Epic Records/CBS: USA (ref. 34-03759) & UK (ref. EPC A 3184), March 1983
Chart position: USA Pop No. 1, R&B No. 1 / UK No. 3
RIAA: certified Platinum on 14 February 1989

THE SONG

Genesis

The goal with the album *Off the Wall* had been to excel in various different genres, such as soul, funk, and R&B, while at the same time giving a nod to pop (*Girlfriend*) and to jazz influences (*I Can't Help It*). When Michael Jackson and Quincy Jones went into the studio to record *Thriller*, the producer wanted to add a hint of rock, hitherto absent from the output of the leader of the Jacksons. With his eclectic background, the former jazz musician had, throughout his career, championed a vision of music, and in art in general, without no-go areas. He asked Michael Jackson to write a lively song inspired by the rhythm and tone of *My Sharona* by The Knack.

As so often when asked to describe his art, the singer found it difficult to explain the birth of a song that became a landmark in his career. He said: "I wanted to write a song, the type of song that I would buy if I wanted a rock song. That is how I approached it and I wanted the kids to enjoy it. The next thing I can recall is the song being there. I think the gift is there naturally but the songs come through me."[56]

One of the few clues to analyzing the birth of *Beat It* is the demo released in 2009 on the two-CD version of the original soundtrack to the documentary *Michael Jackson's This Is It*. It is a version recorded by the artist in his private studio at the Jackson family home in Encino. Take after take, he performs with each instrument and plays each arrangement. The lyrics are still embryonic, so much so that the melody, which is already fully formed, is scatted without words. The mix released on this quite rare CD is in fact cleverly put together from each of the tracks recorded at the time by Brent Averill, Michael Jackson's personal recording engineer, in order to create a multitrack version.

With the lyrics for *Beat It,* Michael Jackson tackles a theme that was important at the time, namely, violence among young people. Certain rap artists, such as Grandmaster Flash, had dealt in quite a fatalistic way with the lives of marginalized young people living in underprivileged areas. Violence, drugs, and many other problems afflicted the young in the early 1980s. Jackson, though, offers a message full of hope and common sense: when violence is on the prowl, you should extract yourself from the situation without risking your life. "It

Michael Jackson performs *Beat It* onstage during the *Victory* tour, 29 July 1984, at Giants Stadium, East Rutherford, New Jersey.

tells kids to be smart and avoid trouble. I don't mean that you should turn the other cheek while someone kicks in your teeth, but, unless your back is against the wall and you have no choice, just get away before violence breaks out."[2] Although since the age of ten he had known only the affluent areas of Hollywood, the singer had remained sensitive to the problems young people encounter the world over. This human, even humanitarian, strand was to develop even further later in Jackson's career, with songs such as *We Are the World* and *Heal the World*.

Although the recording sessions for *Thriller* were completely occupying all the teams at Westlake during the summer of 1982, Quincy Jones was impatient and put pressure on his young protégé: he wanted to hear this famous rock song that he had asked for several weeks earlier. After a protracted game of cat and mouse, the producer tracked down the artist in his mini recording studio in Encino. With the help of Brent Averill, the two men reviewed several tracks on which Michael Jackson had set down some ideas. On finally hearing the track that contained a demo version of *Beat It*, Quincy Jones exclaimed that it was just the song they needed[55]. So it was that *Beat It* became one of the most iconic tracks on *Thriller*, while at the same time reinforcing Michael Jackson's reputation as a versatile songwriter.

Production

The recording of *Beat It* became such an intense process that the studio ended up feeling the heat, as the recording engineer Matt Forger recalled: "Yes, *Beat It* was particularly tricky. It was a song that constantly challenged the entire team. Michael wanted a punchy sound to match the emotion of the track, so everyone was constantly being pushed to the limit. The studio equipment seemed to sense the struggle and fought back in its own way. At one time during a playback of the song, the monitor speakers actually caught on fire and smoke came pouring out of the wall. It's as if the studio was fighting back, but we prevailed and beat the song into form and the result speaks for itself."[57]

The backbone of the band given the task of creating *Beat It* was mainly composed of the Toto team. Steve and Jeff Porcaro, plus Steve Lukather, shared the keyboards and drums between them, as usual. As well as these three virtuoso musicians, Michael Jackson and Quincy Jones brought in other big names from Californian studios: Greg Phillinganes, a faithful partner to the Jackson family since the album *Destiny* (1978), helped Steve Porcaro on keyboards; Paul Jackson supported Steve Lukather in the rhythm guitar parts; and Bill Wolfer, who like Phillinganes had worked with Michael Jackson in the studio and on stage, contributed his synthesizer expertise, honed by having worked with Stevie Wonder on many occasions.

The guitarist Eddie Van Halen shares the stage with Michael Jackson during the *Victory* tour concert at the Texas Stadium in Dallas, 14 July 1984.

The intro to *Beat It* enabled the song to become a musical institution, a classic recognizable from the first note. The gloomy gong that opens the song was the idea of the arranger Tom Bähler. He was one of the few people at the time who owned a Synclavier, a revolutionary machine in the recording studio. It was the first digital synthesizer designed by Vermont company New England Digital (NEDCO), and its sole competitor was the Fairlight, made by the Australian company CMI. The proud possessor of a Synclavier II, a model launched in 1980, Tom Bähler identified a sound that was factory-programmed into the machine and suggested it to Quincy Jones as the sound for the intro to *Beat It*. The gong's dramatically dense sound appealed to the producer. And so began the love affair between Michael Jackson's music and the Synclavier.

The snare drum on *Beat It* possesses a punch that sets it aside from the other songs that were played on FM radio at the time. Energetic and spare, it accentuates the violence of the soundtrack, which contrasts with the shrill, almost childlike, voice of the singer. This stark effect was the result of an accident: although a large bass drum had been delivered to the Westlake studio, something fell accidentally onto its protective case. Michael Jackson stopped dead, and asked where that sound had come from. He called over the recording engineer, Bruce Swedien, who positioned a microphone in such a way as to properly capture the resonance of the case. The artist then recorded the sound of this singular drum, and ended up being credited as "drum case beater" on the album.

Pete Townshend had been Quincy Jones and Michael Jackson's first choice for the guitar solo on *Beat It*. However, as he was on tour with The Who, he was not able to fit the album's recording sessions into his timetable. So Eddie Van Halen was invited and, as was so often the case with Michael, the manner in which contact was made had an element of comedy. When Quincy Jones called him to suggest he record a guitar solo for Michael Jackson, the leader of the Van Halen band thought it was a prank phone call and hung up several times. Eventually Van Halen realized it was not a joke. The next day he met Quincy Jones and Bruce Swedien at the Westlake studios. After hearing the song, he suggested some changes to allow him to play his solo in the best possible way, as he told CNN in 2012: "I listened to the song, and I immediately go, 'Can I change some parts?' I turned to the engineer and I go, 'OK, from the breakdown, chop in this part, go to this piece, pre-chorus, to the chorus, out.'"[58] It took ten minutes to make the changes. Eddie Van Halen then plugged in his Frankenstrat V2 guitar (not a Kramer, a brand he played only from 1983) into the Gibson speakers in the studio. Armed with two packs of beer and his most rock'n'roll energy, he recorded two solos and doubled the bass line played by Greg Phillinganes on the Moog synthesizer. At that point Michael Jackson was working in another studio, recording the vocal takes for the album *E.T. Storybook*. The famous guitarist was worried how Michael would respond to him changing a few measures in the song. But the singer listened to the two takes and gave his verdict: "Wow, thank you so much for having the passion to not just come in and blaze a solo, but to actually care about the song, and make it better."[58]

Van Halen honestly believed that this guest appearance would go unremarked and that his band, who were reluctant to see him work with other artists, had not even been informed. Simply credited in the sleeve notes to *Thriller*, and without any fee having been negotiated, the collaboration between Jackson and Van Halen is an example of the successful crossover that was gaining popularity in the 1980s.

Producer Bob Giraldi, Michael Jackson and choreographer Michael Peters going over the details for the short film *Beat It*.

THE SHORT FILM

Director: Bob Giraldi
Producers: Mary M. Ensign and Antony Payne
Leading actor: Michael Jackson
Supporting actors: Michael Peters and Vincent Paterson
Shooting dates: 9 to 20 March 1983
Shoot locations:
• 560 South Gladys Avenue, downtown Los Angeles (shots in the street);
• Green Apple Market (formerly the Hard Rock Cafe), 300 East 5th Street, Los Angeles (pool scene);
• Intersection of East Fifth and Seaton Street, downtown Los Angeles (manhole cover scene);
• Special Cafe, 416 East Fifth Street, downtown Los Angeles (bar scenes);
• Jing San Food, Inc., 458 South Alameda Street, downtown Los Angeles (final scene in the hangar).
Duration: 4'58

Genesis

"You know, two gangs coming together...and the song is so self-explanatory that it's so easy to make the short film..."[59] That is how Michael Jackson summed up the birth of the idea for the video that would illustrate *Beat It*. Unlike *Billie Jean*, this time he had a budget of $150,000, which he had been paid as an advance on royalties. After talks with CBS and its managers, it was decided that *Beat It* would be the third single taken from *Thriller*. In February 1983, just back from a trip to London, the artist saw Bob Giraldi's demonstration video. Impressed by the precise, flowing editing of a McDonald's commercial he had made, he planned to hire him to shoot *Beat It*. Bob Giraldi, who was of Italian descent, was one of that generation of young creatives working in advertising. He worked for the agency Della Femina and Partners before founding his own company, Bob Giraldi Productions. When the singer asked him to come and discuss the *Beat It* project, Giraldi had just one clip to his name: *Pieces of Ice* by Diana Ross.

His collaboration with Michael Jackson, which was highly productive throughout 1983 to 1984, enabled the foundations of the musical short film envisaged by the artist to be laid: a clever fusion of a commercial and a musical from the golden age of Hollywood. For *Beat It*, the two wrote down on paper a story inspired by the street fights in *West Side Story*. The singer wanted a dance sequence as the finale. The choreographer Michael Peters, who had also worked on *Pieces of Ice*, was a natural choice to join the team, and together with Michael Jackson put together the main choreography for the song.

Michael Jackson surrounded by dancers in *Beat It*—some of them members of real-life street gangs.

The legendary dance sequence on the short film *Beat it*. To the star's right is Vincent Paterson, the leader of one of the gangs.

During shooting of the café scenes, in which Michael Jackson dances behind a pool table, journalists from *Ebony* visited on-set to do a story on the making of the clip. As so often, the star gave the famous African-American monthly privileged access to certain pivotal moments in his career. Shooting proceeded without incident, and the singer took advantage of a break to go with his sister La Toya to the premiere of the musical *Dreamgirls* on 20 March in Hollywood.

It was decided that Peters would play one of the gang members. But he needed a rival, so a casting was organized. Among the hundred or so hopefuls there was a dancer who showed up dressed like a real hoodlum: Vincent Paterson, who had also worked on *Pieces of Ice*. He had trained with Shirley MacLaine and had begun to make a name for himself in Hollywood. The casting for *Beat It* allowed him to work for the first time with Michael Jackson, who saw him as an ideal partner; he was to join him on his greatest short films, such as *Smooth Criminal*, *Black or White*, and *The Way You Make Me Feel*. In a French interview with Richard Lecocq, the dancer recalled the casting in these terms: "I arrived...dressed as if I were already a character in the movie. I wasn't dressed like the dancers, with all the accessories that go with it. Above all, that made Michael Jackson notice me. I had worked with my character, I'd written him a story, and I knew what I had to do with it."[60]

Production

On 9 March 1983 the *Beat It* team met for the first day's shooting in the Skid Row area, one of the most dangerous in Los Angeles. As well as the 25 dancers that had been cast, 50 youths from local gangs, the Crips and the Bloods, were hired as extras and for the final choreographed section. There was a police presence at the shoot, but several times tensions between the two gangs came within a hair's breadth of bringing down the whole project. On the first evening, Bob Giraldi was on the point of giving up. Far removed from the studio setting of the clip for *Pieces of Ice* with Diana Ross, the *Beat It* shoot, out in the street, brought him out in a cold sweat. To restore calm, the director suggested shooting one of the dance sequences right away. Michael Jackson backed the idea. Vincent Paterson succeeded in bringing the artist out of his shell and urged him to go even closer to the dancers and young extras. "All of a sudden, real magic happened—I'll never forget the look on the faces of the Crips and the Bloods while they watched, in awe, their brothers—most of whom were black and Hispanic gay men—dancing with such beauty, rhythm, macho, and cool—something the gang members must have known instinctively they would, or could, never be able to do. When I surprised the actors and replaced the rubber knife with a real switch-blade, the set went wild,"[55] Bob Giraldi recalled.

As well as with Michael Peters and Vincent Paterson, Michael Jackson worked with the hip-hop dancer Popin' Pete and the Electric Boogaloos dance crew, who had, notably, made some fine appearances on the TV show *Soul Train*. The fusion of group dancing created by Michael Peters and the street dance sequences was to be repeated in later short films by the singer in the 1980s and 1990s.

While the clip for *Billie Jean* had been produced to a tight budget and schedule, with *Beat It* Michael Jackson succeeded in playing a part in the editing studio and approved each shot with Bob Giraldi's team. When the short film was shown for the first time on MTV in April 1983, it sent the song shooting up the *Billboard* singles chart, reaching the Top 5, where *Billie Jean* remained at No. 1.

Michael Jackson on the set of the short film of *Billie Jean*, early February 1983.

Images from the *Victory Tour* were used for a *Billie Jean* promo video. It was published in January 1985 but to date has not been commercially released in any form.

BILLIE JEAN

Michael Jackson / 4'57

Musicians
Michael Jackson: lead and backing vocals
Greg Phillinganes: Rhodes piano
Greg Smith: synthesizer
Bill Wolfer: synthesizer
Dean Parks: guitar
Louis Johnson: bass guitar
Ndugu Chancler: drums
Michael Boddicker: emulator
Recording
Westlake Recording Studios, Los Angeles: 14 April to 8 November 1982
Technical team
Producers: Quincy Jones and Michael Jackson
Recording engineer: Bruce Swedien
Synthesizer programming: Bill Wolfer
Vocals, rhythm, and synthesizer arrangements: Michael Jackson
Strings arrangement: Jerry Hey
Strings conductor: Jeremy Lubbock

USA
A-side: *Billie Jean (single version)* / 4'50
B-side: *Can't Get outta the Rain* / 4'02
UK
A-side: *Billie Jean (single version)* / 4'50
B-side: *It's the Falling in Love (album version)* / 3'46
Released by EPIC Records: USA, 22 January 1983 (ref. 34-03509) / UK, 17 January 1983, (ref. EPC A 3084)
Chart position: USA R&B No. 1, Pop No. 1 / UK No. 1
RIAA: certified Gold 4 April 1983 / certified Platinum on 14 February 1989 / twice Double Platinum (digital) 9 May 2013

1982

THE SONG

Genesis

"It all starts with the song. And Michael wrote *Billie Jean*, that stuff you know it was just highly highly personal. According to him, he said it was about a girl that climbed over the wall and the fellow was lounging...hanging out, shades on...just like invaded the place, a stalker almost...and Michael says she accused him of being the father of *one* of her twins!"[61] said Quincy Jones when describing *Billie Jean*. On the basis of this rather surprising paternity issue, the singer prepared to make the whole planet dance.

In 1981 the song was playing endlessly in the young prodigy's head while he traveled by car along the Ventura freeway in California. He was so absorbed by his new creation that he did not notice the smoke pouring dangerously out of the engine. He remained equally calm while waiting for the breakdown truck, for the creative process of *Not My Lover* (the song's original title) tirelessly occupied his mind.

Billie Jean is, first and foremost, a reflection of his highly unusual everyday life. In the song, the artist tackles the subject of groupies, who enter his apartment or hotel room and then invent love stories or even children. *Billie Jean* is one of these young women, prepared to do anything to secure an acknowledgment of paternity or some money. Michael Jackson explains in his autobiography:

> The girl in the song is a composite of people we've been plagued by over the years...I couldn't understand how these girls could say they were carrying someone's child when it wasn't true. I can't imagine lying about something like that. Even today there are girls who come to the gate at our house and say the strangest things, like, "Oh, I'm Michael's wife," or "I'm just dropping off the keys to our apartment." I remember one girl who used to drive us completely crazy. I really think that she believed in her mind that she belonged with me. There was another girl who claimed I had gone to bed with her, and she made threats. There've been a couple of serious scuffles at the gate on Hayvenhurst, and they can get dangerous.[2]

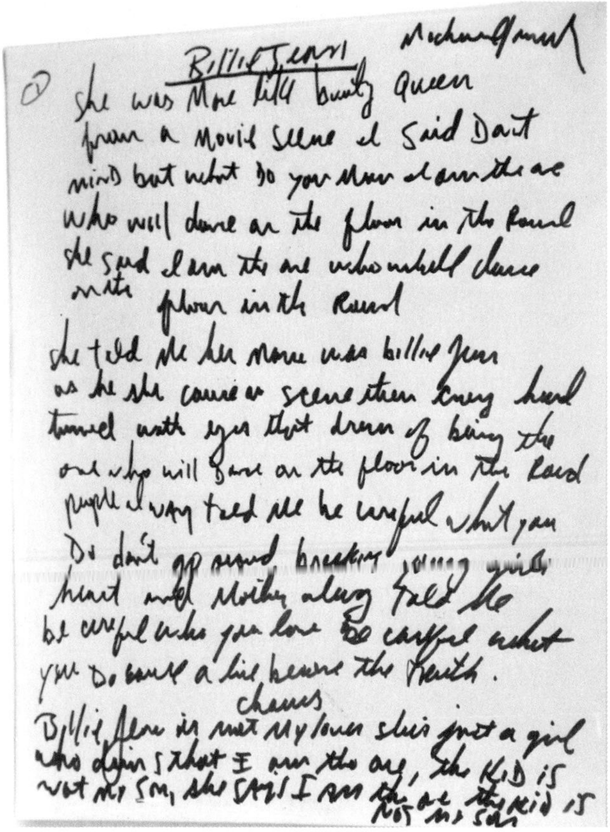

Manuscript of the lyrics of *Billie Jean* by Michael Jackson.

Ndugu Chancler used a Yamaha "Jacaranda" drum kit to record the beat for *Billie Jean*. Bass drum: 22" x 18"; Snare drum: 14" x 5,5"; Toms : 12" x 8", 13" x 9"; Bass toms : 14" x 14", 16" x 16"; Cymbals : 14" (Twenty Hi-Hat), 18" (Twenty Crash), 20" (Twenty Ride), 223 (2002 Novo China).

FOR JACKSON ADDICTS

A second version of *Billie Jean* was recorded to honor the Jacksons' first advertising contract with Pepsi, included on the 1996 Vox Records CD *Great Cola Commercials 2.*

Production

Michael Jackson often used to relate how the music, lyrics, and whole structure of his songs first came into being in his head. He would then call on the best musicians to transcribe the exact sound or melody that had come to life inside him. It was not an easy task; however, everyone enjoyed recreating his songs and giving them a musical existence. In the early 1980s Bill Wolfer, the keyboard player on the *Triumph* tour (among others), presented himself at the family studio to help transcribe the artist's ideas.

> *Billie Jean* started out at Michael's house in Encino. He had turned the guest house into a 16-track studio, and we made demos there of the three songs that I eventually recorded with Quincy for the album. Michael and I started by sitting down at a Rhodes piano, and Michael sang me the bass line. I started playing it, and then he sang the top notes of the three chords that ascend and descend over that ostinato bass. At that point, we spent maybe an hour or more trying out different harmonies for the rest of the chords. There are a million ways you can harmonize those notes, and I tried them all before I landed on the one he was looking for. The amazing part about that is that, to me, several of the combinations I tried sounded very hip to me—they worked—but Michael never lost sight of what he had been hearing in his head. He didn't play an instrument, but he was definitely a musician. He could work out entire arrangements in his head, and hang onto them, even when he was hearing something very close.
>
> The next step was recreating the sound Michael had heard me experimenting with sometime during the tour. I didn't even remember it at first. There was a CS-80 there, and eventually I remembered a sound where I was trying to get something like French horns and strings simultaneously, but this other weird aspect, almost like human voices, crept in. Once I had the sound programmed, we recorded the demo.[42]

This recording, *Billie Jean* (home demo, 1981) appears on the 2001 special edition of *Thriller.*

When Michael Jackson played him the song, Quincy Jones felt something was missing. The singer then continued to develop its various sections until Louis Johnson introduced the bass line that would transcend the song and make it the most incredible track in the history of pop music. *Billie Jean* contains unique DNA that the signature bass line renders immediately recognizable even today. The producer thought this 30-second introduction was far too long and would need to be cut. But the artist insisted, assuring him that it gave him an irresistible urge to dance. Fortunately, it remained intact, for the maxi single pressing.

Greg Phillinganes was on keyboards, and Jerry Hey did his best to make the string arrangements sparkle. They brought their sensitive and expert touch to the song. Bruce Swedien at the controls, like an orchestral conductor, selected the tracks, blended them, and mixed them until he had given substance to the whole:

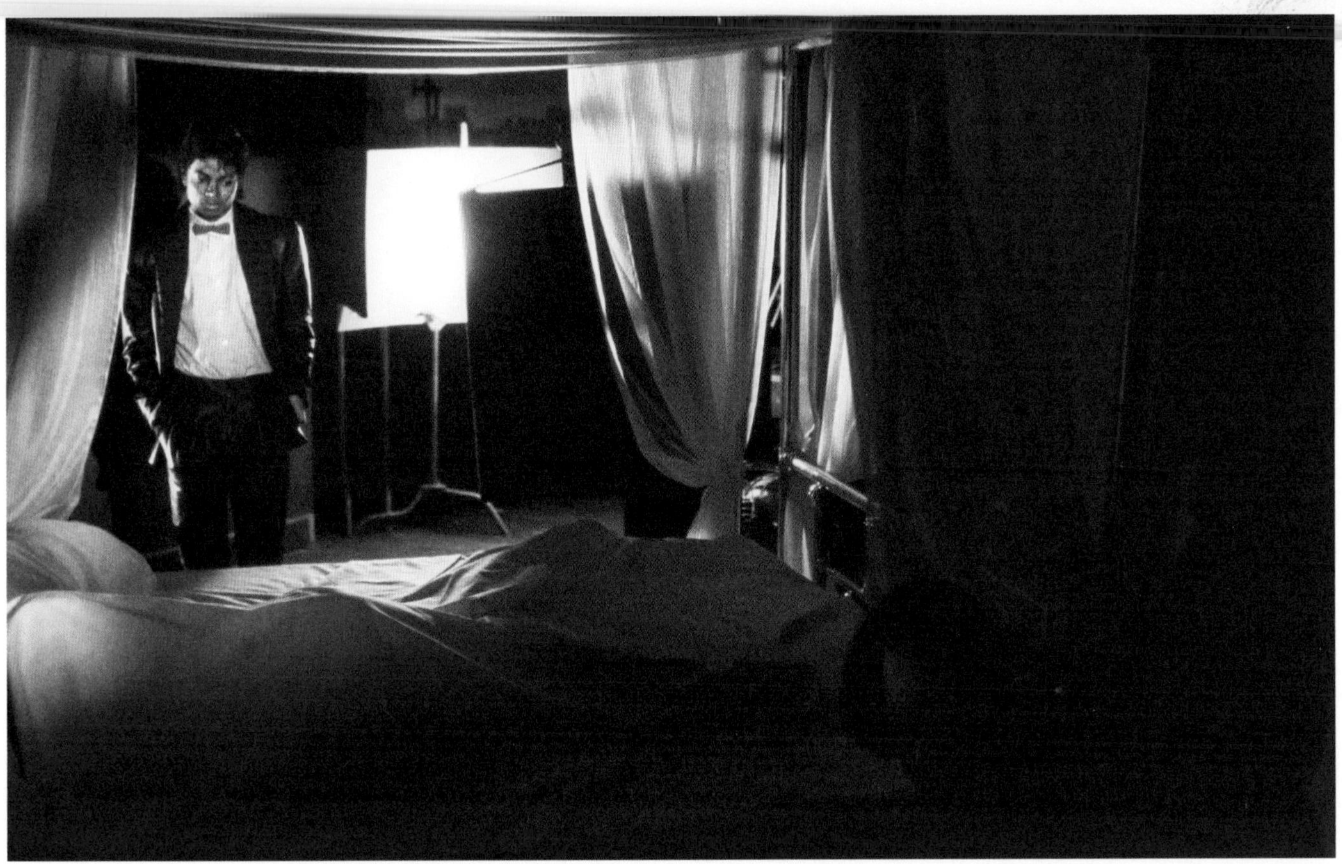

Michael Jackson looking sad in the soft lighting of the short film of *Billie Jean*.

The year is 1982. The song is *Billie Jean*. The sonic image of Michael Jackson's *Billie Jean* is a perfect example of what happened when I sat around dreaming awhile, about combining different recording techniques to produce a unique musical canvas with a tremendous "sonic personality." …I recorded the drums (played by the fantastic drummer, N'Dugu) with as tight and powerful a drum sound as I could come up with. Of course I put N'Dugu's drum set on my plywood drum platform. Also at this time, I had a special kick drum cover made that covers the whole front of the kick drum. There's a slot with a zipper in it that the mike fits through. When the kick drum mike is in place, in the slot in my drum cover, I zip the opening tightly shut around the mike. I brought in my old pal George Massenburg's spectacular-sounding, portable, 12-channel recording console and used it to record the rhythm section. With it I recorded the bass, drums, and guitars on my analog 16-track, with no noise-reduction equipment in the way of that fantastic sound! In my estimation, the result of the song *Billie Jean* is a perfect example of what I call "sonic personality." I don't think there are many recordings where all you need to hear is the first few drums beats and you instantly know what song it is...I called MJ, Quincy, and Rod into the control room and played mix 2 for them. They loved it!!! They were all dancing and carrying on like crazy!!! Smiles all around! Then Michael slipped out of the control room, turned around, and motioned to me to follow him...Then he whispered to me, "Please Bruce, it's perfect, but turn the bass up just a tiny bit, and do one more mix, please..." I said to him... "OK Smelly, no problem"...Well, this went on for about a week. Soon I was up to mix 91!!! I had a stack of ½ inch tapes almost to the ceiling!!!..I played Mix 91 for the boys... Everybody smiled...but Quincy had one of his funny looks on his face…Quincy said "You know Svensk, just for the fun of it, can we listen to one of your earlier mixes???" My heart jumped because I knew that my earlier mixes were dynamite!!! Then Quincy said, "Let's hear mix number 2!!!" Oh WOW!!!! Hallelujah!!! I love mix 2!!!! We listened to mix 2... IT WAS SLAMMIN'!!! EVERYONE IN THE STUDIO WAS GROOVIN' AND DANCIN' and HAPPY, and actin' IGNORANT!!!! Well, here's the deal. When *Thriller* was released to the whole world by Epic Records, on Tuesday, November 30, 1982, it went to Tower Records with MIX 2 OF *Billie Jean* on it!!! The REAL Story of *Billie Jean*...[62]

Michael Jackson with Steve Barron, director of the short film.

THE SHORT FILM

Director: Steve Barron
Producer: Siobhan Barron
Lead actor: Michael Jackson
Supporting actor: Simon Fields
Shoot date: February 1983
Shooting location: Ren-Mar Studios, 846 North Cahuenga Blvd, Hollywood, California
Duration: 4'54

Genesis

With *Billie Jean*, Michael Jackson redefined the very foundations of his music: from now on, it was to be as visual as it was auditory. He invented the short film, and in so doing opened up new artistic perspectives but also a new economic lifeline for music, which was going through a bad patch as regards record sales. Moreover, *Billie Jean* marked the singer's total, committed emancipation, with a view to the future, and without his brothers. The myth of the artist surely has its roots here.

In 2014, Steve Barron recalled the shooting of the *Billie Jean* clip in his book *Egg n Chips & Billie Jean: A Trip through the Eighties*. The film director had just completed the video *Don't You Want Me* for the group the Human League when he was contacted directly by Michael Jackson, who liked the video's atmosphere and movie-like quality. His requirements were quite simple: the artist wanted a short film that told a story, not just a video. The budget allocated by CBS for making this video was $50,000, the biggest Steve Barron had ever worked with at that time.

The director returned to an idea he had originally meant for Joan Armatrading: "the Midas touch thing."

He suggested to Michael Jackson the idea that he would move around a set, with the ability to light up everything he touched, and even to turn it into gold. The singer liked it, and the two met a few weeks later on the set of Ren-Mar Studios in Hollywood.

Production

Michael Jackson was met by a storyboard consisting of two blank sections, destined to contain the dance sequences he wanted to incorporate. In the video, he would pass in front of a store displaying mannequins in the window. The singer suggested that he bring them to life and dance with them. Already he was introducing the idea of a group choreography, like those that would appear later in the short films of *Thriller* and *Beat It*. However, CBS refused to provide the extra $5,000 this sequence would require.

Billie Jean sparked a true revolution of people's attitudes and marked a watershed moment for African-American artists on MTV.

Steve Barron was completely at ease on the set, until, he humbly admitted, Michael Jackson started dancing. For the young man's talents as a dancer astonished him, and the steps followed each other at such speed that the director was afraid of missing them. The planned dance sequence involved 11 paving stones lighting up as Michael passed by. However, on the day of filming, some were not working. Michael immediately adapted his moves, and launched into an unrestrained performance. Barron was stunned. He described this as a surreal moment; he had never before seen anything like that dance.

The scenes were soon in the can, and it was time for post-production. The director took advantage of the fact that Michael Jackson was passing through London to work with him. At this point, Barron was still keeping secret his plan to divide the screen into three sections, to show several images simultaneously of the artist dancing, thus reinforcing their effect. This sequence was to become iconic.

A few weeks later MTV broadcast the video. It was something completely new and it would change an era.

Human Nature

Steve Porcaro, John Bettis / 4'05

Musicians
Michael Jackson: lead vocals
David Paich: synthesizer
Steve Porcaro: synthesizer and programming
Steve Lukather: guitar
Jeff Porcaro: drums
Paulinho Da Costa: percussion
Michael Boddicker: emulator
Recording
Westlake Recording Studios, Los Angeles: 14 April to 8 November 1982
Technical team
Producer: Quincy Jones
Recording engineer: Bruce Swedien
Assistant recording engineer: Steve Bates
Technician engineer: Matt Forger
Arrangements: David Paich, Steve Porcaro, and Steve Lukather

In 1983, Miles Davis recorded *Human Nature*. His legendary trumpet overlays the vocal parts originally sung by Michael Jackson.

In 1993 the song was sampled and made popular once again by the group SWV with its remix hit *Right Here/Human Nature Remix* (by Teddy Riley).

A-side: *Human Nature (7-inch edit)* / 3'46
B-side: *Baby Be Mine (album version)* / 4'20
Released by Epic Records: USA, 18 July 1983 (ref. 34-04026) / The Netherlands, August 1983 (ref. EPC A 3681)
Chart position: USA R&B No. 27, Pop No. 7 / The Netherlands No. 11

1982

For Jackson Addicts

The single pressings of *Human Nature* reveal another version, with synthesizer arrangements that differ in the break. It is also available as a 3-inch Japanese CD released in 1987 (Epic ref. 10-8P-3047).

Genesis

At the end of the summer of 1982, the hits that were to form the backbone of the album *Thriller* had already been recorded: *The Girl Is Mine, Wanna Be Startin' Somethin', Thriller*, and *Billie Jean*. Quincy Jones took some time to think about the project while work continued on the other songs: *Carousel, Got the Hots, Nightline, Hot Street, She's Trouble, Baby Be Mine*, and *The Lady in My Life*, all of which were in the process of being put together or recorded. Jones was still in search of new material, chiefly with a pop quality. He called on David Paich of the group Toto, a session musician and arranger with Steve Porcaro on the recording sessions for *Thriller*, and asked him for some suggestions. Toto were in the process of finishing the mixing of their album *Toto IV* (1982)—which included the global hit *Africa*—and Steve Porcaro took on the task of putting David Paich's various ideas on cassette. He used a cassette on which he had himself recorded a preliminary demo of a ballad entitled *Human Nature*. This song had not been retained by his group, who preferred, in the context of live performance, to concentrate on punchier, more rock numbers. Some time later, Quincy Jones was quietly listening to the cassette in his office. At the end of the first side the auto/reverse system kicked in, starting to play the second side. After a moment of silence, a melody made itself heard, with the provisional lyrics "Why? Why? Why?..." It gave Quincy Jones goosebumps, and he felt the song would suit Michael Jackson perfectly. In his role as synthesizer programmer, Steve Porcaro was disinclined to make musical suggestions, as the roles in Quincy Jones's teams were clearly defined and left little room for maneuver. But chance had decided otherwise, much to the annoyance of David Paich, whose suggestions in the end were not considered.

In September 2015, for the KLCS documentary series *Composers on Composing*, directed by Bambi Moé, Steve Porcaro recalled the genesis of the song. One day, having picked up his daughter from school, he noticed that the little girl was upset; she complained that a boy had hit her. The girl, who was barely five years old, asked her father what had motivated her attacker: "Why?" Steve Porcaro could not come up with an answer to the question—and it was at this moment that the theme of *Human Nature* began to take shape in his mind.

At Quincy Jones's request, John Bettis completed the lyrics, retaining the questioning of complex human relation-

A promotional photo from the shoot for the single's sleeve.

ships and preserving all the melody's sensitivity. *Human Nature* evokes a sadness that is far removed from the desired rock quality originally suggested by the producer.

Production

The musical richness of *Human Nature* is a distillation of the impressive output of melodies produced by Toto during their career. It is comparable to another of the group's hits, *Rosanna,* produced at the same time. Four of Toto's members recorded *Human Nature*: David Paich and Steve Porcaro on synthesizers, Steve Lukather on guitar, and Jeff Porcaro on drums. The close teamwork between the two keyboard players adds to the song's unusual, sad sound. Their song was impeccably imitated by Greg Phillinganes during Michael Jackson's tours.

As was his wont, during recording sessions the young singer watched and listened but did not interfere with the group's creativity. Sessions were fairly short. David Paich said in an interview in 2015: "Michael was very involved in it, and he's a perfectionist...He was always in the room with us, privately, saying, 'I just want you to have total freedom to do whatever you want. Just think of Michelangelo painting the Sistine Chapel—do whatever you need to do here. Sky's the limit.'"[54]

In 2009, Michael Boddicker recalled the details of the production of synthesized string sounds for this song:

> The *Human Nature* signature synth string part. That was Steve Porcaro's track. He used a Yamaha CS-80 with glide (chromatic instead of portamento) at the head—it's got that nice little CS fuzz around the sound. That fuzz was also part of a multilayered sound I used for the four-chord basic string vamp on *Billie Jean*—Michael Jackson himself played that part on a CS-80 in one take. No punches. No repairs. No sequencers or time correction. Seven minutes. Perfect performance....the line that counters the vocal on the second half of the first *Human Nature* chorus is my sound playing a line written by Rod Temperton. The sound and part were later supplanted by background vocals, but the basic, main lines, solo, and most layers are from Steve Porcaro.[63]

Bruce Swedien mixed the song to fit the sound of the other originals on the album, with Steve Porcaro helping the editing.

Michael Sembello's song *Carousel*, which originally was to have been included, was eventually dropped in favor of *Human Nature,* much to the regret of its writer, who would have to wait until 2001 for it to be included on a special edition of the album.

The song was released as the fifth single, only in the US and a handful of European countries. It did not benefit from a video, but it was to come into its own on stage. Throughout his career, Michael Jackson developed powerful imagery around this song, combining dancing with meticulous stage direction. Beneath a simple, warm light, he would dance languorously, then break, using gestures that could have been borrowed from the mime Marcel Marceau or Charlie Chaplin. He highlighted notes in the chorus with vocal arrangements prepared for live performance.

The first demo of *P.Y.T.* can be heard on the compilation *Michael Jackson—The Ultimate Collection* (2004).

P.Y.T. (Pretty Young Thing)

James Ingram, Quincy Jones / 3'58

Musicians
Michael Jackson: lead vocals
Greg Phillinganes: synthesizer and programming
Michael Boddicker: vocoder and emulator
James Ingram: Portasound keyboard
Paul Jackson Jr.: guitar
Louis Johnson: electric bass
Ndugu Chancler: drums
Michael Jackson, Louis Johnson, Greg Phillinganes, James Ingram, Steven Ray: clapping hands
Janet Jackson, La Toya Jackson, Becky Lopez, Bunny Hull: P.Y.T.s /backing vocals
James Ingram, Howard Hewett: additional vocals
Recording
Westlake Recording Studios, Los Angeles : 14 April to 8 November 1982
Technical team
Producer: Quincy Jones
Recording engineer: Bruce Swedien
Assistant recording engineer: Steve Bates
Technician engineer: Matt Forger

Genesis

The idea of a song on the theme of P.Y.T. (Pretty Young Thing), supposedly came to Quincy Jones after his wife, Peggy Lipton, brought some underwear home which bore these words.

Some time before *Beat It* and *The Lady in My Life*, Michael Jackson and Greg Phillinganes made an initial demo. Suave, languorous, and syrupy, it did not appeal to the producer, who felt it lacked energy in both the lyrics and the music: "I was alone at dawn, she woke me / She was asleep and tired…" Jones decided to revise it completely with James Ingram, his protégé on the project *The Dude* (1981). Together, they injected more arrogance into the song, by calling out to the young girl in the story directly: "You know you, you make me feel so good inside / I always wanted a girl just like you / Such a P.Y.T., pretty young thing." Perfectly in tune with the youth and energy of the performer, the Jones / Ingram version turned out to be much more punchy and dynamic.

In 2008, as part of a promotion for the 25th anniversary of the album *Thriller*, will.i.am, leader of the Black Eyed Peas, and Quincy Jones met to make a promotional video. will.i.am questioned the older man about working on making the record. When the young musician referred to the first demo version of *P.Y.T.*, the producer replied curtly that it had never existed, and that he had only ever worked on the one he wrote with James Ingram. Regardless of this argument between songwriters, Michael Jackson was to use the harmonies on his demo for other songs, such as *Someone Put Your Hand Out*.

Production

James Ingram remembered vividly the explosive energy that Michael Jackson gave off in the studio: "This was the very first time I had seen [him] sing. I had quite simply never seen anyone move like that! Everyone I know tries to control their breathing so it's not heard at the microphone.…Michael came out bathed in sweat and asked me, 'Did I sing well?' I answered, 'Michael, you were awesome singing that song.' Michael didn't worry about controlling his breath at the microphone. He was a genius."[64]

The singular brilliance and sound of *P.Y.T.* were the result of the excellent work of Michael Boddicker, the only person at the time who could master the variations of analog synthesizers. He programmed the Minimoog that provided the music for the

USA
A-side: *P.Y.T. (Pretty Young Thing) (album version)* / 3'58
B-side: The Jacksons: *Working Day and Night (live)* / 4'26
UK
A-side: *P.Y.T. (Pretty Young Thing) (album version)* / 3'58
B-side: The Jacksons: *This Place Hotel (live)* / 4'40
Released by Epic Records: USA, 8 October 1983 (ref. 34-04165) / UK, 19 March 1984 (ref. A 4136)
Chart position: USA R&B No. 46, Pop No. 10 / UK No. 11

Michael Jackson at the Black Radio Exclusive convention at the Hyatt Regency Hotel in Los Angeles, 1 July 1983.

The Korg VC-10 Vocoder made it possible to control synthesized sounds using the voice or instruments connected to the system.

song: "Those were my two Richie Walbourn-modified Minimoogs, set side by side, with engineer Bruce Swedien's special multiple-mono compression."[63]

In 2009, with regard to synthesized sounds that answered the backing vocals, Michael Boddicker recalled:

> That was a Roland Jupiter-6 "wang bar"-style pitch bend doubled with, and controlling, a Sequential Circuits Prophet-5, thus the sort of smear you can hear on the "wobble" between the top two notes. I recall the keyboards were set on the very top of a stand so they were practically at ear level!...It sounds multitracked, but really, it's not. It's a single-track sample of Michael Jackson's voice, done on an E-mu Emulator I—serial number 1, in fact! We then used this mode the Emulator had where you could sample the sound twice, then detune one of the voices while in "unison" mode. It was recorded with lots of top end added, and Bruce Swedien's special reverb known as "spit." Quincy Jones would say, "Sven, put some spit on it!"[63]

Four "P.Y.T.s" accompanied the backing vocals, including Michael's two sisters, Janet and La Toya. "In the intro to *Pretty Young Thing*, I sounded a bit more confident than I had on the last album. I liked the 'code' in the lyrics, and 'tenderoni' and 'sugar fly' were fun rock'n'roll-type words that you couldn't find in the dictionary. I got Janet and La Toya into the studio for this one, and they produced the 'real' backup vocals. James Ingram and I programmed an electronic device called a Vocoder, which gave out that E.T. voice."[2]

P.Y.T. was the sixth single to be released, just before the single *Thriller*. It entered the charts, without performing spectacularly, but it remained a particular favorite with fans of the artist.

FOR JACKSON ADDICTS

The singer Monica sampled *P.Y.T. (Pretty Young Thing)* in *All Eyez on Me* (2002), and used some unreleased vocals by Michael Jackson. Released as a single, it was produced by Rodney "Darkchild" Jerkins.

THE LADY IN MY LIFE

Rod Temperton / 4'57

Musicians
Michael Jackson: vocals
Greg Phillinganes: Rhodes piano
David Paich and Steve Porcaro: synthesizers
Paul Jackson: guitar
Louis Johnson: bass guitar
Jeff Porcaro: drums
Michael Boddicker: emulator
Recording
Westlake Recording Studios, Los Angeles: 14 April to 8 November 1982
Technical team
Producer: Quincy Jones
Recording engineer: Bruce Swedien
Arrangements: Rod Temperton

FOR JACKSON ADDICTS

In 2002, Chrysalis, which owned the rights to Rod Temperton's work, released a double CD under the sober title *The Songs of Rod Temperton*, which included the long version of *The Lady in My Life*. A noticeable background noise comes through on this—proof that access to the master was not easy, even for the song's composer!

Genesis

She's out of My Life had allowed Michael Jackson to leave behind his childlike image of the Motown years by finally performing a song with adult lyrics. *The Lady in My Life* rammed the point home and added a touch of sensuality hitherto absent in the young artist's repertoire.

Rod Temperton outdid the song by Tom Bähler, composing a languorous, slow number, deliberately placed at the end of the album, as if heralding the end of the evening on an imaginary dance floor, where the only people left were a few lovers looking for each other.

Where Gamble and Huff (who nevertheless wrote ballads of undeniable sex appeal for Teddy Pendergrass) failed, Rod Temperton succeeded. The composer managed to produce, at just the right time, a song that could mix it with the great crooners, but which remains a rarity in Michael Jackson's work. In *The Lady in My Life* he sings a declaration of love that combines romanticism with sensuality, all in the cause of a promise of eternal marriage.

Rod Temperton was accustomed to writing dance numbers and, at Quincy Jones's request, ventured into ballad territory with panache. In 1981 he had written *Somethin' Special* for his album *The Dude*. This song, performed by Patti Austin, who at times sang in the same register as Michael Jackson, sounded like a rough draft for *The Lady in My Life*, which was put together in an intimate setting made to measure for the young singer within the Westlake studios. The end of the song, as written and arranged, had to resonate plaintively, a supplication by the lover asking his chosen one to yield to his advances.

Production

Michael Jackson, under the guidance of Quincy Jones and Rod Temperton, recorded take after take, but the results were unconvincing. The sadness of *She's out of My Life* had touched him so deeply that he had been in tears at the end of every performance. *The Lady in My Life* made life more difficult for him, as if he had difficulty immersing himself in the ambiance of love tinged with sensuality that is peculiar to the song.

Having failed to achieve the desired effect, Quincy Jones took the young artist to one side and gave him a simple instruction: he should imagine he was begging someone, literally.

Michael Jackson enjoys the sunset in Miami, Florida, November 1984.

Michael agreed, on condition that all the lights were turned out. His pathological shyness in the studio was gaining the upper hand, and it was only in such darkness that he felt he could express himself and produce the desired vocal sounds.

The results were staggering: in the final measures of *The Lady in My Life*, the young singer transformed himself into a veritable soul crooner. His performance gave a distant nod to his performance of *Who's Loving You*, recorded in 1969 with The Jackson Five. At that time, he sang the blues with a youthful abandon that left Smokey Robinson, the song's composer, open-mouthed. Thirteen years later, performing a similar exercise, he seemed less at ease letting himself go at the microphone.

The first mix of *The Lady in My Life* lasted 6'08. Listening to the album's first master, the producer, singer, and recording engineer all decided to cut the song. The second verse and chorus were removed, thus changing the song's dynamic. Although a good third was cut in the final version, *The Lady in My Life* succeeded in retaining its dramatic intensity. The new edit even managed to give more power to the song's final minutes, during which Michael Jackson "improvised."

The band put together to accompany him was reduced to the minimum. *The Lady in My Life* was the result of pared-down sessions, in which skillful dosing of the synthesizers lent the song an unexpected melancholy quality. Steve Porcaro's drums worked effectively, seemingly following the rhythm of a couple slow dancing.

As a postscript to *Thriller*, Rod Temperton said his goodbyes to Michael Jackson and Quincy Jones: the composer would not figure on *Bad*, and would never again work with the artist. *The Lady in My Life* was thus to remain a rare gem, never released as a single and which, despite being included on the best-selling album of all time, has managed to retain an intimate, precious quality down the years.

OUTTAKES

THRILLER OUTTAKES

The making of *Thriller* was the result of a song selection process for which Michael Jackson and Quincy Jones took complete responsibility. The songs below are some of the rejects, which did not have the honor of inclusion on the album that sold more than 60 million worldwide. It should be noted that *Carousel, Hot Street, Nightline,* and *She's Trouble* have all been on the bootleg circuit since the early 1990s. Although some of these songs have enjoyed official release since, others continue to exist only through this unofficial Michael Jackson discography.

CAROUSEL

Michael Sembello, Don Freeman / 4'08

Musicians: (unknown) / **Recording: Westlake Recording Studios, Los Angeles**: 14 April to 8 November 1982 / **Technical team: Producer**: Quincy Jones / **Recording engineer**: Bruce Swedien

Carousel was on the shortlist for but, at the last minute, failed to make it onto *Thriller.* Composed by Michael Sembello and his acolyte, the musician Don Freeman, it is a light, romantic, mid-tempo number that describes the unrequited love of a young man for a circus artist passing through town. Rod Temperton recalled that *Carousel* was put aside in favor of *Human Nature*:

> When we first went in the studio to make the real album, we, I believe, did nine cuts as the tracks and did some vocals on them. At that point we kind of stepped back for a minute and had a listen and we realized that three or four of the cuts—not that they were bad—but were just not fitting in with where the album appeared to be going. Right from the beginning, Michael had written *Billie Jean,* and everybody knew that that was going to be a cornerstone of the album. And the style of that and *Wanna Be Startin' Somethin'*, another track Michael had written for it, plus what was to become *Thriller,* were kind of giving the whole thing an edge and a direction, that some of the other tracks didn't have. They seemed a little too poppy, and too straightforward for where we appeared to be going. So that's why those tracks never made the album—and one of them was *Carousel.* It was a great song, a slowish song by Michael Sembello. It was beautiful but, lyrically and at that point in time, it didn't seem that that was where the album was heading to...Eventually they were all replaced with *Beat It*, *The Lady in My Life*, *Human Nature*, which were some of the best things on the album so I don't think it was a mistake in the end."[61]

Missing out must have plunged Sembello and Freeman into justified dejection...The look on Sembello's face during the Grammy Awards ceremony in Los Angeles on 28 February 1984 said it all: he was in the room when Michael Jackson and his colleagues made a clean sweep of the most coveted awards. That evening, *Thriller* dominated the record industry. The guitarist-composer consoled himself with the hit *Maniac*, which figured on the original soundtrack of the movie *Flashdance* (1983) and opened the door to well-deserved commercial success.

Carousel began to do the rounds amongst fans in the early 1990s, as poor-quality cassette copies under the title *Circus Girl*. In 2001, Michael Jackson reissued his first four solo albums with Epic, in parallel with the release of his final work, *Invincible*. *Carousel* reappeared on *Thriller: Special Edition* that year, in a frustratingly truncated version (1'49). In the mid-2000s Sembello released the complete version, lasting 4'08, on his site, MichaelSembello.com. At the end of 2008, to celebrate Michael Jackson's 50th birthday, Sony Music launched the King of Pop project, in which a series of compilations were released, voted for by the public. On 3 October 2008, Sony Music Italy released its volume, securing the right to publish a 3'40 version of *Carousel*.

Hits from *Thriller* made up the setlist for the *Victory* tour, which crisscrossed the US from July to December 1984.

Got the Hots

Michael Jackson, Quincy Jones / 4'27

Musicians: (unknown) / **Recording: Westlake Recording Studios, Los Angeles**: 14 April to 8 November 1982 / **Technical team: Producer**: Quincy Jones / **Recording engineer**: Bruce Swedien

Along with *Can't Get outta the Rain*, *Got the Hots* brought Quincy Jones and Michael Jackson together as songwriters. This funk number, punctuated by synthesizer chords and riffs with electric overtones, was in line to figure on *Thriller* in place of *P.Y.T.* The singer mentioned the existence of the number during sworn statements in court on 8 and 10 November 1993 in Mexico, during the course of a legal action over plagiarism. The song's lyrics are a declaration of love that remains close to the themes and ambiance of *Off the Wall*. *Got the Hots* did not make an official appearance until 2001, when it featured on *Thriller: Special Edition*. At the time, Michael Jackson was on bad terms with Tommy Mottola, CEO of Sony Music. This conflict had consequences for the artist's planned releases. Most of the bonus tracks planned for the reissues of these major albums (*Off the Wall*, *Thriller*, *Bad*, and *Dangerous*) were canceled. *Got the Hots* was one of the victims of this artistic and financial power struggle between the two men. It was not until February 2008 that the demo version of *Got the Hots* timidly succeeded in gaining a place on a Japanese pressing of *Thriller 25*. In the meantime, however, the song had been reincarnated in the form of another number on the album, *Kiss of Life* by the singer Siedah Garrett, released in 1988. The melodic line of *Got the Hots* had been given to Rod Temperton, who rebooted the song and gave it a new title: *Baby's Got It Bad*. Thanks to some ingenious legal and financial arrangements reached between artists and musicians, this new work was jointly signed by Siedah Garrett and Rod Temperton.

Hot Street

Rod Temperton, Michael Jackson / 3'55

Musicians: (unknown) / **Recording: Westlake Recording Studios, Los Angeles**: 14 April to 8 November 1982 / **Technical team: Producer**: Quincy Jones / **Recording engineer**: Bruce Swedien

Baby Be Mine ended up winning out over *Hot Street*. Michael Jackson made no secret of his liking for this song during the famous sworn statement filmed in Mexico in November 1993. Composed by Rod Temperton, the song was initially entitled *Slapstick*. The lyrics describe a femme fatale with whom the singer falls in love. He is transported by this girl, who leads him to dream. The term "slapstick" alluded to slapstick comedy, such as that by Charlie Chaplin, the Marx Brothers or Laurel and Hardy.

The song has a solid musical base: driven on by a rhythm programmed on the ever-present Linn M-1, it has a droning synthetic bass played on the keyboard that gives it an effective groove. But the lyrics were too sensible and lacked boldness. Temperton wrote some new ones with the King of Pop. The theme was a darker one: the beautiful heroine changed into a part-time prostitute who conquered the heart of the young Michael. This presence of a femme fatale in his musical universe was to be developed in later years, but during the making of *Thriller*, Quincy Jones felt that *Hot Street* did not chime with the rest of the album. To this day the song, which has been doing the rounds of the bootleg circuit since the early 1990s, has still not been officially released.

Nightline

Glen Ballard, Davey Faragher, Brie Howard / 4'47

Musicians: (unknown) / **Recording: Westlake Recording Studios, Los Angeles**: 14 April to 8 November 1982 / **Technical team: Producer**: Quincy Jones / **Recording engineer**: Bruce Swedien

For the first time in his career, Glen Ballard worked with Michael Jackson when he suggested *Nightline* (also known as *Nite-Line*) to Quincy Jones for the album *Thriller*. Once the rumor was about that the duo were heading into the recording studio to work on a new album, the cassettes began to pile up on the legendary producer's desk. Since he had formed his label, Qwest, Jones had sought out the best composers and performers. He hired Glenn Ballard, whom he advised to make sure he remained in control of his own musical destiny. The young songwriter dealt with the disappointment of not seeing his song included on *Thriller* by telling himself it would be on the next album. He succeeded in having one song included on *Bad* in 1987 (*Man in the Mirror*), and another on *Dangerous* in 1991 (*Keep the Faith*). When *Nightline* was officially dropped from the *Thriller* project, Ballard suggested the song to the Pointer Sisters, who included it on their album *Break Out* in November 1983. However, it was replaced on pressings made in 1984 by *I'm So Excited*, which became one of the group's greatest hits. At the same time, Randy Crawford released an album also entitled *Nightline*: Ballard managed to recycle his composition on two projects.

She's Trouble

Terry Britten, Billy Livsey, Sue Shifrin / 4'08

Musicians: (unknown) / **Recording: Westlake Recording Studios, Los Angeles**: 14 April to 8 November 1982 / **Technical team: Producer**: Quincy Jones / **Recording engineer**: Bruce Swedien

This song, also known under the title *Trouble* on the bootleg circuit, numbered Tony Britten among its composers. He was one of the architects of the triumphant return of Tina Turner to the public eye with the song *What's Love Got to Do with It* (1984), cowritten with Graham Lyle. *She's Trouble* took Michael Jackson back to the carefree pop sound of his Motown years. The adult, sophisticated image that he had created and developed since *Off the Wall* was entirely absent. The chorus of *She's Trouble* was reminiscent of the theme tune of a TV series for teenagers. Quincy Jones and Michael Jackson rejected the song, but it would bring success to younger stars who were more in tune with the song's lyrics and musical character. Thus Scott Baio, the young American actor who played Chachi in *Happy Days* before becoming the protagonist of his own series, *Charles in Charge*, salvaged *She's Trouble* and recorded it for his album *The Boys Are Out* (1983). In the UK, Musical Youth, a ska version of The Jackson Five, also used the song, which figures on the group's album *Different Style* (1983) and reached 25th place in the US R&B charts.

Sunset Driver

Michael Jackson / 4'03

Musicians: (unknown) / **Recording: Hayvenhurst, Encino, Yamaha Studios Glendale, California:** 1982 / **Technical team: Producer**: Michael Jackson / **Recording engineer**: Keith Seppanen / **Mixing**: Bill Bottrell

With Michael Jackson, a good idea never went to waste: it just needed time to mature. *Sunset Driver* was written at the end of the 1970s for the album *Off the Wall*. An initial demo was recorded in 1978 in the family studio in Encino. The artist then took the decision, together with Quincy Jones, not to keep the song for that project. He reworked it at home in 1982. The bass line displays a rhythm similar to the supercharged groove of *Can't Get outta the Rain*. However, the song didn't make it to the definitive tracklist for *Thriller*. It lay forgotten during the sessions for *Bad*, but it resurfaced at the start of the 1990s during the recording of the album *Dangerous*. Michael Jackson used the melodic base of the verses for an early version of *Blood on the Dance Floor*. This intermediate version, a sort of improbable hybrid between the two songs, was recorded and filed away in the studios of the producer Teddy Riley under the reference *Blood on the Dance Floor Mix 6 No. 24*. The young singer was not satisfied with the result, and left *Sunset Driver* to lie dormant in his archives. In 2001 Michael Jackson wanted to include the 1978 version as a bonus on the reissue of *Off the Wall* that year, but disagreement with the label scuppered the plan. In November 2004, *Sunset Driver* finally saw the light of day, in its 1982 version, on the box set *The Ultimate Collection*.

Michael Jackson with E.T., the extra-terrestrial. This photo was distributed as a poster with the box set *E.T. Storybook.*

E.T. STORYBOOK

Every masterpiece has its antechamber, its dark zone, which paradoxically can also charge it with positive energy. It is as if limits and constraints set off electric shocks that drive a project in a new direction. *Thriller* is no exception. Quincy Jones and Michael Jackson had four months to get the album in the can. Epic was exerting pressure, driven by its financial goals—which were logical given that *Off the Wall* had won ten million fans.

Quincy and Steven

While they were engaged in this marathon, the producer accepted a proposal from his new friend Steven Spielberg. Spielberg had just released *E.T. the Extra-Terrestrial*, a film that was to become emblematic of the 1980s and heartwarming family movies. Driven by a ferocious desire to capitalize on the film's success (*E.T.* was patented and spawned an almost endless number of spin-off products), the movie director decided to adapt his feature-length film to produce a record album for children. The idea was to release a box set containing a record that told the film's story, together with a booklet and some goodies. To flesh out the concept, Spielberg asked Quincy Jones to produce a song for him that would be the record's opening and closing theme.

Seduced by the siren calls of Hollywood and the world of movies, the producer agreed, and suggested Michael Jackson record the song. The young man jumped for joy at the idea of taking part in an adaptation of the biggest movie of the year. The director had thus managed to place his project in the hands of two kind souls who were already on side, and the two musicians began work on the song without delay. A few weeks later, Spielberg asked Quincy Jones whether he would be prepared to produce the entire album. Even though he was already engaged in the epic marathon of recording *Thriller*, the producer agreed—his ego, like Michael Jackson's, was flattered by the proposal. From that moment on, passion prevailed over reason.

How *E.T.* almost killed off *Thriller*

When Quincy Jones looked at the tapes supplied by Spielberg and his editor, Bruce Cannon, he realized that the director had underestimated the amount of work involved: transforming a two-hour movie into a 40-minute audio album was no easy task. What was needed was a veritable rewrite, which demanded both cohesion and a sense of rhythm. It was a matter of conveying the emotion in the film to a listener who had not seen it on the big screen.

In the space of six weeks, Quincy Jones succeeded in giving the project shape, with the invaluable help of his team. He juggled *E.T.* and *Thriller* to the point that some felt he unintentionally neglected some technical and artistic aspects of Michael Jackson's album. *E.T.* took on more importance than expected and encroached upon the concentration needed to create the successor to *Off the Wall*.

All the more so since Michael Jackson allowed himself to become totally tied up in the project. Reading the story, relating each scene, he gives the impression of being in the forest, not far from E.T., as if he were guiding him in his adventures. Of all the recordings published during his career, *E.T. Storybook* is the one that allows his candor and spontaneity to burst forth naturally, without any filter. The singer is more than a narrator—he plays a role in his own right. Recorded with a skillfully controlled reverb effect, his voice soars over the action as if in a waking dream.

Breaches by MCA

As far as the project's business aspects were concerned, Quincy Jones went ahead with the recording sessions before the legal details had been settled. Unfortunately the situation became complicated. The *E.T.* project was to be released by MCA, a record label that was one of CBS's competitors. MCA's legal department failed to contact Michael Jackson's label to check whether he was free to contribute to the project and, if so, on what conditions. [65]

When Walter Yetnikoff, CEO of CBS, heard about the storybook album, he wasn't happy: How could they allow MCA to commercially exploit the image of their bestselling artist? Legal action was taken in a New York court. Clarence Avant, an old friend of Quincy Jones and a man with many interests

in the entertainment industry, took on the role of mediator. Yetnikoff demanded $500,000 from the label. It is said that if the label failed to pay up, he would simply order that the storybook be banned.

After many weeks of negotiations, which monopolized Quincy Jones's attention during the recording sessions for *Thriller* and *E.T.*, agreement was finally reached the day after Thanksgiving: MCA could sell the album by producing 500,000 copies of a deluxe version of the box set. In return, Sheinberg had to pay CBS half a million dollars for the use of Michael Jackson's image within this extremely limited framework.

The box sets were released on 7 November 1982; collectors pounced on them. The theme song recorded by Michael Jackson, *Someone in the Dark*, was made available as a single to US radio stations, but its commercial release was eventually canceled—again, for legal reasons. To this day, this promotional pressing has remained the star's rarest record.

During the summer of 1982, Quincy Jones, Michael Jackson, and Steven Spielberg work on the *E.T. Storybook* project.

A fragile, short-lived friendship

On 28 February 1984 the album *E.T. Storybook* won a Grammy Award for best children's album. In hindsight, it was an ironic recognition, given that the project has been under a curse ever since. Over the years, aside from the serious legal issues that dogged the storybook album, relations between the singer and the director got progressively worse.

Michael Jackson was hopeful of landing the role of Peter Pan in a future movie. But in the end it was Robin Williams who played the character, in *Hook* (1992), something Jackson saw as a betrayal. In 1995 the singer released a song entitled *They Don't Care About Us*, in which he deals with the theme of oppression. Certain lyrics were deemed to be anti-Semitic. The film director condemned the singer and the song in the media. Despite a tentative reconciliation on the set of the film short *Michael Jackson's Ghosts* in 1996, the two former friends no longer saw each other.

In 2002, Steven Spielberg celebrated the 20th anniversary of *E.T.* by releasing the film once again to movie theaters. This new commercial venture spawned an unprecedented range of merchandising, including the rerelease of certain flagship items. TV shows paying tribute to the movie were also broadcast the world over. *E.T. Storybook* was conspicuously absent from all these celebrations.

E.T. Storybook was thus erased from the glorious history of the movie *E.T.*, as if the storybook album was the awkward cousin in a family that needed to continue to shine and appeal to millions all over the world. The conditions attached to the album remained strict: even the record label's reproduction rights were charged at an exorbitant rate. Quincy Jones and Rod Temperton, respectively the producer and cowriter of the song *Someone in the Dark*, managed to lift certain legal restrictions, so that the number could be included in the 2001 reissue of *Thriller*. Condemned to a forced removal from all distribution channels, whether physical or digital, adapted to new modes of consumption, *E.T. Storybook* remains a rare pearl that has gone to waste, like an abandoned brother, without whom the creation of *Thriller* would not have been the same.

Someone in the Dark

Alan and Marilyn Bergman, Rod Temperton / 4'58

From the album: *E.T. Storybook* / **Released by MCA Records:** USA, November 1982 / UK, January 1983 (ref. MCA 70000) **Chart position:** USA Pop No. 37 / UK No. 82 / **Musicians:** (unknown) / **Recording: Westlake Recording Studios, Los Angeles:** August 1982 / **Technical team:** / **Producer:** Quincy Jones / **Recording engineer:** Bruce Swedien / **Arrangements:** Jeremy Lubbock

Genesis

Neil Diamond released *Heartlight*, a pop song inspired by *E.T.*, which Steven Spielberg considered using for the *E.T. Storybook* project, but it did not fit with the otherworldly atmosphere that was desired for the box set. Steven Spielberg suggested to Quincy Jones that he write a song for the storybook album, and once he heard *Someone in the Dark*, *Heartlight* was definitively dropped.

Rod Temperton surpassed himself in writing the song. He had already composed several ballads for Jones's album *The Dude* in 1981, but when the producer commissioned him to write music to accompany the *E.T. Storybook*, he managed to find the perfect tune. In the key of C major, *Someone in the Dark* succeeds in conveying the unique friendship between Elliott and E.T., and the sadness of the parting that ends the film. The British musician wrote a score that brought to mind the innocence of *Over The Rainbow*, the song in the movie *The Wizard of Oz*, written by Harold Arlen and E.Y. Harburg and brilliantly performed by Judy Garland.

Quincy Jones decided to give his friends Alan and Marilyn Bergman the task of writing the lyrics. This famous duo had worked with the biggest names in Hollywood, from Frank Sinatra and Barbra Streisand to Fred Astaire and Ray Charles. From the late 1960s, the couple had had a string of successes for both film and television. Michael Jackson's producer had met them on the set of the movie *In the Heat of the Night* in 1967—a film that won them and their colleagues public acclaim.

Someone in the Dark is the opening and closing theme of *E.T. Storybook*. The Bergmans wrote three verses and two choruses. The first two verses, contained in the opening version, describe the friendship between Elliott and the creature from outer space. The last, logically occurring at the start of the closing version, crystallizes the movie's final scene, where the two friends bid each other goodbye, and follows on perfectly from the last sequence of the album.

Production

Quincy Jones enlisted the services of Jeremy Lubbock to conduct the orchestra brought in to play Rod Temperton's score. Bruce Swedien adjusted his redoubtable Harrison console to make the song sound like a logical sequel to the original film soundtrack, composed by John Williams.

The subtle mixing of the song, in which the fretless bass heightens the sadness of the words, is worthy of the greatest productions in cinema. Bruce Swedien and Quincy Jones's strength lay in their adaptability: their huge experience on many original movie soundtracks and other pop albums enabled them to approach this recording session with equanimity.

The drummer Ndugu Chancler was present: "Steven Spielberg and Quincy Jones were at the console. The control room was lit, and the studio plunged into darkness. As I went in I heard music, and assumed they were listening to a playback. But suddenly a voice said, 'Can I sing that phrase again?' Michael Jackson was recording a vocal take in the dark. Here was a guy who knew the lyrics by heart, without needing a sheet of paper or a music stand in front of him. Here was a guy who went beyond the words and made the song his own, the way John Coltrane could do."[66]

For Jackson Addicts

The promotional single for *Someone in the Dark* contains both versions of the song: the opening (4'58) and the closing ones (3'04), renamed the "long" and "short" versions. Although the first version is available on several CDs, the second has not, to date, been re-pressed for any other project.

JOE "KING" CARRASCO

DON'T LET A WOMAN (MAKE A FOOL OUT OF YOU)

Joe "King" Carrasco, Johnny Perez / 3'49

From the album: *Synapse Gap (Mundo Total)* / **Released by MCA Records:** USA (ref. MCA-5308) & UK (ref. MCF 3143), 1982 / **Single: Released by MCA Records:** USA (ref. MCA-52081) & UK (ref. MCA 803), 1982 / In 1985, another single of the song was released in France and Spain for the promotion of the EP *Viva San Antone*. This new version did not make use of Michael Jackson's harmonies / **Michael Jackson:** vocal harmonies / **Recording: Paramount Studios (studio 55), Los Angeles:** 16 October 1981 / **Tony Ferguson:** producer

In *Don't Let a Woman (Make a Fool out of You)*, Michael Jackson humbly put aside his voice and supplied the harmonies for the only reggae number he ever took part in. Joe "King" Carrasco was a crazy, bewitching character, and the king of Tex-Mex rock'n'roll. In 2015 he recalled his short but providential collaboration with the young singer:

Michael Jackson and Joe "King" Carrasco at the recording session for the song at Studio 55, Los Angeles, October 1981.

> In the fall of 1981, the band Joe "King" Carrasco and The Crowns had signed a recording contract with MCA Records to make their second album, *Synapse Gap (Mundo Total)*. The studio, consisting of two rooms, was owned by producer Richard Perry. We recorded our second LP at Studio 55 at Paramount Studios in Los Angeles. The Jacksons came in next door and that's when I met Michael. Michael was sitting in the studio next door...We started talking about how he hung out with Bob Marley in Jamaica and he told me how Bob would cook over an open fire. We talked more about African music, reggae, and Bob Marley than we did about The Jackson Five. That's how we became friends.
>
> One day, when we were starting work on *Don't Let a Woman (Make a Fool out of You)*, we had no one who could sing the harmonies. So I asked Michael: "Hey! Michael, would you agree to sing the harmonies on this song?" He replied: "Yes!" He came and sang four or five parts for verses and bridges, and then we quickly wrapped up the song...He was amazing. Michael Jackson was a real professional in the studio. He was perfectly in control of the mic; he understood the mic. Then his father started to panic, because he absolutely didn't expect his son to be singing with Joe "King" Carrasco, a new wave group. So we handed him a check for $135...In my view, Michael's voice should have been mixed high. However, the producer felt that the public would think we were trying to take advantage of Michael Jackson. I also think that those four or five harmonic lines were a real creative effort, and we could have released a much better song. Anyway, we were musicians above all, and Michael was one too. We were both music fans! That was the root of our friendship. He was a good guy, and very humble...If Michael ever heard that song, he probably thought: "Where did my harmonies go?" Somewhere at home, under a pile of tapes, I have the recordings of this session with Michael Jackson, which were never released.[67]

Michael Jackson's discreet involvement in *Don't Let a Woman (Make a Fool out of You)*, which was both improbable and brilliant, tells us about his extreme generosity and consuming passion for all styles of music.

Bill Wolfer

Papa Was a Rollin' Stone

Norman Whitfield, Barret Strong / 5'17

So Shy

Bill Wolfer / 4'36

From the album: *Wolf* / **Released by Constellation Records:** USA (ref. 60187) & Europe (ref. 96.0187-1), 1982 / **Chart position:** USA R&B No. 50 / **Single: Released by Constellation Records:** USA (ref. 7-69849) & UK (distributed by Solar, ref. E 9849), 1982 / **Michael Jackson, Oren Waters, Maxine Waters, Julia Waters:** backing vocals / **Recording: Allen Zentz Recording, Los Angeles**: (unknown) / **Bill Wolfer:** producer and arranger

An assiduous pupil of Stevie Wonder, discreet and engaging, Bill Wolfer observed Michael Jackson's artistic coming of age first hand. Over the space of a few years he traveled all over America with the *Triumph* tour and helped the singer at the keyboard during the creative process for his greatest hits. He was already present in *Can You Feel It,* and then rejoined the team for *Wanna Be Startin' Somethin'*, *Beat It*, and *Billie Jean* in the album *Thriller*. He also put the finishing touches to other Michael Jackson songs, such as *Muscles* (Diana Ross) and *Say Say Say* (a duet with Paul McCartney), which he brought to life, often at the singer's Encino home.

In 1981, Bill Wolfer recorded his first solo album, *Wolf*, at the Allen Zentz studio, where Michael Jackson had recorded his demo for *The Girl is Mine*:

> Since it was the first solo album by an unknown, I certainly wasn't shy about asking a few of my friends to help out. Michael and I got to the point where we got along very well, and we respected each other, and enjoyed each other's company. I didn't know if he would do it, but I thought, why not ask? I was delighted that he immediately accepted...I just wanted him to fill out the background vocals, adding a fourth voice to the great family group, The Waters. If I had tried for some sort of solo thing from him, then it would have been complicated. But it was a classic Motown song and he was from that era. I hadn't told The Waters anything other than I had invited someone to sing with them. I didn't want them to be disappointed if for some reason Michael couldn't make it. But he did, right on time, and you should have seen their faces when they saw who was going to be singing with them! Michael loved doing the session. He loved being in the studio, and working, and it was fun for him to just be a studio singer for the day. No pressure, just sing, blend in with the group, and be professional, and he had fun doing that. They knocked it out so fast, that Michael was disappointed that it was over, and asked if I had anything else they could sing on. I told the engineer to put *So Shy* on the machine, and we did that in no time. It was a fun, relaxed session.[42]

Michael Jackson and Bill Wolfer pose in this rare photo from the time of the *Triumph* tour in 1981.

The album *Wolf* was reissued in CD format by the Canadian label Unidisc in 2006 (ref. AGEK-2566).

From left: Lionel Richie, James Ingram, Michael Jackson, and Stevie Wonder. The quartet were among the stars providing the backing vocals in Donna Summer's *State of Independence* (1981).

FOR JACKSON ADDICTS

Released in 2015, the box-set collection *Donna Summer—Singles...Driven by the Music* contains a number of remixed versions of the song (ref. DBT MSNGBOX 01).

DONNA SUMMER

STATE OF INDEPENDENCE

Vangelis, Jon Anderson / 5'50

From the album: *Donna Summer* / **Released by Geffen Records:** USA (ref. GHS 2005) and UK (ref. K 99163), August 1982 / **Chart position:** USA R&B No. 6, Pop No. 20 / UK No. 13 / **RIAA:** certified Gold 21 September 1982 / **Single: Released by Geffen Records:** USA (ref. 7-29895) and UK (ref. K 79344), November 1982 / **Chart position:** R&B No. 31, Pop No. 41 / UK No. 14 (1990 No. 45 / 1996 No.13) / **Dara Bernard, Dyan Cannon, Christopher Cross, James Ingram, Michael Jackson, Peggy Lipton Jones, Kenny Loggins, Michael McDonald, Lionel Richie, Brenda Russell, Donna Summer, Dionne Warwick, Stevie Wonder (All Star Choir):** backing vocals / **Recording: Ocean Way Studios, Los Angeles:** (unknown) / **Quincy Jones:** producer

At the beginning of the 1980s, just when disco was fizzling out, Donna Summer, who had been the queen of the preceding decade, left Casablanca Records for the giant label Geffen. From then on, the diva wanted to orientate her work towards a more rock sound—and her new label sought out Quincy Jones to produce the star's next album. Initially he turned down the proposal, explaining that he had been given too many projects since the blockbusters *Off the Wall*, *Give Me the Night* (George Benson), *Light Up the Night* (The Brothers Johnson), *Just Once* (James Ingram), and *Razzamatazz* (Patti Austin).

The entire team of *Off the Wall* and the future *Thriller* was engaged in the project: Rod Temperton, Greg Phillinganes, Paulinho Da Costa, Michael Boddicker, Jerry Hey, David Paich, Steve Porcaro, Steve Lukather, and Louis Johnson. Professional production, together with the use of such talented session musicians, was a first for Donna Summer, who recorded some quality songs, such as *Love Is in Control* and *Livin' in America*.

The recording session for *State of Independence* was the last that Michael Jackson and Quincy Jones took part in before starting work on *Thriller*. The number was a cover of a song by Jon Anderson and Vangelis (*The Friends of Mr Cairo*, 1981) and retained all its original reggae/Afro-Caribbean style in this new version. The producer strongly intensified the lyrics' message of love and unity by bringing in a spellbinding "All Star Choir" which contained so many famous names that Michael Jackson's voice cannot clearly be picked out. The sessions were filmed and used as a preamble to another project that would take shape a few years later: *We Are the World*.

The single *State of Independence* was a particular success in Europe. It repeatedly took the European charts by storm in multiple remixed versions, thus constantly reiterating its universal message.

Diana Ross arrives at the Oceans ceremony with Michael Jackson (Los Angeles, 31 March 1981).

FOR JACKSON ADDICTS

A live version of *Muscles* can be heard on the 1989 album *Diana Ross—Greatest Hits Live*. In 2014, the 1982 album *Silk Electric* was reissued in the collection *The Soul Funk Classics* with several bonus tracks including *Muscles (edited version)* (4'03) and *Muscles (12-inch version)* (6'38).

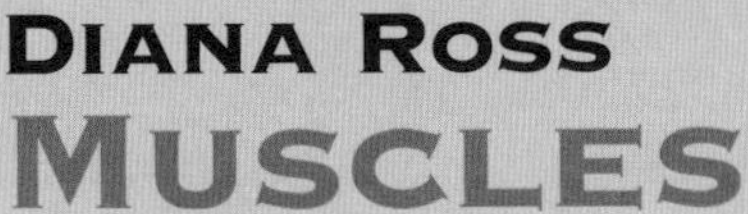

DIANA ROSS
MUSCLES

Michael Jackson / 4'36

From the album: *Silk Electric* / **Released by RCA Records:** USA (ref. AFL1-4384) and UK (ref. EAST 27313) September 1982 / **Chart position:** USA R&B No. 5, Pop No. 27 / UK No. 33 / **RIAA:** certified Gold 14 December 1982 / **Single: Released by RCA Records:** USA, 17 September 1982 (ref. PB-13348) / UK, October 1982 (ref. CL 268) / **Chart position:** USA R&B No. 4, Pop No. 10 / UK No. 15 / **Recording: Hollywood Sound Recorders, Los Angeles:** (unknown) / **Michael Jackson:** producer (Mijac Music)

Michael Jackson wrote *Muscles* especially for his musical godmother, friend, and confidante, Diana Ross. "I was coming back from England working on Paul McCartney's album, zooming along on the Concorde, and this song popped into my head," he recalled in 1982. "I said, 'Hey, that's perfect for Diana!' I didn't have a tape recorder or anything so I had to suffer for like three hours. Soon as I got home I whipped that baby on tape."[68] The artist asked his colleague and friend Bill Wolfer to join him in the studio to make the song. Speaking to *Invincible Magazine* in 2015, Wolfer recalled:

> Michael called me, told me he was producing a song for Diana Ross, and could I come play some synthesizer. Of course, I was happy to do it, I'd been a fan of hers from way back. Sadly, she wasn't at the studio that day. It was Michael and I, the engineers, and Michael's assistant, Nelson Hayes, and Muscles, Michael's enormous boa constrictor. Yes, the song was inspired by and named for his pet snake. For most of the session, Muscles was sleeping in this big pillowcase, but then Michael got him out, and asked me if I wanted to hold him. This snake was so big and heavy, it took both Michael and Nelson to lift it up and drape it around my shoulders. It must have weighed close to 70 pounds. After a minute, the snake started squeezing my neck, getting a tighter grip on me. I told Michael, "Get this thing off of me!" They laughed, and took him off. They thought it was very funny, I wasn't so sure. As far as the work that day, I was coming in after the basic tracks had been laid, and overdubbing some synthesizer parts. As always, it was fun to work with Michael, but I remember that snake more than anything else.[42]

Diana Ross recorded her voice during another session. The song does not refer to a snake, but to a man: indeed, to the man of Miss Ross's dreams. She doesn't want to know whether he will be young or old; she just wants him handsome and with muscles the whole length of his body, as the song's lyrics put it.

A video directed by Paul Justman visually portrayed the diva's dreams of seduction. The musical clip was judged to be a little too provocative in comparison with other productions of the early 1980s.

Nevertheless, the song earned Diana Ross a Grammy Awards nomination in the best female R&B vocal performance category.

When performing *Muscles* on tour, the singer did not hesitate to have a few men come on stage alongside her. She would willingly rip open their T-shirts and encourage them to flex their muscles to show them off.

PORTRAIT

PAUL MCCARTNEY
THIS IS THE MAN

James Paul McCartney was born in Liverpool, United Kingdom, on 18 June 1942. After the premature death of his mother, he was very soon encouraged by his father to play music—initially the trumpet, which he eventually dropped to switch to the acoustic guitar. He wrote a few songs before he met John Lennon in 1957. Their duo was soon enlarged with the arrival of George Harrison and Ringo Starr, and thus The Beatles were born. The group's popularity soon grew beyond the Liverpool city limits, becoming a worldwide phenomenon in the mid-1960s. From then on, the music of The Beatles entered the collective unconscious, with songs such as *Strawberry Fields Forever, Something, Hey Jude, Let It Be, Yesterday*, and *Come Together*. The group broke up in September 1969, when John Lennon decided to leave. Paul officially announced The Beatles' breakup when he embarked on his solo career in April 1970, launching the band Wings.

Meeting

Michael Jackson and Paul McCartney met for the first time on 24 March 1975, on board the *Queen Mary*, which was moored at Long Beach, Los Angeles, and where Paul was celebrating the completion of Wings' fourth album, *Venus and Mars*. The ex-Beatle was struck by how the young singer radiated energy and talent. They met again a year later, on 24 June 1976, at a party in Beverly Hills, to which all the Jackson brothers had been invited. McCartney told Michael Jackson that he had written a song for him: *Girlfriend*. "We shook hands amid a huge crowd of people, and he said, 'You know, I've written a song for you.' I was very surprised and thanked him. And he started singing *Girlfriend* to me at this party. So we exchanged phone numbers and promised to get together soon, but different projects and life just got in the way for both of us and we didn't talk again for a couple of years. He ended up putting the song on his own album *London Town*."[2]

The song finally found its way to Quincy Jones, who felt it was an obvious choice for Michael Jackson, who included it on his album *Off the Wall*.

Hitting it off together

Girlfriend was just the start of a dazzling collaboration, and the songs Paul McCartney and Michael Jackson wrote together during the first half of the 1980s have gone down in musical history. The came together again at the end of the 1980s, when the young prodigy decided to call the older musician to declare his artistic passion: "Let's get together and write some hits."[69] *The Girl Is Mine* (*Thriller*, 1982), *Say Say Say*, and *The Man* (*Pipes of Peace*, 1983) sealed a strong artistic friendship, the first two becoming worldwide hits. As for *The Man*, it was not released as a single and had a lower profile.

The ATV catalog

In 1985, Michael Jackson consolidated his dominant position on the musical scene by investing in the rights to various songs. He acquired some of the ATV catalog, which included most of The Beatles' songs. The shrewd businessman that he had become overshadowed the friendly relations he had with the ex-Beatle. Ironically, it had been Paul McCartney himself who had shown him it was worth investing in rights, by speaking highly of the work of his new music publishing venture, MPL Communications.

"I was staying with Paul and Linda at their house in the country when Paul told me about his own involvement in music publishing. He handed me a little book with MPL printed on the cover. He smiled as I opened it, because he knew I was going to find the contents exciting. It contained a list of all the songs Paul owns and he'd been buying the rights to songs for a long time. I had never given the idea of buying songs any thought before. When the ATV music publishing catalog, which contains many Lennon-McCartney songs, went on sale, I decided to put in a bid."[2]

Nevertheless, Paul McCartney took this with dignity and was always unstinting in his praise when speaking of Michael Jackson's genius and commitment to work. In 2009, on TV with David Letterman, he even laughed at the fact that his advice had backfired, saying: "He was a lovely man, massively talented, and we miss him."[70]

Paul McCartney poses in the streets of New York in 1982.

Michael Jackson was always protective of his share of the Sony/ATV catalog, which he bought for $47.5 million in 1985 and firmly refused to sell. However, in 2017 the executors of his will, attorneys John Branca and John McClain, proceeded with the sale of his most precious asset, which realized $750 million.

The finest tribute

Today Paul McCartney has the distinction of having paid Michael Jackson the finest of all the artistic tributes since his death. In October 2015, on the bonus DVD with the deluxe reissue of his album *Pipes of Peace*, he included a montage of images shot by his wife, Linda, in 1981 when Michael Jackson visited them at their country house in Sussex. The reissue's promotion was based on a completely new mixing of the hit *Say Say Say* (*Say Say Say 2015 Remix*), in which the two singers' voices have changed places in comparison to the original version, and Michael Jackson's is brought into the foreground delicately and with subtlety. The video clip jumps back a generation, showing a child gliding, twirling, and dancing through city streets like a future mega star in the making.

Michael Jackson's collaboration with Paul McCartney remained the most productive of his career. It was an inspired meeting between two geniuses who became friends, and went beyond the rules of mere business.

PAUL McCARTNEY AND MICHAEL JACKSON

SAY, SAY, SAY

Paul McCartney, Michael Jackson / 3'55

From the album: *Pipes of Peace* / **Released by Columbia Records:** USA, 31 October 1983 (ref. 39149) / **Released by Parlophone Records:** UK, 31 October 1983 (ref. 1652301) / **Chart position:** USA R&B No. 49, Pop No. 15 / UK No. 4 / **RIAA:** certified Gold 9 January 1984 / certified Platinum 17 February 1984 / **Single: Released by RCA Records:** USA (ref. 38-04168) and UK (ref. R 6062), 3 October 1983 / **Chart position:** USA R&B No. 2, Pop No. 1 / UK No. 2 / **Musicians: Michael Jackson:** lead vocals / **Paul McCartney:** lead vocals and bass guitar / **Bill Wolfer:** keyboard / **Gary Herbig:** saxophone / **Ricky Lawson:** drums / **David Williams:** guitar / **Chris Smith:** harmonica / **Jerry Hey, Ernie Watts, and Gary Grant:** brass / **Recording: AIR Studios and Odyssey Studios, London:** May to September 1981 / **Cherokee Studios, Los Angeles, and Sigma Sound Studios, New York:** (unknown) / **AIR Studios, London: mixing,** 15 February 1983 / **Technical team: Producer:** George Martin / **Recording engineers:** Geoff Emerick, assisted by Jon Jacobs (AIR Studios), and Jon Kelly, assisted by Teri Reed (Odyssey Studios) / **Arrangements:** Paul McCartney and George Martin / **Mixing:** Geoff Emerick, assisted by Jon Jacobs

THE SONG

Genesis

Paul McCartney admitted, with amusement, that he thought he was dealing with a pestering fan the first time Michael Jackson called him on his private line. Initially suspicious, he refused to believe it was Michael on the line. It was an unusual introduction, and typical of the jokes and teasing that punctuated the short film of *Say Say Say*.

Mary McCartney, Paul's daughter, recalled how her idol visited the family home when she was a child and she almost fainted when she was told he was coming. She relates how her parents welcomed Michael Jackson, and reminisces about the precious moments she shared with him, riding on horseback in the family paddock: "Mum took lots of pictures. He and Dad were going to write together and see what happened."[71]

For a long time, little was known about the writing of *Say Say Say*. Secrets began to be gradually revealed from 2014, when Bill Wolfer gave an interview to the French magazine *Invincible*. In 2015, more information was forthcoming, revealed by Paul McCartney's technical team in the booklet accompanying the deluxe reissue of the album *Pipes of Peace*. Accounts varied regarding the degree of creative and musical commitment on the part of the two artists, depending on whether they came from the Jackson or McCartney camp. This partnership still has its fair share of mystery as regards the two artists' exact input.

At the start of 1983, Michael Jackson was ubiquitous on the world musical scene. Following the success of the first duet with Paul McCartney in *The Girl Is Mine*—which became the first single released from the album *Thriller*, in October 1982, and a Gold record in January 1983—*Billie Jean* followed suit, with its unique, original clip. The children's album *E.T. Storybook*, which the singer made with Quincy Jones and Steven Spielberg, entered the Top 100 albums the following month. It was a favorable moment for Michael Jackson and Paul McCartney, who publicly announced their artistic collaboration for the first time at the British Record Industry Awards, on 8 February 1983 at the Grosvenor House Hotel, London. The ex-Beatle received several awards, and the American accepted an award on behalf of Barbra Streisand, who was unable to attend.

In *Say Say Say*, the two artists came together on one of their favorite subjects: love. Thwarted love, difficult love, unrequited love: the protagonist laments and then begs his beloved to return to his side. The context of his fiancée's leaving is left vague, which makes the protagonist seem like a smooth talker who is trying to make amends. His pleas come one after another: "Don't leave me with no direction"; then intensify: "You know I'm crying," "You can never say that I'm not the one who really loves you"; and finally become almost funny, or laughable: "Standing here, baptized in all my tears." This is the secret of the light touch of this piece, sung as a duet. The verbal sparring of the two singers reinforces the echo of this lament. The passage of the singing from one to the other disconcerts the listener, and increases the confusion and credibility of the singers' appeal to this woman.

This photo appeared on the back of the single's sleeve. Paul McCartney and Michael Jackson pose for Linda McCartney at a studio console.

Production of the original version

On 14 October 2015 the official Paul McCartney website published a filmed interview in which the British singer recalls the beginning of their musical collaboration, when Michael Jackson first visited him in 1981:

> We went upstairs, there's a little piano upstairs, and we just sat around, like, a guitar, the piano, and we just said right, so what shall we do? So we just started, like you do, and…I was on the piano…but I had the guitar in case I wanted to show some line or something. Yeah, so, we just did it upstairs, and it came very easily. 'Cos I was quite excited to write with him, he was quite excited to write with me, so we were poppin' off each other and, um, so we just did it, as I say. It was quite a short session, and we were in the same room, face to face…it was live and…I just wrote the lyrics down, you know, and said: "OK, that's it."[69]

In October 2014, Bill Wolfer, the keyboard player on the song, was the first to share his recollection of the making of *Say Say Say*. He related how Michael Jackson called to ask him to make a finished demo using a cassette on which he and Paul McCartney had recorded their two voices plus a single guitar line. Bill Wolfer described in detail the process of making the demo, explaining how the rhythm had been worked out on a Linn LM-1, before a basic version was laid on a four-track recorder using a Rhodes piano, with bass notes and percussion played on a synthesizer. This initial demo was used in the studio a few days later to lay Nate Watts's bass line and Ricky Lawson's drums. Those same lines had originally been given to the drummer Jonathan Moffett and bass player Mike McKinney, who were regulars on the Jacksons' tours, but their experience of live performance did not suit the more rigorous discipline of the studio. David Williams came on the scene later to overdub some guitar. Little by little the demo was completed, with the addition of further overdubs on the synthesizer, a brass track, and a harmonica solo by Chris Smith. The harmonica player remembered his astonishment at finding himself in the studio with Michael Jackson, who was standing close to him and began to sing into his ear. Nevertheless, he still managed to wrap it up in one take. Gradually, the young star began to admit to Bill Wolfer that he wanted to produce a complete 24-track recording, in the hope that Paul McCartney would use this version. All that would remain was to add their voices and mix everything. And this sophisticated demo did indeed become the final version, just as he'd hoped—with the difference that the bass line by Nate Watts was replaced by a new track played by the ex-Beatle.

FOR JACKSON ADDICTS

In 1983 the song was published as a cassette in Germany, in unique packaging, probably the first of its kind in the history of the single. The format was identical to that of a maxi single but in a 12-inch cutout cardboard (ref. Odeon–1C K 262-1653994).

John "Jellybean" Benitez produced two remixes for *Say, Say, Say*: a long version (5'40) and an instrumental version (7'00) available on maxi singles released at the time.

When the cassette with this demo on it reached Paul McCartney's team and they listened to it, they were very surprised at how well finished it was. The British team then decided to fly to Los Angeles to rework the brass with Jerry Hey, Ernie Watts, and Gary Grant. At the same time, work began on *The Girl Is Mine*. According to Gary Herbig, who played saxophone in the session at the Cherokee Studios, "Ernie Watts, Gary Grant, and Jerry Hey made for a fabulous horn section."[71] The recording engineer Jon Jacobs told how, when they returned to Abbey Road Studios in London to resume work, the box containing the Ampex tape with the recording was missing from the trolley. He recalled that a veritable gale of panic swept through the studio, before it was found in a corridor a few minutes later.

After this, it was Michael Jackson's turn to visit London to record in the studio. According to Jon Jacobs, when the new version was played to him, the American was extremely satisfied with the result and danced for joy. He took part in the mixing with George Martin, Geoff Emerick, and Jon Jacobs. At the time, it was impossible to perform this operation automatically. The studio console was so large that the singer joined in manipulating the controls, to help Jacobs with this complex task.

Paul McCartney recalled: "Me, Michael, and George Martin, we sort of all produced *Say Say Say* ...Michael was big, but he was not as big as he was going to be. He'd done *Off the Wall* when I met him, but it was pre-*Thriller*. It was kind of an early period for him. So it was mutually beneficial, and it was good fun..."[71]

Production of the 2015 version

In 2015, for the deluxe reissue of the album *Pipes of Peace* from the *Paul McCartney Archive Collection*, the big surprise was a new mix of the song that turned out to be completely different. At the ex-Beatle's request, Steve Orchard, the engineer responsible, had made use of the previously unused vocal parts and switched the verses that the two singers sang. He had decided to use as the instrumental base the remix by the DJ John "Jellybean" Benitez, which was longer than the original version and had been pressed, at the time, on a maxi single. But the biggest novelty was a technical one: the mix had never been given the multitrack treatment. Steve Orchard had been forced to recreate it from scratch. In the end, the backing vocals from the original multitrack had been used to optimize the instrumental mix. The final mix had been entrusted to Spike Stent in order to give a new dimension to the resounding bass notes that had suffered in earlier CDs featuring the song. Mastering was carried out by Alex Wharton, using a 1972 EMI TG 1.2k analog console with a 91Hz sharp EQ coupled with a Shadow Hills compressor, to produce a very clear compression with excellent bass conversion. Digitization was carried out on a Junger Accent 2.

THE ORIGINAL SHORT FILM

Director: Bob Giraldi
Producer: Antony Payne
Lead actors: Paul McCartney and Michael Jackson
Supporting actors: Linda McCartney and La Toya Jackson
Cameos: Bob Giraldi, Art Carney, and Harry Dean Stanton
Shooting dates: October 1983
Shoot locations:
- Antique Depot in Los Alamos, California (vaudeville sequences);
- Union Hotel in Los Alamos, California (bar scene and room where the protagonists shave);
- Sycamore Valley Ranch in Los Olivos, Santa Barbara County, California (numerous sequences, including those of the intro and in the orphanage).

Duration: 4'58

Genesis

The short film's vaudeville atmosphere is charming in its freshness and light touch. The two biggest stars of pop play opposite each other, and their rapport shines through. The script was designed to convey the friendship and camaraderie that then existed between Paul McCartney and Michael Jackson. While the former is impressive in his maturity, the latter's candor and innocence shine through, bringing balance to the duet

Contrary to rumours, Jackson and McCartney remained friends over the years. They are shown here backstage on the Beatle's World Tour in late 1989.

On 7 October 2015 the official Paul McCartney website published an exclusive video of the song's new mix. It features impeccable photography directed by Ryan Heffington, and has a freshness thanks to the young dancers. The video's connecting thread is a young boy wandering through a poor city neighborhood. He dances and glides like a budding Michael Jackson, meets some friends and taunts a group of girls. A series of dance-offs follow, culminating in a "battle" in the final sequence, reminiscent of the clip *Love Never Felt So Good*.

and forging a link between the 1960s legend and the 1980s pop icon.

In a rural Americana setting, Mac and Jack (McCartney and Jackson) play traveling conmen who sell potions that, they claim, endow people with the colossal strength of a raging bull. After staging a fake demonstration of this, they pocket the public's cash and promptly sneak off. However, their misdeed is excusable, because the money obtained by dishonest means is destined for a nearby orphanage. Their adventures later lead them to perform in a cabaret, with the help of a charming Linda McCartney, who is sometimes at the piano to accompany the company's performances and at other times an accomplice in their mischief, crying "Fire!" to disperse the crowd as fast as possible. La Toya Jackson plays the part of a beautiful young woman whom Michael has spotted in the crowd. In the backstage scene, they get ready in a room of the Union Hotel in Los Alamos, which today has been kept as it was during the shooting and can be visited, much to the joy of fans. The video ends in the back of a pick-up truck, as they head off for further exploits. Most of the short film was shot at Sycamore Valley Ranch in Los Olivos, Santa Barbara County, California, which Michael Jackson would buy in the late 1980s and there build his dream home, Neverland.

Production

The budget for this cinematic adventure has been estimated at almost $327,000. Bob Giraldi recalled the atmosphere of camaraderie on the set of *Say Say Say*. The actors really seemed to enjoy working together, and the director captured this friendship on film: "Paul decided to dab Michael's unsuspecting face with shaving cream. The look on Michael's face said it all. I used it in the final edit. Nice memories."[71]

Jeffrey Hornaday, who choreographed the video, also remembered this bond. He related how, while the film crew was setting up, Paul picked up an old acoustic guitar, which was there in all probability because of its old-time appearance rather than its musical quality; it was fretless, with just some hand-cut ridges on the fingerboard. Nevertheless, he got hold of some strings and strung it in order to play. Michael gave a great big smile and started singing with him an improvised, acoustic version of *Say Say Say*.

Choreography is not a major element of this clip. Nevertheless, Michael Jackson and Paul McCartney execute a few steps that are half 1930s swing and half cabaret in American Western style—and are soon followed by the pop star's unique style of dancing.

Paul McCartney, his wife, Linda, and Michael Jackson at the British Record Industry Awards in London, 16 February 1983.

PAUL McCARTNEY AND MICHAEL JACKSON

THE MAN

Paul McCartney, Michael Jackson / 3'54

From the album: *Pipes of Peace* / **Released by Columbia Records:** USA, 31 October1983 (ref. 39149) / **Released by Parlophone Records:** UK, 31 October 1983 (ref. 1652301) / **Chart position:** USA R&B No. 49, Pop No. 15 / UK No. 4 / **RIAA:** certified Gold 9 January 1984 / certified Platinum 17 February 1984 / **Musicians: Paul McCartney and Michael Jackson:** lead vocals / **Dave Mattacks:** drums / **Linda McCartney:** backing vocals / **Recording: AIR Studios, London:** May to September 1981 / **Sigma Sound Studios, New York:** (unknown) / **AIR Studios, London**: mixing, 8 June 1983 / **Technical team: Producer:** George Martin / AIR / **Arrangements:** Paul McCartney and George Martin / **Recording engineers:** Geoff Emerick, assisted by Jon Jacobs (AIR Studios) / **Mixing:** Geoff Emerick, assisted by Jon Jacobs

Paul McCartney's album *Pipes of Peace* contains a second duet with his friend Michael Jackson. Linda McCartney accompanies them on backing vocals, as if to affirm all their happiness in sharing these moments of creativity. Work on the song shuttled back and forth between the UK and the US several times before being completed, almost two years after it was first written. This ballad, with its simple pop sound, describes a new start in a man's life, without really telling the listener the cause. Less well known than *Say Say Say*, *The Man* was meant to be released as a single, but CBS decide to cancel the release so as not to overshadow the success of *Thriller.* A handful of countries, such as Peru, did, however, see the single's release. An acetate master disc (used to create metal "stamper" molds for pressing vinyl) was even sold at auction in the early 2000s, proof that there had indeed been plans for such a single. The acetate disc's label listed a new version of the song, lasting 5'58; this version remains unreleased to this day.

On the bonus DVD with the 2015 deluxe edition of the album *Pipes of Peace*, *The Man* is the soundtrack to the video of Michael Jackson's visit to Paul McCartney's home in 1981.

FOR JACKSON ADDICTS

In Mexico, a superb promotional single was released. The sleeve showed Paul McCartney and Michael Jackson in the short film *Say Say Say* (the shaving scene). The title on the sleeve, in Spanish, reads: *Paul McCartney con Michael Jackson—El Hombre–The Man* (EMI SEC-229).

Michael poses with Rockwell during the *Victory* tour on 2 December 1984.

FOR JACKSON ADDICTS

The instrumental version of this song on a maxi single extended the song to 5'26.

ROCKWELL
SOMEBODY'S WATCHING ME

Rockwell / 5'01

From the album: *Somebody's Watching Me* / **Released by Motown Records:** USA (ref. 6052ML) and Europe (ref. ZL 72147), 26 January 1984 / **Chart position:** R&B No. 5, Pop No. 15 / UK No. 52 / **RIAA:** certified Gold 29 March 1984 / **Single: Released by Motown Records:** USA (ref. 1702 MF) and UK (ref. TMG 1331), 14 January 1984 / **Chart position:** USA R&B No.1, Pop No. 2 / UK No. 6 / **RIAA:** certified Gold 29 March 1984 / **Musicians: Michael Jackson:** backing vocals (his name does not officially appear in the song's credits for contractual reasons) / **Recording: Mars Recording Studios, Los Angeles:** (unknown) / **Technical team: Producers:** Curtis Anthony Nolan and Rockwell / **Arrangements:** Curtis Anthony Nolan and Rockwell / **Recording engineers:** Arne Frager / **Mixing:** Arne Frager, Curtis Anthony Nolan and Rockwell

Kennedy William Gordy, known as Rockwell, is the son of Berry Gordy, founder of Motown Records (see page 22). He is believed to have used a pseudonym so as to approach Motown incognito and avoid accusations of nepotism being leveled at his father—who reportedly was surprised at his son securing a contract.

He wrote *Somebody's Watching Me* in two days. The song is based on a personal memory of a neighbor who constantly watched him from his window. It also mentions an ex-girlfriend whom he liked to scare, as a joke, by stealing silently into the bathroom while she was washing her hair in the shower and suddenly pressing his face against the shower's side.

Rockwell, whose sister Hazel is married to Jermaine Jackson, then traveled to Encino to play his new creation his brother-in-law's family. Speaking to *Rolling Stone* magazine in 2016, he said: "I performed it about eight or nine times... Michael says, 'Hey Rebbie! Hey Janet! You gotta hear this song Kennedy did.' Every time we stopped the song, Michael called three more people down. Afterwards, Michael pulled me to the side and says, 'Kennedy, I gotta talk to you for a second. Who are you going to get to sing background vocals?' I said, 'Why don't you do it?' It worked just like that."[72]

Rockwell added that Jermaine also added his voice to the song's final version. Bizarrely, though, only Michael Jackson's voice can be heard in *Somebody's Watching Me*. The song, considered an example of "paranoid pop," was released as a single and was a resounding success. A video, made by Francis Delia, supported the song's theme and promotion. The clip followed in the spooky, creepy footsteps of the *Thriller* short film.

VICTORY

1. TORTURE*
2. WAIT*
3 ONE MORE CHANCE
4. BE NOT ALWAYS*
5. STATE OF SHOCK*
6. WE CAN CHANGE THE WORLD
7. THE HURT*
8. BODY

* Only those songs with which Michael Jackson was significantly involved are covered in the following pages.

Victory **ALBUM**

Released by Epic Records: USA and UK, 2 July 1984
(US ref. QE 38946 and UK ref. EPC 86303)
Chart position: R&B No. 3, Pop No. 4 / UK No. 3
RIAA: certified Platinum on 30 October 1984

Tito, Marlon, Jermaine, Randy, and Michael in the finale of *Wanna Be Startin' Somethin'* on the *Victory* tour, 1984.

VICTORY, SIX BROTHERS REUNITED BUT DIVIDED

For the TV show *Motown 25: Yesterday, Today, Forever*, which aired on 25 March 1983 to celebrate the 25th anniversary of Berry Gordy's record label, the Jackson brothers prepared a special number. The group was joined on stage by Jermaine for the first time since 1975 (other than the somewhat fleeting appearance alongside his brothers for the televised performance of *Destiny* on the late-night show *Midnight Special* in 1979). He had just quit Motown for Arista, the record label managed by Clive Davies, and he was working on a new album.

The "comeback" performance given by the six brothers certainly made an impact: America rediscovered its much-loved kids performing a set masterfully controlled by Michael, who danced his first moonwalk to *Billie Jean*. Behind the scenes, Katherine and Joe Jackson had tears in their eyes, with Joe seeming the most affected. The head of the family realized that there was still business to be done with his talented offspring, and he planted the seed of a final mammoth project. Once the show was recorded, he gathered his sons together to sell them the idea of a family tour. It was likely to be an uphill struggle. The breakdown of the relationship between Michael and his brothers, which dated from *Off the Wall*, seemed irretrievable once *Thriller* started beating all the records. The weeks passed, and the discussions were going well. Initially, Michael refused. Joe asked Katherine to step in. As a loyal wife, she did so, and persuaded her son to help his brothers on the stage one last time.

The plan for a world tour called *Victory* slowly and painfully took shape. So began the various power struggles, culminating in Michael's decision to fire his manager, Ron Weisner. The result was that, in early summer 1983, the young star found himself with no one to turn to when it came to making important choices in his solo career.

Genesis of the *Victory* album

The release of the second-to-last album that The Jacksons were contracted to record with Epic was postponed on numerous occasions due to the success of *Thriller*. It was finally slated for release in late 1983. Michael Jackson was completely preoccupied by his solo activities, and announced right from the start that he would not be as involved in the family project as he had been with previous albums.

The album was named after a song composed by Michael Jackson that he had originally recorded with Freddie Mercury. But Michael had found it difficult to reach any sort of creative agreement with the Queen frontman, as the two men had very different artistic visions. At the 16th International Convention of Queen's fan club at Prestatyn in Wales in 2001, Greg Brooks, Queen's archivist, confirmed the existence of this mysterious track. The two singers also worked together on other compositions that were not officially published in their lifetimes.

Victory was the only record that officially reunited the six Jackson brothers. For the occasion, the group dropped the "The" and simply called themselves "Jacksons" on the album sleeve. Nelson Hayes, a long-standing friend and assistant to the artists, was responsible for coordinating the recording of the album. But behind the reunion that brought the original group back together lay many conflicts of interest, which were amplified by Michael's growing solo success. The recording sessions took place between November 1983 and May 1984. The pre-

1984

Marlon and Michael Jackson during one of the many breaks in *Working Day and Night* on the *Victory* tour, 1984.

paration and design of the record ended up being a legal and artistic tug-of-war in which the siblings tried to grab a slice of the cake. Each brother included one of his own compositions, ensuring that he was credited as producer and arranger. *Victory* was essentially a lawyers' and financiers' album whose sales ensured substantial royalties for the Jackson brothers. The days when the boys from Gary were happy just to sing were long gone. The hard-won artistic independence of *Destiny* was replaced by protocols and contracts signed by each participant.

Marketing and promotion of the album was a total headache. Michael Jackson made it clear that he wanted to remain in the background, and even asked the artist Michael Whelan to ensure that his image on the album sleeve was kept discreet. He refused to film the videos that had been planned for the singles. And to top it all, during rehearsals for the tour, it was decided—unbelievably—that none of the songs from the album would be performed on stage.

When *Victory* appeared in stores on 2 July 1984, fans discovered a Tetris consisting of eight tracks strung in a row like pearls without a unifying thread. Thanks to the Jacksonmania generated by *Thriller*, the album nevertheless managed to go double Platinum in the United States after four months. Final worldwide sales peaked at four million, ten times less than *Thriller*.

6 July 1984, Kansas City: the *Victory* tour begins

In 1984, the Jacksons copied the Rolling Stones' strategy by producing an album as a pretext for a tour. It was the last tour that Michael Jackson would do with his brothers. Hot on the heels of the Fourth of July festivities, the American public were treated to the Jacksons' new concert. At the Arrowhead Stadium in Kansas City, more observant audience members noticed that the show was just a variation of *Triumph*, the previous tour. The hits from *Off the Wall* were replaced by the hits from *Thriller*, although Michael refused to perform the title track for fear of attracting the wrath of Jehovah's Witnesses.

Like the album, the show highlighted the huge abyss between the singer and his brothers. Jermaine managed to slip in a solo set at the concert, but struggled to arouse the crowd. *Tell Me I'm Not Dreamin'*, the only post-*Thriller* song performed, brought Michael and Jermaine together in a duet. The group's former lead singer launched into the first verse, but some found his performance lacking, and felt that he had to be saved by his younger brother's abilities on stage.

The charts showed a similar trend: *State of Shock*, the first single from the album, was certified Gold, and reached No. 3 on *Billboard*. But apart from *Torture*, which slipped into the Top 20 at No. 17, the other tracks went unnoticed.

A family in conflict

The lengthy *Victory* tour continued throughout the summer and fall of 1984. Every public appearance confirmed Michael as an artist in his own right, a star with his family meekly trailing along in his wake. The Jacksons were now a group in name only, and the issues dividing the brothers could only be resolved through the intervention of the various lawyers. Michael poached Epic's head of promotion, Frank DiLeo, to become his manager in April 1984. DiLeo was a marketing genius who became the King of Pop's staunch right-hand man, helping him to negotiate the *Victory* project in his best interests.

On 9 December 1984, at the Dodger Stadium in Los Angeles, The Jacksons gave their last concert. After the finale,

During the *Victory* tour, Michael Jackson performed the greatest hits on *Thriller* live for the first time. Here, he sings *Beat It* (1984).

Shake Your Body, Michael took the opportunity to make the split official: "This is our farewell tour, you've all been wonderful, it's been a long twenty years and we love you all!" The brothers looked surprised, but the show went on for the last time. When he slipped discreetly off the stage, the pop prodigy was finally free to devote himself entirely to his own projects.

Victory and the first issues

The *Victory* project would cause Michael Jackson a great deal of stress and anxiety. When his father first got the ball rolling on the family tour, he hired the services of Don King, the boxing promoter with a controversial past, known for his brash sense of humor and tendency to bluff with tragi-comic results. This so-called businessman was utterly unscrupulous and dreamt up a preposterous ticket sales system that forced fans to pay $120 upfront for four tickets that they were not even certain of winning in a draw set up for the purpose. Unlucky fans would end up with no ticket and no money (although not everyone involved was a loser!). The singer insisted that these dubious ticket sales had to stop, and he announced the day before the first concert that his tour proceeds would be donated to charity.

Several months earlier, on 27 January 1984, at the Shrine Auditorium in Los Angeles, the Jacksons had filmed a commercial for Pepsi-Cola, sponsor of the *Victory* tour. The director Bob Giraldi asked Michael to stand at the top of a staircase, where smoke and special-effects machines were being used to create a screen of sparks, while the cameraman got the best angles. The star did so, but one machine was too close to him and a huge spark hit his heavily gelled hair. As the singer danced down the staircase, he realized his hair was on fire. His brother Tito and his assistant Miko Brando rushed to help. The singer sustained second and third degree burns to the top of his head and was scarred for life. Despite numerous operations, he suffered from frequent pain, which began his need for painkillers. However, Pepsi paid the singer $1.5 million in damages, which he used to open a Michael Jackson Burn Center, in existence for three years.

FOR JACKSON ADDICTS

The music video only featured Jackie, Tito, Marlon, and Randy Jackson. Jermaine refused to appear, instead working on the release of his album *Dynamite*. Michael also declined. So with no flesh-and-blood star on set, the producer Jeff Stein hired a Michael Jackson waxwork from Madame Tussauds Nashville, which appeared twice.

[THE JACKSONS]

TORTURE

Jackie Jackson, Kathy Wakefield / 4'51

Musicians
Michael and Jermaine Jackson: lead vocals
Jackie, Jermaine, Marlon, Michael, Randy, and Tito Jackson: backing vocals
Randy Jackson: keyboards, synthetizers, and percussion
John Barnes: Fairlight synthesizer
Michael Boddicker: keyboards, synthesizers, digital brass, and programming
Jeff Porcaro: drums
Jack Wargo: solo guitar
Jerry Hey: trumpet
Recording
Soundcastle Studios, Silverlake: November 1983 to May 1984
Technical team
Producer: Jackie Jackson
Recording engineer: Bill Bottrell
Assistant recording engineers: Paul Ericksen, Mitch Gibson, Bino Espinoza
Brass arrangements: Jackie Jackson and Jerry Hey
Programming additional synthesizers: David Ervin
Mixing: Bill Bottrell
Project coordination: Nelson Hayes

1984

Single

A-side: *Torture* (*single version*) / 4'30
B-side: *Torture* (*instrumental*) / 4'59
Released by Epic Records: USA, 30 September 1984 (ref. 34-04575) / UK, August 1984 (EPC A 4675)
Chart position: USA R&B No. 12, Pop No. 17 / UK No. 26

Genesis

Cowriting *Can You Feel It,* a noteworthy track in The Jacksons' discography, gave Jackie Jackson increased confidence in his own abilities. Although the song did not excel in the charts, it became one of the group's anthems, a rallying cry at concerts. With this success behind him, the eldest Jackson brother continued the momentum and worked on other tracks. He composed pieces that would mostly be used for his solo album *Be the One* (1989). For *Victory*, he wrote a futuristic funk piece that reused the rhythmic beat of *Can You Feel It*, but with an additional bass line that traced a long decrescendo theme, as if plunging into a world of darkness.

The lyrics were written by Kathy Wakefield. She had learned the ropes at Motown in the late 1960s, and, in 1981, she cowrote *One Hundred Ways* for Quincy Jones' album *The Dude*. The song tells the story of the breakup of a relationship seen through the eyes of a deceived and emotionally tortured boyfriend. Taken literally, the text feels like a fantasy story, somewhere between a dream and a nightmare, where the hero is trapped in the clutches of a fiendish woman.

Jackie had hoped to record *Torture* as a duet with Michael. But Jermaine's return to the group, which was officially announced at the last minute just as the contracts for the *Victory* tour were being drawn up, changed everything. *Torture* was one of the songs presented to Larkin Arnold, an executive at Epic Records, at a meeting held at Epic's headquarters to select the initial tracklist. The record label felt that a Michael-Jermaine duet would appeal to the public in general and to those who were nostalgic for the Motown years. A demo with Jackie and Michael is said to have existed, but no evidence for this has ever been produced.

Production

Randy Jackson helped out during the *Torture* sessions, playing keyboards and percussion to accompany Jeff Pocaro's drums that in turn created a white-hot rhythm. Synthesizer overdubs were laid over the drum track. John Barnes on the Fairlight synthesizer created and distilled some unusual sounds, like the cracking of whips and horrifying shrieks that reinforced the track's fantasy atmosphere.

In addition to all these synthesizers and machines, the producer Bill Bottrell, working with Michael Jackson for the first

Randy, Marlon, Michael, Jermaine, Tito, and Jackie pose for the sleeve of the single *Torture* (1984).

time, called on the services of the king of brass, Jerry Hey, to play the short motif that appears at the end of the chorus, among other places.

Jermaine and Michael shared out the verses between them, creating a contrast that listeners had not heard since The Jackson Five had quit Motown. Ironically, while the two brothers once sung about fraternity and loyalty on *I'll Be There*, they were now singing about a love story with an unhappy ending.

Jackie performs some ad-libs in the last minute of the song. These were not in the album version, but ended up appearing in the mix for the 4'30 single as well as the maxi 45 rpm that ran to 6'15.

[**THE JACKSONS**]

WAIT

David Paich, Jackie Jackson / 5'24

Musicians
Jackie Jackson: lead vocals
Jackie, Jermaine, Marlon, Michael, Randy, and Tito Jackson: backing vocals
David Paich and Steve Porcaro: keyboards and synthesizers
Jeff Porcaro: drums
Steve Lukather: guitar
Lenny Castro: percussion
Recording
Record One Studios and Sunset Sound Recorders, Los Angeles, and Hog Manor Studios (unknown): November 1983 to May 1984
Technical team
Producers: David Paich, Steve Porcaro, and Jackie Jackson
Recording engineer: Tom Knox
Assistant recording engineers: Niko Bolas, Stuart Furusho, Shep Longsdale, and Terry Stewart
Mixing: Greg Ladanyl and Niko Bolas (Record One Studio)
Project coordination: Ivy Skoff (for Toto) and Nelson Hayes (for The Jacksons)

FOR JACKSON ADDICTS

The version pressed as a British single contains an extra synthesizer arrangement played by Paich and Porcaro.

A-side: *Wait (single version)* / 4'17
B-side: *She's out of My Life (Live Triumph Tour 1981 edition)* / 4'49
Released by Epic Records: UK, 10 December 1984 (ref. EPC A 6105)

Genesis

Following the success of *Thriller*, Michael Jackson asked Steve Porcaro from the group Toto to produce two tracks for *Victory*. These were *Wait* with Jackie Jackson, and *The Hurt* with all the brothers. Porcaro, a keyboardist, helped Jackie with the production of *Wait* while David Paich worked on the text with him.

The song was inspired by a complicated relationship that Jackie had with a girl he met in Paris. He invited her to dinner on the Champs-Elysées, but she rejected his advances. In the song, Jackie expresses the impatience of a captivated would-be lover, and incites the listener to hope for a sign of encouragement from the woman. The methodical rhythm sounds like strangled sobs, fueling the lamentation.

Production

All the musicians from Toto were involved in the production, and the tracks were laid down in three different studios. However, despite the immense talent of the instrumentalists, the result is fatally disjointed. Everyone involved clearly worked hard on creating great music on the composition, but somehow no one managed to visualize the overall mix.

A horn sounds out, immediately followed by Jeff Porcaro's drums superimposed over David Paich's and Steve Porcaro's synthesizers. The rhythmic ostinato carries on throughout the piece to the extent that it becomes nerve-shattering. At the first bridge, Steve Lukather plays a wonderful guitar riff, which is unfortunately smothered by the same obstinate line. The song finally takes off at the second bridge. Not a moment too soon, the lyrics "My Pride!" and "Any longer..." sung by Michael Jackson lift the song, saving it from this infernal tempo.

This song features Jackie's vocals but other tracks showcasing each of the brothers' vocals pop up here and there on the album. The lack of coherence and solid production is clearly audible on *Wait*, the fourth and last song on the album to be released as a single. It was only issued in the United Kingdom, where it failed to make the charts.

FOR JACKSON ADDICTS

As well as *Be Not Always*, Michael and Marlon Jackson worked on other songs that were not used on family or solo projects. *Slipped Away* and *Doing Dirty* were two of these tracks that have never been released to date.

BE NOT ALWAYS

Michael Jackson, Marlon Jackson / 5'36

Musicians
Michael Jackson: lead and backing vocals
Greg Porée: acoustic guitar
Robin Renee Ross: viola
Gayle Levant: harp
Recording
Image Recorders and Evergreen Studios, Los Angeles: November 1983 to May 1984
Westlake Recording Studios: mixing, November 1983 to May 1984
Technical team
Producer: Michael Jackson
Recording engineer: Bruce Swedien
Technical director: Matt Forger
Assistants: John Van Nest and Mike Hatcher
String arrangements: Jerry Hey
Conductor: Murray Adler
Mixing: Bruce Swedien
Project coordination: Nelson Hayes

Michael Jackson rested for a few days at the Caribou Ranch, Colorado, in September 1984.

Genesis

Be Not Always originated in 1979 in the family home in Encino. Michael Jackson composed this ballad, with Marlon cowriting the lyrics. This ode to compassion depicts intense scenes of human misery. Michael Jackson sings for those left by the wayside, "Mothers cry, babies die / Helplessly in arms." The ravages of war are described very explicitly. Michael and Marlon denounce the actions of politicians that always leave the weakest paying the price. This labored and excessive outburst is the logical sequel to *Man of War*, an antiwar piece that Gamble and Huff wrote for the group in 1977 (see page 109).

While preparations for *Victory* were in full flow, the artist had some songs up his sleeve that stood to bring some real added value to the project. In a documentary filmed in early 1984 by his personal cameraman, Steve Howell, he cites two tracks, *Buffalo Bill* and *Liberian Girl*. He hints that they could be used on the tracklist for the album. But in the end, quite unexpectedly, he dropped these two compositions, despite his belief that they had great potential, in favor of *Be Not Always*. This was a dreamy ballad at the completely opposite end of the scale to the hits especially created for *Off the Wall* and *Thriller*. *Be Not Always* was probably an outtake from *Triumph*, and was discreetly slotted into *Victory* where it was quietly treasured by hardcore fans of the creator of *Billie Jean*.

Production

The guitarist Greg Porée joined the Jackson brothers in the studio to record *Be Not Always*. He had already contributed to *Time Waits for No One* by The Jacksons and *Night Time Lover* by La Toya in 1980. Michael Jackson summoned Porée to his home in spring 1981, along with the violist Robin Ross. Assisted by his sister Janet, he led the musicians in a jam session recorded on a radio cassette player. The artists were called back in 1983 to finalize *Be Not Always* in the studio. The singer wanted only his vocals, Porée's guitar, and Ross' viola to stand out. The final mix contains a violin score composed by Michael Jackson and conducted by Murray Adler, a versatile violinist who had worked with artists from Dee Dee Bridgewater to Harry Nilsson.

Bruce Swedien added the finishing touches, recorded in the Image Recorders (vocals, guitar, and alto violin) and Evergreen (orchestra and strings). Ross knew nothing about the additional strings until she heard the song on the radio.

FOR JACKSON ADDICTS

The maxi single pressing of *State of Shock* was extended to create a long version of 5'40 and an instrumental version of 4'35. In the UK, the single was released as a picture disc.

[THE JACKSONS]

STATE OF SHOCK

Michael Jackson, Randy Hansen / 4'30

Musicians
Michael Jackson: lead vocals and handclaps
Mick Jagger: lead vocals
Jackie Jackson, Marlon Jackson, Michael Jackson, and Johnny Ray Nelson: backing vocals
David Williams: guitar and bass guitar
Paulinho Da Costa: percussion
Recording
Westlake Recording Studios, Los Angeles, and A&R Recording, New York: November 1983 to May 1984
Technical team
Producer: Michael Jackson
Recording engineer: Bruce Swedien from Brent Averill's 16-track source
Assistant recording engineers: Matt Forger (Los Angeles) and Ollie Cotton (New York)
Technical director: Matt Forger
Linn programming: Michael Jackson
Mixing: Bruce Swedien
Project coordination: Nelson Hayes and Shari Dub

FOR JACKSON ADDICTS

***State of Shock* was the first song issued after the success of *Thriller*. The release of the song was seen as such a major event that a DJ on KIQQ-FM radio (Los Angeles) played the track nonstop for 24 hours.**

1984

A-side: *State of Shock (single version)* / 4'05
B-side: *Your Ways (album version)* / 4'32
Released by Epic Records: USA, 18 June1984 (ref. 34-04503) / UK, June 1984 (ref. EPC A 4431)
Chart position: USA Pop No. 3 / UK No. 14
RIAA: certified Gold 31 August 1984

Genesis

In the early 1980s, Michael Jackson became enthralled by the group Queen and its charismatic frontman Freddie Mercury. He was fascinated by the singer's artistic vision and the theatrical imagery in his stage performances, which marked a milestone on the rock scene. Jackson made multiple visits backstage at Queen concerts. He was seen hanging out with members of the band at the Forum in Los Angeles in July 1980 and September 1982.

The young singer drew inspiration from Queen's set decor for the design of the Jacksons' *Triumph* tour in 1981. He composed a song, *State of Shock*, that he wanted to record with Freddie Mercury. The song is constructed around a heady guitar riff and tells the story of two friends who fall in love with the same girl, pitching them both literally into a state of shock. The concept is the same as *The Girl Is Mine*, but this time it is a rock version. The simple theme is merely a stage setter for a duet between two spectacular voices.

In spring 1983, Freddie Mercury and his personal assistant, Peter Freestone, met the singer at his home in Encino. During a session that lasted six hours, the two artists recorded two demos: *State of Shock* and *There Must Be More to Life Than This*, a ballad for piano and vocals written by Freddie Mercury.

Brent Averill, Michael Jackson's personal recording engineer, recorded this first version of *State of Shock* on a 16-track console. The session was fairly cobbled together as Peter Freestone recalls: "At the start of the track they needed a drum track to keep the beat, and then they added music and instruments to this. Michael had a clever idea for the bass drum beat. He and Freddie were in the control room with the technician, and I spent five minutes banging a toilet door in perfect time!! Somewhere in Michael's vaults there is a tape of me!"[73]

After the session, the two singers kept in touch, but their busy schedules meant that their version of *State of Shock* was never released.

Several months later, in a bid to conquer the pop scene, Michael Jackson resurrected *State of Shock* to record it with another big name on the British rock scene, Mick Jagger. Following on from his musical adventures with Paul McCartney, the artist pulled off a second coup by recording with the lead singer of another great band in the annals of rock music.

Mick Jagger was well aware of the opportunity that this pre-

Mick Jagger and Tina Turner perform *State of Shock* at the Live Aid concert, 13 July 1985, in the John F. Kennedy Stadium, Philadelphia.

sented for him. Although the success of *Tattoo You* in 1981 had guaranteed the Stones a prominent place in the public eye, the group's future was uncertain. At a time when his relationship with Keith Richards was not at its best, the singer had begun working on solo projects—he was already putting together his first album *She's the Boss* when he agreed to sing on *State of Shock*. This partnership with Michael Jackson happened at just the right time for him, and he saw it as a possible springboard.

And so as if by magic, these two heavyweights of the music scene appear together on the sleeve of a 45 rpm, to the delight of Jackson's record label, which was looking for a strong single to launch the *Victory* album.

Production

In early 1984, Brent Averill delivered the 16-track tapes to Bruce Swedien, who was overseeing the production of *State of Shock*. Michael Jackson's vocals were recorded in the Westlake studios. Seth Riggs, his voice coach, helped him to produce notes in an aggressive tone but without destroying the melody.

The fundamentals of the recording as had been designed with Freddie Mercury in Encino were retained. David Williams' bass guitar line and riff were then added. Williams based his sound on the rhythmic tracks to infuse the kind of rock energy similar to that of The Rolling Stones' numbers.

Michael Jackson was seeking a plain raw sound without any particular flourish. The only musicians other than David Williams to contribute to the piece were Paulinho Da Costa and the backing singers. The overall effect may seem a little caricatural, but the sound delivered in *State of Shock* did its job, meeting the requirements of FM radio stations at the time. Bruce Swedien traveled to New York to record Mick Jagger's vocal contribution. Once the mixing had been done, Michael Jackson was disappointed by the vocals contributed by the lead singer of the Stones. He felt that Jagger sang flat and wondered how he had ever made it as a singer: "How did he ever get to be a star? I just don't get it. He doesn't sell as many records as I do."[8] The brief encounter between the two stars generated a few promotional photos for the single.

The song had great commercial potential, but Michael Jackson refused to film a video to promote it. Mick Jagger achieved his highest *Billboard* position ever (No.3) with *State of Shock*. However, despite several attempts, the shadow of The Rolling Stones always loomed large over his solo career.

Michael and his younger brother Randy on stage during the *Victory* tour.

[THE JACKSONS]

THE HURT

Michael Jackson, Randy Jackson, David Paich, Steve Porcaro / 5'20

Musicians
Randy Jackson: lead vocals, keyboards, and synthesizers
Michael, Jackie, Tito, Jermaine, Marlon, and Randy Jackson: backing vocals
David Paich: keyboards and synthesizers
Steve Porcaro: keyboards and synthesizers
Recording
Soundcastle Studios and Can-Am Recorders, Los Angeles, and Hog Manor Studio (unknown): November 1983 to May 1984
Technical team
Producers: The Jacksons, David Paich, and Steve Porcaro
Arrangements: Michael Jackson, Randy Jackson, David Paich, and Steve Porcaro
Recording engineers: Tom Knox and Bill Bottrell
Assistant recording engineers: Shep Longsdale, Paul Ericksen, Bino Espinoza, Brian Malouf, and Ann Calnan
Mixing: Bill Bottrell (Soundcastle Studios)
Conductor: Murray Adler
Project coordination: Ivy Skoff (for Toto) and Nelson Hayes (for The Jacksons)

Toto, craftsmen of the Jackson sound: Jeff Porcaro, David Paich, Steve Lukather, Steve Porcaro, David Hungate, and Bobby Kimball.

Genesis

Randy Jackson was always the most accomplished musician in the family. Having gained his qualification as a bass guitarist, he tried out several instruments and acquired a taste for composition. Although Michael and Randy's composing partnership was less prolific after the release of the album *Triumph* (1980), the two brothers nevertheless continued to share their musical ideas. Over time, Michael Jackson built up a strong relationship with the musicians from the group Toto, who Randy met on several occasions. Regarding how *The Hurt* came into being, the youngest of the Jackson brothers would recall: "I'd be playing one concept for days on the keyboard at David Paich's house, with the drum machine going. One day Michael started singing to it. Jackie joined in, and we worked it until it became a song."[23]

Randy and Michael Jackson, Porcaro, and Paich agreed to develop the song in the studio. Michael left his younger brother to perform the verses and chorus, preferring to sing backing vocals with his other brothers.

The lyrics of *The Hurt* describe a painful relationship. But despite being treated badly, the hero cannot forget the woman he loves. The text contains some of Michael Jackson's typical expressions such as "quench my desire" that he would later use in his solo projects including *Give In to Me* (1991), another tale of unrequited love.

Production

The Jacksons' sound was never as close to electro-funk as it was on *The Hurt.* On this track, Randy Jackson, David Paich, and Steve Porcaro have clearly enjoyed themselves, programming multiple synthesizers to create a dense sound canvas for the tune.

The openly mechanical production gives rise to a cold industrial groove, which comes to life and exudes warmth thanks to Randy's vocals and the filtered backing vocals of the Jackson brothers. *The Hurt* gives an idea of what the *Victory* album would have been like if the group had decided to work with the Toto team on the whole project. Porcaro's and Paich's expertise, along with the Jacksons' intuitive talent, would have created a winning chemistry, which unfortunately does not fully come to fruition anywhere else except on this track.

DUETS WITH OTHER STARS

In the first half of the 1980s, Michael Jackson was very keen to meet and work with other artists, which led to some wonderful collaborations, some with family members and others with music legends or popular contemporary artists. As a songwriter, producer, or just a backing singer, he was constantly analyzing the music scene worldwide, which at the time was rich, eclectic, and extremely prolific. He always enjoyed developing different styles outside the context of his own albums.

FREDDIE MERCURY AND MICHAEL JACKSON
THERE MUST BE MORE TO LIFE THAN THIS

Freddie Mercury / 3'27

From the compilation: *Queen Forever* / **Released by Virgin Records:** USA and Europe, 10 November 2014 (US, ref. 4704085 and UK, ref. 0602547040831) / **Chart position:** USA Top Hard Rock Albums No. 4, Top Rock Albums No. 11 / UK No. 5 / **BPI (British Phonographic Industry):** certified Gold 10 June 2014 / **Musicians: Michael Jackson:** lead vocals / **Freddie Mercury:** lead vocals and piano / **Brian May:** guitar / **Roger Taylor:** drums and percussion / **John Deacon:** bass guitar / **William Orbit:** synthesizers / **Recording:** Family studio in Encino (Michael Jackson vocals), summer 1983 / **Technical team: Producer:** William Orbit / **Recording engineer:** William Orbit / **Assistant recording engineers:** Mack, Brent Averill, Justin Shirley Smith, Joshua J. Macrae, and Kris Fredriksson / **Synthesizer programming:** William Orbit / **Mixing:** William Orbit

In the summer of 1983, Freddie Mercury came to the studio in Encino for a recording session with Michael Jackson. For several hours, they worked together developing the songs *State of Shock, There Must Be More to Life Than This*, and *Victory*. Freddie Mercury's assistant Peter Freestone, who was there that day, said: "[*There Must Be More to Life Than This*] was a Freddie piece he was just working on at this time...Freddie sat at the piano and let Michael try the singing. Where there were no words written, Freddie told Michael to ad-lib, which he did with words about love."[74]

The song celebrates life and denounces all the shortcomings and hatred in our world, including racism, wars, and violations of human rights. It ends with a positive moral message: "A living hope for a world filled with love." Unfortunately for the history of contemporary music, the two men never finalized the joint project. According to the British specialist Chris Cadman, the track was nearly included in the tracklist for Queen's album *Hot Space* (1982, without Michael Jackson), then on the album *The Works* in 1984 (it is not known whether the idea of including a version with Michael Jackson was ever envisaged). Freddie Mercury ended up recording a solo version for his album *Mr Bad Guy* (1985).

In the early 2000s, with the advent of the internet, the recording of the work session that the two men did together, in which the Queen frontman plays the music and Michael Jackson sings, was leaked. Ever since, fans have been hoping for an official release of the song. In 2014, for the compilation album *Queen Forever*, the former members of the group nego-

Freddie Mercury worked on three songs with Michael Jackson during the 1980s: *State of Shock*, *There Must Be More to Life Than This*, and *Victory*.

tiated with Michael Jackson's estate and were granted authorization to use the song. *There Must Be More to Life Than This* (William Orbit Mix) was published in an attempt to bring this virtual duet to life using a number of available sources. This mix, which is now recognized as official, includes only minimal participation by Michael Jackson; it is more of a guest appearance than a real duet between the two legends. As for the original Queen mix, it remains in the group's archives.

FOR JACKSON ADDICTS

In 2014, David LaChappelle produced a video in which the graceful movements of dancer Sergei Polunin contrast with the harsh war scenes that start and end the film.

JERMAINE JACKSON AND MICHAEL JACKSON

TELL ME I'M NOT DREAMIN' (TOO GOOD TO BE TRUE)

Michael Omartian, Bruce Sudano, Jay Gruska / 4'22

From the album: *Jermaine Jackson* (USA and Japan) / *Dynamite* (Europe) / **Released by Arista Records:** USA, 14 April 1984 (ref. AL 8-8203) / UK, start May 1984 (ref. 206317) / **Chart position:** USA R&B No. 1, *Billboard* Dance Club Songs No. 1, Pop No. 19 / UK No. 57 / **RIAA:** certified Gold 10 July 1984 / **Musicians: Jermaine Jackson:** lead and backing vocals / **Michael Jackson:** lead vocals / **Nathan East:** guitar / **John Robinson:** drums / **Michael Omartian:** keyboards / **Ray Parker Jr.:** guitar / **Jermaine Jackson and Michael Omartian:** percussion / **Recording: Soundcastle Recording Studios, Santa Monica**: 1984 / **Technical team: Producer:** Michael Omartian / **Recording engineer:** Bill Bottrell / **Arrangements:** Michael Omartian

Between 1976 and 1982, Jermaine Jackson published no less than seven solo albums at Motown while his brothers released only four. His productions varied enormously in musical quality. Stevie Wonder hailed his genius on the excellent *Let's Get Serious* (1980), his biggest success at Motown. It reached No. 1 on the *Billboard* R&B, and sold two million copies around the world. To his fans' great regret, the next three albums did not recreate the same magic. Jermaine's career was stagnating. In 1981, he made an almost desperate appeal to his brother on the album *I Like Your Style*. The track *I'm My Brother's Keeper* is a melancholic and mawkish ode in which he urges his brother not to forget him.

In 1983, he made up his mind to leave Motown and signed a contract with the Arista Records label, founded by Clive Davies and Barry Manilow. His career took a new turn.

He started studio recording in the middle of Thrillermania, and staked everything on his new production. He was working so hard that he initially refused his father's invitation to join his brothers on the *Victory* project. On the TV show *Friday Night Videos*, Jermaine declared: "Michael and I have sung so many songs together over the years that I thought we should do something on this album. So I was gonna sing the whole song myself and then I thought well maybe this would be a great song for us to sing...He did the second verse, I did the first verse, and we did the bridge switching off and on like we used to do on stuff like *I Want You Back* and *The Love You Save*. That's what people wanted to hear and the song came out so great!"[75]

Jay Gruska, cowriter of the song, recalled the genesis of the song and how it was produced, in the French magazine *Invincible*:

When we started writing it, it was only for Jermaine. Very quickly, within a few weeks, Michael Omartian [cowriter and musician] told me of the possibility that Michael Jackson would do it as a duet and I was excited beyond belief. When the news was confirmed a little while later, we were all very happy. Michael Jackson, by that point, was easily the biggest musical artist in the world, so to have him sing one of our songs was as good as it gets...Since the song was written for one point of view, it is one man singing to one woman. When it became a duet, it is two men singing to either the same woman or each to their own woman, it doesn't really matter. When the rhythm track was recorded, the people in the studio were just Michael Omartian (keyboards), Nathan East (bass), John Robinson (drums), and myself doing the work vocal. (Michael Landau, who was in the band Maxus with me, played guitar but did it at a later date). Jermaine and Michael Jackson were not at that tracking session. My work vocal was basically used to teach them the song. Unfortunately I was not able to attend the vocal session with Michael J. and Jermaine J., which they did together at the same time a few weeks later."[76]

Jermaine Jackson's album was released in April 1984 in the United States and Japan before being issued in Europe under the title *Dynamite*. It has a great musical identity: the first tracks on the album are very energetic, with electro-funk sounds that sparkle, resonate, and delight. The keyboards played by John Barnes, Michael Omartian, and Greg Phillinganes are hugely impressive, and make the album an absolute benchmark in terms of keyboards. The album has many other wonderful gems, including Whitney Houston sing-

Michael and Jermaine together again, on stage at the *Victory* tour.

ing the lead-in backing vocals in *Sweetest Sweetest*, and only just failed to go Platinum. It sold almost 900,000 copies in the United States, nearly two million copies worldwide, and featured on the *Billboard* 200 charts for 49 weeks. The *Victory* tour phenomenon detracted from its success in the United States, while in Europe it continued to be popular after the release of the single, *When the Rain Begins to Fall*, a duet with the singer Pia Zadora (which featured on the soundtrack of the film *Voyage of the Rock Aliens*). The tune was so successful that it was included in subsequent editions of the album.

CBS Records were protective of the success of *Thriller* and refused to allow *Tell Me I'm Not Dreamin' (Too Good to Be True)* to be released as a single. Many promotional versions were in circulation all over the world, which meant the track got a lot of airtime. As an alternative to CBS' refusal to release the track, the song found a slot on the B-side of the single *Do What You Do*. In 1985, *Tell Me I'm Not Dreamin' (Too Good to Be True)* was nominated for a Grammy Award in the category of best R&B performance for a duo or group with vocals.

FOR JACKSON ADDICTS

The instrumental version appears on the B-side of the single *Dynamite*. Strangely, it was not on the 2012 album rerelease.

Rebbie Jackson promotes her first album on the set of the Christmas special of the show *American Bandstand*, 22 December 1984.

On the back of the single, Michael Jackson wrote a rather enigmatic dedication: "To my mannequin friends."

FOR JACKSON ADDICTS

In 2012, Funky Town Grooves USA rereleased an expanded album with 12-inch and instrumental versions (ref. FTG 318).

REBBIE JACKSON
CENTIPEDE

Michael Jackson / 4'25

From the album: *Centipede* / **Released by Columbia/CBS Records:** USA (ref. 39238) and Europe (ref. 25926), 10 October 1984 / **Chart position:** USA *Billboard* 200 No. 63, Top R&B/Hip-Hop Albums No. 13 / **Single: Released by CBS Records:** USA (ref. 38-04547) and UK (ref. A4528), 11 September 1984 / **Chart position :** USA R&B No. 4, Pop No. 2 / **RIAA:** certified Gold 5 May 1992 / **Musicians: Rebbie Jackson:** lead vocals / **Michael Jackson and The Weather Girls:** backing vocals / **John Barnes:** synthesizers / **David Williams:** guitar / **Jerry Kaye:** bugle / **Recording: Yamaha International Recording, Glendale, and Widetrack Recording Studio, Los Angeles**: 1984 / **Technical team: Producer:** Michael Jackson / **Recording engineer:** Matt Forger / **Arrangements:** Michael Jackson / **Drum programming:** John Barnes

Rebbie Jackson made her stage debut alongside The Jackson Five in 1974, during a series of shows that the group performed at the MGM Grand Hotel in Las Vegas, and on the CBS TV variety show, *The Jacksons*, first broadcast in 1976. The show's producer suggested that she should launch a solo career, but the young woman decided against it as she was expecting her second child. At the time, she remained a discreet presence, singing backing vocals on the tracks of some of the big stars of the time such as Betty Wright, The Emotions, Kool and The Gang, and Crystal Wilson.

But at the age of 34, she decided to launch a solo career. Michael Jackson wrote, produced, and did the backing vocals for the song *Centipede* on his sister's very first album. The electro-funk tune, after which the album was named, became a pop-funk classic in the 1980s. The song follows a tradition of tunes like *Muscles* and *Eaten Alive*, composed for Diana Ross. The lyrics take the listener on a crazy journey into a world of hocus-pocus involving strange insect- and reptile-like beasts as metaphors for a very bizarre kind of love. John Barnes' synthesizers go wild throughout the whole tune, David Williams' guitar is languid, and The Weather Girls' (*It's Raining Men*, 1983) vocals make the chorus sound even more intense.

A music video was filmed in support of the single. In the video, Rebbie, visiting a museum, is suddenly transported inside a painting, and her personality abruptly changes. Wearing a striking red dress, she looks demonic and dominating. She embodies desire and has the ability to tame wild animals and charm all the men she comes across. The imagery is quintessentially 1980s in style. The sparkling laser effects were modeled on the ones in The Jacksons' *Torture* video.

With over 500,000 copies sold, *Centipede* was Rebbie Jackson's biggest success. The track unfortunately failed to get off the ground in Europe.

Janet Jackson surrounded by her elder brothers for the recording of the backing vocals in *Don't Stand Another Chance* in Los Angeles, 1984.

JANET JACKSON

DON'T STAND ANOTHER CHANCE

Marlon Jackson, John Barnes / 4'14

From the album: *Dream Street* / **Released by A&M Records:** USA (ref. SP-4962) and UK (ref. AMA 4962), 23 October 1984 / **Chart position:** USA R&B No. 19, Pop No. 147 / **Single: Released by CBS Records:** USA (ref. AM-2660) and Europe (ref. AMS 9782), 13 August 1984 / **Chart position:** USA R&B No. 9 / **Musicians: Janet Jackson:** lead vocals / **Michael Jackson, Jackie Jackson, Tito Jackson, Bino Espinoza:** backing vocals/ **John Barnes:** keyboards / **John Barnes:** Moog bass guitar / **Jonathan Moffett:** Simmons drums / **Recording: Soundcastle Recording Studios and Can-Am Recorders, Los Angeles:** 1984 / **Technical team: Producer:** Marlon Jackson for V.B.M. Productions / **Associated producer:** John Barnes / **Recording engineer:** Bill Bottrell / **Rhythmic arrangements:** Marlon Jackson and John Barnes

After making her debut in the Jackson family shows, Janet appeared in several TV series. In 1982, she signed a four-album contract with the label A&M Records. Her first album, entitled simply *Janet Jackson*, was coproduced by Bobby Watson, and written by Rene Moore and Angela Winbush. The funk numbers *Say You Do* and *Young Love* showcase the young star's vocal talent.

In 1984, for her second album, *Dream Street*, her brother Marlon tried his hand at writing and production (V.B.M Productions). With John Barnes (composer, arranger, and keyboardist on *Victory*), he composed the powerful *Don't Stand Another Chance* mostly with synthesized sounds. The lyrics, about the singer's adolescent issues, contain no real surprises. She sings that she does not want to give a second chance to people who try to take her boyfriend away from her. Michael, Jackie, and Tito offer their support in the form of backing vocals that echo their sister's warning. A video was made of Janet recording the song in the studio to promote the track and the album. The single became well known in the United States and the rest of the world even though it did not make it into the Hot 100. In November 1984, the single *Dream Street* also met with success alongside a music video featuring guest appearances from actors from the TV series *Fame*.

FOR JACKSON ADDICTS

***Don't Stand Another Chance* (*specially remixed version*) 6'52 and (*dub version*) 6'52 are only available on maxi 45 rpms (USA, ref. SP-12105 and Europe, ref. 12-9782).**

Olivia Newton-John, Jennifer Holliday, and Michael Jackson at the première of *Dreamgirls* at the Shubert Theatre in Century City, 20 March 1983.

Jennifer Holliday

You're the One

Michael Jackson, Buz Kohan / 4'35

From the album: *Say You Love Me* / **Released by Geffen Records:** USA and UK, 19 August 1985 (US ref. GHS 24073 and UK ref. GEF 26564) / **Chart position:** USA R&B No. 34, Pop No. 110 / **Musicians: Jennifer Holliday:** lead vocals / **John Barnes:** keyboards, synthesizers, synthesized bass guitar / **Earl Klugh:** acoustic guitar / **Israel Baker:** first violin / **Recording: The Power Station, New York:** 1985 / **Technical team: Producer:** Michael Jackson / **Arrangements:** John Barnes / **Synclavier programming:** Craig Huxley / **Musician hire:** Ben Barratt / **Recording engineer:** Bruce Swedien / **Additional engineers:** Ric Bultz, Matt Forger, Chris Bellman

In early March 1983, Michael Jackson was working on the *Beat It* video in close collaboration with the choreographer Michael Peters. At the time, Peters was also working for Michael Bennett on the choreography for the musical comedy *Dreamgirls*, an adaptation of The Supremes' story. In the musical, the three singers, Deena Jones, Effie White, and Lorrell Robinson, are called The Dreamettes. On 20 March 1983, Peters invited Michael to the opening night. That evening, the singer met Jennifer Holliday, who was playing the role of Effie White.

The singer from Texas made a major impression on Michael, so much so that he gave her his track *You're the One*, composed with his friend Buz Kohan (scriptwriter of the 1971 TV special *Goin' Back to Indiana* and writer of some of the most beautiful odes in Michael Jackson's musical career, including *You Were There, Gone Too Soon, Elisabeth I Love You*, and *Scared of the Moon*). Buz Kohan made some alterations to the lyrics and the melody on the version sung by Jennifer Holliday.

Michael Jackson also produced the song. John Barnes did the arrangements and brought some warm and gentle synthesized sounds to the mix. Bruce Swedien polished the overall production and delivered a perfectly balanced track that excellently showcases the singer's superb vocal variations.

You're the One is perfect for Jennifer Holliday's magnificent vocals. In her album acknowledgments she wrote: "To Michael Jackson. I don't know why you chose me, but I'm deeply touched, very honored, and mighty thankful to you for writing *You're the One* for me. Thank you for such a beautiful experience!"

For Jackson Addicts

The album *Say You Love Me* by Jennifer Holliday has never been released as a CD and is not on any streaming platforms. It is a rare gem only available on vinyl press and cassettes from the time.

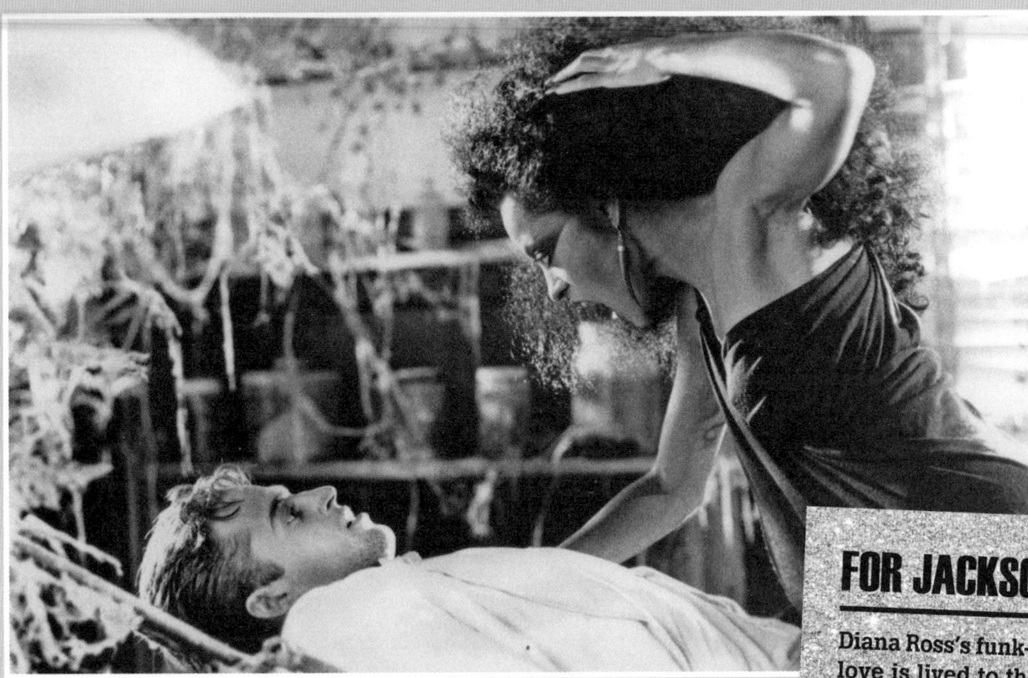

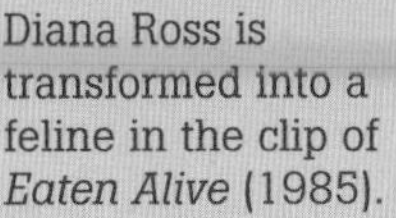

Diana Ross is transformed into a feline in the clip of *Eaten Alive* (1985).

FOR JACKSON ADDICTS

Diana Ross's funk-rock poetry style, where love is lived to the fullest, is idealized in a black-and-white video inspired by H.G. Wells' *The Island of Dr. Moreau*, produced by David Hogan. Diana Ross plays a feline creature who captures a shipwrecked man.

DIANA ROSS
EATEN ALIVE

Barry Gibb, Maurice Gibb, Michael Jackson / 3'50

From the album: Eaten Alive / **Released by RCA Records:** USA (ref. AFLI-5422), 24 September 1985 / **Released by Capitol Records:** UK (ref. EJ 24 0408 1), 24 September 1985 / **Chart position:** USA R&B No. 27, Pop No. 45 / UK No. 11 / **Single: Released by Capitol Records:** USA (ref. PB-14181) and UK (ref. CL 372), 13 August 1984 / **Chart position:** USA R&B No. 10, Pop No. 77 / UK No. 71 / **Musicians: Diana Ross:** lead vocals / **Michael Jackson and Barry Gibb (and unknown):** Backing vocals / **Recording: Bill Schnee Studio, Los Angeles, Middle Ear Studio, Miami** / **Technical team: Producers:** Barry Gibb, Karl Richardson, Albhy Galuten, and Michael Jackson / **Recording engineer:** Humberto Gatica

Diana Ross had a rather mixed solo career since leaving Motown for RCA, Except for *Muscles* in 1982, most of her singles had gone no further than the Top 30. In 1985, she was working on the follow-up to the album *Swept Away*, which features the tribute song to Marvin Gaye, *Missing You* (US Top R&B No. 1).

She called upon Barry Gibb, who had already worked with Diana's idol and longtime rival, Barbra Streisand. The Bee Gees singer offered her several tracks, including *Eaten Alive*. He finished a first version of the composition in March 1985. Michael Jackson heard the demo and suggested several additional elements. *Eaten Alive* then became a collaborative project between three men (Barry Gibbs, his brother Maurice, and Michael Jackson), and so was effectively a creation of some of the biggest-selling stars in previous years. Diana Ross was in seventh heaven, and made the very most of this unexpected pop dream team.

In July 1985, Michael Jackson delivered his demo, which included new ideas that were well received by the Gibb brothers. The team got together at the Bill Schnee Studio in Los Angeles and at the Middle Ear Studio in Miami. Although he had vowed to stay out of the limelight until the release of his new album, Michael bent the rules a little in this case. He agreed to sing backing vocals and finish off the chorus with the lyrics "I don't ever wanna be eaten alive" in his own inimitable vocal signature.

On the version intended to open the album, the work on the breaks and percussion kits unveiled a new style in the artist's composition technique: more dynamic, industrial, and hypnotic than ever, with the rhythm moving away from the soul and R&B style that had characterized his work up until then. *Eaten Alive* was the opening salvo for some more ambitious tunes, where jerky, breathless verses alternated with crystal-clear melodies in the choruses.

The chemistry between the Gibb brothers' and Michael Jackson's harmonies worked miracles, giving *Eaten Alive* a dark and mystical groove. However, this unique formula made very few waves in the United States. Worse still, *Eaten Alive* was the last time Diana Ross appeared in the American Top 40. Her biggest fan base from then on was in Europe.

Michael Jackson and Lionel Richie at the Lion Share Recording Studios, Los Angeles, in 1985.

We Are the World

Michael Jackson, Lionel Richie / 7'02

From the album: USA for Africa—*We Are the World* / **Released by Columbia Records:** USA and UK, 28 March 1985 (USA ref. 40043 and UK (ref. USAIDF 1) / **Chart position:** USA Pop No. 1 / UK No. 1 / **RIAA:** certified Triple Platinum on 24 June 1985 / **Single: A-side:** *We Are the World (single version)* / 6'22 / **B-side:** *Grace (album version)* / 4'30 / **Released by Columbia Records:** USA and UK, 7 March 1985 (US ref. US7-04839 and UK ref. CBSA 6112) / **Chart position:** USA Pop No. 1 / UK No. 1 / **RIAA:** certified Quadruple Platinum on 1 April 1985 / **Musicians: Lionel Richie, Stevie Wonder, Paul Simon, Kenny Rogers, James Ingram, Tina Turner, Billy Joel, Michael Jackson, Diana Ross, Dionne Warwick, Willie Nelson, Al Jarreau, Bruce Springsteen, Kenny Loggins, Steve Perry, Daryl Hall, Huey Lewis, Cyndi Lauper, Kim Carnes, Bob Dylan, Ray Charles:** lead and backing vocals / **Dan Aykroyd, Harry Belafonte, Lindsey Buckingham, Mario Cipollina, Johnny Colla, Sheila E., Bob Geldof, Bill Gibson, Chris Hayes, Sean Hopper, Jackie Jackson, La Toya Jackson, Marlon Jackson, Randy Jackson, Tito Jackson, Waylon Jennings, Bette Midler, John Oates, Jeffrey Osborne, The Pointer Sisters, Smokey Robinson:** chorus / **John Robinson:** drums / **David Paich and Michael Boddicker:** synthesizers / **Paulinho Da Costa:** percussion / **Louis Johnson:** synth bass / **Michael Omartian, Greg Phillinganes, Steve Porcaro, Marcus Ryles, Ian Underwood:** keyboards / **James Ingram, Cathy Worthington, Greg Phillinganes, Marcel East, Khaliq Glover, Elaine Phillinganes, Karla Phillinganes, Steven Ray, and Mark Ross:** handclapping / **Recording: A&M Studios, Los Angeles:** 28 to 29 January 1985 / **Technical team: Producer:** Quincy Jones / **Coproducer:** Tom Bahler / **Recording engineers:** Humberto Gatica and John Guess / **Assistant recording engineers:** Larry Fergusson and Khaliq Glover / **Vocal arrangements:** Tom Bahler, Quincy Jones, and Michael Jackson / **Allocation of solos:** Quincy Jones and Tom Bahler / **Synthesizer arrangements:** David Paich, Michael Omartian, Quincy Jones, John Barnes, and Ian Underwood / **Rhythm arrangements:** Quincy Jones and John Barnes / **Synthesizer programming:** John Barnes, Michael Boddicker, and Steve Porcaro / **Synclavier programming:** Kevin Maloney and Mark Ross / **Oberheim-8 programming:** Marcus Ryles / **Mixing:** Humberto Gatica

Genesis

In late 1984 Harry Belafonte and producer Ken Kragen decided to launch a charity project in response to Band Aid, the group Bob Geldof had created a few months before. Band Aid had released a single called *Do They Know It's Christmas?* in the UK, and its proceeds had gone toward humanitarian aid for the famine in Ethiopia. Forty-six American artists—from Bob Dylan to Kim Karnes and Diana Ross—came together as a super-group, which was named USA for Africa. Harry Belafonte suggested hiring Quincy Jones to produce the song. Jones accepted and asked Lionel Richie to write it. Richie's manager was none other than Kragen himself. Stevie Wonder was supposed to join his former Commodore colleague, but he was tied up with the making of *In Square Circle*, so Quincy Jones recommended replacing him with Michael Jackson.

Michael, who had just finished the grueling *Victory* tour with his siblings, wanted to recover in private. But as soon as Quincy explained the charitable purpose of the project, Michael jumped on board. So Lionel Richie and Michael Jackson found themselves working together: their task was to create a song with a universal melody. Richie already had something in mind when he met Michael at his place in Encino and the two former Motown students got down to working day and night and putting in extra hours. Soon their song began to take shape.

When it came time to divide up the lyrics between each singer, Michael suggested singing the song with Lionel Richie while the rest of the group provided backing vocals. Quincy had to explain that some of the other stars wouldn't be too happy with that arrangement.

The first version of the song was, of course, not bad, but Quincy knew they could do better. Michael decided to take a few days to work alone on the demo, which he largely sang using improvised lyrics. One particular sentence created a problem because it was too morbid for a charity project that was supposed to bring hope. The lyrics "There's a chance we're taking / We're taking our own lives," were thus replaced with "There's a choice we're making / We're saving our own lives."

On 22 January 1985 the three men, plus Stevie Wonder as their guest, met at the Lion Share studios owned by Kenny Rogers. John Robinson was on drums and Louis Johnson on bass. This bare bones team recorded a rudimentary version of the song. Two days later, the song was finalized on tape and sent to the 46 artists participating in the project.

Production

Kragen, Belafonte, and Jones scheduled the recording session for the night of the American Music Award ceremony on 28 January 1985 in the Shrine Auditorium in Los Angeles. The idea was to funnel all 46 singers to nearby A&M Studios once the awards were over. At 10 p.m., everyone in the group met up at the studios. Michael had arrived a few hours earlier to prep the work alongside Quincy Jones and the technical crew. Two days earlier, Quincy had found the perfect location with Kragen, Belafonte, and recording engineer Humberto Gatica. The team was well aware that with all the top stars involved, the session could easily devolve into a battle of the egos, so they planned accordingly. To avoid any skirmishes, they adopted strategic technical measures, like ensuring each person had their own microphone. When the 46 artists arrived for the big event, they found a note Quincy had left for them on the studio door saying "Check your egos at the door." Quincy meant business. Recording went on until dawn. The producer had demanded a silence of the grave while recording the main voices, as the smallest of sounds could have disrupted the flow and schedule of the session.

When it was time for the chorus to come in, Quincy Jones recorded everyone at once. When listening to one of the playbacks, one can hear a slight, continuous metallic sound coming from the mix: Cyndi Lauper's many bracelets jingled at the start of each bar. She removed her jewelry during the session, but some of these sounds were left in the final take anyway.

Michael Jackson had planned on freestyling some lyrics in Swahili, but when the 46 singers started to rehearse this part, it became as clear that many of them couldn't memorize the words. Plus, Bob Geldof, who was participating as a special consultant, wondered whether this tribute would be well received by Africans. Other variations were attempted, but none of them stuck. However, the team spirit that had dominated at the beginning of the evening prevailed, and the singers agreed to sing the last words of the chorus in English.

Once the lead and backing vocals were taken care of, Quincy Jones asked some of the singers to stay for some additional ad-libs. First, he had Diana Ross, James Ingram, and Stevie Wonder sing together. Largely unconvinced by the result, he tried other combinations. He then chose some soloists for the song's final fadeout. This is how Bob Dylan ended up singing some improvised lines before giving way to Ray

On 28 January 1985, Michael Jackson arrives early to prepare for the recording of *We Are the World*.

Charles, who recorded several takes as the studio cleared out. When he realized Bruce Springsteen was still hanging around, Quincy decided to pair the Boss' husky voice with Stevie Wonder's luminous one. The contrast was stunning. James Ingram and Ray Charles sang the last few ad-libs, dotting the song with blues-infused notes and variations.

All the additional vocals recorded on the evening of 29 January and the following day added a joyful intensity to the song. Clearly, Jones knew how to combine the talents at his disposal to achieve top-notch vocal fireworks.

Prince, who was also at the Shrine Auditorium that night to receive several American Music Awards, did not join his colleagues at A&M Studios. Quincy Jones had invited him a few days before, but as Prince's recording engineer, Susan Rogers, explained in an interview, "I only heard Prince's side of the conversation—I was in the control room waiting—but he declined it. It was a long conversation, and Prince said, 'Can I play guitar on it?' And they said no, and he ultimately said, 'Okay, well, can I send Sheila?' And he sent Sheila. Then he said, 'If there's going to be an album, can I do a song for the album?' And evidently they said yes."[77]

The single came out on 7 March 1985 and knocked several records out of the park: within three days, about 300,000 copies had been sold in the United States alone. As for global sales, they surpassed four million copies. In 1985, USA for Africa was able to raise about $60 million in aid for the famine in Ethiopia. This rush of solidarity, which the media called charity business, convinced the American government to increase its humanitarian aid disbursement to $800 million.

The USA for Africa Foundation hired a film crew to shoot the recording session. The footage was used in a documentary about the making of the song, which aired on HBO on 12 May 1985 and was later released on VHS. A reedition also came out on DVD in 2004 in honor of the 20th anniversary of *We Are the World*.

Quincy Jones directs the group of artists assembled under the name USA for Africa at the A&M Studios, Los Angeles, 28 January 1985.

FOR JACKSON ADDICTS

In April 1985, Sonny Melendrez created a new version of *We Are the World*. Michael Jackson immediately praised it and threw his support behind it. He also included an excerpt in a 1988 documentary about his career called *The Legend Continues*. The Children of the World choir recorded this take under the masterful eyes of Stanley Clarke and George Duke, who had also brought in a few future stars, including a certain Stacy Ferguson, now known as Fergie of the Black Eyed Peas, and Drew Barrymore, the young heroine from *E. T.*

The first page of the original score of *We Are the World*, autographed by many of those who took part.

The poster for *Captain EO*, the Disney movie made in collaboration with Kodak (1986).

CAPTAIN EO
AN INTERLUDE IN 3D

Michael Jackson skipped out on the *Live Aid* concert, held on 13 July 1985 to promote the humanitarian effort against the famine in Ethiopia. He had a good reason: he was busy negotiating the details of a new film venture. After working on *The Wiz* in 1978, his next cinematic project would be a video Disney was producing for its theme parks.

On 1 October 1982, the Epcot Center at Disney World in Florida launched a new attraction called *Magic Journeys*. Produced in collaboration with Kodak, this film used state-of-the-art, three-dimensional technology that combined two 70mm cameras. By filming the same scene from two slightly different angles, these cameras recreated a realistic 3D effect that the human eye could capture with the use of special glasses. This technology, called Kodak-Disney 3D, laid the foundations for modern 3D techniques later developed for movie and home theaters.

The attraction was a smashing success. It encouraged Disney executives to make more videos like it and continue to develop cutting-edge technology. In 1984, Michael Eisner was named CEO of Walt Disney Company. A former Paramount Studios executive, he breathed new creative life into the role and did not hesitate to call upon his network of film contacts.

When Michael met Mickey

In September 1984, Frank Wells, an old hand at Warner Studios, and Michael Eisner, were scouting filming locations in Disneyland. Thrillermania was at its peak, and the idea of associating Michael Jackson's name with Disney's parks made a lot of sense. So Wells asked Walt Disney Imagineering, which was responsible for developing and creating attractions, to come up with ideas that would involve Michael.

Michael had never hidden his admiration for the world of Walt Disney, so he was eager to follow the advice of his friend and advisor David Geffen and meet with Disney Pictures' president Jeffrey Katzenberg. Michael happily accepted the lead role in the film, which would air in Florida, California, and Japan. He said he wanted to work with Steven Spielberg or George Lucas. Spielberg, already busy filming *The Color Purple*, declined. But Lucas, the creator of *Star Wars*, accepted the mission.

Wells and Eisner were excellent marketers and knew how much American families loved the science fiction of *Star Wars*: this was a time when family entertainment was losing interest in fairy tales and increasingly turning to the adventures in space of Luke Skywalker and friends. Lucas agreed to produce the film in 3D, but was clear about the fact that his own special-effects studio, Industrial Light and Magic (ILM), and the *Star Tours* attraction (another Disney project) were taking up a lot of his time. Long before Disney bought the *Star Wars* franchise, Lucas had already begun to develop its storyline in the theme park's Tomorrowland area. Lucas' name appeared in the credits, but most of the film's executive production was conducted by Rusty Lemorande.

Francis Ford Coppola, who was one of Michael Eisner's contacts, produced the film. George Lucas, who'd met Coppola during the shooting of *Finian's Rainbow* (a musical comedy starring Fred Astaire and Petula Clark), readily approved of this choice. Coppola's artistic sensibility and passion for music ended up convincing Disney executives to hire him.

The making of *Captain EO*

Rick Rothschild, of Walt Disney Imagineering, worked on the film's concept. It took him a few days to come up with three ideas for Michael Jackson: in the first, the singer would be walking through the park before being suddenly swallowed up by the ride attraction, Pirates of the Caribbean. A series of spectacular scenes would ensue before he could to return to the real world. The other two ideas took inspiration from the same theme: Michael must save the inhabitants of a planet ruled by an evil queen. For this, two different ambiances were proposed: one would be similar to Peter Pan's world and be equipped with a cast of unlikely characters such as elves and fairies. The other would take place in the future, with Michael playing a spaceship captain. Michael Eisner, George Lucas, and Michael Jackson took a particular liking to the futuristic

A photo session during the shooting of *Captain EO* in 1985.

scenario, which was a great way to combine the unique worlds of Disney and *Star Wars*. The working titles were *The Intergalactic Man* and *Space Knights*. In April 1985, Michael Jackson, Francis Ford Coppola, Rusty Lemorande, and William Ellenshaw of Disney met at George Lucas' offices in San Anselmo and settled on *Captain EO* as the final title from the Greek Eos, the goddess of dawn.

The premise was simple: Michael Jackson must save a world where an evil queen (played by Anjelica Huston) rules with fear and oppression. He thus brings light to a lost planet fated to live in darkness. This story, which Elvis Presley wouldn't have passed up during his Hollywood years, was an excuse to reveal two new songs to the public: *We Are Here to Change the World* and *Another Part of Me*. Michael wanted to promote

Michael Jackson, Anjelica Huston, and the cast of *Captain EO* in one of the scenes that was cut from the movie.

them right after the video, but pressure from his label to work on a follow-up to *Thriller* forced him to shelve them. In the end, Michael would include *Another Part of Me* in *Bad*. *We Are Here to Change the World* would have to wait until 2004 to be officially released as part of *The Ultimate Collection*.

More than a million dollars a minute

The preproduction for *Captain EO* started in March 1985 and shooting began on 15 July of the same year. The filming and postproduction of this 17-minute film ended up taking more than 18 months to make. Instead of assigning the choreography to his friend Michael Peters, Michael Jackson worked with Jeffrey Hornaday, who had already designed the choreographies for *Flashdance* and the video for *Say Say Say*. As for the soundtrack and background music, they fell to James Horner, who brilliantly executed Disney's plans.

In addition to the complicated filming techniques, which required patience to control the heavy 3D cameras, a second team was asked to build a movie theater that would create the best possible conditions for airing a film and soundtrack of this type. As with *Magic Journeys*, the audience would have to wear special glasses to experience the 3D effect. As for the sound, it was mixed in multichannel, making *Captain EO* the first film in history to be made in 5.1 surround sound.

The initial budget of $17 million (more than a million dollars a minute) was soon surpassed. The number of planned special effects was multiplied by three. The theater installation took longer than expected: it was supposed to be functional by April 1986, but delays kept piling up, and Disney finally announced that it would open by September 1986. Costs skyrocketed, and the team started to talk about figures reaching $25 million.

When the attraction opened on 12 September 1986 at Epcot, and on 18 September at Disneyland, the figure of Michael Jackson was glaring in its absence. Busy recording *Bad*, he had to settle for reading about the public's reaction in the papers and hearing about them from Disney.

Captain EO in space and time

Thanks to *Captain EO*'s huge success, Disney finally broke with its reputation of being outdated. Freed from the shadow of its creator, who died in 1966, and of the often austere policies he had imposed, the company was able to take a new direction and commit to ambitious projects that were more in line with the time. In addition to the 3D adventure of *Captain EO*, George Lucas was working on *Star Tours*, a simulated experience inspired by the famous saga. Disney's artists were turning to the production of new original films, including *The Little Mermaid* in 1989, which supplanted commercial flops like 1986's *The Great Mouse Detective*.

Captain EO remains a gem among Michael Jackson's productions. The film, which was part music video and part attraction, only ever saw the light of day within the confines of Disney's theme parks. MTV was able to air it on television in 1996, but, to this day, the film remains officially unpublished,

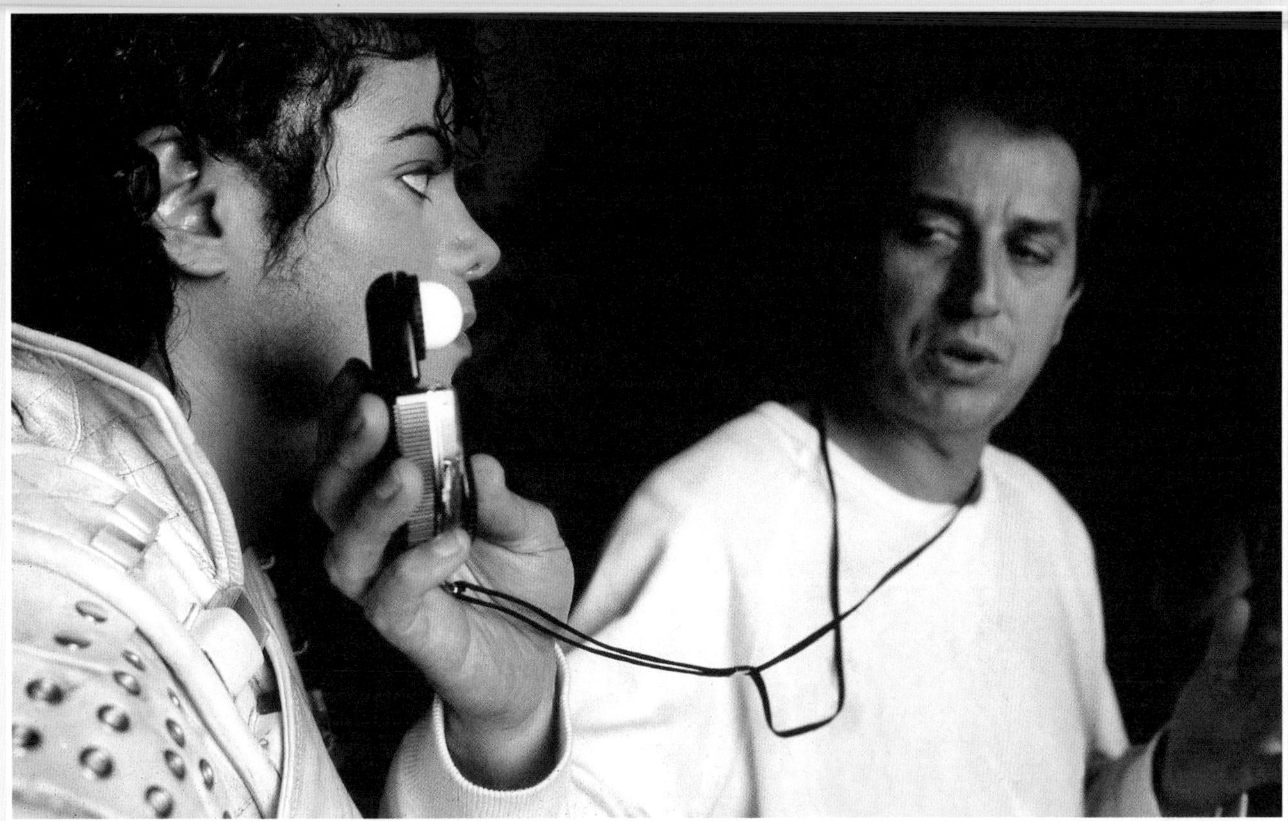

With *Captain EO*, Kodak and Disney reinvented 3D and opened it up to the widest possible audience by associating themselves with Michael Jackson.

including on VHS and DVD. This is due to the film's financial and legal setup, which is a bureaucratic nightmare of contracts involving Lucas, Coppola, Jackson, and all the dancers and actors who appeared in the film. Not to mention that Disney has always refused to market the content of its attractions.

The film's operating licenses expired in 1994 at Epcot and in 1997 at Anaheim, but after Michael Jackson's death in 2009, the public requested that the attraction return by popular demand. *Captain EO* ran between 2010 and 2015, but Disney said this would be the last voyage of the brave captain and consigned this ambitious work to the annals of history.

FOR JACKSON ADDICTS

On 30 July 1985, Michael Jackson fell and injured his right hand while filming *Captain EO*. He was taken to Brotman Memorial Hospital, where he took the time to visit children being treated there.

THE SHORT FILM

Director: Francis Ford Coppola
Producer: Rusty Lemorande
Executive Producer: George Lucas
Lead actors: Michael Jackson, Anjelica Huston, Dick Shawn
Extras: Tony Cox, Debbie Lee Carrington, Cindy Sorenson, Gary DePew
Shoot date: July 1985
Shooting location: Culver City Studios, California
Duration: 17'44

We Are Here to Change the World

Michael Jackson, John Barnes / 2'53

1985

From the album: *The Ultimate Collection*
Released by Epic/Legacy: USA (ref. EPC 5177433) and UK (ref. 5177433), 16 November 2004
Musicians
Michael Jackson: vocals
John Barnes: drum machine and synthesizer programmer, keyboards
Recording
Westlake Recording Studios (studios A and D), Los Angeles: 1985
Technical team
Producer: Michael Jackson
Recording engineer and mixing: Matt Forger
Assistant recording engineers: Bruce Wildstein, Ric Butz

The final scene of *Captain EO*: Michael Jackson watches Anjelica Huston changing into a queen.

Genesis

Michael Jackson saw in John Barnes a loyal musical ally, someone he could work with to create songs quickly and efficiently. After contributing to *Victory*, Barnes struck up a friendship with the Jackson siblings. In September 1984, he spent a few days with Michael at the Caribou Ranch in Colorado. Many artists, including Elton John, had used the property's studio. There, the two men quietly started to develop their song ideas, many of which Michael would later use in side projects.

We Are Here to Change the World was intended to promote peace. It is a somewhat regimented-sounding march, but one that was meant to spread love throughout the world. Compared to previous songs, like *Wanna Be Startin' Somethin'*, the hectic bass line is reined in. Michael wanted a complicated rhythmic track and dance steps that would emulate the moves of a warrior.

Like Diana Ross' *Eaten Alive*, the verses are tightly packed with melodic lines, giving the song a staccato effect, like the one Rod Temperton had already given to *Off the Wall*. The chorus, which is liberating, appears to be literally reaching for the stars with its crescendo, as if it were paying tribute to the concept of *Starlight*, which was the working title for *Thriller*.

Production

Matt Forger, John Barnes, and Michael Jackson met in the A and D studios at Westlake to record *We Are Here to Change the World* and *Another Part of Me,* the two songs that would appear in *Captain EO*. The first contains a futuristic rhythm so groovy that even hip-hop and electro funk artists of the time couldn't help but love it.

John Barnes programmed the drum machine by adjusting settings that hadn't been changed since The Jacksons had recorded *Body* the year before.

The song's minimalism gives it a short and punchy sound, which aptly represents *Captain EO's* mission of peace. Matt Forger used both right and left channels to create a balance rich enough to capture and maintain the listener's attention. Like Michael, Matt knew the song would be played at high volume in Disney's specially created theaters. The goal was therefore to deliver a science-fiction soundtrack rather than a radio or club tune.

Michael Jackson is accidentally whipped on the head by one of the "warriors" in the fight scene of *Captain EO.*

The drum machine was mixed to give the bass drums a deep and muted resonance. Long before QSound Labs created the QSound audio technique, which consists of creating a 3D sound from a stereo source, Forger created an immersive and realistic soundtrack that paired perfectly with the background music composed by James Horner.

The version that ended up in the film includes a number of breaks that follow Captain EO's journey into the kingdom as he fights the evil queen and her soldiers. Once again, Michael and his dancers filled these instrumental sections with choreographies inspired by breakdancing. After keeping it close to his chest for many years, the singer finally released a studio version of *We Are Here to Change the World* as part of *The Ultimate Collection* (2004). Forger's uplifting and catchy mix unleashed all the energy this space groove could muster, setting the stage, in a way, for Michael's future stylistic choices.

1. BAD
2. THE WAY YOU MAKE ME FEEL
3 SPEED DEMON
4. LIBERIAN GIRL
5. JUST GOOD FRIENDS
6. ANOTHER PART OF ME
7. MAN IN THE MIRROR
8. I JUST CAN'T STOP LOVING YOU
9. DIRTY DIANA
10. SMOOTH CRIMINAL
11. LEAVE ME ALONE (BONUS CD TRACK)

Bad **ALBUM**

Released by Epic Records: USA (ref. 40600) and UK (ref. EPC 450290), 31 August 1987
Chart position: USA R&B No. 1, Pop No. 1 / UK No. 1
RIAA: certified six-time Multiplatinum 1 June 1988 / certified ten-time Multiplatinum 16 February 2017

A shot by Sam Emerson, from the photo shoot for the final sleeve of the album *Bad* (1986).

BAD, MICHAEL VERSUS JACKSON

1987

How does one top an album that broke all records and helped a declining music industry bounce back? How can a young man establishing himself as a solo artist in his own right, to the point of outshining his family's group, overcome the notorious "difficult second album" syndrome and reinvent himself? How can Michael Jackson, in short, break his own records to become the King of Pop?

In 1983, as Michael Jackson was promoting *Thriller*, he put in countless media appearances. The following year, the effects of this significant artistic and human investment reverberated throughout the world: like a shockwave across the planet, Jacksonmania was reaching countries that had barely even heard of the artist previously. It was Michael Jackson's global coronation as king of the music industry. The moniker King of Pop had not yet taken hold, but the media noticed Michael's ability to turn everything he touched into gold and called him The Gloved One. But soon after a smashing success at the 1984 Grammys, an American tour would expose the palpable tensions within the Jackson clan.

The King and the Prince

Michael's rising success was starting to annoy reporters, who thought the young singer might be overrated. The economic and political flop of the *Victory* tour only added fuel to their fire. One thing followed another and soon all the rock critics were praising Prince for releasing *Purple Rain* in the heat of the summer of 1984: in lieu of a rivalry like the one between The Beatles and The Rolling Stones, columnists of all sorts were more than happy to overthrow the King of Encino and install the Prince of Minneapolis in his stead. This predictable reaction was illustrative of the limited perspective that journalists had at the time, as if two talents of equal measure couldn't possibly coexist. Especially since Prince—even though he reveled in the joys of 1980s stardom and knew how to milk it for all it was worth—was following a very different career path from Michael's. One was working with Hollywood legends who thought of him as a son, the other was pursuing his rock heritage with a far simpler musical style. One took four years to release an album that would feature on training programmes for recording engineers, the other was constantly recording to produce immediate results that would immortalize his emotional state at the time. They had two schools of thought and two styles, but in the end, they were both talented musicians.

The two leading men accepted the competitive relationship that had been imposed on them. Only once did they appear together in front of a camera, at a James Brown concert in 1983. The godfather of soul called each of them to the stage, one after the other, for a surprise tribute. Michael Jackson started off with a blues cry before sliding on stage with an impulsive and dynamic moonwalk. He whispered into James Brown's ear that Prince was also in the audience. The Minneapolis Kid took the stage with measured enthusiasm, as if he'd wanted to remain hidden. After performing a guitar solo and dancing a few frenzied steps, he returned to the audience. While doing so, he grabbed onto a lamppost, causing it to fall off the stage.

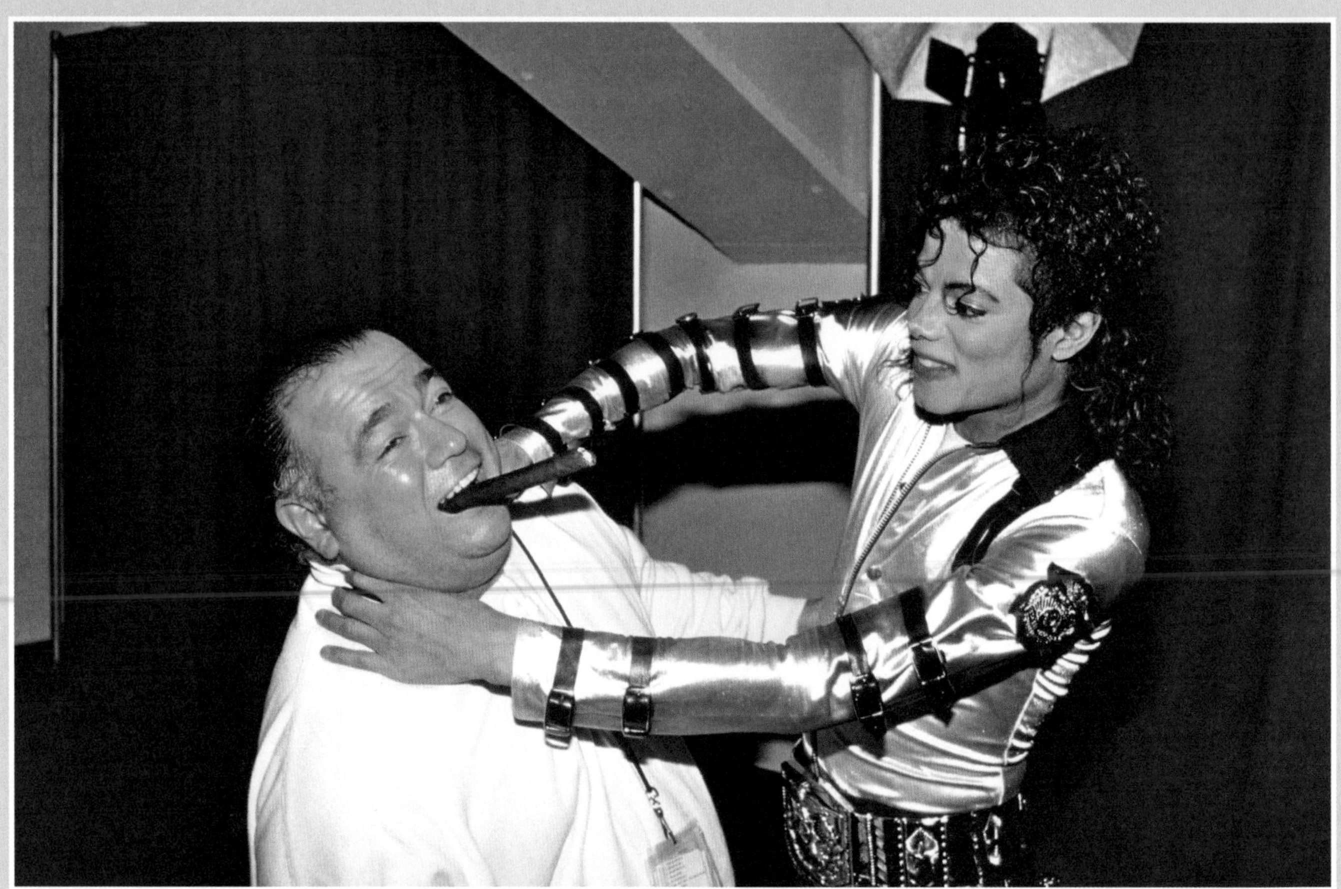

Michael Jackson and his manager Frank DiLeo backstage on the *Bad* tour in 1988.

1987

The two artists fueled a conflict that divided and enthralled both the public and the critics. In fact, Prince sold fewer records than Michael Jackson, but both were part of a generation of charismatic and extremely popular 1980s stars. They were dominating global charts alongside the likes of Bruce Springsteen and Madonna.

This Jackson-Prince rivalry highlighted the media's obsession with the creator of *Thriller*, whose success was starting to irritate them. When the *Victory* tour came to an abrupt end in Los Angeles in December 1984, even though the family had wanted to go global with this one last tour, the media started ripping into the Jackson family by denouncing its greed, all the while taking care to lay the blame specifically on Michael. Aware of this image problem, Michael tried to protect himself by avoiding the public eye. Aside from recording *We Are the World* and filming *Captain EO*, he kept to himself and stopped releasing music, even singles. During this long hiatus, he went on an unexpected trip to Australia from 19 to 21 October 1985. One can look to The Beatles' catalog to understand why.

ATV and the purchase of The Beatles

In the early 1980s, while working with Paul McCartney, Michael Jackson discovered the fascinating and lucrative world of music editing. The former Beatle assured him this was a sound investment and a great way to pay tribute to his favorite songs by other artists. Michael, charmed by the idea, almost jokingly suggested that he'd one day end up with The Beatles' songs. McCartney laughed good-naturedly, never guessing just how right he was.

Revenue from *Thriller* allowed Michael to collect a $53 - million royalty check on 14 March 1985 from his record company, CBS. The young multimillionaire was beginning to understand that he could now use his money to make sound investments. In addition to bricks-and-mortar investments, he became interested in the music catalogs that were available on the market.

At the time of The Beatles, Lennon and McCartney had entrusted the rights to their songs to publisher Dick James under the aegis of Northern Songs. In 1969, after problems arose with unpaid taxes, James sold the company to ATV, which belonged to Sir Lew Grade. The Beatles, now robbed of the rights to their songs, discovered that their publisher did not have their best interests at heart. In 1982, ATV was acquired by Bell, which was owned by Australian millionaire Robert Holmes à Court. In September 1984, Michael Jackson's lawyer, John Branca, told him that the ATV catalog was for sale. It now contained The Beatles' songs from Northern Songs as well as a few others by Little Richard and Pat Benatar. Michael asked him to negotiate the purchase of this ideal investment.

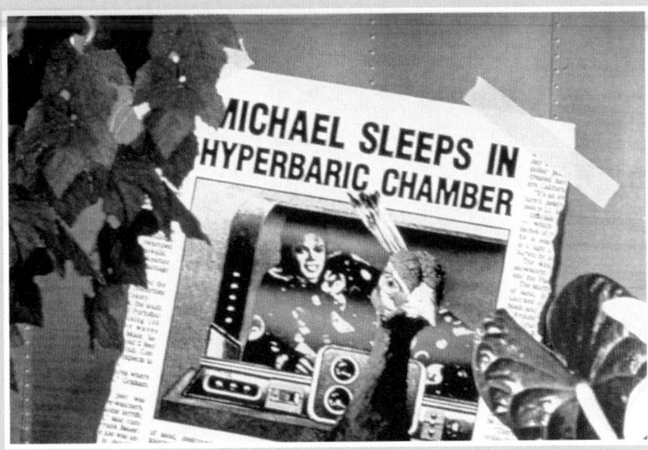

In *Leave Me Alone*, Michael Jackson settled his scores with the press.

McCartney and Yoko Ono had hoped to buy the songs as a joint offer in 1981, but negotiations had come to naught. McCartney didn't think he should have to spend a fortune to get his own songs back. In 1985 he and his lawyer stood by this position. Michael Jackson, for his part, continued to negotiate with businessmen Martin Brandier, Charles Koppelman, Charles Knapp, Samuel J. LeFrak, and with Virgin Records. The singer would meet some of these opponents again. After lengthy negotiations lasting eight months, Michael became the owner of ATV Music for 47.5 million dollars. But Holmes à Court imposed one condition of sale: the buyer would have to make one appearance on Australian television during a telethon aired on Channel 7. Michael accepted and fulfilled his obligation in Perth between 19 and 21 October 1985.

As of 10 August 1985, The Beatles' songs belonged to Michael. The news sent the media into a frenzy. It was still denouncing the "Michael Jackson machine," scrutinizing the *Victory* tour's accounting problems, and criticizing the proliferation of promotional products, but Michael's acquisition of ATV only caused the media to further demonize him. The rock media—which was mostly white—took offense at seeing a 27-year-old black man acquire the pop heritage of the 1960s. Fears ran wild that the songs belonging to the "four boys in the wind" would be used for purely lucrative ends. Between mountains of glitter and suitcases full of cash, Michael Jackson was being painted a suspicious character ready to use The Beatles' rich repertoire for nefarious ends. But as time and facts have shown, Michael approached his new treasure with caution and wisdom. Some of The Beatles' songs were used in commercials for famous brands, like Nike, but the singer did not hesitate to axe a Beastie Boys cover of *I'm Down* that he thought too irreverent: it was for their 1986 album *License to Ill*. And when the CD market was in full swing, Jackson and his team at ATV were careful to reissue the groups' prestigious songs in good condition.

However, by acquiring the ATV catalog, Michael Jackson set in motion an unfortunate series of events that would eat away at his career and at his life. The move formalized his divorce from a large part of the media, and from the 1990s onward he would become bogged down in constant conflicts with a long list of partners, managers, and supposed friends who tried to buy the famous catalog from him, as if it were the holy grail of art and money.

The rumor mill

At the same time as The Beatles' catalog incident, coverage of Michael Jackson transitioned from the music media to the tabloids. In 1986, as the launch of *Captain EO* was nearing, Michael redoubled his public appearances while wearing a surgical mask. The *National Enquirer* published on its cover a picture of him lying in an oxygen chamber designed to keep him alive until he was over 150 years old. Michael's fan base was perplexed, but did not waver in its support. Journalists, however, saw these pictures as gifts from heaven. The irony was that Michael was the one who put together this photo shoot with his manager, Frank DiLeo. He'd wanted to gauge just how far the media would follow him into his madness. The boomerang effect turned out to be far more intense than expected. That was the moment when Michael Jackson shed his clean image for that of an eccentric young man who firmly preferred the company of animals to that of humans. The absence of a wife or girlfriend in his life did nothing to temper this impression.

As rumors continued to spread, Michael was soon given an insulting nickname. In 1986, the British press began to call him Wacko Jacko, which the tabloids soon shortened to Jacko. The moniker stuck, and Michael complained about it during an interview on ABC on 13 September 1997 in Paris. The prince of the 1983 and 1984 charts was becoming a joke for a growing number of people. Behind all this was a flawed but useful idea: bad press is better than no press at all.

The album of living dangerously

As all this unfolded, Michael Jackson continued to seek inspiration for a follow-up album to *Thriller*. The musical landscape had changed since 1982. Rap was starting to gain ground, notably through artists who'd signed with Def Jam, such as LL Cool J. The carefree nature of funk was giving way to darker music supported by even more machines. Electronic music was continuing its ascent alongside the inevitable rise of house and techno.

FOR JACKSON ADDICTS

For the cover of his new album, Michael Jackson asked photographer Greg Gorman to take a picture similar to the one that had made Gloria Swanson: her serious and piercing gaze appears from behind a lace veil that hugs the contours of her face. Walter Yetnikoff, the CEO of CBS, rejected this image and called for a new one. Sam Emerson, Michael's personal photographer, took the definitive photo during the shooting of the *Bad* video.

Michael returned to the studio with Quincy Jones, who'd just written the score to *The Color Purple* for Steven Spielberg. The producer knew that with each passing day his protégé was becoming an artist in his own right. While Michael had only written three songs for *Off the Wall* and four for *Thriller*, he wrote nine out of 11 songs for *Bad*. This third solo album, to be released by Epic, became a pet project in which the artist let his imagination run wild. He created songs that oscillated between the feverish rock of *Dirty Diana* and the timeless ballad of *I Just Can't Stop Loving You*.

The album's surprising working title was *Pee*. Quincy Jones and Michael Jackson agreed to develop a harder image in the style of rock used in *Beat It*. Some of Michael's lyrics spoke of a dark world inhabited by groupies (*Dirty Diana*) or by paparazzi who were chasing him (the lover he was pushing away in *Leave Me Alone* was a metaphor for his love-hate relationship with the media).

1987

The two men worked together despite having different artistic visions. Unlike Michael, Quincy believed rap was the music of the future and wanted to write a song with Run DMC, the leading hip-hop group of the day. In the summer of 1986, the group sang *Walk This Way* with Aerosmith, which reached No. 4 in the US charts. So Michael wrote a song that talked about the devastating effects of crack cocaine while Run DMC recorded a demo busting rhymes on the same theme. But the meeting between the two artists came to nothing, and the *Crack Kills* project was dropped.

To cap off their collaboration, Michael and Quincy wrote a piece borrowing from the magic formulas that had given them *Thriller*, trying to perfect them as much as possible. The analog recording techniques that had given *Thriller* its intense and precise sound gave way to a digital method. Recording engineer Bruce Swedien, a true craftsman who wasn't intimidated by technological advances, found a way to give *Bad* a musicality that the critics would love. He worked at Westlake's studio D with a new Harrison MR-2 console with 56 inputs, which was similar to digital recorders like the 32-track Mitsubishi X 850. Other tracks were made more traditionally, on Neve V consoles attached to 16-track tape recorders.

Meanwhile, Michael was discovering the joys of the Synclavier, the amazing synthesizer that was responsible for the miraculous sounds in *Thriller*. Thanks to musician and technician Chris Currell, Michael learned to play this instrument, which allowed him to fine-tune and give shape to his new song ideas.

Michael wanted to create a sound that would make his songs twice as successful but take half the time to produce. He came up with a clever technique that everyone could agree on: each fast piece on the album was raised in pitch by five percent in order to reach high tonalities and establish an ever more captivating rhythm. The differences were most noticeable when the songs were played on the radio. *Bad* stood out as an oddity in the record industry: it was written and performed by an artist who was breaking free of some of the norms while continuing to promote his own, a tactic that he'd set in motion with *Thriller*.

While *Bad* impressed with its surgical precision, it never managed to fully win over its audience. The singer and his producer spent months fine-tuning the album, racking their brains as to how to improve it, or at least how to match it. Michael Jackson wrote "100 million" on his bathroom mirror, which was the number of record sales he wanted to achieve with his new album. Michael's race to beat his own record ultimately failed to win over the public and the media: *Bad* would remain that "second album," condemned to live in the shadow of its more glorious predecessor.

The album came out on 31 August 1987. In the United States, it sold 10 million copies, compared to 25 million for

Michael Jackson and his boa constrictor Muscles. This was a promotional photograph for the official line of soft toys called "Michael's Pets" (1986). Part of the profits were donated to charitable causes.

Thriller. The American public increasingly turned away from Michael Jackson, who reacted by promoting his image in other countries and expanding to new markets. In the end, *Bad* sold more than 20 million copies worldwide, making it the second most widely sold album of all time. Michael and his manager Frank DiLeo achieved this by taking the risk of releasing nine of the 11 songs as singles. In the only promotional stunt for the album, a tenth single was released exclusively for a French audience. The first five singles squeezed into No. 1 on the US *Billboard*, a first in the history of music charts. *Bad* was a musical work of art that was promoted over the course of 18 months. It was rare for an album's record promotion strategy to be so successful. Not satisfied with making videos for his singles, Michael set off on his first solo world tour.

A tour and a video

On 12 September 1987, Michael Jackson performed at his first concert for the *Bad* tour. During the 123 days of the tour, he appeared before his audience as a fully formed artist, for the first time alone on stage without his siblings. This inspired tour broke records and contained all the resilience and energy of the best rock concerts of the time. Michael Jackson worked with Vincent Paterson to perfect performances that would later become the basis for Michael's subsequent tours. This 16-month journey—a more than effective promotion for the album—made Michael the undisputed king of showbusiness and of the music world. When the tour ended on 27 January 1989 in Los Angeles, the numbers spoke for themselves: after taking four continents and 15 countries in 123 concerts, the

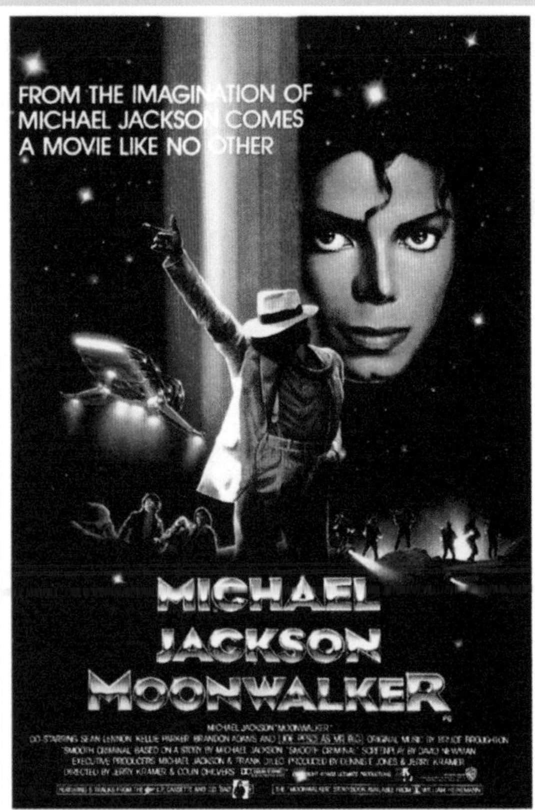

The poster for *Moonwalker* (1988), the feature-length movie produced and financed by Michael Jackson.

On 20 April 1988, just before his 30th birthday, Michael Jackson published his memoirs, which he dedicated to his idol Fred Astaire. Known as *Moonwalk*, the book was the result of lengthy negotiations between Doubleday and its editor, Jackie Onassis. Within a few months the book sold 450,000 copies throughout the world. For the first time, with the help of writer Stephen Davis, Michael opened up about what it was like to live in the spotlight from such an early age. To promote the book, Michael produced a documentary called *The Legend Continues*, which appeared on television and was distributed in VHS. It included the best moments of Michael's career and was narrated by James Earl Jones.

Bad tour had garnered 4.4 million fans and generated $125 million in revenue. But in the United States, the gap was widening and became difficult to fill. While the public was happy to gather across the globe to fawn over Michael, this was not the case for the media and music professionals at home: at the 30th Grammy Awards at Radio City Music Hall in New York on 2 March 1988, Michael Jackson had to sit and watch as each award slipped away right in front of him. While *Thriller* had won eight Grammys, *Bad* only won one for best recording engineer. That evening, though unhappy, Michael followed Frank DiLeo's advice and performed a combination of *The Way You Make Me Feel* and *Man in the Mirror*. Energized by the rage and frustration that he was experiencing at the hands of his peers, Michael delivered a performance that was so electric that he proved himself a born leader, someone who was able to enthrall an entire audience with one improvisation. The air of discomfort that reigned after this performance spoke volumes about the disenchantment and lack of understanding that was affecting the media and part of the music industry at the time.

To raise the stakes for *Bad's* promotional campaign, Michael launched production of a feature film called *Moonwalker*. Far from being a classic, the film is a patchwork of scenes that depict Michael's world. Its pinnacle comes at *Chicago Nights*, a medium-length film within the feature where Michael is a superhero flying to the rescue of a group of children being threatened by a drug lord. This good-and-evil plot is what set the backdrop for the *Smooth Criminal* video, which would turn out to be one of Michael's emblematic pieces.

The rest of *Moonwalker* is made up of a series of scenes, through which the only connecting thread is Michael Jackson. It was an opportunity to give the public three videos in addition to *Smooth Criminal*. The first one, *Speed Demon*, was a cartoonish chase where the artist, dressed as a rabbit, tries to escape his groupies and the photographers hunting for their latest scoop. The second one, *Leave Me Alone*, shows a world inspired by *Gulliver's Travels*, in which Michael debunks the many rumors about him. The last one, *Come Together*, the first Beatles cover, was recorded by producer Bill Bottrell, which heralded the end of Michael Jackson's collaboration with Quincy Jones.

Moonwalker was released to great acclaim in European and Japanese theaters. American distributors were not interested, so Frank DiLeo released the film directly to video, which meant it would never be projected in cinemas on American soil. This misstep caused the end of DiLeo's professional relationship with Michael, who let him go on 14 February 1989. Now the only captain of his ship, Michael closed his *Bad* years, and the 1980s, by setting his professional relationships and affairs in order.

Hanging onto the barrier to greet his fans, Michael Jackson reaches out to the crowd at one of his *Bad* tour concerts in Tokyo in 1987.

The artist of the decade and the birth of the King of Pop

Michael Jackson's tireless approach finally bore fruit: *Bad* became a seminal album in the second half of the 1980s, and when reckoning time came, Michael was crowned artist of the decade by MTV, not to mention his own record company.

Bad marked the end of Michael's collaboration with Quincy Jones and cemented his status as a singer-songwriter who would remain, paradoxically, underestimated in his lifetime. But he was the one largely responsible for this, as he always remained tight-lipped about his creative process. While he allowed himself to be filmed and photographed throughout his professional career as if he were an emperor exalting the grandeur of his rein, the fruits of his labor remained locked away in his personal vault.

When meeting his fans for the first time as a solo artist during his *Bad* tour, Michael realized how much of an impact he had on the public, which worshipped him unconditionally. That's when he cemented his status as worldwide idol. The sometimes excessive hysteria he provoked during his public appearances powered the legions of admirers who followed him throughout the world. It was these fans who ended up nicknaming him the King of Pop, an expression he later took control of by trademarking it.

In May 1988, thanks to profits from his solo career, Jackson left his family home in Encino and bought Sycamore Ranch, an enormous property in Santa Ynez, where he created a world of his own. The property sold for an estimated $20 million. This world, far from Hollywood society, was where the singer took refuge after the *Bad* tour.

Bruce Swedien ensured continued support for album sales at the time by producing a series of additional mixes. Many vocal takes that don't appear in the album were thus mixed and released as part of the version entitled *Dance Extended Mix Includes False Fade* (8'24).

BAD

Michael Jackson / 4'06

Musicians
Michael Jackson: lead and backing vocals, vocal percussion ("How now, brown cow")
Jimmy Smith: Hammond B3 organ with MIDI (solo)
Greg Phillinganes: synthesizer and synthesizer (solo)
John Barnes, Michael Boddicker: synthesizers
John Robinson: drums
David Williams: guitar
Kim Hutchcroft, Larry Williams: saxophones
Gary Grant, Jerry Hey: brass
Paulinho Da Costa: percussion
Christopher Currell: Synclavier, digital guitar, washboard
Recording
Westlake Recording Studios (studio D), Los Angeles: 1986
Technical team
Producers: Quincy Jones and Michael Jackson
Recording engineers: Matt Forger and Bruce Swedien
Rhythmic arrangements: Michael Jackson, Christopher Currell, and Quincy Jones
Vocal arrangements: Michael Jackson
Brass arrangements: Jerry Hey
Synthesizer programming: Larry Williams and Casey Young
Drums programming: Douglas Getschal
Mixing: Bruce Swedien

1987

Single

A-side: *Bad* (single) / 4'05
B-side: *I Can't Help It* (album) / 4'28
Released by Epic Records: USA (ref. 34 07418) and UK (ref. EPC 651100), 2 September 1987
Chart position: USA R&B No. 1, Pop No. 1 / UK No. 3

THE SONG

Genesis

Halfway through the song, *Bad* lets rip a roaring bass line of undeniable R&B accents. It resembles, and may even give a nod to, the one heard in Barrett Strong's classic Motown hit *Money (That's What I Want)*.

The similarities end there. *Bad* was inspired by a strange incident Michael experienced in 1984: while on tour with his siblings in Atlanta, he stopped at an antique shop to buy a present for his mother. When the owner saw him arrive, he chased him away saying, "You are bad! You are bad!" without giving an explanation. This phrase stayed in Michael's head, and he used it to write the song.

Lyrics aside, Michael Jackson believed that *Bad* went beyond the message from *Beat It*. When he sings "If you don't like what I'm saying, then won't you slap my face," he highlights the importance of demanding respect without giving in to violence.

In 1984, the public and media split into two camps: Michael Jackson versus Prince, with the more demanding rock critics preferring Prince's records. Michael Jackson and Quincy Jones ignored these media intrigues and even considered a duet with the Kid from Minneapolis. They thought a musical confrontation would be the perfect way to stage a street fight on video. It would be sure to make a splash. But the project never took shape, to the disappointment of the stars' respective fan bases.

Nevertheless, Michael and Quincy invited Prince to a meeting in Encino. Bruce Swedien was also present. "Prince was always competing with Michael," recalled Quincy Jones in an interview. "So I told Michael, 'You sit there and Prince sits there, so it won't look like we're ganging up on him to do the record.' It was a beautiful meeting, a funny meeting, and [Prince] said, 'You don't need me on this, it's going to be a number one anyway'—which it was. Prince did not leave without handing 'a lot of funny presents' to Jackson, cryptically addressed to 'Camille.'"[78] And that will remain a mystery because this Camille, whoever he or she was, was never spoken of again.

For his part, the *Purple Rain* singer told Chris Rock in an interview on VH1 that "The first line in that song is 'Your butt is mine' so I was saying, 'Who gonna sing that to whom?

Michael Jackson and the *Bad* dancers in action at Hoyt-Schermerhorn Street station on the New York subway in 1986.

Because you sure ain't singing it to me, and I sure ain't singing it to you.' So right there we got a problem."[79]

Production

Bad was the standard by which Michael and Quincy measured all the songs they created for this last album together. Bruce Swedien had found a new console Harrison MR-2 equipped with 56 inputs and had had it installed in Westlake's brand new studio D. John Robinson, who'd featured heavily in *Off the Wall* but nowhere in *Thriller*, made his big comeback. He played the first rhythmic track, which was mimicked by a drum machine programmed by Douglas Getschal. To top it all off, Michael recorded a beatboxing segment that Bruce Swedien nicknamed "How now, brown cow." Michael often used his vocal percussion abilities to write songs. They allowed him to recreate the sound of certain instruments. His preference for this mode of expression showed just how well he was able to memorize, digest, and sometimes repurpose interesting sounds for the final versions of his songs.

In *Bad*, the digital coexists with the analog: Jerry Hey's intricate brass arrangements merge with a digital guitar embedded with a Fairlight played by Chris Currell. The song is a tribute to the R&B of the 1950s and 1960s, which is how *Shamone*, a phonetic adulteration of the expression "Come on," became a nod to Mavis Staples, who says it in *I'll Take You There*. What's more, Quincy Jones decided to bring on board the famous jazz organ player Jimmy Smith (1928–2005), who'd been dubbed the "eighth wonder of the world" by Miles Davis. Smith used his Hammond B3 MIDI organ to perform a solo. A short version of it appears on the song's album (the full solo only appears in the video). Old hand Smith starts off the song, while newbie Greg Phillinganes finishes it at the synthesizer. The sequence bore the mark of Quincy Jones.

Martin Scorsese directs Michael Jackson on the set of *Bad* in New York in 1986.

1987

THE SHORT FILM

Director: Martin Scorsese
Producers: Quincy Jones, Barbara De Fina
Executive producers: Michael Jackson, Harry Ufland, Frank DiLeo
Leading actors: Michael Jackson, Wesley Snipes
Extras: Adam Nathan, Pedro Sanchez, Greg Holtz Sr., Jaime Perry, Paul Calderon, Alberto Alejandrino, Horace Bailey, Marvin Foster, Robert Flack, Dennis Price, Edgard Mourino
Choreography: Michael Jackson, Gregg Burge, Jeffrey Daniel
Shooting dates: November 1986
Shoot locations:
• The Masters School, 49 Clinton Avenue, Dobbs Ferry, New York (school scene)
• West 122nd Street, between 7th and 8th Avenues, Harlem, New York (scenes in Daryll's home neighborhood)
• Hoyt Schermerhorn Station, Brooklyn, New York (subway station in the final scene)
Duration: 18'06

Genesis

Michael Jackson knew that everyone was expecting something big from him, so as with *Captain EO*, he wanted to work with a great director like Steven Spielberg or George Lucas. He believed this would ensure his comeback. Quincy Jones, along with his manager Frank DiLeo, steered Michael away from those directors, arguing that he actually needed a director able to capture the tougher, more "street," image that was befitting of *Bad*. So DiLeo reached out to his friend Martin Scorsese, another film legend, who had shot a vast repertoire of films set in New York.

Scorsese asked Richard Prince to write the script, since he'd already worked with him on *The Color of Money*. The scriptwriter was intrigued. "This was when music videos were just becoming a big thing," he explained in an interview. "So Jackson wanted to show people that he's 'down.' Think about it: Richard Price, Scorsese, Michael Jackson, who the hell is going to say no? Of course I was going do it. And everybody did their job."[80] Price created an eight-page script based on a clip from *Newsweek*. The video features Edmund Perry, a young African-American college student from Harlem who's come home for the holidays to be confronted with a choice: follow his studies or join up with the old gang. He ends up getting killed. The message of nonviolence, in the vein of *Beat It*, prevails.

In *Bad*, the young Wesley Snipes made his first major screen appearance, New York, 1986.

The video opens with images of a New England University campus and ends with singing and dancing at a subway station in New York.

A casting call was put out to fill the role of the student's childhood friend, the one who had stayed behind in Harlem. The young Wesley Snipes passed the difficult selection process with flying colors: he knew not to overact. This was his first appearance on screen, and it would become a stepping stone toward a brilliant Hollywood acting career.

Production

Jackson, Scorsese, Jones, and DiLeo decided to film the scenes on location, so the film crew set up shop in New York in November 1986. Michael had never seen Harlem's streets before. As he roamed them, he was constantly amazed by the tension emanating from this urban environment, to the point where he kept asking the film crew if people really lived in those dreadful conditions. The first part of the story was filmed in black and white in order to highlight the workaday nature of the young protagonist's life.

The final dance scene takes place on the platform of an abandoned subway station. When he arrived on location, Michael was visibly excited about filming in such an authentic spot. He even pointed out that the smell of urine made it more realistic. This scene, filmed in color, was a tribute to street dancing and to musical comedies like *West Side Story*. Michael worked with two assistant choreographers to combine these two styles: Jeffrey Daniel, whom he'd known since the 1970s, and Gregg Burge. Geron "Casper" Candidate, closing dancer for *Soul Train*, also contributed. Together, the team choreographed the routines during intense rehearsals at Helmsley Place. Michael Jackson filmed these sessions so that the three of them could choose which routines would appear in the final cut.

Notably, Jeffrey Daniel suggested including some of Michael's iconic dance steps in the choreography. These steps would end up canonizing Michael's dance style: they have since inspired dance companies to teach similar moves to students.

Gregg Burge's choreography focused on the technical scenes where Michael and his dancers performed a series of steps inspired by the musical comedies of Hollywood. Scorsese set up his camera to follow the movements of the dancers, especially Michael's.

In the final scene, Michael Jackson and his gang intone a song reminiscent of African-American gospel music. It's the moment in which Michael connects with his roots, and his a capella singing makes him sound like a modern-day James Brown. In defying the character played by Wesley Snipes and his henchmen, Michael delivers the song's original message: *Bad* isn't making a case for violence, nor is it an excuse to shoot gang scenes—it is an appeal for us all to respect ourselves and others.

Bad aired for the first time on CBS on 31 August 1987, on a program called *The Magic Returns*. It was overseen by Larry Stessel, head of marketing at Epic Records, and it surprised the general public: Michael Jackson's image had changed radically. His increasingly androgynous look divided opinion and delighted those journalists who were trying to minimize the impact of his musical comeback. But *Bad* stood the test of time, and has since become a musical and visual reference point for many pop musicians.

PORTRAIT

Matt Forger and Michael Jackson in 1982 during the recording sessions for the album *Thriller*.

MATT FORGER
SOUND ARCHITECT

Matt Forger began his music career as a recording engineer for rock groups based out of northeastern United States. Unsatisfied with the materials and techniques that were available at the time, he set out to create his own audio system by assembling the components himself. A firm believer in self-education, he knew the importance of learning and adapting new technologies.

He built a solid reputation within the local music scene because he understood the need for specific sounds that would fit a group's style and the venue in which they were performing. He decided to move to Los Angeles, site of the country's biggest recording studios, and began to collaborate with more and more producers, including Giorgio Moroder and George Duke. Forger's life changed the moment he met Quincy Jones and Bruce Swedien and discovered their incredible skills and work ethic. He soon joined this prestigious team and recorded several songs with them. In 1982 he worked on the album *Donna Summer*, which included *Love Is in Control*.

The King of Pop's right-hand man

The first time Matt Forger worked with Michael Jackson was in 1982, when he helped create *Thriller* and *E.T. Storybook*. His work on this last piece was especially striking: he devised a working schedule and technical system that would yield the best possible recording sessions in the smallest amount of time. Michael considered Matt Forger a trustworthy partner and a music lover, someone who understood that his songs would be played on home stereo systems as well as on stage.

Forger was soon put in charge of some of the team's most impressive projects, such as the opening music to the *Victory* tour (*Kreeton's Overture*) and the songs used in *Captain EO*. And when Michael Jackson was working on *Bad*, they both put in extra work and increased the number of test sessions.

The two men worked on Michael's solo albums together, and when Michael and Quincy's partnership came to an end, Matt Forger became someone the King of Pop could lean on for support, along with Bruce Swedien. During this time, Michael was writing songs that had a lot of visual potential, so Matt Forger, propelled by new technological advancements, began to sharpen his cutting-edge techniques to make high-quality recordings, which very often became models for future work.

A partner as loyal as he was discreet

Over the years, Matt Forger became a living memory keeper, an archivist, and documentarian, who was often solicited when Michael's record company needed help with an anthology. He worked on the rerelease of Michael's solo albums in 2001 and on the release of *The Ultimate Collection* in 2004. Forger was consulted when Michael and his lawyer, Peter Lopez, signed a contract with Sony Music to celebrate the 25th anniversary of *Thriller*.

Forger was also lending his talents to other artists, notably a Japanese singer known as Yuming (full name Yumi Matsutoya). Once again, Forger used his expertise as a recording engineer and coproducer—and his constant quest for originality—to create a new sound for Yuming, who wanted to redefine herself. As a result, the singer was able to make a musical comeback: she achieved strong commercial success, which allowed Forger to win two Gold Disc Awards, the Japanese equivalent of the Grammys.

Although Michael was less productive during the 2000s, he and Matt Forger stayed in touch. In addition to their artistic relationship, Michael was fond of Matt and his family and regularly invited them to Neverland, where he and Matt would work while Matt's wife and daughter enjoyed the estate's relaxing, idyllic setting. Matt Forger was a real trooper. His professionalism matched his legendary discretion, and he remains a key figure within Michael's circle. Forger took care to respect the artist's legacy and continued to defend the strong values he shared with Michael, Quincy Jones, and Bruce Swedien. They were the mentors who had believed in him at the start of his career.

From left: Vincent Paterson, Michael Jackson, and Joe Pytka on the set of *The Way You make Me Feel* (1987).

JOE PYTKA
THE MAGIC EYE

Joe Pytka was born on 4 November 1938 in Pittsburgh, where he studied fine arts and chemistry at Carnegie Mellon University. He started out his film career at WRS Motion Pictures while still a student and, upon graduation, decided to move to New York, where he joined the postproduction team at MGM. As Pytka worked on more and more projects, he collected the contacts he would later draw upon to develop his own business. He then threw himself into directing an ambitious documentary about Steve McQueen and desert motorcycle racing. The film never came to fruition, but Pytka managed to complete a short called *High Flying Bird*, which contained images of the actor riding one of his hot rods.

Joe Pytka was a great lover of music. He incorporated songs by artists he admired into his works. Bob Dylan gave him permission to use his songs in the documentary *Maggie's Farm*. Later, Pytka moved on to producing commercials. In 1984, he directed Ronald Reagan's reelection campaign ad, which depicted the United States of the mid-1980s with a certain romanticism and a well-balanced sense patriotism. It was the perfect instrument for swaying the race against Reagan's Democratic opponent, Walter Mondale.

Pytka's role in creating the Jacksonian image

In 1983, Michael Jackson worked on several projects with Italian-American film director Bob Giraldi, who had previously produced and directed videos for *Beat It* and *Say Say Say*, and was familiar with Michael's tastes and preference for blending different sounds. But things changed on 27 January 1984: the director stood by helplessly as an unfortunate filming accident unfolded right before his eyes on the set of a Pepsi commercial (see page 263). Although Michael survived the event, his relationship with Giraldi did not. Michael wanted a new director for the first *Bad* videos, someone modern and attuned to public preferences. He fell in love with Joe Pytka's style, especially after watching the official campaign ad for Ronald Reagan's 1984 presidential race. From 1987, Joe Pytka would regularly make Michael's original ideas a reality while still developing ads for Pepsi, which was sponsoring the *Bad* and *Dangerous* tours. His style was easily recognizable: he enhanced each shot with lighting and filtering techniques that infused his images with a sense of magic. This was ideal for the big cathode ray tube TV screens of the 1980s. Pytka captivated the audience with simple scenes, and his editing skills, quick and in tune with the musical rhythms he used, were a perfect match for Michael Jackson's enigmatic image.

Stand-out commercials

During the *Bad* years, Pytka directed the videos for *The Way You Make Me Feel* and *Dirty Diana*. He also directed *The Chase*, a concept developed by Michael and his manager, Frank DiLeo. In this series of four commercials, Michael Jackson tries to lose a horde of fans and journalists. Shot as part of an ad campaign for Pepsi, these were the first US ads to ever be aired on Russian television.

In 1992, the two men teamed up again to create two new Pepsi commercials. The first one, called *Dreams*, saw Michael come to life on the cover of *Dangerous*, as if he were springing forth from the album cover, which had been painted by Mark Ryden. The second one, *I'll Be There*, depicted an imaginary meeting between an adult Michael and his teenage self. Special effects allowed both adult and teen MJs to perform a piano-voice version of the famous Jackson Five song at the same time. The commercial was broadcast during the 1993 Super Bowl half-time—a TV slot Pytka had often claimed, as his commercials were given pride of place each time the massive event was televised.

Pytka also helped develop the image of the second most famous MJ in the United States: Michael Jordan. In addition to the many commercials for his famous Air Jordan sneakers, Jordan and Jackson teamed up in *Space Jam*, a film that encapsulated Pytka's skills. However, Pytka dropped off the radar after that and stopped working with Michael Jackson, who from the mid-1990s onward was making videos with other artists.

THE WAY YOU MAKE ME FEEL

Michael Jackson / 4'58

Musicians
Michael Jackson: lead and backing vocals, finger snapping
John Robinson: drums
Eric Gale, David Williams: guitars
Kim Hutchcroft, Larry Williams: saxophones
Gary Grant, Jerry Hey: brass
Ollie E. Brown, Paulinho Da Costa: percussion
Christopher Currell: Synclavier, finger snapping
John Barnes, Michael Boddicker, Greg Phillinganes: synthesizers
Recording
Westlake Recording Studios (studio D), Los Angeles: 1987
Technical team
Producer: Quincy Jones
Coproducer: Michael Jackson
Recording engineers: Bruce Swedien and Matt Forger
Brass arrangements: Jerry Hey
Rhythm and vocal arrangements: Michael Jackson
Drum machine programming: Douglas Getschal
Synthesizer programming: Larry Williams
Mixing: Bruce Swedien

1987

FOR JACKSON ADDICTS

Before its release, the song was subtitled *Hot Fever*, but this was left out of the final album and single releases. It didn't show up again until 2001 on CDs promoting the US rerelease of *Bad*.

Single

A-side: *The Way You Make Me Feel* (*single*) / 4'26
B-side: *The Way You Make Me Feel* (*instrumental*) / 4'26
Released by Epic Records: USA (ref. 34-07645) and UK (ref. EPC 651275), 23 November 1987
Chart position: USA R&B No. 1, Pop No. 1 / UK No. 3

THE SONG

Genesis

Katherine Jackson had asked her son to write her an R&B song with a shuffle rhythm, so Michael wrote a piece that combined a funky and catchy rhythm with an ethereal melody, a nod to the classic Motown hits of the 1960s.

Michael's three-note bass line established a solid foundation for the song, giving it an intense backdrop that emphasized the melody and the arrangements. He wrote this song one step at a time, laying down the main melody and then the backing vocals one by one. In this way, he made it seem as if each part were responding to the other during the refrain. *The Way You Make Me Feel* was the positive version of *Billie Jean*. Instead of singing a sad love song, Michael Jackson indulged in the overused but enjoyable trope of the declaration of love.

Production

John Robinson's rendition of Michael's shuffle rhythm was a veritable last stand. Michael capped it off with the sort of beatboxing only he could produce, then set it on tape. Robinson's drums, equipped with digital pads, let rip a heavy and rich beat. The other elements were added later. Standing firm behind his instrument, the drummer did one session after another, playing nonstop rhythms for up to 12 minutes in a row.

As with *Bad*, Michael Jackson's moves became instruments to be added to the mix: by snapping his fingers throughout the song, Michael retained the human touch, which had risked being erased by Douglas Getschal's programming effects.

For his part, Quincy Jones amplified the R&B, even jazzy, tone of *The Way You Make Me Feel* by bringing in Jerry Hey and his unmatched talent for brass instruments. The final mix was slightly sped up in order to make the song more danceable and attractive to radio stations.

Bruce Swedien created various mixes for the maxi single. In the process, he had a revelation: he would let the rhythm run on and only keep the rich backing vocals. These included multiple harmonies stretched over 10 different tracks, but also finger snapping and the sound of Michael dancing behind the microphone. The result was hypnotic, and it can be heard on the long version of the maxi single, among other places. DJs were more than happy to add this version to their playlists.

FOR JACKSON ADDICTS

In 1987, the CD was setting in slowly and *The Way You Make Me Feel* was the first CD single commercialized in the UK. It helped launch the lucrative CD single market of the 1990s. Surprisingly, UK releases contained mono versions of the song, with similar timings and arrangements to those released on vinyl in the USA and Europe.

Michael Jackson and the actor Tatiana Thumbtzen kiss during the *Bad* tour concert on 3 March 1988 at Madison Square Garden, New York.

Early editions contain a 4'58 version ending with the backing vocalists singing the refrain on a loop. This was replaced in 1989 by a variation that revisited the same arrangements seen in the 4'26 single, but drawn out to 4'58. Ad-libs that Michael Jackson sings at 3'40 appear again at 4'30 on this version and are laid over the backing vocals repeating the chorus.

The Way You Make Me Feel was a tribute to musicals, a genre of which Michael Jackson was so fond.

THE SHORT FILM

Director: Joe Pytka
Producer: Michael Nesmith
Leading actors: Michael Jackson, Tatiana Thumbtzen, Joe Seneca
Extras and supporting actors: La Toya Jackson (extra), LaVelle Smith (dancer), other unidentified extras and dancers.
Shooting date: June 1987
Shoot location: Skid Row, Los Angeles
Duration: 14'22 / 9'22 / 6'43

1987

Genesis

Michael Jackson's manager Frank DiLeo and Quincy Jones reached out to Joe Pytka, who a few months before had created a series of Pepsi commercials with Michael. They asked him to create a video that would make Michael seem more masculine.

As with *Bad*, Jackson, Jones, and DiLeo wanted the video to have a long introduction. Pytka asked August Wilson to write the intro but he declined. The director showed Michael a documentary he had made about gangs harassing girls in the street. Michael liked his style, and the idea was adapted to the storyline of this second video excerpted from *Bad*.

The story they chose was simple: neighborhood boys try to get the attention of passing girls. Michael breaks away from the gang and places himself in front of a girl to try to win her over.

A casting call was put out to find new talent. Tatiana Thumbtzen, a 27-year-old model who'd already appeared in several commercials in Japan, stood out because of her uncanny resemblance to Michael Jackson, as if she were his female alter ego.

Production

The Way You Make Me Feel was filmed in June 1987, a few weeks before the *Bad* tour began in Japan. Michael insisted on the authenticity of the shots and asked the team to use the Los Angeles neighborhood of Skid Row. Like with *Beat It*, Joe Pytka took it one step further: he suggested recruiting real gang members.

Michael Jackson and Tatiana Thumbtzen were the main characters. The dance sequence was supposed to focus on Michael's moves as he followed the young woman down the street. It was agreed that this would be the only dance number, but Michael changed his mind and asked his choreographer, Vincent Paterson, to come up with a ballet finale. The two men put together a short dance inspired by Gene Kelly and Fred Astaire's musical comedies. The director learned of this plan at the last minute and had to adjust the filming schedule accordingly. Michael surrounded himself with dancers he'd worked with a few months before on the *Smooth Criminal* video, including LaVelle Smith. They rehearsed again and again.

Back in the writing room, Joe Pytka gave free rein to his love for documentaries. He created a 14'22 montage that provided context and introduced the film's secondary characters:

Michael Jackson performs *The Way You Make Me Feel*,
reproducing on stage the choreography of the short film.

the hooligans who hung around the block and their daily lives, which were marked by frequent acts of vengeance and arrests; and the girls, princesses lost in the dirty, sad streets who nevertheless continued to hope for a better future, one they fantasized about day after day. At 4'40, Michael Jackson appears on screen and confronts some of the neighborhood folk. After being put in his place by an intimidating shopkeeper, he runs into an old man who is surveying the scene from afar. The old wise man gives Michael a life lesson that inspires him to distance himself from the gang and find his own identity. This is the moment where the singer meets the character played by Tatiana Thumbtzen.

This version, though Michael approved it, couldn't be aired on television, especially on MTV, which had become a video factory churning out shorter and shorter music videos. Two other versions were prepared and submitted: the first one, lasting 6'43, starts at the point where Tatiana meets Michael on the corner. The second, 9'22 long, was a provisional version that had even more flair and introduced Michael's character earlier in the film.

FOR JACKSON ADDICTS

While rehearsing for the *Bad* tour in Pensacola, Florida, in February 1988, Michael Jackson recorded a new version of *The Way You Make Me Feel* in his hotel room. He planned on performing it at the 30th Grammy Awards on 2 March 1988 at Radio City Music Hall. He would later perform it again at a special concert for the Sultan of Brunei on 16 July 1996 and at Madison Square Garden on 7 and 10 September 2001. These latter two shows marked the 30th anniversary of Michael's solo career.

Speed Demon

Michael Jackson / 4'01

Musicians
Michael Jackson: lead and backing vocals, synthesized vocals
Larry Williams: MIDI saxophone (solo)
Miko Brando, Ollie E. Brown, and John Robinson: drums
Bill Bottrell and David Williams: guitars
Kim Hutchcroft: saxophone
Gary Grant and Jerry Hey: trumpets
Paulinho Da Costa: percussion
Christopher Currell: Synclavier and special effects
John Barnes, Michael Boddicker, and Greg Phillinganes: synthesizers
Recording
Westlake Recording Studios (studio D), Los Angeles: 1986
Technical team
Producers: Quincy Jones and Michael Jackson
Recording engineers: Matt Forger and Bruce Swedien
Sound arrangements: Ken Caillat and Tom Jones
Rhythmic arrangements: Michael Jackson and Quincy Jones
Synthesizer and horn arrangements: Jerry Hey
Vocal arrangements: Michael Jackson
Drum machine programming: Douglas Getschal
Synthesizer programming: Eric Persing
Mixing: Bruce Swedien

1987

Single

A-side: *Speed Demon (single edit)* / 4'01
B-side: *Speed Demon (single edit)* / 4'01
Released by Epic Records (as promo maxi-single only): France, 4 September 1989 (ref. PRO 548).

THE SONG

Genesis

"*Speed Demon* is a machine song," said Michael Jackson, in brief, in his autobiography *Moonwalk*. The song opens with the sound of an engine revving at full force, as if to announce that something electrifying is coming. At first, the lyrics are about the motorcycle driver wanting to arrive somewhere on time. Then the melody turns, driven by a strange heat. The motorcycle ride becomes a complex metaphor: is Michael channeling his intense and electrifying rhythm as a superstar or, as the video suggests, is he acting out his permanent escape from the paparazzi and his more maniacal fans? "Speed demon, you're the very same one / Who said the future's in your hands? / The life you save could be your own / You're preachin' 'bout my life like you're the law / Gonna live each day and hour like / For me there's no tomorrow." This very visual song evokes the figure of James Dean in *Rebel Without a Cause*.

Bruce Swedien recalls a funny story in his book *In the Studio with Michael Jackson*: whether intentionally or not, while on the way to the studio to record this song, he got a speeding ticket, which gave him the inspiration he needed to give the piece the intoxicating rhythm it demanded.

Production

Speed Demon is characterized by the percussive use of synthesizers. Louis Johnson was familiar with the piece, and his legendary bass could have provided a very nice musical line. But the team opted for a completely digital method. Michael Jackson's voice became an integral part of the percussive sound layering, to the point where his breathless and gimmicky style have never been complemented as well as they were in this piece.

The Synclavier digital synthesizer was the star of the song. The team used this computerized system to synthesize the myriad sampled sounds that Christopher Currell had created beforehand in Michael's studio. "On *Speed Demon*," explained Currell, "the original demo had a synthesizer sound doing a sweep up in the break before the solo. I thought that this was not very creative or interesting and had nothing to do with the song's content. My idea was to replace it with a race car shift-

The director Will Vinton and Michael Jackson on the set of *Speed Demon* in Los Angeles, March 1988.

ing through gears. I dropped the sounds into the Synclavier, made a patch, which included the gear shift sound, and I played the race car shifting through the gears in the right timing with the groove. Michael loved it, so it is what you hear in the final song."[81]

Midway through the song, a jazzy improvisation joins the synthesizer melody and the right-hand part, interrupting the frenzied rhythm. The tonality begins to rise, accompanying the mechanical theme with a crescendo that accentuates the shifting of gears and supports the music's increasingly frenetic speed. Various genres join in and blend together: a frenzied funk sets in before giving way to a metallic rock that is at times infused with warm, round blues tones. The musical sections are so different from each other in terms of rhythm and nuance that they almost lose the listener, which is likely the intention of this musical oddity.

In the *Bad 25* documentary, Michael can be seen giving Will Vinton precise instructions regarding the identities of the various characters in the California Raisins commercial, which included an animation of Michael's image (filmed a year after *Moonwalker*).

FOR JACKSON ADDICTS

Unlike the album, the French promotional maxi single of *Speed Demon* remains the only version of the song that doesn't fade into the beginning of *Liberian Girl*. New generations can enjoy a remix by Nero, rereleased for *Bad*'s 25th anniversary.

The final dance sequence of *Speed Demon* was overseen by Vincent Paterson.

Speed Demon was a parable about the people who harassed Michael Jackson.

THE SHORT FILM

Directors: Jerry Kramer and Will Vinton
Producers: Jerry Kramer, Will Vinton, Michael Jackson, Frank DiLeo
Claymation production: Will Vinton Productions, Inc.
Leading actor: Michael Jackson
Extras: Clancy Brown, Bill Bray, Miko Brando, and Eddie Garcia
Conception and execution: Will Vinton
Head animator: Doug Alberle
Head set designer: Bryan Jones
Director of photography: Crescenzo Notarille
Original score: Bruce Broughton
Choreography: Michael Jackson and Vincent Paterson
Motorcycle: Harley Davidson
Shooting date: March 1988
Shoot location: Warner Studios, Los Angeles
Duration: 10'10

Genesis

The video, which was folded into *Moonwalker*, was made in Claymation, a technique that experienced a revival in the 1970s and 1980s, and which was popularized by Will Vinton in commercials. Here, it was used in live action shots.

The scene is frenetic: a horde of people chase Michael's character, Spike the biker rabbit, through the sets at Warner Studios (renamed MJJ Studios for the video). During the chase, Spike runs into other celebrities being animated by Claymation: Sylvester Stallone, who appears as a construction worker showing off his muscles, Tina Turner, and Pee-Wee Herman.

After escaping from the paparazzi and his pestering fans, the biker takes a moment to rest in the California desert (reminiscent of the desert from the Wile E. Coyote and Road Runner cartoons by Warner Studios). He removes his suit, leaves it by the side of the road, and gets ready to ride off again, this time as Michael Jackson. As he's about to set off, someone taps him on the shoulder: it's Spike, who miraculously came to life again to challenge Michael to a dance-off. Only animation could have pulled off such improbable effects. All of a sudden, the camera pans to a surrealist road sign that bans dancing in the area! A passing police officer (Clancy Brown) issues Michael a ticket before Spike's character gives his accomplice one last wink and the video comes to an amicable end.

Production

Speed Demon was filmed in March 1988 and was integrated into *Moonwalker*, a larger project directed by Jerry Kramer. At Michael's request, the director hired Will Vinton to create the special effects for the animated high-speed chase scene where Michael plays Spike. "We shot the speed demon chase scene two days after Michael appeared on the Grammy Awards and did that remarkable hit where he dropped his knees," said Jerry Kramer of the filming of *Speed Demon*. "He bit the floor so hard, the whole world asked, 'How did he do that?' Well, he did that by hurting both knees! So we filmed the chase scene two days later with a guy who couldn't run. We worked around it."[82]

LIBERIAN GIRL

Michael Jackson / 3'52

Musicians
Michael Jackson: lead and backing vocals
Letta Mbulu: Swahili singing
John Robinson: drums
Paulinho Da Costa: percussion
Christopher Currell: Synclavier
John Barnes, Michael Boddicker, David Paich, Larry Williams: synthesizers
Recording
(Unknown): first version made for *Victory*, 1983
Westlake Recording Studios (studio D), Los Angeles: work started again under the working title *Pyramid Girl*, 1986
Technical team
Producers: Quincy Jones and Michael Jackson
Recording engineers: Matt Forger and Bruce Swedien
Drum machine programming: Douglas Getschal
Synthesizer programming: Steve Porcaro
Rhythmic arrangements: Michael Jackson, John Barnes, and Quincy Jones
Synthesizer arrangements: Jerry Hey, John Barnes, and Quincy Jones
Vocal arrangements: Michael Jackson and John Barnes
Swahili song arrangements: Caiphus Semenya
Mixing: Bruce Swedien

Single

A-side: *Liberian Girl (edit)* / 3'39
B-side: *Girlfriend (album version)* / 3'04
Released by Epic Records: UK, 3 July 1989 (ref. EPC 654947)
Chart position: UK No. 13

1987

THE SONG

Genesis

Liberian Girl was a favorite among the nine songs Michael wrote for *Bad*. He was already talking about composing the piece back in early 1984, during an interview filmed by his cameraman, Steve Howell. The interview was released in 1991 under the name *Unauthorized*. In it, Michael's smile spoke volumes about how much he loved working on new personal projects. Originally meant to appear on The Jacksons' *Victory* album, the song was shelved and replaced by *Be Not Always*. There was no doubt that Michael had bigger plans for *Liberian Girl* and wanted to keep it under his hat.

After the phenomenal success of *Bille Jean*, Quincy Jones had the brilliant idea to ask Michael to write most of the songs for *Bad*. *Liberian Girl* came out of the woodwork in 1986, under the working title *Pyramid Girl*. In 1987, the pop star said of the birth of the piece: "I wrote that at my house in the game room, I think I was playing some pinball or something and the song just popped into my head and I think I ran upstairs, put it on tape and it became *Liberian Girl*."[83]

The song is Michael Jackson's most beautiful tribute to Africa. The mysterious girl represents both his awareness of his origins and his hopes of understanding Africa. The theme progresses and unfolds as a declaration: "You know that you came / And you changed my world / Just like in the movies / With two lovers in a scene." Moved by the romanticism and tenderness of the piece, Quincy Jones and Bruce Swedien agreed to produce it. They overlaid its delicate embellishments, transforming the song into an ode to Africa and to the Liberian muse that inspired it.

Production

"*Naku penda piya / Naku taka piya / Mpenziwe*" ("I love you, too / I want you, too, my love"). South African singer Letta Mbulu opened the song with these few words in Swahili, which she sang beautifully. This was Michael's second time using Swahili in his work, after *Wanna Be Startin' Somethin'*. Quincy Jones, who traced his origins to East Africa, was particularly drawn to this language: in 1955, he famously put together the beautiful jazz arrangements for Clark Terry's song *Swahili*.

The image on the sleeve of the single *Liberian Girl*.

In 2015, Letta Mbulu spoke of her collaboration with Michael: "I was playing a concert in Senegal, and I got a call from my husband saying Quincy was doing a song and wanted someone who could sing in Swahili. I don't speak Swahili, but I was his go-to African voice [Quincy Jones and Letta Mbulu, *Many Rains Ago* (*Oluwa*), A&M Records, 1977] and I had a friend from Kenya who was able to help me write the words. It went something like '*Nakupenda*,' meaning 'I love you.' And I chanted 'ah-ah-ah-ah' at the end because I knew what Michael liked. He was very fascinated by me coming from Africa, but he was quite shy. It was an honor that he chose me—you couldn't get bigger than that."[84]

To create the introduction's unique atmosphere, Michael Boddicker added animalistic cries to the synth's sounds. He immediately followed these with an exotic bar that complemented Letta Mbulu's opening lyrics. The song's preponderance of blended sounds required the intervention of an army of experts, such as John Barnes, David Paich, Larry Williams, and Steve Porcaro. To this day, John Barnes is surprised at how quickly the song was recoded, given the clean, natural sound it achieved.

In the studio, everyone teamed up to bring this wonderful song to life. Bruce Swedien couldn't contain himself when it came to talking about *Liberian Girl*: "*Liberian Girl* is one of my absolute favorites of all the music that I've done with Michael...Michael's vocals on *Liberian Girl* are absolutely stellar!"[85] In 2012 he added that, "I'm a great believer of sonic fantasy, not sonic reality. Sonic fantasy means creating a soundscape that exists only in your imagination...*Liberian Girl* is a perfect example."[86] The song's atmosphere was so enthralling that many have asked Bruce Swedien for permission to create their own mix. Only recording engineer Russ Ragsdale, with Paulinho Da Costa, secured authorization. Nevertheless, former studio assistant Brad Sundberg, who still teaches seminars to fans, loves to have them listen to a percussive jungle mix version of the song. This mix could very well have come from Paulinho Da Costa.

Michael Jackson on the set of the short film *Liberian Girl*.

The South African singer Letta Mbulu recorded the Swahili words heard in *Liberian Girl* (1989).

THE SHORT FILM

Director: Jim Yukich
Producer: Paul Flattery
Leading actor: Michael Jackson
Extras (in order of appearance): Beverly Johnson, Malcolm-Jamal Warner, Sherman Hemsley, Brigitte Nielsen, Paula Abdul, Carl Weathers, Whoopi Goldberg, Quincy Jones, Jackie Collins, Amy Irving, Jasmine Guy, Rosanna Arquette, Billy Dee Williams, Lou Diamond Phillips, Olivia Newton-John, John Travolta, Corey Feldman, Steven Spielberg, Debbie Gibson, Rick Schroeder, Blair Underwood, Weird Al Yankovic, Bubbles, Suzanne Somers, Lou Ferrigno, Don King and his son, Mayim Bialik, Virginia Madsen, David Copperfield, unknown mystery person, Richard Dreyfuss and his daughter Emily, Danny Glover, Olivia Hussey, Dan Aykroyd, and Steve Guttenberg
Shooting date: 18 April 1989
Shoot location: A&M Chaplin Stage, Los Angeles
Duration: 3'49

Genesis

Exhausted from previous videos, Michael Jackson did not want to appear in this one. So director Jim Yukich, hired by CBS, came up with a new idea: he would have a group of celebrities await Michael's arrival on set. The singer liked the idea, and filming started without precise specifications. Richard Dreyfuss, who'd just finished filming a special program with Yukich, was the first to accept the role. He suggested inviting Steven Spielberg along, and as bigger and bigger names joined the project, the guest star cast grew. Michael's chimp, Bubbles, joined in as well. He was a stand-in for the anticipated arrival of his famous owner.

Production

The video was filmed in two days. Jim Yukich quietly moved about the set, filming the actors mingling with only a few script lines to go on. He captured John Travolta and Olivia Newton-John, who hadn't worked together since *Grease*, and Steven Spielberg, who was annoyed at having to be on the other side of the camera for once. Scriptwriter Rob Schneider wrote a few lines of dialogue, but on the whole, Yukich got a continuous shot of the general good mood and eagerness to meet the star. To lend further legitimacy to the video, Michael was finally persuaded to participate, however minimally. He agreed to a cameo in the last scene, which was shot in 15 minutes and in a single take. "OK everybody, that's a wrap," he announced after suddenly appearing behind a camera, as if he were the video's director of photography. The video for *Liberian Girl* was only broadcast in Europe from July 1989.

FOR JACKSON ADDICTS

***Liberian Girl*, the ninth single from *Bad*, was only released in Europe, Japan, and Australia, as a radio edit without the fade-out from *Speed Demon*, which precedes *Liberian Girl* on the album. The instrumental version did not appear on the single, only on a 10-inch acetate disc.**

Michael Jackson and Stevie Wonder on stage during the *Bad* tour in Brisbane, Australia, 28 November 1987.

Just Good Friends

Terry Britten, Graham Lyle / 4'05

Musicians
Michael Jackson, Stevie Wonder: lead and backing vocals
Stevie Wonder: synthesizer (solo)
Ollie E. Brown, Humberto Gatica, and Bruce Swedien: drums
Michael Landau: guitar
Kim Hutchcroft and Larry Williams: saxophones
Gary Grant and Jerry Hey: brass
Paulinho Da Costa: percussion
Christopher Currell: Synclavier
Michael Boddicker, Rhett Lawrence, Greg Phillinganes, and Larry Williams: synthesizers
Recording
Westlake Recording Studios (studio D), Los Angeles: 1987
Technical team
Producer: Quincy Jones
Coproducer: Michael Jackson
Recording engineers: Bruce Swedien and Matt Forger
Synthesizer and vocal arrangements: Terry Britten, Graham Lyle, and Quincy Jones
Brass arrangements: Jerry Hey
Vocal arrangements: Michael Jackson
Drum machine programming: Cornelius Mims
Mixing: Bruce Swedien

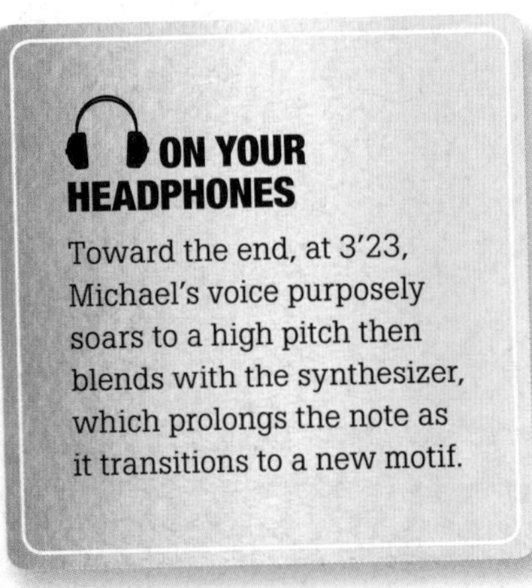
ON YOUR HEADPHONES
Toward the end, at 3'23, Michael's voice purposely soars to a high pitch then blends with the synthesizer, which prolongs the note as it transitions to a new motif.

Genesis

In 1984, Terry Britten and Graham Lyle resurrected Tina Turner's musical career with *What's Love Got to Do with It*. Quincy wanted *Bad* to have something very special: a combination of *The Girl Is Mine* and *P. Y. T.*, a poppy yet funky duet that would unite two legends of African-American music: Michael Jackson and Stevie Wonder.

These elements might seem like the perfect ingredients for a spectacular and memorable song, but things didn't turn out that way. The making of *Just Good Friends* drowned in its own ambitions, or rather, in its lack of ambition: without a strong and original idea, the song became mired in the same old story of two men fighting over a woman.

Just Good Friends was one of only two songs that Michael didn't write for *Bad*. It appears at the end of the A-side, as if to give Michael time to breathe before moving on to the rest of the record, which still has some tasty morsels to offer. The collaboration between the two friends was promising, but the expected fireworks didn't materialize. Thirty years after the release of the album, Quincy Jones admitted to having poorly managed this collaboration between the two Motown prodigies: "I made a mistake on the duet with him and Stevie [*Just Good Friends*, written by Terry Britten and Graham Lyle]. That didn't work."[87]

Production

Just Good Friends was an interesting collaboration between Michael and Quincy's regular studio musicians, Chris Currell's Synclavier, and Stevie Wonder's synthesizer, which gave the piece a solo like no other. In the manner of *P. Y. T.*, the groove created by the bass line is totally distinct from the melody. Coupled with Ollie E. Brown's rhythmic tracks and supplemented by a drum machine, the synth layers add a modern but perhaps too artificial touch to the piece. The guitar and brass arrangements give it a more conventional funk feel.

Just Good Friends was among the first songs to combine 1980s R&B with pop, though it did so in a somewhat wonky manner. Quincy Jones would later fine-tune this sound for his album *Back on the Block* (1989).

The 1985 recording session at Westlake was filmed and included in *Captain EO*. Matt Forger and John Barnes can be seen behind the console as Michael Jackson records *We Are Here to Change the World* in the booth.

ANOTHER PART OF ME

Michael Jackson / 3'53

Musicians
Michael Jackson: lead and backing vocals
Paul Jackson Jr. and David Williams: guitars
Kim Hutchcroft and Larry Williams: saxophones
Gary Grant and Jerry Hey: trumpets
Christopher Currell: Synclavier
Rhett Lawrence and John Barnes: synthesizers
Recording
Westlake Recording Studios (studio D), Los Angeles: 1985 to 1986
Technical team
Producers: Quincy Jones and Michael Jackson
Recording engineers: Matt Forger and Bruce Swedien
String arrangements: Jerry Hey
Rhythmic and vocal arrangements: Michael Jackson and John Barnes
Mixing: Bruce Swedien

1987

FOR JACKSON ADDICTS

As well as maxi single and instrumental versions, Bruce Swedien made four other versions, released on various maxi singles: extended dance mix (6'18), radio edit (4'24), dub mix (3'51), and a cappella (4'01).

A-side: *Another Part of Me* (*single*) / 3'47
B-side: *Another Part of Me* (*instrumental*) / 3'47
Released by Epic Records: USA (ref. 34-07962) and UK (ref. EPC 652844), 11 July 1988
Chart position: USA R&B No. 1, Pop No. 11 / UK No. 15

THE SONG

Genesis and production

After finishing his lengthy *Victory* tour in 1985, Michael met with recording engineer Matt Forger at his family studio to lay the foundation for his new album. Much like the inconspicuous Bill Wolfer, who worked on *Thriller*, Matt Forger was the true creator behind *Bad* (see page 304). The sound specialist spent almost a year thinking about the songs he would present to Quincy Jones.

The first few songs he worked on were *Another Part of Me* and *We Are Here to Change the World*, which had to be quickly included in Disney's 3D film *Captain EO* (released on 12 September 1986). *Another Part of Me* stuck out from the album like a sore thumb and came at the worst possible moment because of how closely the lyrics matched the theme from the film: "This is our planet / You're one of us...The planets are linin' up / We're bringin' brighter days." Captain EO spread a universal message of love, rallying people to a just cause. The universe, space, and interstellar friendship were all ideas that had already been developed and included in *Can You Feel It* (*Triumph*, 1980).

After recording *We Are Here to Change the World*, Michael Jackson gave Matt Forger his musical and rhythmic instructions for *Another Part Of Me*. Forger followed them to the letter. Bruce Swedien took over the song in 1986 and added clinking and other sound effects needed to incorporate it into *Captain EO*. He also used Matt Forger's initial takes to mix the album version and create adaptations for the maxi singles.

When it came time to select the songs for *Bad*, *Another Part of Me* was pitted against *Streetwalker*. "It's funny because he really wanted this song to be on the album," recalled Quincy Jones in an interview. "I was in the studio that day and DiLeo was there, too—he was asking us to choose the songs that would be on the album...Michael had his heart set on *Streetwalker* while I preferred *Another Part of Me*, which had an ambiance I was particularly interested in. We spent a lot of time debating and bickering over this."[88] In the end, *Streetwalker* was dropped and didn't come out until it appeared on the album's special edition in 2001.

Another Part of Me was the sixth single to be released, but unfortunately, it didn't reach No. 1 in the Pop charts unlike the first five singles.

Michael Jackson visits China during the *Bad* tour in 1987.

THE SHORT FILM

Director and producer: Patrick Kelly
Leading actor: Michael Jackson
Extras: Frank DiLeo, the musicians from the *Bad* tour, and various characters
Shooting dates: May to July 1988
Shoot locations:
• Wembley Stadium, London
• Parc des Princes, Paris
Duration: 4'45

Genesis

By the late 1980s, music videos were evolving. Janet Jackson's *Control* (1987) launched a new genre: the sensitive and immersive video that allowed television viewers to become privileged witnesses to events unfolding on screen. Cameras were capturing dance moves, closely following them from live on stage to the pit before diving straight into the details of the moves.

Production

The music video was created by combining shots from *Bad* tour concerts in Europe, especially those from Parc des Princes in Paris and Wembley in London. Patrick T. Kelly assembled the images by starting with pan shots of jubilant fans, then punctuated them with images of celebrities coming to watch the latest stage phenomenon. Michael's graceful swaying was well received and his breaks and resumptions perfectly complemented the music. In the background, Greg Phillinganes created an infectious enthusiasm and a natural freshness by whirling and twirling frenetically at his keyboards. Images of fans fainting by the stage added to the singularity of the event. They were quickly hauled out of the pit by an army of security guards. The first version of the video was released on Saturday 30 July 1988 on MTV as part of a show called *Michael Jackson: Around the World.* A second version, which became the official one, was released with added sound effects and a few new shots.

In his *Bad 25* documentary, Spike Lee used a whole new set of high-definition images from the *Bad* tour. In so doing, he proved that very high-quality sources did exist, unlike those from Michael Jackson's personal VHS recording, which served as a bonus for the collector's anniversary edition of *Bad*.

FOR JACKSON ADDICTS

On 19 September 1988, one week before the *Bad* tour returned to the United States, MTV aired a 30-minute documentary, *Another Part of Me,* showing images from the European tour. It still has a cult following.

Man in the Mirror

Siedah Garret and Glen Ballard / 5'18

Musicians
Michael Jackson: lead and backing vocals
Siedah Garret: backing vocals
The Winans (Carvin Winans, Marvin Winans, Michael Winans, and Ronald Winans): backing vocals
Andraé Crouch and the Andraé Crouch Choir (Sandra Crouch, Maxi Anderson, Rose Banks, Geary Faggett, Vonciele Faggett, Andrew Gouché, Linda Green, Francine Howard, Jean Johnson, Perry Morgan, Alfie Silas): backing vocals
Ollie E. Brown: clap
Dann Huff: guitar
Greg Phillinganes: keyboards
Glen Ballard and Randy Kerber: synthesizers
Recording
Westlake Recording Studios (studio D), Los Angeles: 1987
Technical team
Producers: Quincy Jones and Michael Jackson
Recording engineer: Bruce Swedien
Rhythmic arrangements: Glen Ballard and Quincy Jones
Synthesizer arrangements: Glen Ballard, Quincy Jones, and Jerry Hey
Vocal arrangements: Andraé Crouch
Mixing: Bruce Swedien

1987

On the cover of her single *I Don't Go for That*, Siedah Garrett is wearing a blue jacket sewn with leather musical notes that represent the melody in *Man in the Mirror*.

Single

A-side: *Man in the Mirror* (*single*) 4'55
B-side: *Man in the Mirror* (*instrumental*) 4'55
Released by Epic Records: USA,16 January 1988 (ref. 34-07668) / UK, 8 February 1988 (ref. EPC 651388)
Chart position: USA R&B No. 1, Pop No. 1 / UK No. 2

THE SONG

Genesis

To complete the song selection for *Bad*, Michael and Quincy went looking for something that "would spread some sunshine on the world"[86] and bring a certain seriousness to the project. Quincy asked the singer-songwriters from his Qwest label to write some original productions. Siedah Garrett rose to the challenge with a touching and unusual track: "All I wanted to do was give Michael something he would want to say to the world, and I knew it couldn't be another 'Oh baby, I love you' song. It had to be a little bit more than that. It needed to have some substance. He hadn't recorded anything like this to that point. I was just taking the risk that he might not get it, you know...It was a huge privilege for me when Quincy decided that the song was good enough to play for Michael—to consider recording for the *Bad* album."[89]

During a July 2014 trip to Paris, Siedah Garrett spoke at a seminar organized by Dorothy's Gallery: "*Man in the Mirror*, wow, this song changed my life...I'd been signed for two and half years of my five-year contract with Quincy Jones and I hadn't written anything of note...he gave me an idea of what he wanted the song to be."[90] She spoke at length about the origins of the song's title (the story of which started long before she wrote it), during a session with John Beasley. The pianist had answered a phone call in a mysterious way, and Siedah had asked herself "What kind of man could he be? A man in the mirror?" Much later, when Quincy assigned her to work with writer Glen Ballard, the expression "man in the mirror" popped into her head. Words came to her all by themselves, in such a flood, she insisted, that her hand couldn't keep up with the writing. She finished the first two verses and the chorus within 15 minutes.

Glen Ballard finished writing as Siedah Garrett got ready to record the song's first demo. She was so overwhelmed with enthusiasm that she stopped by Quincy's place in the middle of the weekend to drop off the tape. She didn't have to wait long for a response: two to three hours later, Quincy called to say "Sid, this is the best song that I've heard in ten years!"[86]

Later, Michael Jackson called her to finish writing the piece. "I'd never spoken to Michael before...and inside I'm like 'Oh my God, it's Michael Jackson!' [laughing] but on the phone [com-

Michael Jackson performs *Man in the Mirror* at the Grammy Awards in Radio City Music Hall, New York, 2 March 1988.

posed] 'How can I help you?'...He told me he wanted the chorus to be longer...but I didn't want him to write it. So I gave him six different stanzas to choose, and he chose 'You gotta get it right, while you got the time / 'Cause when you close your heart, then you close your mind.'...Michael begins to tell me 'I love your song.' The second thing he said to me was 'I love your voice.'"[90]

The pitch Siedah used to record her first demo was too high for Michael's voice. She reworked it in his presence, in Westlake's studio D, while he filmed her.

Man in the Mirror is the backbone of the *Bad* album. The first few verses of the song give off a sense of helplessness: they dwell on how the world ignores the suffering of others, and on its lack of awareness concerning their needs. Then comes a resolution that is full of energy and hope: "If you wanna make the world a better place / Take a look at yourself and then make a change!"

Michael didn't want to just accept the values espoused by the piece. He wanted to make them shine with conviction. During both the *Bad* and *Dangerous* tours, fans shed tears each time Michael sang *Man in the Mirror*. On stage, he would spin around frantically—as if to create the winds of change—before kneeling to beg the world to hear his message and act on his request. He continued to raise awareness at each concert that he performed. With time, he became one with the song, as was illustrated by his performance of it at the 1988 Grammys.

Production

"*Man in the Mirror* to me totally represents that place that Michael started directing his energy to," said Matt Forger in a 2012 interview with *Time* magazine. "You start to really see where Michael's heart is, where his soul is, what his intent was for, what he would like to accomplish with his music."[91]

Part of the proceeds from the single were donated to Camp Ronald McDonald, an association that helps children with cancer. The record was dedicated to Yoshiaki Hagiwara, a five-year-old Japanese child who was kidnapped and killed in 1987. As the *Bad* tour traveled across Japan, the singer dedicated it to the young boy and said he would pay for the funeral.

A second *Man in the Mirror* video, directed and produced by Patrick Kelly (director of the *Another Part of Me* video), was filmed during the *Bad* tour. It was used in the opening song of the film *Moonwalker*.

Greg Phillinganes, Glen Ballard, and Randy Kerber's keyboards and synthesizers gave the song a heavenly sound, as if to gradually elevate its message to the skies. The sounds ring out, bewitch, captivate. The guitar comes in at the first refrain, allowing the song to reach a whole new emotional level. The melody, now enriched, starts to build up, inviting the listener to focus even more on the intended message. Then comes a clap (a percussion instrument imitating the sound of hands clapping) from Ollie E. Brown. His drummer, John Robinson, later explained that the sound was made by overlaying two parts, one of which was denser and speeded up to 15 percent of its tempo. This gave a more powerful sound when it was played at regular speed. He thought it was the most beautiful clap ever recorded. Bruce Swedien said he played and recorded the snare drum track at home. He added the sound of two plywood planks being struck one against the other.

This flood of musicality drove Michael to release wild, staccato sounds and give off more and more energy as the music and lyrics progressed.

Michael made Andraé Crouch listen to the working version of *Man in the Mirror.* Crouch suggested putting his chorus on the word "change," which Michael agreed to immediately. Bruce Swedien then spread the members of the Andraé Crouch Choir throughout the Westlake studio in order to create an extremely powerful effect. He used two Neumann M-49 microphones positioned at 90 degrees and as close to one another as possible (the Blumlein technique). The recording was natural and very impressive—the piece literally ignited. The music and the choir exploded, reaching the type of quality that Quincy Jones and Michael Jackson were looking for. The song comes to an end on a calm and confident high point. Then the singer finishes it off with his soft voice: "Make that change."

Man in the Mirror was the fourth single to reach No. 1 on *Billboard* and remains among Michael's fans' favorite songs.

THE SHORT FILM

Director: Don Wilson
Producers: Chuck Haifley and Seth Blair
Executive producer: Larry Stessel
Editing: Archival footage and images of Michael Jackson (from the *Bad* tour, Japan, 1987)
Shoot date: (unknown)
Shooting location: (unknown)
Duration: 5'03

Genesis

For the video, Larry Stessel, the CEO of Epic, reached out to Don Wilson—who also directed the CBS special *Michael Jackson: The Magic Returns*—and told him Michael wanted to tell a really harrowing story. "This was the day after Thanksgiving," explained the director. "We met in the attic of [Jackson manager] Frank DiLeo's home in Encino...So, Michael and I sat down and just started making a list of things that we could think of. I had two or three handwritten pages of ideas. Michael wasn't the kind of guy who told you what to do, he would inspire you to go do it with his backing."[33]

Production

"I went to all these places that have archival news footage and said, 'Give me all your worst stuff,'" explained Don Wilson. "And by the end of the day, I'd looked at dead bodies and massacres and famine. After a while, I would go to a bar—immediately. It was brutal. I probably had 200 hours of footage."[33] The video was full of images of the greatest figures in the history of humanity: Gandhi, Martin Luther King, Mother Theresa, JFK, Lech Wałęsa. Wilson wanted to make a reversible video: "What I mean is if one were to play the video in reverse they'd notice that it begins with purity and innocence, and man's inaction and injustices create chaos, hopelessness,

1987

During the *Bad* tour, Michael Jackson visits the Nagatacho Elementary School in Tokyo, 30 September 1987.

and war."[92] Michael didn't ask for any changes—the images had moved him to tears.

I Just Can't Stop Loving You

Michael Jackson / 4'23 (with spoken intro)

Musicians
Michael Jackson and Siedah Garrett: lead vocals
Michael Jackson: spoken intro
Nathan East: bass
Ndugu Chancler: drums
Dann Huff: guitar
Paulinho Da Costa: percussion
John Barnes: piano
Christopher Currell: Synclavier
David Paich and Greg Phillinganes: synthesizers
Recording
Westlake Recording Studios (studio D), Los Angeles: 1987
Technical team
Producers: Quincy Jones and Michael Jackson
Recording engineer: Bruce Swedien
Rhythmic arrangements: Quincy Jones
Synthesizer arrangements: David Paich and Quincy Jones
Vocal arrangements: Michael Jackson and John Barnes
Synthesizer programming: Steve Porcaro
Sound effects: Hugo Zuccarelli
Mixing: Bruce Swedien

1987

On his Facebook page, Brad Sundberg wrote that the song's intro was cut in new editions of the album because DJs found it too long. Thankfully, its full length was reinstated for *Bad 25*.

Single

A-side: *I Just Can't Stop Loving You* (*with spoken intro*) (*single*) / 4'17
B-side: *Baby Be Mine* (*album version*) / 4'14
Released by Epic Records: USA (ref. 34-07253), 22 July 1987 / UK (ref. EPC 650 202), 27 July 1987
Chart position: USA R&B No. 1, Pop No. 1 / UK No. 1
RIAA: certified Gold 28 September 1987

Genesis

This love song had the monumental task of launching the promotion of the *Bad* album. To everyone's surprise, after the success of the high-octane *Thriller* and the wild *Victory* tour, Michael returned to the stage with a song that was calm and strangely sensual. It was unlike anything in the repertoire he'd amassed until then. Nothing, or almost nothing, had yet been leaked about the *Bad* project. Only one single and the image on its cover had been released by July 1987. The images stood out in their simplicity: the singer looks serene, has mid-length hair, his arms are folded in front of him, and his face is ensconced in shadows, so that his eyes are barely visible. *I Just Can't Stop Loving You* has a mystery about it, a strange calm before the storm. It might seem trivial that Michael was recording a love song given how many he'd recorded in his Motown days...except that now—and this changes everything—the song was written, composed, and produced with his tender loving care.

In the song, Michael whispers tender words to his beloved and declares his love for her: "I just want to lay next to you for a while / You look so beautiful tonight / Your eyes are so lovely / Your mouth is so sweet / A lot of people misunderstand me / That's because they don't know me at all / I just want to touch you / And hold you / I need you / God I need you / I love you so much." This 30-second introduction was a marriage of love between the *Thriller* years and those that started off *Bad*: while girls were now swooning to his lyrics, the boys still remembered the hunk from *Thriller*, a perfect sex symbol to emulate.

The piece is followed by a beautiful duet, which Michael planned on singing with Barbra Streisand or Whitney Houston before Quincy Jones decided on Siedah Garrett. As she recalled,

> Quincy called me back two days later, and I thought we were gonna finish *Man in the Mirror*. I went there and it was just Bruce Swedien (an engineer), Quincy, Michael, and me, and I sat in the back of the studio waiting for Quincy to be ready for me to do whatever I was gonna do...I remember walking to the room, in the recording studio, and opening the doors seeing two music stands, and two microphones. On each music stand was a lyrics sheet and on the lyrics sheet it said

Siedah Garrett and Michael Jackson record *I Just Can't Stop Loving You* at Westlake Recording Studios, Los Angeles, in 1987.

"Michael / Siedah / Michael / Siedah," and it was in that moment that I realized: Oh my God, I'm singing a duet with Michael Jackson—with the King of Pop—unreal! It was so unreal. While recording it, Michael recorded his part, but when it came to me singing my verses, he began tossing popcorn in my face in an effort to make me mess up. Quincy Jones, not seeing this, began to chastise me for flubbing the takes. Michael, on the other hand, was just cracking up![89]

Using trusting words, Michael declares his passion for his new love in the song. Shy and charming, he expresses his feelings with a crescendo, accompanied by Siedah Garrett's unique voice, soft but powerful and tinted with blues.

Production

Speaking of the recording, assistant recording engineer Brad Sundberg mentioned "pillow talk." The plan was to bring Michael's voice as close to the listener as possible, to emulate an intimate conversation. The methods used were impressive. For the spoken intro, Bruce Swedien had Michael whisper the lyrics into the ear of a mannequin, whose head was covered in microphones. After they switched to the QSound processor, the product was impressive. There are many photos of Michael lying in bed with this head covered in microphones and a nylon stocking. "I was in a bed when I was doing that. I was lying under covers and everything. I did that whole rap in the dark. I say, 'A lot of people misunderstand me, that's because they don't know me at all.' And I guess that's true. People believe a lot of crazy stories they read. And some are true, some not."[83]

Sheryl Crow sang the song on stage with Michael Jackson during the *Bad* tour, standing in for Siedah Garret, who was recording her *Kiss of Life* album (1988).

Michael Jackson and the young Sheryl Crow on the *Bad* tour in London, July 1988.

From a musical standpoint, David Paich said he was glad to have worked on this song, which he thought resembled a 1960s song. His and Greg Phillinganes' synthesizers lightly back the spoken intro, creating the bridge that softly introduces the main theme. The rhythm, which is almost metronomic, never overdoes it. It discretely accompanies the positive vibes given off by the two singers, and seems to disappear entirely in the second part of the piece. Nathan East's bass beautifully highlights the vocal variations with a regular changing of chords. John Barnes' piano adds an echo that emphasizes the romance of the theme.

Quincy Jones and Michael Jackson decided to make a Spanish and a French version of the song, both of which reinforced the message of love.

1987

Todo mi amor lo eres tu

(***I Just Can't Stop Loving You***, Spanish version)
Michael Jackson, Rubén Blades / 4'10

Rubén Blades, the king of salsa, was asked to write the Spanish version. "Quincy Jones called to ask me to help him with a request from Michael Jackson," he explained. "He wanted to sing in Spanish for the first time in his professional career. I adapted *I Just Can't Stop Loving You (Todo mi amor lo eres tu)* into Spanish and I spent three days with Michael, Quincy, and Humberto Gatica's sound engineer, teaching him how to pronounce the words, taking the role of coach during the recording. I think he did a spectacular job. He was extremely professional, an excellent student, and thrilled to be singing in Spanish."[93] Initially relegated to the Spanish-speaking market (as a single and as a bonus track for vinyl or CD editions), this version was made available more widely in 2001 for the special edition of the *Bad* album.

Je ne veux pas la fin de nous

(***I Just Can't Stop Loving You***, French version)
Michael Jackson, Christine "Coco" Decroix / 4'07

The French version was created by a Belgian friend of Quincy Jones, Christine Decroix. The weak translation, and Michael and Siedah's sometimes glaring struggles with turning the lyrics into French, may explain why the song wasn't released at the time. It came out on the *Bad 25* album. It remains a hidden gem nonetheless.

Like with the first single from *Thriller*, *The Girl Is Mine*, *I Just Can't Stop Loving You* was promoted without a video, as per Michael's request. The song reached No. 1 on the US *Billboard*, staying there for 14 weeks, gradually building up expectations for the new album.

FOR JACKSON ADDICTS

An exclusive promotional maxi single in Spanish has the words *"Canta en español"* on its cover. The verses are sung in English, the refrain in Spanish (ref. ARI 2059).

PORTRAIT

JOHN BARNES
THE PIANIST OF THE GREATS

Michael Jackson and John Barnes: a trusting partnership that stood the test of time.

John Barnes' immense modesty shouldn't distract from the fact that he was an incredibly talented musician and a major, long-lasting influence on Michael Jackson. In the first hours of the 1970s, at the beginning of his career, the pianist and keyboardist played his Fender Rhodes piano for Marvin Gaye's album *I Want You* (1976). Motown's greatest artists enlisted his valuable talents: The Four Tops, The Miracles, and Edwin Starr. John's subsequent partnerships were equally prestigious: Bill Withers, Minnie Riperton, Shalamar, Herb Alpert, and so on.

His position as arranger, composer, and instrumentalist allowed him to join the Jackson family fold: he worked on *Victory* in 1984, he accompanied Jermaine Jackson as he made his comeback after leaving Motown, and he supported Janet Jackson's *Dream Street* album that same year. Before setting up shop as part of Michael Jackson's solo career, John Barnes participated in several side projects with Diana Ross (*Eaten Alive*) and Jennifer Holliday (*Say You Love Me)*, most notably, as well as *We Are the World*.

He could have boasted, though he never did, of being part of the musical dream team that allowed Michael to pursue his talent as a composer at Hayvenhurst. Alongside Matt Forger and Bill Bottrell, John Barnes recorded, accompanied, and edited the myriad demos produced for *Bad*. He continued to advise the King of Pop during the making of *HIStory* too.

Rarely interviewed, the pianist continues to quietly share his passion and expert advice. Recently, he helped to develop Soft Mozart 2.0, an innovative and fun piece of piano software.

DIRTY DIANA

Michael Jackson / 4'52

Musicians
Michael Jackson: lead and backing vocals, claves
Steve Stevens: guitar (solo)
John Robinson: drums
Paul Jackson Jr. and David Williams: guitars
Christopher Currell: Synclavier
John Barnes, Michael Boddicker, and Randy Waldman: synthesizers
Recording
Westlake Recording Studios (studio D), Los Angeles: 1986
Technical team
Producer: Quincy Jones
Coproducer: Michael Jackson
Recording engineers: Bruce Swedien and Matt Forger
Synclavier programming: Denny Jaeger
Vocal arrangements: Michael Jackson
Rhythmic arrangements: Michael Jackson, John Barnes, and Jerry Hey
Synthesizer arrangements: Michael Jackson, Quincy Jones, and John Barnes
String arrangements: John Barnes
Drum programming: Douglas Getschal
Mixing: Bruce Swedien

1987

Single

A-side: *Dirty Diana (single version)* / 4'42
B-side: *Dirty Diana (instrumental version)* / 4'42
Released by Epic Records: USA (ref. 34 07739) and UK (ref. EPC 651546), 12 April 1988
Chart position: USA R&B No. 5, Pop No. 1 / UK No. 4

THE SINGLE

Genesis

"Michael's songs, even if they have some abstract basis, they always somehow are autobiographical," said Quincy Jones.[88] *Dirty Diana* is the perfect example of this. "I love *Dirty Diana*, that's one of my favorites...Because it's a life story of a groupie. I hate to say the word 'groupie' but that's what it is and it's something that I've experienced and a lot of people who grew up on the road experienced."[83]

Dirty Diana was the logical follow up to *Beat It*. It continued to build up Michael Jackson's strong relationship with rock. The singer had written a plaintive ballad full of bitterness and built around three rotating chords that increased in pressure, culminating in a rage-filled refrain.

Upon the release of the song, many wondered who this famous Diana was, this easy young woman Michael was talking about. Everyone's attention landed on Diana Ross, Michael's fairy godmother and muse, who on 23 October 1985 had married successful Norwegian businessman Arne Næss. Michael was visibly saddened by news of this marriage. Although he never publicly spoke of his reasons for using this name, all signs pointed to the former leader of The Supremes as the subject of this sad love song.

Michael Jackson was looking for a guitarist to accompany him for this song. *Beat It* had inadvertently caused Van Halen to break up. The other members of the group had never forgiven Eddie for playing for such a mainstream artist as Michael. When he was working on *Dirty Diana*, the singer had set his sights on Steve Stevens, Billy Idol's longtime musical partner since the days of Generation X. Unlike Van Halen, Idol and Stevens had broken up well before *Dirty Diana*, just after the release of *Whiplash Smile* in 1986. Michael's unexpected proposition was perfect timing for the guitarist: he was on the verge of releasing his solo work—an audio tape of his first songs was included in the May 1986 edition of *Guitar World*.

In 2012, for the 25th anniversary of *Bad*, Steve Stevens spoke of his first meeting with Michael and Quincy:

> Quincy Jones called me, and I had just been signed to Warner Brothers directorates, and my A&R guy was Ted Templeman, who was the producer of Van Halen. And

Every concert by Michael Jackson had its fair share of fans on the verge of fainting.

Ted and Quincy were friends so that's how Eddie Van Halen ended up doing *Beat It*. So when it came time for the next record, Quincy called Ted and said, "Who can we get, we don't want to do the same thing again." And Ted suggested me, and then I got a phone call—I was living in New York at the time—and I got a phone call from Quincy Jones. So the phone rang and I thought somebody was f**king with me, so I hung up the phone, and then the phone rings again and he goes, "Don't hang up, because this is the real deal. I got your number from Ted Templeman and we're working on Michael's follow up to *Thriller*, and would you be interesting in coming in and playing on the track." So that's how that came about.[94]

Production

Equipped with a Jackson guitar (you can't make this stuff up), Steve Stevens arrived at the Westlake studios to record his solo for *Dirty Diana*. He had one condition: he wanted the singer to be there. In fact—as irony would have it—he'd already worked on a record with Diana Ross, the likely subject of *Dirty Diana*, but she wasn't there on the day of the recording. She was sorry to miss it.

While the other rhythmic guitars were being played by Paul Jackson Jr. and David Williams, Stevens plugged in his Jackson and dove into the captivating world of *Dirty Diana*: "I had made some prior assumptions about this song. The first thing that hit me was that it was much darker and heavier than I'd expected. It looked like it had a lot of character, with a strong dose of malice, which was great for me, because as a guitarist you want to go deep and play aggressively."[94]

Bruce Swedien recorded the session. With Michael and Quincy's support, he began to prepare alternative versions and mixes that could be used for the single.

"The version that I played on was about seven minutes long," recalled Stevens. "They recorded much the same way that we did with Billy Idol. We always prepared for dance remixes, extended versions, and we always knew that this kind of stuff would be played in dance clubs. So you needed material to do remixes, etc. They explained to me that the song was gonna be edited down, but they were gonna give me this full version to play on, and it was maybe two minutes of guitar solo there and then the actual song itself...It was not a big entourage or anything, it was four guys in a studio [Michael Jackson, Quincy Jones, Bruce Swedien, and Steve Stevens] just trying to make great music. That kind of put me at ease. But then you realize we're all just here to make music and once we got down to it that other stuff kind of fell away and it just spoke in musical terms. Michael was really very musical. The things he requested and asked for were all really cool ideas, he understood what I was about and was trying to get the best out of my performance. It was a great session.[94]

This brilliant partnership resulted in *Dirty Diana* and gave it a huge, heavy sound similar to the heavy metal of the 1980s.

The production for this song proved just how well the technical team from *Bad* knew how to adapt to different registers. The Synclavier, played once again by the talented Chris Currell, worked miracles without undermining the dramatic force of the song. In fact, the synths' subtle textures, and the sound effects produced by this diabolical machine, added to the dramatic intensity of the lyrics.

When the single came out on 12 April 1988, only the edit and instrumental versions were used: Steve Stevens' many outtakes are still gathering dust in the archives.

Michael Jackson and Steve Stevens pose for the photograph on the back of the sleeve of the single *Dirty Diana* (1988).

Michael Jackson and Princess Diana talk backstage at the *Bad* tour concert in Wembley Stadium, London, 16 July 1988.

THE SHORT FILM

Director: Joe Pytka
Producer: Larry Stessel
Leading actors: Michael Jackson, Steve Stevens, and Lisa Dean
Shoot date: March 1988
Shooting location:
Long Beach, California
Duration: 5'06

Genesis

When the video hit the screens, Michael Jackson was busy with his first solo tour. As he traveled across America for the new version of the *Bad* tour, he would air a simple video: as he performs *Dirty Diana* on stage, a mysterious young woman—of whom we only see the slender legs—gets out of a car and slowly walks through dark streets before getting into the back of Michael's limo. After his performance ends, he goes backstage and gets ready to leave. When he opens the door to his limo, he discovers the femme fatale who's been following him.

Lisa Dean plays opposite Michael in this video, after becoming famous for modeling in a commercial for Levi's 501. For the *Dirty Diana* video, she earned a modest $300 per day.

The script also left room to portray the momentous meeting between Steve Stevens and Michael Jackson. In the video, the famous guitarist becomes, in the course of one song, Michael's ideal acolyte, clad in a black leather outfit and proud of his gravity-defying hairstyle.

Production

Filming took place in Long Beach in March 1988. Michael Jackson was filmed with two cameras that captured his dance moves and sensual poses. He slipped and hurt himself during one of the takes and didn't come back to finish the last shots until a few days later. Joe Pytka filmed continued to film events on set and captured the famous close-ups that show "Diana" walking through the streets.

Director and film editor Larry Bridges worked on the first edits. Bridges had already worked with Bob Giraldi on the final cut of the *Beat It* video. He suggested making another version with the concert scene, using a second narrative arc involving groupies lurking backstage. Lisa Dean's character is still there, but she comes across as the ultimate temptress, the one who stands out and gets what she wants by acting alone.

Larry Stessel, who produced this video for Epic, didn't hide his dissatisfaction with the edit in his meeting with Pytka and Bridges. He criticized the director for having completely skated over the sensual, rock, and subversive aspects of the song. The afterword of the Larry Bridges' version shows fans waving their lighters at Michael Jackson as he strikes a signature pose under the magical, grandiose light of the reflectors.

When the producer told Michael and his manager Frank DiLeo that the edit was unusable, the two men asked him to take the lead. But Stessel refused to replace Pytka, an important and well-known director. Following closed talks, Joe Pytka ended up giving in and created the 5'06 version that we know today, and which was sent to television channels throughout the world. In this final version, the remote duel between Michael and the malevolent Diana is highlighted by dynamic yet subtle editing. The groupies from the first edit have disappeared. Michael can only find respite on stage, surrounded by his musicians and his fans. When he leaves the stage to go home, he is seized by the demons represented by this torturous woman.

Michael Jackson and Vincent Paterson swap ideas on the set of *Smooth Criminal* in Los Angeles, 1987.

PORTRAIT

VINCENT PATERSON
THE MAN BEHIND THE THRONE

Vincent Paterson started off as a comedian before taking an interest in dance. A true jack-of-all-trades, he was endowed with an eye for originality and a primordial talent for using it persuasively. He signed his first major stage contracts in the 1970s, after which he accompanied Shirley MacLaine on one of her world tours.

A winning pair

Vincent's first collaboration with Michael Jackson came in 1983 with the *Beat It* video. Michael understood his rare and instinctive talent: Paterson was not just a dancer, but someone who knew that each character in a choreographed piece had his or her own story to tell.

While dancing, Paterson played a role, like a comedian. Michael loved this strong narrative approach. Over the years, they worked together more and more. Both as choreographer and director, Paterson would help Michael develop the concepts for his biggest videos. He also directed them: *Beat It*, *Thriller*, *The Way You Make Me Feel*, *Smooth Criminal*, *Black or White*, *Will You Be There*, and *Blood on the Dance Floor*. This long and fruitful partnership also saw them work together on special projects, such as the 1993 Super Bowl half-time show. When the King of Pop agreed to perform for this televised event, he worked with Paterson to create a mini-show that would become a starting point and model for shows to come.

By working with Michael, Paterson also fought for the status of dancers in the United States. While the idea of intellectual property still didn't apply to choreographies, the rights and social protection cover of these artists improved under Michael. Vincent supported this campaign, allowing many dancers to gain a foothold in a world dominated by fierce competition.

The art of the tailor-made

A versatile hand, Vincent Paterson worked with Michael to devise the staging for the second part of the *Bad* tour (1988 to 1989). The resources they used established a practically permanent foundation for the tours that would come later. Vincent found a balance between rock concert and Hollywood show, which revived Michael's unique and highly visual performances to their full splendor. Their ambitious sets widened horizons for pop artists everywhere: videos came to be part of the staging itself.

In 1990, he decided to take a dance routine that Diana Ross had rejected and adapt it to *Vogue*, by Madonna. The result was a dance inspired by Marie Antoinette. When Madonna performed the song on stage during the MTV Music Awards in 1990, she blew everyone away.

In 1999, Paterson was working with Lars von Trier and Björk when he came up with the choreography for *Dancer in the Dark*. During filming, he discovered that the Icelandic singer was also a great fan of the King of Pop.

Vincent Paterson remains one of Michael's few colleagues able to carry on an authentic, sincere, and disinterested conversation with him throughout the years. He asked a lot of himself and the artists he worked with, and in so doing, was able to reinvent Michael Jackson's image in 1997 for the video of *Blood on the Dance Floor*. Michael knew he could count on his trusty right-hand man. He asked him to help promote the reedition of *Thriller* in 2008. When the video and its "making of" were aired during the Tribeca Film Festival created by Robert De Niro, Vincent promoted the video during the event.

Vincent Paterson's humility condemned him to an unjust oblivion, at least for a large part of the public. But his work speaks for itself, and by itself it represents some of the most beautiful examples of pop culture at the end of the 20th century. His lengthy collaboration with Michael not only enriched the singer's repertoire, but also yielded some iconic images, often imitated but never duplicated, which are now part of the entertainment industry's heritage.

Smooth Criminal

Michael Jackson / 4'16

Musicians
Michael Jackson: lead and backing vocals, handclapping, and finger snapping
Bill Bottrell, John Robinson, Bruce Swedien: drums
David Williams: guitar
Kim Hutchcroft, Larry Williams: saxophones
Gary Grant, Jerry Hey: brass section
Kevin Maloney: muted Steinway piano
Christopher Currell: Synclavier
Denny Jaeger and Michael Rubini: Synclavier effects
John Barnes, Michael Boddicker: synthesizers
Bruce Swedien: additional rhythms and police chief announcement
Recording
Westlake Recording Studios (studio D), Los Angeles: November 1986 to April 1987
Technical team
Producer: Quincy Jones
Coproducer: Michael Jackson
Recording engineers: Bruce Swedien and Matt Forger
Michael Jackson's heartbeat: Dr. Eric Chevlen, digitally processed on the Synclavier
Rhythmic arrangements: Michael Jackson and John Barnes
Vocal arrangements: Michael Jackson
Brass section arrangements: Jerry Hey
Synclavier effects: Denny Jaeger and Michael Rubini
Special sound effects: Hugo Zuccarelli
Mixing: Bruce Swedien

1987

Single

A-side: *Smooth Criminal* (*single*) / 4'10
B-side: *Smooth Criminal* (*instrumental*) / 4'10
Released by Epic Records: USA (ref. 34-08044) and UK (ref. EPC 653026), 14 November 1988
Chart position: USA R&B No. 2, Pop No. 7 / UK No. 8

THE SONG

Genesis

Michael Jackson recorded a demo called *Al Capone* at his studio in Encino. The dark lyrics told the story of a woman who was murdered, and whom the singer promised to avenge: Al Capone tries to reason with the singer, but in vain. The same story was used and developed under a different angle for *Smooth Criminal*: for this, Michael hardened his tone and sang about a real chase followed by a tragic ending. Here, the woman, Annie, is again the target of a man who wants her dead. For once, Michael had inverted the roles: the female character didn't represent evil or vice, like the character from *Billie Jean*.

The name Annie, which is repeated in the chorus, has long intrigued listeners. Matt Forger revealed the identity of this unlucky woman in the *Bad 25* documentary directed by Spike Lee in 2012: it is the nickname of the CPR-training mannequin (also called Rescue or Resusci Annie) on which Michael Jackson had practiced in the 1980s.

The song was written in C major, with a crescendo bass line that alternated with silences, creating a syncopated effect. The style already used for *Speed Demon* was fine-tuned: the staccato, breathless verses are almost rapped as the singer narrates the fast-paced action with precision. These give way to a chorus and a diminishing bass line, which creates a striking contrast with the rest of the song. The lead and backing vocals then take off into a falsetto that suggests a fatalistic tone, as if to illustrate poor Annie's last minutes on Earth.

Production

Smooth Criminal's spectacular introduction breaks the silence like the opening of a Hollywood film. In the first few seconds, a heartbeat rings out and speeds up until the rhythmic track comes in. Michael Jackson wanted to capture the sound of his own heart for this opening sequence. "I don't remember whose idea it was to record Michael's heartbeat for *Smooth Criminal*," recalled Chris Currell. "It was an interesting project. Michael contacted Dr. Eric Chevlen and flew him down to Westlake from the Bay area. Dr. Chevlen had special equipment for recording the human heart. I recorded Michael's heartbeat directly into the Synclavier in stereo. I digitally processed it in the Synclavier to give it a bit more clarity. I then controlled the

Michael Jackson's white suit was a tribute to the one worn by Fred Astaire in the movie *The Band Wagon* (1953).

speed of his heart digitally, slowly speeding it up. You can hear it in the beginning of *Smooth Criminal*."[81]

The song and video for *Smooth Criminal* were recorded and filmed concurrently. Michael was traveling back and forth between studios to work on the elements that would be used for the video and the album. He asked Bruce Swedien to prepare some mixes, and Vincent Paterson, the choreographer for *Smooth Criminal*, came up with the breaks and group dances that would appear in the video.

The video arrangements feature a sharper and more forceful drum sound. The song loses its dark and funky identity and adopts sounds that are closer to pop. At Michael's request, the recording engineer also created other versions. Michael Jackson and his manager Frank DiLeo chose seven of these for the single.

In the album version, at 2'45, a male voice yells something into what sounds like a megaphone: "OK, I want everybody to clear the area right now!" It is Bruce Swedien in the role of a police officer evacuating a crime scene. In addition to this unexpected appearance, the recording engineer contributed to the rhythmic track by overlaying additional sounds over John Robinson and Bill Bottrell's drums.

When *Smooth Criminal* finally came together, the balance for the mix was quite heavy: the bass drum failed to keep time in a resounding way, unlike in other songs, such as *Bad* or *Another Part of Me*. The mix was approved for the album anyway and released in September 1987 on vinyl, cassette, and CD.

In late February 1988, Michael Jackson was in Kansas City for his first American concert for the *Bad* tour. Chris Currell was among the artists to join Michael on stage, and recalled:

Michael Jackson in the final scene of *Smooth Criminal (aka Chicago Nights)*, the medium-length music video that tells the story of three young children who take on a drug dealer; the video also appears in the film *Moonwalker* (1988).

Just an hour or so before the last Kansas show, Michael called me into his dressing room. He said since there was over a week before the next shows in New York, I had to fly to New York in the morning and go to the Hit Factory to rerecord *Smooth Criminal*! He told me to please tell everyone so they can arrange everything. Of course everyone freaked out! My tech Mitch was planning on going home for a few days but he would have to cancel it. The Synclaviers would have to be taken out of the trucks and sent separately to New York that evening after the show! Michael always seemed to have me do these kinds of communications so management did not like me very much!

1987

In New York, when I arrived at the Hit Factory, Mitch and Bruce Swedien were there. The Synclavier was set up, ready to go and Bruce had *Smooth Criminal* all cued up. He turned to me and said, "I have already recorded this twice. I don't know what Michael wants to hear." Michael was supposed to come to the studio but changed his mind. He was off playing with some friends. I told Bruce that I know what Michael wants to hear. So Bruce said, "You mix it then."
We rerecorded the Synclavier and I mixed the song. Michael said he would be at his penthouse so we should bring the tape recorder, amps, and speakers to the penthouse for him to hear the final mix. Everyone was nervous about how Michael would respond to the new mix. I was confident that I got it the way he would like it, because of our work at his house. We had to rent a lot of equipment and send it over to Michael's penthouse. His penthouse had a dance studio with high ceilings so we set up the equipment there. Everything was ready to go when Michael walked in.

He said hello and wanted to hear the song. Bruce started the song. Immediately Michael started to dance! This was a good sign! He danced all the way through till the end. Then he said, "This is great! It sounds the way it is supposed to sound!" Then he turned around and left! Everyone breathed a sigh of relief. This mix was used on later pressings of the *Bad* album. Basically it has more punch than the first version. I never got credit for the remix.[81]

FOR YOUR HEADPHONES

The American promo CD of *Smooth Criminal* (ref. ESK 1274) used the same mixes as the commercial editions of the maxi single. But further inspection reveals the remix arrangements are different: the sharp snare drum, which is normally only heard in the chorus, is used throughout the special extended dance mix and extended dance mix radio edit versions. There are also differences between the drum and percussion tracks in the Annie mix.

Robert De Niro pays a visit to Michael Jackson on the set of *Smooth Criminal* in 1987. Frank DiLeo is on the right.

THE SHORT FILM

Director: Colin Chilvers
Producers: Michael Jackson, Frank DiLeo
Leading actor: Michael Jackson
Extras (and supporting roles): Kellie Parker, Sean Lennon, Brandon Quintin Adams
Shooting dates: mid-February to mid-April 1987
Shoot locations: Culver City and Universal Studios, California
Duration: 9'48

Genesis

Michael Jackson wanted to put this song to a video that paid tribute to Western movies. He shot a few test images near his home; they were released to the public for the first time in *Michael Jackson's Private Home Movies*, a program he produced for Fox in 2003. He can be seen walking through a prairie dressed in a red shirt and wearing a black hat. He strikes a few poses and executes a few brief and precise dance steps.

After realizing that this environment didn't match the theme of *Smooth Criminal*, he gave his choreographer Vincent Paterson the tape containing the song's instrumental version and asked him to follow his instinct and come up with something that would represent the music. Paterson came up with a dark setting inspired by 1930s and 1940s gangster movies, all the while keeping in mind that Michael was a big fan of Fred Astaire. As discussions progressed, *Smooth Criminal* soon became a tribute to the legendary dancer. Many sequences were direct nods to *The Band Wagon*, directed by Vincente Minnelli in 1953. Michael Jackson designed his own outfit for the video. He wore a black armband on his right arm, an insignia he would regularly use for his stage costumes later on.

As *Smooth Criminal* took shape, Michael decided to produce a feature film: *Moonwalker*. The dance sequence for *Smooth Criminal* was dusted off and used in a medium-length film called *Chicago Nights*, which tells the story of three young children faced with a dealer who wants to sell them drugs. This storyline, directed by Colin Chilvers—known for having mastered special effects in *Superman* (1978)—became the cornerstone of *Moonwalker*, a hybrid film made up of sequences exalting Michael on the dawn of his 30th birthday. Vincent Paterson didn't participate directly in the making of this film, limiting himself to the staging and the choreography of the musical sequence. In the end, *Smooth Criminal* and *Moonwalker* together cost Michael Jackson the pretty sum of $27 million, which he only managed to pay off thanks to the film's release in VHS.

Production

Michael Jackson bounced back and forth between the Westlake and Universal studios to create *Smooth Criminal*. Over the course of six weeks, Vincent Paterson and a troop of artists gave everything they had to making this video. Their number would get bigger and bigger each time Michael saw the images on film. In order to make the choreography even more spectacular, a second floor was added to the set. Michael spent extra-

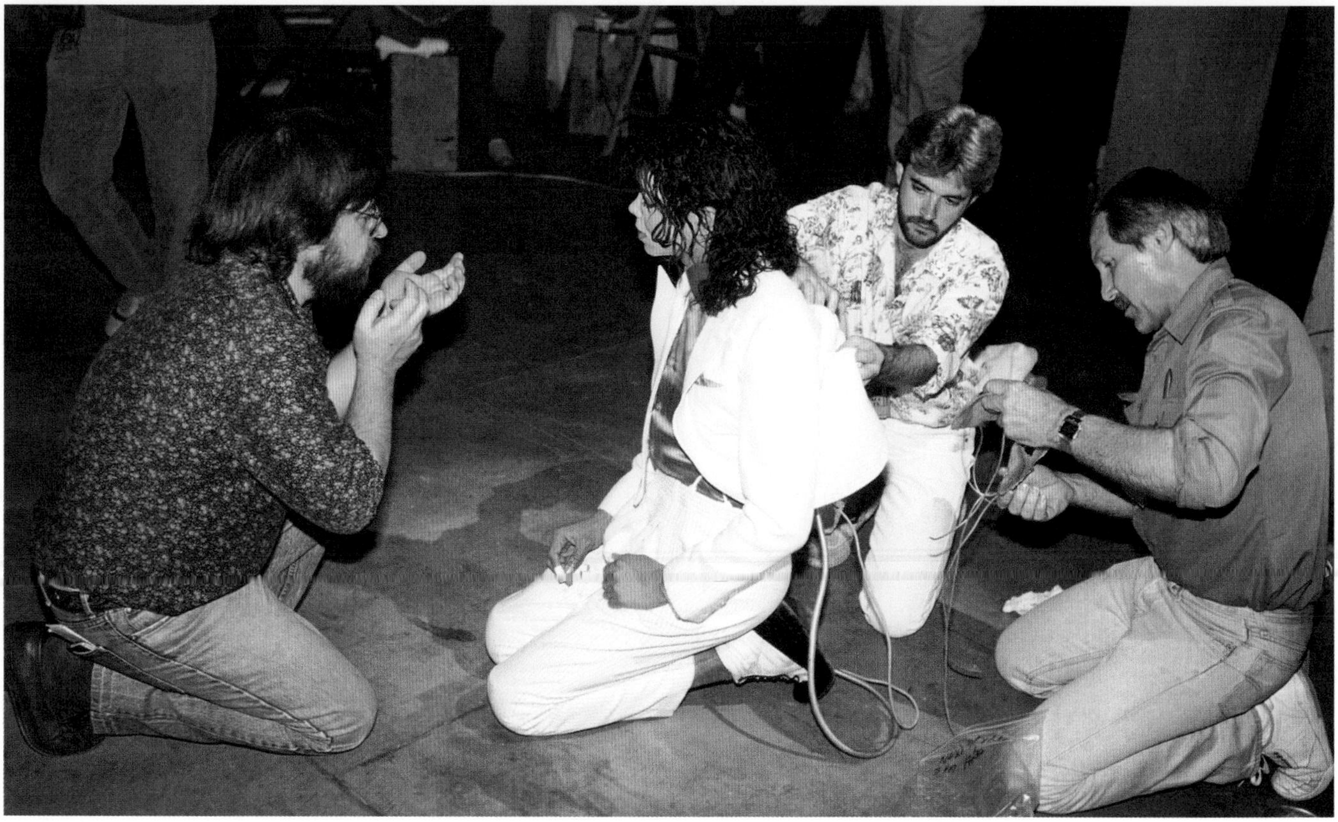

The director Colin Chilvers with Michael Jackson on the set of *Smooth Criminal* in 1987.

vagant amounts on *Moonwalker*. This project fed his passion for film.

Vincent Paterson initially directed the group's choreography and the famous scene known as "lean," where Michael and the dancers leaned 45 degrees toward the ground before standing upright again, as if by magic. This optical illusion was made possible by harnesses attached to the dancers' outfits and tied to transparent strings. These were pulled by operators guiding and holding each dancer from above. The video owed a big part of its success to this dance step, which soon became an iconic Michael Jackson move.

Jeffrey Daniel oversaw the transitions between the group dances and Michael's solos. For the scene where gangsters chase Michael into the bar, where the action takes place, Daniel took inspiration from *Bugs Bunny* cartoons, where characters hop and move jerkily instead of walking.

In the end, Michael Jackson worked with him to create the shots of him dancing alone on the mini-set installed in the background. This is the scene where he tries to escape, but the gangsters engage in hot pursuit.

Many of Michael's friends watched the filming at Culver City and Universal Studios. Among them was choreographer Hermes Pan, who had worked with Fred Astaire on a number of films. At the time, the musical comedy hero was suffering from the pneumonia that would end up killing him on 22 June 1987. Pan assured Michael that Astaire would be very proud of the tribute. Shortly before he passed away, Astaire said, "I didn't want to leave this world before meeting my successor. Thank you Michael."[95]

In 1989, this video received two prestigious awards: a Grammy Award for best music video (short format) and an MTV Video Music Award for best special effects.

[BONUS TRACK]

Leave Me Alone

Michael Jackson / 4'40

Musicians

Michael Jackson: lead and backing vocals, synthesized vocals
Larry Williams and Greg Phillinganes: synthesizers
Paul Jackson Jr.: guitar
Casey Young: Synclavier

Recording

Westlake Recording Studios (studio D), Los Angeles: 1985 to 1986

Technical team

Producers: Quincy Jones and Michael Jackson
Recording engineers: Matt Forger and Bruce Swedien
Rhythmic and vocal arrangements: Michael Jackson
Synthesizer programming: Larry Williams and Casey Young
Mixing: Bruce Swedien

For Jackson Addicts

Epic decided not to market the five remixes Bruce Swedien produced. A few acetate disks that came from Bernie Grundman's mastering studios have made it possible for fans to listen to them, but they still haven't been officially released. They are: extended dance mix (7'10), extended dance mix radio edit (5'29), dub version (5'43), instrumental (4'25), and a cappella (4'10).

A-side: *Leave Me Alone* (*single*) / 4'40
B-side: *Human Nature* (*album*) / 4'05
Released by Epic Records: UK, 13 February 1989 (ref. 654672)
Chart position: UK No. 2

The Song

Genesis

Leave Me Alone was one of the first songs created by Matt Forger and John Barnes in the family studio in Encino. The piece, which wasn't on the album's original tracklist, was released as an exclusive bonus for the CD edition. For some time, it remained inaccessible to the many fans who did not yet own a CD player. While in *The Way You Make Me Feel* Michael was chasing a girl, in *Leave Me Alone* he was imploring people to let him go: "The song is about a relationship between a guy and a girl. But what I'm really saying to people who are bothering me is: 'Leave me alone.'"[2] He was talking about the media, which in the second half of the 1980s was pursuing him with more zeal than ever. It was a long overdue settling of scores with the press. The video ridiculed the stupid rumors circulating about him, from the oxygen chamber in which he slept, to his alleged attempt to buy the bones of Joseph Merrick, the Elephant Man. The irony was that many of these absurdities had come from Frank DiLeo, Michael's manager, who'd been trying to maintain Michael's omnipresence in the media. Some of them still hold stock today. *Leave Me Alone* was trying to be a voice of reason.

Production

From a musical standpoint, *Leave Me Alone* had a synthetic funk sound. Larry Williams and Greg Phillinganes had fun with it. They were the only ones pulling the strings, and their synthesizers imposed their purely digital laws on the piece. The rich chords created interesting sound reverberations that Michael's voice enhanced once it was layered up and made into an echo. The only real instrument was Paul Jackson's guitar, which skillfully and steadily led the piece through the song's musical space-time delirium.

Leave Me Alone was released as a single in Europe, notably in the UK, where tabloids were particularly aggressive toward Michael. The eighth single of the album no doubt pleased fans, who hadn't yet given up on their record players. Ireland celebrated the piece with a No. 1 in the charts while in the UK, where *Belfast Child* by Simple Minds still clung to No. 1, the song only reached No. 2.

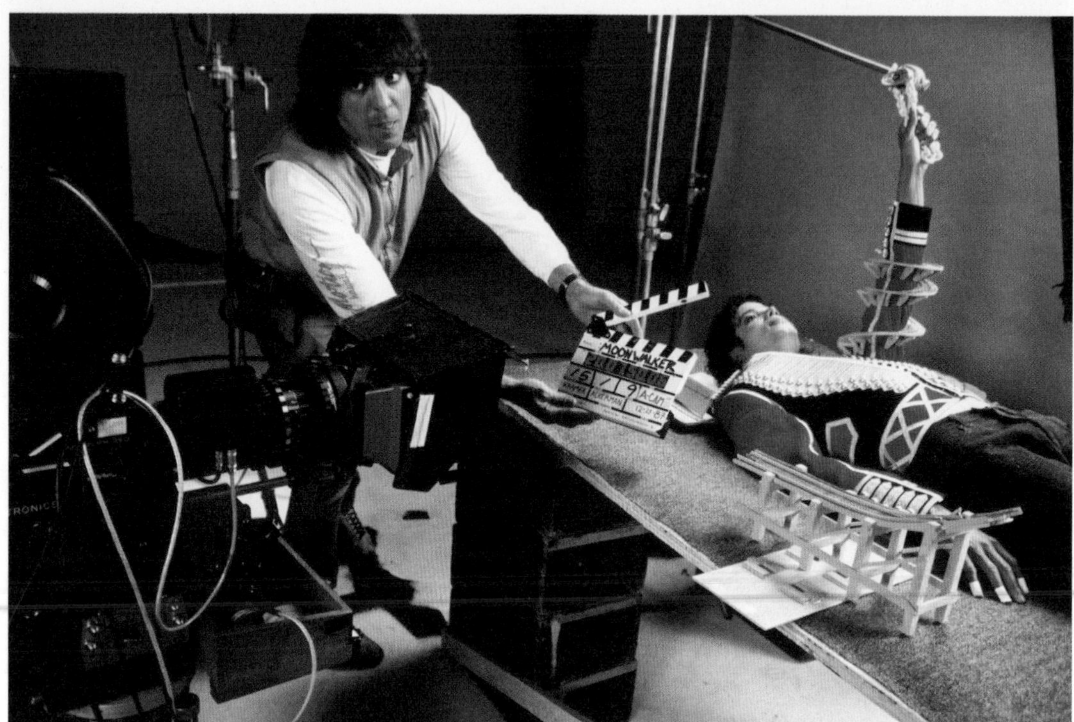

Michael Jackson, his pet snake Muscles, and his pet chimpanzee Bubbles on the set of *Leave Me Alone* in 1987.

Made using often basic techniques, the short film *Leave Me Alone* won a Grammy Award for best music video, short form, in 1989.

1987

THE SHORT FILM

Director: Jim Blashfield
Producers: Jim Blashfield, Paul Diener, Michael Jackson, Frank DiLeo
Leading actor: Michael Jackson
Extra: Bubbles
Shoot date: January 1988
Shooting location: Culver City, California
Duration: 4'39

Genesis and production

Director Jim Blashfield, known for his surrealist worlds and animation techniques, was asked to stage the freakish atrocities Michael Jackson had supposedly committed, according to the media. While it only took three days to shoot the video's various sequences, nine months of postproduction were needed to create the imagery, designs, and effects. Behind the scenes, small hands were busy using X-Acto knives to cut out characters, animals, and objects from the original 35mm film. They were used to animate the rich and strange world depicted in the video.

In 2014, Jim Blashfield explained:

> Michael was really very open to this [idea]. The fact that he would think it would be OK to represent his plastic surgery, with the nose and the scalpel, it was just pretty great. I heard through the grapevine Michael's mother didn't like that particular image that much...If you wanna know how come it took nine months, we're down on an animal preserve photographing llamas and peacocks. And then we're off at Oak's Park, the local amusement park, photographing things there...Each and every bit of it is made up of still images that are all stacked on top of one another on a piece of glass. Look in any one scene and look at how many different things there are going on, so each one of those had to have its own shoot. There's a splash that shows up throughout the entire video, and that was so time consuming to cut out that we just had one and it was passed around...There was a guy, he specialized in that splash, and I think he worked on it for weeks. He also was responsible for hair...He sat on this tall stool kind of hunched over, with these odd glasses that jewelers or somebody wears. Just cutting one 32nd of an inch after another.[33]

Metaphors abound and are superimposed on each other, with the dance of the Elephant Man's skeleton being the most famous. Bubbles, Michael's chimpanzee, suddenly appears and flies around in a ridiculous plane that takes Michael through the theme park, where he is at once spectator, background, and circus freak. At the end of the video (which is also a fervent tribute to Elizabeth Taylor), a giant Michael Jackson comes alive, smashes through the park walls that enclose him, and frees himself from the grip of this skillfully created hallucination.

In order to honor the impressive quality of this work, the video was included in *Moonwalker*, where it accompanies the two main sequences.

[BONUS TRACK]

Come Together

John Lennon, Paul McCartney / 5'27

From the film: *Moonwalker* / B-side of the single *Remember the Time* / 5'27
From the album: *HIStory* / 4'02

Musicians
Michael Jackson: lead vocals
Bill Bottrell: guitar and drums
Recording
Westlake Recording Studios (studio D), Los Angeles: 1986 to 1987
Technical team
Producers: Michael Jackson and Bill Bottrell
Recording engineer: Bill Bottrell

Come Together conveyed a message of peace and brotherhood befitting The Beatles.

1987

THE SONG

Genesis

In 1969, the year The Jackson Five signed with Motown and The Beatles broke up, psychologist Timothy Leary asked John Lennon to write him a song for his campaign to become governor of California. The song's title was taken from his slogan: "Come together, join the party." Marred by a dark history of drugs, Leary soon dropped out of the race. So Lennon reworked everything that he'd put into the campaign song, which he wrote with George Harrison, and *Come Together* was the result. The song opened *Abbey Road*, the last album of The Beatles, which was released in September 1969. The lyrics gave significant air time to the "nonsense-speak" so dear to John Lennon, and promoted a unifying theme: "One thing I can tell you is you got to be free...Come together, right now, over me."

Since 1985, with his purchase of the famous ATV catalog, Michael Jackson became the owner of the rights for a long list of Beatles' songs. Some might see the cover of *Come Together* as a jab at his friend Paul McCartney. Indeed, Michael did make off with a large part of the rights to Paul's works. But more than anything, it's a tribute. As the video's director Jerry Kramer explained, "*Come Together* is a testament to the message of unity that The Beatles spread throughout their careers."[82]

The recording was conducted as a side project, since Michael's albums hadn't included covers since the days of *Thriller.* Michael assigned the project to recording engineer Bill Bottrell, who would lead the whole operation. *Come Together* was recorded without Quincy Jones, but in his shadow. The illustrious producer would likely see this as a first betrayal, given that the title, *Come Together*, could be interpreted as the rallying cry of a star looking for new artistic partnerships.

The song struggled to fit into the career of the future King of Pop. Initially presented as a stage recording at the end of *Moonwalker*, the song was first released in stores on the B-side of the *Remember the Time* single in 1992. A shorter version of the song would later appear on *HIStory* (1995).

Production

Recording engineer Bill Bottrell wasn't completely unknown in Jackson's circle, and he had stood by the Jackson children

Sean Lennon, Michael Jackson, and Brandon Adams on the set of *Moonwalker* in 1987.

throughout their solo careers. In 1984, he'd already had a hand in *Torture* and *The Hurt*, which was in *Victory*. Lacking a permanent studio, Bottrell worked as a freelancer through the mid-1980s. He was listed in the credits for Jermaine's *Tell Me I'm Not Dreamin' (Too Good to Be True)* and Janet's *Don't Stand Another Chance*. Michael was never far from these projects.

Bottrell was in full control of this cover, which was one of his first coproductions. This collaboration would be the first test of a career that would include *Monkey Business*, *Black or White*, *Give in to Me*, and *Earth Song*. In the second half of the 1980s, he remained by Michael's side through most of the Hayvenhurst sessions that led to the *Bad* album. It is very possible that the foundations for this piece were initially built in the family studio before being perfected in another one.

In the era of the sacred Synclavier, most musicians adopted completely digital recording methods. Michael Jackson, trained in the system's use by Christopher Currell, likely put his experience to use here.

The mix that appeared in *Moonwalker* was slightly different from the one that was released on records: it was more rock, more scenic, and used sonorities that were less round and more crude.

On the *HIStory* tour, Michael used the song and its unifying message in a medley with the song *D.S.*, but everyone seems to have forgotten about this mix.

In *Come Together*, Michael Jackson, looking the part of a rocker, moves around the stage surrounded by his musicians (1988).

The short film *Come Together* concluded the film *Moonwalker* and heralded a new chapter in the career of Michael Jackson (1988).

FOR JACKSON ADDICTS

The long version of *Come Together* (5'27) can be found on maxi singles of *Remember the Time* (ref. 657774 2) or in the collections *Michael Jackson—Tour Souvenir Pack* (Europe, MJ4) and *Michael Jackson—Tour Souvenir CD Single* (Japan ESCA 5703-7).

1987

THE SHORT FILM

Directors: Jerry Kramer and Colin Chilvers
Producers: Dennis E. Jones, Michael Jackson, and Frank DiLeo
Leading actor: Michael Jackson
Extras: Jennifer Batten (guitar), Don Boyette (bass), Greg Phillinganes (guitar-keyboards), Frank DiLeo, Sean Lennon, Kellie Parker, Brandon Quintin Adams
Shoot date: 1988
Shooting location: California (unknown)
Duration: 5'41

Genesis and production

Jerry Kramer and Colin Chilvers' video was adapted to resemble Joe Pytka's *Dirty Diana*. An audience was called into the studio to create the illusion of a concert. Except for the brief appearance of the three child stars from *Moonwalker* (including Sean Lennon, John's son) announcing the end of the film, there was no story to accompany the stage performance, which makes the video a little long. Fans were happy to see Michael Jackson acting like a real rocker: he was coming and going from one side of the stage to the next, more or less to the tune of Jennifer Batten's electric guitar solos or Don Boyette's bass. Greg Phillinganes, Michael's star keyboardist, also gave a breathtaking performance. The editing did not follow a chronological timeline: Michael's t-shirt is ripped in one scene but not in the next, his shirt is tucked into his pants and then out again...and the unnatural progression of the live show is evident and inconsistent. Perhaps this was done on purpose?

Michael Jackson's outfit on stage was identical to the one he wore on the cover of the *Liberian Girl* single: leather pants, white t-shirt under a yellow shirt, and a belt decorated with a large buckle. This accessory, which Michael had commissioned from designers Michael Bush and Dennis Tompkins, was definitely one of the stars of the video. The two designers took ten months to create this symbol of power, possibility, and freedom. The silver plate, which was disproportionately large, was almost the size of a suit of armor. It was decorated with carved birds of prey, including the American bald eagle and a two-headed Germanic eagle. The *Bad* logo, set in 18-carat gold, further enhanced the design.

PORTRAIT

CHRISTOPHER CURRELL
THE SYNCLAVIER MAN

Christopher Currell was a guitarist by training. Like Bill Wolfer or John Barnes (see page 329), he was a very inconspicuous figure within Michael's 1980s circle. In March 2015, on the site headphone.guru, he suggested for the first time that his mastery of the Synclavier had a powerful impact on the *Bad* album and on the rest of Michael Jackson's career.

Quests for new sounds

Although he performed with many groups throughout the 1970s, Currell soon realized his guitar's musical range was limited and decided to go in search of different, more abstract sounds. He initially gave the Moog synthesizer a try, but it revealed itself to be impractical. In May 1980 he discovered the Dartmouth digital synthesizer, better known as the Synclavier, a technology that came with digital syntheses of polyphonic samplings and more. His dream suddenly came true, even though mastering this technology turned out to be a bit harder than mastering the guitar. He dedicated himself to learning how to interact with this revolutionary system. Unable to afford the $40,000 machine at the time, he practiced at his friend Denny Yeager's place. He was able to purchase his own first system in 1982.

A patient teacher

Having become a specialist, Christopher Currell taught master classes and spoke at conferences to show the world the Synclavier's value as a marketing tool. As the system evolved, Currell became increasingly engaged in production and consolidated his abilities as a programmer. Michael Jackson called him hoping he could teach him how to use the machine:

> It was in the summer of 1985...He [Michael] had heard about me from the New England Digital company. Michael had a huge Synclavier system and he asked me if I would teach him how to use it. Apparently he had had many programmers operating his Synclavier but not being musicians...I put together a nice learning program and schedule for Michael to learn the Synclavier...I went to his personal studio at his house on a Sunday morning...We sat down in front of the Synclavier and began his first lesson. He told me, "I don't know anything about computers." I said, "No problem, first, you insert this floppy disk." He said "time out" and said he did not know what a floppy disk was. I realized Michael barely knew how to operate a cassette recorder! His hands-on with technology was very limited! So I got more simple and we continued. After three hours, I had taught Michael how to power up and boot up the Synclavier, call up his sound library, and showed him how to call a sound down to the keyboard for him to play. He said, "That's all I can take for today, can you come back tomorrow for a session?" I said, "Sure!" Little did I know that this would be the beginning of the most interesting four years of my life![81]

Hayvenhurst to Westlake

In 1986, as work was slowly progressing on *Bad*, Chris Currell spent long weeks, from ten to eleven hours a day, configuring Michael Jackson's system and arranging his repertoire of sounds. They worked on several songs together while preparing for *Bad*. Michael introduced Currell to Bruce Swedien, who was also teaching himself to use the Synclavier. One week before recording for the album began, Michael asked his secretary to inform Chris Currell that he'd be part of the Westlake team. Michael's personal Synclavier and everything in it were thus transferred to the famous studio. Quincy Jones, for his part, was barely familiar with the new benefits of this complex instrument, which had been used sparingly in *Thriller*. However, the producer knew that Michael used the Synclavier in his demos. Chris Currell was ushering in a new musical era as the two creative geniuses, Quincy Jones and Bruce Swedien, learned a new way of doing things.

Greg Phillinganes' keyboards and John Robinson's drums were digitalized, tailored, and magnified by the magic touch of the Synclavier. The synchronizations and arrangements were simplified and mastered to the point where Bruce Swedien became visibly excited by the prospect of creating the wonderful single mixes, dubs, and extended versions of the *Bad* songs.

Without Chris Currell, the sound of *Bad* would not have been the same.

The use of the system became automatic for *Bad*. Chris Currell said that he received a cold welcome from the group of studio musicians Quincy Jones had assembled for *I Just Can't Stop Loving You*. Someone even said, "So YOU'RE the reason why no one was being called."[82]

The Synclavier on the *Bad* tour

Speed Demon, *Bad*, and especially *Smooth Criminal*, were all given their energy levels and unique sonorities by the Synclavier. The imposing musical device, with Chris Currell at the reins, was brought along for the *Bad* tour and used on stage starting on 12 September 1987. Wearing a costume that looked like something out of *Star Wars*, Currell danced around the Synclavier's control screens and overlapping keyboards. He appeared on stage with an unlikely red guitar that looked like it came from outer space.

His effects were phenomenal and innovative: this time, all the musicians were able to recognize the good this machine could do for the tour. Michael Jackson's new friend couldn't stop talking about the precious moments he experienced with Michael and his group in the late 1980s during the *Bad* tour. Thanks to him, Michael Jackson's music shifted to more avant-garde directions driven by new choices of sound, and to the systematic use of striking rhythms, as in *Bad's* main songs. By allowing him to formalize the creation of his demos, the Synclavier became a definite means of creative emancipation for Michael.

One wonders, however: did the widespread use of the Synclavier in *Bad* ultimately influence Michael Jackson's decision to break with Quincy Jones for the remainder of his career?

OUTTAKES

BAD OUTTAKES

Bad generated many outtakes, some of which have never been released to the public. The first ones, chosen by Michael, appeared in 2001 in the special edition version of the album. In 2012, Matt Forger had the responsibility of choosing brand-new outtakes as bonuses for the 25th anniversary edition of the album. The posthumous album *Xscape* would later include eight of these in 2014. The *Bad* outtakes are full of clues about Michael's creative preferences and his musical thought process.

STREETWALKER

Michael Jackson / 5'53

Musicians: Michael Jackson: lead and backing vocals / **Jason Martz:** harmonica / **Recording: Hayvenhurst, Encino, California**: 1986 to 1987 / **Technical team: Producer:** Bill Bottrell / **Recording engineer:** Bill Bottrell

When it was time to finalize *Bad*, Michael Jackson voted that *Streetwalker* be included in the album. Quincy Jones gave it up in favor of *Another Part of Me*. Nevertheless, Michael knew that he would use it again one day. The song elicited passionate reactions from his admirers when he revealed its existence for the first time in a deposition before a court in Mexico in 1993. *Streetwalker* then became one of the most coveted outtakes of the album.

Recording engineer Bill Bottrell said he reworked the song while Michael was traveling the world on the *Bad* tour. He explained that Michael had rejected Jason Martz' harp line, calling it foolish. Nevertheless, the line was kept, meaning Michael either returned to his previous position on the matter or had it modified. The song was included in the *Bad 25* anniversary edition released in 2012.

From a musical standpoint, *Streetwalker* was clearly a prequel to *Dangerous*. The theme unfolds around a young prostitute who lives in a dangerous and oppressive world. Michael pursues her incessantly, trying to declare his admiration and love for her: "My every thought is you / And that's a fact, yeah yeah / I'd like to take you places / How about New York City / Or Paris, France?"

Michael Jackson in the intro to *Smooth Criminal* during the *Bad* tour in 1988.

Fly Away

Michael Jackson / 3'27

Musician: Michael Jackson: lead and backing vocals / **Recording: Hayvenhurst, Encino, California:** 1987 / **Technical team: Producer:** Michael Jackson / **Recording engineer:** (unknown)

Fly Away is likely to have been developed in the family studio. It was Michael's timid attempt to forge his own career path. He first tried it in *Bad*, then in *Dangerous* and *HIStory* before finally shelving it. Like *Streetwalker*, the song found its home as a bonus track to the 2001 and 2012 reeditions of *Bad*.

In 1998, even before his own version was released, Michael Jackson decided to give the soft ballad to his big sister Rebbie, who used it in her album *Yours Faithfully*. While on the *HIStory* tour, Michael supervised its recording remotely and advised his sister on how to perform the song. The mid-tempo refers to an abusive love where forgiveness is spoken of in saccharine tones. The King of Pop backs up Rebbie's voice in the refrain, reinforces the chorus, and adds some beautiful ad-libs. Their duet is in perfect harmony, and Michael's vocal variations—for which, bizarrely, he wasn't credited as second or backing vocalist—transport and intensify the piece's flights of lyricism.

Cheater (Demo)

Michael Jackson and Greg Phillinganes / 5'09

Musicians: Michael Jackson: lead and backing vocals / **Greg Phillinganes:** piano, synthesizers / **David Williams:** guitar / **Recording: Hayvenhurst, Encino, California**: 1986 / **Technical team: Producer:** Michael Jackson / **Recording engineers:** Matt Forger and Bill Bottrell / **Single A-side:** *Cheater* (*demo*) / 5'09 / **B-side:** *One More Chance* (*R. Kelly remix*) / 3'50 / **Released by Epic Records as a promo 12-inch:** UK, 14 September 2004 (ref. XPR 3829) (CD promo ref. XPCD2989)

Written by Greg Phillinganes and Michael Jackson, *Cheater* was first and foremost proof of the unbreakable friendship between the two artists. The sounds of the Synclavier, which appear everywhere in the demos for *Bad*, were enriched by David Williams, who brilliantly embellished the piece with his guitar as Greg Phillinganes added warm and dynamic piano chords.

The lyrics depict the corrupt world of gambling. The singer, vindictive, accuses a liar of having cheated, tricked, and manipulated. Taking on the stance of a real macho guy, he slowly reveals his gambler character. The piece could easily have been set in the famous 1930s club from *Moonwalker*.

In 2004, the King of Pop included *Cheater* in the *Michael Jackson: The Ultimate Collection* compilation. The song was supposed to be a single, but in the end it was not distributed. A maxi single—whose cover is indisputably the most beautiful one from the 2000s—was released in the UK to support the song's promotion on the radio.

The promotional schedule closed with the release of a promo CD that included a radio edit of the song. Another video was produced using archival images and aired on MTV.

DON'T BE MESSIN' 'ROUND (DEMO)

Michael Jackson / 4'19

Musician: Michael Jackson: lead and backing vocals / **Recording: Hayvenhurst, Encino, California / Westlake Recording Studios, Los Angeles:** 1986 to 1987 / **Technical team: Producer:** Michael Jackson / **Recording engineers:** Brent Averill and Bruce Swedien / **Single:** second track of the 2012 CD single *I Just Can't Stop Loving You* / **Released by Epic Records:** USA, 5 June 2012 (limited numbered edition, ref. 88725414922) / Europe, 1 June 2012 (ref. 88725414922)

According to Matt Forger, who chose and adapted the *Bad 25* outtakes, *Don't Be Messin' 'Round* could have gotten its bossa-nova influences and light pop accents from Stevie Wonder's *Don't You Worry 'Bout a Thing* (*Innervisions*, 1973). The recording engineer completely reworked Brent Averill's song from the early 1980s. Having been forgotten after the *Thriller* days, the song reappeared in 1986 or 1987. It was improved upon with new recordings, this time done by Bruce Swedien. For *Bad 25*, Matt Forger, who had privileged access at the time, gathered the song's various tapes scattered between Hayvenhurst and Westlake and selected their most accomplished elements, which he used to create the piece for the anniversary compilation. Matt Forger's mixing was very true to the original, and the song was purposely left in its demo state. One can hear Michael Jackson giving musical directions: "bridge," "guitar." In the lyrics, he asks a girl to dance and tries to avoid making any mistakes in his attempts to charm her. The star decided to stop production on the song, which is why it was never released on any album.

Don't Be Messin' 'Round appeared on the CD single of *I Just Can't Stop Loving You* (2012), which launched the promotion of *Bad 25* and started off the slew of surprises coming out of this new edition.

I'M SO BLUE (DEMO)

Michael Jackson / 4'07

Musicians: Michael Jackson: lead and backing vocals / **John Barnes:** synthesized harp / **Recording: Hayvenhurst, Encino, California:** 1986 / **Technical team: Producer:** Michael Jackson / **Recording engineers:** Matt Forger and Bill Bottrell

"What most artists would consider finalized recordings, Michael Jackson would call them demos,"[96] recalled Matt Forger referring to *I'm So Blue*. The song is the perfect example of the kind of work they did at Hayvenhurst to later present to Quincy Jones for use in *Bad*. Here, Michael sings about a love story that ends badly: "She left me for another man." In the lyrics, as in the music, his melancholy and sadness are palpable in each version of the piece: "Here I am, so all alone / And I am so sad and lonely / Tell me, what will I do?" The Synclavier sounds a repetitive bass line and gives the rhythm the weight of a broken heart that no longer wants to go on beating. The piece's atmosphere is as melancholic as it is timeless. In each refrain, John Barnes plays a delicate melody on the synthesized harp, which reinforces the bleakness of the piece. The ballad is full of soft and light arrangements: calls to abandon all hope of ever being loved again.

Michael Jackson rehearsing for the *Bad* tour in Tokyo, September 1987.

Song Groove (aka Abortion Papers) (Demo)

Michael Jackson / 4'26

Musician: Michael Jackson: lead and backing vocals / **Recording:** (unknown): 1986 / **Technical team: Producer:** Michael Jackson / **Recording engineers:** Brian Malouf and Gary O.

The song was created and recorded by Brian Malouf and Gary O., two recording engineers who had only just started working with Michael. Matt Forger, who was well acquainted with Michael's working habits, knew how to make the piece come alive with what they had. The production required them to combine two tapes, each containing half of the piece. *Song Groove* was a technical title Michael had given the song. *Abortion Papers* was the title that fit the theme at hand. For the first time in his career, Michael was taking up a social issue, abortion, by telling the story of a Catholic family devastated by the drama, shame, and judgement of others. The lyrics make a statement without imposing judgement. The subject was sensitive but wasn't meant to shock puritanical and religious America or defenders of civil liberties. Anyone could interpret the words in their own way. The aim of the song was to raise awareness of an important problem in society.

"Much of these styles you can hear in the songs included in *Bad 25* are developed in later albums,"[96] said Matt Forger when introducing *Song Groove's* musical texture and subdued but tense atmosphere, which were also used in *Dangerous*. The recording engineer insisted on the aggressive quality of the style, mostly made so by an ensemble of metallic sound effects. Well aware of his fame, Michael Jackson was trying to turn his music into a vehicle for social and humanitarian expression.

FOR JACKSON ADDICTS

Intentionally or not, Stevie Wonder also recorded a song called *Free* around the same time. Included in his album *Characters*, it was a huge success, especially in France.

Free (Demo)

Michael Jackson / 4'25

Musician: **Michael Jackson:** lead and backing vocals / **Recording:** (unknown): 1986 / **Technical team:** **Producer:** Michael Jackson / **Recording engineer:** Bill Bottrell

Once again, Stevie Wonder's influence is very evident in this song. Michael Jackson's ballads were often inspired by harmonies created by Stevie Wonder, including *Blues Away* in 1976, all the way to *Beautiful Girl* in 2004. *Free* is as fresh a song as any The Jacksons had produced in the late 1970s. Matt Forger said it was one of his favorite songs. Michael's emotion clearly comes through, and one can easily feel his joy and happiness. His voice induces an automatic smile and creates a pleasant sensation of inner joy.

Sometimes it helps to let one's soul drift along to the sounds of simple and pure words accompanied by a fresh and playful melody. Here is the song's humble proposition: "Free, free like the wind blow / To fly away just like a sparrow / To feel letting my hair blow / To take my time wherever I go."

Punctuated with the sound of the Synclavier, the harmonies are light and wonderful complements to Michael's colorful vocal variations. The lyrics, recorded in various layers, bring warmth to the piece. The song was unveiled in 2012 for the anniversary reedition of the album.

Price of Fame (Demo)

Michael Jackson / 4'33

Musician: **Michael Jackson:** lead and backing vocals / **Recording:** **Hayvenhurst, Encino, California:** 1986 / **Technical team:** **Producer:** Michael Jackson / **Recording engineers:** Bill Bottrell and Matt Forger

Price of Fame is well known among Michael Jackson fans. The song was slated as the main theme for a Pepsi commercial, but producers ended up using a special edition of *Bad* with the words adapted to highlight the merits of the drink. The version of *Price of Fame* that came out in *Bad 25* had been recorded in Hayvenhurst. It was meant as a sequel to *Billie Jean* and a prequel to *Who Is It*, all the while maintaining its own identity and originality. It was built around a smooth ska/reggae rhythm and was one of Michael's rare incursions into this genre. The lyrics perfectly reflected Michael's state of mind when *Thriller* became a top-selling album and he reached a popularity that remains unrivaled to this day. His fame was so great that he could no longer go out in public. "I want a face no one can recognize in disguise... / They thought of taking pictures, autographs, then they grab." The jumpy music creates an oppressive atmosphere that only relents at the cry "you pay the price of fame."

After the Pepsi version of *Price of Fame* was leaked online, it became possible to see how much work Michael had put into it.

Michael Jackson uses a submachine gun to drive back the troops pursuing him in a scene from the short film *Smooth Criminal*, Los Angeles, 1987.

AL CAPONE (DEMO)

Michael Jackson / 3'34

Musician: Michael Jackson: lead and backing vocals / **Recording: Hayvenhurst, Encino, California:** 1986 / **Technical team: Producer:** Michael Jackson / **Recording engineers:** Matt Forger and Bill Bottrell

The rather crude *Al Capone* was the first iteration of what would become the much more sophisticated *Smooth Criminal* (see page 336). It was a reflection of Michael's love for storytelling and songs with strong cinematographic potential. The star chose a different story from the one lived by the real Al Capone. The idea was original, fresh, and adapted to Michael's codes. Both songs seemed to come from a different piece called *Chicago 1945*, which Michael had recorded some time before, but which remains unreleased.

LOVING YOU (DEMO)

Michael Jackson / 3'02

Musician: Michael Jackson: lead and backing vocals / **Recording: Red Wing Studio, San Fernando Valley, California:** 1985 to 1986 / **Technical team: Producer:** Michael Jackson / **Recording engineers:** Matt Forger and Chris Desmond

The *Loving You* demo was recorded in the Red Wing studio in the San Fernando Valley while Michael's personal studio in Hayvenhurst was being renovated. "He'd sneak away to these smaller studios and it would just be a place where he could work and experiment and add different layers,"[97] explained Matt Forger. Work had just started on *Bad*, and the song became another testament to Michael's preference for pretty and soft ballads. Its melodious and airy accents were reminiscent of the three solo albums from the Motown days or of *Farewell My Summer Love*. Its warm hints and vocal variations were again overlaid. Michael had a particular preference for this technique, which would remain a key element in his music. The sounds resound, the effects twirl like clouds of butterflies. Like in a rainbow, the colors all appear at the same time, reinforcing the state of perfect love. The song ends with a tune that sounds strangely similar to that of *The Girl Is Mine*. *Loving You* may be a logical continuation of the success Michael had shared with his friend Paul McCartney. It was scrapped for the anniversary reeditions and belatedly chosen for inclusion in the 2014 *Xscape* compilation.

Michael Jackson rehearses with his musicians in Tokyo, a few days before the start of the *Bad* tour in September 1987.

FOR JACKSON ADDICTS

Get It **was produced in several versions: an instrumental edit (4'13); extended version (6'44); and extended instrumental (6'44). A single "edit" version (4'22) was released as a CD as part of a Motown promotion.**

Stevie Wonder and Michael Jackson

Get It

Stevie Wonder / 4'31

From the album: *Characters* / **Released by Motown Records:** USA (ref. 6248ML) and UK (ref. ZL72001), 6 November 1987 / **Chart position:** USA R&B No. 1, Pop No. 17 / UK No. 33 / **RIAA:** certified Platinum 8 January 1988 / **Musicians: Michael Jackson and Stevie Wonder:** lead vocals / **Mary Lee Evans and Stevie Wonder:** backing vocals / **Stevie Wonder:** synthesizers, bass guitar, drums, and synthesized percussion / **Ben Bridges:** guitar / **Recording:** CBS/Sony Studio, Tokyo (Michael Jackson's voice), and Wonderland Studio, Los Angeles: September 1987 / **Technical team: Producers:** Stevie Wonder, Gary Olazabal, and Quincy Jones (Michael Jackson's voice) / **Recording engineer:** Gary Olazabal / **Single A-side:** *Get It (edit version)* / 4'22 / **B-side:** *Get It (instrumental edit)* / 4'13 / **Released by Motown Records:** USA, 5 May 1988 (ref. 1930 MF) / UK, 16 May 1988 (ref. ZB 41883) / **Chart position:** USA R&B No. 4, Pop No. 80 / UK No. 37

Genesis

After having sung *Just Good Friends* with Michael Jackson on *Bad*, Stevie Wonder in turn invited his friend to perform a duet on the *Characters* project, which was to appear at the end of 1987. *Get It* was the last musical testament to the indestructible friendship between the two artists. This final collaboration almost failed to see the light of day, due to the busy schedules of these two musical giants.

At the beginning of September 1987, Stevie Wonder performed a series of concerts in London that had been rescheduled, after several cancellations in May that year. At the same time, Michael Jackson was about to start his first world tour as a solo artist, beginning in Japan. It was impossible for the two artists to record in the studio together, so they agreed to create their duet remotely: Stevie Wonder would work in Los Angeles, while Michael Jackson would sing in Tokyo. The song deals with a young woman who has cut herself off from all loving feelings, while the two singers are determined to get her to change her mind: "Gonna get it, her love / Gonna get it, her kisses / Gonna get it, her heart." The tune is conventional and had been recorded many times. The song would not become a landmark in musical history, nor in the career of either artist. There was no magic at work: the song suffered from the fact that the two singers were at a distance from each other, and it showed no trace of their usual affinity.

Production

Stuck in London, Stevie Wonder recorded a few vocal lines to send to Quincy Jones as a base to work on. By the time the Motown genius had finished his session, it was too late to send the tapes to the producer on the other side of the Atlantic. That same evening, during his concert at Wembley Arena, he had the astonishing idea of asking for a member of the audience's help with a very special mission: to do an extremely urgent favor of the highest importance, all expenses paid. An individual immediately came forward and set off for Los Angeles without delay, tasked with handing the tapes over to Quincy Jones in person. At that exact moment, Michael Jackson was about to leave for Japan, where he was to give his first concerts in Tokyo from 12 to 14 September 1987. It was therefore in that city that his vocal parts were worked on and recorded, in the CBS/Sony studio, which then sent the tapes to Stevie Wonder's team.

After being hastily mixed and mastered, the duet was pressed and included in the album, which appeared on 6 November 1987.

In *Get It*, the overblown synthesizers struggle to create a melodious, solid musical framework. This is far from the quality to which Stevie Wonder's audiences were accustomed, and the overall effect is one sorely lacking in subtlety. Even Ben Bridges' discreet guitar has trouble making its repetitive notes heard, drowned as they are in an electronic frenzy. This was a great disappointment, given that this classical and jazz musician, a faithful friend to Stevie Wonder, usually recorded his guitar in masterly fashion in the Motown singer's greatest hits.

Get It was released as a single on 5 May 1988, while the *Bad* tour was under way in the United States, and then in Europe on 16 May, as Michael Jackson arrived in Rome—as if the song wanted to follow the star's progress on his world tour. No video promoted the single, and the sleeve omitted to give due prominence to the duo. With good reason, the song did not distinguish itself in the charts, and remains unknown to the general public.

The Jacksons
2300 Jackson Street

Jermaine, Jackie, Tito, and Randall Jackson, Gene Griffin, and Aaron Hall / 5'05

From the album: *2300 Jackson Street* / **Released by Epic Records:** USA (ref. EK 40911) and UK (ref. EPC 463352), 28 May 1989 / **Chart position:** USA R&B No. 14, Pop No. 59 / UK No. 39 / **Musicians: Jackie, Janet, Jermaine, Marlon, Michael, Randy, Rebbie, and Tito Jackson:** lead vocals / **The Jackson Family and Children: Stacee, Yashi, and Austin Brown (Rebbie's children); Siggy, Brandi (Jackie's children); Taj, Taryll, and Tito (T J) Jackson (Tito's children); Jermaine Jr., Autumn, Jaimy, Jeremy, and Jourdyn Jackson (Jermaine's children); Valencia, Brittany, and Marlon Jr. Jackson (Marlon's children):** backing vocals / **Teddy Riley:** all instruments / **Rhett Lawrence**: synthesized samples / **Paul Jackson Jr.:** guitar / **Don Myrick:** saxophone / **Recording:** Westlake Recording Studios (studio D), Los Angeles, and several others (unspecified): 1989 / **Technical team: Producers:** The Jacksons, Teddy Riley, Gene Griffin / **Recording engineers:** Dennis Mitchell, Jeff Lorenzen, Larry Fergusson, David Ahlert, and Marlon Jackson / **Assistant recording engineer:** Pee Wee Jackson / **Mixing:** Keith Cohen and Larry Fergusson / **Arrangements:** Teddy Riley and The Jacksons / **Single A-side:** *2300 Jackson Street (edit version)* / 4'05 / **B-side:** *When I Look at You* (never before released) / 4'20 / **Released by Epic Records:** USA (ref. 34-69022) and UK (ref. EPC 655206), 16 April 1989 / **Chart position:** USA R&B No. 9 / UK No. 76

THE SONG

Michael Jackson had been resting since 27 January 1989, after his marathon world tour and the frenzied time of the *Bad* years. At this point, The Jacksons decided to return to the fray and begin promoting a completely new project. Five years after *Victory*, the single *Nothin' (That Compares to You)*, written by L A Reid and Babyface, discreetly heralded the arrival of the album *2300 Jackson Street*. The song was effective and made an impact without, however, rising high in the charts in any country. Michael Jackson did not take part in the recording, and his fans snubbed the single, while waiting to hear more about his new project. It was almost summer when the album finally made it into the record stores—its sleeve showing only Jermaine, Tito, Jackie, and Randy posing in front of their little childhood home in Gary. The image confirmed the idea already put forward by the single *Nothin' (That Compares to You)*: the album was a project featuring just four Jacksons, not six. It was ten years since Michael had left the circle of his siblings, without ever having announced this officially. It seemed the time had come for Marlon to strike out on his own and realize his dream of a solo career.

Jermaine, who deep down hoped to keep the group going, took control of the album's production. The Jacksons enlisted the help of Michael Omartian, a longtime collaborator of the family, and of a young newcomer, Teddy Riley (who was to unleash the surging new jack swing in half the songs on *Dangerous* at the start of the 1990s). In featuring the Riley sound for the first time and on a large scale, *2300 Jackson Street* set out to be its pioneer with *She*, one of the album's real gems.

Promotion continued with the release of a second single, *2300 Jackson Street*, which extolled the family's cohesion. Teddy Riley coproduced the song, which displays a clearly expressed collective melancholy that is both nostalgic and a touch weepy, laying a solid foundation for Jermaine's idea of an inseparable Jackson clan. With the passing years he would unceasingly, and with monotonous insistence, call for a return to the original lineup, as if he wanted to ignore or deny the glaring artistic gulf that had opened up between Michael Jackson and his brothers. In *2300 Jackson Street* the whole family, Michael and Marlon included, showed up to celebrate childhood, sacrifice, and the hard work of the Jacksons' parents. The recording functioned as a showcase for the family's musical genius, which they certainly saw more as a way of honoring their parents than as a reunion of the group. La Toya was not invited to take part, because her scandalous adventures had alienated her from the family for some time. Janet shone, and Rebbie also enjoyed joining in the song. All the brothers' and sisters' children were invited to join in the backing vocals, all of whom already showed promise that they would carry the Jackson torch.

Teddy Riley is celebrated as a one-man orchestra, being credited as playing almost all the instruments, with the excep-

2300 Jackson Street remains a mythical place where the history and the career of the king of pop began.

tion of a few notes on the guitar and the saxophone from Paul Jackson and Don Myrick, brought in to heighten the sadness of the tune. This little family party struggled to sell, and the single passed almost unnoticed by the public.

THE SHORT FILM

Director: Greg Gold
Producer: Phil Rose
Leading actors: Katherine, Jackie, Janet, Jermaine, Marlon, Michael, Randy, Rebbie, and Tito Jackson
Extras: Joseph Jackson; Stacee, Yashi and Austin Brown; Siggy, Brandi, Taj, Taryll, Tito (TJ), Jermaine Jr., Autumn, Jaimy, Jeremy, Jourdyn, Valencia, Brittany, and Marlon Jr. Jackson
Shooting dates: spring 1989
Shoot location: Hayvenhurst, Encino, California
Duration: 4'32

In the heat of a spring Sunday afternoon in California, the video of *2300 Jackson Street*, directed by Greg Gold, presents the Jackson children in honeyed tones. Katherine Jackson, like a good matriarch, opens the sequence of candid images of a family out in force, gathered together at Hayvenhurst. Everyone mingles casually, plays in the garden, and seemingly waits for the barbecue to become hot enough for the usual annual family banquet to begin.

The presence and sweet vocal variations of Michael and Janet naturally stand out from the whole, lending the film a clear credibility.

FOR JACKSON ADDICTS

The little-known remix *2300 Jackson Street (The Family Mix)* 5'45, and its instrumental version (5'00), made by Jackie Jackson and Cornelius Mims, appeared on a promotional US 12" record (EAS 1795). The song was also performed on stage in 1994, without Michael Jackson, during a TV show made by the family, *The Jackson Family Honors*. The video clip was not included in the DVD box set *Michael Jackson's Vision*, which contains a retrospective of all the star's short films.

A galaxy of stars pay homage to Sammy Davis Jr. for the special show *Sammy Davis, Jr. 60th Anniversary Celebration*, broadcast 4 February 1990 on ABC.

MICHAEL JACKSON
YOU WERE THERE

Buz Kohan, Michael Jackson / 2'00

TV show: Sammy Davis Jr.'s 60th Anniversary Celebration / **Date:** 13 November 1989 / **Location:** Shrine Auditorium, Los Angeles

At the end of 1989, Michael Jackson performed *You Were There* on the TV special *Sammy Davis Jr.'s 60th Anniversary Celebration*. The show paid homage to Davis, bringing together many of his friends, all praising the exceptional career of the African-American star who, already ill, would pass away a few months later.

It was the writer and composer Buz Kohan, a friend of both singers, who had the idea for this magnificent musical tribute, which, as it turned out, Michael Jackson paid just once in his career. Although at first reluctant to make a television appearance, he yielded to the composer's pleas. Buz Kohan persuaded him that this was his last chance to recognize publicly his artistic debt to Sammy Davis Jr., who had been a trailblazer for black artists. *You Were There* was a solemn hymn bearing the message of a rising African-American generation, of which Michael Jackson was the mouthpiece that evening. The day before the show, the singer learned the song and rehearsed at the piano in the huge concert hall where the musical tribute would be held. After he had changed a few notes and words, and pronounced himself satisfied with the song, the minor changes were given to an arranger tasked with writing the orchestral version for the following day. A few hours before the show, the pop idol showed up to hear how the new version sounded, and took the opportunity to fine-tune some stage moves. On the night, his performance began simply yet charismatically: the effects were sober and solemn, and never before had Michael Jackson's voice varied with such fragility, subtlety, power, or dignity. Moved to tears, Sammy Davis Jr. climbed on stage and embraced Michael Jackson as his spiritual son.

Ralph Tresvant of the group New Edition, enjoyed a solo career during the early 1990s.

RALPH TRESVANT

ALRIGHT NOW

John Barnes, Michael Jackson / 4'17

From the album: *Ralph Tresvant* (included on the CD version only) / **Released by MCA Records:** USA, 27 November 1990 (ref. CD MCAD-10116) / UK January 1991 (ref. CD DMCG 6120) / **Chart position:** USA *Billboard* 200 No. 17, R&B, Hip-Hop Albums No. 1 / UK No. 37 / **Musicians: Ralph Tresvant:** lead vocals / **John Barnes:** Synclavier / **Charles Fearing:** guitar / **Recording:** John Barnes Studio, Los Angeles / **Technical team: Producers:** John Barnes, Vassal Benford (additional production) / **Recording engineer:** Jack Rouben / **Assistant recording engineer:** Eugene Dixon / **Mixing:** Louis Silas and Peter Arata (mixing engineer) / **RIAA:** certified Gold and Platinum 23 January 1991

At the beginning of the 1980s the producer Maurice Starr formed a group modeled on The Jackson Five which, he believed, would emulate the success of the brothers from Gary, Indiana, 10 years on. Five African-American teenagers—Ralph Tresvant, Bobby Brown (the group's leader), Ricky Bell, Michael Bivins, and Ronnie DeVoe—were picked for the lineup, which went by the evocative name of New Edition. It had some great hits, notably *Candy Girl* in 1983. The model proved effective, to the point that fans and the press compared Ralph Tresvant's head voice to that of Michael Jackson, because its smooth variations of tone were enchanting and captivating. In 1984, having been fired by the band, Maurice Starr repeated the experiment with the now well-known New Kids on the Block.

In 1986, Bobby Brown left New Edition and was replaced by Johnny Gill. The new lineup took a different turn artistically with the release of the album *N.E. Heart Break* (1988), one of its biggest hits, in which the avant-garde sounds of the incipient new jack swing already heralded the shattering musical revolution of the 1990s. It was produced by Jimmy Jam and Terry Lewis, the magicians of Minneapolis who were already working with Janet Jackson.

Meanwhile, Bobby Brown pursued his solo career, releasing his first album, *King of Stage*, in 1986. A battle between egos, as pointless as it was out of proportion, filled the pages of the musical press, which wanted to establish whether Bobby Brown or Ralph Tresvant might receive Michael Jackson's musical endorsement.

At MCA Records, the label of both musicians, the competition was internalized. In January 1991, Ralph Tresvant released his first album, which soberly bore his name as its title. Its first three songs, which included the incredible *Sensitivity*, were produced by Jimmy Jam and Terry Lewis. L A Reid, Babyface, and Richard Wolf finished the job, resulting in a work that was a veritable bulldozer aimed at the puncturing the arrogance clearly displayed by Bobby Brown. It looked to be game over when the song *Alright Now*, written by John Barnes and Michael Jackson, was included on Ralph Tresvant's album—discreetly, and only on the CD version. Should this be taken to mean that the master had chosen his disciple? Too few details are known to establish how this song found its way on to Ralph Tresvant's album. It is certain that the King of Pop worked on a demo of the song, but here, too, precise details are sketchy: it is almost completely unknown when it was written and developed.

Thanks to hard work and talent, Bobby Brown gained the ascendant, with many highly successful hits. Over the years, he asserted his own style, becoming a well-known and popular rapper, and marrying the singer Whitney Houston.

In the 1990s the press tried to ignite a new media contest, this time between Bobby Brown and Michael Jackson. It did not last a long time, fortunately...Because sometimes common sense wins the day.

FOR JACKSON ADDICTS

A fairly rare version in Spanish of *Do the Bartman* was recorded by Sara Vivas for the series and pressed as a promotional single. This version, mixed by John Boylan, is available only on this single.

BART SIMPSON
DO THE BARTMAN

Bryan Loren / 5'10

From the album: *The Simpsons Sing the Blues* / **Released by Geffen Records:** USA (ref. GHS 24308) and Europe (ref. GEF 24308), 4 December 1990 / **Chart position:** USA Pop No. 3 / UK No. 6 / **Single: A-side:** *Do the Bartman* (7" house mix/edit) / 3'54 / **B-side:** *Do the Bartman* (LP edit) / 3'59 / **Released by Geffen Records:** USA (réf. PRO A 4179) and UK (réf. GEF 87), November 1990 / **Chart position:** UK No. 1 / **Musicians: Bart Simpson (Nancy Cartwright):** lead vocals / **Homer Simpson (Dan Castellaneta), Marge Simpson (Julie Kavner), Lisa Simpson (Yeardley Smith), and Maggie Simpson (Matt Groening):** additional voices / **Bryan Loren and Michael Jackson (the latter not credited):** backing vocals / **Bryan Loren:** instruments / **Paul Jackson Jr.:** additional guitar / **Laurie Ros, Bart Stevens, and Richard Voltrop:** background shouting / **Recording:** Record One Studios, Sherman Oaks, California: 1990 / **Technical team: Producers:** Bryan Loren and Michael Jackson (the latter not credited) / **Recording engineer:** Richard Cottrell / **Assistant recording engineers:** Julie Last and Bart Stevens / **Mixing:** Bryan Loren at Larrabee Sound Studios, Los Angeles

THE SONG

The Simpsons, the famous series satirizing the American way of life created by Matt Groening, was first broadcast on television in December 1989. The main character in Fox's weekly program was the incorrigible Bart Simpson, a little rascal who loves to play nasty tricks and is especially fond of the music of Michael Jackson. He is a farcical character and appears at the end of the clip *Black or White*, reiterating the passion he has for the artist.

That same year Michael Jackson, himself a great admirer of the show, quietly recorded the song *Do the Bartman* for the album *The Simpsons Sing the Blues*. The piece was written jointly with the composer and producer Bryan Loren, with whom the singer had recorded some lines for the album *Dangerous*. With him Michael Jackson endeavored, as always, to make demos and develop innovative, creative styles. As it turned out, the star set his heart on Teddy Riley's new jack swing, consigning the work done with Bryan Loren to near oblivion (some of it appears here and there in other related projects). *Do the Bartman* is unquestionably the best-known and most successful result of their collaboration.

The song's lyrics begin by drawing a portrait of the teasing Bart Simpson before inviting the listener to follow his mischievous instructions for executing a few dance steps: "Shake your body turn it out if you're bad, man / Ah front to back to the side yes you can, can / Everybody in the house do the Bartman."

As the period and style demanded, the music is governed by a rounded, regular digital sound, with just the guitar of Paul Jackson Jr. lending a welcome warmth and a great deal of musicality. Bryan Loren was at the console, like an orchestral conductor playing all the instruments at once. The producer sang the backing vocals himself, and Michael Jackson joined him in the harmony of the chorus—for which he received no mention in the credits, because Epic/Sony still did not want him to put his name to music released by other labels. His presence on the recording was revealed over the years in interviews with Matt Groening and Bryan Loren.

Do the Bartman was released as a single only in Europe. Various pressings featured numerous remixes, and among the most sought-after were a British picture disc and an American promotional CD with a flip book, the latter containing almost all the versions produced. The album was a great success, riding on the popularity of the TV series, and became a Double Platinum record. The single, meanwhile, did very well in Europe, even spending three weeks at the top of the British charts.

To celebrate the show's 20th anniversary, in 2009 a figurine of Leon Kompowsky, voiced by Michael Jackson, went on sale.

Matt Groening poses proudly with the characters he created. Left to right: Lisa, Maggie, Marge, Bart, and Homer Simpson.

THE SHORT FILM

Director: Brad Bird
Producers: Larina Jean Adamson, Matt Groening, Sam Simon, James L. Brooks (executive producer), Sherry Gunther (animation producer), Gábor Csupó (animation executive producer), András Erkel, Richard Sakai, Szávó Sztilkovics, Ken Tsumura, Csaba Varga (associate producers)
Leading actor: Bart Simpson (Nancy Cartwright)
Supporting actors and extras: Homer Simpson (Dan Castellaneta), Marge Simpson (Julie Kavner), Lisa Simpson (Yeardley Smith), Principal Skinner (Harry Shearer), Milhouse Van Houten (Pamela Hayden), Edna Krabappel (Marcia Wallace)
Shooting dates: late 1990
Shoot location: Varga Studios, Hungary
Duration: 6'02

The clip was directed by Brad Bird, created by the Hungarian Varga Studios, and choreographed by Michael Chambers. The action takes place during a performance at the school in Springfield. Bart Simpson bursts in, rapping, dancing, and leading his young friends with the aim of cheekily breaking up the boredom and solemnity of the occasion. The dance steps burst forth, very much inspired by Michael Jackson, and all the characters follow Bart, all over the town, to the sound of his singing, which eventually fills the entire world. As always, the boy is brought back into line: his frenzied dance ends on the stage where it began and Bart is thrown out of the performance.

The video clip was included as a bonus with the DVD of the series' second season.

In 1991, the first episode of the third season of *The Simpsons* gave pride of place to Michael Jackson. The singer lent his voice to the character of Leon Kompowsky, and also wrote the little tune *Happy Birthday Lisa,* which was released on the album *Songs in the Key of Springfield* (Rhino Records, 1997). Sony Music still had control of all the artist's appearances, and he was credited under the pseudonym John Jay Smith for his voice, and as W A Mozart for writing *Happy Birthday Lisa.* In order that he should not be recognized, a vocal mimic even had to second him to perform the few sung passages in the episode. Nevertheless, the star recorded his own version of *Happy Birthday Lisa*: the song, which lasts barely more than 1'30, was to be included as a bonus on the special edition of the album *Dangerous* in 2001, of which the second record was canceled. The short piece eventually found its way to fans via the unauthorized route of the internet in 2007.

DANGEROUS

1. JAM
2. WHY YOU WANNA TRIP ON ME
3 IN THE CLOSET
4. SHE DRIVES ME WILD
5. REMEMBER THE TIME
6. CAN'T LET HER GET AWAY
7. HEAL THE WORLD
8. BLACK OR WHITE
9. WHO IS IT
10. GIVE IN TO ME
11. WILL YOU BE THERE
12. KEEP THE FAITH
13. GONE TOO SOON
14. DANGEROUS

Dangerous **ALBUM**

Released by Epic Records: USA (ref. 454) and UK (ref. EPC 465802), 26 November 1991.
Chart position: USA R&B No. 1 / UK No. 1
RIAA: certified six times Multiplatinum 29 September 1994 / certified seven times Multiplatinum 30 May 2000

The release of the album *Dangerous* on 26 November 1991 was a global event. Sony Music devoted impressive resources to its promotion. Opposite, the window of A&A Records in Yonge Street, Toronto, Canada.

1991

DANGEROUS, THE FLIGHT OF ICARUS

Without Quincy Jones by his side, Michael Jackson approached the 1990s by reinventing himself, both musically and visually. *Dangerous* established his emancipation: from now on, he wished to be known as the King of Pop. Aged 33, Michael Jackson bought Neverland, the setting of his dreams, and proved that he could manage his career by himself. He also treated himself to total freedom—both professionally and in his private life—which, alas, would eventually cost him dear.

Once promotion of the album *Bad* was complete, Michael Jackson took stock of his solo career and decided that it deserved to be celebrated with the first compilation of his best solo work at Epic. With CBS, he began work on a project entitled *Decade—1979–1989*, comprising his best songs, enlivened with a few unreleased ones. The sessions for the new songs took longer than expected; the timetable shifted and the future opus ended up being renamed *Decade—1980–1990*. A tracklist was drawn up and circulated internally among the label's project bosses:

Volume 1: *Don't Stop 'Til You Get Enough / Rock with You / Off the Wall / She's out of My Life / This Place Hotel / Someone in the Dark / Wanna Be Startin' Somethin' / The Girl Is Mine / Thriller / Beat It /Billie Jean / P.Y.T. (Pretty Young Thing) / State of Shock*

Volume 2: *Bad / The Way You Make Me Feel / Man in the Mirror / I Just Can't Stop Loving You / Dirty Diana / Smooth Criminal / Come Together / I'll Be There (adult version) / Never Can Say Goodbye (adult version) / Black or White / Heal the World / Who Is It*

A proposed sleeve design showed Michael Jackson's eyes in close-up, framed by two horizontal black bands, as in a CinemaScope frame. However, months passed and the singer was slow to make the recordings of the new songs that were to be part of the project. CBS became concerned that it may not be able to release this time-sensitive compilation in time for the New Year celebrations, first for 1989 and then 1990. Eventually, the King of Pop announced that he had written too many good songs and preferred to devote himself to making a new album. The *Decade* project was dropped. As for the sleeve design, it was put to one side and reworked for the single *In the Closet*, which was released in spring 1992.

CBS becomes Sony Music

While the *Decade* project was being worked on and then abandoned, CBS's situation changed. Ever since the mid-1980s, the Japanese giant Sony had made clear its desire to buy the record label. At the time, Sony boasted some of the biggest names in international music: Barbra Streisand, Bruce Springsteen, Bob Dylan, Simon and Garfunkel, part of Miles Davis's catalog and, of course, all the work of Michael Jackson and The Jacksons since 1976.

Negotiations dragged on, hindered by the misgivings of the label's founder, William S Paley, who had bought the Columbia label before renaming it CBS Records in 1938. The businessman wanted to retain the catalog's heritage and identity. However, the links with Sony became ever closer when the Japanese company launched the CD. Its factories manufactured CBS's discs. With an ever-increasing role in the running of the label, Sony became a legitimate and credible partner

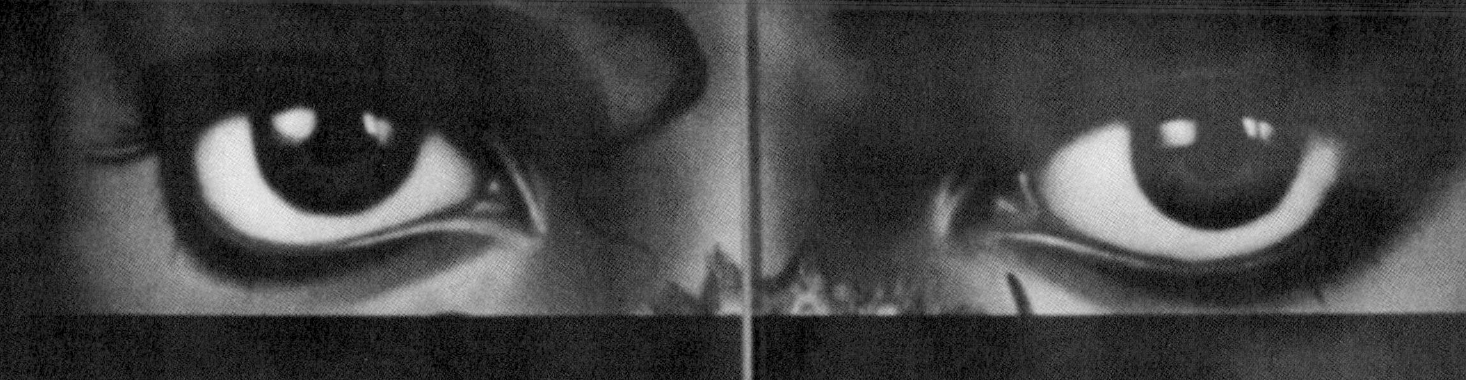
Sony Music
MICHAEL JACKSON
MICHAEL JACKSON
MICHAEL JACKSON
DANGEROUS

Michael Jackson is presented with a Grammy Legend award by his sister Janet at the 35th Grammy Awards ceremony at the Shrine Auditorium, Los Angeles, 24 February 1993.

through acquisition. It finally bought CBS on 17 November 1987, for the tidy sum of $2 billion. The label changed its name to Sony Music on 1 January 1991. This merging of two giants of the entertainment industry had direct consequences for Michael Jackson's relationship with the label that had supported him ever since The Jackson Five left Motown in 1975.

The new contract

On 20 March 1991, Sony Music announced that it had signed a new contract with Michael Jackson: the singer committed himself to recording six new albums. Although most artists were paid royalties at the rate of around 18 percent, he negotiated 25 percent. On top of this, he received an advance of $18 million on signing the contract, as well as $5 million more, payable on the release of each new album. It has been estimated that the star earned a total of $1 billion from this collaboration.

Sony's record company and its hardware division, which produced audio and video equipment for domestic and professional use, understood that the way consumers used music and images was changing. In that sense, at the start of the 1990s Michael Jackson embodied the archetypal multimedia artist, capable of reaching a wide audience. This new working relationship was announced under the leadership of Akio Morita, cofounder of Sony and inventor of the famous Walkman, who became good friends with the star.

Alongside these multimedia projects, Michael Jackson's new record company allowed him to launch his own label. Initially called Nation Records, it was definitively renamed MJJ Music, starting out in 1993 with the release of the soundtrack of the movie *Free Willy*. It remained active until 2001, riding the wave of 1990s popular music. The all-female group Brownstone recorded two high-quality R&B albums for it, reaching No. 8 on *Billboard* with the mid-tempo song *If You Love Me*. The label also released the first album by 3T, the sons of Tito Jackson and nephews of Michael. Their profile in the US was almost nonexistent, but the trio found a receptive audience in Europe, at a time when boy bands were highly popular—a bandwagon that 3T jumped on with gusto.

Michael and Janet

Although he helped out his nephews by giving them a break with his new label, Michael Jackson definitively burned his musical bridges with his brothers. In 1989 The Jacksons released one last album, entitled *2300 Jackson Street*. This album, on which Michael Jackson featured only in the title track, marked the end of the contract between the brothers and Epic Records.

However, for all that, Michael Jackson retained a sense of family allegiance; in the late 1980s and early 1990s he supported, either closely or at arm's length, his brothers in their various solo album projects. For example, he worked behind the scenes to ensure that Marlon secured a contract with Capitol Records. Jackie and Randy also launched their careers with the star's support. The one and only solo album by the youngest of the brothers, with the low-key title *Randy and the Gypsys*, was bursting with good ideas developed with the producer Bryan Loren.

The Neverland Ranch, conceived by Michael Jackson as a true haven of peace, was decorated with sculptures on the themes of play and innocence.

The sibling who continued to make a name for herself independently of her famous surname was Janet. Her album *Control*, released in 1986, started a competition with her brother Michael. From then on, they tried to outdo each other with their records, alternating with tours. When Janet released *Rhythm Nation* on 19 September 1989, Michael was fascinated by the album, which was structured on a series of songs, one after the other, that had the issue of social inequality and access to education at its heart. He repeatedly declared he was a fan of certain songs, such as *The Knowledge*, which he used for practice in his private dance room.

Rhythm Nation turned out to be a forerunner to *Dangerous*. Its industrial sound and refined, classy production by Jimmy Jam and Terry Lewis—not to mention the presence of ballads such as *Livin' in a World*, with its fair-minded, inspired humanitarian streak—haunted the singer when he was working on the successor to *Bad*.

While Janet asserted herself as a rival to Michael, engaging in healthy competition, Jermaine responded with the bitterness of an elder brother and former leader of the group that had been pushed into the background. His career at Arista had been in decline since the (largely European) success of *Dynamite*, and he released one last album, *You Said, You Said*. One of the songs on the album, *Word to the Badd!*, created controversy. In this funk number with swingbeat overtones, produced by L A Reid and Babyface, Jermaine settled his scores with Michael: "Reconstructed / Been abducted / Don't know who you are / Think may love you / They don't know you / Lonely superstar / Never think about who you love / Only think about number one." Thus begins this polemical song, which was released in August 1991, a few months before *Dangerous*. It sent Michael Jackson into a mad fury and caused a profound rift between the two brothers. Jermaine tried to justify himself by explaining that the song was a declaration of love for his young brother. But the media, like the person whom the song addressed, had difficulty believing his explanation.

A man alone

If Jermaine was right on any point, it was certainly on the artistic and professional solitude Michael Jackson wrapped himself in from the early 1990. Having fired the charismatic Frank DiLeo, he hired a new manager, Sandy Gallin, a discreet right-hand man who was tasked with carrying out his employer's orders.

As if to distance himself from the world of Hollywood, the singer retreated to Santa Ynez where, in 1988, he bought Sycamore Ranch, promptly renamed Neverland Ranch in homage to the story of Peter Pan. He had come across the property in 1983, during the shooting of the short film *Say, Say, Say*, and had vowed to settle in this peaceful part of California. Thirty million dollars was the price to pay for a place that he was to shape to his taste and transform into a haven. Major works were carried out to make the site into an amusement park, which the singer would open to his closest friends and to disadvantaged children.

On the business side, the star put in place an administrative team based at the offices of his company MJJ Productions, who took care of the business and were responsible for running it day to day. Larry Stessel, who had been in charge of promotion of the albums *Thriller* and *Bad* for Epic, oversaw the launch of *Dangerous* before leaving the label. In the studio, ever since the departure of Quincy Jones, the King of Pop found himself at the center of a frenzied court of producers and musicians, all seeking a coveted, strategic position.

Producers for hire

When the sessions for the album *Bad* were complete, Michael Jackson, who had discovered the talent of Bill Bottrell, declared himself satisfied with the alchemy they had created together. Having made a modest debut on The Jacksons' album *Victory*, the recording engineer had produced *Come Together*, the cover of The Beatles' song that ended the movie *Moonwalker* and heralded a new musical direction. The singer had promised to turn him into an important figure, a producer with a central role in his next album. He kept his word, and entrusted him with producing songs such as *Black or White*, a classic that, like *Billie Jean*, spent seven weeks at No. 1 on *Billboard*. Bill Bottrell had gained the confidence of the King of Pop, with whom he would work regularly during the 1990s.

At the very start of that decade, the singer also made use of the services of Bryan Loren, a talented young producer who put machines and drum machines at the heart of his productions. The two men worked on several songs and released the song *Mind Is the Magic* for the magicians and lion-tamers

Siegfried and Roy, who would use it as the soundtrack to one of their acts. Bryan Loren did not work only with Michael at the time, but also with Marlon, Janet, and Randy Jackson on their respective solo projects. Nevertheless, he was to be sidelined, a victim no doubt of the struggles for influence raging within the star's entourage. Although he was a musician on *Black or White* and *Who Is It*, this promising producer was finally excluded from the *Dangerous* project.

Bill Bottrell, meanwhile, managed to secure his place alongside the singer for the album's pop-oriented songs. However, the King of Pop wanted a producer from the funk and R&B scene to make songs with a relentless groove. He was in search of a rare beast and interviewed numerous candidates. The few songs recorded with Bryan Loren were definitively shelved. The same went for the producers L A Reid and Babyface, who had been hitmakers in the late 1980s, helping The Jacksons on their album *2300 Jackson Street* and propelling Bobby Brown into the charts.

1991

Teddy, are you ready?...

Ironically, the solution came from Quincy Jones. During the recording sessions for *Bad*, the celebrated producer had noticed the young Teddy Riley, inventor of new jack swing and leader of the group Guy (see page 374). At the time, he was under the thumb of Gene Griffin, an autocratic manager who took a dim view of the collaboration between his protégé and the creator of *Billie Jean*, for he feared Riley might be snapped up by the Jackson/Jones team. Two years later, just like L A Reid and Babyface, the young man was working on *2300 Jackson Street*. In 1990, he made remixes of the song *I Don't Go for That* (with Siedah Garrett), from the album *Back on the Block* by Quincy Jones. Teddy Riley embodied that modern vision of African-American music that combined hip-hop beats and soul melodies with ease and skill. From the rapper Kool Moe Dee to the crooner Keith Sweat, many were those who sought his services to produce hits bearing the hallmark of new jack swing.

In 1990, Michael Jackson's entourage contacted him to organize sessions on *Dangerous*. From their first meetings, the pop star had fairly clear ideas for songs, and the young musician suggested grooves and rhythm tracks which, in his view, fitted with the singer's style. There was a chemistry between the two men, and they cowrote certain songs, such as *Remember the Time*.

Teddy Riley was a product of new technology, but he did not forget the importance of a natural, musical approach once in the studio: "We recorded it in California, at Record One, and then we ended up in Larrabee Studios. I was using a lot of vintage stuff to get the sound we needed. Reeds and SSL XLs were mainly the boards we used—I always loved vintage better than digital. It's way better...much warmer."[98]

As well as Bill Bottrell and Teddy Riley, the recording engineer Bruce Swedien was also promoted, holding the reassuring position of coproducer alongside Michael Jackson of four songs on the album. He thus ensured that a more classic sound was retained, preserving the continuity with Quincy Jones's productions.

Michael, Macaulay, Slash, and David Lynch

Confident in the team that had been assembled in the studio, the singer then made sure that the promotion campaign would spring its fair share of surprises. He decided to create an event for each single, calling on an impressive list of stars to appear in each of his short films. Macaulay Culkin, the young star of *Home Alone*, started the ball rolling in *Black or White*, closely followed by the comedian Eddie Murphy, the basketball player Magic Johnson, and the fashion model Iman in *Remember the Time*. Appearing with these three personalities, plus the statuesque Naomi Campbell, who played opposite him in *In the Closet*, enabled the star to show himself to be entrenched in the African-American community. This image was set in stone by the video of *Jam*, in which another MJ appeared, one who had made history in American basketball: Michael Jordan.

Michael treated himself to some established directors: David Lynch made the teaser for the album and David Fincher displayed his impeccable esthetic in *Who Is It*. Michael Jackson also brought in up-and-coming directors, such as the young John Singleton, fresh from the success of his first feature-length movie, *Boyz N the Hood*. The credits for the album's short films read like an ideal filmography that many actors would be proud of.

The best mixers of the time made singles taken from the album: from C+C Music Factory to Tommy Musto and Moby, many tried their hand at this stylistic exercise which, inevitably,

The short film *Black or White*, which marked the start of Michael Jackson's return to the screen, revealed a feline, instinctive choreography in its second part.

distorted the original song. Although unimpressed, Michael Jackson nevertheless went along with this process, which was a condition of his new contract with Sony Music.

The amount of celebrity name-dropping rolled out for the promotion of *Dangerous* was breathtaking. But at the end of this long commercial exercise, which was concluded in December 1993, it was Slash, the Guns N' Roses guitarist, who came out on top, appearing in two songs released as singles: *Black or White* and *Give in to Me*. He then embarked on a professional relationship with the King of Pop that was to last more than ten years.

An album becomes an event

The release of *Dangerous* was a wide-ranging marketing operation that was conducted as if it was an affair of state, for the album naturally aroused keen interest. When the master of the single *Black or White* was sent to Europe, Sony Music made sure the tape was conveyed by two bodyguards, who flew to London on Concorde. On 20 November 1991, 30,000 copies of the record were nevertheless stolen from a warehouse at Los Angeles airport. But this security lapse did no harm to the success of *Dangerous*, and when the album arrived in the record stores on 26 November 1991, it took off spectacularly, selling five million copies outside the United States in one week! However, the US market was increasingly losing interest in the music of Michael Jackson: in his home country, the record sold only around two million in November and December 1991, and sales eventually stagnated the following year. The artist and his record label, sensing clearly which way the wind was blowing, focused promotion on other continents, above all Europe and Asia.

The sleeve also broke new ground. Michael Jackson was no longer shown in a conventional photograph, as on *Off the Wall*, *Thriller*, and *Bad*. Instead, he asked the American painter Mark Ryden to portray his world in an intriguing picture, where all the symbols associated with the King of Pop were juxtaposed with images that evoked the modern world. Thus the singer put forward his view of the world, without offering any explanation or comment in the interviews he granted to carefully chosen media. The album's sleeve notes contained two texts that excited the imagination of buyers: *The Dance*, which summed up his philosophy and relationship with physical movement, and *Planet Earth*, a recorded poem, which he preferred to keep under wraps.

Visually, Michael Jackson reinvented himself, adopting new styles appropriate to his status as King of Pop—a name that, from this period onward, was routinely used in all his official communications.

A new tour for a good cause

By way of after-sales for *Dangerous*, Sony Music asked its artist to go on tour once more. The singer had declared that the *Bad*

Flanked by his guitarist Jennifer Batten, Michael Jackson performs *Black or White* at Super Bowl XXVII in the Rose Bowl Stadium, Pasadena, California, 31 January 1993.

1991

tour was his farewell one, and that he wished to devote himself to other art forms, such as movies. However, the financial demands of the album were enormous, and the *Dangerous* tour eventually became unavoidable. To motivate himself, the King of Pop went back on the road in aid of a charitable foundation he had just launched, Heal the World—which he announced during a press conference in New York on 3 February 1992. He took advantage of this opportunity to sign a new contract with the Pepsi company, which sponsored the charity tour.

The movie director Kenny Ortega was given the job of creating the new *Dangerous* production, which was a variant of the *Bad* tour. In terms of stagecraft, the singer went from a classic rock concert configuration to a meticulously scripted show, which relied on numerous special effects and video sequences. Musically, the use of playback tapes became ever more prevalent. Between 27 June 1992 and 11 November 1993, the star performed 69 concerts in front of a total audience of more than four million people. The tour had no dates in the United States, and the American public only had access to this concert via exclusive TV broadcast onto HBO, which paid the artist the tidy sum of $20 million for the privilege.

Out to reconquer the United States

The excellent TV ratings achieved by the Bucharest concert were the springboard for a campaign to reconquer the American market. From late 1992 to May 1993, Michael Jackson made multiple public appearances in his native country, aimed at reviving sales of *Dangerous*. On 18 and 19 January he was among the guests of honor at the gala for the inauguration of President Bill Clinton. On 31 January 1993 he performed at half-time at the Super Bowl, with a number written together with Vincent Paterson, which contained highlights from the *Dangerous* tour. On 10 February the TV presenter Oprah Winfrey interviewed him live from his ranch, Neverland. In the course of a very long conversation, the singer revealed to the world that a skin condition, vitiligo, was responsible for his increasingly white skin color over the years.

The weeks passed in a media marathon that enabled Michael Jackson to make himself visible to the general public once again. He was showered with nominations at the most prestigious musical award ceremonies, such as the American Music Awards and the Soul Train Music Awards. On 24 February 1993 the Recording Academy paid tribute to him, bestowing on him a Legend Award, which was the crowning distinction of his career.

Accusations and attempted extortion

Michael Jackson concluded this long series of appearances in Monaco, where the World Music Awards had decided to honor him with three awards. He appeared together with a stepfamily he had met some months earlier. The mother of two children was not on good terms with her ex-husband, Evan Chandler, a Californian dentist whose dream was to become a movie director. When Chandler learned that his children and ex-wife were rubbing shoulders with Michael Jackson, he tried to contact the latter to seek his help in financing a film project. The star refused, which angered the father, who then created a nightmarish situation. He placed his son, Jordan Chandler, under sedation and made him recount a story of sexual abuse

Stevie Wonder, Michael Jackson, and Diana Ross on the steps of the Lincoln Memorial in Washington, DC, on the occasion of the gala for the inauguration of President Bill Clinton, 18 January 1993.

supposedly at the hands of Michael Jackson. He threatened to make the matter public. Michael Jackson and his attorneys did not give in to this blackmail, and on 24 August 1993, as the second leg of the *Dangerous* tour was starting in Asia, the young boy's revelations did the rounds in the media. From that point on, the King of Pop tried to honor his concert commitments, but in vain: one after the other, they were cancelled, and his entourage began to fear for his health. On 11 November 1993 he gave the last performance of his tour in Mexico City, the fifth in the city to a full house, with an audience numbering almost 100,000. The next day, he announced via an audio link that he was canceling the rest of the *Dangerous* tour, and declared that he was addicted to painkillers, notably as a result of the intense stress caused by the tour.

Michael Jackson then vanished from the radar and underwent treatment at a London clinic. Profoundly affected by the legal proceedings that the media dubbed the "Chandler Affair," he reappeared on 22 December on live TV, reading out a statement at his ranch. In it he asserted his determination to fight the accusations and thanked all those who had supported him.

Divorce complete

This pledge to fight to the end to clear his name did not materialize. On 26 January 1994 attorneys for the two sides announced they had reached agreement to settle this sexual assault affair. The singer's insurance company paid financial compensation to the young boy, in return for a halt to the proceedings, in order to avoid a legal case that would make headlines. The sum paid was not disclosed. Sony Music and the other partners of the King of Pop had counseled this course of action, so that he could bounce back and resume his work where he had left off. But the damage had been done: Pepsi, long-standing sponsor of Michael Jackson's tours, brought the advertising contract, signed just before the start of the tour, to an abrupt end. And in the minds of much of the public and the media, this financial agreement, the details of which had remained confidential, was seen as proof of the singer's guilt. Few journalists, after all, took an interest in the personal details and motivation of the plaintiffs. This very clumsy means of escape opened up a breach into which other fraudsters jumped, trying to make money from the creator of *Thriller.*

On 24 September 1994 the Santa Barbara county prosecutor's office issued a press release—it received low-key media coverage—which stated that there were no charges against Michael Jackson. On 22 December 2009 the FBI announced that the case file was void and contained no basis for charges to be brought. Nevertheless, this unexpected affair in a hitherto immaculate career was not without aftereffects: as well as its financial consequences for the life and career of Michael Jackson, its shockwave made itself felt in his creative output.

On 10 October 1992, HBO broadcast its footage of the *Dangerous* concert given on 1 October in Bucharest, Romania. That day the network secured the best audience rating in its history, with a market share of almost 34 percent.

PORTRAIT

TEDDY RILEY
THE KING OF NEW JACK SWING

Teddy Riley was born on 8 October 1967 in Harlem. He showed an interest in music from the age of five, and thanks to his diligence in the classes he attended at church, learned to play several instruments. The producer Gene Griffin took him under his wing and recorded his first album in 1984, as leader of the group Kids at Work, with Clurel Henderson and Timmy Gatling. Riley, then aged 16, played keyboards on the album, which met with limited success and the group split up very quickly. Teddy then started the band Guy, with Gatling and Aaron Hall, still under the control of Gene Griffin. The group had begun work on its first album when Timmy quit, being replaced by Aaron's brother, Damion Hall: this was to be the group's definitive lineup. At the same time, Teddy Riley got himself noticed when he produced *Go See the Doctor* by the rapper Kool Moe Dee in 1986.

Guy and new jack swing

When the group released its self-titled album *Guy* in 1987, it made a huge impact on the world of funk. The genre—which was aging and struggling to adapt to the rise of synthesizers and other studio machines—found a new lease of life thanks to the music of Riley and his friends. The journalist Barry Michael Cooper named this new style "new jack swing." The formula developed by Teddy Riley was simple: he combined hip-hop beats with soul melodies to produce a more catchy, modern sound. The group made hit after hit, and Riley collaborated with many others. With Keith Sweat he created the hit *I Want Her*, which became a new jack swing anthem, as did *Just Got Paid*, which the producer oversaw for Johnny Kemp.

Teddy Riley realized that he had talent, and that Gene Griffin was getting the credit for his work. On top of that, there was some shady business regarding contracts that were to the young musician's disadvantage, as well as unpaid royalties. Nevertheless, the two continued to work together until the end of the 1980s. The songs *She* and *2300 Jackson Street* on The Jacksons' eponymous album of 1989 were among the last they worked on together. Teddy Riley finally rid himself of this troublesome manager and producer, and worked alone on Guy's second album, also made with the Hall brothers.

The Future went on sale on 13 November 1990. The sound had hardened, and Guy, assisted by Wreckx-N-Effect, a rap group led by Markell, Teddy's brother, settled its scores with Gene Griffin in the song *Total Control*. When the album was released, Quincy Jones was impressed and advised Michael Jackson to work with Teddy Riley on *Dangerous*.

The partnership between the two men was a milestone: they adjusted their personal styles to each other's in order to create numbers that became standards of modern R&B. *Remember the Time* is the finest example—it plunged the King of Pop back into a groovy style that he had somewhat neglected since the *Off the Wall* years.

New jack swing conquers the world

Dangerous stunned not just the general public, but devotees of the new jack swing style as well. Never before had Riley's machines sounded so bold and inventive. The collaboration between the young producer and Michael Jackson took priority over Guy and Riley realized that the group's ambitions were now too modest for him. In 1992 they went their separate ways, to the dismay of their fans, but the producer bounced back and made the album *Hard or Smooth* with Wreckx-N-Effect. On it, he gave a break to two young artists who would find their own fame: Pharrell Williams and Chad Hugo, future members of the Neptunes, took part in the recording of the song *Rump Shaker*.

The global success of the album *Dangerous* enabled Teddy Riley to assert his style before an ever larger audience.

Although he had already produced *My Prerogative* for Bobby Brown in the late 1980s, he revived it for his album *Bobby*, released by MCA in 1992. For this flagship work by the ex-member of New Edition, he compiled a series of songs that performed respectably in the charts. The record's backing vocals were provided by Riley's new group, Blackstreet, consisting of Chauncey Hannibal, Levi Little, and Dave Hollister. The release of the album *Blackstreet* in 1994 signed the death warrant of new jack swing and marked the birth of a new style, known as "heavy R&B."

Teddy Riley at his keyboards in New York on 14 December 1990.

Blackstreet and heavy R&B

A few months before the release of *Dangerous*, Teddy Riley met with Michael Jackson to work on a song that was to feature in an ambitious short film on the subject of *The Addams Family*. However, the project was postponed, and although the two partners kept in touch regularly, the King of Pop turned to producers Jimmy Jam and Terry Lewis for the next album after *Dangerous*: *HIStory*.

Teddy Riley persevered with Blackstreet. In 1996 the single *No Diggity*, recorded with Dr. Dre, achieved classic status and earned the group widespread popular appeal. Meanwhile, Teddy Riley founded his own label, Lil' Man Records, which was distributed by Interscope. Through it he launched the careers of several artists, such as Queen Pen, who had a decent hit in *All My Love*, but his sometimes baffling sense of judgment led him to block the release of the album by Tammy Lucas, a singer from New York who came from the house music scene and who had successfully established herself as one of the legendary divas of new jack swing with the song *Is It Good to You*.

At the end of the 1990s, Riley and his faithful acolyte Chauncey Hannibal continued the Blackstreet story with the album *Finally* (1999). However, disagreements between the group's members strangled the record's promotion campaign at birth. Teddy Riley then decided to reunite Guy for a third album entitled simply *III*. It found success only among people who were nostalgic for the days of new jack swing.

Unfortunately things went from worse to worse for Riley in the early 2000s. His productions had difficulty keeping up with Rodney Jerkins, a young musician whom he had mentored. The master was being overtaken by a new generation of hitmakers who were calling the shots of R&B. Nevertheless, he recorded his first solo album, *BlackRock*, whose planned release by Virgin Records in 2001 was cancelled. In fact, the team tasked with the album's launch was also managing Mariah Carey's *Glitter* project, but following *Glitter*'s spectacular failure, the entire team was fired and all work in progress abandoned.

Turning a corner in the 2000s

During the 2000s, Teddy Riley attempted several tours that fell through and announced several projects that failed to materialize. While he was working on the beginnings of *Invincible*, Michael Jackson nevertheless turned to him once more. The two men worked mostly on ballads, which were often sad, making a break from the frenzied rhythms of *Dangerous*. When the King of Pop died in 2009, the inventor of new jack swing paid him homage by performing some of the songs they had created together, such as *Remember the Time*, singing the tune through the tube of his talk box.

At the end of 2010 the executors of the star's will asked Riley to complete work on some songs for the first posthumous album, *Michael*. One of the songs he produced, *Breaking News*, caused controversy, because a large proportion of the public and fans did not recognize Michael Jackson's voice in the song and protested that a fraud had been perpetrated. Condemned to silence by a contract signed with the attorneys for the King of Pop, Teddy Riley mismanaged this sad affair, which was to tarnish his reputation among purists.

He rehabilitated himself musically in the early 2010s by visiting South Korea, where he produced some songs for several artists on the K-pop scene. In 2011, in South Korea he produced the song *The Boys*, a hit by the group Girls' Generation that attained popularity in the United States.

Riley's output in the rest of the world stagnated during the 2010s, and his name ended up being forgotten by the general public, who worshipped artists such as Pharrell Williams, oblivious to the fact that they had learned the ropes with Riley.

A legendary producer and an enigmatic character, Teddy Riley is one of the people who undeniably had an effect on the music of Michael Jackson. He can also claim to have created a musical style, new jack swing. During his lifetime Jackson found in him an ally for pushing back certain musical boundaries. Having worked with the King of Pop for more than ten years, Teddy Riley without a doubt made a brilliant successor to Quincy Jones.

JAM

Rene Moore, Bruce Swedien, Michael Jackson, Teddy Riley / 5'39

Musicians
Michael Jackson: lead and backing vocals
Heavy D: rap
Teddy Riley: keyboards, synthesizers, drums, and guitar
Rene Moore and Brad Buxer: keyboards
Rhett Lawrence, Michael Boddicker, and Brad Buxer: synthesizers
Bruce Swedien: keyboards and drums
Recording
Ocean Way Recording, Record One Studios (studio 2) and Larrabee North, Los Angeles: 25 June 1990 to 30 October 1991
Technical team
Producers: Michael Jackson, Teddy Riley, and Bruce Swedien
Recording engineers: Bruce Swedien and Teddy Riley
Arrangements: Michael Jackson, Bruce Swedien, Teddy Riley, and Rene Moore
Vocal arrangements: Michael Jackson
Mixing: Bruce Swedien and Teddy Riley

1991

USA
A-side: *Jam* (*7-inch edit*) / 4'03
B-side: *Rock with You* (*Masters at Work remix*) / 5'29
UK
A-side: *Jam* (*7-inch edit*) / 4'03
B-side: *Beat It* (*Moby's submix*) / 6'11
Released by Epic/Sony Music Records: USA (ref. 34-74333), 13 June 1992 / UK (ref. EPC 658360), 26 September 1992
Chart position: USA R&B No. 3, Pop No. 26 / UK No. 13

THE SONG

Genesis

The producer, writer, composer, and performer Rene Moore worked on the bare bones of the song *Jam* with Bruce Swedien, and planned to record it for his new Motown album *I'll Be Good*, before finally suggesting the song to Michael Jackson. Bruce Swedien recalled in 2013: "Both of us thought to ourselves, 'Wow, we'd better play this for Michael, this is screamin',' so we did and Michael loved it."[99] The King of Pop added words that were radical and hard-hitting, a loud call to become aware of the worsening state of the world: "Nation to nation, all the world must come together / Face the problems that we see." Not since *Beat It* had Michael Jackson been so vindictive. His was a unifying call, intended to be a thunderous opening to the album *Dangerous*: "False prophets cry of doom," "I'm conditioned by the system." Over a base of powerful snare drums as well as more complex sounds created by the duo of Moore and Swedien, Teddy Riley set to work to polish and soften the song's rich material.

Production

The producer and musician introduced the musical trends he had developed with his group Guy. From hip-hop to new jack swing, *Jam* brought his style to a bigger stage. In 1992, recalling the production of the song, Teddy Riley related: "*Jam* was brought to me as just a drum beat. Rene Moore and Bruce Swedien came up with the idea and gave it to Michael as a beat, so you can't take that credit away from them. But it was just a stripped tune until Michael did his vocals and I came in with the icing. I actually added most of the keyboard parts, all of the percussion elements, all of the horn parts, and all of the guitar parts to make the tune what it is today."[100] In 2009, he completed the picture: "He [Michael] told me to see what I could do with it so I took it and created some more instruments and reproduced the record—and he loved it. That's the way it worked a lot of the time...It was my idea to get the rapper Heavy D to perform on there as well. He was Michael's favorite rapper at the time."[101] Heavy D's rap is inseparable from the song, as it gels with the harshness of the subject matter.

At the beginning of summer 1992, *Jam* was released as a single in the United States, while *Who Is It* was released in

Michael Jordan gives Michael Jackson a basketball lesson. The two stars exchanged a few passes for the shooting of the short film *Jam* on 20 April 1992.

Europe. Countless remixes, some overseen by Teddy Riley himself, appeared on numerous regular or promotional pressings. These productions, of uncertain quality, flooded the airwaves and were played by DJs in nightclubs. The market for remixes ballooned, targeting urban audiences in America and dance or techno devotees in Europe. *Jam* entered the charts all over the world, but made the Top 10 only in France, Spain, and New Zealand.

Michael Jackson chose the song to open concerts on his *Dangerous* tour, because its percussive sound allowed an electrifying choreography that drove fans wild from the first few minutes.

The famous leader of the Chicago Bulls' Dream Team, Michael Jordan helped to popularize basketball and the NBA worldwide, from the mid-1980s to the early 2000s.

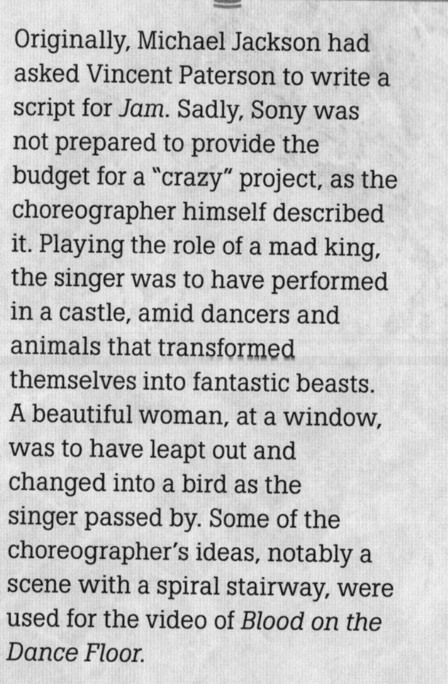

Originally, Michael Jackson had asked Vincent Paterson to write a script for *Jam*. Sadly, Sony was not prepared to provide the budget for a "crazy" project, as the choreographer himself described it. Playing the role of a mad king, the singer was to have performed in a castle, amid dancers and animals that transformed themselves into fantastic beasts. A beautiful woman, at a window, was to have leapt out and changed into a bird as the singer passed by. Some of the choreographer's ideas, notably a scene with a spiral stairway, were used for the video of *Blood on the Dance Floor*.

THE SHORT FILM

Directors: David Kellogg and Michael Jackson
Producer: Phil Rose
Leading actors: Michael Jackson and Michael Jordan
Extras and supporting actors: Heavy D, Kris Kross, and Naughty by Nature
Shooting date: 20 April 1992
Shoot location: Chicago
Duration: 7'50

Genesis

Without a clearly defined script, it fell to David Kellogg to create the clip's urban atmosphere. He was a specialist in the genre, having made numerous commercials. He and the producer, Phil Rose, decided to shoot in a disused hangar on Chicago's South Side, for the simple reason that Michael Jordan, one of the video's two stars, had some important engagements at the time with the Chicago Bulls' famous Dream Team. Phil Rose recalled: "We started looking into what was available in the city...there weren't many industrial warehouses there that had a ceiling high enough. Then we noticed that there was this bombed-out old armory, and we just came in and had a look around, and it was perfect. It has a huge open space...It was a dump and the production designer, Rob Pearson, put in a full-sized basketball court. I mean, it was surreal to just be in this sort of completely old building and have this gorgeous basketball floor set up there."[102] The producer told an amusing anecdote: "I had to meet with the local police chief and everything else without revealing who was in the video, so we portrayed it as a Hellmann's mayonnaise commercial, so we wouldn't draw any attention to ourselves. The call sheet itself, we kept [the actual video details] off there; we kept it off of the crew lists. Anything that had any kind of printed material on it was basically listed as a mayonnaise commercial. With any typical shoot or making a commercial, you don't really advertise it, but you do have street signs up directing equipment and crew."[102]

Production

Although shooting proved problematic because of the busy schedules of the two Michaels, Jackson and Jordan, the video's plot was simple: the two characters shared their respective specialisms. One taught the other how to make basketball passes, while the other taught a few dance steps. Michael Jackson arrived on set first, and the chief of police thought he was going crazy when he found out this wasn't in fact a mayonnaise commercial. He became even more concerned when, two hours later, the basketball mega-star also showed up. Phil Rose said: "There was a lot of improvisation, especially when you're working with two people like that whose schedules are what

Michael Jackson on the basketball court specially built in a Chicago hangar for the April 1992 shooting of the short film *Jam*.

they are. Michael [Jackson]'s strength is performance, of course, and the other Michael's strength is sports. Jordan was a bit clumsy dancing, I have to say, and I would say Michael's jump shot was probably as weak as Jordan's dancing. So it was really just about capturing moments between them and then using the footage we gathered. It felt very natural. I mean, it really was kind of more documentary filmmaking than composed filmmaking."[102]

David Kellogg remembers that special care was taken over the lighting: "Michael Jackson and his team were really concerned about lighting. There was no secret about that. There were no rules with the two of them together, but it was only when [Jackson] performed that they cared a lot about the lighting. They really didn't like any side lighting because I think he felt that his face was really angular and the shadow he didn't really like…He preferred a silhouette or straight-front lighting and pretty soft, so behind the camera there would just be sort of a wall of light."[102]

Other stars also appeared on the video, such as the rapper Heavy D, who featured in the original song. The two young vocalists of the Atlanta hip-hop group Kriss Kross, who were the darlings of the public at the time, also made a brief appearance. The huge figure of Michael Jordan almost stole the show from Michael Jackson, so great was the basketball player's stardom. Another symbol of African-American success, Jordan, naturally, executed perfect dribbles. And although Michael Jackson managed some sporting feats, it was because his shots owed everything to digital special effects. The camera moved fast, and the sequences mirrored the jerky rhythm of the music.

A short version of the video, lasting 4'10, was distributed chiefly in the United States. Another version, lasting 7'50, allowed the time to include more footage of the dance lesson Michael Jackson gave Michael Jordan.

The King of Pop retained a vivid memory of his meeting with the sporting idol, as he demonstrated on the TV program *Michael Jackson's Private Home Movies,* broadcast by FOX on 24 April 2003, where he explained that a very large number of shots were not used in the video's final edit.

A third, much rarer video, which can be seen on the Japanese LaserDisc *UntouchaBulls,* shows an exclusive edit of *Jam* punctuated by images of legendary passes made by Michael Jordan on the basketball court.

Why You Wanna Trip on Me

Teddy Riley, Bernard Belle / 5'25

Musicians
Michael Jackson: lead and backing vocals
Teddy Riley: keyboards, synthesizers, and guitar
Paul Jackson Jr.: guitar (intro)
Recording
Cherokee Studios (studio 3), Los Angeles: strings
Allen Zentz Recording, Los Angeles: rhythm tracks and vocals
Westlake Recording Studios, Los Angeles: brass and mixing
4 December 1978 to 3 June 1979
Technical team
Producers: Teddy Riley and Michael Jackson
Recording engineer: Bruce Swedien
Arrangements: (unknown)
Mixing: Teddy Riley and Bruce Swedien

1991

This was not released as a single, but used in the closing credits for the video compilation *Dangerous: The Short Films* (1993).

The faithful Paul Jackson, shown here in Chicago, 12 October 1993, worked with Michael Jackson in the studio and saw the star's career develop over the years.

Genesis

Michael Jackson was offered this made-to-measure song by Bernard Belle and Teddy Riley. The two worked together regularly in the early 1990s and created some of the biggest hits of the new jack swing movement. *Why You Wanna Trip on Me* could be seen as following on directly from *Leave Me Alone*, hardening that song's tone. Riley said: "We knew people were after him, people were talking about him. But we didn't get too direct, we didn't say anybody's name, 'cause when you're too direct it gets boring."[23]

The style of syncopated couplets and melodious refrains, which first appeared in some of the songs on *Bad*, is fully developed here. "They say I'm different / They don't understand," Michael Jackson cries as soon as he takes the microphone. After the urban, pacifist hymn of *Jam*, he settles scores with those who are persecuting him. This theme of paranoia was to reappear regularly in the artist's work. It inevitably widened the gap between his fans—who were right behind the King of Pop, sympathized with him, and supported him in his battle with the press—and the media, which frequently mocked his use of records to settle scores.

Production

Paul Jackson Jr. opens the fiendish intro to *Why You Wanna Trip on Me* with a swirling guitar solo that sounds like a descent into hell. A working CD, containing 30 different tracks of this intro, documented the guitarist's recording session; recorded at Teddy Riley's Future Records studio, only 61 are in existence. There are many variations of the riffs, but what stands out from all of them is the urge to make the instrument resound like a whirlwind that carries the listener away to a dark, suffocating place.

Teddy Riley is the second guitarist playing. He provides a rhythmic line, a real funky force fused with blues, which injects that dose of heavy, insistent groove that permeates the song. Riley recalled: "The element I'm most proud of in this song is my guitar playing. I thought he [Jackson] was going to get another person to play on it but he wanted my good self playing! That was something special to me. I was using an acoustic Ovation guitar."[101]

The spare, striking production does away with a bass line, leaving the limelight to the synthesizers, mostly played without

Michael Jackson on the set of the Pepsi commercial Dreams, directed by Joe Pykta, on 13 May 1992. Some sequences used *Why You Wanna Trip on Me* as the soundtrack and were included at the end of the compilation *Dangerous: The Short Films.*

programming. *Why You Wanna Trip on Me* embodies that rare, effective combination of the cutting-edge sounds of electronic music of the time with an intuitive, soul-inspired approach that reconnects with the authentic groove of the 1970s. Riley recalled: "The whole song didn't take long to produce, actually. I think the longest part was writing everything and getting everything formatted. There's no studio trickery either, really. When you're doing analogue it's pretty much, you know, getting everything on tape, you know? It's very warm. That's basically it."[101]

FOR JACKSON ADDICTS

The intro, played by Paul Jackson Jr., opened Michael Jackson's half-time Super Bowl performance on 31 January 1993 in California.

In the Closet

Michael Jackson, Teddy Riley / 6'32

Musicians
Michael Jackson: lead and backing vocals
"Mystery Girl": second lead vocals
Teddy Riley: keyboards and synthesizers
Recording
Ocean Way Recording, Record One Studios (studio 2), and Larrabee North, Los Angeles: 25 June 1990 to 30 October 1991
Technical team
Producers: Michael Jackson and Teddy Riley
Recording engineers: Bruce Swedien and Teddy Riley
Rhythm and synthesizer arrangements: Teddy Riley
Vocal arrangements: Michael Jackson

1991

Single

A-side: *In the Closet* (7-inch edit) / 4'29
B-side: *In the Closet* (The Mission Radio edit) / 4'28
Released by Epic Records: USA (ref. 34-74266) and UK (ref. 657934), 27 April 1992
Chart position: USA R&B No. 1, Pop No. 6 / UK No. 8
RIAA: certified Gold 9 June 1992

THE SONG

Genesis

While recording *Bad,* Michael Jackson came close to performing the track as a duet with Prince. For the song *In the Closet*, it was with Madonna that he failed to team up. He conceived the song as a scandalous shared duet but, as soon as the artists began work on the project together, their divergent views became apparent. Madonna wanted to impose a vision that was unquestionably more provocative, whereas the King of Pop was intent on retaining his basic idea. No common ground was found...This meeting between two of pop's biggest stars, which the world of music would sorely miss, would without a doubt have had a colossal impact.

In the Closet is about a secret relationship between two lovers. Never before in his career had Michael Jackson tackled such a sexual, scandalous, and torrid subject. The song's theme made a clean break with everything he had produced in the past; the composition was self-assured, brilliant, and it admirably complemented the rest of his work. The song played upon an interesting ambiguity because, although it dealt with adultery, the expression "out of the closet" usually refers to a gay person "coming out." But while some tried to see a paradox, the lovers' torrent of impatient desire soon drowned out such questioning. Fans, who were unaccustomed to hearing the singer deal with this kind of subject, welcomed the song with a certain amount of pride: their idol had revealed himself not to be such a prude after all, even though he usually seemed a little reserved!

Production

"Now, *In the Closet* was something Michael came up with, and it came out exactly as he wanted the track to be. He kind of put his vocals on a Dictaphone when he was in another room. He'd often record the vocals on a Dictaphone and take them into the studio and then see how it would all work out,"[101] recalled Teddy Riley in 2013. What the producer did was boost the sounds the artist had imagined and add some funky, explosive, nefarious elements. The sound effects and rounded nature of the sounds that accompany the tune magnificently come on top of the erotic crescendos that mark the love story, even the lovemaking, of the two.

Princess Stephanie of Monaco presents an award to Michael Jackson at the World Music Awards ceremony, 12 May 1993.

The introduction is sung by an unknown woman, who is credited as "Mystery Girl" and aroused great curiosity among fans until it became known that it was Princess Stéphanie of Monaco. At the beginning of the 1990s the Monaco royal was trying her hand at being a singer, and Sony financed, at great expense, the promotion of her second album—her first in English. When she was passing through Los Angeles, the princess recorded her voice in the studio. Its timbre is almost unrecognizable, it is so filtered through various devices.

There are few acoustic instruments; only the intro features the sound of violins, which do justice to the words whispered by Stéphanie of Monaco. The up-tempo arrangements are percussive and industrial, and perfectly fit the style and principles introduced by Teddy Riley.

The single's release led to many remixes, all geared to the markets at which they were aimed, sometimes dance or hip-hop. The song performed decently in the charts, without causing any surprise, despite the scandalous vigor Michael Jackson showed for the first time in a song. *In the Closet* went to No. 1 only in the US Top R&B, and made a few Top 10s around the world.

FOR JACKSON ADDICTS

Using the same images, a second video was made with the song's club mix version. Shown almost exclusively on MTV, it accompanied the promotion of multiple recordings featuring various remixes.

THE SHORT FILM

Director: Herb Ritts
Producer: Jane Reardon
Leading actor: Michael Jackson
Supporting actor: Naomi Campbell
Extras: two flamenco dancers (not credited)
Shoot date: March 1992
Shooting location: the eastern part of the Salton Sea, California
Duration: 6'16

Genesis

Michael Jackson immediately liked the original idea that the photographer Herb Ritts had for the song. The release of *Who Is It* as the third single from *Dangerous* was even postponed to give priority to this video project, such was the impatience of the King of Pop.

In September 1990, Herb Ritts had made the magnificent clip of Janet Jackson, *Love Will Never Do (Without You)*, which MTV named best video of the year by a female artist. The set was spare, lacking eye-catching visual elements, in order to give priority to the movements and forms of the characters. A desert landscape, some youths with astonishing muscles, a few dance steps, and oscillating camerawork to trigger the energy completed the picture. The photographer approached her brother with a similar idea. The video of *In the Closet* scrupulously copied that of *Love Will Never Do (Without You)*, with the notable difference that the young men were replaced by the most fashionable model of the time: the irresistible Naomi Campbell.

The fashion model Naomi Campbell and Michael Jackson dance in the video *In the Closet* in March 1992. Their closeness on screen went down in history.

From left: Michael Jackson, Herb Ritts, and the American actor Red Skelton on the set of the short film *In the Closet* in March 1992.

Production

On the set, which featured a tiny model of a colonial or Spanish baroque church in the scenery, Herb Ritts explained: "It's really about bringing Michael's energy out in a new way"[103]

Wearing a dirty, white T-shirt and dusty black jeans, his hair slicked back, Michael flaunts an improbable but realistic look. The divine Naomi oscillates languorously around him, adopting suggestive poses, and embraces, caresses, wraps herself around him, charming him. Their bond is touching and sincere; it illustrates the words of the song wonderfully. The King of Pop wore a big smile during shooting. He felt confident and greatly enjoyed himself between takes. Naomi Campbell, a protégée of Quincy Jones, recorded the intro in her own voice, as the producer had succeeded in getting her deeply involved in the project. Her version was never made available on CD.

The photography is impeccable, and the natural light exceptional. As a final touch, the video was given a sepia tone, a process appreciated by the director, which brought warmth and sensuality. The last scene is devoted to a wild dance by Michael.

The video was first broadcast on 23 April 1992, except in South Africa, where it was deemed too suggestive. *In the Closet* also won an MTV award for best cinematography in a video.

Cindy Crawford delivered MTV's report on the shooting of the video. The channel, a major partner in the promotion of the album *Dangerous*, invited 35 winners of the "My Dinner with Michael" competition to come and meet the singer and Naomi Campbell on location.

She Drives Me Wild

Michael Jackson, Teddy Riley / 3'41

Musicians
Michael Jackson: lead and backing vocals
Wreckx-N-Effect: rap
Teddy Riley: keyboards and synthesizers
Recording
Ocean Way Recording, Record One Studios (studio 2), and Larrabee North Studios, Los Angeles: 25 June 1990 to 30 October 1991
Technical team
Producers: Teddy Riley and Michael Jackson
Recording engineer: Bruce Swedien
Rhythm and synthesizer arrangements: Teddy Riley
Vocal arrangements: Michael Jackson
Mixing: Bruce Swedien and Teddy Riley

1991

Aqil Davidson and Markell Riley, members of Wreckx-N-Effect, at the fourth *Billboard* Music Awards in the Universal Amphitheater, Universal City, Los Angeles, on 8 December 1993.

Genesis

Rather like a logical continuation of *Speed Demon*, *She Drives Me Wild* gives a further glimpse of the fantastic relationship captured on tape between Michael Jackson and machines. In his world, and the images shown of him, the King of Pop very rarely appeared at the wheel of an automobile. He was often being driven by a chauffeur, and he was not known for his passionate love of motorcycles or other fast machinery, unlike some stars. But this theme of speed and horsepower seems to be a framework within which the star projected his stories, based either on real events or on emotions experienced in dreams. *She Drives Me Wild* contains the heady refrain "She got the look," a reply to the emblematic phrase of the song *U Got the Look*, written by Prince in 1986. In the second verse the reference to a "paisley-cut top" naturally denotes a precise style of fashion garment, but the word "paisley" also, of course, evokes the studios of the creator of *Purple Rain*, which bore that name. Thus, in a subtle, indirect way, the owner of Neverland sent a message to the Kid from Minneapolis, who not only had declined his invitation to feature on *Bad* but had also hired Frank DiLeo, Michael's former manager, to run his affairs, starting with the ambitious promotion campaign for the album *Diamonds and Pearls*, one of Prince's greatest successes of the 1990s.

The lyrics of *She Drives Me Wild* tell the simple story of a bashful lover transfixed by the beauty of a femme fatale, who is full of self-assurance and aware that the world is at her feet. The rap that intervenes, by way of a break in the middle of the song, was written by the duo Wreckx-N-Effect, consisting of Aqil Davidson and Markell Riley, brother of Teddy. At the time, the two young men were finishing work on their third album, *Hard or Smooth*, which was a milestone on the new jack swing and hip-hop scenes. Far from deserving the famous black-and-white rectangle with the words "Parental Advisory / Explicit Content," which was applied to many rap records in the early 1990s, the rap text of Aqil and Markell kept within a certain moral framework.

Production

Teddy Riley was bursting with inventiveness when he produced *She Drives Me Wild*. The Synclavier was set aside, to make way for his samplers and programming skills. Instead of cap-

Michael Jackson shooting a commercial entitled Waves, which promoted the album *Dangerous* in Europe and Sony television sets in Japan in 1991.

turing sounds from real life, recorded outside, Riley proceeded in a more traditional fashion. He said: "My biggest memory from that recording was that we used all car sounds as drum sounds and it came out perfectly. I didn't go out into the field and record actual car sounds and take back to the studio—I had a sample CD that was really cool. It wasn't something I'd done before; it was the first time I went for unusual sounds in the place of drums."[101]

The heavy artillery let loose by Riley on the tracks of the Ocean Way studio manages to make the listener forget that there is no rhythm guitar in a song which, nevertheless, possesses a groove worthy of James Brown himself. On the other hand, the chords that begin each measure create the hypnotic effect that some critics at the time compared to that in the song *Thriller*.

Destined to remain on the album without the benefit of being released as a single, *She Drives Me Wild* was recycled on stage as musical transition between *They Don't Care about Us* and *In the Closet* during the HIStory tour in 1996 and 1997.

Remember the Time

Teddy Riley, Michael Jackson, Bernard Belle / 4'00

Musicians
Michael Jackson: lead and backing vocals
Teddy Riley: keyboards and synthesizers
Recording
The Hit Factory, Miami: 1991
Technical team
Producers: Michael Jackson and Teddy Riley
Recording engineers: Bruce Swedien and Teddy Riley
Rhythm and synthesizer arrangements: Teddy Riley
Vocal arrangements: Michael Jackson
Mixing: Bruce Swedien and Teddy Riley

1991

FOR JACKSON ADDICTS

The 7-inch main mix version (3'59) of *Remember the Time*, released as part of *Michael Jackson—Visionary: The Video Singles* (2006), contains an alternative mix.

USA
A-side: *Remember the Time (album version)* / 4'00
B-side: *Black or White (The Underground Club mix)* / 3'33
UK
A-side: *Remember the Time (album version)* / 4'00
B-side: *Come Together (unreleased* / long *version)* / 5'27
Released by Epic Records: USA (ref. 34-74200) and UK (ref. EPC 657774), 14 January 1992
Chart position: USA R&B No. 1, Pop No. 3 / UK No. 3
RIAA: certified Gold 16 March 1992

THE SONG

Genesis

Of all the songs produced by Teddy Riley on the album *Dangerous*, *Remember the Time* pulled off the feat of combining styles: the number blends old-style, electrifying funk with a sustaining modern, incisive beat. Written with Bernard Belle, who worked at Motown before joining the new jack swing movement, the song allows considerable room for Michael Jackson's vocal variations, which are reminiscent of those from his early years. It is a nostalgic recollection of a love story: "Do you remember when we fell in love / We were young and innocent then / Do you remember how it all began / It just seemed like heaven so why did it end?" In 2009, Teddy Riley recalled the marvelous way Michael welcomed his suggestions:

> I was working on *Remember the Time* with him and we actually stopped. I played the music; that was actually the fifth song, the fifth track, that I played for him. And he stopped me. I thought I was going to be kicked off the project! He took me to the back, and I thought he was going to lecture me, you know, like I did this chord wrong, or something, and he was like, "Play that on the piano." And he took me in the back just to see if I'd play, and I played it on the piano, and he just went, "That melody, everything, everything, is just great about this song, and what I want to do to this is, I want it to be full of love. I can't tell you who I'm writing this about, but I know this is gonna be our second single." He said this when we were playing the track…I know who it's for, but I can't say. I would never. [104]

What the producer seemed to be forgetting was that on the back of the single's sleeve, the King of Pop had had these words added: "Dedicated with love to Diana Ross." Was this a way for the singer to apologize for *Dirty Diana*? Surely no one other than the Motown diva could awake so many loving memories—so dear, sweet, and precious—in the singer's heart.

Production

A perfect blend of the brilliance of R&B and the bewitching rhythm of new jack swing, *Remember the Time* was calibrated

On 9 March 1993, Michael Jackson electrified the audience at the Soul Train Music Awards in the Shrine Auditorium, Los Angeles. Because he had a wounded leg, he performed his choreography seated. The song, and the stage routine, were never performed live.

for its mission of seduction. The breaks and reprises give a crazy energy to the song, which was always very popular with audiences. In 2009, Teddy Riley revealed some details of its production: "The elements on this song that give it that new jack swing sound are the ones that I used when I recorded with Guy and Bobby Brown to pioneer it. Sort of like the twisted samples I brought in. There were no samples of other people on that; what I did was make the sounds myself—I was sampling myself."[101]

Teddy Riley had the freedom to develop his own creative inspiration by making additional versions, which were released as various 12-inch and CD maxi singles. The rhythmic combinations were modulated and became richer, as the mood took him, but without ever betraying the piece's spirit. Teddy Riley said: "For me, that song was true R&B. I didn't put hip-hop into it until the remix. For that, I used a real upright jazz bass on a hip-hop beat. I really like that one. I also changed the organ part on the remix and did it with my voice through a vocoder."[100]

The single was a resounding success worldwide, even if it did not emulate the repeated No. 1 hits of years gone by.

In 1993, to celebrate winning the best R&B/Soul single by a male at the Soul Train Music Awards, Michael Jackson performed the song live, although he was obliged to do so seated on a chair because he had an injured leg. The stage effects echoed elements of the short film, and the performance was unique: even sitting down, the King of Pop brought it to life with his charismatic presence, and the guests were thrilled when he tried to get up to support the song's effective breaks, which had been specially mixed for the occasion.

John Singleton, who directed the short film of *Remember the Time*, at the MTV Movie Awards held at Walt Disney Studios, Burbank, California, 5 June 1992.

1991

THE SHORT FILM

Director: John Singleton
Producer: Reid Shane
Leading actor: Michael Jackson
Supporting actors: Eddie Murphy, Iman, The Pharcyde, and Magic Johnson
Choreography: Fatima Robinson
Shoot date: January 1992
Shooting location: Universal Studios, Los Angeles
Duration: 9'16

Genesis

Michael Jackson put his confidence in the up-and-coming generation of American movie directors, and for the short film of *Remember the Time* he hired John Singleton, the 24-year-old director of the movie *Boyz N the Hood* who, at that time, was unaccustomed to filming with such ample resources. Singleton recalled: "He said, 'Whatever you want to make this as cool as possible, let's do it. Let's get Eddie Murphy. Let's get Magic Johnson...' Magic Johnson was going through his thing where he'd just revealed he had HIV. Michael said, 'We have to put Magic in this video.' I'll always remember that. He was a very visual guy. They weren't videos to him. They were short films—visualizing the funkiness of what he was trying to accomplish in the music. He was always trying to set the bar higher."[105]

The action is set in ancient Egypt, and the model Iman, the wife of David Bowie in real life, is the center of all attention in the first part of the video. As queen of Egypt, she is the incarnation of desire, and her pharaoh, Eddie Murphy, does his utmost to try to entertain her.

Production

Magic Johnson, the resigned MC, announces the acts of the jugglers and fire-eaters that are supposed to amuse the queen, but who end up being thrown to the lions or beheaded. A man wearing a long coat then comes slowly forward and performs a magic trick that hits the target. He suddenly disappears, then reappears from some gravel that he had previously scattered on the ground. In a morphing effect borrowed from the movie *Terminator 2*, Michael Jackson appears; he has an androgynous look, radiant in his golden costume. Infuriated by the singer's charm, which seems to be having an effect on the queen, the pharaoh sets his guards in pursuit of him. As if in homage to the movie *Cleopatra*, starring Elizabeth Taylor, the Pharaoh of Pop moves through the magnificent stage scenery of Universal Studios until he finds the queen again, and exchanges a kiss with her. The video swings to a dancing rhythm by Fatima Robinson, a young, 21-year-old choreographer and friend of the director, who perfected one of Michael Jackson's finest group performances of the 1990s. In 2010, she recalled: "As a choreographer, you're so used to counting for an artist and Michael didn't like to count at all; he liked for you to kind of repeat the rhythm of a song. So, in a normal setting, I would count, 'Okay, here we go: 5-6-7-8 and 1-2-3-4,' whereas Michael, he would like you to go, 'Uhn-Ah-Uhn-Ah, Uhn-Ah-Uhn-Ah,' and so you would dance to the rhythm of the song as opposed to counts, because it made you feel the song more."[106]

Caught in a vise by the pharaoh's guards, Michael the magician dematerializes again and leaves the palace before the short film comes to an end. The camera effects are subtle and refined, and the video was a landmark in the annals of the King of Pop.

FOR JACKSON ADDICTS

Can't Let Her Get Away was not released as a single to promote *Dangerous*, but in 1992 was pressed as a maxi-single in Costa Rica.

CAN'T LET HER GET AWAY

Michael Jackson, Teddy Riley / 4'59

Musicians
Michael Jackson: lead and backing vocals
Teddy Riley: keyboards and synthesizers
Recording
Ocean Way Recording, Record One Studios (studio 2), and Larrabee North Studios, Los Angeles: 25 June 1990 to 30 October 1991
Technical team
Producers: Teddy Riley and Michael Jackson
Recording engineer: Bruce Swedien
Rhythm arrangements and synthesizers: Teddy Riley
Vocal arrangements: Michael Jackson
Mixing: Bruce Swedien and Teddy Riley

Can't Let Her Get Away was Michael Jackson's homage to James Brown (seen here in London on 9 March 1971).

Genesis

Can't Let Her Get Away was one of the song ideas that Teddy Riley worked on first before suggesting them to Michael Jackson. Here the young producer paid homage to James Brown with an incisive rhythm inspired by the song *Blues and Pants* by the Godfather of Soul. He said: "This was mostly from a sample CD that I just put together myself, and it kind of reminded me of the James Brown sound. I could feel it. I thought I'd bring a shadow of some of the greatness of the James Brown production sound to this. I made the sample CD myself—that was me playing instruments, then looping them up and having them lying around for potential projects. Back then I just had them lying around and I hadn't used them...But I really wanted to use them! ...Throughout the album I was drawing off a lot of CDs I had hanging around, all played by myself. I'm a multi-instrumentalist."[101]

For the first time in his career, the King of Pop sang a rap verse in the middle of a song by way of a break. The way it was written and the influences it shows, *Can't Let Her Get Away* makes it a song that pays homage to the rhythm and blues that played such a significant part in the singer's early years.

Production

Teddy Riley put together the instrumental track using synthesizers and samplers in sequence. After a spectacular intro, which gives the feeling the listener is carried away in a whirlwind, some drum kicks, reminiscent of the beginning of *Sex Machine*, herald the start of the rhythmic section.

The brass kicks at the start of each measure use a sample from *Get Up Offa That Thing* by James Brown, recorded in 1976. The sound extracted and recycled by Riley can be heard at 0'20 on that original recording. Although the guitar riff that is repeated as background pays tribute to the famous *Blues and Pants* by James Brown, the young producer avoided sampling that song's rhythmic base. For *Can't Let Her Get Away* he played an original guitar line, inspired by Brown's musical style.

Michael Jackson's rap was incorporated into the song with a chopped-up delivery, as if his voice were affected by tiny power cuts that followed the song's rhythm. This skillful editing served as his introduction into the world of hip-hop. In singular fashion, the singer finally recognized a musical style in which, during the sessions for the album *Bad*, he had placed little faith.

FOR JACKSON ADDICTS

Part of the instrumental version of *Heal the World* features in the credits of the video compilation *HIStory Volume I* (1995).

Heal the World

Michael Jackson / 6'25

Musicians
Michael Jackson: lead and backing vocals
Christa Larson: lead vocals (intro and finale)
John Bahler Singers: backing vocals
David Paich and Brad Buxer: keyboards
Michael Boddicker, David Paich, and Steve Porcaro: synthesizers
Jeff Porcaro: drums
Recording
Ocean Way Recording, Record One Studios (studio 2), and Larrabee North Studios, Los Angeles: 25 June 1990 to 30 October 1991
Technical team
Producer: Michael Jackson
Coproducer: Bruce Swedien
Recording engineers: Bruce Swedien and Matt Forger
Rhythm arrangements: Michael Jackson
Vocal arrangements: Michael Jackson and John Bahler
Orchestral arrangements: Marty Paich
Mixing: Bruce Swedien and Matt Forger

1991

Single

USA
A-side: *Heal the World (album version)* / 6'25
B-side: *She Drives Me Wild* / 3'41
UK
A-side: *Heal the World (7 inch edit)* / 4'31
B-side: *She Drives Me Wild* / 3'41
Released by Epic Records: USA (ref. 34-74708) and UK (ref. EPC 658488), 23 November 1992
Chart position: USA R&B No. 62, Pop No. 27 / UK No. 2

THE SONG

Genesis

Heal the World was among the first songs Michael Jackson wrote after the sessions for *Bad*. Initially, it was earmarked for the *Decade 1980–1990* compilation as a bonus track.

We Are the World and *Man in the Mirror* had enabled the King of Pop to take a humanitarian turn musically, an extension of his commitment on the ground to the cause of the underprivileged. But *Heal the World* aimed to go farther, and establish itself as the new anthem for the 1990s.

Originally the song was entitled *Feed the World*. The similarity with the song on the B-side of Band Aid's single *Do They Know It's Christmas*, released in late 1984, is without doubt what led the singer to change the title to *Heal the World*, like a promise to cure humanity once and for all.

The song's prelude was written by Marty Paich, father of David Paich, of the group Toto. The composer wrote this introduction specially, taking into account the suggestions and recommendations of the person who had commissioned him. This collaboration set the tone for the song, and confirmed Michael Jackson's growing propensity for increasingly longer intros to his songs.

Careful listeners also noticed a subtle relationship between *Heal the World* and *Livin' in a World (They Didn't Make)* by Janet Jackson, released two years earlier on the album *Rhythm Nation*. Almost as if they were having a competition by means of ever more innovative songs, clips, and concerts, the two youngest Jackson siblings mutually inspired each other during much of the 1980s and 1990s. Whereas *Livin' in a World* looks with sadness and despair upon a world that is enduring urban and social violence, *Heal the World* takes the opposite view, dreaming of a radiant future for generations to come.

Production

Heal the World was Michael Jackson's first song as producer for one of his solo albums. The symbolism was powerful, as the artist chose to take the senior role on a work that offered his manifesto for peace and environmentalism. Put together in a traditional fashion, the song's production bears that timeless stamp that calls to mind some of the greatest standards from Disney movies.

Michael Jackson, forever concerned about unhappy childhoods, set himself a challenge: to heal the world. The singer put his fame at the service of children, like here in Bucharest on 30 September 1992.

This similarity is reinforced when, in the first few seconds of the song, the young singer Christa Larson gives a brief address which, in a few lines, sums up the song's aim. A regular presence at Disney, she was the first child singer to be signed up by the Walt Disney Records label. In *Heal the World* she adopts a more solemn tone than usual, as Michael Jackson gave her the mission of conveying a message that took on a completely different magnitude when delivered by a child.

Rather than calling on the Andraé Crouch group for the backing vocals, the artist turned to John Bahler, brother of Tom, with whom he had already worked during the early 1970s at Motown. The idea came to him as a result of a phone call from David Paich. After a brief conversation about the song, the musician set to writing the backing vocals, which were then submitted to the star for approval. The day of the recording session Michael Jackson was home with a fever. The composer played him the final version over the telephone. The singer was happy with the result, and completed *Heal the World*, making sure that the choir led by John Bahler was showcased.

Between the first demos, entitled *Feed the World*, and the final version of *Heal the World*, seven months passed, during which a long series of alternative versions was produced. To this day, these remain in the archives of Michael Jackson's heirs.

FOR JACKSON ADDICTS

A special version of *Heal the World* was pressed into a promotional CD by Sony Music to promote its new range of portable CD players (Discman) in 1993. On it, Michael Jackson explains his charitable aims. This campaign, entitled *Signature Series*, was cancelled at the last minute, and the discs have since become coveted collectibles as a result.

Every time he performed *Heal the World* on the *Dangerous* tour, Michael Jackson welcomed children onstage, as here, in the Volks Stadium, Bayreuth, Germany, 2 September 1992.

Michael Jackson announces he will appear at half-time at the Super Bowl, at a press conference in Pasadena, 26 January 1993. The singer performed his anthem *Heal the World* and drew a giant mural interactively with the crowd, to boost the song's message.

A SONG FOR A CHARITABLE FOUNDATION

As well as being the title of the song on the album *Dangerous*, Heal the World was also the name of a charitable foundation launched by the singer at a New York press conference on 3 February 1992. He announced that he had agreed to set off on tour once again, with the sole aim of raising funds for this new charitable organization.

For ten years Heal the World was active on the ground, running many aid projects for disadvantaged children. The star donated the takings of his *Dangerous* tour to the charity and set in motion a number of operations—which were barely reported by the media. In late 1992 a consignment of humanitarian aid was sent to Sarajevo, then besieged by Serbian forces. In 1997 the King of Pop agreed to give a British newspaper exclusive use of the first photographs of his son, Prince, for $3 million, which he paid into his Heal the World foundation.

However, Heal the World ceased its activity in 2002 because of lack of funds. Since the star's death in 2009, a possible relaunch is in the hands of those managing his estate. His three children have not yet revived their father's organization, although they have inherited his charitable disposition. Prince and Paris Jackson regularly give their time to philanthropic operations on the ground, both in the United States and other countries.

THE SHORT FILM

Director: Joe Pytka
Producers: Suellen Wagner and Vincent Joliet
Lead actor: none
Extras: only Michael Jackson's niece, Brandi Jackson, is identifiable
Shoot date: 1992
Shooting locations: (unknown)
Duration: 6'25

Genesis

Michael Jackson's aim was not to interfere with the message of the song. He therefore proceeded as with *Man in the Mirror* and did not take part in the short film that accompanied *Heal the World*, leaving it instead to Joe Pytka to create a video that could do maximum justice to his words.

The director came up with a script consisting of two sections: the first shows children living in a war zone surrounded by troops; they then manage to escape and spread a message of peace and brotherhood across the world.

Production

In this clip, shots with distorted perspectives, which give a flattened effect, alternate with images in neutral tones, as if to bring out a certain reality of war—another demonstration of Joe Pytka's skill in creating images that are as simple as they are effective.

Like the song, the short film aims to be timeless, showing imaginary war scenes, characters, and situations in a time and place that are indefinable yet remain contemporary. Faced with the ever-present reality of the world, visible on TV networks, the happy ending of *Heal the World* may seem naive, but it is simply echoing the message of the song.

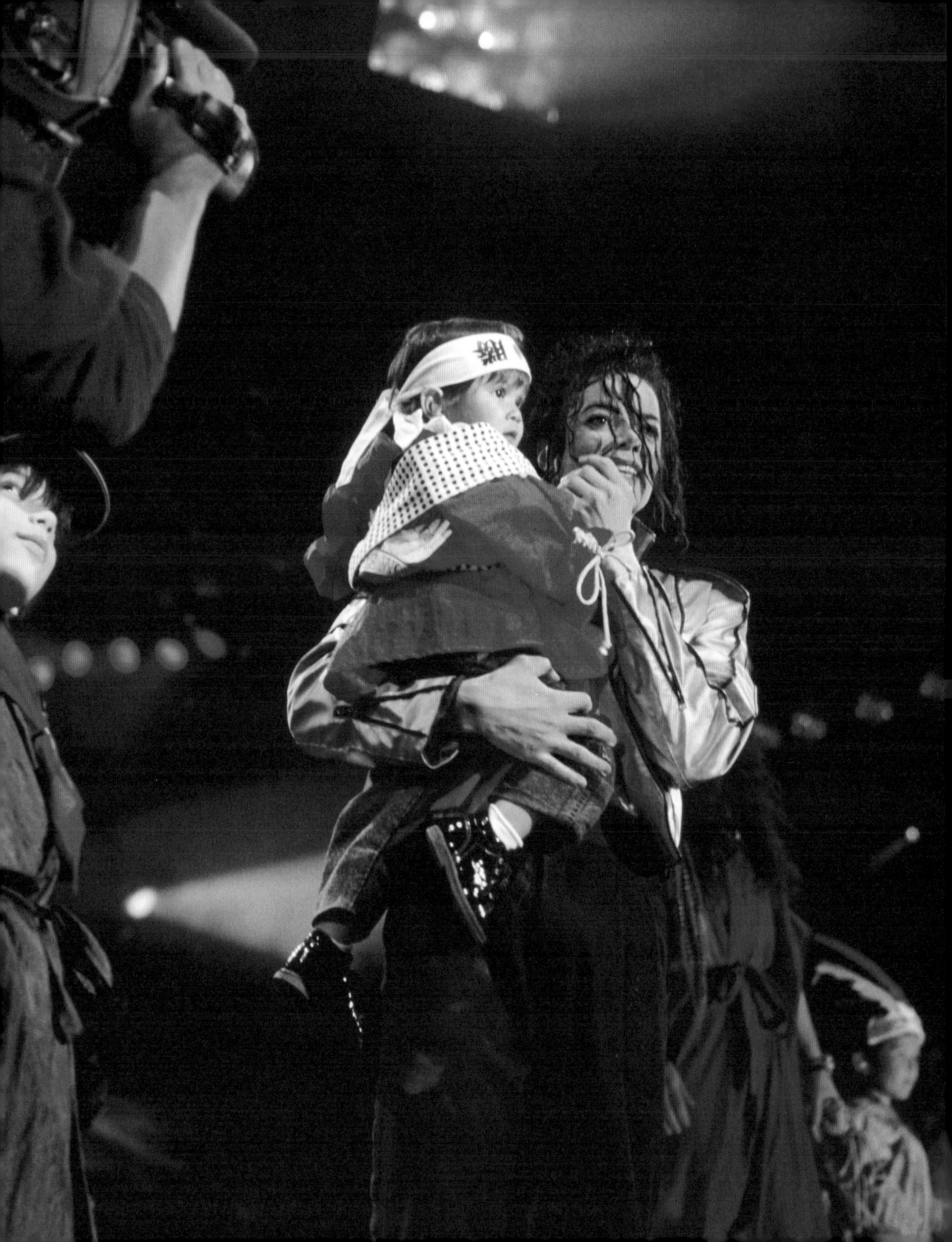

Black or White

Michael Jackson, rap by Bill Bottrell / 4'16

Musicians
Michael Jackson: lead and backing vocals
Bryan Loren: drums and Moog synthesizer
Brad Buxer: percussion
Terry Jackson: bass guitar
Brad Buxer, John Barnes, and Jasun Martz: keyboards
Bill Bottrell: percussion and guitar
Tim Pierce: heavy metal guitar
Michael Boddicker and Kevin Gilbert: speed sequencer synthesizers
Scott Frankfurt: sound effects (morphing)
L.T.B. (Bill Bottrell): rap
Slash: guitar (intro)
Recording
Ocean Way Recording, Record One Studio (studio 2), Larrabee North Studios, and Westlake Recording Studios, Los Angeles: 1987, 1989 to 1990
Technical team
Producers: Michael Jackson and Bill Bottrell
Recording engineer: Bill Bottrell
Arrangements: (unknown)
Mixing: Bill Bottrell
Intro:
Composition: Bill Bottrell
Production: Michael Jackson
Recording engineer and sound design: Matt Forger

1991

Single

A-side: *Black or White* (single version) / 3'22
B-side: *Black or White* (instrumental version) / 3'22
Released by Epic Records: USA (ref. 34-74100) and UK (ref. EPC 657598), 11 November 1991
Chart position: USA R&B No. 3, Pop No. 1 / UK No. 1
RIAA: certified Platinum 6 January 1992

THE SONG

Genesis

The sessions for *Bad* were barely over when Michael Jackson began to turn his attention to new ideas for songs. *Black or White* was the first he worked on when he returned to the studio. In the initial phase, he wrote an intro with a guitar riff played over a white-hot metal rhythm. He recorded this part at home in 1987, and asked Bill Bottrell to rework it in August 1989. "He had in mind to use it as the intro to *Black or White*,"[23] the musician explained.

Drawing inspiration from the rock energy that had enabled him to create *State of Shock* in 1984, the King of Pop composed a song with a captivating melody and rhythm, and peaceful lyrics. He was sending a message of peace at a time when the world was changing rapidly: in Germany, the Berlin Wall eventually fell; in Eastern Europe totalitarian regimes were disappearing one after the other. In the Middle East, the situation in Iraq was concerning the international community and monopolized the media, which were engaged in a frenzied pursuit of news.

Black or White sent out its message of hope using all the resources at the disposal of the "Jacksonian" style. The way *Black or White* was written was a perfect synthesis of the star's skills. Musically, the song effected the transition between those used on *Bad* and those that would define *Dangerous*.

At first, Michael Jackson planned to release the song on the *Decade* project. When he decided to drop the compilation to concentrate on a new, original album, this song became one of the cornerstones on which the record would be built. The artist decided to release it as a single, but wanted above all to release a duet to launch the promotional campaign of his new work. This tradition, which was started on *Thriller* with *The Girl Is Mine* (sung with Paul McCartney) was impeded when Madonna refused to sing with him on *In the Closet*. Not wishing to break this golden rule of having a duet open the proceedings, the singer invited Slash, the guitarist of Guns N' Roses, to play the intro to *Black or White*. The plan for the singles' release was changed: *Black or White* became the first song on *Dangerous* to be revealed to the public, marking the return of the King of Pop to center stage.

Michael Jackson and the guitarist Slash perform *Black or White* on *MTV's 10th Anniversary Special,* broadcast on 27 November 1991.

Production

The appearance of Slash in the intro marked the start of an artistic collaboration and friendship that would defy the passing years. The guitarist said in 2014: "The first time we met, it was probably for a total of ten minutes. He left me in the studio, gave me free rein to do what I wanted with the track, and just took off. But it was on the road that a relationship developed."[107]

The long introduction was conceived like a scene in a movie: it features a father (played by Bill Bottrell), who is arguing with his son (Andres McKenzie) because the latter is listening to music too loudly in his bedroom. The youth ends by taking against his father, and decides to send him a fatal blast of sound by playing another song even louder. At this point, *Black or White* begins.

The sequence was written by Bill Bottrell and put together by Michael Jackson, who was already visualizing the opening scene of the short film that would illustrate the song. Matt Forger handled the technical side. His experience on the album *E. T. Storybook* and other hybrid projects, such as *Captain EO,* enabled him to perfect this intro, which immediately put images into the listener's mind.

When the opening measures of *Black or White* are heard, the drums played by Bryan Loren announce the timbre: precise, cracking, and supported by clinking from each snare drum, it functions as a skeleton for a song in which every detail was polished for months on end. The musician, who worked on many other songs that were ultimately dropped from the album, also plays the bass line on a Moog synthesizer, which is doubled by Terry Jackson's bass guitar.

The power of *Black or White* lies in the richness of its multiple guitars. Bill Bottrell plays the two parts that are heard throughout the song. For the main riff, he plugged a Kramer guitar into a Beyer M160 amp to produce a keen sound that fits with the star's voice. The acoustic guitar chords that punctuate each phrase of the verses are played on a Gibson LG2 dating from the 1940s.

In the middle of the song, a third guitar comes in: it is Tim Pierce, not Slash, who plays the guitar heard in the bridge section. At the time, Michael Jackson was fascinated by Mötley Crüe, and asked his guitarist to draw inspiration from the group's sound. During the rap, the rhythm guitar that plays the funky chords again comes from Bill Bottrell.

The rest of the team take care of the radio-friendly sound. Michael Boddicker and Brad Buxer play the synthesizers that quietly sound the chords at the end of each chorus. Kevin Gilbert joins them with the speed sequencer just before the rap, which is reminiscent of the sound effects created by Chris Currell on *Speed Demon*.

At 2'41, a rapper named as L.T.B. comes in with some anti-racist prose, ending with the emblematic sentence "I'm not gonna spend my life being a color." This punchline fascinated

FOR LISTENERS

At 3'25 in the song, two faint sounds can be heard on the left- and right-hand channels, when Michael Jackson sings: "It don't matter if you're black or white." This is not a fault in the recording, but simply the sound of his hands tapping his thighs, marking the rhythm.

FOR JACKSON ADDICTS

In 1992, a mix of *Black or White* with new lyrics praising the Pepsi-Cola brand was played at the end of the *Dangerous* tour, broadcast on HBO and other TV networks around the world. It remains unreleased.

Michael Jackson prepares to turn himself into a panther in the last scene of the short film *Black or White*.

1991

admirers of Michael and excited the curiosity of journalists, who saw in it a hidden message connected to the physical changes the star had undergone in recent years.

The rap attributed to the famous L.T.B. was the idea, and the work, of Bill Bottrell, who recalled: "After the first few days of working on it, we really had the core of the song, the verses, the chorus, and Michael sang it really early on. All we had was this big gaping middle section, that sort of just sat and that was and on our minds for many months."[108] The producer woke up one morning with the idea of adding a rap with words that would sustain the song's message. He recorded this section and played it to the singer, who was thrilled with it and suggested he include his performance in the final version of the song. Bill Bottrell, embarrassed at taking on a rap, given that he was a songwriter, not a rapper, tried to persuade Michael Jackson to have another artist recite those lines. At the time, stars of the genre, such as Heavy D, LL Cool J, and the group Wreckx-N-Effect, were already taking part in recording sessions. But the singer insisted: he wanted Bottrell's voice. Mindful of the fact that at the time rap was still the exclusive preserve of African-American artists, the talented—but white—recording engineer adopted, humorously, a pseudonym that in no way called to mind a hip-hop artist: L.T.B., short for *Leave It to Beaver*, a TV series from the late 1950s whose protagonist is a white youth who lives in the suburbs.

THE SHORT FILM

Director: John Landis
Producers: Red Shane for Propaganda Film
Leading actors: Michael Jackson, Macaulay Culkin, George Wendt, Tyra Banks, and Bart and Homer Simpson
Extras: Brandi Jackson, John Landis
Shoot date: September to October 1991
Shooting locations:
• Vasquez Rocks Natural Area Park, Agua Dulce, California (dance scene with Native Americans)
• 11779 Sheldon Street, Sun Valley, California (scene in which Michael Jackson and the Native American dancer appear on the freeway)
• Other, unspecified film studios
Duration: 11'02

Genesis

In 1991, the Propaganda agency signed a contract with Sony Music for the production of Michael Jackson's short films for the album *Dangerous*. *Black or White* was the first project the artist worked on with this new team. Having failed to set up an attention-grabbing duet with Madonna to announce his return, the singer worked on an original script built around this rock song. Some weeks passed, and the project managers at Propaganda struggled to keep things moving in their conversations with the star. Several directors, such as David Lynch and David Fincher, were considered, but all ended up refusing the commission. The King of Pop, meanwhile, missed some rehearsals, was slow in

The dance scene with Native Americans occurs in the first part of the *Black or White* music video (1991).

finishing songs for the album, and took time off to treat himself to some trips, notably with his young friend Macaulay Culkin. Propaganda contacted John Landis, knowing that he knew Michael Jackson well and would be able to get him to focus. The director agreed, but demanded to be paid weekly. This powerful incentive—the short film's budget was funded by the singer and Landis had a strong bond with Michael Jackson—enabled shooting of *Black or White* to pass off without major hitches.

John Landis had not worked with the King of Pop since 1983. When they got together again in late 1991 for *Black or White*, he realized that the young man had become an artist completely in control of his work, who had little time for deadlines and financial demands with regard to his projects. On *Thriller* they had worked jointly, but this quickly gave way to a setup where the singer, now mature and self-assured, gave instructions to a collaborator with whom he had already written an important chapter in the history of music videos.

The *Black or White* clip was made like a true short film. Lasting 11', this mini-movie consists of two parts. The first conveys the song's message of humanism and brotherhood. The second, which is darker, shows the artist, alone and left to his own devices in a dark street, performing a dance through which he rebels against racism and intolerance.

Michael Jackson turned to his long-standing choreographer, Vincent Paterson, for help in writing and developing the sequences for the short film. To increase the video's impact on its release, a first-class cast was assembled: as well as Macaulay Culkin, star of the movie *Home Alone*, Michael called on the actor George Wendt (from the TV series *Cheers*), the young model Tyra Banks, and cartoon characters Bart and Homer Simpson.

Production

When the first scenes were being shot, Michael Jackson was not happy with John Landis' idea of making him dance in front of a gray background inspired by the photographs of Irving Penn. He therefore asked Vincent Paterson to help him rewrite the way the sequences followed on from each other, in order to retain a strong narrative thread throughout the film. The star and his choreographer put together a script in which the artist was shown visiting different countries and cultures in the world, in the manner of the "It's a Small World" attraction at Disney amusement parks. John Landis allowed himself to be persuaded. From that point on, *Black or White* was above all the work of Michael Jackson and Vincent Paterson, with the director contributing only his expertise in the technical sense of the term.

The first sequence shows the singer in natural settings, or such settings recreated in the studio. He is filmed in the depths of the Californian desert, surrounded by Native Americans,

After shooting his second video with Michael Jackson, John Landis poses with the star and the young actor Macaulay Culkin. The end of shooting was celebrated in style! This whipped cream battle can be seen in footage of the making of *Black or White,* included in the video *Dangerous: The Short Films.*

FOR JACKSON ADDICTS

When the short film of *Black or White* was officially released in late 1993, on the video compilation *Dangerous: The Short Films,* racist messages were added, using a graphics tablet, to the windows of buildings and car windows, which the singer smashes during his solo dance number. This new version reinforced very emphatically, even excessively, the video's message of tolerance and peace.

At the end of 1991, *Black or White* was used for a TV commercial entitled *Waves,* in which Michael Jackson promoted Sony's Kirara Basso television sets for the Japanese market.

evoking the memory of the original inhabitants of the North American continent. He also executes a few steps of a Russian dance (with dancers that are all of American background). From one tableau to the next, he extends the hand of friendship to peoples who have often had conflicted relations with the United States, and he emphasizes universality. In a panoramic shot with a blue background, his figure dances on the top of the Statue of Liberty which, thanks to the magic of digital effects, shares an imaginary space with the biggest monuments on the planet.

1991

This image is followed by a sequence that, at the time, was revolutionary, in which the faces of extras appear one after the other, with a realistic effect that makes each melt into the next: this succession of men's and women's faces of all ethnicities reinforces the song's anti-racist message. This part of the film was made using a technique that heralded the use of digital effects in movies: morphing. Developed in the late 1980s, it was initially used in a few commercials, as well as by George Lucas in *Willow* and *Indiana Jones and the Last Crusade*, two movies that Lucas cowrote and produced.

When the song ends, with the last face of the morphing sequence on the screen, a black panther appears on the set and guides the viewer toward the second part of the short film. The animal eventually descends a staircase and crosses over into a dark place. Another morphing effect transforms the panther into Michael Jackson, who then heads into a deserted street where he launches into a singular dance routine. Trusting his instinct, the King of Pop improvised the various highlights of this second part during shooting. But he also wanted to show off some of his legendary dance steps. John Landis recalled: "By that time, I was saying, 'Mike, you're such a great dancer,' but he insisted on doing the same twelve moves everyone loved. He could really tap, so we did a wonderful tap dance number. The only thing left of it in the video is you see him do two steps and then kick a bottle in slow motion."[109] During this sequence, the artist wanted above all to perform a dance punctuated by sensual, suggestive movements that would get people talking.

Michael Jackson liked to reuse certain situations and dance steps. With *Black or White*, he embarked on an increasingly blatant process of self-quotation. Thus the first moments of the second part of the short film are a remake, shot by shot, of the commercial he took part in for the L.A. Gear brand of trainers in 1990.

The first TV broadcast of *Black or White*, announced as a major event, took place on 14 November 1991 in 27 countries. More than 500 million television viewers saw the video, which marked the star's triumphant return. Long before the arrival of the internet and viral marketing, Michael Jackson managed to cause a great deal of ink to be spilt with the second part of the video. The public, which had always had an image of him as immaculate, even aseptic, was scandalized. His body language, which was judged to be shocking by the media and some bodies representing TV viewers, drowned out the song's pacifist message.

The day after the first broadcast, the artist responded, releasing a press statement in which he apologized and gave his assurance that his intention was in no way to upset television viewers. There was speculation that this note was written several days before the clip's release, ready to be sent to newsrooms all over the world. Whether a lapse of judgment or a marketing masterstroke, either way *Black or White* entered the pantheon of the most memorable short films made by the King of Pop.

> **FOR JACKSON ADDICTS**
>
> Michael Jackson commissioned a video edit of *Who Is It* from producer Bob Jenkins. Using images from throughout Michael's career, this version was added to the list of official videos on the YouTube account michaeljacksonVEVO in 2009.

Who Is It

Michael Jackson / 6'34

Musicians
Michael Jackson: lead, soprano, and backing vocals
Linda Harmon: soprano vocals
Bryan Loren: drums
Bill Bottrell: drums and synthesizers
Louis Johnson: bass guitar
Brad Buxer, Michael Boddicker, David Paich, Steve Porcaro, and Jai Winding: keyboards
Endre Granat: first violin
Larry Corbett: cello
Recording
Ocean Way Recording, Record One Studio (studio 2), and Larrabee North Studios, Los Angeles: 25 June 1990 to 30 October 1991
Technical team
Producers: Michael Jackson and Bill Bottrell
Recording engineer: Bill Bottrell
Vocal arrangements: Michael Jackson
Keyboard arrangements: Brad Buxer and David Paich
String arrangements: George Del Barrio
Keyboard programing: Brad Buxer, Michael Boddicker, David Paich, Steve Porcaro, and Jai Winding
Mixing: Bill Bottrell

Single

A-side USA: *Who Is It (7-inch edit)* / 3'59
B-side USA: *Wanna Be Startin' Somethin' (Brothers in Rhythm House mix)* / 7'40
A-side UK: *Who Is It (7-inch edit with intro)* / 4'10
B-side UK: *Rock with You (Masters at Work remix)* / 5'29
Released by Epic Records: USA (ref. 34-74406), March 1993 / UK (ref. EPC 658179), July 1992
Chart position: USA R&B No. 6, Pop No. 14 / No. 1 / UK No. 10

THE SONG

Genesis

"Michael's songs, even if on some abstract base, to me were always somehow autobiographical, you know. It always felt that way, knowing him really well and the complexities in and out of his life...I always felt it was autobiographical; even if it was something he was resisting, it would come out in a song. And I think he's very lucky to have that, that ability to be such a good songwriter and a singer too, to get it out. It's cathartic,"[88] Quincy Jones said on the reissue of the album *Bad* in 2001.

Originally destined for the "best of" project *Decade*, *Who Is It* is one of the gems on *Dangerous*, in which Michael Jackson sings of unhappiness in love. The song acted as an echo of *Billie Jean* and *Dirty Diana*, and the King of Pop revealed himself with unprecedented maturity and selflessness. The song's theme is loaded with unusual mystery, with a darkness and resignation that cannot be expressed unless they have been experienced personally. The lyrics are filled with sadness: "I gave her everything / Inside one heart could find / I gave her passion / My very soul / I gave her promises / And secrets so untold." The song was written in 1990 in collaboration with the producer Bill Bottrell, who had witnessed Michael Jackson's most intimate emotions. No song since *Be Not Always* had displayed so much palpable suffering. According to his former producer Quincy Jones, the singer, without a doubt, intended this song to be a release in which he would open his soul and his heart, turning to his audience as his confidant.

Production

An army of keyboard players features in *Who Is It*, accompanying the song's resigned tone. A myriad of skillfully mixed sounds materialize and burst forth, sometimes disconcerting or troubling the listener. Bryan Loren creates and drives the wonderful sonority of the drums, which lend their rhythm to the weight of the lament, while the short, metronomic notes of Louis Johnson's bass guitar are superimposed, masterfully distilling the song's melancholy.

In March 1993, when *Give in to Me* was destined to be a new single for the US market, its short film was given an exclusive screening during the TV show Michael Jackson shared

A still from the video made by David Fincher for *Who Is It*. The short film was not released in the US, being replaced instead by a collection of archive images approved by the star.

Like *Billie Jean* and *Bad*, *Who Is It* was used for a Pepsi advertising campaign. The video *Dreams* was shot on 13 May 1992 by Joe Pykta. In a graphic setting that resembles the scenery on the sleeve of *Dangerous*, Michael Jackson pursues the gorgeous Vanessa Sandin from the Elite agency and performs a few dance steps. Unlike other advertising songs, *Michael* did not sing the lyrics ringing the praises of the drinks brand.

with Oprah Winfrey. On that occasion, the singer performed *Who Is It* with some beatboxing which was so incredible that the record label canceled the release of *Give in to Me* and replaced it with *Who Is It*. The exclusive version from this a cappella performance goes by the title *The Oprah Winfrey Special Intro*. The single did not take the world's charts by storm, nor did it leave a mark in the collective unconscious, but it nevertheless retains a very special place in the hearts of the singer's admirers.

THE SHORT FILM

Director: David Fincher
Producers: Gregg Fienberg and Reid Shane
Leading actor: Michael Jackson
Supporting actors: (unknown)
Shoot Date: 1992
Shooting location: Los Angeles / Neverland (helicopter scene)
Duration: 6'37

Genesis

The seventh of the nine short films for the album *Dangerous* was entrusted to the skilled director David Fincher, after he had finished shooting the movie *Alien 3* and before he made the fabulous *Seven* and *Fight Club*. A video-maker to the stars, he enlisted the services of Jordan Cronenweth, the distinguished director of photography who had worked on, among others, Ridley Scott's movie *Blade Runner*. Together, they were to create the most photographically striking and mysterious short film in the career of the Michael Jackson.

The director did not want to show Michael in his glittering outfits. In the video his clothing is sober, and only his pants, slightly short and allowing a glimpse of his socks, could be said to be faintly reminiscent of the artist's usual dress code. Neither was there any question of his seducing the camera with his devastatingly effective dance steps or other gimmicks: he was to be manly, a dandy, and highly respectable.

Production

The video begins with the camera skimming the Art Deco façades in Los Angeles. A golden but paradoxically cold light highlights the rough or carved stonework, which appears to move thanks to the subtle play of shadows. The camera sweeps through this stony environment as if it were the gaze of a distraught person. In a Gotham City where the singer could, without a doubt, bump into Bruce Wayne, he laments and rages, seated on his sofa. The source of his distress gradually takes on the features of a ravishing young woman with whom he is deeply in love until he learns that she is, in fact, a prostitute who goes under various false identities. Assisted in her activities by incredibly well-oiled logistics, this beautiful woman charges for her services to numerous rich notables. The frequency of her assignations is shown by a collection of magnificent images. Weary of being miserable, the singer decides to seek a change of scene and boards a helicopter, then a private jet, to flee and try to soothe his pain. The young woman, who has seen the error of her ways, visits his home to try to reconquer his love, but he is already far away. This adventure in CinemaScope comes to a halt with a wide shot, which neither resolves nor soothes the malaise. The video ends in great solitude, as coldly as it began.

The short film was shown exclusively on the British TV channel BBC2, but Michael Jackson rejected the final result and demanded that it be withdrawn immediately from all program schedules. A new version was edited and included in the compilation *Dangerous: The Short Films*. The single was released in the United States in March 1993, without a video broadcast on TV.

Give in to Me

Michael Jackson, Bill Bottrell / 5'30

Musicians
Michael Jackson: lead and backing vocals
Bill Bottrell: drums, bass guitar, mellotron, and guitar
Slash: guitar (special performance)
Recording
Ocean Way Recording, Record One Studio (studio 2), and Larrabee North Studios, Los Angeles: 25 June 1990 to 30 October 1991
Technical team
Producers: Michael Jackson and Bill Bottrell
Recording engineer: Bill Bottrell
Guitar recording: Jim Mitchell
Guitar recording assistant: Craig Brock
Mixing: Bill Bottrell

1991

Single

A-side: *Give in to Me* (*vocal version*) / 4'43
B-side: *Dirty Diana* (*edit*) / 4'40
Released by Epic Records: Europe, 15 February 1993 (ref. 658946)
Chart position: UK No. 2

THE SONG

Genesis

Michael Jackson, Bill Bottrell, and the assistant recording engineer Brad Sundberg met for an impromptu work session. For two hours, Jackson and Bottrell exchanged ideas and looked for inspiration to write a rock song. Ensconced in the studio with CDs of Van Halen, AC/DC, and other hard rock groups to hand, they began to sketch out the bare bones of a ballad. A large part of this session would sadly be leaked on the internet after Brad Sundberg presented a copy of the recording during one of his seminars in the early 2010s. On this fascinating document the King of Pop can be heard exchanging ideas with his colleagues while letting his imagination run free. He launches into vocal improvisation and has fun with expressions, in the style of The Beatles' song *Dig It*, such as "like CIA," "like FBI," "like a rolling stone," and "like B B King."

Little by little, the tune of *Give in to Me* takes shape around three chords which, though they are reminiscent of those of *Dirty Diana*, give a strong, singular identity to the song, the main theme of which is hopeless love. Michael Jackson plays the neglected antihero, abandoned in a one-way love story. The depressive romanticism of *Give in to Me* definitively deprives the album *Dangerous* of a song that pins all its hopes on love.

Production

In a work setting where everything seemed to be measured and weighted down to the last decibel, Michael Jackson felt the need to take the pressure off by making *Give in to Me* a song conceived with a certain spontaneity. Bottrell says of the recording session:

> In fact, on *Give in to Me,* he looked to me for those looser, more instinctive vocals. These contrasted with what was achieved by the other people he was working with, because in that case he had the same agenda as I had. Still, we took that song too far. We had a live take of me sitting on a stool, playing guitar, and him singing, with a very simple drum loop running throughout. Michael loved that, but it was me who got insecure and started layering things. Eventually, he had Slash come in and add loads of guitars, and the song was

Michael Jackson is received by the mayor of Munich, who handed over a check for 40,000 deutschmarks (about $25,000 today) for his foundation Heal the World, 26 June 1992. The singer took advantage of this stay in Germany to shoot the short film *Give in to Me.*

transformed; not for the better, in my view. And that had nothing to do with Slash, but by virtue of the production that went into it.[110]

The result was a darkly romantic ballad that was ultimately underestimated in the discography of the King of Pop.

THE SHORT FILM

Director: Andy Morahan
Producers: Michael Jackson, John Landis, and George Folsey Jr.
Leading actors: Michael Jackson and Slash
Extras (or supporting actors): Living Colour
Shoot date: 25 June 1992
Shooting location: 166 Landsberger Strasse, Munich, Germany
Duration: 5'31

Genesis

Made when the infernal marathon of the *Dangerous* tour was already under way, the short film of *Give in to Me* reflects the spirit of spontaneity in which the song was created in the studio. Michael Jackson reached agreement with Sony to make a simple, low-budget video. From the record label's point of view, the first three singles from *Dangerous* had already enabled the album to do satisfactorily well in the charts, and this latest video was now not a marketing priority.

Michael tried to take advantage of this situation. In Chris Cadman's book *The Maestro,* he is quoted as saying: "We had no time at all to shoot it. We wanted it to be exciting and fantastical and fans, you know, like it's a rock concert and that's how it ends up, that's the result."[23]

Production

On 25 June 1992, Michael Jackson was in Munich for the first concert of the *Dangerous* tour. He managed to find a few hours in his crowded schedule to make the short film of *Give in to Me.* Slash and the members of the group Living Colour met him at 166 Landsberger Strasse, where a rock concert stage had been set up for the film. Fans and extras were recruited a few days before the shoot.

The director Andy Morahan, who had already worked with Slash and Guns N' Roses on the clip of *November Rain,* directed the cameras to capture wide shots and close-ups of the King of Pop as he performed the song on the temporary stage. This simple shooting set-up was just one aspect of the project. Like the song, which had benefited from ambitious post-production including, notably, input from Slash, the rushes shot that day in Munich were put together and amplified using digital effects. These give the impression that the rock concert is transformed into a firework display, with a series of explosions and bolts of electric lightning which shoot through the singer's moving body and those of his partners on stage.

Will You Be There

Michael Jackson / 7'40

Musicians
Michael Jackson: lead and backing vocals
The Andraé Crouch Singers: backing vocals
Greg Phillinganes: keyboards
Michael Boddicker and Rhett Lawrence: synthesizers
Brad Buxer: keyboards, drums, and percussion
Bruce Swedien: drums and percussion
Paulinho Da Costa: percussion
Prelude
Beethoven, *Symphony No. 9 in D minor,* opus 125, Fourth movement: presto, beginning at *Adagio ma non troppo, ma divoto* (measure 33)
Interpreted by: The Cleveland Orchestra / **Conductor:** George Szell / **Producer:** Robert Shaw
Recording
Ocean Way Recording, Record One Studio (studio 2), Larrabee North Studios, and Westlake Recording Studios, Los Angeles: 25 June 1990 to 30 October 1991
Technical team
Producer: Michael Jackson
Coproducer: Bruce Swedien
Recording engineers: Bruce Swedien and Matt Forger
Vocal arrangements: Michael Jackson
Rhythm arrangements: Michael Jackson and Greg Phillinganes
Choral arrangements: Andraé and Sandra Crouch
Orchestral arrangements: Johnny Mandel
Synthesizer programing: Michael Boddicker, George Duke, and Rhett Lawrence
Mixing: Bruce Swedien

Single

USA
A-side: *Will You Be There (radio edit)* / 3'39
B-side: *Will You Be There (instrumental)* / 3'44
UK
A-side: *Will You Be There (radio edit)* / 3'39
B-side: *Girlfriend (instrumental)* / 3'04
Released by Epic Records: USA (ref. 34-77060) and UK (ref. EPC 659222), 24 May 1993
Chart position: USA R&B No. 53, Pop No. 7 / UK No. 9
RIAA: certified Gold 3 December 1993

1991

THE SONG

Genesis

"I wrote *Will You Be There?* at my house Neverland in California...I didn't think about it hard. That's why it's hard to take credit for the songs that I write, because I just always feel that it's done from above. I feel fortunate for being that instrument through which music flows. I'm just the source through which it comes,"[111] the star said in an interview with *Ebony* in 1992. Yet again, when asked about his creative process, Michael Jackson cites divine forces that are beyond his comprehension. It was Quincy Jones who instilled in him this modesty, which allowed him to remain humble about his work throughout his life.

With *Will You Be There*, he conceived a song with a structure consisting of several parts: a long and ambitious tapestry of sound, with an ever-greater taste for narrative. In it, he explores subjects his work had not touched on until then: spirituality, faith, and the questions all human beings grapple with when faced with the doubts sown by life's trials.

The theme, played on the piano as a series of chords in the finest gospel tradition, is supported by a jerky rhythm that nevertheless still soars. The song ends with a monologue by Michael Jackson, who wonders aloud whether someone will be there when he faces difficulties alone. These lines are a touching and sincere echo of the questions he asked himself from his lofty status as a global star. Behind the universal message, the star in fact reveals far more of himself than in any of his previous songs.

Production

As producer, Michael Jackson managed to record his compositions, giving them a timeless sound that is difficult to categorize, and which was far removed from the influences of fashion that affected his contemporaries. At the start of the 1990s, the marriage—or more accurately cohabitation—of traditionally produced music and digital music played tricks on a number of artists. Stevie Wonder, for example, succumbed to the artificial magic of synthesizers to such an extent that compositions from that time struggled to recapture the carefreeness and lightness that were typical of his early work. For his part, the King of Pop knew that the two approaches could coexist if each element was carefully weighted and integrated. From Stevie Wonder's team, he took on the young Brad Buxer, who installed his syn-

Like the choreography in the show *MTV 10th*, the routine for the performance of the song *Will You Be There* on the *Dangerous* tour featured an angel that embraced the singer at the end of the number.

thesizer in the Ocean Way studio. The singer teamed him up with the faithful Greg Phillinganes, a stalwart of the old school and of a type of sound that first appeared in the late 1970s with The Jacksons. Rhett Lawrence, who was already present at the time of *Bad*, oversaw the programing of the synthesizers.

Assisted by Bruce Swedien, Brad Buxer programed the singular rhythm that wavers between a ragga beat and African rhythms. At the time, the rhythm tracks that were in fashion were mostly made from looped samples. George Michael, to name but one, proceeded in this way with the song *Soul Free*, from his album *Listen Without Prejudice, Vol. 1* (1990). Michael Jackson, however, refused to yield to this easy option and chose instead to create original sounds.

As the song progresses, there is a crescendo: after the singer has performed two verses and a bridge, a gospel choir backs up his questioning. Andraé Crouch's group, who already featured at the start of the song, just before the first chords on the piano, delivers a performance that lets its gospel power burst forth, unlike their contained and balanced performance in songs such as *Man in the Mirror*.

In the song's epilogue the star recites a moving text, his throat clenched with what appears to be sincere emotion. During a seminar held in Pierre-Bénite, near Lyon, France, on 26 November 2016, the choreographer Vincent Paterson related how the King of Pop, overcome by the text, shed real tears when he recited these lines during the recording of the show *MTV 10*, on 15 November 1991 in Santa Monica.

When the album *Dangerous* was released, the Italian singer Al Bano considered that Michael Jackson had plagiarized his song *I Cigni di Balaka*. He filed a complaint in 1993 and embarked on a long legal battle. The American star lost initially, in 1995, but eventually won the case in 1999 in civil court and in 2001 in criminal court. The verdict was that both his song and Al Bano's bore similarities with the song *Bless You for Being an Angel* by The Ink Spots (1939).

The long intro to *Will You Be There* features a passage from Beethoven's Ninth Symphony, performed by the Cleveland Orchestra. The album's credits failed to mention this, so the orchestra asserted its rights, and in December 1992, an American judge ordered that *Dangerous'* sleeve notes mention the source of the extract.

Poster for the film *Free Willy*, released in the US on 16 July 1993, whose theme tune was the song *Will You Be There*.

Michael Jackson performs *Will You Be There* onstage during the *Dangerous* tour in Japan, December 1992.

FOR JACKSON ADDICTS

The *DVD Vision* box set (2010), contains an alternative edit of the classic version, with different shots at the end of the clip. This version was earmarked for the video compilation *Dangerous: The Short Films* in 1993, but was dropped at the last minute.

The soundtrack to *Free Willy*, the first album released by MJJ Music, contains two versions of *Will You Be There*—lasting 5'53 and 3'40.

1991

THE SHORT FILM

Director: Vincent Paterson
Producers: Joel Gallen, Ute Leonhardt
Leading actor: Michael Jackson
Shoot date: 1991 to 1993
Shooting locations
Classic version:
- Santa Monica airport, Los Angeles (*MTV 10* TV show scenes)
- *Dangerous* tour (shots on stage)

***Free Willy* version:**
- *Dangerous* tour (shots on stage)
- Images from the movie *Free Willy*

Duration: classic version: 6'05 / *Free Willy* version: 3'36

Genesis

Before *Dangerous* had even been released, Michael Jackson decided to create a choreography and screenplay for *Will You Be There*. He contacted Vincent Paterson, who responded sensitively to the song's spiritual side. He suggested a series of dance steps devised for him, and a screenplay in which he brings about meetings between men, women, and children, who all carry within them the message of the lyrics. As an epilogue, the choreographer suggested that an angel could descend from the sky and envelop the singer in its wings.

This rich, ambitious number was first broadcast on the show *MTV 10*, which celebrated the 10th anniversary of the famous music channel. The audience who attended the recording that took place on 15 November 1991 in Santa Monica therefore heard the song as a preview, before its release.

The song was shot and edited by Jackson and Paterson, who were keen to produce an effective sequence. This performance was used as the basis for the clip Vincent Paterson was asked to make in 1993.

Production

At the request of Michael Jackson, who had complete confidence in him, Vincent Paterson made two versions of *Will You Be There*. The first one consists of shots taken from the *MTV 10* performance and images from the *Dangerous* tour, during which the King of Pop sang the song on stage each evening.

The second version of the clip fulfilled a marketing and promotional function: Michael Jackson authorized the use of the song as the main theme of the movie *Free Willy*, which Warner released in the summer of 1993. To promote the film, another clip was put together using images from the *Dangerous* tour and the movie.

The young singer Shanice Wilson, who at the time was topping the charts with her song *I Love Your Smile*, released by Motown, shared the backing vocals in *Keep the Faith* with Siedah Garrett

KEEP THE FAITH

Glen Ballard, Siedah Garrett, Michael Jackson / 5'57

Musicians
Michael Jackson: lead and backing vocals
The Andraé Crouch Singers: backing vocals
Siedah Garret and Shanice Wilson: backing vocals
Jai Winding: piano and bass guitar
Rhett Lawrence: drums, percussion, and synthesizers
Bruce Swedien: drums and percussion
Michael Boddicker: synthesizers
David Williams: guitar
Recording
Ocean Way Recording, Record One Studio (studio 2), Larrabee North Studios, and Westlake Recording Studios, Los Angeles: 25 June 1990 to 30 October 1991
Technical team
Producer: Michael Jackson
Coproducer and recording engineer: Bruce Swedien
Arrangements: Glen Ballard, Jerry Hey, and Rhett Lawrence
Vocal arrangements: Andraé and Sandra Crouch
Mixing: Bruce Swedien

After *Man in the Mirror*, Siedah Garrett wrote a second song for the singer. Here, she is seen singing on the *Oprah Winfrey Show* on 27 September 1990.

Genesis

Michael Jackson asked Siedah Garrett to write a new song for him. However, the young woman's music publisher thought that the King of Pop would never commission a songwriter to write two songs on two different albums—she had already worked on *Bad*, writing *Man in the Mirror*. But, far from discouraging the composer, this warning galvanized her, and she turned the challenge into creative drive. She polished the preliminary version of *Keep the Faith* with her friend Glen Ballard before playing it to the star. The three then met at the Record One studio in Sherman Oaks. During that session, Glen Ballard began to improvise on the piano. "I played my best approximation of gospel piano and Michael and Siedah were improvising over either shoulder—Michael was dancing, stomping, jumping. It was exhilarating and in the spirit of the song—we were feeling it."[23]

Keep the Faith picks up where *Man in the Mirror* left off. Like a little brother to that classic (cowritten by Glen Ballard and Siedah Garrett, and included on *Bad*), *Keep the Faith* develops the theme of resilience: a message of hope to young people and all those who realized that, in the early 1990s, the world was not yet finished with inequality and conflict. However, unlike *Man in the Mirror*, Michael Jackson intervened to contribute to the lyrics.

Man in the Mirror calls out to the listener, suggesting that he or she change themselves in order to make the world around them a better place. *Keep the Faith* also speaks of working on yourself to resolve your problems and move forward, but this time the message focuses on acquiring the confidence necessary to start the process of change deep within.

Production

For this song, almost the entire team that worked on *Man in the Mirror* was called upon. Andraé Crouch's group came back to sing the backing vocals, which reach a climax in the second part of the song. Quincy Jones was not in the studio to assist in producing this new hymn, but Michael Jackson could count on the skills and expertise of Bruce Swedien to see the project through. He used the same formula as for *Man in the Mirror* and *The Places You Find Love* on Quincy Jones's album *Back on the Block* (1989). The stereo sound he managed to capture enabled each instrument to take its place and be singled out.

Michael Jackson greets his fans from the balcony of his hotel room in Tenerife on 25 September 1993, during the *Dangerous* tour.

The recording of Michael Jackson's vocals made life difficult for Swedien, because the singer struggled to find the tone the song demanded. After several takes, he finally broke down. Bruce Swedien: "I found him standing in the corner of his office, crying his eyes out. He was totally heartbroken—cut to the quick…We went to the studio, cut a whole new demo, and recorded a scratch vocal all the way through…We didn't leave the studio until dawn."[23]

During these long sessions the Michael adjusted the way he placed his voice, and took the opportunity to refine the lyrics at the end of the song. One of these versions was leaked onto the internet in 2002. It came from a series of cassettes belonging to Rob Disner, one of the assistant recording engineers. The vibes and variations in the singer's voice were definitively deleted from the version included on *Dangerous*.

Produced by Michael Jackson with help from Bruce Swedien, *Keep the Faith* became a peaceful hymn which, despite everything, fell short of the gospel power of *Man in the Mirror*.

PORTRAIT

BUZ KOHAN
A BENEVOLENT SOUL

Alan "Buz" Kohan was born on 9 August 1933 in New York, in the Bronx. His family was Jewish; his father worked in textiles and his mother was a housewife. As a teenager he quickly developed an interest in writing. After doing a series of odd jobs, he got into screenwriting and wrote several episodes of the cartoon series *Barney Google and Snuffy Smith* for Paramount in New York. From 1965, he wrote several TV shows for Sammy Davis Jr., and in 1967 joined the team of the *Carol Burnett Show*. This experience taught him the magic and conciseness required when writing for television.

Very soon, fashionable crooners called upon his services: Perry Como and Bing Crosby asked him to work on their Christmas broadcasts. Buz Kohan became a paragon in the world of American entertainment: the biggest studios and most prestigious institutions turned to him. In 1976 he took part in writing the 48th Academy Awards ceremony. He then moved from television to movies, via the theater, where the biggest stars benefited from his talents. He became a versatile, reliable all-rounder who could create every detail of the projects he worked on clearly, simply, and with originality.

Buz and Michael

Buz Kohan worked with Michael Jackson for the first time in 1971, when Motown asked him to write the show *Goin' Back to Indiana*, which celebrated the return of The Jackson Five to their native city. Buz Kohan was introduced to a promising young teenager, with whom he was to develop a professional relationship and friendship that was to last until the death of the person who, by then, had become the King of Pop.

Buz Kohan realized that the character of the young Michael, like that of Sammy Davis Jr., was unique and out of the ordinary. He had promised himself that he would no longer "give his soul" as he had done with the performer of *I've Gotta Be Me*, but the charisma of the young artist, who saw in him a second father who was sensitive to his dreamy, optimistic nature, led him to drop his guard.

The artist and the writer regularly came together on projects that were veritable landmarks in the career of Michael Jackson. When the young singer agreed to take part in the TV show celebrating Disneyland's 25th anniversary, Buz Kohan created a number for him that was as innocent as it was magical, and in which the admiration he had for Walt Disney leapt off the screen. The following year, the author was backstage when Diana Ross invited her young protégé to celebrate the success of her latest album, produced by the band Chic, on a special show tailor-made for her.

In 1983, on the occasion of the legendary *Motown 25*, Buz Kohan wrote the few lines that made the transition between the song Michael Jackson had just performed with his brothers and the song he was about to sing, *Billie Jean*. The writer was one of the lucky people who witnessed, live, the young performer's first moonwalk.

Unswerving loyalty

As the 1980s were drawing to a close, on 13 November 1989, Buz Kohan brought together the two artists who had left the biggest mark on his life as a writer: Michael Jackson and Sammy Davis Jr. He managed to convince the pop star, who was then frail and suffering from severe pain in his scalp—the result of an accident he had had when shooting a commercial for Pepsi—to pay homage to the towering figure of the crooner in a special TV show celebrating his 60-year career. Sammy Davis Jr. was extremely ill, and did not have long to live. Michael Jackson performed a song that had been written specially for this ceremony, which brought together the biggest names in the world of entertainment. Entitled *You Were There*, it made explicit the bond between the two artists, who had fought decisive battles on behalf of the African-American community, and also how much the younger artist owed to his senior.

In 1997, Buz Kohan and Michael Jackson presented Elizabeth Taylor with an ode that did justice to her legendary stature and to the friendship she had with the singer since the mid-1980s. This was to be the last significant collaboration between the two friends, though they continued to stay in close touch over the years. Kohan was very often to be found ens-

Buz Kohan, a writer and lyricist who worked with Michael Jackson over more than three decades.

conced in his discreet office in Hollywood's quiet streets. There, he kept all Michael Jackson's handwritten notes; the singer had found in him an unusually willing and disinterested listener.

Aside from TV shows, the two men worked together on songs that highlighted the singer's love for ballads that seemed made for musicals or for animated films in the highest tradition of the Disney studios. Their most iconic collaboration remains the song *Gone Too Soon*, which Michael Jackson recorded to pay homage to the young Ryan White, who died at the age of 17 from the effects of AIDS. It was this infinite love and respect for people dear to their hearts, and the essential values they shared, that kept Buz Kohan and the King of Pop close until the latter's premature death. Kohan's sadness was equaled only by his discretion and integrity. He was one of the few people who had the ability to stay close to, and understand, the artist and unique individual that was Michael Jackson.

Gone Too Soon

Larry Grossman, Buz Kohan / 3'22

Musicians
Michael Jackson: lead vocals
David Paich: keyboards and synthesizers
Steve Porcaro and Michael Doddicker: synthesizers
Abraham Laboriel: bass guitar
Recording
Ocean Way Recording, Los Angeles: 1990
Technical team
Producer: Michael Jackson
Coproducer and recording engineer: Bruce Swedien
Rhythm arrangements: David Paich
Orchestral arrangement: Marty Paich
Mixing: Bruce Swedien

1991

On 19 January 1993, Michael Jackson was among the guests at the gala for the inauguration of President Bill Clinton. After giving a moving speech that paid homage to Ryan White and raised the issue of AIDS, he performed *Gone Too Soon*, the first and only time in his career he did so in public.

Single

A-side: *Gone Too Soon* / 3'22
B-side: *Gone Too Soon (instrumental)* / 3'22
Released by Epic Records: USA (ref. 34-77312), December 1993 / UK (ref. EPC 659976), 1 December 1993
Chart position: UK No. 33

THE SONG

Genesis

Ever since the recording of *Thriller*, Michael Jackson stuck to this rule: not to include covers on his albums. When he bought The Beatles' catalog, he broke this rule with a muscular version of *Come Together*. Against all expectations, he agreed to record a song on *Dangerous* that had already been used by other artists. Composed by Larry Grossman and Buz Kohan in 1983 for the TV show *Here's Television Entertainment*, *Gone Too Soon* was the accompaniment to a sequence that paid homage to artists who had died. Dionne Warwick was the first to perform this gentle ballad, which celebrated the memory of a panoply of stars who were "gone too soon," as in the title. During her performance the faces of Elvis Presley, Karen Carpenter, John Belushi, Cass Elliott, John Lennon, Bobby Darin, Minnie Riperton, Sam Cooke, Harry Chapin, Buddy Holly, Otis Redding, Jimi Hendrix, Jim Croce, and Bobby Van appeared in the background.

Dionne Warwick intended to record the song for one of her albums, but the project failed to materialize. Patti LaBelle and Donna Summer also performed it live and hoped to immortalize it in the studio, but these plans too were abandoned. When Michael Jackson and Buz Kohan met up in 1990, *Gone Too Soon* came up in conversation. The artist said he was worried about singing a song that already had a history, but admitted that he was captivated by the lyrics and the message that they conveyed. Buz Kohan told him that the song was waiting for him, and it was his to record. At the time, the health of his friend Ryan White, a young teenager suffering from AIDS, was deteriorating. The singer knew that the young man would die soon. He was one of the first young AIDS sufferers to talk openly to the media about his illness. After a brave battle against the disease, he died on 8 April 1990. Michael Jackson had promised him that he would appear in his next short film, but they did not manage to meet in time to realize this project.

The King of Pop then asked Buz Kohan and the archivist Paul Surrat to create an homage in video that would immortalize the moments he had been fortunate to share with his friend. Paul Surrat, who for several years had saved footage of all Michael Jackson's television appearances, put this together, using the soundtrack from Dionne Warwick's performance.

Ryan White at age 16. The young hemophiliac had become infected with HIV through a blood transfusion. He fought his battle in the media spotlight and became a close friend of Michael.

Michael Jackson was pleased with the result and, since the song had never been released on record, was prepared to record his own version. For the first time since *Off the Wall* he agreed to relax his own rule and he transformed *Gone Too Soon* into a farewell message to Ryan White.

Production

Surrounded by the team from the group Toto, Michael Jackson settled into the producer's chair and went on to demonstrate that he had remembered the lessons of Quincy Jones. The combination of keyboards and meticulously dosed layers of synthesizer sounds complements the discreet bass guitar line played by Abraham Laboriel.

As in *Heal the World*, Marty Paich composed the song's introduction: a series of chords played on the violin leads to the first notes on the electric piano, which gently launch the beginning of the song. The sound quality of *Gone Too Soon* follows on logically from the songs *Grace* (1984) and *Prelude to the Garden* (1989), both by Quincy Jones. The spare arrangements are the result of the skill and style that were characteristic of the star's long-standing producer. Its cinematic approach places this composition in the noble category of Hollywood movie soundtracks.

Buz Kohan went to the Ocean Way studios to be present at the recording sessions for the song. As usual, Michael Jackson sang in the dark, while Bruce Swedien oversaw the session, comfortably ensconced behind the console. "He put his soul into it," recalls Buz. "There was no exaggeration or affectation. It was real emotion."[112] In 2002, an alternative version of *Gone Too Soon* found its way onto the bootleg market. It was clear that the interpretation differed little on this other recording, and that Michael Jackson had managed to find the right intensity to immortalize this farewell to his friend Ryan White.

THE SHORT FILM

Director, versions 1 and 2: Bill DiCicco
Producer: Paul Surrat
Leading actors: Ryan White and Michael Jackson
Shoot date: 1993
Shooting location: archive footage
Duration: Version 1: 4'07 / Version 2: 3'39

The video made by Paul Surrat with Dionne Warwick's performance as a soundtrack remained unreleased, but served as the basis for the short film that would be sent to TV stations to promote *Gone Too Soon*.

Bill DiCicco made a discreet video in which Ryan White was the main protagonist. The archive footage shows the battle the young man fought and immortalizes a radiant, positive image of him. Michael Jackson appears just twice in the clip, which is certainly one of his less significant ones, but no less heavy with meaning for all that.

In 2006, the online media store iTunes revealed an unreleased version of *Gone Too Soon*. This second edit, also by Bill DiCicco, had been made at the request of Michael Jackson, who wanted to screen it in his private movie theater at his ranch, Neverland. After Jackson's death, it was released in the DVD box set *Vision* (2010).

Gone Too Soon was released as a single on 1 December 1993, World AIDS Day.

DANGEROUS

Michael Jackson, Bill Bottrell, Teddy Riley / 6'59

Musicians
Early Version (6'40)
Bill Bottrell: drums, synthesizers
Final version:
Michael Jackson: lead and backing vocals
Teddy Riley, Brad Buxer, Rhett Lawrence: synthesizers
Recording
Ocean Way Recording, Record One Studio (studio 2), and Larrabee North Studios, Los Angeles: September 1990 to October 1991
Technical team
Early Version (6'40)
Producers: Bill Bottrell and Michael Jackson
Recording engineer: Bill Bottrell
Mixing: Bill Bottrell
Final version
Producers: Teddy Riley and Michael Jackson
Recording engineers: Jean-Marie Horvat, Bruce Swedien, Teddy Riley, and Thom Russo
Rhythm and synthesizer arrangements: Teddy Riley
String arrangements: Ben Wright
Vocal arrangements: Michael Jackson
Mixing: Bruce Swedien and Teddy Riley

1991

FOR JACKSON ADDICTS

Two versions of *Dangerous* (*radio English*, 4'23 and *radio Spanish*, 3'37) were released in Mexico in 1993 as part of a Sony Music promotional CD (ref. PRCD- 95910).

Genesis

Michael Jackson used the rhythm base of *Streetwalker*, which he had written in 1985 for the album *Bad*, to create another song, entitled *Dangerous*. In 1994, he explained:

> Okay, like I said before, I wrote the song *Streetwalker* and I wasn't completely satisfied with it, I was frustrated that, you know, it wasn't exactly what it should be. I have a lot of songs like that, like kinda unfinished. And I…So I gave the song to Billy and he fooled around with it, he put some drum sounds and put it through, you know, computers and things. And he gave the tape back to me with the bass lick, the drums, and everything on it. And I'd listen to it quite often and I liked what I heard, but it didn't really have a melody yet, a vocal melody. And eventually the melody just came, just hearing the music the whole composition as itself…Well like I said before, the bass lick was there ready from the previous song that I had written. Billy Bottrell had taken the bass sound and he put chords from a keyboard, chords on top of that, and drum sounds. And that's what inspired the melody, what he did is what inspired me to write the melody, cause out of that whenever I hear the chords, you need to have that progression, I hear a million melodies in my head and hearing that, that's what inspired me to write that, what Billy did.[113]

This is how the demo of the *Dangerous* dubbed *Early Version* came into being in September 1990. The lyrics return to the theme of a vicious woman, prepared to do anything to get what she wants. The song's heavy, urban atmosphere brings to mind that of *Smooth Criminal*. The listener can imagine that the heroine of the song on *Bad*, Annie, seeks revenge, and gets it in *Dangerous*.

The phrased verses, somewhere between rap and slam (rap poetry), gave the singer the opportunity to play the role of the narrator of a story that seemed like a distant memory. The pre-choruses raise the tension with a series of phrases built around chords that crescendo toward the chorus, which is liberating and typical of those that the star wrote: based on the repetition of the word "dangerous", they are rebukes that the singer aims directly at this woman who is tormenting him.

On 7 February 1994, Michael Jackson attended court in Denver, Colorado, to give evidence in a plagiarism case

Michael Jackson performs *Dangerous* live for the penultimate time on 20 April 2002 for the special show *American Bandstand 50th Anniversary*, which was broadcast on 3 May 2002.

brought by the singer Crystal Cartier. This artist claimed to have written a song entitled *Dangerous* in 1985 and to have recorded it in 1990. She did not copyright her work until October 1991, a few weeks before Michael Jackson's version was released. The King of Pop explained to the court the genesis of his song. For the first time in his career, in response to close questioning by attorneys, he revealed details about his method for writing songs: "Well, usually when I write the songs I get I…I vocally, I orally, use a melody into a tape recorder. And for instance with the song *Streetwalker*, which has a driving bass lick that I just spoke about, which I'll have a tape recorder and I'd just sing the bass part into that tape recorder. And for *Streetwalker* the bass melody went ahh [sings]. And I've taped that bass lick and put the chords of the melody over the bass lick. And I…And that what inspires the melody or the other sounds that I'm hearing in my head, but that is the bass lick and I use the Moog and a bass guitar to create that sound that I'm hearing in my head."[113]

Production

Michael Jackson was not satisfied with the first version of *Dangerous*, so he asked Teddy Riley to rework the song. He told the court in Denver: "I had Teddy going and kinda update the sounds…So we kinda shaped and modeled and sculpted till I got what is on the *Dangerous* album."[113]

Teddy Riley applied his expertise and refined the version created by Michael and Bill Bottrell so as to breathe some new jack swing energy into it that was as hard-hitting as it was innovative. The producer recalled: "The track evolved: Michael came in with the hook, I did the music and then we finalized the song. We used a drum machine, the Akai MPC-60, and a lot of the sounds from that and samples I had on my sample CDs. There's no science to it, I just feel my way through the production. I always feel my way—I never do anything the same."[101]

Teddy Riley took the bold decision of removing the bass line, which had been taken from *Streetwalker*, and building a new rhythm track. He incorporated a bass drum that was similar to those used in some techno music at the time and evoked the one he had already used in the song *Her* by his group Guy (1990). The snare drum, compressed and forceful, added that striking contrast which made the rhythm even more aggressive and insistent. The dark atmosphere created by Bill Bottrell became even more dense and bleak in the hands of Teddy Riley. The young producer deployed his entire arsenal of sounds and stuffed the song full of industrial sounds. The long

The song *Dangerous* was added to the setlist for the second part of the *Dangerous Tour* (1993).

Michael Jackson and his dancers rehearse the precisely scripted choreography of *Dangerous*. The stage direction was to evolve over the years.

1991

0'22 intro is a rumble of machines, like a hellish factory toward which the listener is headed before being seized by the incessant, infernal rhythm, which comes to an end only after 7'00 and three false endings—excuses for prolonging the digital groove that spins like clockwork.

Dangerous illustrates perfectly how Michael Jackson applied the same working techniques as his long-time mentors, Berry Gordy and Quincy Jones, who always relied on healthy competition, or rather stimulation, between those they worked with in order to obtain the best results. The handing over of *Dangerous* from Bill Bottrell to Teddy Riley did not cause an ego crisis in the studio. Bill Bottrell recalled: "I never felt competition with Teddy, and when MJ suggested Teddy do a version, I had no problem. Hey, it's all about the writing. Teddy's version rocks and sounds like the '90s, where mine was stuck in the '80s."[114]

Like a work that he had trouble finishing, *Dangerous* was a song that Michael Jackson constantly modified and adapted throughout his career. The singer and his record label aimed to release it as the tenth and last single from the album, with a promotional and marketing impact comparable to that of *Thriller* and *Smooth Criminal*. However, the "Chandler Affair", an attempt at extortion disguised as a moral issue, and the hasty ending of the *Dangerous* tour put paid to those plans.

In early 1993 the King of Pop decided to perform *Dangerous* live. The first performance took place at the American Music Awards, held in the Shrine Auditorium, on 27 January 1993. The studio version was completely altered, which produced a new mix. This contained new sound effects and breaks to fit the ultra-technical choreography the artist had created with the dancer LaVelle Smith. This soundtrack was developed further, making clear the connection with *Smooth Criminal* when an extract from that song was included in the performance at the MTV Music Awards on 7 September 1995. Finally, in the *MJ and Friends* concerts in Seoul and Munich, on 25 and 27 June 1999 respectively, a third version of *Dangerous*, even more spare, hard-hitting, and mechanical, was presented to the audience, who understood that their idol had decided to make this song a high point of his live performances. The King of Pop continued to modify the song right up until the planning for the *This Is It* concerts in 2009. This enabled him to pay tribute to the works that had inspired him by incorporating into the song short extracts from film soundtracks, such as *The Good, the Bad and the Ugly*, and the horrific, strident strings of Alfred Hitchcock's *Psycho*.

In the intro to the first version of *Dangerous*, made by Bill Bottrell, a muffled sound followed by a cry is clearly audible. This is due to a section of wall falling on Michael Jackson's head when recording had begun. This amused the singer, who decided to retain the sounds captured at the start of the song.

The front cover of the *Dangerous* tour program.

[**BONUS TRACK**]

Someone Put Your Hand Out

Michael Jackson, Teddy Riley / 5'25

Musicians
Michael Jackson: lead and backing vocals, keyboards, and strings
Brad Buxer: keyboards and strings
Paulhino Da Costa: percussion
Jonathan Moxie: synthesizers
Oscar Castro-Neves: guitar
Recording
Studio (unknown): April 1992
Technical team
Producers: Michael Jackson and Teddy Riley
Recording engineers: Bruce Swedien and George Mayers Jr.
Assistant recording engineers: Tim Roberts, Brad Sundberg, Thom Russo, John Chamberlin, and Rail Rogut
Additional Pro Tools: John Hanes
Digital editing: Michael Prince
Mixing: Serban

Someone Put Your Hand Out had already been worked on at the time of *Bad*, and was reworked by Teddy Riley in 1991, but this song was not included on the album *Dangerous*. It was finally recorded in April 1992 and became part of a marketing exercise, being released through a promotion—a unique case in the career of the King of Pop.

In the summer of 1992 the *Dangerous* tour started in Europe, in partnership with Pepsi-Cola. To mark the event and fulfill his commitment to advertising the brand, Michael Jackson granted the beverage corporation this unreleased song, which would be distributed in the first instance as an audio cassette handed out at press conferences. Pepsi, using a proven marketing strategy, offered this coveted treasure to customers in certain countries who bought a certain number of bottles of soda. The existence of this unreleased song, which was only broadcast by radio stations with tie-ins to the *Dangerous* tour, soon became common knowledge worldwide, leading to impatience where supermarkets did not display the offer. In those pre-internet days, the rumor soon took hold that it was possible to buy the tape in the United Kingdom. Eventually, all Europe's record stores managed to get hold of it and put it on sale. Although it was not widely known at the time, Japan had already abandoned the cassette format and released a magnificent 3-inch CD, which would be the only digital pressing of the song for a long time. It finally became available to all in 2004, on the compilation *Michael Jackson—The Ultimate Collection*.

Someone Put Your Hand Out is both plaintive and languorous; the artist sings of his hope of finding love one day. The song is touching in its sincerity. It is pure, solemn, and heady, conveying an innocent, brave emotion unlike any other song by the King of Pop. Bruce Swedien produced it with Michael Jackson, and mixed the medley on the B-side, made up of a selection of songs from the album *Dangerous*.

Exclusive *Dangerous* tour cassette / Pepsi-Cola promotion
A-side: *Someone Put Your Hand Out* / 5'25
B-side: *Dangerous Medley* / 6'15
Released by Epic Records/Pepsi-Cola: Europe (ref. 982789), May 1992 / Japan (ref. TDDD 90052), 1992

DANGEROUS OUTTAKES

When he returned to the studio to record *Dangerous*, Michael Jackson freed himself from the charismatic but sometimes authoritarian presence of Quincy Jones. Left to himself and finally free to make his own decisions, he worked with numerous other producers and sought to find an identity that would enable him to begin the 1990s with a groundbreaking sound. The preparation for *Dangerous* was littered with forgotten or rarely heard songs, which, had they been included in place of those the star chose, would have given a completely different picture of his musical world.

MONKEY BUSINESS

Michael Jackson, Bill Bottrell / 5'45

Musicians: Michael Jackson: lead and backing vocals / **Bill Bottrell:** bass guitar, drums, guitar / **Greg Phillinganes:** Wurlitzer piano / **Jim Keltner, Lenny Castro:** drum machine / **Jim Horn:** saxophone / **Recording: Westlake Recording Studios, Record One Studios, Larrabee North Studios, Los Angeles**: 1989 / **Technical team: Producers**: Michael Jackson and Bill Bottrell / **Recording engineers**: Bill Bottrell, Matt Forger, Kevin Gilbert / **Assistant recording engineers:** Rail Rogut, Bart Stevens, Brad Sundberg, Julie Last, John Chamberlin / **String arrangements:** George Del Barrio / **Mixing:** Bill Bottrell / **Single recording:** Matt Forger / **Box set:** *The Ultimate Collection* / **Released by Epic:** USA and UK, 16 November 2004 (US ref. ESK 92600 and UK ref. 517743)

This was the second song whose title referenced a song by Elvis Presley (the first was *Heartbreak Hotel*). Initially entitled *Too Much Monkey Business*, this song was worked on for many months in various studios. Michael Jackson was keen to finish it, and for a long time kept it among the top contenders for inclusion on *Dangerous*. In 1991, *Monkey Business* was included on a very rare CD, of which only about ten copies were made and handed out to Sony Music management who had come to Neverland to hear some songs on the new album.

Matt Forger had the heavy responsibility of recording the monkey cries heard in the intro. Bubbles, Michael Jackson's pet chimpanzee, was recruited for the task: the star would splash water on him to make him cry out. When the music starts, the atmosphere of soul and blues from the American South goes wonderfully with Michael Jackson's voice, which is deep in the verses and rises to falsetto as it approaches the chorus. The interpretation is reminiscent of the jazzy vocalization in *You Can't Win*, his first solo number produced by Quincy Jones.

All the same, there remains a hint of pop in this song, and the presence of the saxophonist Jim Horn, who worked on some of the ex-Beatles' solo projects, confirms this. As in the Elvis song, Michael Jackson bemoans the disappearance of moral values and condemns the loose morals of his day.

Although he is not credited, Teddy Riley contributed a few overdubs to bring the song into line with the rest of the output. Despite its musical quality, *Monkey Business* did not make it into the select tracklist of *Dangerous*. It was destined to be included on the bonus CD of the reissued album in 2001, but that project fell through under pressure from Tommy Mottola, the head of Sony, with whom the King of Pop was at war. During the battle, a few test CDs dated 12 January 2000 were nevertheless made, sending collectors into a frenzy. The passage of time eventually granted *Monkey Business* modest exposure on the box set *Michael Jackson: The Ultimate Collection*, which the star agreed to release to honor his contract with the record company.

Michael poses in the dance room of his ranch, Neverland, in 1991.

Work That Body

Michael Jackson, Bryan Loren / 3'29

Musicians: Michael Jackson: lead and backing vocals / **Bryan Loren:** synthesizers, keyboards, drums / **Recording: Westlake Recording Studios, Record One Studios, Larrabee North Studios, Los Angeles**: 1989 / **Technical team: Producers**: Michael Jackson and Bryan Loren / **Recording engineer**: (unknown) / **Mixing:** Bryan Loren

Bryan Loren wanted to make songs with Michael Jackson that would return to the carefree, funk spirit of the album *Off the Wall*. *Work That Body*, an unpretentious synthetic groove, fitted the bill. Loren applied all his talent as a musician and skills as a synthesizer programmer. The rhythm allows the riffs of well-oiled synthesizers, which sound similar to electric guitars, to resound. The singer's plaintive, harsh voice is reminiscent of his performance of certain songs during his last years at Motown. Indeed, Michael gives a nod to his first record label: at 1'54 he repeats, 20 years on, the famous words "Sit down girl! I think I love you!" that are heard on *ABC*. Always looking to the future and ready to return to old ideas as long as they served an innovative purpose, Michael Jackson preferred to leave *Work That Body* to one side in favor of productions by Teddy Riley, such as *She Drives Me Wild*. Intended for inclusion on the bonus CD on the reissue of *Dangerous* planned for 2001 but eventually scrapped, the song remains unreleased to this day on the official market. As well as the famous test CD of *Dangerous*, which was leaked on the internet, Bryan Loren posted the song on his MySpace page in the mid-2000s.

If You Don't Love Me

Michael Jackson, Bill Bottrell / 4'13

Musicians: Michael Jackson: lead and backing vocals / **Bill Bottrell:** bass guitar, drums, guitar / **(unknown):** keyboards and synthesizers / **Recording: Westlake Recording Studios, Record One Studio, Larrabee North Studios, Los Angeles**: 1989 to 1990 / **Technical team: Producers**: Michael Jackson and Bill Bottrell / **Recording engineer**: (unknown) / **Mixing:** Bill Bottrell

A real oddball from the *Dangerous* sessions, *If You Don't Love Me* is a vigorous rock number whose aggressiveness springs from a story of thwarted love. In the choruses, the rhythm is hammered out in the manner of a hit from the heyday of Motown. The guitar riff, simple and typical of the early 1990s, a period that saw the rise of grunge, marks the song in a very—perhaps too—repetitive way. At 3'34, a break allows the listener to draw breath a little. Michael Jackson has just enough time to continue complaining and begging his beloved before launching even more intensely into the last choruses, which are delivered with the same energy. In the early 2000s a first version was leaked on the internet that was almost the definitive version. A few guitar arrangements were missing, and the mixing of the vocals was not yet complete. The definitive version, authorized by the singer, figured on the test CD of the reissue of *Dangerous* planned for 2001. *If You Don't Love Me* stands out on it as an unlikely rock nugget, unique in Michael Jackson's repertoire.

Serious Effect

Michael Jackson, Bryan Loren, LL Cool J / 4'18

Musicians: Michael Jackson: lead and backing vocals / **LL Cool J:** rap / **Bryan Loren:** synthesizers, keyboards, drums / **Recording: Westlake Recording Studios, Record One Studios, Larrabee North Studios, Los Angeles**: 1990 / **Technical team: Producers:** Michael Jackson and Bryan Loren / **Recording engineer:** (unknown) / **Mixing:** Bryan Loren

The rapper LL Cool J was one of the hip-hop artists popular in the United States at the end of the 1980. Having finally accepted rap, and keen to include some guest appearances in his songs, Michael Jackson recorded several numbers with him. *Serious Effect* was one of these. Built around a rhythm put together by Bryan Loren, the song describes the beauty of a woman who has an effect on every man she meets. This very simple theme is an excuse for a flowing mid-tempo, somewhere between funk and rap, which Michael Jackson tries to bring to life. LL Cool J interjects a verse delivered in very classic style. At the end of the song, Michael follows suit, launching into some ad-libbing that flirts with rap. For reasons of his own, very likely because the song lacks a strong melodic line, the singer decided not to release the song, preferring *Can't Let Her Get Away*, a discreet but effective new jack swing number—much to the displeasure of Bryan Loren, who declared that he liked it more than the other songs he had worked on for *Dangerous*.

An intimate moment: Michael Jackson on the phone during the making of the album *Dangerous* (1991).

She Got It

Michael Jackson, Bryan Loren / 4'28

Musicians: Michael Jackson: lead and backing vocals / **Bryan Loren:** synthesizers, keyboards, drums / **Recording: Westlake Recording Studios, Record One Studios, Larrabee North Studios, Los Angeles:** 1989 to 1990 / **Technical team: Producers**: Michael Jackson and Bryan Loren / **Recording engineer:** (unknown) / **Mixing:** Bryan Loren

This song is driven by a metallic, industrial beat over which plays a spare electric guitar riff, not dissimilar to the opening measures of *Blood on the Dance Floor,* coproduced by Michael Jackson and Teddy Riley. *She Got It* is based on simple, repetitive motifs. Bryan Loren abandoned the shattering snare drums with which he had attempted to build his reputation to put together a rhythm redolent of the late 1980s. The funky synthesizer chords make groovy arrangements worthy of Prince but here, again, in too repetitive a fashion. The King of Pop seems to be enjoying himself in this song when he lets loose a few vocal utterances and ad-libs, and then spontaneously bursts out laughing. Also earmarked for inclusion on the legendary 2001 *Dangerous* bonus CD, which was never released, this almost-completed song has remained in the archives to this day.

OUTTAKES

Michael Jackson opened Neverland to the public for the first time and granted a long interview to the star presenter Oprah Winfrey on 10 February 1993.

MEN IN BLACK

Michael Jackson, Bryan Loren / (unknown)

Musicians: Michael Jackson: lead and backing vocals / **Bryan Loren:** synthesizers, keyboards, drums / **Recording: Westlake Recording Studios, Record One Studios, Larrabee North Studios, Los Angeles:** 1990 / **Technical team: Producers**: Michael Jackson and Bryan Loren / **Recording engineer**: (unknown) / **Mixing:** Bryan Loren

Also featuring on the CD handed out to Sony management during their stay at Neverland, the song *Men in Black* was mentioned for the first time in the British fanzine *Off the Wall*. The piece by the editor, Adrian Grant, published in 1990, described a dark and fascinating number. Michael Jackson wrote this song when he learned that Steven Spielberg was planning to make a movie with that title. Completely unreleased on the official market, this song was one of those Jackson/Loren coproductions that could have helped to build a different musical identity for *Dangerous*. The producer, who was decidedly left out of this album, presented at his seminars a version of this song without lyrics, containing only the backing vocals sung by the star. In early 2017, a few measures of the song were leaked on the internet, revealing the inspiration behind this number that generations of fans had fantasized about. *Men in Black* turned out to be a gem of new jack swing that could have featured on Janet Jackson's *Rhythm Nation 1814*. As for the bass line, it echoes motifs that Teddy Riley was so fond of in the early 1990s, for example in *Tell Me How You Feel* for the group Wreckx-N-Effect.

FOR ALL TIME

Steve Porcaro, Michael Sherwood / 4'03

Musicians: Michael Jackson: lead and backing vocals / **Steve Porcaro, David Paich:** keyboards / **Steve Lukather:** guitar / **Jeff Porcaro:** drums / **Angelikson Productions:** additional keyboards (2007 version) / **Recording: Westlake Recording Studios, Record One Studios, Larrabee North Studios, Los Angeles**: 1990 / **Technical team: Producer:** Michael Jackson / **Recording engineer:** Bruce Swedien / **Assistant recording engineer:** Tom Bender / **Mixing:** Mick Guzauski/ **Box set:** *Thriller 25* **/ Released by Epic:** USA and UK, 8 February 2008 (ref. 88697220962)

In a fairly vague attempt to rewrite or reformulate his story, Michael Jackson released *For All Time* as a bonus on the reissued *Thriller 25*, which in 2008 marked the 25th anniversary of this landmark album. The sleeve notes and the sales literature sent to stores by the record label said that the song was written during the sessions for the mythical album. Many doubted this, especially as the song appeared on the bootleg market together with several other songs from the *Dangerous* sessions. The voice heard on this working version and on the version released in 2007 is the same, and does not resemble the voice the star sang with during the *Thriller* years. A lingering doubt remained for some time, as the King of Pop liked to rework songs that had been put aside. But Steve Porcaro, in 2014, reset the context and confirmed the origin of *For All Time*: "The song was actually written during the *Dangerous* era, and then Michael recorded it for the first and only time."[115] Michael Sherwood, who cowrote the song with the keyboard player, confirmed this: "Steve Porcaro and I had written a track for Michael Jackson called *For All Time* for the *Dangerous* album. Michael Jackson wanted another sort of *Human Nature* track and reached out to Steve Porcaro—but, in the 11th hour, the song was bumped for Michael's track, *Gone Too Soon*."[116]

The cheerful chords of the Monkees' song *Daydream Believer* were the inspiration for those of *For All Time,* though the latter are sadder. In the chorus, Steve Porcaro combined three different vocal takes to get Michael to pronounce the words "for," "all," and "time,". This effect gives the impression that the words are coming out in a vague way, as if in a dream. A timeless ballad that allows the star's voice to float above a melody and words that describe an eternal love, *For All Time* is the fruit of a successful reunion of part of the team that created *Thriller*.

Slave to the Rhythm

L A Reid, Babyface, Daryl Simmons, Kevin Roberson / 4'35

Musicians: Michael Jackson: lead and backing vocals / **L A Reid:** keyboards and drums / **Babyface:** keyboards / **Kevin "Kayo" Roberson:** bass guitar / **Recording: Can Am Studios, Larrabee North Studios, Los Angeles**: 1990 / **Technical team: Producers**: L A Reid & Babyface / **Recording engineer:** Bruce Swedien / **Assistant recording engineer:** Thom Russo / **Mixing:** Bruce Swedien, Paul McKenna / **Album:** *Xscape* / **Released by Epic:** USA and UK, 14 May 2014 (ref. 88843066762)

On 8 May 1990, Michael Jackson went to the Regent Beverly Wilshire Hotel in Los Angeles to receive a prize from the BMI (Broadcast Music Industry) organization, which protected the rights of American musicians. During that event he briefly met the duo of Antonio "L A" Reid and Kevin "Babyface" Edmonds. A few weeks later the star invited them to his ranch, Neverland, to discuss the possibility of working together.

Going by the name of L A Reid and Babyface, the duo turned everything they touched to gold. For example, the two friends had helped the young Bobby Brown to refine his style after he left the group New Edition to embark on a solo career. The musician then went on to have a series of hits, including *On Our Own*, theme of the movie *Ghostbusters II*, and *Every Little Step*. L A Reid and Babyface also launched their own record label, LaFace, distributed by Arista. Intrigued by the two men's commercial success, Michael asked them to write some songs for him.

During the conversation, he spent many long minutes with them dissecting the sound of two other producers who were fashionable at the time: Jimmy Jam and Terry Lewis. This duo, who were from Minneapolis, were then producing a hard-hitting urban sound that can be heard on the *N.E. Heartbreak* by New Edition and *Rhythm Nation 1814* by Janet Jackson. They were regular producers for Michael Jackson's younger sister, who recorded songs such as *The Knowledge,* which her brother played continuously during long dance practice sessions, with them. Describing his attachment to this song, with its overpowering bass line, Michael Jackson told Reid and Edmonds: "I am a slave to the rhythm."[117]

This sentence, which he repeated during an interview with Oprah Winfrey in 1993 and to the magazine *Gold* in 2002, stayed in the minds of the two musicians. They played him several songs on which they were working, and the singer set his heart on a track with a throbbing, funky beat, which he asked them to complete. With the help of Kevin Roberson, the musician who had written the first bass line, this was to become *Slave to the Rhythm*.

The star and the two producers, plus Bruce Swedien and Paul McKenna, recording engineer for the LaFace label, met at Larrabee North Studios to record the song. Michael Jackson recorded take after take to achieve not only the right tone but also the vocal intensity that would bring the song's story to life. He took the song to heart, and described with passion the life of this woman subjected to a daily routine that demanded the best of her, while offering her little gratitude in return. Although carried along by a lively rhythm and a catchy tune, *Slave to the Rhythm* did not make it onto the tracklist for *Dangerous*. The King of Pop decided not to continue working with the famous duo who, at the same time, had signed Jermaine Jackson to their label. The former leader of The Jackson Five could not bear the idea that his younger brother worked with producers he was also keen on. In 1991, he teamed up with Reid and Edmonds to release a mocking song, *Word to the Badd!!,* in which he settled scores with Michael. This song destroyed what little confidence and respect remained between the two brothers, and sounded the death knell for Jermaine's career with big record labels. Meanwhile, the King of Pop continued on his way and kept *Slave to the Rhythm* among his work in progress. He planned to rework the song for the albums *HIStory* and *Invincible*, but each time it remained in the pipeline.

After Michael Jackson's death, the song was earmarked for inclusion on *Michael*, the first compilation of unreleased tracks drawn up by the star's beneficiaries in 2010. It was dropped from that project and was finally released in 2014 on *Xscape*: L A Reid, who by then was CEO of Epic Records, decided to produce and each song for this compilation of unreleased material. He thus gave well-deserved exposure to this work that had partly been leaked on the internet during the early 2010s. He even envisaged releasing a version as a duo with Justin Bieber. The fans of the King of Pop reacted with anger when the idea was made public, so much so that the ex-producer withdrew it.

Michael Jackson dances in the gardens of Neverland Ranch in 1991.

Do You Know Where Your Children Are

Michael Jackson / 4'39

Musicians: Michael Jackson: lead and backing vocals / **David Williams:** guitar / **John Barnes:** keyboards and Synclavier / **Recording: Can Am Studios, Larrabee North Studios, Los Angeles**: 1990 / **Technical team: Producer:** Michael Jackson / **Recording engineers:** Matt Forger and Bill Bottrell / **Mixing:** Matt Forger and Bill Bottrell / **Album:** *Xscape* / **Released by Epic:** USA and UK, 14 May 2014 (ref. 88843066762)

Ever since the late 1970s, Michael Jackson had worked on songs that dealt with subjects linked to current affairs and which reflected the state of society. The title of *Do You Know Where Your Children Are* was inspired by advertisements that were broadcast by American television networks from the 1960s to the 1980s. By asking viewers this question just before the 10 p.m. or 11 p.m. news bulletins, the public services sent out a reminder to parents, who were responsible for their children's education and safety. Throughout his career, the artist wrote texts in which he revealed his pain at the world's problems, and especially that of unhappy childhood. Some of these writings were adapted for songs, while others remained in the form of prose or poems. *Do You Know Where Your Children Are* deals with the future of children in large cities. The singer could not turn a blind eye to this issue when crossing Los Angeles by car, or when he watched news channels that sensationalized certain human interest stories broadcast during prime time.

Michael Jackson worked on this song with Matt Forger and Bill Bottrell during the sessions for *Bad*. He made a first demo in the Encino studio with John Barnes on Synclavier. David Williams, the second musician he called on, supplied the guitar solo. The song did not win the support of the famous "A-Team" at Westlake, consisting of Quincy Jones and Bruce Swedien. It resurfaced during the sessions for *Dangerous*, but was no match for *Why You Wanna Trip on Me* which, in a certain way, describes the problems afflicting our society. The singer preferred to retain this vigorous, dark song coproduced by Teddy Riley. *Do You Know Where Your Children Are* continued its journey through time and various recording sessions. In the mid-1990s it was considered for the album *HIStory*, with a hip-hop rhythm different from that created with John Barnes in Encino. At the end of 2010 a version that featured a contribution from the guitarist Steve Lukather was leaked on the internet. The rhythm track incorporated a sample from *Synthetic Substitution* by Melvin Bliss, which had already been used in 1991 by the group Naughty by Nature on *O.P.P.* Considered for the posthumous compilation *Michael* (2010), the version of *Do You Know Where Your Children Are* dating from the *Bad* sessions appeared on the Deluxe pressing of the posthumous album *Xscape* (2014).

In 2004, on NBC, the song was included in the soundtrack for the animated series *Father of the Pride*, which tells the story of the white lion of Siegfried and Roy.

Siegfried Fischbacher and Roy Horn
Mind Is the Magic

Michael Jackson / 6'21

From the album: *Siegfried and Roy—Dreams and Illusions* / **Released by Edel Records:** Germany, (ref. 0028972EDL) (Album), 29 March 1995 / **Single: Released by ZYX Music:** Germany, 26 February 2010 / **Musicians: Michael Jackson:** lead and backing vocals / **Arrangements:** Michael Jackson and Bryan Loren / **Recording:** (unknown): 1989 / **Technical team: Recording engineer**: Richard Cottrell / **Mixing:** Bryan Loren and Richard Cottrell

Genesis

The duo Siegfried Fischbacher and Roy Horn escaped the gloom of postwar Germany and settled in the United States, where they made a name for themselves with an original show that combined magic with wild animals. The two artists met the teenage leader of The Jackson Five when they were all performing at the MGM Grand in Las Vegas. The then very young Michael was an honored audience member, faithfully attending all their shows. Over the years, the singer of *Thriller* continued regularly to attend the various performances that the Masters of the Impossible gave all over the world, and he was always happy to meet up with them, as they had now become friends. In the late 1980s the magicians returned to Las Vegas, staying at The Mirage, where a special complex had been built to accommodate their extraordinary logistics. From 1990, they settled there permanently.

As luck would have it, Thomas Bähler, a constant presence in Michael Jackson's career, was the music director and composer of the music for the permanent show at the The Mirage. In 2014 he told the French magazine *Invincible* that the King of Pop had written *Mind Is the Magic* himself, and that all he had done was incorporate it into the show's soundtrack. His recollection of the song's history was valuable and detailed. He knew, for example, that Siegfried had worked on a stage effect for the singer's *Bad* tour, a magic trick that consisted of making the star disappear at the end of his performance of *Working Day and Night*, and then to cause him to reappear a few seconds later at the top of a crane, where he would then sing *Beat It*. The illusionist teased Michael Jackson, saying Michael could never pay him a fee for this little magic favor, but that all he needed to do was give him something in return. This repayment quickly took the form of a song to introduce the new show of the magicians and lion-tamers. Thus the *Mind Is the Magic* project came into being.

In the lyrics, Michael Jackson describes a magical garden where orchids and violets disappear mysteriously. He then goes on to pay fervent homage to the talents of Siegfried and Roy. The song, tailor-made for the two performers, expresses all the admiration the star had for the magic and the artistic world conjured up by his two friends.

In 2001 the new stars of Las Vegas signed a contract with The Mirage, which was sadly to come to an end two years later, after Roy was very severely injured by one of his white tigers.

Production

Searching for original musical ideas, the star undertook several work sessions with the talented producer and musician Bryan Loren, and gave him the job of producing *Mind Is the Magic*. In 2014, speaking to *Invincible* magazine, the writer of *Do the Bartman* admitted he hated the recording. He insisted that the King of Pop had written *Mind Is the Magic* unaided; all he had done was shape it, as he had been asked to do. Musically, the rhythm is impeccable, and the sounds are bewitching, transporting the listener instantly into a strange parallel world. It is surprising that Bryan Loren rejected this song, for it fits well with his meticulous, melodious style, delivered effectively and rich in astonishing sounds. Having completed the mixing, the producer entrusted the task of finishing the song to recording engineer Richard Cottrell, who seems to have added his own voice to some parts of the backing vocals.

Unfortunately, too few technical details are available for an in-depth knowledge of the production of this song.

Thomas Bähler recalls playing *Mind Is the Magic* to Quincy Jones, who by then was no longer working with Michael Jackson. The producer reportedly recognized the bare bones of a song that had been dropped from an album, probably *Bad*. With total honesty, Quincy Jones admitted that *Mind Is the Magic* was a very impressive song.

Michael Jackson visiting his friends Siegfried and Roy backstage at their 6 August 2002 show at the Mirage Hotel.

In 1995, in the duo's homeland, Germany, where the magicians were national stars, the soundtrack of the show *Siegfried and Roy—Dreams and Illusions* was released as a CD by the Edel label. The original version of *Mind Is the Magic* was also released as a single in 2010 by ZYX Music. A series of Inaudible remixes completed this CD of four songs.

FOR JACKSON ADDICTS

The documentary *This Is It*, made by Kenny Ortega in 2009, shows Jackson rehearsing new dance steps, called the Drill, which was to open his stage performance of *They Don't Care About Us*. This was mixed with an extract from *Mind Is the Magic*.

Bryan Loren
To Satisfy You

Bryan Loren / 5'58

From the album: *The Music from the New World* / **Released by Arista Records:** Japan, 21 August 1992 (ref. BVCA-144) / **Musicians: Bryan Loren:** lead vocals / **Michael Jackson:** backing vocals (not credited) / **Bryan Loren:** all instruments / **Recording: The Closet (unknown):** 1990 to 1992 / **Technical team: String arrangements:** Clare Fischer

In 1984, the electro-pop-funk album *Bryan Loren* revealed a talented young musician, originally from Long Island, and propelled the song *Lollipop Luv* to No. 23 in the *Billboard* R&B chart. The composer and arranger went on to make a name for himself during the second half of the decade on albums by Barry White and The Brothers Johnson. In 1987, for A&M Records, Loren produced the album *Discovery* by Shanice Wilson, a young and talented singer of the up-and-coming generation. He gradually began to acquire a role working with the Jackson family, first with Marlon (*Life*, *Baby Tonight*, 1987), then with Randy (*Gigolo* and *I Need You*, *Randy and The Gypsys*, 1989). In 1989, he suggested the song *Work* to the youngest Jackson sibling, who recorded it for *Rhythm Nation 1814* (1989). The song was not, in the end, selected for the final tracklist of this successful work and became known only in the early 2000, on the writer's MySpace page.

In 1990, the great George Benson bestowed on Bryan Loren the Sony Innovators Sound Award, which showcased his talent and acted as a springboard for his career. It opened the door to the musician, bringing him together with the prodigy of the Jackson family, who was in search of new sources of musical inspiration after having made three albums with the star producer Quincy Jones. After a few work sessions, though, the collaboration with Bryan Loren failed to generate a musical spark that was strong or charismatic enough. The hopes expressed by Sony in the pages of the July 1990 issue of *Ebony* magazine did not, after all, seem to bring the label's superstar on board. Nevertheless, the work produced by the two men would find a place, as a second choice, on a few peripheral projects or various compilations of the star's songs.

To Satisfy You was one of the songs Bryan Loren suggested to Michael Jackson in preparations for the album *Dangerous*. Although the singer had a particular soft spot for syrupy ballads, he did not like this song, so it remained at the demo stage. Bryan Loren kept some tracks recorded by the King of Pop and used them as part of the backing vocals for his own version, which was released only in Japan on the album *Music from the New World*.

In this version, Michael can be heard singing the tune in his soft voice: "My only wish is to satisfy you / I want to make this the best I can do / To keep you happy with all my might / You'll want for nothing both day and night." The rhythm, unchanging but brilliant, and adorned by rich, crafted sonorities, is softened by magnificent violins that plunge the listener into a passionate musical theme.

For Jackson Addicts

In 1994, Damion Hall, of Guy, recorded the number in a version rearranged and produced by Bryan Loren, with Chanté Moore taking Michael Jackson's' place on backing vocals (*Straight to the Point*, Silas Records, 1994). A few promotional CDs of the time include the original instrumental version by Loren (ref. LSJ5P-2920 and LSJ5P-2972).

In 1998, Bryan Loren was one of a plethora of producers on Rebbie Jackson's fourth album, released by the label MJJ Music. His songs *What You Need* and *Play Your Game* open the album *Yours Faithfully*.

Shot entirely against a blue background in April 1993, the clip of *Whatzupwitu* shows Michael and Eddie Murphy moving through the scenery that features on the sleeve of the album *Love's Alright*.

Eddie Murphy
Whatzupwitu

Eddie Murphy, Trenten Gumbs / 3'21

From the album: *Love's Alright* / **Released by Motown Records:** USA and Europe, 23 February 1993 (US ref. 374636354-2 and Europe ref. 530 136-2) / **Chart position:** USA R&B No. 80 / **Musicians: Eddie Murphy and Michael Jackson:** lead vocals / **Audrey Wheeler, Sandy Barber, Sophia Bender, Boys Choir of Harlem:** backing vocals / **Recording: Bubble Hill Studios, Englewood, New York, and Ocean Way Recording, Record One Studios and Larrabee North Studios, Los Angeles:** early 1992 / **Technical team: Producers:** Eddie Murphy and Trenten Gumbs / **Recording engineers:** Andre Jackson, Eric Stark, and Keith Evans / **Assistant recording engineer:** Kim James / **Keyboard and drums programming:** Eddie Murphy and Trenten Gumbs / **Mixing:** Jon Gass (Power Station) / **Single: Track 1:** *Whatzupwitu (album version)* / 3'21 / **Track 2:** *Whatzupwitu (instrumental)* / 3'21 / **Released by Motown Records:** USA, March 1993 (ref. cassette single 3746322054) / France, July 1993 (ref. CD single 860 116-2) / **Chart position:** USA R&B No. 74 / R&B/Hip-Hop Airplay No. 74 / France No. 36

THE SONG

Genesis

In 1989, at their first meetings in public, the American actor Eddie Murphy handed over two successive prestigious awards to Michael Jackson. First came the Achievement Award at the American Music Awards, and then the very first Sammy Davis Jr. Award in history, at the Soul Train Music Awards. The two artists grew closer, and there followed a fruitful artistic exchange at the time of *Dangerous*.

In 1992, Eddie Murphy played the pharaoh tirelessly trying to entertain his charming queen in the short film *Remember the Time*. The video, shot with sumptuous scenery depicting an idealized ancient Egypt, courtesy of Universal Studios, was a landmark.

At the same time, the actor-singer was working on his album *Love's Alright* for Motown and recorded *Whatzupwitu* with Michael Jackson. In 1993 the *Beverly Hills Cop* revealed the song's theme on MTV: "We did a duet together on a song called *Whatzupwitu*, and that's the next single. It's me and Michael and the Harlem Boys Choir. It's all about the world, and asking the question: What's up with you?"[118]

Michael Jackson graciously agreed to sing this positive, environmentally aware, and brotherly message, with its slightly silly tone: "Sun is gonna shine / Flowers gonna grow / Clouds'll sprinkle showers / Rivers gonna flow / Man ain't got the power / To kill nothing but himself / Man is a creation / Man is nothing else…"

Production

To date, no details about the making of the song have been made available. A glance at the album's credits shows that several studios on the East and West Coasts of the US are mentioned, which might indicate that the duet was recorded by the artists in two different places.

The second single from Murphy's album (after *I Was a King*), *Whatzupwitu* was released on the promotional circuit in the United States in March 1993, and only a single cassette found its way into the record stores. In July, France, the Netherlands, and Australia were the only countries where the song was given a chance as a single and commercially exploited. In France, *Whatzupwitu* made it into the Top 50, reaching No. 36. So the success of this musical treat of the summer was somewhat muted. Sony imposed a blanket of silence on the duet. For legal reasons, the French pressings could not mention Michael Jackson's name on the single sleeve. This explains the sticker reading: "*En duo avec …*" ("A duet with"), which was illegible for the general public.

With a knowing twinkle in his eye, Michael Jackson goes along with the jokes of his friend Eddie Murphy on the set of the video of *Whatzupwitu* in 1993.

Michael Jackson makes a second vocal contribution to *Love's Alright* on the track *Yeah,* together with countless other volunteer artists, an original concept dreamed up by Eddie Murphy. The song features a simple tune in which the title is sung as a slogan. A rare pressing of the song *Yeah* was released in very small numbers (ref. Motown W021582-4). The aim was to publicize a charity of the same name: the Yeah! Foundation, whose mission was to raise money for educational or health organizations.

FOR JACKSON ADDICTS

In 1997, Japan included the clip of *Whatzupwitu* on the DVD *Music Video Clip Dance 4* (ref. Pony Canyon PCBP-0005) and on its reissue in 1998, *Promo Lights Clip! Back To...Dance 2* (ref. Columbia COBY-90154). This was the first time that a clip featuring Jackson had made it into a DVD. Both are highly sought after by collectors.

THE SHORT FILM

Director: Wayne Isham
Producer: (unknown)
Leading actors: Eddie Murphy and Michael Jackson
Extras: Boys Choir of Harlem
Shoot date: April 1993
Shooting location: (unknown, but in all probability New York)
Duration: 3'25

"Have you seen my album cover? Clouds and all that stuff? It's us, me and Michael, in the sky and the clouds, with hearts, doves, and kids floating around, lots of special effects. Very psychedelic,"[118] said Eddie Murphy, durign the promotion of the single. The video was filmed entirely with a blue-screen background in order to embed these countless visual elements.

In 1999, MTV's viewers voted *Whatzupwitu* the third-worst video clip in history, the last straw for the singer of *Thriller*, whose videos were legendary! Ultimately, it was decided to withdraw the video from the chain's distribution network. In February 2015, asked by a *Guardian* journalist about the fact that his video had often been derided, Eddie Murphy replied: "There's not a lot of people that have footage of themselves dancing around in the clouds with Michael Jackson. I do have that forever."[119] Paradoxically, the admirers of the King of Pop were particularly appreciative of this clip, which was the last example of the star's innocent energy before the terrible Chandler affair, which was to make him lose that unique spark that lit up his eyes.

For his part, Eddie Murphy pursued his brilliant career as an actor, director, and producer. We are indebted to him for *Trading Places*, *Shrek*, and *The Nutty Professor* movies (the second of which, *The Klumps,* he starred in with Janet Jackson).

> **FOR JACKSON ADDICTS**
>
> A sample of Jackson's *I Can't Help It* features on *Upton Joy*, one of many remixes of *Joy*.

BLACKstreet

JOY

Teddy Riley, Tammy Lucas, Michael Jackson / 4'38

From the album: *BLACKstreet* / **Released by Interscope Records:** USA, 21 June 1994 / UK, 9 July 1994 (ref. 92351) / **Chart position:** USA R&B No. 7, Pop No. 52 / UK No. 35 / **Single: Released by Interscope Records:** USA and UK 21 March 1995 (ref. 95769) / **Chart position:** USA Pop No. 43, R&B No. 12 / UK No. 56 / **Michael Jackson:** backing vocals / **Recording: Future Recording Studios, Virginia Beach, Virginia**

Teddy Riley and Michael Jackson planned only one love song on top of the seven up-tempo numbers already chosen for *Dangerous*: *Joy*. Using a musical idea of the young producer's as the base, the King of Pop composed a melody that fitted its jazzy, slightly sensual chords. The song's dreamy atmosphere was the ideal setting for lyrics worthy of a declaration of love. As the work sessions for *Dangerous* progressed, Teddy Riley submitted the music for *Joy* and *Remember the Time* to Tammy Lucas, daughter of the jazz and soul musician Ray Lucas, whom he had met at the Uptown Records label a few months earlier. He had taken her under his wing and included her in his pool of artists. As well as being an accomplished singer, the young woman had a talent for writing. She struggled to find lines she felt were strong enough to complement the nostalgic groove of *Remember the Time*. On the other hand, the tune of *Joy* inspired her, and her text paid homage to Michael Jackson, her childhood idol. She created a declaration of love that Michael could sing. Her timeless, angelic vision of happiness fitted marvelously with the music composed by Teddy Riley and the King of Pop. The star recorded and finished the song, but decided not to include it on *Dangerous*. The album was thus released without any positive breath of love sustained by hope, and retained its pessimistic vision of romantic relationships.

The members of the group BLACKstreet in Chicago in June 1994. From left: Chauncey Black, Teddy Riley, Dave Hollister, and Levi Little.

When Teddy Riley worked on the first album by his new group, BLACKstreet, he asked Michael Jackson whether he could use *Joy*. The singer agreed, and also authorized him to retain his backing vocals. However, because Michael Jackson's contract with Sony prevented him from appearing freely on other projects, his discreet participation was not mentioned in the credits. The lead role was given to Levi Little, who delivered a glittering performance in a falsetto that at certain moments called to mind the vocals of the King of Pop. Sadly, he was to stay with the group for only two years. When *Joy* was released as a single in March 1995, the clip changed the meaning of the song: the ballad had now become a fathers' declaration that Teddy Riley and his colleagues made to their daughters. Seen from this angle, *Joy* takes on a transgenerational dimension that Tammy Lucas had not been thinking about when she wrote the lyrics. However, it is clear that both approaches work and, without a doubt, make this song one of very few that tell of absolute love.

HISTORY

1. SCREAM
2. THEY DON'T CARE ABOUT US
3 STRANGER IN MOSCOW
4. THIS TIME AROUND
5. EARTH SONG
6. D.S.
7. MONEY
8. COME TOGETHER*
9. YOU ARE NOT ALONE
10. CHILDHOOD
11. TABLOID JUNKIE
12. 2BAD
13. HISTORY
14. LITTLE SUSIE
15. SMILE

*Song presented on page 344

HIStory: Past, Present & Future - Book I **ALBUM**

Released by Epic Records: USA (ref. 59000) and UK (ref. EPC 474709), 15 June 1995
Chart position: USA R&B No. 1, Pop No.1 / UK No. 1
RIAA: certified 5 times Multi-Platinum on 16 August 1995 / certified seven times Multiplatinum 12 October 1999

Filmed in August 1994 in Budapest, Hungary, the teaser *HIStory* promoted the album. It was first broadcast 22 May 1995 on MTV.

1995

HISTORY, THE KING'S FURY

Following the Chandler affair (see page 372), which shook his kingdom to the core, Michael Jackson somehow found the strength to bounce back and deliver a highly personal album. It was misunderstood by critics at the time of its release, and the tracks took on a completely different meaning after the star's death in 2009: *HIStory* as the journal of a king despised in his home country and revered by the rest of the world.

Several weeks after the Chandler affair finally concluded, Michael Jackson decided to head back to the studio. He had been frustrated by the premature end to the promotion of the *Dangerous* album and felt that an injustice had been done. He set out to repair the damage by doing what he did best, making music.

From early January 1994, with his longtime partners including Bruce Swedien and Matt Forger among others, he started working on some new songs in the Record One studio. But the King of Pop was traumatized by the earthquake that hit Los Angeles on 14 January. He needed peace and quiet to give free rein to his creativity. Two weeks later, he decided to fly to New York with his team.

HIStory was created within the walls of the prestigious Hit Factory studio. Michael took possession of the same premises that had inspired Paul Simon for his album *Graceland* in 1985 and Bruce Springsteen the previous year when he recorded the legendary *Born in the USA*. He was also aware that Stevie Wonder had created his iconic double album *Songs in the Key of Life*, in which each song tells the story of a different life experience, in the very same studio. Jackson was determined to record an album on which he could express his profound anger and deep sadness at being misunderstood, as he perceived it, as a man and as an artist. Being in the New York studio gave him renewed energy.

Sony Music had to grit their teeth when he announced that he wanted to hire the Hit Factory. The multinational company possessed its own studios in the Big Apple with all the latest state-of-the-art equipment. But Michael Jackson stood his ground and recorded most of his new songs in the studios that were steeped in history.

The initial concept behind *HIStory* was to market a best-of album with five additional original tracks. As with the *Decade* project, the idea was to celebrate Michael Jackson's career, while bringing in a few new numbers. Once again, the King of Pop created a much larger batch of songs than initially envisaged. In the first half of 1994, when it became obvious that the best-of album was turning into a new record, marketing meetings were held to refine the concept. Dan Beck, who was then senior product manager at Epic Records, suggested the title *HIStory*. The word referred to both his history and his version of the story. Michael Jackson liked the idea of a one-word title, as it was a natural follow-on to his previous album titles. The name *HIStory* was approved in June 1994, several months after Jackson had already planned the visuals for his new opus.

An album sleeve that made history

Jackson once again chose to work with David Coleman, artistic director of CBS and subsequently Sony Music, with whom

For the promotion of *HIStory*, the statue of Michael Jackson that appears on the album's sleeve is carried up the River Thames in London.

1995

he had collaborated on every album since he first signed at Epic with The Jacksons in 1975. During a trip to Russia, the singer had come across the statue of the *Motherland* in Volgograd. It had been erected back in the days of the USSR in homage to the fighters of Stalingrad (as Volgograd was formerly known). A woman representing the Motherland holds a raised sword aloft, threatening anyone who dares attack her children. Michael Jackson decided that he too wanted to be immortalized as a giant statue, as if symbolizing his status as King of Pop.

David Coleman was well aware of the star's tendency to constantly alter details in the drawings and illustrations that he commissioned for album covers. So to save time and money, he called on the services of Diana Walczak and Jeff Kleiser, two highly talented computer graphics experts who had started revolutionizing the way album covers were produced in the mid-1990s. Their portfolio already boasted the new Columbia Pictures logo. Walczak and Kleiser suggested creating a sculpture that would then be digitized point by point on an IT database. This digital version could then be altered and finalized with the material of Jackson's choice. Diana Walczak proposed versions in marble and gold. The first was chosen to illustrate the album, the second would be used on the video compilation *HIStory on Film* that went on sale in 1997.

This megalomaniac vision of himself that Michael Jackson unself-consciously embraced led to a promotional campaign the likes of which had never before been seen in the world of pop. The singer asked Sony's marketing services to display giant replicas of the album cover statue in the biggest cities in the world. On 15 June 1995, the album's release date, nine giant *HIStory* statues appeared in different countries. The media, of course, jumped at the opportunity to criticize the star's megalomania and egocentricity. In London, a steel-and-fiberglass sculpture was floated down the Thames. In France, the operation was canceled following the terrorist attacks on the Paris train network in July 1995.

A teaser for the album *HIStory*. Michael parades with an army equipped with dummy weapons, in a very Soviet-style setting and ambiance.

Teaser and controversy

The King of Pop appeared to be suffering from delusions of grandeur. Whereas the teaser for the *Dangerous* album had been an enigmatic 30-second commercial directed by David Lynch, the one for *HIStory* was a 3'57 mini film directed by Rupert Wainwright. To background music from the soundtrack to *Red October*, Michael Jackson appears as an emperor making a triumphant return home to be greeted by a crowd of adoring fans fully signed up to his cause, amid a strong military presence and workers busily preparing the festivities. Partly shot in Budapest and completed with cutting-edge special effects, this promotional film had an astronomical budget of $4 million. It provoked a media outcry when it was first broadcast on MTV on 22 May 1995. Some journalists saw in it similarities to the Nazi propaganda film *Triumph of the Will*, directed by Leni Riefenstahl in 1935, which chronicled the Nazi Party Congress in Nuremberg in 1934. The King of Pop denied any connection between the two in an interview with the journalist Diane Sawyer on ABC's *Primetime Live* on 15 June 1995. He said that his intention was just to fool around with the media and capture their attention by provoking them. The last semblance of any kind of relationship between the singer and the media crumbled, as it became abundantly clear that the mutual misunderstanding was now entrenched.

Best-of and new songs

This episode somewhat overshadowed what *HIStory* was really all about, namely the music. By working from New York, Michael Jackson had completely changed his usual modus operandi. He had previously worked with Teddy Riley to develop a new sound for *Dangerous*, but had decided not to involve him on the new songs. He was fascinated by the album *Rhythm Nation 1814* (1989) by his younger sister Janet Jackson, so he set up a meeting with the album's two producers, Jimmy Jam and Terry Lewis. The duo, both experienced creators of smash hits, joined the *HIStory* team in October 1994 and coproduced four tracks with the singer. Michael Jackson produced five tracks for the album himself, and called on the services and expertise of other partners such as Bill Bottrell and David Foster on four others. In an effort to keep up with the times, he asked the young Dallas Austin and the King of R&B, R. Kelly, to each create a track for him.

This resulted in an album that was more disjointed musically than previous ones, even though the artist sequenced all the different songs himself, like so many pearls on a string. The album expressed his fury with the media and his heartache due to his lost childhood, which had been sacrificed on the altar of celebrity. Although *HIStory* occasionally loses direction in disparate musical textures, it generally stays on course and

Michael Jackson performs *Earth Song* at the Brit Awards in London, 19 February 1996.

1995

achieves what no other album in Jackson's career had set out to do. It reveals his darkest feelings, his fears, his pain, and his disillusionment.

Pre-listening

In spring 1995, the album was finally ready. It was presented as a double CD and triple vinyl with 30 songs in two parts. The first part consisted of 15 of the star's greatest hits, chosen by different Sony Music offices around the world. The second part comprised 14 new songs and a cover version of The Beatles' *Come Together*, recorded during the *Bad* years.

Jim Morey and Sandy Gallin, the King of Pop's managers, organized a pre-listening session of the album in the Larrabee North studio in Los Angeles. Michael Jackson and Bruce Swedien, who was operating the tapes, were both there. Around 30 managers from Sony took their seats in the main room. After listening to the new album in its entirety, it is said they stood up and left without applauding or making a comment. It is believed that the artist had thought that this might happen but was nevertheless shocked by such indifference.

Public support had not waned

The album was released with great fanfare on 15 June 1995. Although the staff at Sony Music in the US perhaps no longer saw Michael Jackson as a priority, the singer could still count on the discreet unwavering support of Sony's founder, Akio Morita, who had become a staunch friend. Tommy Mottola, CEO of Sony Music, was forced to toe the line and finance the album's launch campaign, estimated at $30 million. *HIStory's* spectacular success from the outset reaffirmed its author's status as the King of Pop. In its first week, almost 400,000 copies of the album were sold in the US, and it hit the top of the charts in over 18 countries. In the United Kingdom, 100,000 copies flew off the shelves in the first two days. However, during the initial release period, American sales did not exceed four million copies. But worldwide, *HIStory* finally clocked up 15 million copies sold, making it the best-selling double album in history. The slow sales on American soil led Michael Jackson to rethink his communication strategy.

A media marathon

When the album was released, Michael Jackson followed his managers' advice and resumed the promotional campaign that had been initiated in 1993 to restore his image with the American public. Just as this media crusade had started bearing fruit with the *Dangerous* album returning to the top spots in the US charts, the Chandler affair shot it down in flames.

The King of Pop supported the release of *HIStory* with numerous appearances on popular TV shows. Festivities kicked off on 22 June 1995 at the VH-1 Awards, a week after the album was released. Morgan Freeman presented Michael Jackson with a special award for his humanitarian work. Boyz II Men, who sing a few lines of the song *HIStory* on the album version, performed *Heal the World* and *We Are the World* onstage at the Shrine Auditorium in Los Angeles, where the awards ceremony was held. In the middle of their performance, the King of Pop put in a surprise appearance and finished singing the anthem *USA for Africa* with them.

On 17 August, the singer participated in one of his first-ever live online chats with his fans via AOL, CompuServe, and Prodigy. But the pièce de résistance was saved for MTV. The legendary music channel held its famous Video Music Awards in New York on 7 September. Michael Jackson was nominated seven times for *Scream*, and walked away with three trophies. For the occasion, he and his dancers, led by LaVelle Smith, choreographed a 15-minute-long number comprising a series of short excerpts from his greatest hits. It was performed at the opening ceremony and was promptly criticized by the media

At the MTV Video Music Awards ceremony, on 7 September 1995, Michael Jackson performed a medley that lasted at least 15 minutes.

for being too attention-grabbing and giving the singer too big a platform. But in retrospect the performance has become a role model for artists who have followed in the star's footsteps. Beyoncé, Chris Brown, Britney Spears, and Justin Timberlake are some of the many artists who have adopted the same concept of increasingly sophisticated choreography and stage sets to accompany their songs.

On 23 September 1995, the King of Pop continued his media crusade on BET (Black Entertainment Television), which was then celebrating its 15th anniversary. He became the first artist to be inducted into the BET Walk of Fame. He performed his latest single, *You Are Not Alone*, which was riding high on the American Top 40.

Following this series of public appearances in the US, Michael Jackson flew to Germany. His friend and promoter, Marcel Avram, had negotiated a TV appearance for him on *Wetten, Dass… ?*, the primetime show on the ZDF channel. The King of Pop appeared on this popular TV show to present his new single, *Earth Song*, which ended up selling one million copies in Germany and another million in the United Kingdom. He performed the song, with a stage show reminiscent of others that he had previously used on his tours. He also performed a medley of the song *Dangerous*, that he would continue polishing and perfecting onstage up right until the early 2000s.

Back in the US after the trip to Germany, the singer began preparing for a TV show on HBO. The channel had previously

Prince Albert of Monaco presents an award to Michael Jackson at the World Music Awards, 8 May 1996.

negotiated broadcasting rights for the 1992 *Dangerous* tour. This time around it commissioned an original show called *Michael Jackson: One Night Only*. The intimate concert event was due to take place at the Beacon Theater in New York, in front of a carefully chosen audience. The recordings of the two shows planned for 8 and 9 December 1995 would be used as the basis for a final edit that was due to be aired by HBO and re-broadcast on foreign TV channels. A series of numbers were written, the star's usual stage decor was partially redesigned, and rehearsals began. The mime artist Marcel Marceau was invited to accompany the singer in a pared-down and poetic version of *Childhood*. But on 6 December, after rehearsing the song *Black or White*, the King of Pop collapsed on stage and lost consciousness. He was rushed to the Beth Israel Medical Center. The doctors diagnosed gastroenteritis and severe dehydration. The concert was cancelled. The same evening, he was due to receive a special award at the *Billboard* Awards ceremony. Tina Turner stood in for him at the last minute. Several days after the incident, Michael flew to Disneyland Paris where he decided to spend Christmas.

After a short convalescence, the King of Pop resumed his promotional activities in Europe. Following the cancellation of the HBO show and the scant promotion of the single *Earth Song* in the United States, he realized that the continued sales of *HIStory* were more likely to be outside the States than within it. On 19 February 1996, he attended the Brit Awards to receive several honors, including Artist of a Generation, presented to him by Bob Geldof.

The King of Pop's media marathon finally ended at the World Music Awards in Monaco on 8 May 1996, where he received five awards. On this occasion, he delivered a tamer version of *Earth Song*. He was also reunited with his professional godmother, Diana Ross, who was there to receive a Legend Award for career achievements.

Reluctant to tour

After this tour of European cities, Michael Jackson's image was well and truly imprinted on people's minds in Europe, but it had much less impact on sales than a concert tour would have had. The King of Pop had no interest at all in spending months on the road doing a world tour, and made every effort to delay or even cancel the *HIStory* tour. But Sony Music was determined to continue selling the artist's double album to recoup its huge initial outlay of $30 million for the launch budget. In the mid-1990s, although the CD market was doing rather well, a project like *HIStory* could only be profitable if it included a world tour.

Kenny Ortega and others who had previously worked with Michael Jackson on the *Dangerous* tour got together at San Bernardino in California in summer 1996 to rehearse for the show. Jonathan Moffet, who had not played in the *Bad* and *Dangerous* tours, made his big comeback as drummer, a key position that Michael considered highly important.

As a warm-up for the main tour, Michael Jackson and his troops gave a concert in Brunei on 16 July 1996 for the Sultan's 50th birthday. He played to an audience of 60,000 invited guests at the Jerudong Amusement Park. The fee for this royal show remains a secret. This was arguably Jackson's best concert of the 1990s. The staging and choreography was similar to the *Dangerous* tour, with additional songs from *HIStory*, such as *You Are Not Alone* and *Earth Song*, as well as the legendary jazz version of *The Way You Make Me Feel*, which he had only ever performed once, at the Grammy Awards in 1988. Pirate copies of the concert recording, which eventually appeared on the market, show the singer looking radiant and delighted to be performing.

When the *HIStory* tour started for real on 7 September 1996 in Prague, the Czech Republic, the atmosphere was quite different. The show was impressive for its precision and

Michael Jackson in concert at Jerudong Park, Brunei, 16 July 1996.

meticulous attention to detail. It was a rock and pop extravaganza, in which the songs were interspersed with videos depicting the singer's universe. The King of Pop gave his all when it came to the dancing, but 90 percent of the time he simply mimed the singing. Despite this somewhat low-octane performance in comparison to his greatest tours, the *HIStory* tour was headline news everywhere it went. In Eastern Europe, Asia, and Australia, the artists met his fans, many of whom were seeing him on stage for the first time. On 7 October 1996, he gave a concert in Tunis, donating the profits to local charities. On 31 December, he returned to Brunei for a special New Year's Eve concert. The sales of *HIStory* were doing well almost everywhere except the US, where promotion of the album had been put on the back burner since late 1995. Michael Jackson was not one to bear grudges and agreed to honor two concert dates on American soil that ended the first half of the *HIStory* tour. On 3 and 4 January 1997, he played to full houses at the Aloha Stadium in Hawaii. The 70,000 tickets sold out in less than a day. However, this limited comeback was not enough to relaunch his career in his home country.

Loss of control

Forced to continue the tour and often ignored when it came to decisions about the promotion of his album and the choice of singles, Michael Jackson gradually lost control of certain aspects of his career. The 1990s was a time of aggressive sales strategies by record labels aimed at short-term profitability. In the US, the King of Pop was counted among the stars who had peaked in the 1980s, having already enjoyed huge popularity in previous years. Although Walter Yetnikoff, former CEO of CBS, would put his foot down on occasions, he usually ended up going along with the artist's wishes. But Sony Music was now run by Tommy Mottola. A native of the Bronx, appointed by Yetnikoff in the late 1980s to manage the American division of CBS, Mottola became Chairman CEO of the company when it changed its name to Sony Music in 1991. Under his

Michael Jackson and Lisa Marie Presley backstage at the TV show *Jackson Family Honors* at the MGM Grand Hotel, Las Vegas (19 February 1994).

management, spectacular successes alternated with scandals. He was responsible for spotting such talents as Shakira and Destiny's Child, but was also involved in disputes with some of the label's headline artists such as George Michael and Terence Trent D'Arby as well as his own wife, Mariah Carey.

During the 1990s, the relationship between Tommy Mottola and Michael Jackson deteriorated. The two men struggled to find common ground when it came to producing and marketing music. As the tension between them grew, their relationship nevertheless remained cordial, mostly thanks to Sony's founder Akio Morita, who protected Jackson and guaranteed him a certain peace of mind. But when Morita died of pneumonia on 3 October 1999, there was no longer anyone between Michael Jackson and the Sony Music chief. The rules of the game were shortly to change.

The wedding of the century

On 19 February 1994, Michael Jackson made his first public appearance after the Chandler affair, when he agreed to participate in a live performance organized by his family, The Jackson Family Honors. The ceremony was held at the MGM Grand in Las Vegas. It was a tribute to Berry Gordy and Elizabeth Taylor, with performances by Celine Dion, Smokey Robinson, and a few members of the Jackson family.

The King of Pop attended with a very special guest on his arm: Lisa Marie Presley. They had been dating for several months but their presence at the event did not arouse any particular suspicion among the attending press.

However, news that they were a couple broke several months later, in early summer 1994. The press ran various stories claiming that the star had married the daughter of the King, Elvis Presley. The rumors spread over the next few weeks, and their marriage was finally made public on 1 August. Michael Jackson and Lisa Marie Presley had wed on 26 May 1994 in the Dominican Republic.

The two lovers had rarely been seen together. The tabloids published endless stories about this unlikely pairing, although given their respective past histories it seems quite natural that they should end up together. Their very unusual status would have made it hard for either of them to find a partner capable of understanding their very particular lifestyles, and without an ulterior motive. The Presley–Jackson pairing, somewhere between a marriage of convenience and a royal alliance, captured the popular imagination.

Michael Jackson flanked by Mickey Schulhof (to his right) and Tommy Mottola (to his left) at the signing of the Sony/ATV contract in 1995.

In December 1995, Michael Jackson agreed to sign over half the rights to his ATV catalog, including The Beatles' songs, to Sony for $100 million. In return, he became a 50 percent shareholder in the tracks owned by Sony. This merger led to the creation of Sony/ATV, which has since become the world's leading music publishing catalog. This decision strengthened Jackson's connections with the music giant. It also left him sitting on a goldmine that never stopped growing. In 2002, Sony/ATV acquired the Acuff-Rose catalog that included many country standards. In 2007, it purchased the catalog of composers Jerry Lieber and Mike Stoller, who wrote the legendary *Hound Dog* for Elvis Presley. But the true masterstroke that made Sony/ATV market leader came in 2012, when the company spent $2.2 billion on the acquisition of EMI Music Publishing. Michael Jackson played an active role in the group's expansion. World sales of his own records and earnings from his tours continued to generate income, and the investment in Sony/ATV allowed him to leave his assets untouched. But many were keen to get their hands on Jackson's 50 percent stake. Until his dying day, Michael Jackson fought to keep hold of his shares in this catalog that symbolized an alliance between an artist's business acumen and the cold, efficient strategy of a multinational company bent on surviving the record industry crisis. While the merger gave rise to an increasingly prosperous financial empire, it also caused endless personal and professional headaches for Michael Jackson.

In early August 1994, Lisa Marie accompanied Michael Jackson to Budapest to film the teaser for the *HIStory* album. On 12 September, they opened the MTV Video Music Awards ceremony where they were seen kissing in front of the cameras for the first time. When the album was released in stores, the keenest observers noticed that Michael referred to his new family in *They Don't Care about Us*. "I have a wife and two children who love me," he sings in reference to his new wife, who had a son and daughter from her previous marriage to Danny Keough.

The release of *HIStory* put Michael back in the spotlight. Once again absorbed in his work and delighted to rediscover his public, he resumed his life as an artist. It is hard to know what the relationship between husband and wife was really like. But on 19 January 1996, news of their divorce was made public. Their spokespeople cited irreconcilable differences. The couple went their own ways, but they were seen together again in South Africa where the King of Pop was ending his *HIStory Tour* on 15 October 1997. However their relationship went no further, as in the meantime the singer had made plans to start a family with his nurse and long-standing friend, Debbie Rowe.

PORTRAIT

JIMMY JAM AND TERRY LEWIS
THE MAGICIANS OF MINNEAPOLIS

Minneapolis is, of course, known as Prince's hometown, but it was also the starting point for two other record industry heavyweights. Jimmy Jam and Terry Lewis were the golden duo who accompanied funk music as it metamorphosed during the 1980s.

The Time

The two men first struck up a friendship while attending a TRIO Upward Bound program at the University of Minneapolis. Their shared passion for music led to the creation of the group Flyte Tyme, which became The Time in 1981 when singer Morris Day and then guitarist Jesse Johnson joined the band. The four men developed their own original and distinctive funk sound, which also acknowledged Minneapolis' rock heritage. On stage in their simple stylish outfits, consisting of suits and long coats, they looked like movie gangsters.

In 1981, The Time were the opening act for Prince, who also surreptitiously produced their first records under the pseudonym Jamie Starr. In 1982 Jam and Lewis's destinies suddenly changed. Diana R. Andrews, who was then working for the Solar label, took them under her wing. As their manager she opened the door to many fruitful projects. The pair produced songs for various artists including the S.O.S. Band, who enjoyed well-deserved commercial success with the track *Do It*. The manager looked after her protégés well, introducing them to the biggest producers and artistic directors in the country, including John McClain, a long-standing friend of the Jackson family.

Control

In 1985, John McClain became the manager of the youngest member of the Jackson family, Janet, in an attempt to give her career a new lease of life. Up until then, the young singer had been handled by her father, who had been content to have her record uninspiring funk albums entirely lacking in ambition. She had managed to diversify into acting on a few TV series such as *Fame*, but her songs were a long way off the top *Billboard* spots. That was until Jam and Lewis started working with her on her next solo album. It was called *Control* and was released on 4 February 1986. It made Michael Jackson's spine tingle as he listened to it on repeat, vowing to do better on his next album. With just nine songs and seven singles, Janet made a name for herself as a singer in her own right and sold more than ten million copies. It was an achievement to rival Madonna, who on many occasions was inspired by Janet's stage setup.

The hitmakers

The global success of *Control* put an unexpected rocket under Jam and Lewis's career. From then on, an ever-growing list of artists sought to work with them. They created an urbane and modern sound that openly admitted using drum machines such as the legendary Roland TR-808, and synthesizers such as the Yamaha DX7.

In 1988, they helped the group New Edition to polish the sound on their album *N.E. Heartbreak*, as well as giving them a mature ballad that Boyz II Men would cover in the 1990s: *Can You Stand the Rain*. It featured new sounds and textures that the duo would recycle and develop on their second album with Janet Jackson: *Rhythm Nation 1814*. Consisting of 20 tracks (11 songs and nine interludes), it is a plea for equality and education. The young woman's sudden social awareness raised a wry smile among certain critics who felt that her lifestyle was somewhat removed from reality, but the album appealed to the public, who gave her standing ovations during her first world tour. Michael Jackson fell in love with the record and it numbered among his influences when he was working on *Dangerous*.

From Janet to Michael

By the early 1990s, the two men's reputations were firmly established. As early advocates of swingbeat with L A Reid and Babyface, Jam and Lewis could legitimately claim to have paved the way for Teddy Riley, the inventor of new jack swing, the genre that rescued funk from the doldrums (see page 374).

After fleetingly re-forming the group The Time to record the album *Pandemonium* in 1990, they resumed their work as

The two producers Jimmy Jam and Terry Lewis first took Janet, the youngest of the Jackson siblings, under their wing before working with Michael on the album *HIStory*.

producers. In 1993, the album *Janet* continued on from the work with their protégé that they had started with *Control* in 1986, while placing greater emphasis on the young singer's femininity.

Michael Jackson contemplated working with Jam and Lewis on the *Dangerous* album, but in the end, it was with Teddy Riley with whom he found the magic formula that would make his songs popular both on the streets and on major radio stations. In October 1994, with the recording sessions for *HIStory* already underway in New York, the King of Pop asked the duo to suggest some tracks. He had not forgotten the musical fury and intensity of *Rhythm Nation 1814* and he was looking for some bold and sleek productions in which to wrap his vindictive lyrics. As well as *Scream*, which he recorded with his younger sister, the two men helped him develop *Tabloid Junkie*, *2Bad*, and *HIStory*. The Jam and Lewis sound certainly left its mark on the productions of the creator of *Billie Jean*, but never quite generated the kind of timeless song that would remain engraved forever in people's minds. The producers' musical adventure with the King of Pop ended with the development of *Is It Scary*, one of the tracks in the short film *Ghosts*. The overall outcome of this short but intense collaboration was positive but it failed to match the impact of productions by Quincy Jones, Bill Bottrell, and Teddy Riley. Jimmy Jam and Terry Lewis are both extremely gifted men who can turn their hand to anything while remaining attentive to an artist's needs. They unwaveringly supported and helped Michael Jackson at a time when his empire was looking decidedly unsteady and he was struggling to find new inspiration.

Scream

Jimmy Jam, Terry Lewis, Michael Jackson, Janet Jackson / 4'37

Musicians
Michael Jackson: lead vocals, backing vocals, percussion
Janet Jackson: lead and backing vocals
Jimmy Jam, Terry Lewis: percussion and keyboard
Recording
Hit Factory, New York: Michael Jackson's vocals
Flyte Tyme Studios, Edina, Minnesota: Janet Jackson's and Michael Jackson's vocals:
October 1994 to December 1994
Technical team
Producers: Jimmy Jam, Terry Lewis, Michael Jackson, and Janet Jackson
Recording engineers: Bruce Swedien and Steve Hodge
Arrangements: Jimmy Jam, Terry Lewis, Michael Jackson, and Janet Jackson
Mixing: Bruce Swedien and Steve Hodge

1995

Single

USA
A-side: *Scream (clean album version)* / 4'37
B-side: *Childhood* (theme tune from *Free Willy 2; album version*) / 4'27
UK
A-side: *Scream (single edit)* / 4'01
B-side: *Childhood* (theme tune from *Free Willy 2; album version*) / 4'27
Released by Epic Records: USA (ref. 34 78000) and Europe (ref. 662022), 31 May 1995
Chart position: USA Pop No. 5, R&B No. 2 / UK No. 3
RIAA: certified Platinum 31 July 1995

THE SONG

Genesis

HIStory opens with a howl of exasperation. The singer is incensed by all the terrible things published about him on a daily basis in the world's press. *Scream* begins with a mass of electronic and rocket engine sounds that seem to propel the singer far from the stupid and preposterous scandals doing his tour of the globe. Up in space, he yells out, expressing the full force of his fury, hoping that from up high it will be heard by the whole world. The unequivocal warning in *Leave Me Alone* had not sufficed to calm the deluge of unfounded nonsense about him. So he deliberately adopts a harsher, more offensive, and vulgar tone. Michael Jackson is looking to settle a few scores. The tabloids' efforts to portray him as a monster had been so effective that they led to the kind of accusations that could annihilate a man. In 1993, a gullible public was not in the least surprised when the Chandler affair hit the headlines, and worse still, took great pleasure in reading the stream of salacious stories that appeared in print. The singer's life was destroyed, and his anger could not be contained. The *HIStory* album was his only possible outlet, and it was both necessary and frank. *Scream* was the first well-placed punch and the first single released from the album.

The track revived the tradition of presenting a duet as the first single, and signaled Michael Jackson's return to the music scene. For the only time in his career, the singer chose to do a duet with a member of his family. And the person he picked was his youngest sister Janet. Since the mid-1980s, Janet had notched up an impressive list of chart hits and awards, carving a place for herself in American and global pop culture with *Control* (1986), *Rhythm Nation 1814* (1989), and *Janet* (1993). The youngest of the Jackson siblings, considered the other prodigy of the family, became one of the biggest female stars of her era. She appealed to American youth in search of an identity at a time when her brother had abandoned the States, touring the rest of the world and achieving chart success in Europe.

Janet asked her two favorite producers, Jimmy Jam and Terry Lewis, to compose several tunes to present to her brother. Neither man was entirely comfortable with this request from their muse, as they were both aware of the potential con-

The duet was historic. For the very first time, Michael teamed up with his little sister to work together at the top echelon of pop music.

flict of interest between two such talented singers working together. Janet herself was completely fine with it. She played her trump card: the King of Pop himself wanted Jam and Lewis to be in charge of the track.

In the warm spring of 1995, the announcement that the pair were to sing a duet came like a bombshell. The world's music press went crazy, portraying it as a championship match between the two Jackson styles to see who was the best entertainer. Hopes for that outcome were rapidly dashed when the theme of the song was revealed.

In June 2016, many years after the media frenzy had died down, the journalist Mike Smallcombe asked Jimmy Jam how the song had come about. Jam replied:

Michael didn't really give us any direction. He just said, "Come with a bunch of tracks and I'll listen to what you come up with." So over a period of three or four days we began creating about five different tracks at our studio in Minneapolis. We had Janet come over because we wanted her here for inspiration; we felt it was important for the tracks to have a Janet vibe. So Janet listened to the tracks and, for one of them, she said, "This is the one he will like." So Terry and I were like, "How do you know?" And she just said, "I know my brother!" And then after listening to another one of the tracks, she said, "I hope he doesn't like this one, because I want it!"[120]

The track she was referring to became *Runaway*, the standout song on her compilation *Design of a Decade: 1986–1996*. Janet and her producers traveled to the Hit Factory in New

FOR JACKSON ADDICTS

With the remix business at its height, a multitude of reworked versions were produced on different media by Dave "Jam" Hall, Naughty by Nature, and David Morales: from R&B to dance music, there was something for everyone in nightclubs. Fans can have fun tracking down all the profitable remixes and versions produced by the major labels that are scattered across the United States, Japan, Europe, and Australia. Like Teddy Riley, who polished his musical choices on the maxi-single versions of *Jam* and *Remember the Time*, Jimmy Jam and Terry Lewis produced *Scream Louder (Flyte Tyme remix)*, which samples *Thank You (For Letting Me Be Myself Again)* by Sly and The Family Stone.

When performing concerts on the *HIStory Tour,* Michael removed his space armor before singing *Scream.*

York to play their creations to Michael Jackson. He listened carefully to each of their proposals before choosing the track that Janet had said he would like.

The following day, the King of Pop started working on the melody and rhythm for the duet, in a low key that was more suited to his voice than to Janet's, according to Jimmy Jam. Janet had resigned herself to a mere guest appearance on her brother's album, but she had not counted on the talent and devotion of the two Minneapolis producers. As they were the ones ultimately responsible for the track, they worked hard to ensure that the final result achieved perfect harmony between the vocals and charismatic personalities of each singer. Any sign of rivalry on Michael's part was entirely unintentional and simply the result of his utter absorption in his own way of doing things.

The King of Pop rapidly wrote lyrics for the song. The tone was aggressive and scathing and for the first time in his career he used the f-word: "Stop f**kin' with me." This was not enough to require the album to carry the famous Parental Advisory logo, although some singles released in America still bore the following warning: "This recording contains language that may be offensive to some listeners."

The general tone of *Scream* is hard-hitting but interspersed with melodious choruses: "Tired of injustice / Tired of the schemes / Your lies are disgusting / What does it mean?" In the end, Jimmy Jam and Terry Lewis' composition surfs a musical wave of resonances tailor-made for Janet Jackson's vocal range.

Production

Jimmy Jam, Terry Lewis, and Janet Jackson were all in the Hit Factory studio in New York when the King of Pop recorded his vocals. Jimmy Jam recalls:

> He definitely had things to get off his chest and that's what it was about. Recording the song was probably one of the most mind-blowing experiences ever. He walked into the studio, very nice and very kind: "OK, I'm going to try my part now." So Michael goes in and the moment the music starts, he turns into the Tasmanian devil. He's a whole different person, stomping, clapping, he's got jewelry jinglin'—all the stuff you're not supposed to do in the studio. Me and Terry are sitting there going "Oh my God!" [Teddy Lewis adds, "Screaming like fans."] He totally nails the song start to finish. Janet leans in and goes, "I'll do my vocal in Minneapolis." She wanted no part of following that. I don't blame her. So we do Janet's vocal, we send it to him. "Oh, Janet sounds really good. Where did you record her?" Minneapolis. "Oh, I want to come to Minneapolis and do my vocal." What you got was this sibling rivalry between brother and sister who are also competitive.[121]

The track was then mixed partly by Michael Jackson's longtime recording engineer Bruce Swedien and partly by Steve Hodge, who was used to working with Janet Jackson.

Michael is calm before exploding into song in *Scream*. In the short film the two protagonists move through different compartments of their spaceship, used for sport, dancing, games, meditation, and so on.

Mike Smallcombe's interview with Jimmy Jam included an amusing anecdote about an incident that allegedly occurred at a party in Neverland (we only have the producer's word for this). Janet asked Jimmy Jam if the version of *Scream* that she had just heard, in which she felt her vocals had been toned down, had been included in the final master tape for the album. The producer went and asked Michael Jackson, who pretended not to understand what he was talking about. Janet's teams then requested the immediate return of the mix in order to tweak her vocals and add a few handclaps. Whatever the truth of the matter, the result is convincing. The duet is both tender and moving, and marks a milestone in the careers of both singers. *Scream* alternates harshness and melodious moments, heightened by programming effects and heavy synthesizers, setting the pace for the rest of the *HIStory* album, which would appeal to a broad public.

The launch of the album took the unusual form of a double single containing the tracks *Scream* and *Childhood*. The song blazed its way into the Hot 100, immediately climbing to No. 5, although failing to make No. 1. The clean album and single edit singles were both censored versions that lacked all the shock value. The second single edit version and the remixes managed to shake off the "what-will-people-say" attitude about the offensive language for the first time in one of Michael's songs.

Michael Jackson is radiant on the set of *Scream*, before launching into a dancing battle with his sister Janet.

In order to conceal the finger gesture unsuitable for public consumption, various edits hide or blur Janet Jackson's defiant flipping the bird to camera. With regard to lyrics, words that should not really be heard are sometimes censored by a horrendous jarring noise. For a long time, the star's official Vevo account omitted these details and broadcast the only uncensored version of the video.

FOR JACKSON ADDICTS

In 2005, a DVD in the *Director's Series (Volume 4)* collection, *The Work of Director Mark Romanek*, included a director's cut of *Scream* with two very short extra shots that even most informed fans would find hard to spot (ref. Palm Pictures DIRDVD4).

1995

THE SHORT FILM

Director: Mark Romanek
Producer: Ceán Chaffin
Leading actors: Michael Jackson and Janet Jackson
Shoot date: 17 May 1995
Shooting location: Universal Studios, Los Angeles
Duration: 4'47

Genesis

The short film transports Michael and Janet into outer space. Both are fleeing media pressure on Earth, but remain connected with their culture through a selection of artworks onboard their spacecraft, including paintings, sculptures, video games, and Japanese animated films. In space, they are free to enjoy their favorite hobbies in the gym and the virtual gallery. They even rediscover a certain peace of mind in a special meditation zone. The decor is futuristic and bathed in dazzling and cosmically cold light.

Production

Seven stages were erected in hangar number 24 at Universal Studios for the various sets that were used to shoot the video. The interstellar expedition was directed by the renowned director Mark Romanek, who relies here on his precise and sophisticated photographic techniques. He had previously directed *Free Your Mind* by the group En Vogue and *Are You Gonna Go My Way* by Lenny Kravitz, and would later go on to direct Janet Jackson's *Got 'til It's Gone*. *Scream* is generally considered the most expensive short film in the history of music videos. MTV gives the official expenditure for this galactic escapade as $7 million. The director was a fan of the singer of *Thriller* and very nervous about meeting his idol. He recalls his conversations with Michael Jackson on set, "I remember getting to chat with Michael between takes of shooting *Scream*.... He just seemed like a cool, easy-to-talk-to guy. He really focused his attention on you, which is something that very charming people do. We talked about our favorite movies. I was impressed with his knowledge of foreign cinema. When it came time to perform for the cameras, the transformation from this relatively regular guy to some sort of divinely possessed super-being was really astounding, metaphysical—hard to fully comprehend. The chance to experience the phenomenon of his gift from only a few feet away gave me chills. It was the treat of a lifetime."[122]

Michael and Janet Jackson arrived on set with their respective choreographers, Travis Payne and LaVelle Smith for the King of Pop, and Sean Cheesman and Tina Landon for his sister. Each artist carefully observed the other, performing precisely choreographed pieces aimed at creating exactly the kind of high-quality video that everyone would expect from two artists at the top of their game. The world impatiently awaited the result.

Scream was released, and the awards piled up: Mark Romanek received the Grammy Award 1996 for best music video (short form), and the short film won three MTV Video Music Awards for best dance video, best choreography, and best art direction. Not to mention the *Billboard* Music Video Award 1996.

They Don't Care about Us

Michael Jackson / 4'44

Musicians
Michael Jackson: lead vocals, backing vocals, percussion, keyboards, and synthesizers
Los Angeles Children's Choir: backing vocals
Trevor Rabin: guitar
Slash: additional guitar
Brad Buxer: percussion, keyboards, and synthesizers
Chuck Wild, Jeff Bova, Jason Miles: keyboards and synthesizers
Recording
Hit Factory, New York: 1990, 1994, 1995 (rerecording to remove the controversial lyrics)
Technical team
Producer: Michael Jackson
Recording engineer: Bruce Swedien
Assistant recording engineers: Eddie De Lena, Matt Forger, and Rob Hoffman
Synthesizer programming: Brad Buxer, Chuck Wild, and Michael Jackson
Choral arrangements: Annette Sander
Vocals, rhythm, and string arrangements: Michael Jackson
Mixing: Bruce Swedien and Eddie De Lena

Single

UK
A-side: *They Don't Care about Us (single version)* / 4'43
B-side: *They Don't Care about Us (Love to Infinity's Walk in the Park radio mix)* / 4'46
Released by Epic Records: UK, 18 March 1996 (ref. EPC 662950)
USA
A-side: *They Don't Care about Us (single version)* / 4'43
B-side: Rock with You (*Frankie Knuckles radio mix*) / 3'47
Released by Epic Records: USA, May 1996 (ref. 34 78264)
Chart position : USA R&B No. 10, Pop No. 30 / UK No. 4

THE SONG

Genesis

Michael Jackson composed *They Don't Care about Us* while he was preparing *Dangerous*. He did something that was rare for him at the time, namely writing lyrics that unequivocally expressed his outrage and indignation. His words were matched with a terse tribal rhythm that he developed with Matt Forger. Whether consciously or not, the King of Pop appeared to draw inspiration from a John Lennon song, *Give Peace a Chance*. To a rudimentary rhythm, the ex-Beatles singer enumerated the world's evils in the verses, and followed up with a cathartic response in the chorus: "All we are saying is give peace a chance." This anthem of hope is taken and turned on its head in *They Don't Care about Us*. Where Lennon evokes peace, Jackson expresses resignation and the cold facts of the era in which he lives: "All I wanna say is that / They don't really care about us."

Production

When the team started recording *They Don't Care about Us* in the Hit Factory studios in New York, Michael Jackson and Matt Forger went back to the drafts written in the early 1990s. The rhythmic structure was totally reworked. The singer, assisted by Brad Buxer, fed sounds one by one into the terse hard-hitting rhythm of the song. Stripped of any bass line, *They Don't Care about Us* stands out in particular for its guitar scores that alternate between suppressed violence and high-wattage explosions. Trevor Rabin and Slash divide up the guitar parts between them, bringing heavy rock sounds to the track. Brad Buxer controls the synthesized layers that rise to a crescendo throughout the song before harmonizing with the extended backing vocals in the chorus.

Then Chuck Wild adds the icing to the cake with sounds from a sound library built for the King of Pop by Andrew Scheps. He packs the song with sound effects that disguise certain words considered too vulgar, or give a bit more punch to the rhythm track at the end of certain bars. Wild's grasp of detail reinforces the musical identity and expands the spectrum of the song. The pared-down final product is the result of a great deal of work. The singer did numerous takes with his musicians, ending up with around a hundred workable tracks.

Michael Jackson and the director Spike Lee on the set of the "prison" version of the short film *They Don't Care about Us*.

He and Eddie De Lena selected the best ones, and passed them on to Bruce Swedien for the final mix.

Controversial lyrics

When the *HIStory* album was released on 15 June 1995, *They Don't Care about Us* created uproar. In the lyrics, Michael Jackson uses the terms "Jew me" and "kike me" to condemn religious, racial and other discrimination. Some accused Jackson of anti-Semitism. The matter blew up to such an extent that the singer was forced to issue an explanation. In a comment inserted into subsequent pressings of *HIStory*, he apologized and assured people that his lyrics were intended to condemn rather than incite racism. He then rerecorded the song, replacing the incriminating expressions with "do me" and "hike me", respectively. A similar written message advocating respect for others appears at the start of the prison version short film. This affair had unfortunate consequences for the album's promotion, which had significantly slowed since the cancellation of the planned HBO channel concerts in New York. The movie director Stephen Spielberg added his voice to those who suspected the singer of anti-Semitism. The two men were briefly reconciled in front of the cameras during the filming of the longer music video *Ghosts* in 1996, but their relationship remained strained.

FOR LISTENERS

On subsequent pressings of the *HIStory* album, Michael Jackson hid the controversial lyrics behind loud electronic sounds. This self-censorship stands out like a sore thumb compared to the rest of the production, which is measured down to the last decibel.

Michael Jackson on the roof in the favelas of Rio de Janeiro, for the Brazil version of *They Don't Care about Us.*

FOR JACKSON ADDICTS

The group of percussionists that accompanied Michael Jackson in the streets of Rio de Janeiro are called Olodum. A Brazilian promotional CD (PRCD 96720) contains the long version of *They Don't Care about Us* (7'07) used in the short film in which Olodum appears, as well as a shorter version (4'42).

1995

THE SHORT FILM

Brazilian version
Director: Spike Lee
Producer: Butch Robinson
Leading actor: Michael Jackson
Shoot date: February 1996
Shooting location: Rio de Janeiro
Duration: 7'17

Prison version
Director: Spike Lee
Producer: Butch Robinson
Leading actor: Michael Jackson
Shoot date: March 1996
Shooting location: New York
Duration: 4'54

Genesis

When *HIStory* came out in stores, the movie director Spike Lee fell in love with the song *Stranger in Moscow*, and was very keen to direct the short film. In September 1995, Michael Jackson was in New York and set up a meeting with the movie director at Lee's home in Brooklyn. The King of Pop wanted him to direct one of his upcoming videos. Spike Lee told Jackson that he would love to do *Stranger in Moscow*, but the star initially offered *They Don't Care about Us*.

The man who had directed *Malcolm X* suggested shooting the film in Brazil among the residents of the favelas in Rio de Janeiro. The star was enthusiastic about the idea, but was not wholly satisfied with the final version that came out in March 1996. This motivated him to produce a second short film in a prison reconstructed in a New York studio.

Production

When they landed in Rio de Janeiro, Spike Lee and Michael Jackson had not the slightest inkling of the sheer number of obstacles that they would encounter. The singer wanted to make the short film indisputably authentic, and insisted that the extras were actual residents of the favelas. The Brazilian media got wind of the story. At the time, they were keen to promote a clean image of the city to increase the prospects of selection to host the 2004 Olympic Games. By claiming that the King of Pop would have to bribe gangs to gain entry into the favelas, they hoped to prevent the filming that would shine a spotlight into the city's poorest neighborhoods. It was a wasted effort. The American singer and his team were welcomed into the favelas by delighted residents.

The MTV teams produced a mini "making-of" documentary that was broadcast on MTV. The short film uses the original album version of the song that contains the controversial, allegedly anti-Semitic lyrics (see page 456). Jewish associations that had already spoken out the previous year once again expressed their displeasure. This particular controversy did little to help matters between Michael Jackson and the US media, which decided to boycott the song and the accompanying short film.

Back from Brazil, the singer and the director reconvened on a film set in New York to shoot the second version of *They Don't Care about Us*. This time around, Spike Lee's militant vision, with the artist's full support, spawned a video in which the action takes place in a prison. From behind the bars of a prison cell, the King of Pop voices his outrage through song. As he and his fellow prisoners are eating their meal together, they rise up against injustice, with the singer leading the revolt. Michael Jackson reuses the concept from *Man in the Mirror* to speak out against injustice through the medium of images. But the archive montage used was so violent that MTV and other channels decided not to broadcast the short film.

ODUM

Stranger in Moscow

Michael Jackson and Brad Buxer (not credited) / 5'44

Musicians
Michael Jackson: lead and backing vocals, beatbox, and percussion
Steve Lukather: guitar
Brad Buxer: guitar, keyboards, synthesizers, percussion, and strings
David Paich, Steve Porcaro: keyboards and synthesizers
Andrew Scheps: Synclavier
Recording
Sony Music Studios and Hit Factory, New York: January 1994
Technical team
Producer: Michael Jackson
Recording engineer: Bruce Swedien
Synthesizer programming: Steve Porcaro
Arrangements: Michael Jackson and Brad Buxer
Mixing: Bruce Swedien

1995

Europe
CD track 1 : *Stranger in Moscow* (*album version*) / 5'43
CD track 2 : *Stranger in Moscow* (*Tee's in House Club Mix*) / 6'53
USA
A-side: *Stranger in Moscow* (*radio edit*) / 4'04
B-side: *Stranger in Moscow* (*Tee's radio mix*) / 4'21
Released by Epic Records: Europe, November 1996 (ref. 663352) / USA, August 1997 (ref. 34 78012)
Chart position: USA R&B No. 50, Pop No. 9 / UK No. 4

THE SONG

Genesis

> *Stranger in Moscow* was written when I was in Moscow on the *Dangerous* tour, and it was just a strange, eerie, lonely time for me. Outside my hotel was just a sea of faces of fans, chanting and screaming, but I was inside my room and I felt like a stranger in Moscow, so all alone, like I was the last person on the planet, and in the song I say, "How does it feel when you're all alone, you're cold inside?" I say, "It's like a stranger in Moscow." That's pretty much how I felt...and the people were lovely and they were some of the nicest people I've ever met and the concert was very successful, but that day I just felt this different feeling and the song *Stranger in Moscow* just came to me and that's how that was written.[123]

Between 12 and 18 September 1993, Russia hosted the major international star for the first time in its history. The concert was announced with unprecedented fanfare, but the organization was chaotic and the press not very inclined to cover the arrival of the Michael Jackson phenomenon. Despite all evidence to the contrary, he was perceived as a complete unknown. In the fall of 1993, the weather was gray and gloomy in a Russia that was undergoing immense social and political change. The country rejoiced and fretted in equal measure about the arrival on its soil of the first Western megastar. The lyrics of *Stranger in Moscow* echo this sentiment: *"Here abandoned in my fame / Armageddon of the brain / KGB was doggin' me / Take my name and just let me be."* All of Michael's movements were planned down to the last detail and he was accompanied everywhere. The forces of law and order were overwhelmed. Never before had so many people gathered in front of the Hotel Metropol in Moscow.

In the few days leading up to his concert in the Russian capital, the singer visited orphanages and participated in military processions. On 15 September 1993, he gave his performance in the pouring rain at Loujniki Stadium, which was full only because numerous free tickets had been distributed. The King of Pop was both astonished and delighted by the warmth of the reception that he got from his Russian fans, who until then had been surreptitiously swapping his albums among themselves.

Michael Jackson comes onstage at his first concert in the Russian capital, 15 September 1993.

This unique experience produced a song on which Jackson's melancholy is more apparent than on any of his other numbers. It is also pervaded by a sense of deep sadness that had never before been expressed. For the second time on the album, Michael Jackson uses the first person, revealing much of his personal and private feelings. *Stranger in Moscow* is heartrending. This highly emotional song invites the listener into the artist's intimate thoughts. It is an autobiographical track, and one of the clearest messages Michael Jackson ever gave.

Production

Stranger in Moscow is also an act of resilience, with its rich and dazzling tonalities lifting the music above the general pathos of the lyrics. It is a rough diamond that Brad Buxer polished with his digital instruments. The delicate musicality of the piece both exposes and conveys the author's deepest feelings.

Brad Buxer coauthored the song but was not credited. This is probably because Michael Jackson wanted to claim sole credit on this piece, which reveals his most intimate feelings about his experiences during his trip to Russia. In 2009, in an interview with the French magazine *Black & White*, Brad Buxer recalled that *Stranger in Moscow* followed on from the music that he and the King of Pop had discreetly worked on for the video game, Sonic 3. "We used a series of chords that we had composed for the game as the basis for *Stranger in Moscow*. More than any other song I worked on with Michael, *Stranger in Moscow* is the one most stamped with my artistic imprint. I'm not credited as cowriter, but I worked closely with Michael on the composition and structure of the song...I also played nearly all of the instruments."[124]

Stranger in Moscow was the first song to be prepared for the *HIStory* album, and was developed in several Los Angeles studios once Jackson returned to the States. However, it was in New York at the Sony Music Studios and the Hit Factory that it gradually took shape. Brad Buxer spent a long time coming up with different chords to get the key and rhythms that Michael Jackson wanted, but it took them less than two hours to actually write the piece.

Stranger in Moscow begins with the sound of pouring rain, placing the listener directly in the nostalgic atmosphere of the theme. Then comes a plaintive and haunting rhythm that surprises with its unusual cadence. It was built on the singer's beatboxing that was then put through a compression filter to produce its own instrumental sound.

The digital sounds of the strings played by Brad Buxer rise with the music and gradually merge into the narrative. The musical structure is simple and unique. It works perfectly with the despondent feel of the song and varies very little, giving a

An exceptional and unprecedented police presence was deployed to welcome Michael Jackson to Moscow. The concert took place in driving rain.

constant, sometimes agonizing, and melancholic feel to the piece.

In 1995, in an interview on the French website totofanfrance.free.fr, Steve Porcaro, who was always there to support Michael Jackson as his creative ideas gradually took shape, talked about his minor contribution to the song. This involved superimposing a drum loop from a CD sampler that someone had bought him from Europe, and using the resonances of a Korg WS synthesizer and some old Oberheim Matrix 12 analog synthesizers connected to the ever-dependable Minimoog. David Paich provided bass input with a Korg M1.

Accompanied by a few notes on the piano, the song ends with a KGB interrogation, completing what the musician David Paich calls the "sound design" of the piece. It was recorded by his Russian brother-in-law: "Why have you come from the West? Confess! To steal the great achievements of the people, the accomplishments of the workers." The highly experienced Bruce Swedien perfected the mixing on what he believed was one of the best songs that Michael Jackson had ever composed.

So as 1996 drew to a close, *Stranger in Moscow* joined the star's many other successful tracks, becoming his last masterstroke in the European charts. In hindsight, the lyrics sound like the prediction of a waning career: "Here abandoned in my fame." In 1997, the song was released as a single to promote the *Blood on the Dance Floor—HIStory in the Mix* compilation in the United States, where it went totally unnoticed.

THE SHORT FILM

Director: Nick Brandt
Producer: Bridget Blake-Wilson
Leading actor: Michael Jackson
Shoot date: 2 July 1996
Shooting location: hangars at Van Nuys airport, Los Angeles
Duration: 5'33

Genesis and production

The short film, *Stranger in Moscow,* was the last of the trilogy that photographer and director Nick Brandt produced for the *HIStory* album. He chose to make a simple, uncluttered video with unusual photography shot on a blue-screen background: "I suggested the idea to Michael and he agreed. That's how it always was. I only ever made one suggestion, and if that didn't suit him, I had nothing else. So I was very lucky to work with him so many times."[124]

Michael Jackson and a few extras all appear to be shut in behind a wall of solitude. They are moving at normal speed in a world where everything else is in slow motion. The contrasting visual effects are superb. They dramatically render the theme of nostalgia and the very intimate message that the singer is sending. On this project in particular, the director showcases his photographic skills. The images are so meticulously reworked and sophisticated that a kind of gloomy stillness and timeless aura seems to emanate from them. The

Before leaving Moscow, Michael asked to linger a few minutes in Red Square, to take a few photographs.

FOR JACKSON ADDICTS

The documentary *Michael Jackson—Moscow Case 1993: When the King of Pop Met the Soviets* (MVD5694D), about his trip to Moscow in September 1993 is worth a view.

one-time rebel of *Beat It* had minimal involvement in the video, no longer appearing to want to contribute new and visionary ideas to his short films, content merely to go along with the director's vision and approach. In this black-and-white film, Michael Jackson wanders the city streets like a normal person. The camera captures specific moments on his journey, with several scenes that are subtly reworked to turn ordinary everyday events into works of art. The melancholic and downbeat feel is expressed in the rhythm of the singer's steps, which were filmed on-set on a baggage belt in a hangar at Van Nuys airport. His hands in the pockets of his long black coat, he looks haggard, as he endlessly roams the streets, destination unknown.

A purifying rain then falls, bringing to life all the characters trapped in their solitude. One by one, they raise their faces skyward, as if there they can somehow see a solution to their angst. The artist also comes to life and stamps on the wet ground as if rebelling against his depression: "Michael…was singing in the fake rain, in front of a blue background. As he sang, he stamped on the ground. But he stamped so hard that the artificial asphalt disintegrated under his foot! He demolished the stage set."[124]

Stranger in Moscow is a visual confession like no other in Michael Jackson's career. Both the video and the song are quite different from anything else Jackson has done, and are a part of his *HIStory* that still moves his most ardent fans.

A video of *Stranger in Moscow* that accompanies the *Tee's in House club mix*, luckily rarely broadcast, destroys all the symbolism of the piece.

This Time Around

Michael Jackson, Dallas Austin, Bruce Swedien, Rene Moore, The Notorious B.I.G. / 4'21

1995

Musicians
Michael Jackson: lead and backing vocals
The Notorious B.I.G.: rap
Dallas Austin: keyboards and synthesizers
Rene Moore: percussion, keyboards, and synthesizers
Bruce Swedien: percussion
Michael Thompson: guitar
Keith Rouster and Colin Wolfe: bass guitar
Recording
Larrabee North, Los Angeles: 1995
Technical team
Producers: Michael Jackson and Dallas Austin
Recording engineers: Bruce Swedien and Rene Moore
Assistant recording engineer: John Van Nest
Arrangements: Michael Jackson, Dallas Austin, Bruce Swedien, and Rene Moore
Mixing: Bruce Swedien

FOR JACKSON ADDICTS

A US 12-inch maxi promo instrumental version of this is available (ref. Epic EAS 7606).

Single

CD track 1 USA: *This Time Around (album version)* / 4'21
CD track 1 Europe: *This Time Around (D.M. radio mix)* / 4'05
Released by Epic Records: USA, December 1995 (ref. 7602 S1) / Europe, February 1996 (ref. SAMPCD 3598)
Chart position: USA R&B Airplay No.23

Genesis

Dallas Austin was one of the promising African-American producers in the early 1990s. He first became known after producing two tracks on an album called *Attitude* by the new jack swing group, Troop. He also produced some songs for Motown artists such as Boyz II Men. He was spotted by L A Reid and Babyface and asked to produce part of TLC's first album. Austin also released an album with his short-lived group, Highland Place Mobsters, and one of the tracks, *Dirt Road White Girl*, became an underground hit, boosting his reputation even more. Michael Jackson noticed him and expressed a desire to work with him on the production of a track with urban and hip-hop resonances. The young musician suggested a rhythm based on one that he had already used on a song called *Hollywood*, produced for George Clinton the previous year. Michael Jackson altered the melody and lyrics to suit his style, and Renee Moore and Bruce Swedien worked with Austin to polish the structure of the song.

The King of Pop wrote an autobiographical text in which he speaks of his insecurity and the constant and overwhelming impression of being spied on and exploited by his entourage. This tale of paranoia, which one could vaguely sense in earlier tracks like *Wanna Be Startin' Somethin'*, now became an open wound that was an obvious echo of his difficulties of the previous few years.

Production

Dallas Austin joined Michael Jackson and his team in the Larrabee North studios for several days of recording. The idea of adding a rap to the middle of the song was mooted. At the time, the hip-hop community was embroiled in a feud between East and West Coast rivals; 2Pac Shakur represented California rap while Notorious B.I.G., riding high at Puff Daddy's Bad Boy label, was the face of New York rap. The dark, full-on dense rap flow from the man nicknamed Biggie fitted with the gloomy atmosphere of *This Time Around*. The rapper was duly contacted and he agreed to write two texts, one with completely uncensored lyrics and another more restrained version. Dallas Austin thought that Michael Jackson would prefer the second version, but surprisingly the singer opted for the uncensored rap. Assistant sound engineer John Van Nest recalls the session:

Dallas Austin was one of the promising producers on the R&B scene in the early 1990s.

Notorious B.I.G. accepted the invitation from the King of Pop and contributed his inimitable flow to *This Time Around.*

> So, Dallas and I were expecting him any minute, and pretty much on time, Notorious strolls in. He was quite an imposing figure when he walked in, as he was quite popular at the time. I had no idea what to expect from him in terms of attitude, but he seemed nice when he walked in. No problem. But almost immediately, he blurted out, "Yo, Dallas, can I meet Mike?" To which, Dallas replied that he thought so. Biggie went on to talk about how much this opportunity meant to him, as Michael was his hero. Anyway, Dallas tells him that we're going to lay down the rap first, so Biggie heads in the booth, we get some headphone levels and get ready to start recording.[125]

In one take recorded on the Sony 3348 multitrack tape recorder, Notorious B.I.G. laid down the rap that Dallas Austin was looking for. To err on the side of caution, the producer asked him to do it again. After the second take, the rapper once again asked to meet the King of Pop. "Michael came in," recalls Van Nest. "Biggie nearly broke out in tears…I could tell how much this meant to him. Well, Michael could have this effect on anyone, even the most hardcore rappers!"[125]

After listening to the recording together, Biggie and Michael Jackson spoke briefly and immortalized their meeting with a photo. The rapper had come especially from Philadelphia for a session that lasted only a few minutes, but he had no regrets.

The finished song became part of the *HIStory* album, giving it an R&B tonality that was very much in keeping with the times. Despite the flawless production and a successful balance between Michael Jackson's and Dallas Austin's styles, *This Time Around* failed to make it as a standout track. It was mainly distributed on the US promotional circuit as a CD and a maxi vinyl bearing stickers publicizing the Michael Jackson HBO Special concert, which in the end never happened. David Morales, Maurice Joshua, and Uno Clio complete the long list of Dallas Austin remixes that covered all tastes on the dancefloor.

On 7 September 1995, Notorious B.I.G. and Michael Jackson met up again on stage at the MTV Video Music Awards. The rapper presented the best dance video award to the singer and his sister Janet.

NICK BRANDT
DESTINED TO BE A HUMANIST

Nick Brandt was born and raised in London, where he studied painting and film at Central Saint Martins College of Art and Design. In 1992, he emigrated to the United States and became a director of the short films that would leave their mark on 1990s music history. Whitney Houston's video *I Will Always Love You*, which he directed in 1992, became iconic on the back of the global success of the film *Bodyguard*. The video about exploring someone's feelings was certainly original, although the singer's producer Clive Davis felt that Houston had become a spectator in her own film. Nick Brandt's style became internationally recognized, with Whitney Houston's version of the song outstripping the popularity of Dolly Parton's original. Houston's version sold almost 20 million copies, scooped two prestigious Grammy awards (record of the year for 1994 and best female vocal performance) and amassed many other awards around the world—enough to vie with Michael Jackson's unequalled track record and leading to Michael immediately expressing an interest in working with the director. Nick Brandt's love of storytelling combined with his introspective style and flawless photographic work meant that he ended up directing the largest number of short films in Michael Jackson's career: *Childhood*, *Earth Song*, *Stranger in Moscow*, *Cry*, and the unfinished *One More Chance*.

Nick Brandt and Michael Jackson in deep discussion on the set of the short film *Childhood* in1995.

Focusing on Africa

After his partnership with the King of Pop ended, Nick Brandt gradually returned to photography, which became his main activity. He works exclusively in Africa, portraying the continent as a work of art. The photographer's highly charismatic style brought Africa into art galleries the world over. For Michael Jackson fans, the work of the British photographer echoes the humanitarian and environmental concerns of the star himself. Nick Brandt first became interested in Africa when he was filming some images in Tanzania to complete the *Earth Song* video. So in a small but significant way, his subsequent career and the work he did with the King of Pop are connected.

As a photographer, Brandt is mainly concerned with art as altruistic, sublime, and emphatically powerful. He quite literally transcends the documentary style of animal photography and continues to open up new unexplored avenues. He has been exhibiting his work in major galleries around the world since 2004. In 2010, he established the Big Life Foundation, which actively contributes to the preservation of ecosystems and species in Kenya and Tanzania.

EARTH SONG

Michael Jackson / 6'45

Musicians
Michael Jackson: lead and backing vocals, keyboards, and synthesizers
Andraé Crouch, Sandra Crouch, and Andraé Crouch Choir: backing vocals
Steve Ferrone: drums
Michael Thompson and Bill Bottrell: guitars
Guy Pratt: bass guitar
David Foster: keyboards and synthesizers
David Paich: piano, keyboards, and synthesizers
Recording
Ocean Way Recording, Record One Studio and Larrabee North, Los Angeles; Hit Factory, New York: 1990, 1994, 1995
Technical team
Producers: Michael Jackson and David Foster
Coproducer: Bill Bottrell
Recording engineer: Bruce Swedien
Orchestration: Bill Ross
Synthesizer programming: Steve Porcaro
Orchestral arrangements: David Foster
Vocal and rhythm arrangements: Michael Jackson and David Foster
Mixing: Bruce Swedien

Single

UK
CD track 1: *Earth Song (radio edit)* / 4'58
CD track 2: *MJ Megaremix* / 10'33
USA
Maxi single: *Earth Song (Hani's around the World Experience)* / 14'47
Released by Epic Records: UK (ref. EPC 662569), 9 November 1995 / USA (ref. EAS 7605), December 1995
Chart position: UK No. 1

THE SONG

Genesis

Michael Jackson composed *Earth Song* in his hotel room in Vienna, Austria, while on the road during the *Bad* tour. He was motivated by a need to put down on paper his emotions about the world that he saw on his travels: a world increasingly disfigured by the ravages of industrialization and pollution. He produced a poignant piece, in which a series of grievances culminates in an avalanche of questions, bringing to the listener's attention human absurdity and the catastrophic decisions that harm nature.

Earth Song was part of Michael Jackson's idea for an ambitious trilogy in homage to the "blue planet." He wrote a suite comprising a poem *Planet Earth*, *Earth Song*, and an epilogue in the form of a symphony that remains unpublished.

The King of Pop recorded the poem *Planet Earth* during the *Dangerous* sessions. This recording was eventually scaled down to a printed text in the album booklet. It would later also be published on the *This Is It* bonus CD as a recital without background music. He produced a finished version of *Earth Song* for the *Dangerous* album, but ended up choosing to replace the environmental anthem with *Heal the World*, which conveyed a more global humanitarian message.

Production

Michael Jackson produced the first version of *Earth Song* intended for the *Dangerous* album with Bill Bottrell in 1990. The long intro leads into the theme played on the piano. The Toto team worked with Michael to give the song its timeless sound, falling somewhere between impeccably polished Californian pop and an imposing piece for a movie soundtrack.

When he decided not to include *Earth Song* in *Dangerous*, Michael Jackson left this particular version, which was more developed than a demo, untouched. In 1994, when he returned to the tapes to finalize the song for *HIStory*, he polished the arrangements in the Hit Factory studio with the help of the composer David Foster. It was Foster who wrote the orchestral arrangements that accentuate the crescendo at the end of the song. Bruce Swedien used a Neumann M 49 static multi-pattern large diaphragm tube microphone to record Michael

Michael Jackson poses for a series of photos destined for the sleeve of the single *Earth Song* (1995).

Jackson's vocal track. The microphone gives unparalleled warmth to the voice.

The song ends with the singer ad-libbing questions; the response "What about us?" comes in the best gospel tradition from Andraé and Sandra Crouch's backing vocals. In the last part of the song, Jackson sings falsetto, although his original intention was to produce angry and harsh lyrics, like the ad-libs on *Bad* and *Who Is It*. A few days before the *HIStory* recording sessions ended, he rerecorded this sequence and strained his vocal cords to the point of risking damaging his voice.

The recording of *Earth Song* from 1990 and the final 1995 version have very few noticeable differences. The rhythmic track is one of those timeless gems that show absolute genius. Over the years, the King of Pop's lyrics, unfortunately, have become increasingly relevant.

On 25 and 27 June 1999, Michael Jackson performed *Earth Song* at the MJ and Friends concerts. For the occasion, he asked his friend Slash to join him on the stage. The musician's guitar shrieked out notes that enhanced the song's dramatic intensity.

At the end of the routine of *Earth Song* in concerts on the *HIStory Tour*, a child offered the soldier a flower as a token of peace.

THE SHORT FILM

Director: Nick Brandt
Producer: Bridget Blake-Wilson
Leading actor: Michael Jackson
Extra: Slobodan Dimitrijević
Shoot date: November 1995
Shooting locations:
- Amazon forest
- War zone in Karlovac, Croatia
- Tanzania
- Warwick, New York State

Duration: 6'45

Genesis

Michael Jackson wanted to produce a short film that would fully convey the power of the lyrics in *Earth Song*. He spoke to Sony Music and suggested shooting a video set in real locations across the globe. The company agreed. The young British director Nick Brandt was awarded this exciting contract (see page 466). He had already directed the music video for Whitney Houston's *I Will Always Love You*, but had refused to have his name attached to it after Clive Davis, chief executive at the Arista label, decided to alter the editing. He instead chose to use the pseudonym Alan Smithee. This particular video used images from the movie *Bodyguard* combined with shots filmed against a blue-screen background. The director filmed Whitney Houston singing her version of the Dolly Parton song on an empty stage. When the camera zooms in on her eyes, the decor changes, transitioning to a snowy scene where the diva really works her vocal range. Michael Jackson was drawn to Nick Brandt's visual capabilities and his original staging.

Brandt presented his ideas for a video that would portray the wretched state of planet Earth. The script for *Earth Song* is simple, portraying a range of characters in different parts of the planet at a time when the environment is under threat The characters all pick up handfuls of soil, as if attempting to reconnect with the Earth and re-establish peace and order in the world.

Production

The filming of *Earth Song* was a low-key epic that led to the creation of an archive of authentic images of the planet in the mid-1990s. Shots by Nick Brandt are interspersed with images from documentaries.

The King of Pop appears in the cornfield sequence filmed in Warwick in New York State. Dressed in a ripped red-and-black suit, he performs in an apocalyptic setting, which appears to have been recently devastated. In the second half of the song, immensely powerful wind machines and camera effects simulate a life-giving storm that symbolizes a return to a safe and healthy world. The singer puts his heart and soul into this part of the performance. Once all the images were in the can, Michael Jackson supervised the editing with Nick Brandt, and was very exacting about the rhythm of the images.

The *Earth Song* short film became one of MTV's most popular music videos in the 2000s, with Michael Jackson dominating the British and German charts, and selling one million singles in each country. In the US, the song was only released as a single on the promotional circuit, and went largely unnoticed.

PORTRAIT

BILL BOTTRELL
A PURVEYOR OF GOOD POP MUSIC

Bill Bottrell was born in Los Angeles in 1952. He attended school in Germany for a short period before returning to California to study music at university. After graduating, he went from studio to studio in the state, gradually learning his chosen profession of recording engineer. His first real work was in the United Kingdom with Jeff Lynne from the British group Electric Light Orchestra, before he went on to join Sandcastle Studios in Silverlake, California, where he mixed *The Hurt* and *Torture* by The Jacksons. The ambitions of the 30-something recording engineer were gradually realized as he began to be better known in the industry: He supported both Jermaine Jackson (*Tell Me I'm Not Dreamin'*) and Janet Jackson (*Don't Stand Another Chance*) at crucial turning points in their careers in the early 1980s.

In 1985, Bill Bottrell entered the inner circle of the Jackson family studio in Hayvenhurst where he worked with Michael Jackson, painstakingly polishing the sound arrangements for the *Bad* album. Bill Bottrell produced and recorded *Streetwalker* with Michael, a song that the singer loved but which was not included in the final selection for the album. As Bottrell had first-hand experience of the English rock scene, he was the obvious choice to direct the cover version of *Come Together* by The Beatles. His remarkable work on this piece paved the way for his participation on the *Dangerous* album some time later. Bill Bottrell was the man who discreetly built the bridge that took Jackson's career into the 1990s.

The right man for the situation

On *Dangerous*, Bottrell shouldered the major responsibility of accompanying Jackson as he took his first artistic steps without Quincy Jones. He helped secure Jackson's great comeback with the incredible *Black or White*, one of the truly memorable tracks of the King of Pop's career. Bill Bottrell's influence can be felt on all the album's iconic pieces: *Dangerous, Give in to Me*, and *Who Is It* all bear the unmistakable signs of his rock/fusion sound.

The recording engineer ended his collaboration with the singer by producing the anthem to the planet, *Earth Song*. He set up his own studio in 1990 to become a talent spotter and work with new artists. He was behind the first solo album by the American singer Sheryl Crow, originally the charming backing vocalist from the *Bad* tour. Her quadruple Grammy award-winning album, *Tuesday Night Music Club* was the high point of their close collaboration.

With Bill Bottrell, Michael Jackson expands his musical field and delivers pop compositions that make history.

In the mid-1990s, Bill Bottrell set up a new studio in Northern California that worked with many artists, such as Seal, before the 2000s brought him back to Los Angeles, where he now writes and composes songs. More recently, he has been sharing his expertise with schoolchildren in Europe and the US, training the next generation of recording engineers, while continuing to contribute to a number of soundtrack projects for films and documentaries.

D.S.

Michael Jackson / 4'49

Musicians
Michael Jackson: lead and backing vocals
Brad Buxer: keyboards and synthesizers
Chuck Wild: synthesizers
Slash: guitar
Recording
Larrabee North, Los Angeles, and Hit Factory, New York: 1994 to 1995
Technical team
Producer: Michael Jackson
Recording engineer: Bruce Swedien
Vocal and rhythmic arrangements: Michael Jackson
Mixing: Bruce Swedien

Genesis

When the Chandler family brought a lawsuit against Michael Jackson in 1993 for sexually molesting their son Jordan, district attorney Tom Sneddon was put in charge of the file on behalf of Santa Barbara County. He ended up taking the case personally, devoting his energy to an inquiry that, in the end, provided no evidence of guilt that would justify a prison sentence. As part of the investigation, the district attorney served Jackson with a warrant to take photographs of his body. These would be used to verify if the boy's statements about the singer's genitals were true. In mid-December 1993, Michael Jackson was back in the United States after spending time in a London clinic in an attempt to shake off his dependence on painkillers. This is when the district attorney and his men came to Jackson's home to take the photos. On 22 December, Michael Jackson appeared live on television, claiming that he was innocent and complaining about the humiliation that he had suffered at the hands of the forces of law and order. Tom Sneddon's involvement with the singer continued into the 2000s when he prosecuted another case of child molestation brought against him.

The King of Pop expressed his rage and frustration in *D.S.*, a rock number reminiscent of the hard-hitting riffs of *State of Shock* and the marked binary rhythm of *Come Together*. It paints the portrait of a lawman and exposes the failings in the judicial system.

Production

D.S. was a classic production by the singer himself, which draws its quiet strength from the attention to detail that he had learned from Quincy Jones. Following Jackson's instructions, Brad Buxer and Chick Wild programmed the synthesizers and created a clinically cold and clean rock framework on which Slash laid his guitar section. The Guns N' Roses guitarist played the rhythmic lines, as well as a gut-busting solo in the middle of the track.

Since the departure of Chris Currell in the late 1980s, Michael Jackson had felt that he needed someone who truly mastered the synthesizers and could bring a touch of originality to his production. Following Bruce Swedien's advice, he hired Chuck Wild from the Californian group Missing Persons. As well as the Synclavier, Chuck Wild also used Hyperprism and MetaSynth software to transform samples from CD databases into unique sounds that the King of Pop decided to include in several of his productions.

At a time when the hip-hop scene was unashamedly sampling beats from the great soul and funk standards, Michael Jackson used just a small fragment from *Owner of a Lonely Heart* by Yes. He reused the kick that can be heard at 0'19 on this classic, originally recorded in 1983. Michael Jackson's voice is full of rage and almost at saturation point as he hammers out his enemy's name throughout the chorus. If one listens closely to the song, the singer appears to say the real name of the attorney. The low sales potential of *D.S.* meant that it would not be released as a single, and in any case Sony

The artist alone onstage, ready to face his audience, at the start of a concert on the *HIStory* tour.

Music felt that it was too subversive. But the artist fought tooth and nail for his rage-filled song and even included it in the setlist for the 1996 *HIStory Tour*. Although he usually performed his major hits and No. 1s at his concerts, he decided for once to reserve a special place for this lesser-known song.

Money

Michael Jackson / 4'42

Musicians
Michael Jackson: lead and backing vocals
Brad Buxer: synthesizers and keyboards
Nile Rodgers: guitar
Recording
Hit Factory, New York: 1994
Technical team
Producer: Michael Jackson
Recording engineer: Bruce Swedien
Vocal and rhythmic arrangements: Michael Jackson
Mixing: Bruce Swedien

Nile Rodgers, founder member of the group Chic.

FOR JACKSON ADDICTS

Money was long scheduled to be released as a single from *HIStory*, but only appeared as a few remixes by Fire Island. One was included on *The Greatest Dance Album in the World* (1997) compilation. When *HIStory* came out, Sony Music was ready to release *Money* as a single, but Michael Jackson went with *They Don't Care About Us*.

Genesis

While he was busy recording songs about his personal demons, Michael Jackson decided to examine toxic issues in the world in general as well as those that affected his own life. This song decries the power of money over people. The King of Pop chose a pattern reminiscent of *Dangerous*: spoken rap-style verses and sung choruses. The rounded and hypnotic bass line that he wrote appears to draw its inspiration both from *Billie Jean* and *The Knowledge*, a Janet Jackson song of which he was particularly fond.

Michael Jackson's initial aim was to indirectly point the finger at all those who were seeking to destabilize his empire, and he wrote a long text that featured the word "murder." Although as an artist he had already tackled the theme of horror and zombies with *Thriller*, he had not yet referred to death so explicitly.

Production

He recorded the full text at the Hit Factory. Due to timing constraints and self-censorship, the 5-inch track was reduced to a duration of 4'42. The length of the CD planned for Michael Jackson's 15 new tracks could not be extended, and *Money* was one of the songs that was cut to leave sufficient room for the others.

The session was recorded spontaneously, which comes through when listening to the tune. The King of Pop was searching for a specific rhythmic guitar line for the track but was struggling to find the elusive gem. Rob Hoffman, one of Bruce Swedien's freelance assistants, suggested that he call Nile Rodgers, the cofounder of the group Chic, famous for his timeless funk chords. Rodgers accepted the invitation. In just a few minutes, he got his guitar to produce exactly the sound the singer was seeking.

Following Michael Jackson's instructions, Brad Buxer combined three different bass lines to create the sound that we hear on the final mix. The efficient, uncluttered sound of *Money* is the result of a subtle mix of ingredients that show that the star was still more than capable of creating a distinctive funk track reminiscent of the groovy soul textures of *Off the Wall*.

Diana Ross performed a cover version of *You Are Not Alone* on her album *Voice of Love* in 1996. R. Kelly did likewise in 2010, with his version appearing as a hidden track on his CD *Love Letter.*

You Are Not Alone

R. Kelly / 5'44

Musicians
Michael Jackson: lead and backing vocals
R. Kelly, Steve Porcaro: synthesizers and keyboards
Recording
Chicago Recording Company, Chicago: rhythmic and vocal tracks
Hit Factory, New York: vocals, backing vocals, and overdubs: **1994**
Technical team
Producers: R. Kelly, Michael Jackson
Recording engineer: Bruce Swedien
Vocal and rhythmic arrangements: Michael Jackson
Synthesizer programming: Peter Mokran, Andrew Scheps, Steve Porcaro
Mixing: Bruce Swedien

1995

For Jackson Addicts

A 6'01 version of *You Are Not Alone* with additional ad-libs was published in *The Ultimate Collection* (2004) box set. It features the version that was finalized in 1995 but shortened at the time in order to fit the 15 tracks of *HIStory* onto a single CD.

USA
A-side: *You Are Not Alone* (*album edit*) / 4'54
B-side: *Scream Louder* (*Flyte Tyme remix*) / 5'30
France
A-side: *You Are Not Alone* (*radio edit*) / 4'29
B-side: *Scream Louder* (*Flyte Tyme remix*) / 5'30
Released by Epic Records: USA (ref. 34-78002) and Europe (ref. EPC 662310), 15 August 1995
Chart position: USA R&B No. 1, Pop No. 1 / UK No. 1
RIAA: certified Platinum 13 October 1995

The Song

Genesis

R. Kelly composed the basis for *You Are Not Alone* in a hotel. "The spirit of the song was so powerful. I could block anything out," he recalls. "In my imagination, I was in a room with that light and piano alone. I can hear melodies like that…"[23]

At the time, the singer/producer had split with his group Public Announcement and was enjoying a successful solo career. His first album, *12 Play*, featured 12 tracks, as the name suggests. All together they resembled an R&B instruction manual for the 1990s. He introduced a genre that would spread across the whole music industry, namely the schmaltzy ballad with interminable vocalizing.

You Are Not Alone is a song he wrote about a person that he had loved and lost. He produced an initial version in his recording studio in Chicago, where the King of Pop met up with him to listen to it. Michael Jackson loved what he heard and invited Kelly to the Hit Factory in New York to finalize the track.

In September 1995, the music and melody of *You Are Not Alone* caught the attention of two Belgian songwriters, brothers Eddy and Danny Van Passel. They had spotted that the song was remarkably similar to a composition they had written in 1993, despite R. Kelly's claims of quasi-divine inspiration. Their composition was entitled *If We Can Start All Over.* The matter ended up before the Brussels courts. After a 12-year legal battle, the judge ruled in favor of the claimants, and R. Kelly was found guilty of plagiarism. The ruling only applied in Belgium, where *You Are Not Alone* was withdrawn from sale. In 2011, when Michael Jackson's beneficiaries published the soundtrack for the Cirque du Soleil show The Immortal, the Belgian pressing contained all the songs except this one.

Production

R. Kelly was invited to the Hit Factory in New York to develop *You Are Not Alone* with Michael Jackson. The tapes that he had recorded in Chicago were transferred to the King of Pop's team in New York. "*You Are Not Alone* was kind of a basic R&B groove with a verse and chorus," recalls assistant recording engineer Rob Hoffman. "The rest of the arrangement came from MJ, and lots of overdubs by Steve Porcaro with programming by Andrew Scheps. I like to think R. Kelly's subse-

Michael Jackson always had a young girl come on stage while he was performing *You Are Not Alone* – here, when the *HIStory Tour* resumed in Bremen, Germany, 31 May 1997.

FOR LISTENERS

At 4'35, Michael Jackson holds a note on the word "heart." Attentive listeners will notice that this is in fact the same note held for 12 seconds over three bars.

quent success with ballads came from watching what MJ did with his initial track idea."[474]

At a time when US R&B production was all about the "gangsta" attitude, notably with the group Jodeci and its producer DeVante Swing (who had created a raw and sensual sound that wowed the charts), *You Are Not Alone* adopted the more understated style characteristic of other groups like Boyz II Men. The King of Pop chose not to step over into the dark side of R&B, laying down his vocals on what was rather predictable instrumentation that offered no real surprises. Once again, he was accompanied by the Andraé Crouch Choir.

This reassuringly safe track, adapted for the US market, achieved a unique feat in the record industry: it went directly to No. 1 in the *Billboard* charts. It was also the star's last No. 1 released in his home country during his lifetime.

THE SHORT FILM

Director: Wayne Isham
Producer: Joey Plewa
Leading actors: Michael Jackson and Lisa Marie Presley
Shoot date: July 1995
Shooting locations:
• Pantages Theatre, Hollywood (on stage in the theater)
• Raleigh Stages, New York (scene near the swimming pool)
• Death Valley, Monterey, California, and Lake Powell, Utah (natural backdrops filmed and embedded in a green-screen)
Duration: 5'35

Genesis

After the futuristic short film for *Scream* and the starry-eyed fable of *Childhood*, Michael Jackson hired Wayne Isham to create the images for *You Are Not Alone*. The director was known for his long and productive collaboration with Bon Jovi, Megadeth, and Metallica, as well as his occasional incursions into the world of pop. In 1993, he worked with Michael Jackson for the first time on the duet *Whatzupwitu* with Eddie Murphy.

Jackson contacted him to produce a music video that would portray the true beauty of his relationship with Lisa Marie Presley. The marriage between these big names in American showbiz was a source of endless fascination, with many believing that it was a sham and a mere business arrangement.

Production

Wayne Isham and Michael Jackson filmed the shots of the star dancing in an empty theatre at Pantages Theatre. The slow-motion effects and angelic light make his dance moves seem sublime. Following instructions from Michael Jackson, the director captured some spontaneous shots of the two lovers that were used in the final edit. The scene that set the gossip machine in motion is the one where Lisa Marie Presley and the singer appear semi-nude in a setting that replicates the painting *Daybreak* (1922) by Maxfield Parrish, an American cultural icon. Jackson saw it as an homage to the painting's classical Greek inspiration.

Two versions of *You Are Not Alone* were completed in ten days (five for filming, five for editing). The first focuses on Jackson and Presley, as well as the singer dancing in the desert. The second shows the singer as a cherub pierced by love's arrow.

FOR JACKSON ADDICTS

The instrumental version of *Childhood* appears on the soundtrack of the movie *Free Willy 2 (The Adventure Home)*—Original Motion Picture Soundtrack (USA Epic/ MJJ Music ref. EPC 480739 / Europe Epic/ MJJ Music ref. BK 67259).

Childhood

Michael Jackson / 4'28

Musicians
Michael Jackson: lead vocals and percussion
New York City's Children's Choir (Tracy Spindler, Natalia Harris, Jonathon Ungar, Brandi Stewart, Reeve Carney, Caryn Jones, and Brian Jones)
New York Philharmonic Orchestra conducted by Jeremy Lubbock
David Foster: percussion, keyboards, and synthesizers
Brad Buxer: keyboards and synthesizers
Recording
Hit Factory, New York: March 1995
Technical team
Producers: Michael Jackson and David Foster
Recording engineer: Bruce Swedien
Synthesizer programming: Michael Boddicker and Brad Buxer
Arrangements: Michael Jackson, David Foster and Bruce Swedien
Orchestration: Jeremy Lubbock
Mixing: Bruce Swedien

1995

Single

USA
A-side: *Scream (clean album version)* / 4'37
B-side: *Childhood* (theme tune from *Free Willy 2; album version*) / 4'27
UK
A-side: *Scream (single edit)* / 4'01
B-side: *Childhood* (theme tune from *Free Willy 2; album version*) / 4'27
Released by Epic Records: USA (ref. 34 78000) and Europe (ref. EPC 662022), 31 May 1995
Chart position: USA Pop No. 5, R&B No. 2 / UK No. 3
RIAA: certified Platinum 31 July 1995

Genesis

"People wonder why I always have children around," Jackson said in the Oprah Winfrey interview in 1993. "It's because I find the thing that I never had through them. Disneyland, amusement parks, arcade games—I adore all that stuff because when I was little, it was always work, work, work."[476]

His message, which was both naive and troubling in its sincerity, became the central point of a vicious circle that would literally ruin his life.

Childhood appears on the reverse side of the single *Scream*. Whereas *Scream* was a direct blow aimed at the media, *Childhood* is gentler and more balanced in tone. It is a ballad that expresses his affection for the magic and purity of childhood, and is one of the most personal confessions that Michael Jackson ever recorded in his career. *Childhood* is a musical statement that is as gullible and honest as the one he made to Oprah Winfrey two years previously. It is in no way a justification. The singer simply bares his soul with hitherto unseen honesty and sincerity, devoid of any filters, withholding nothing. "Have you seen my childhood? / I'm searching for the world that I come from / 'Cause I've been looking around / In the lost and found of my heart / No one understands me." Here he excels in the art of the ballad that he so loved. His voice is crystal clear and produces long decrescendos that reinforce the melancholy of the theme like sighs: "People say I'm not okay / 'Cause I love such elementary things / It's been my fate to compensate / For the childhood / I've never known."

The simplicity of the lyrics and the harmonious vocal variations are moving both for their purity and, to a certain extent, for their disconcerting wisdom. The song should have put an end to the insane machinations around Michael Jackson but the world turned out to be just too crazy a place.

Production

Childhood stands out musically because, like *Smile*, it was recorded by a string orchestra. The pure sound of the violins and the resonance of the notes comes from a technique that recording engineer Bruce Swedien exceled at. He explains how he used his impressive tube traps to harness the full potential of the acoustic pressure areas in the corners of a room. The tube trap converts changes of pressure into air movements. The energy is regulated and absorbed independently of the

Michael Jackson and the mime Marcel Marceau rehearse *Childhood*,
4 December 1995, for the HBO concert, which was eventually canceled.

soundwave: "I have 14 ASC Tube Traps that I use in a variety of situations. On Michael's new album, I used them recording the two big orchestral pieces. I used all 14 spaced around the studio mainly for dispersion [of the sound], not for absorption. There was a slight edginess that I heard in the room, and I wanted a very wide open and very smooth, silky string sound."[127]

In the 1960s, the recording engineer had spent a long time experimenting on recording major string sections, mostly with the works of Gustav Mahler. With *Childhood*, he was continuing the experimentation by carefully placing his equipment to try and obtain a wide and dramatic stereophonic sound: "So I used my two Neumann M 50s above the conductor and then the first and second violins are set up to his left and right… Some composers specify that set-up; it seems to fit the music so well with a big string orchestra."[127] The positioning of the orchestra is crucial to achieve the best sound recording: "I set up the first violins on the left, with the second violins on the right side," Bruce Swedien says. "I set up the violas on the left behind the first violins, with the cellos on the right behind the second violins. The basses are in the middle to the rear of the room…I then set up the main orchestral mikes 30 feet above the conductor's head so that these mikes will hear the orchestral balance in the conductor's perspective."[128]

For this unique moment in his career, Michael Jackson recorded from a darkened booth in the Hit Factory. Watching through the glass, he waited for the violins from the New York Philharmonic Orchestra to strike up before singing live with them. His vocals deliver a sensitive response to the strings. Brad Sunberg, the assistant recording engineer, often shows the video of this recording session at the talks he gives to select fans. At the end of the song, Michael Jackson is like an excited child. He seems completely and utterly satisfied; his Peter Pan side has never been so apparent.

The composer and pianist David Foster plays the melody on the piano, backed by Brad Buxer's and Michael Boddicker's assured and confident keyboards and synthesizers.

Michael Jackson lost in thought on the set of *Childhood* in 1995.

Night shot of Neverland Ranch, the haven of peace that Michael Jackson had built to his specification, down to the smallest detail.

1995

THE SHORT FILM

Director: Nick Brandt
Producer: Bridget Blake-Wilson
Leading actor: Michael Jackson
Extras and supporting roles: Francis Capra, Erika Christensen, Jena Malone, Jason James Richter
Shoot date: 30 May to 2 June 1995
Shooting location: Los Padres National Forest, California
Duration: 4'29

Genesis

The short film for *Childhood* is a melancholic fable directed by Nick Brandt. It was inspired by Eugene Field's poem *Wynken, Blynken, and Nod* (see the 1938 Disney short-film adaptation). Some scenes also seem to draw their inspiration from the world of *Peter Pan* (1953), another Disney production—Michael Jackson was particularly fond of this story and of the main character, to whom he was often compared.

In the video, the singer sits in a forest bathed in the light of a superb moon. He is alone, gazing nostalgically up at the stars. As an adult, to his huge disappointment, he is not allowed onboard the magic boats that are full of children journeying around the sky. Unable to participate in the fun and games or share the wonderful views with the children, the star sings about his lost childhood. Jason James Richter and Francis Capra, the two young actors from the movie *Free Willy*, are among the children up in the sky. The video is pure and simple, a magical treasure in Michael Jackson's work.

Production

This dreamlike film took several days to complete, during which Michael Jackson and the film crew communed with nature in Los Padres National Forest, north of Los Angeles. The director Nick Brandt recalled in an interview for the French magazine *Black & White* in 2009: "We shot the video in a forest in the middle of a national park, one hour's drive north of Los Angeles. The whole shoot took a week. We spent four nights outside in the forest, then two days in the studio, filming the flying boats against a blue-screen background. But Michael wasn't there for those shots...It was a metaphor for childhood dreams. Michael very much believed in the idea of always pursuing your dreams...He left the directing and editing up to me. I showed him the final version and he accepted it."[124]

The video ends with the sound of children's laughter, and a paper plane gliding toward the singer like a message of hope.

Tabloid Junkie

Michael Jackson, James Harris III, Terry Lewis / 4'32

Musicians
Michael Jackson: lead and backing vocals, beatbox
James Harris III, Terry Lewis: synthesizers and keyboards
Recording
Hit Factory, New York: 1994
Technical team
Producers: Michael Jackson, James Harris III, Terry Lewis
Recording engineer: Bruce Swedien
Vocal and rhythmic arrangements: Michael Jackson
Mixing: Bruce Swedien

1995

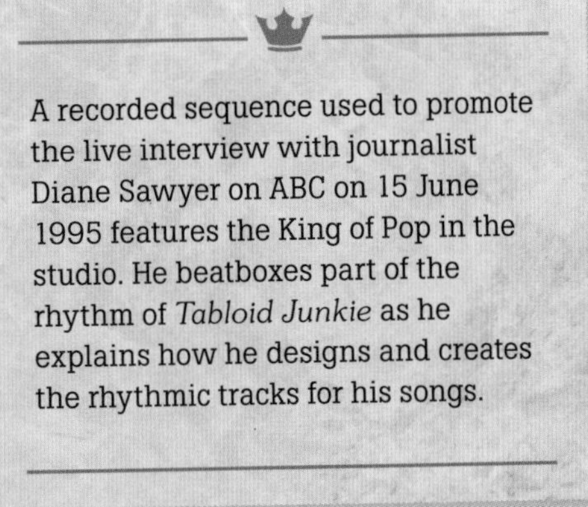

A recorded sequence used to promote the live interview with journalist Diane Sawyer on ABC on 15 June 1995 features the King of Pop in the studio. He beatboxes part of the rhythm of *Tabloid Junkie* as he explains how he designs and creates the rhythmic tracks for his songs.

Genesis

While they were in New York discussing *Scream*, the duet with Janet Jackson, Jimmy Jam and Terry Lewis got Michael Jackson to listen to some other songs. The King of Pop's finely tuned ear picked out some syncopated industrial rhythms reminiscent of *The Knowledge*, a track recorded by his younger sister Janet Jackson for her album *Rhythm Nation 1814*. Michael Jackson composed a melody and wrote some lyrics in which he once again sought to settle his score with the tabloid press. The initial working title was *Tabloid Jungle*, intended to show that Michael Jackson was the prey being hunted down by the media. It ended up becoming *Tabloid Junkie,* to portray the idea of the public's addiction to the media.

The lyrics are surprising for their frankness and for the way that they play with the headlines and rumors dreamt up by journalists. The singer ends each chorus with statements such as "They say he's homosexual," in reference to the rumors in the late 1970s that he was gay, or "She's blonde and she's bisexual," a headline that took aim at Madonna.

Production

Tabloid Junkie is a natural follow-on from the up-tempo pieces on Janet Jackson's famous album *Rhythm Nation 1814,* which at the time of its release in 1989 completely changed the rules of R&B. Michael Jackson wanted to use similar sound techniques to those on *Rhythm Nation*, which worked well, but by then were six years old. By asking Jimmy Jam and Terry Lewis to finalize *Tabloid Junkie*, he was effectively accepting that sonically it would be somewhat old hat by the time *HIStory* was released in June 1995.

The first-class production brings to the fore the insistent rhythm of the chorus. The rhythmic base is enhanced by beatboxing tracks that the artist recorded and stacked up like layers of clouds. Unlike *The Knowledge*, the Janet Jackson track that he had in mind while he was recording, *Tabloid Junkie* has many thematic variations and breaks, which at certain points are reminiscent of the interludes between the songs in *Rhythm Nation*.

Planned for a while as a single release, *Tabloid Junkie* kept its place in the album as a slightly outdated gem, but one that did the job it set out to do.

FOR JACKSON ADDICTS

2Bad was never released as a single, but was remixed by Wyclif Jean, the rap performed by John Forte. This version featured on the remix album *Blood on the Dance Floor.*

2BAD

Michael Jackson, Bruce Swedien, Rene Moore, Dallas Austin, Shaquille O'Neal / 4'49

Musicians
Michael Jackson: lead and backing vocals, beatbox
Rene Moore: synthesizers and keyboards
Recording
Hit Factory, New York: 1994
Technical team
Producers: Michael Jackson, James Harris III, Terry Lewis, Bruce Swedien, Rene Moore
Recording engineer: Bruce Swedien
Synthesizer programming: James Harris III, Rob Hoffman, Michael Jackson
Brass arrangements: Jerry Hey and Michael Jackson
Vocal arrangements: Michael Jackson
Mixing: Bruce Swedien

The basketball player Shaquille O'Neal executed a 180-degree turn when he embarked on a highly successful musical career.

Genesis

2Bad is a complex track that brings together some of the big names in the music world. It is the umpteenth ode to Michael Jackson's struggles with his persecutors. "I'm standin' though you kickin' me," he writes in an aggressive funk style. This is addressed at a woman who wishes him harm, but the parallel with the media is immediately obvious and is more pronounced and emphatic than on *Leave Me Alone* in 1987.

Having previously invited the two biggest basketball stars of the early 1990s (Michael Jordan and Magic Johnson) to appear in his short films, on this occasion the King of Pop invited the basketball player/rapper Shaquille O'Neal to write a verse for the middle of the piece. The text is an homage to Michael Jackson's career, with Shaq eagerly mentioning *Thriller* and *Bad* in his verse.

Production

The intro samples Run-DMC's *King of Rock*. Released in 1985, *King of Rock* was accompanied by a music video in which the members of the group are cheerfully stamping on a sequined glove in an imaginary museum of white music. Run-DMC were following the trend of openly criticizing Michael Jackson's global success, despite the fact that he had paved the way for black artists on MTV. Not one to bear a grudge, and apparently suffering from the same syndrome that had led Ronald Reagan to appropriate the anti-establishment lyrics of Bruce Springsteen's *Born in the USA* for his second presidential campaign, Michael Jackson used the first lines of this song to build the atmosphere of resistance that can be felt in the lyrics of *2Bad*.

The heavy-handed production, overloaded with drum machines that end up caricaturing the new jack swing of the early 1990s, leaves little room for Jerry Hey's horns, which are nonetheless very much present.

Michael Jackson spent hours listening to multitrack versions of songs by Sly and The Family Stone to find rhythmic ideas and incorporate the sound into *2Bad*.

Shaquille O'Neal's participation brought a somewhat superfluous rap credibility to the tune. This guest appearance was removed when *2Bad* was reedited for the short film *Ghosts*.

HIStory

Michael Jackson, Jimmy Jam and Terry Lewis / 6'37

Musicians
Michael Jackson: lead and backing vocals
Andraé and Sandra Crouch, Andraé Crouch Choir, and Boyz II Men: backing vocals
Leah Frazier: child soloist
Other musicians: (unknown)
The Philadelphia Orchestra conducted by Eugene Ormandy: excerpt from the *Great Gate at Kiev* taken from *Pictures at an Exhibition* by Modeste Moussorgski; orchestral version arranged by Maurice Ravel
Recording
Hit Factory, New York; Flyte Tyme Studios, Edina, Minnesota; Ocean Way Recording, Record One Studios, and Larrabee Studios, Los Angeles: mainly 5 February 1994 to 28 March 1995
Technical team
Producers: Michael Jackson, Jimmy Jam, and Terry Lewis
Recording engineers: Jimmy Jam, Terry Lewis, and Bruce Swedien
Arrangements: Michael Jackson, Jimmy Jam, and Terry Lewis
Mixing: Jimmy Jam, Terry Lewis, and Bruce Swedien

Single

Double single
A-side: *HIStory (7-inch HIStory Lesson edit)* / 4'09
B-side: *Ghosts (radio edit)* / 3'50
Released by Epic Records: Europe, 30 July 1997 (ref. 664615)
also published in Japan, Australia, and South Africa
Chart position: UK No. 5

1995

FOR JACKSON ADDICTS

Due to rights issues raised after the release of the album, the *Great Gate at Kiev* performed by The Philadelphia Orchestra was replaced by another similar composition (composition not credited) on pressings of the album from 1996 onward.

Genesis

The promotional teaser for the *HIStory* album was seen by the press as the megalomaniacal delusion of a star who had completely lost touch with reality. After the various affairs that had tarnished his reputation, Michael Jackson reaffirmed his status as leader in the pop world by using images of his many cheering fans, with some even shown fainting in his presence. He had soldiers armed with fake weapons lined up like a battalion ready to defend him from attacks and ensure that his version of the truth was heard.

The singer needed an anthem with plenty of drive and bravado to galvanize his troops and retain his status as King of Pop. He chose Jimmy Jam and Terry Lewis to compose it, instructing the two producers to write a catchy song that everyone could hum along with.

In the first verse, Jackson portrays a beaten and humiliated man, perhaps himself, who, despite all the adversity, still has the courage and aspiration to carve a place for himself in world history. The chorus delivers a call to action as if it were a motto set in stone, a code of conduct applicable to everyone everywhere, an ideal to live up to: "Every day create your history / Every path you take you're leaving your legacy." The message is altruistic, solemn, and utopian. It suggests that everyone is capable, through motivation, will power, and daily actions, of making history and creating a better future.

Production

Michael Jackson chose the *Great Gate at Kiev*, an excerpt from the *Pictures from an Exhibition* suite, as the intro for *HIStory*. It was originally composed for piano by Modest Moussorgski, a famous nineteenth-century Russian composer. The piece Jackson used was a well-known orchestral adaptation by the French composer Maurice Ravel. The solemnity of the intro gives the song the anthem feel that Michael Jackson wanted, and plunges the listener into the kind of atmosphere that one would not expect on a pop record. The orchestral excerpt immediately grabs the attention, making the listener concentrate on the message about to be delivered. For the first time in his career, the King of Pop used themes from classical music in his work. He actively sought prestigious samples that would take his creation to a higher plane. Classical music played an important part in Michael Jackson's daily life. He lis-

Michael Jackson performed *HIStory* as the finale of each concert on the *HIStory* tour.

tened to composers ranging from Claude Debussy to the contemporary composer Aaron Copland.

The musical intro is followed by drums, a sound that continues to be heard throughout the narrative. Voices—of people who worked on the album, according to recording engineer Matt Forger, whose voice can also be heard—announce some dates: 26 March 1827 (death of Ludwig van Beethoven), 28 November 1929 (birth of Berry Gordy). This is followed by a section where the sound of a winding tape symbolizes time being sped up, then a spoken sequence featuring a recording of Michael Jackson as a child: "Whatever I sing, that's what I really mean. Like, I'm singing a song…I don't sing it if I don't mean it." The editing is admirably precise: superimposed on numerous layers, Michael Jackson transports and guides the listener into the theme before the song really gets going. There are so many elements involved that Jimmy Jam remembers how hard it was to manage the tracks. He ended up having to divide them onto four 48-track digital tapes, a very complex process that was carried out at the Larrabee studio in Los Angeles.

Backing vocals by the incredible Boyz II Men, Motown's successful vocal quartet, rise to an initial crescendo, giving off irresistible vibes that are quickly joined and reinforced by the Andraé Crouch Choir, whose powerful voices had already given impetus to many other Michael Jackson compositions.

HIStory concludes with a child soloist Leah Frazier bringing a note of optimism before the narrative thread resumes with well-known quotes from Martin Luther King and Neil Armstrong.

In 1997, Sony Music chose to release the song as a single to promote the *Blood on the Dance Floor—HIStory in the Mix* compilation. This was the first time that a remix version of a track had been directly released. *HIStory* (*7-inch HIStory Lesson edit*), remixed by Tony Moran and accompanied by a minor music video produced by Jim Gable, that does not do justice to the song, attracted scant attention. Rightly so, this video was not included in the 2010 DVD compilation *Michael Jackson's Vision*.

Little Susie

Michael Jackson / 6'13

1995

Musicians
Michael Jackson: lead vocals
Markita Prescott: child soloist
Atlanta Symphony Orchestra and Chorus conducted by Robert Shaw: symphonic orchestra (intro)
Recording
Hit Factory, New York: 1994 to 1995
Technical team
Producer: Michael Jackson
Recording engineer: Bruce Swedien
Synthesizer programming: Brad Buxer, Steve Porcaro, and Andrew Scheps
Orchestration: Brad Buxer and Geoff Grace
Arrangements and mixing: Bruce Swedien

In what was an unusual and inspired choice, Michael sampled the French composer Maurice Duruflé at the start of *Little Susie*.

Genesis

This song is about a lonely little girl who is abandoned, left to her own devices, and ends up murdered. "Somebody killed little Susie / The girl with the tune / Who sings in the daytime, at noon / She was there screaming / Beating her voice in her doom / But nobody came to her soon..." Like a paean to the little girl's innocence, the singer recounts the last moments of her life before going on to describe the ghastly procession of nosy neighbors who come to see her little body "fashioned so slenderly." This poignant, profoundly sad song is based on a true story. It conveys a macabre sense of tragedy that was a surprising inclusion in a Michael Jackson album. Never before had his work shown so much pathos.

Chris Cadman, a British Michael Jackson specialist and author of the book *Michael Jackson,* writes in his book, *The Maestro* (2013), that *Little Susie* could be part of a series of five songs that Michael Jackson wrote down in his personal notebook dating from 1979. According to Cadman, the song's theme is derived from a grisly news story from the early 1970s. Another theory holds that Jackson may have been inspired by the poem *The Bridge of Sighs* by the English poet Thomas Hood, which tells of the drowning of a young prostitute who has been rejected by society.

Production

For the intro to *Little Susie*, the King of Pop used the *Pie Jesus* segment from the *Requiem* by French organist and composer, Maurice Duruflé, performed in 1987 by the Atlanta Symphony Orchestra and Chorus and conducted by Robert Shaw. The musical theme starts with the discreet angelic accompaniment of a choir singing in unison. The original work was cut by around 45 seconds to allow the crescendo, rising theme, and the vocals to come in sooner. The choir gradually becomes more high-pitched as the orchestral sound builds up. This progression is led by a wonderful cello solo. Then comes the decrescendo that reverts to the more serene atmosphere of the start of the song. The *Requiem* stops abruptly with the startling sound of a key being turned in a music box. The whispered singing of a child provides the transition to Michael Jackson's voice, which comes in to a background of plaintive violins, in a risky but intentional juxtaposition of two worlds.

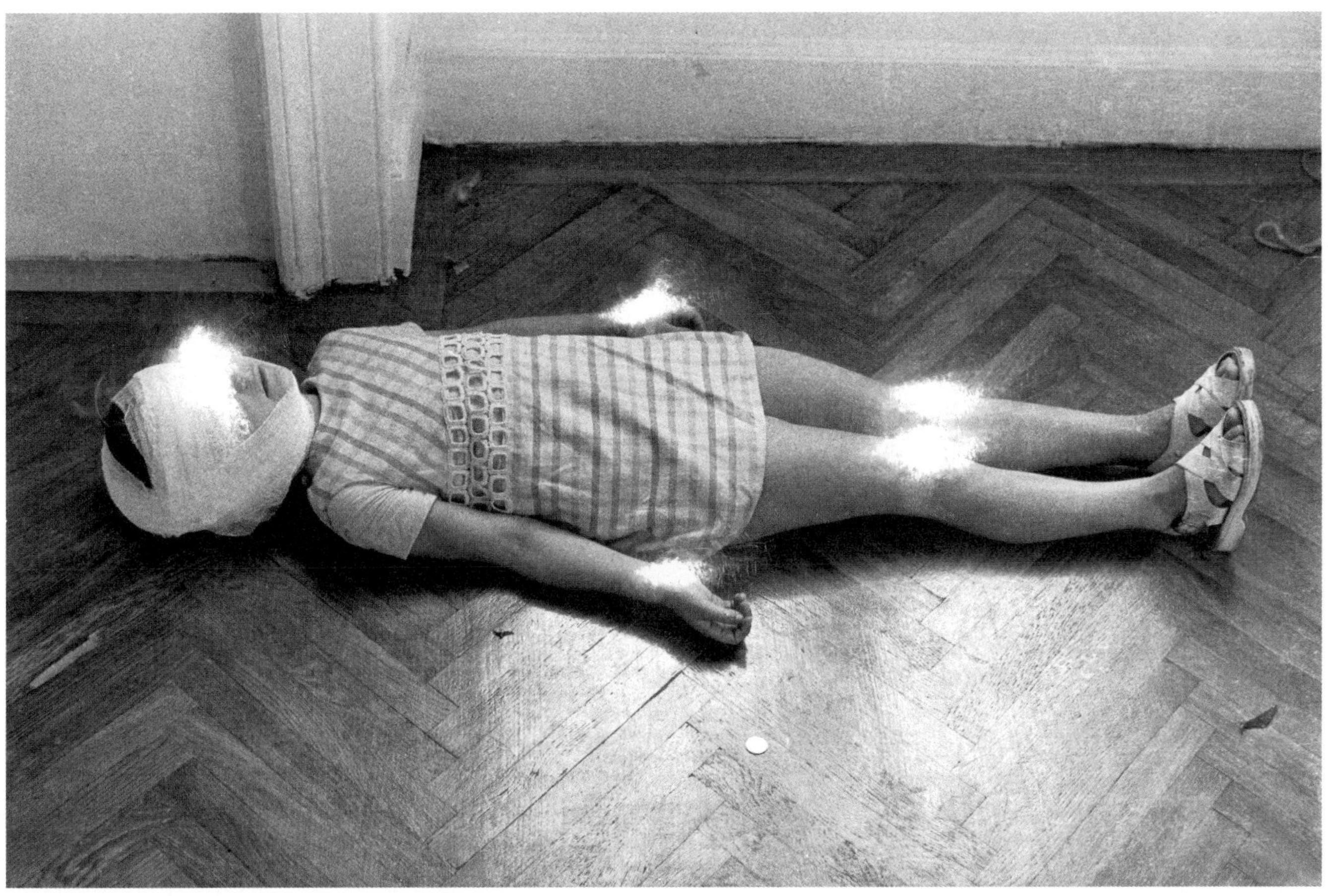

This image by Gottfried Helnwein was used as the illustration for the song *Little Susie* in the booklet for the album *HIStory*.

"*Little Susie* was originally recorded with an orchestra...," explains assistant recording engineer Rob Hoffman. "Then later revamped and re-orchestrated by Steve Porcaro. I think after the track was done MJ decided to change the key or tempo. Not sure which. So Steve was called in to redo it—all synths this time!!! With Andrew Scheps doing the programming."[129]

Rob Hoffman also gives some technical details: "The music box is a sample Andrew and I made. We bought a bunch of music boxes, tore them apart and created a sample set in the EIIIxp [emulator]. [From a microphone] DPA 4006...if I recall correctly. Brad Buxer then played the part in the intro."[129]

Bruce Swedien was responsible for adjusting the musicality of the piece. He used a somewhat unusual technique to bring gloss and charisma to the additional digital strings. Working in studio one at the Hit Factory, he broadcast Steve Pocaro's synthesizer part through the speakers and recorded the sound that came out. The aim was to capture the sounds in a natural environment.

Little Susie, with its dark and violent theme, was yet another melancholic track on the *HIStory* album, adding to the general impression of the singer's troubled state of mind at the time.

SMILE

Charlie Chaplin, John Turner, Geoffrey Parsons / 4'56

Musicians
Michael Jackson: lead vocals
New York Philharmonic Orchestra conducted by Jeremy Lubbock: philharmonic orchestra
Recording
Hit Factory, New York: 29 March 1995
Technical team
Producers: Michael Jackson and David Foster
Recording engineer: Bruce Swedien
Orchestration: Jeremy Lubbock
Arrangements and mixing: Bruce Swedien

1995

FOR JACKSON ADDICTS

On the single sleeve, Michael Jackson poses with a child in a recreation of the famous photo from the Charlie Chaplin movie, *The Kid*. After the single's release was cancelled, fans hunted down the few copies that had been pressed and saved.

Single

Track 1: *Smile (short version)* / 4'20
Track 2: *Is It Scary (radio edit)* / 4'11
Released by Epic Records: Europe, slated for November 1997 but subsequently canceled (ref. EPC 665 130)

Genesis

Besides being an all-time movie great, Charlie Chaplin was also a self-taught musician who composed several soundtrack scores for his films. Prior to the emergence of talking pictures in 1931, Chaplin made some shrewd choices regarding the music that was played live in movie theaters alongside his films. He later went on to compose the music himself. For *Modern Times* (1936), he created a musical theme that later became a song in 1954 with lyrics by John Turner and Geoffrey Parsons. *Smile*, as they entitled it, became an anthem to the smile's ability to dispel sorrow. The great Nat King Cole (1954), Judy Garland (1963), and Diana Ross (1976) popularized the tune before Michael Jackson, in turn, chose to pay public homage to the man he had always idolized.

Charlie Chaplin, a man of vision and an incredibly rigorous artist, was a tremendous influence on Michael Jackson, who replicated Chaplin's professional principles throughout his career. As a child, the young Jackson Five vocalist was constantly drawing Chaplin's famous character, as many photographs show. Later on, Jackson took to appearing at photo sessions dressed up as the Tramp, with his bowler hat, torn jacket, trousers that were too short, oversized shoes, and of course the infinitely bendable bamboo cane.

Just like Michael Jackson, Chaplin had never really received a musical education, but played the piano, the violin, and the cello. His character sometimes played the violin in his films.

Michael Jackson's version of *Smile* is solemn and dignified. Over the years, it has achieved the status of a diamond that has been well polished by the singer's voice.

Production

Following Bruce Swedien's suggestion, the recording of Michael Jackson's version was built on the same framework as *Childhood*. "During the recording of *Smile* on *HIStory*, Bruce thought it would be great if Michael would sing live with the orchestra," recalls assistant recording engineer Rob Hoffman. "But of course, we didn't tell the players that. We set him up in a vocal booth off to the side. They [the musicians] rehearsed a bit without vocals in, then during the first take Michael sang, just about knocked them out of their chairs."[131] The star recorded a complete version of the song with the orchestra in a single take, but was not totally satisfied with the result. So he

Michael Jackson dressed up as Charlie Chaplin in 1995 for the sleeve of the single *Smile,* which was eventually canceled

asked to do a few retakes. Michael did a bunch of takes live with orchestra...In all I think there were 14 takes of *Smile,*"[131] says Rob Hoffman. As was often the case, the first take was the one used on the record, according to Bruce Swedien. At the end of the session, the 50 musicians gave Michael Jackson a standing ovation when he came into the recording studio to greet them.

Smile gave Michael Jackson the opportunity to sing in a more soothing key on the album. *HIStory* therefore ended on a serene note, giving the impression that the singer had finished screaming out his resentment and had perhaps found inner peace again: "Smile and maybe tomorrow / You'll find that life is still worthwhile."

The musician David Foster played the piano part that brings the piece to a close. The singer envisaged himself moving away from the camera in this sequence on the short film that he had planned to accompany the song. But to date, no sign of any such video has been seen. *Smile* should have been the last single from the *HIStory* album. For the video, Michael Jackson was due to perform the track on the German TV show *Wetten, Dass?* and the *Royal Variety Show* in England. Both shows were canceled and the video never appeared..

HISTORY OUTTAKES

Michael Jackson brought out previous drafts of songs such as *They Don't Care About Us* and *Earth Song* for *HIStory*, which he polished for public consumption. During these short sessions, he also worked on new ideas. He frequently composed and shaped these songs on his own, with the help of some of his long-term partners.

Much Too Soon

Michael Jackson / 2'48

Original version: Musicians: Jeffrey Mironov: guitar **/ Recording: Hit Factory, New York:** May 1994 **Technical team: Recording engineer:** Bruce Swedien / **Michael compilation: Musicians: Michael Jackson:** lead vocals / **Tommy Emmanuel:** guitar / **Dean Parks:** kora / **Tommy Morgan:** harmonica / **Suzie Katayama:** accordion / **Charlie Bisharat:** violin / **Technical team: Producers:** Michael Jackson and John McClain / **Arrangements and conducting:** David Campbell

Much Too Soon is a gentle ballad that was recorded in May 1994 during the *HIStory* sessions, but was then relegated to the vaults. Its existence was revealed in 2009 by Bruce Swedien and his assistant Rob Hoffman: "One morning MJ came in with a new song he had written overnight. We called in a guitar player, and Michael sang every note of every chord to him...We then witnessed him giving the most heartfelt and profound vocal performance, live in the control room..."[129]

In their search for more information on the original version of this tune, three fans from the forum MJFrance tracked down the session guitarist that Rob Hoffman had mentioned. He turned out to be Jeffrey Mironov, who appeared to have been contacted directly by Brad Buxer to come and play on *Much Too Soon* at the Hit Factory in New York. "We did a kind of audition," the guitarist explained to the three French fans. "Michael was looking for someone who he felt comfortable with. He turned up and I plugged in various guitars to different amplifiers, and we did an inventory of the sounds that I had...There was...a click track..., a classical guitar, and his vocals. We rehearsed the song and when he felt good, he went into the control room and sung from there while I played in the studio."[130]

The final version was mixed by Bruce Swedien and finished off with a few overdubs. In 2009, the recording engineer posted a note handwritten by Michael Jackson on www.ocala.com, a local news website in Florida. The note read: "Mix No.9 of *Much Too Soon* is great, Love MJ." In 2010, several weeks before its official release on the *Michael* compilation, the track was leaked on the internet with no details of which particular mix it was.

The officially released version was entirely reworked. Jeffrey Mironov's guitar track was replaced by a track recorded in London by guitarist Tommy Emmanuel. There are almost too many string layers stacked up in the new version, and the kora, violin, and guitar struggle to make themselves heard. Suzie Katayama (who plays on *Elisabeth, I Love You)* brings in a mawkish accordion track that considerably weighs down this already very melancholic piece. A few harmonica notes express the singer's forlorn hope that his lost love will return: "And hoping that my prayers will see / The day that you'll come back to me."

In the Back

Michael Jackson / 4'31

Musicians: Michael Jackson: leading and backing vocals / **Linda Harmon:** soprano vocals / **Bill Bottrell, Sekou Bunch, and Neil Jason:** bass guitar / **Paulinho Da Costa and Eric Anest:** percussion / **Lenny Castro:** congas / **Rayford Griffin:** drum and percussion / **Bill Bottrell:** drum, percussion, and guitar / **Tom Langford Scoble:** guitar / **Gayle Levant:** harp / **Billy Preston:** organ / **Suzie Katayama, Bruce Dukov, Joel Derouin, Berj Garabedian, Endre Granat, Ralph Morrison, Michele Richards, Eve Sprecher, Kenneth Yerke, Robert Becker, Mona Newman, Matthew Funes, and Karie Prescott :** strings / **Recording: Hit Factory, New York / Ocean Way Recording, Record One Studios, and Record Plant Studios, Los Angeles**: 1994 to 2004 / **Technical team: Producer:** Michael Jackson / **Arrangements:** Michael Jackson / **String and harp arrangements:** Michael Jackson and Brad Buxer / **Keyboard and synthesizer programming:** Michael Jackson, Brad Buxer, and Michael Boddicker / **Drum programming:** Michael Jackson, Brad Buxer, and Charlie Bryant / **Digital system programming:** Matt Carpenter / **Orchestral arrangements:** George Del Barrio / **Musician hire (strings):** Bruce Dukov / **Pro Tools:** Michael Prince / **Production supervision:** Matt Forger / **Production coordination:** Michelle Bligh / **Recording engineers:** Michael Prince, Brad Buxer, Mick Guzauski, Bill Bottrell, Bobby Brooks, Eddie De Lena / **Assistant recording engineers:** Rob Hoffman, Tony Duino Black, Jeff Demorris, Jon Mooney, Paul Dicato

Released on the compilation *Michael Jackson—The Ultimate Collection*, *In the Back* was developed in two stages: first, 1994 prior to the *HIStory* sessions, then reworked in 2004. Michael Jackson was seeking ideas for his own personal and innovative structure, but did not quite succeed in the end. His creativity resulted in a musically rich and complex piece that was unlike any of his other work. Michael Jackson essentially dictated the notes and rhythms to Brad Buxer by beatboxing and singing the piece over the phone. Brad Buxer was full of praise for this song. At a talk he gave with Brad Sundberg in Los Angeles in 2014, he referred to it as a testament to Michael Jackson's musical genius. The structure is indeed innovative, with a completely "turned around" and reversed structure, as Buxer explained. The song cannot really be defined as any particular style. It needs to be appreciated as a complex acoustic challenge, a personal creative experience. There is no real verse or chorus, and the piece seems to begin directly with the bridge. This destructuring is astonishing and unusual, and either captivates the listener or leaves him wondering. In 2009, Brad Buxer talked about the track for the first time: "[It] is incredible and proves once again how much of a genius Michael was...All the ideas are his. What a shame that he never wrote any lyrics! The track deserved to be fully finished... We recorded a lot of parts that don't appear on the version that you know. Billy Preston, for example, the legendary keyboardist, who has worked with The Beatles and The Rolling Stones, came to the studio one day to play the organ, but Michael didn't keep that part...Michael liked finding original sounds that the human ear had never heard. He often said to me: 'Brad, find me a sound that hurts me, really hurts.' What he meant was that he wanted something that shook him up inside."[124]

3T

Why

Babyface / 5'20

From the album: *Brotherhood* / **Released by Epic Records (MJJ Music):** USA, November 1995 (ref. BK 57450) / Europe, December 1995 (ref. 481694 2) / **Chart position:** USA Pop No. 127 / UK No. 11 / **Single: Released by Epic Records (MJJ Music):** USA (ref. 36 K 78366) and UK (ref. 663538 1), January 1996 / **Chart position:** USA R&B No. 71 / UK No. 2 / **Musicians: Michael Jackson and 3T:** lead vocals / **Recording: Hit Factory, New York** (Michael Jackson's vocals recorded by Bruce Swedien): 1994 to 1995 / **Titan Studio, Los Angeles** (vocals by 3T, recorded by Michael Vail Blum): 1995 / **Technical team: Producer:** Michael Jackson / **Recording engineers:** Bruce Swedien, Michael Vail Blum, Dave Way / **String arrangements:** Jeremy Lubbock / **Mixing:** Dave Way (Larrabee West, Los Angeles)

Taj (1973), Taryll (1975), and T.J. (Tito Joe) (1978) are Tito Jackson's three sons. The trio of young artists began their career in 1992. Their very first, rather modest, composition, *You Are the Ones*, was included in the soundtrack for the series *The Jacksons—An American Dream*. The three boys continued their ascent up the musical ladder when they signed a contract with the Epic label, and two of their numbers, *Didn't Mean to Hurt You* and *What Will It Take,* appeared on the soundtracks for the movies *Free Willy 1* and *2*. In 1995, 3T released their very first album, called *Brotherhood*, on Michael Jackson's MJJ Music label. *Anything,* the first single released from the album, met with global success, notably in Europe where the young stars were later swamped by the wave of boy bands in the second half of the 1990s.

The second single from the album was called *Why*, a mid-tempo composed by Babyface that was offered to Michael Jackson for his *HIStory* album. Jackson recorded it and played it to his nephews. The boys liked it so much that their uncle gave them the piece for their first album, helping them lay down their vocals during the recording sessions and producing the track for them. This simple, fresh, and joyful track also retains the backing vocals from Michael Jackson's original version, thus bringing the harmonies to the fore.

The single was a huge hit in Europe, and the various maxi singles are a compilation of the tracks already released on the *Free Willy* soundtracks. Michael Jackson was reviving his tradition of helping other family members with their music by giving his nephews a great springboard to help them break into a world that was swarming with boy bands. He even went so far as making a video in support of the track.

For Jackson Addicts

The *DW bonus mix*, released only in Europe, adds glossy elements to *Why*'s fresh tones.

A video directed by Ralph Ziman corroborates Michael Jackson's involvement. Filmed in black and white, he is seen smiling as he teases his nephews.

3T pose with their father, Tito Jackson, in front of the family home in Gary, Indiana in 1995.

3T

I Need You

Eric Carmen / 3'54

From the album: *Brotherhood* / **Released by Epic Records (MJJ Music):** USA, November 1995 (ref. BK 57450) / Europe, December 1995 (ref. 481694 2) / **Chart position:** USA Pop No. 127 / UK No. 11 / **Single: Released by Epic Records (MJJ Music):** Europe (ref. 663926 1) and Australia (ref. 663991 2), 18 November 1996 / **Chart position:** UK No. 3 / **Musicians: Michael Jackson and 3T:** lead and backing vocals / **Chuck Anthony:** guitar / **Bjorn Klingvall, Berit Kullberg, Johanna Nystrom, Joakim Sanden:** backing vocals / **Recording: Titan Studio, Los Angeles** (by Michael Vail Blum): 1995 / **Technical team: Producers:** Denniz Pop and Max Martin / **Recording engineers:** Denniz Pop, Max Martin, and Dave Way / **Mixing:** Denniz Pop and Max Martin (Cheiron Studios, Stockholm)

I Need You is the second track from the *Brotherhood* album to which Michael Jackson contributed vocals. In a 1996 interview with the French magazine *Black & White*, 3T explained that on this occasion, the King of Pop's participation came about by sheer chance. After listening to the recording, their uncle suggested that T.J. sing a couple of sentences again. The three brothers immediately went back to the studio to follow the star's valuable advice. They asked Michael Jackson to come and help them, whereupon he took the opportunity to explain exactly what he meant. He suggested that they add vocal inflections to the end of the piece, and recorded his own vocals as a model. The producer was stunned by Jackson's performance and suggested that they kept the track and included it in the final version. The artist agreed, to the producer's great delight, thrilled at seeing his dream of having Michael Jackson sing on one of his tracks come true.

Very much of its time, *I Need You* was a huge success in Europe. British artist Linslee Campbell did several remix versions and a special Christmas version was also released. This time around, Michael Jackson did not appear in the video.

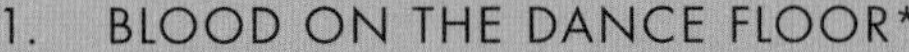

1. BLOOD ON THE DANCE FLOOR*
2. MORPHINE*
3 SUPERFLY SISTER*
4. GHOSTS*
5. IS IT SCARY*
6. SCREAM LOUDER (FLYTE TYME REMIX) (DUET WITH JANET JACKSON)
7. MONEY (FIRE ISLAND RADIO EDIT)
8. 2BAD (REFUGEE CAMP MIX)
9. STRANGER IN MOSCOW (TEE'S IN-HOUSE CLUB MIX)
10. THIS TIME AROUND (D.M. RADIO MIX)
11. EARTH SONG (HANI'S CLUB EXPERIENCE)
12. YOU ARE NOT ALONE (CLASSIC CLUB MIX)
13. HISTORY (TONY MORAN'S HISTORY LESSON)

* Only these unreleased songs will be discussed in this chapter.

Blood on the Dance Floor: HIStory in the mix ALBUM

Released by Epic Records: USA (ref. 68000) and UK (ref. EPC 487 500), 14 May 1997
Chart position: USA R&B No. 12, Pop No. 24 / UK No. 1
RIAA: certified Gold 17 July 1997

Michael Jackson answers questions from the journalist Barbara Walters for the show *20/20*, broadcast on ABC on 12 September 1997.

1997

BLOOD ON THE DANCE FLOOR, OUT OF AMERICA

In early 1996, a lack of support from the US market led to *HIStory*'s sluggish distribution in Europe and other continents. For Sony Music, this wouldn't do: the *HIStory* tour, which started in September 1996, resumed in early 1997 after a break. To ensure the continuation of the tour, the public needed to sink its teeth into a new album. So the King of Pop agreed to subject himself to every artist's worst nightmare: an album remix. *Blood on the Dance Floor* would be his only attempt at this. In addition to remixed versions of some of his latest hits, he released a few new songs that added to *HIStory's* drive for introspection.

Five new releases and eight remixes

When Sony Music asked Michael Jackson to write a new album in order to revive commercial interest, the singer suggested releasing a maxi single or an EP with new songs. At the time, Michael had resumed work on a medium-length film called *Ghosts* and wanted to use videos of its songs for the project.

Sony was skeptical of the potential of a maxi CD, which it believed would seem too cheap and transient. It predicted that the EP format would come off as too dated and unconventional for the music world. Several weeks of negotiations led to a compromise: the new project would take the form of an album of remixed songs, halfway between a traditional album and a compilation. Michael insisted on including new songs as well.

The tracklist was beginning to take shape. Michael took a song that had been left out of *Dangerous* and added it to the top of the list: it was *Blood on the Dance Floor*, and it would give its name to the album. Michael was always in search of new sounds, so he wrote *In the Back*, but didn't finish it by the time the album's tracklist was completed.

A ballad called *On the Line*—which Michael wrote with Babyface, and which was taken from the film *Get on the Bus* by Spike Lee—was also supposed to be included in the album, but Michael ultimately set it aside in favor of *Is It Scary*, produced with Jimmy Jam and Terry Lewis. *Ghosts* also made the final cut, and both songs would renew focus on the main themes presented in the second edit of the eponymous film. To complete the picture, the King of Pop released one of the songs he'd recorded with Bryan Loren, *Superfly Sister*, and added *Morphine*, which he'd created during the making of *HIStory* and in which he revealed a whole new Michael. The rest of the album was made up of remixed songs from the previous album, but they did not add anything to Michael's music, nor did they outlive the originals.

The album came out on 14 May 1997, two weeks before the resumption of the *HIStory* tour in Bremen, Germany. It received a lukewarm response from rock critics, who at the time were focused on English groups like Blur and Oasis and the magical touch of the French electronic duo, Daft Punk. In the United States, *Blood on the Dance Floor* only enticed some 500,000 buyers, a far cry from the numbers Michael had recorded in the 1980s.

Ghosts was released in Europe around the same time. It was the culmination of a project started in 1993 to promote *Addams Family Values*. The Chandler affair had prevented

Michael Jackson and Prince Al-Walid at the press conference in Paris on 19 March 1996, at which the formation of Kingdom Entertainment was announced.

1997

the King of Pop from participating in the filming. Completed in 1996, *Ghosts* was quietly released in the US in November of the same year, ahead of showings of *Thinner*, a movie adapted from Stephen King's best-selling novel. It didn't reach a large audience in the rest of the world until May 1997: previews were broadcast in London, Sydney, and Tokyo. On 8 May 1997, the film was broadcast out of competition at the 50th Cannes Film Festival. This ambitious marketing campaign was run by a new team that had been managing Michael's affairs for several months.

A prince of a sponsor

After Pepsi pulled the plug on its contract with Michael Jackson in 1993, finding a sponsor became a key financial consideration ahead of the new tour. Charles Bobbit, James Brown's former manager and advisor to Michael when the second half of the tour began in Bremen, put the singer in touch with Prince Al-Walid, a businessman whose reputation had been second to none in the mid-1990s. He had famously helped Euro Disney to get back on its feet after it opened its French theme park in Marne-le-Vallée. In the heat of August 1995, Michael was passing through France and staying at the Disneyland Hotel, at the entrance to the park. His lawyer, John Branca, was with him. During this stay in the Hexagone, the singer met with the Saudi billionaire and the two of them brainstormed a few projects that could unite their unique talents.

Al-Walid wanted to work with Michael and realized that the singer, short on partners and sponsors willing to invest in him, was looking to resume his activities and develop new projects. The prince demanded a more in-depth meeting, which took place at the Beverly Wiltshire Hotel in Beverly Hills. The King of Pop arrived with Charles Bobbit, John Branca, and his childhood friend John McClain, an influential man in the music world who at the time was managing Janet Jackson's career. Back then, Branca and McClaine barely knew each other. They didn't yet know that they would become the executors of Michael's estate. As for Al-Walid, he showed up with his friend and partner, Tunisian businessman and producer Tarak Ben Ammar.

The subject of this meeting was the financing of the *HIStory* tour. Not content with sponsoring the concerts, the prince pitched Michael his project ideas in the family entertainment field: theme parks, television channels, movies, hotels, and casinos. Ideas kept pouring out, and they were ambitious. The Saudi businessman was aware that Michael's image was still very lucrative in Europe and Asia, so he did not hesitate to team up with him. The terms of their contract were never disclosed.

Michael and Prince Al-Walid's alliance solidified with Kingdom Entertainment, whose formation was announced at a press conference in Paris on 19 March 1996. Its main activity was to support the *HIStory* tour. Tarak Ben Ammar also invested in this venture under the aegis of his company, Quinta Communications. During the 1996 to 1997 season, Michael thus distanced himself from his US advisors, broke with his manager Sandy Gallin, and, flanked by this new team, dove headfirst into the *HIStory* tour.

The last tour

The tour began in Bremen, to a tight schedule, allowing Michael to cover the four corners of Europe. Like a well-oiled machine, the *HIStory* tour took on the biggest arenas of the Old World, where the King of Pop performed his greatest hits. Far from feeling motivated by this new stage adventure, however, Michael surrounded himself with musicians he trusted implicitly and chose to rely on playback tapes for 75 percent of his shows.

Visually, the *HIStory* tour was top-notch. All of the resources traditionally used in rock concerts were put aside in favor of large-scale scenic productions that could recreate the sophisticated ambiances found in Michael's music videos. Although it had fewer concerts than the *Bad* tour, the *HIStory* tour was able to attract just as many people and yield even more profits: Over the course of 82 showings, the tour sold upward of four million tickets and earned more than $165 million to boot. But Michael's attention was definitely elsewhere. He and his wife Debbie Rowe had recently had a new son, Prince Michael, born on 13 February 1996. His family life had

Michael Jackson performs *Black or White* on the *HIStory* tour in 1997.

FIRST INDUCTION INTO THE ROCK AND ROLL HALL OF FAME

On 6 May 1997, Michael joined his five siblings for a special ceremony: The Jackson Five were inducted into the Rock and Roll Hall of Fame in Cleveland, Ohio. The legendary group took to the stage to give their acceptance speech, which they did in the greatest American tradition. A video of the history of their career played in the background like a time machine running at full speed. Diana Ross and Berry Gordy, mentors from the early days, came to congratulate the stars.

The rare sight of Michael standing alongside his siblings highlighted just how wide the gulf had become between them. Michael had definitively moved on, and now lived in a world with few remaining ties to his family's ambitions. Several years later in 2001, the doors of the Rock and Roll Hall of Fame would open again, but this time, just for Michael as a solo artist.

become the priority. He scheduled his days and breaks according to his son's needs, and would spend as much time with him as possible before taking the stage for the millions of fans awaiting him each evening. As soon as he got off the stage, he would run to his private quarters, which were usually in the main suite of the Disneyland Hotel or at the George V in Paris. During his long European sojourn, he viewed several properties and hoped to move to France, among other places. His plans never took shape, but they showed that he was beginning to feel less and less comfortable in North America, which had long since given him the cold shoulder.

The end of an era

August 1997 also saw its fair share of bad news: on 31 August, Lady Diana passed away in a car accident in Paris. The King of Pop canceled his concert planned in Ostend, Belgium, for that day. He rescheduled it for 3 September and dedicated it to the princess. A few days later, when Mother Teresa died at the age of 87 years old, Michael was devastated. On 7 September he checked into the George V and accepted an interview with Barbara Walters of ABC to pay tribute to the two figures.

After honoring his European concert dates for 1997, Michael ended the tour in South Africa on 15 October. Physically and mentally exhausted from this odyssey—which had been an economic success, but had failed as a real artistic challenge—he took off for Neverland and a well-deserved vacation. He ended his affiliation with Al-Walid and Tarak Ben Ammar, who refused to follow him to the US and wanted to continue their activities in Europe and North Africa. Michael thus found himself alone and learned to manage his daily activities and business.

The *HIStory* tour officially closed at the end of 1997. This long promotional campaign, which unfolded amid significant changes in the music industry, gave Michael some satisfaction: *Blood on the Dance Floor* became the most widely sold remix album in history. It sold some six million copies worldwide. As a parting gift to a long media crusade, Sony Music released a VHS box set that included *Ghosts*, a shortened version of *On the Line*, and a few other goodies.

Blood on the Dance Floor

Michael Jackson, Teddy Riley / 4'13

1997

Musicians
Michael Jackson: lead and backing vocals
Teddy Riley, Brad Buxer: keyboards and synthesizers
Recording
Soundtrack Studios, New York; Mountain Studios, Montreux, Switzerland; Record Plant Studios, Los Angeles: 1991 and 1997
Technical team
Producers: Michael Jackson and Teddy Riley
Recording engineers: Teddy Riley, Dave Way, and Mick Guzauski
Assistant recording engineers: Eddie De Lena, Andrew Scheps
Arrangements: Michael Jackson
Drum programming: Teddy Riley and Brad Buxer
Digital interface programmer: Matt Carpenter
Mixing: Mick Guzauski

Michael Jackson dedicated *Blood on the Dance Floor* to Elton John as a thank you for his valuable help at the end of 1993, when the *Candle in the Wind* singer welcomed Michael into his home after the cancellation of the *Dangerous* tour.

A-side: *Blood on the Dance Floor* / 4'13
B-side: *Dangerous (Roger's Dangerous edit)* / 4'41
Released by Epic Records: USA and UK, 27 April 1997 (US ref. 34 78007 and UK ref. EPC 664462)
Charts: USA R&B No. 19, Pop No. 42 / UK No. 1

THE SONG

Genesis

Blood on the Dance Floor was one of ten rhythmic tracks that Teddy Riley had drafted for Michael Jackson during the making of *Dangerous*. The producer wrote an outline of it on 6 June 1990 after cloistering himself in the Soundworks Recording Studio in Queens, New York. He worked all night and even turned down an invitation to a party where, as he later found out, someone had been killed on the dance floor. Shocked by the news, he continued to work, ending up with a rhythm that was vigorous, dark, and driven by a funky energy only Riley could have mustered.

When Michael heard Riley's song ideas, he chose the one that had been written on that fateful night. Despite being unaware of the context that had given rise to the song, Michael wrote a catchy melody reusing the syncopated verse and ethereal refrain combination that had made the fame and fortune of many of his songs, such as *Smooth Criminal*. Michael named the song *Blood on the Dance Floor* after the initial suggestion of his recording engineer, Bill Bottrell.

Michael recalled in an interview: "Actually I didn't create the title, my engineer [Teddy Riley] thought of the title."[133] The interview's 1997 transcription, attributed to the president of his British fan club, mistakenly identified Teddy Riley as the engineer. In reality, Bill Bottrell had come up with that title: "*Blood on the Dance Floor* was a song I wrote for MJ during the sessions when *Dangerous* was written, sometime in 1988. I thought I'd be a clever salesman and I teased Michael about this great song I had called *Blood on the Dance Floor*. He was out of town and I was trying to tweak the song and this went on for weeks. He was really intrigued, so much so that before he ever heard what I did, he wrote his OWN *Blood on the Dance Floor*."[116]

The lyrics tell the story of a femme fatale trying to ensnare a man. "Blood is on the dance floor, blood is on the knife," sang the King of Pop. Clearly, he was not yet done with the wicked woman narrative. Teddy Riley found the coincidence surprising. "It was like he prophesied that record," he recalled in an interview. "He felt its mood."[134]

The album *Blood on the Dance Floor* went on sale to promote the second part of the *HIStory* tour in Europe.

Production

Several versions of *Blood on the Dance Floor* were made in the studio before the song was released to the public. Michael's initial inspiration had come from a rhythm Riley planned on using in *Sunset Driver*, a song written for *Off the Wall* in the late 1970s. In one of the versions, Michael sang verses from this song before launching into the chorus, which already contained the basis of the final refrain in *Blood on the Dance Floor*. But upon reflection, Michael opted for a darker verse that pushed the limits of phrasing, contrasted with the melodious refrain, and allowed the groove to crescendo until the words "blood on the dance floor."

Michael and Riley worked on the piece but set it aside, even though they only needed a few more vocal parts to complete the mix. During sessions for *HIStory*, the King of Pop unearthed this very advanced draft and, in early 1997, put the final touches on it at the Mountain Studios in Montreux, Switzerland. This allowed him to polish the mix, which had already been produced in 1991, by adding a few of Brad Buxer's overdubs. The mix was produced by Mick Guzauski, who took on the job that was normally performed by Bruce Swedien.

When the song came out, Teddy Riley couldn't hide his disappointment. "But I kind of feel like [my work on] *Blood on the Dance Floor* was kind of like, dated. That's not what I sound like today, but I thank him for giving me the opportunity once again. But what he needs to do is, you know, come back and get some of this heavy R&B and this new funk."[135]

1997

THE SHORT FILM

Directors: Vincent Paterson and Michael Jackson
Producer: Beth Anthony
Lead actors: Michael Jackson and Sybil Azur
Extra: Kevin Stea
Shoot date: 1997
Shooting location: Raleigh Studios, Los Angeles
Duration: 4'17

Genesis

Sony Music's US headquarters in New York had ceased to prioritize the King of Pop to quite the extent that they previously had: the company only allocated a modest budget to produce the *Blood on the Dance Floor* video. In so doing, it hoped to take fewer commercial risks to promote the remix album than it took for *HIStory* two years before.

Michael reached out to longtime collaborator Vincent Paterson to turn his funky and energetic songs into videos. The choreographer remembered that Michael had not been very disciplined during their last collaboration, which had been the 1993 Super Bowl half-time show: Jackson hadn't participated in all the rehearsals, notably because of his very busy work schedule at the time. So Paterson agreed to work with Michael again, but on the condition that the singer work harder. As for the video project, he suggested that Michael should use it to change his image so that he would appear more masculine, almost macho.

The scenario Paterson wrote saw Michael walk into a club packed with a myriad of characters, each with his or her own story to tell and dance to perform. Paterson gave the famous Susie, who is mentioned in the song, a key role in the script: queen of the dance floor, she breaks into a routine with the intent to seduce the singer. Sybil Azur, a dancer who had previously worked with Paterson on other projects, was chosen for the role.

The project's budget was as tight as its deadlines. Paterson recycled ideas he'd had for *Jam* a few years before. This allowed him to introduce the spiral staircases he hadn't been able to use back then. Rehearsals began, and Michael wasn't able to make the time he had planned. Paterson changed his roadmap and adapted his ideas to suit Michael's schedule. The dance routines, full of salsa influences, took shape as Michael and Sybil Azur grew accustomed to each other while rehearsing their dances together. Sessions went back and forth between hard work and moments of respite that left room for a taste of freedom.

Production

Filming took place in Los Angeles. Lighting set up by Conrad Hall, the director of photography, created an ambiance that was full of color without being garish or flashy. Paterson wrote a series of scenes: the group dance routines alternated with those where Michael spontaneously danced alone. In addition to Hall's precise instructions, Paterson asked a producer friend to lend him a super-8 camera. He used it to film his own images, which he set to the song's Fire Island remix. Paterson invested in a saturated and syncopated calibration, creating a marked and assured grain, thus giving the film a tainted feel he thought would be a better fit for the dark ambiance of the song.

Sony Music firmly rejected Paterson's version: the company believed that Michael Jackson's music videos required a cleaner and more classical aesthetic. So Paterson finalized the video based on Conrad Hill's shots. The record company accepted this version and commissioned a second one with the remix made by Wyclef Jean of The Fugees as its soundtrack.

Preliminary drawings for the short film *Blood on the Dance Floor,* from the archives of Vincent Paterson.

Michael Jackson wanted to release *Morphine* as a single but came up against a veto from his record label, which believed the song wasn't appropriate for the wider public. He rehearsed it repeatedly throughout the *HIStory* tour but never performed it onstage.

1997

Morphine

Michael Jackson / 6'28

Musicians
Michael Jackson: lead and backing vocals, percussion, drums, guitar
Brad Buxer, Bill Bottrell, Jon Mooncy, and the Andraé Crouch Singers: backing vocals
Keith Cohen: keyboards
Brad Buxer: keyboards, synthesizers, piano, percussion
Bryan Loren: percussion
Slash: guitar
Robert Chausow: violin
Juliet Haffner: viola
Orchestra
Jorge Del Barrio: conductor
Bill Hughes: band leader
Drew Demboski, Richard Feves, and Frances Liu: stand-up basses
Steve Erdody, Chris Ermacoff, Anne Karam, Tiam Landauer, Miguel Martinez, and Tina Soule: cellos
Dan Lozano and Valerie King: flutes
Katie Kirkpatrick: harp
Carole Mukogawa, Bob Becker, Karen Elaine, Mimi Granat, Renita Koven, Robin Ross, John Scanlon, and Ray Tischer: violas
Endre Granat, Murray Alder, Jackie Brand, Darius Campo, Ron Clark, Kirstin Fife, Julianne French, Armen Garabedian, Marilyn Harding, Marianne Henry, Karen Jones, Natalie Legget, Joy Lyle, Mike Markman, Liane Mautner, Marisa McLeod, Frances Moore, Maria Newman, Barbara Porter, Bob Sanov, Marc Sazer, Haim Shtrum, Olivia Tsui, and Jennifer Walton: violins
Recording
Hit Factory, New York / Record Plant Studios, Larrabee Studios, and Ocean Way Recording (orchestra), Los Angeles: 1995 to 1997
Technical team
Producer: Michael Jackson
Recording engineers: Keith Cohen, Eddie De Lena, Mick Guzauski, and Tim Boyle
Assistant recording engineers: Rob Hoffman, Tony Duino Black, Jon Mooney, Paul Dicato, Steve Baughman, John Rodd, and Greg Burns
Classical, vocal, and rhythmic arrangements: Michael Jackson
Orchestra arrangements: Jorge Del Barrio
Drums and synthesizer programming: Statik
Synclavier programming: Andrew Sheps
Digital interface programming: Matt Carpenter
Mixing: Keith Cohen

Genesis

The history of rock is rife with an infinite number of songs dedicated to drugs. Known simply as "drug songs," they talk about the harmful effects of these illegal substances and the love-hate relationships certain artists have with them. From Bob Dylan's *Rainy Day Women #No. 12 & and 35* to Sixto Rodriguez' *Sugarman*, examples abound of songs that explore this enduring theme.

Bent on escaping the immaculate world he had developed throughout his career, Michael Jackson joined the fray and got his hands dirty with this risky new project. The King of Pop looked deep within himself and in an extreme move, put on tape the intense pain he'd been feeling every day for many years. In November 1993, his fans were shocked to learn, from the horse's mouth, that he was ending the *Dangerous* tour due to an "addiction to painkillers." The announcement, which had been precipitated by the Chandler affair, brought him to his knees. Physically and emotionally exhausted, he followed his friend Elton John's advice and checked into a detox clinic in London. *Morphine* was born of this difficult time. In this fascinating song, Michael likens his painful yet soothing relationship with the drug to a ride on an infernal roller coaster. Alone in a world full of people who only seemed to want to use him, he took refuge in this fool's paradise to protect himself and to allow his body to keep up with his many professional engagements.

The words in the verses and chorus are harsh and hammered out to a rhythm that evokes *Come Together* by The Beatles. But Michael was also inspired by *The Downward Spiral* by Nine Inch Nails. The song's bridge, written for a light piano melody, creates a clean break that Michael uses to illustrate the fleeting and deceptive release associated with Demerol, an intravenous drug derived from morphine. The break ends suddenly, giving way to the return of the harsh verses and chorus, like a painful rude awakening.

Using samples from the soundtrack of David Lynch's movie *The Elephant Man* (1980), Michael Jackson put on record his fascination with the story of Joseph Merrick.

Morphine created a scandal in Malaysia, which banned the song's title being printed on the cover of *Blood on the Dance Floor*, replacing it with *Just Say No*. South Korea decided to censor the song altogether and omitted it from the album's tracklist.

While *Childhood* is about the extent to which Michael sacrificed his youth on the altar of success, *Morphine* talks about the real pain he felt when facing his demons. This song, which has largely been forgotten by the wider public, is a striking and disturbing portrait of a star dropping all pretense and crying out for help through song.

Production

Musically, Michael chose to dedicate himself to *Morphine* body and soul, much more so than for any other song in his repertoire. He wanted it to reflect his feelings as faithfully as possible and was eager to take on several key recording tasks: in addition to singing the chorus, as usual, he supervised the arrangements and played several instruments. This was the first time he'd taken a seat behind a drum set for a song he was planning to release to the public. It was a talent that many of his more attentive fans knew he had, but which he'd chosen not to display until then. He asked Slash to record the guitar tracks to maximum capacity and played along with him.

As for excerpts, Michael drew an interesting parallel between himself and the story of Joseph Merrick, the famous Elephant Man, who had inspired the eponymous film by David Lynch. The King of Pop used the scene from the film where the nurse asks Merrick whether he had listened to the doctor's advice. The press had found comparisons to this tragic character amusing in the late 1980s, especially when a rumor emerged that Michael wanted to purchase the remains of the Elephant Man. But the use of this scene in *Morphine* supported the theory that both men were circus freaks, curiosities that their contemporaries would never fully understand.

From a musical standpoint, the production of *Morphine*'s verses and refrains was heavy, almost stifling. Michael called on reliable talents and values to make this song and set out a precise roadmap for them to follow. Bryan Loren and Bill Bottrell brought Michael's ideas to life. Michael also asked Brad Buxer to help him build the sound pyramid for this ambitious song. *Morphine* is Michael Jackson through and through, completely free of influences from other producers or arrangers.

The highlight of *Morphine* comes during the bridge. Designed as a breather, it acts as a reverie where the song's hero finds himself face to face with the liberating and deceptive power of Demerol. In this sequence, Andrew Scheps recreates the ambiance of a hospital room where respiratory machines are beeping. Brad Buxer's arpeggios sustain Michael's composed voice as he sings and describes how the Demerol manages to sooth him for a while. The orchestra, led by Jorge Del Barrio, was recorded at the Ocean Way studios in Los Angeles, which had already hosted the team from *Dangerous*. All 44 musicians worked hard to create a clip that was both melodramatic and solemn, as if to represent the fragility of a man faced with his addiction.

In addition to creating a strong personal testimony, the King of Pop used *Morphine* to delve into his love of narration. The song was conceived as a soundtrack, though Michael never had a chance to put it on video. Totally ignored, even shunned upon its release, the song was rediscovered and reevaluated by journalists after Michael's tragic death on 25 June 2009.

Superfly Sister was the only song with Bryan Loren that Michael Jackson completed and approved.

Superfly Sister

Michael Jackson, Bryan Loren / 6'27

1997

Musicians
Michael Jackson: lead and backing vocals
Bryan Loren: guitar, keyboards, and synthesizers
Recording
Ocean Way Recording, Record One studios and Record Plant Recording Studios, Los Angeles: 1991
Technical team
Producer: Michael Jackson
Recording engineers: Richard Cottrell and Dave Way
Assistant recording engineers: Bart Steven and Paul Dicato
Arrangements: Michael Jackson and Bryan Loren
Vocal arrangements: Michael Jackson
Drums and synthesizer programming: Bryan Loren
Mixing: Dave Way

Genesis

In 1997, Michael Jackson stole away to his studio to select five new songs for the *Blood on the Dance Floor* compilation. His addition of *Superfly Sister* loaded the tracklist with tons of oppression and darkness and filled it with Michael's personal experiences. In this song, the King of Pop revisits the ghosts of his formative years: the groupies of loose morals hanging out in hotel rooms with his brothers and the nights performing in strip clubs in the 1960s. These moments never stopped worrying his mother: "Mother's preaching Abraham / Brothers they don't give a damn."

Dark love, sex, and its dangers dominate the life of this superfly sister, known as Susie. Her escapades and chaotic relationships embody Michael's lyrics and insinuate themselves into each harsh word he sings. Dry, raw, and sexually daring, the lyrics follow a jolting and regular rhythm created by Bryan Loren. This was the very first time Loren had managed to place one of his completed productions in an official Michael Jackson project. According to him, the song's title was inspired by Heatwave's *Super Soul Sister.*

Production

As he prepared to work on the *Dangerous* album with Michael, Bryan Loren developed his swing beat and presented it to him as a draft musical base. Michael wrote the words and recorded the majority of his vocal tracks in a single day. Synthesized sounds abound, hit hard, and resound to create a dense and striking texture that strongly supports Michael's lyrics. Certain vintage sounds attempt to reconnect with the electric funk techniques of the 1980s and are supplemented with the keyboard calls heard in *Do the Bartman* (see page 362). During a September 2016 conference in France, Bryan Loren explained that Michael had recorded the song's pronounced handclap by clapping his hands really loudly in the bathroom of the Record One studio in Los Angeles.

Superfly Sister was produced by both musicians in equal measure, even though Michael was the only one credited for the production of the piece. It remains one of Bryan Loren's favorite collaborations with the King of Pop.

GHOSTS, THE MAN IN THE MIRRORS

In early 1993, Michael Jackson buckled down on a project that would reconnect him with the big screen. He hadn't been able to commit to an ambitious film since *Moonwalker*, but this new horror-themed video seemed set to be another done deal in the style of *Thriller* and *Smooth Criminal*. The video would be associated with *Addams Family Values*, a feature film Barry Sonnenfeld had directed for Paramount Pictures that same year.

The 1993 version

On returning from the Japanese leg of his *Dangerous* tour in early 1993, Michael set to work on his idea for a horror-themed music video. He decided to ask the master of the genre, Stephen King, to write a screenplay for him. It was February and the writer was busy filming *The Stand*. One day, while on set, King received a call from Michael asking him to work on a project. Always keen on exploring new ideas and happy to change things up, King accepted.

The two men came up with a scenario where the inhabitants of a small village decide to confront a man who lives alone in a strange house and by his own rules. The villagers believe he doesn't belong in their town and that he's a bad influence on their children. King saw this as an example of generational divide, so indicative of the rock industry.

King suggested Michael hire Mick Garris to direct the film, which they were now calling *Is This Scary*. Garris had appeared as a zombie extra in the *Thriller* video and was not unknown to Michael. At this point, *Is This Scary* was still part of the promotional campaign for *Addams Family Values*. Michael and producer David Nicksay decided to include the song from Michael's video in the film's original soundtrack. Christina Ricci, Jimmy Workman, and Kristen Hooper, who played the children in the feature film, were included in the cast of *Is This Scary*.

Once the team was assembled and the storyboard finalized, filming began at CBS/MTM studios in Los Angeles in the first half of 1993, a few weeks before Michael resumed the *Dangerous* tour in Asia. The artist, the director, and the technicians spent two weeks filming the exterior shots, the dialogue, and the last scene with the Addams children. The King of Pop and Teddy Riley had not yet finished the song, so the musical scenes couldn't be filmed. A first draft of the film was created and since the background music hadn't been recorded, the images were accompanied by a few extracts from the soundtrack to *Edward Scissorhands* by Tim Burton.

Michael's imminent departure for Bangkok, where the next concerts for the *Dangerous* tour were due to take place, and news of the Chandler affair contributed to the cancellation of the project. Paramount, who was producing *Addams Family Values*, broke the contract, leaving Michael and Garris with nothing but their drafts.

Is This Scary becomes *Ghosts*

In late 1995, after having shifted focus to recording and promoting *HIStory*, the King of Pop resumed work on *Is This Scary*. He took full control of the film and made it personal, turning it into yet another outlet for settling scores with part of public opinion and with a media that had been harassing him for years. He planned on using *2Bad*, excerpted from *HIStory*, as the lyrics aligned perfectly with the theme, and *Ghosts*, a song he'd recorded with Teddy Riley and which ended up giving its name to the video project.

He got back in touch with Mick Garris to pick up filming where it had left off in 1993, but the director was busy filming *The Shining* miniseries and suggested Stan Winston, who had been in charge of the special effects for the interrupted film. He was an old acquaintance of Michael's: he had been responsible for makeup on the set of *The Wiz* in late 1977.

In April 1996, work resumed with Stan Winston at the reins. The script had changed and the mayor was no longer portrayed by Ken Jenkins. Michael decided to take up this role, along with that of the Maestro (the occupant of the mysterious manor). With help from Rick Baker, Winston designed the impressive makeup that would transform Michael into a paunchy 50-year-old white man. The unrecognizable star also portrayed other characters: the ghoul version of the mayor and

A series of molds made during the shooting of *Ghosts,* corresponding to the stages of one of the transformations undergone by Michael Jackson.

the various superghoul and skeleton versions of the Maestro. For the skeleton version, Digital Domain, a company specializing in digital special effects, scanned Michael's body and reconstituted it as a digital animation, giving the audience a peek at Michael's full anatomy in one of the scenes.

There were other notable changes. In Mick Garris' version, when faced with the rage of the villagers hunting him down, the Maestro disintegrates by hitting the ground with his head and fists until he disappears in a cloud of dust. The village children gather all the particles scattered on the ground and put their friend's body back together again. The hero is reborn from his ashes before the stunned eyes of the mayor, played by Ken Jenkins. In Stan Winston's version, this scene was replaced by a slight of hand: once Michael is reduced to ashes, the villagers go to leave, but when they open the door, the mayor comes face to face with a monstrous version of the Maestro, who scares him into running away. The owner of the manor reappears and the villagers realize that his presence is not a threat to their town. This happy ending gives *Ghosts* a humorous bent, significantly undercutting Michael's initial intention of creating a dark piece.

The dances had been choreographed with *2Bad* and *Ghosts* in mind. With help from the loyal LaVelle Smith and hip-hop dancers such as Popin' Pete (whose real name was Timothy Earl Solomon), Michael fine-tuned a new gothic dance that echoed the one from *Thriller.* He also put together a routine to the music of Nicholas Pike, who had created the film's original soundtrack.

Limited commercial success

Ghosts was released to a limited number of Sony-owned theaters. It ran as a trailer ahead of the new film adapted from Stephen King's *Thinner* between 25 and 31 October 1996. Special showings that included an appearance from Michael were also organized on 15 November in Sydney, Australia, and on 19 December in Tokyo, Japan.

In early 1997, Michael and Stan Winston made a few changes. They first replaced a part of *2Bad* with *Is It Scary*, a new song recorded with Jimmy Jam and Terry Lewis during the making of *HIStory*. The editing remained the same but the music was changed to match Michael's choreography. The color calibration of the scenes was also revisited. In the 1996 version, blue reigned supreme; in the 1997 version, the balance became richer in hues and nuances.

This new version premiered to the European public with great fanfare at the 50th Cannes Film Festival. On 8 May 1997, Michael took his place along the Croisette and unveiled his new film, *Ghosts*. Stan Winston, who had also made the trip, was by his side. On 15 May, it was the British public's turn to watch this 38-minute maxi clip on the big screen.

These free events, however, did not give Michael the opportunity to recover the $17 million budget he had spent on this very personal project. In late 1997, Sony Music released the film in Europe and Asia on VHS, Laserdisc, and Video CD format. But the proceeds were nothing compared to those garnered by the *Thriller* video, which had been cofinanced by MTV and Showtime and had benefited from a global release to the home video market. In the early 2000s the King of Pop started working on a DVD release, but his increasingly strained relations with Sony Music doomed the project. *Ghosts* thus became a rare specimen of which only Michael's fiercest fans were aware. This highly personal medium-length film allowed Michael to fully reveal himself and his wounds on camera, all while denouncing intolerance. The piece was a daring artistic venture that in many respects broke from established marketing norms and would become Michael's last truly inspired video.

In *Ghosts*, Michael Jackson stripped himself bare, denouncing the devastating effect his accusers and the press had had on his private and professional life.

1997

Ghosts

Michael Jackson, Teddy Riley / 5'08

Musicians
Michael Jackson: lead and backing vocals
Teddy Riley, Brad Buxer, and Doug Grigsby: keyboards and synthesizers
Recording
Future Records, Virginia Beach, Virginia / Hit Factory, New York / Ocean Way Recording, Record One and Larrabee Studios, Los Angeles / Dieter Dierks Studio, Cologne, Germany / Wisseidorf Studio, Amsterdam / Air Studios, London: 1994, 1996, and 1997
Technical team
Producers: Michael Jackson and Teddy Riley
Recording engineers: Teddy Riley and Eddie De Lena
Secondary recording engineers: Bobby Brooks, Matt Forger, Andrew Scheps, Armand Volker, and Albert Boekholt
Assistant recording engineers: Tony Black, Mike Scotell, Greg Collins, Gerd Krenz, Patrick Ulenberg, Paul Dicato, Andy Strange, Rob Hoffman, and Tom Bender
Vocal arrangements: Michael Jackson
Drum programming: Matt Carpenter, Doug Grigsby, Andrew Scheps, Rob Hoffman, and Alex Breuer
Mixing: Dave Way

FOR JACKSON ADDICTS

The first mix was not released on disc, but can be found on rare promotional VHS releases of the film, edited in late 1996.

Double A-side single HIStory/Ghosts
Track 1: *HIStory* (*7-inch HIStory Lesson edit*) / 4'09
Track 2: *Ghosts* (*radio edit*) / 3'50
Released by Epic Records: Europe, 30 July 1997 (ref. 664615), single also released in Japan, Australia, and South Africa
Chart position: UK No. 5

Genesis

In 1993, Michael Jackson and Teddy Riley cowrote *Family Thing*, the main song for the *Is This Scary* video. The tune is groovy and driven by a new jack swing rhythm in which Michael's voice soars to the skies as he repeats the words "family thing." The song was all set to be released in December 1993, but was ultimately canceled after shooting for the film was halted a few months before.

In 1994, Michael and Riley met again to write another horror-themed song. The King of Pop already had a few melodies up his sleeve and wanted to develop them with the young musician and inventor of new jack swing, so he adapted his songs to the blended hip-hop rhythms Riley suggested. The chorus was written as a logical continuation to *Who Is It* and included a few lines in which Michael challenges his enemies before ending on a few practically a capella notes, as in *Another Part of Me*.

The lyrics then depart from the horror theme and turn into a paranoid tale where the King of Pop denounces the "ghost" of jealousy that is chasing him and trying to hurt him. Once again, Michael expresses his raw, unfiltered feelings through tunes that invite listeners to dance.

Production

Ghosts was written during the making of *HIStory* in 1994 but wasn't included in the tracklist of the double album. Michael chose *2Bad* instead, relegating the song he cowrote with Teddy Riley to the backburner. In 1996 he finalized the mix for *Ghosts*, which contained a constant rumbling bass. The young producer only used this instrument sparingly when working with Michael, completely leaving it out of other songs, as with *Dangerous*.

In *Ghosts*, Riley relied heavily on the drum machine, which he programmed to syncopate and hint at the funky and reptilian bass lines of *Billie Jean* and *Thriller*. He mixed and foregrounded the backing vocals and added effects and noises that recalled the musical masterpiece *Heartbreak Hotel* (1980). At the end of some refrains, Michael's voice rises as he sings the word "jealousy."

A second mix was created in early 1997 for the *Blood on the Dance Floor* remix album. The bass line was kept in the background and some of the drum machine kicks were left out. Drier and more subdued, this version nevertheless retains the digital cymbal clashing Riley had programmed for each refrain.

Michael Jackson created a classic dance sequence as the climax of the short film *Ghosts*.

1997

Is It Scary

Michael Jackson, James Harris III, Terry Lewis / 5'35

Musicians
Michael Jackson: lead and backing vocals
Jimmy Jam and Terry Lewis: all instruments
Recording
Flyte Tyme Studios, Edina, Minnesota / Larrabee Studios, Los Angeles: late 1994 to early 1995
Technical team
Producers: Michael Jackson, Jimmy Jam, and Terry Lewis
Recording engineer: Steve Hodge
Assistant recording engineers: Brad Yost, Xavier Smith, Ryan Arnold, Steve Baughman, and Steve Durkee
Arrangements: Michael Jackson, Jimmy Jam, and Terry Lewis
Vocal arrangements: Michael Jackson
Drum programming: Jeff Taylor
Keyboard programming: Andrew Scheps
Mixing: Steve Hodge

Genesis

It is clear from the beginning that *Is It Scary* is the logical follow-up to *Ghosts*. The song fingers those who accuse and judge Michael Jackson without really knowing him. The singer was fed up with people spreading lies or absurd ideas about him so his new approach was to wage a full-frontal attack. He wanted to start a fight, he challenged and provoked: "And if you wanna see / Eccentric qualities / I'll be grotesque before your eyes / Let them all materialize." In addition to the media, he was challenging a complicit and intrusive public, exposing its shameful flaws as if he were handing it a mirror. His tone became direct, provoking, and disinclined to forgiveness: "I'm gonna be / Exactly what you gonna see / So did you come to me / To see your fantasies / Performed before your very eyes."

The song is loaded with the language of horror and fantasy, which sounds like a malicious and daring echo to *Heartbreak Hotel* without, however, straying from the poetic. The lilts and directions of the lyrics to *Is It Scary* perfectly match the scenery in *Ghosts*, whose second part is the ideal video for this song.

Production

When Michael went to Minneapolis to record with Jimmy Jam and Terry Lewis during the making of *HIStory*, he told them about his initial plans for the song. "He told us about the lyrics and melody for this song idea he had," explained Jimmy Jam in an interview. "I think he had already worked with Teddy Riley on a track with a similar theme. He asked us to write the music track for this song he had in mind, and we just created this sort of sinister track. We weren't sure if Michael was going to include the song on the album or what he wanted to do with it. Although Michael had done his lyrics, the track wasn't fully finished, so we went in later and finished the track and mix."[120] The melodies of *Ghosts* and *Is It Scary* respond to each other like twins but also express two distinct sensibilities in terms of production material: Teddy Riley's new jack swing versus Jimmy Jam and Terry Lewis' Flyte Tyme sound.

For Jackson Addicts

As with *This Time Around*, *Is It Scary* never came out as a single but had some success in the promotional circuit, especially in Europe. A few promo maxi singles were produced in the UK and France. It was a time of strange marketing laws and some of the remixes had been intended for the *Smile* single before it was canceled.

On the Line / Gotta Put Your Heart on the Line

Kenneth "Babyface" Edmonds / 4'39 (1997 version) and 4'53 (2004 version)

From the film and albums: *Get on the Bus* by Spike Lee / *Michael Jackson—Ghosts (Deluxe Collector box set)* and *Michael Jackson: The Ultimate Collection* / **Released by Sony Pictures Home Entertainment / Columbia Pictures:** USA, 30 January 2001 (DVD ref. 03636) / Europe, 24 October 2006 (DVD ref. 725200) / **Released by Epic Records:** *Michael Jackson—Ghosts (Deluxe Collector box set)*: Europe, 12 December 1997 (ref. EPC 489155) / *Limited Edition minimax C*: UK, 1997 (ref. EPC 665268) / *Michael Jackson: The Ultimate Collection*: USA and Europe, 22 November 2004 (US ref. E5K 92600 and Europe ref. 517743 3) / **Musicians: Michael Jackson:** lead vocals/ **Recording: Hit Factory, New York:** July 1996 / **Technical team: Producer:** Babyface / **Recording engineer:** unknown / **Mixing:** unknown

From *Girl 6* to *Get on the Bus*

In 1996 Spike Lee had an undeniably great year. In March the director of *Do the Right Thing* and *Malcolm X* gave America a new dramatic comedy called *Girl 6*, whose promotion was extended until summer, when it appeared at the Cannes Film Festival. The original soundtrack—which was mainly populated with songs recorded by Prince and topped off with those of the various groups he'd founded—received some attention from the music industry. Around the time of the film's release, Spike Lee directed two music videos for Michael Jackson's *They Don't Care About Us* (see page 458) Lee, who used film as a vehicle for the promotion of African-American values, could boast of directing a respectable double whammy that year, one that would reach the top echelons of the pop world.

Get on the Bus, which came out in late 1996, was about an impressive protest that had taken place a few years before in Washington DC to highlight the socio-economic hardships of African-Americans. Known as the Million Man March, the event was controversial: it had been organized by Louis Farrakhan, the leader of the Nation of Islam and a man whose opinions had been widely criticized. What's more, the method they used to count the number of protest participants was questionable: they did not actually attract the million people they said they did, while there were no women to speak of among the ranks of the protesters.

Spike Lee's film, although fictional, took on the role of a documentary: the plot of *Get on the Bus* unfolds ahead of the rally as 15 very different men ride the bus to Washington DC. The film is not well known, perhaps because in the end, the event's impact wasn't nearly as significant as those that marked the Civil Rights movement. Among the wider public, the film only garnered very localized success, although it did elicit some interest from fans of the King of Pop. Rumor already had it that Michael Jackson would be recording a song written specifically for this project. The first showings of the film confirmed this news: in the introduction, Michael sings a lovely melody called *Gotta Put Your Heart on the Line*, or *On the Line*.

Genesis and production

The production of this song was part of an exchange of good practices between the pop icon and the director of African-American-oriented cinematic works. The eminent Babyface, who wrote the song, might have given it to Michael for inclusion in *HIStory*, as was the case for *Why* before it was given to 3T.

The lyrics are energizing and sound like a hymn: "Don't waste your time on the past, no, no / It's time you look to the future." The tone is confident, peaceful, and notably lacking in vindictiveness—it is rich in bright and melodious sounds, as per Babyface's characteristically pure style. The song inspires people to work toward the common good. Serene and progressive, it expertly accompanies the film's 15 main characters as they begin their journey.

The mix used in the film leaves a lot of room for Michael's voice to shine during the verses, as the soundtrack is softer and lighter. The chorus highlights the backing vocals, which overtake the sound of Michael's voice.

The song didn't appear on the original soundtrack CD but on a very rare promo CD by Columbia Pictures called *Get on the Bus—For Your Consideration*. The hope was that the song would be nominated for an Oscar. It was finally released on the bonus CD for the *Ghosts* film box set, which came out in Europe and Japan in December 1997, as if Michael had wanted to give fans exclusive access to its distribution.

During the 1990s, Babyface was one of the most sought-after composers and producers on the R&B scene.

FOR JACKSON ADDICTS

A longer version of the song reappeared in 2004 in *Michael Jackson—The Ultimate Collection* and lasted 4'53, along with a percapella passage that added to the song's power and potential.

Elizabeth, I Love You

Michael Jackson, Buz Kohan / 3'43

Musicians: Michael Jackson: lead vocals / **Choral and orchestral arrangements:** Suzie Katayama

Birth of a friendship

Michael Jackson and Elizabeth Taylor became friends under the lens of the paparazzi in the mid-1980s. The two stars were regularly seen together during official events, such as at the American Music Awards (1986 and 1993) or the horse races that Elizabeth Taylor loved attending. The two friends were outwardly affectionate toward each other throughout their lives. In 1988 Michael paid an impassioned tribute to his friend in the *Leave Me Alone* video, in which he practically erected a temple in her glory.

As the years passed, and through the gray clouds that darkened Michael's previously immaculate image, Elizabeth Taylor became a solid shoulder for him to cry on. She was a consummate supporter of Michael and concerned about his welfare as he increasingly became the subject of scandalous rumors. She was the one responsible for dubbing him the King of Pop when she publicly did so at the 1989 Soul Train Awards. Two years later, Michael hosted the reception for Elizabeth Taylor's seventh and last marriage at his Neverland ranch. The mark of their indelible friendship continued to deepen throughout the 1990s. In 1994 Michael personally presented Elizabeth Taylor with a special Jackson family prize during a grand fundraising gala: it was the Jackson Family Honor Award. Later, *Michael Jackson's Private Home Movies*, which was edited and broadcast in 2003, included various intimate moments the King of Pop shared with Elizabeth, such as when she gave him a magnificent Asian elephant called Gypsy, or when they opened their presents together at Christmas. At one of their last public appearances in 2001, Liz Taylor was present at Madison Square Garden for the last concert Michael would ever perform with his siblings. Their friendship was unbreakable: both knew what it was like to sacrifice one's childhood on the altar of showbiz.

A tribute song

On 16 February 1997, Michael made his first public appearance since the birth of his son Prince. Like a devoted admirer, he accompanied the famous actress to her 65th birthday party at the Hollywood Pantages Theatre. To celebrate the event, he surprised her with a song he'd written with his songwriting brother-in-arms Buz Kohan, who spoke of the moment in a 2009 interview:

Elizabeth Taylor visits her friend Michael backstage on the *Dangerous Tour* (1993).

> Michael was abroad and we were talking on the phone, late at night, as usual. He was telling me about his friendship with Elizabeth Taylor, and that their similar childhoods had brought them together...He wanted to pay tribute to the strength and courage that had allowed her to go on, just like

Michael Jackson pays tribute to his great friend Elizabeth Taylor by performing *Elizabeth, I Love You* at the Pantages Theatre, Los Angeles, on 16 February 1997.

he had. He'd written a tune and had a few ideas for the lyrics. He sent me what he had so far. I no longer have the original words he'd written, but I have a tape with a version sung at the piano that he'd recorded after we'd finished writing and composing the piece. I edited the words so that they'd illustrate his thoughts and keep the progression. I wanted to be sure that no false rhyme would creep in—I hate those. The version I ended up with was trying to tell a story. I don't really remember the writing process and I didn't take any notes on it. But I will say that this song came about as a 50/50 collaboration. Later, [Michael] told me how touched Elizabeth had been by the song.[134]

In an unusual move, the King of Pop agreed to perform his song live as a tribute to his friend. He sang it on a simple stage with two screens. The song discussed the values Michael shared with Elizabeth and the difficulty of their respective childhoods. His performance was so heartfelt that it brought tears to Elizabeth's eyes. This was Michael's only performance of the song.

FOR JACKSON ADDICTS

Musician Suzie Katayama wrote the orchestral arrangement and chorus for *Elizabeth, I Love You*. To promote her work, she released a CD compilation of her best arrangements in 1997. When fans got their hands on this nine-track album, they found a 1'38 excerpt of the song. It had been recorded in the studio and sounded like the musical accompaniment to the stage performance Michael had given that evening (Suzie Katayama, *Arrangements*, SK9701).

J-Friends

Children's Holiday

Michael Jackson / 4'20

Charity single: *Ashita ga Kikoeru—Children's Holiday* / **Released by the J-Friends Project:** Japan, 21 January 1998 (ref. JFDD-1) / **Chart position:** Japan Top 40 No. 3 / **Musicians: Tokio, KinKi Kids, and V6:** lead and backing vocals / **Suzukane Children's Choir:** children's backing vocals / **Lil' John Roberts:** drums / **Paulinho Da Costa**: percussion / **Doug Grigsby**: bass / **Charles Fearing and Brett Garsed**: guitars / **Michael Jackson, Brad Buxer, Steve Porcaro, and Geoff Grace**: keyboards and synthesizers / **Endre Granat, Murray Adler, Ron Clark, Joel Derouin, Armen Garabedian, Tiffany Hu, Jean Hugo, Karen Jones, Joe Ketendjian, Gary Kuo, Marisa McLeod, Frances Moore, Liana Reynolds, Olma Tsui:** violins / **Doug Davis, Anne Karam, Tian Soule, Cecilia Tsan:** viola / **Recording:** The Gallery, Brooklyn, New York; Ocean Way Recording, Los Angeles; Barking Doctor Studio, Mount Kisco, New York: 1994 to 1995 / Japanese studios: Johnny's Studio; Planet Kingdom; M-Bar Studio; Bunkamura Studio; Sound Inn; Sound Valley: 1997 / **Technical team: Japanese lyrics:** Goro Matsui / **Japanese directors**: Satoshi Shirota and Atsushi Sawamura / **Japanese codirectors:** Fujiyuki Kakayama (Johnny Company), Kaio Tsuruta, Kenichi Kimura (Dragon and Company Inc.) **Producers:** Michael Jackson, Brad Buxer, and Mick Guzauski / **Japanese producers:** Julie K., Jun-ichi "Randy" Tsuchiya, Johnny H. Kitagawa, Masato "Max" Matsuura, Mary Y. Kitagawa, Shinji Hayashi, Katsuro Oshita, and Keiichi Sakurai (Howdy International) / **Recording engineers:** Bobby Brooks and Tal Miller / **Japanese recording engineers (Mixer's Lab):** Maki Kosugi, Toshio Misu, Norihiko Ebihara, Yasuyuki Hara, Hiroshi Shitamiya, and Kenji Matsunaga / **Assistant recording engineers:** Linda Nilsson and Tom Bender / **Japanese assistant recording engineers:** Manabu Yokota (Mixer's Lab), Eiji Kameda (Planet Kingdom), Hirochi Akikubo (Birdie House), and Keiko Yamashita (Mixer's Lab) / **Drum programming:** Michael Jackson and James Allen / **Arrangements:** Michael Jackson, Brad Buxer, and Geoff Grace / **Additional programming:** Brad Buxer, Geoff Grace, and Doug Grigsby / **String coordination and orchestra conductor:** Jorge Del Barrio / **Mixing:** Mick Guzauski

Genesis

On 17 January 1995 at 5:46 a.m. local time, a very strong earthquake shook the entire Kobe region south of the Japanese island of Honshu. At that moment the country experienced one of its most tragic events in recent history. Estimated figures, which were constantly being revised upward, heralded thousands of deaths and injuries as well as considerable material damage. The world was affected by a unique, poignant, and unprecedented emotion. Many countries rallied to help by way of aid groups. They wanted to assist, support, and rehabilitate a city, a region, a hope for the country.

Michael Jackson couldn't help but be affected by this extraordinary situation. As with *We Are the World*, he wanted to use his fame to promote solidarity through humanitarianism. Almost three years after the catastrophe, he wrote two songs for the Japanese group J-Friends, which recorded *Children's Holiday* in 1998 and *People of the World* in 1999.

J-Friends was formed as a charity group in 1998 by Johnny's Entertainment, a famous Japanese male talent agency. Sony Music was among its longtime partners, making it the logical liaison between J-Friends and Michael Jackson. To create J-Friends, the agency united three of its successful groups—Tokio, V6, and KinKi Kids—to create a group totaling 13 singers. Over the course of almost five years, they took over the airwaves and performed one charity concert after another to promote their six singles, all of which were supported by big names in the international music scene: Michael Jackson, Elton John, Jon Bon Jovi, Earth, Wind, and Fire founder Maurice White, American award-winning composer and songwriter Diane Warren, and lastly, Koshi Inaba, the huge Japanese star from the group B'z. In 2003, as the project came to an end, J-Friends had raised ¥874,278,322, which is nearly $8.2 million today. The funds were used to help victims of the earthquake.

Production

The idea for *Children's Holiday* came during recording sessions for *HIStory*. Produced by Brad Buxer and Mick Guzauski, with Michael as executive producer, the piece was largely created by the same team that worked on *Little Susie*. Jorge Del Barrio conducted an orchestra of string instruments, vio-

On 17 January 1995 a violent earthquake left a permanent scar on the region of Kobe, Japan.

lins, and violas—bright sounds that brought weight and solemnity to the piece. Brad Buxer, Geoff Grace, and Steve Porcaro were responsible for setting down the synthesizer tracks and fine-tuning the gorgeous digital arrangements.

Michael, who sang a beatboxing segment in the piece, contributed in multiple ways, particularly in the composition, rhythmic arrangements, and synthesizing. Mick Guzauski recorded and mixed most of the instrumental tracks in the United States before handing them over to the Japanese teams, who added the children's vocals and chorus. Many of the Japanese studios were responsible for the vocal success of these three groups. Postproduction was entirely managed in Japan, building on the musical tracks provided by the US recording engineers.

The single, whose cover does not expressly advertise Michael's participation, sold more than a million copies. The launch was influential and the standard 3-inch double CD was released along with some cute little CD box sets containing a promotional pin and a booklet of the first drafts of the J-Friends project. The song reached No. 3 in the Japanese Top 40 charts and stayed there for nine weeks. *Children's Holiday* did not have an accompanying video, unlike *People of the World*, whose video strengthened promotion of the song.

The *Children's Holiday* and *People of the World* singles included the instrumental versions of the songs. A special mention goes to *People of the World*, which contains beautifully mixed choral tracks.

J-Friends

People of the World

Michael Jackson / 5'20

Charity single: *People of the World* / **Released by J-Friends Project:** Japan, 13 January 1999 (ref. SRCL 4500) / **Chart position:** Japan Top 40 No. 8 / **Musicians: Tokio, KinKi Kids, and V6:** lead and backing vocals / **Bobbi Page, Sally, Stevens, Rose Beattie, Beth Anderson, Monica Mancini, Edie Lehmann Baddicker, Donna Medine, Gigi Worth, Luana Jackman, Walt Harrah, Jim Gilstrap, Ron Hicklin, Cari Graves, Gene Merlino, Josef Powell, Gene Morford, Kevin Dorsey, Louis Price, Sierra Price, Daniec Ahelson, Sabrina Wiener, Heather Bahler, Laura Leavitt, Stefanie Solomon, Chauna Bryant, Christine Schillinger, Laura Jackman, Megan Dodds, Quincy Bahler, Marc Schillinger, and Fletcher Sheridan:** chorus / **Alia Brockert, Laurie Schillinger, Emerson Lee, Hideo Enomoto, Sachika Enamoto, Dara Hiller, Webster Heath, Marquise Brown, Gavin Turek, Alberto Keossian, Jessica Rotter, Laura Lively, Johnny Hall, Justin Hall:** children's chorus / **The Harmony of the World Japan's Mighty Singers:** Japanese chorus / **Kayoko Ishu:** soprano / **Johnny's Junior and Suzukane Children's Choir:** Japanese children's chorus / **Paulinho Da Costa:** percussion / **Doug Grigsby**: bass / **Greg Porée**: guitar / **Michael Jackson, Brad Buxer, Steve Porcaro, Geoff Grace, Isaiah Sanders**: keyboards and synthesizers / **Murray Older, Becky Bunnel, Mario De Leon, Alicia Engley, Armen Garabedian, Tiffany Hu, Gary Kuo, Natalie Leggett, Barbra Porter, Bob Sanov, Kimiyo Takeya, Olivia Tsui:** violins / **Carole Mukagawa, Matt Funes, Renita Koven, Jorge Moraga, Robin Ross, Ray Tischer:** violas / **Doug Davis, Bob Adcock, Chris Ermacoff:** cello / **Chuck Berghofer and Franci Liu:** stand-up bass / **Jerry Folsom, Marnie Johnson, Phillip Yoo:** horns / **Julie Berghofer:** harp / **David Shostac:** flute / **Vanessa Brown:** percussion / **Recording:** Neverland Ranch, Los Olivos, California; The Gallery, Brooklyn, New York; O'Henry Sound Studio, Burbank, California; Matt Hatter Studios, Los Angeles; Barking Doctor Studio, Mount Kisco, New York: 1994 to 1995 / Japanese studios: On Air Azabu Studio assisted by Shinpei Yamada; Johnny's Studio assisted by Momoko Yamaguchi; Delta Studio assisted by Satoshi Noguchi; Sound Inn assisted by Yoichi Kono: 1997 to 1998 / **Technical team: Japanese lyrics:** Yasushi Akimoto / **Japanese directors:** Satoshi Shirota, Atsushi Sawamura / **Japanese codirectors:** Fujiyuki Kakayama (Johnny Company), Kaio Tsuruta, Kenichi Kimura (Dragon and Company Inc.) / **Producers:** Michael Jackson, Brad Buxer, and Mick Guzauski / **Japanese producers:** Cora Endo (Mugen, lead and backing vocals in Japanese), Julie K., Sumihisa Nishi, Shinji Kawahara, Johnny H. Kitagawa, Hiroshi G., Ikuro Meguro, Ryuzo Kosugi, Shinji Hayashi, Tadayuki Kaminami / **Recording engineers:** Bobby Brooks, Rich Breen, Brad Buxer, Mike Ging, Michael Prince / **Japanese recording engineers:** Daiei Matsumoto, Maki Kasugi, Yuki Mitome / **Drum programming:** Michael Jackson, Brad Buxer, James Allen, Doug Grigsby / **Arrangements:** Michael Jackson, Brad Buxer, Geoff Grace / **Vocal arrangements:** Michael Jackson / **Backing vocal arrangements:** Michael Jackson, Tom Bahler / **Additional programming:** Brad Buxer, Geoff Grace, Doug Grigsby, Michael Prince / **String coordination and orchestra conductor:** Jorge Del Barrio / **Mixing:** Mick Guzauski assisted by Tom Bender

A second single based on the same model as *Children's Holiday* was recorded a year later. The same team was in charge, with the addition of Tom Bähler, the respected composer of the magnificent ballad *She's out of My Life*. He was now tasked with directing the piece's backing vocals. While the same musicians from *HIStory* and *Blood on the Dance Floor* were also involved, they never said whether Michael had originally intended to keep the songs for himself or not. For want of more information, an educated guess would be that Michael worked on these pieces with a strictly charitable aim in mind, given that the Kobe earthquake had taken place during recording sessions for *HIStory*. The King of Pop remained fairly quiet about his participation. In 2014, the *People of the World* demo (or *Children of the World*) was a victim of the MP3 format: brutally uploaded online and stripped of any meaningful context. Sung in gibberish by Michael, the song seems to act as a blueprint for layering certain tonalities and textual references. The Japanese version's lyrics, by Yasushi Akimoto, seem to have followed the inflections in this recording.

Promotion for *People of the World* was completely different from that of *Children's Holiday*. This time, Michael's participation was clearly marked on all covers and in global marketing. A music video (without Michael) was produced and released on VHS. Unfortunately, the song only remained on the Japan Top 40 for five weeks, reaching a pitiful No. 8. It was disappointing for a song that championed Michael's humanitarian values.

Ice Cube, Shaquille O'Neal, and Michael Jackson

We Be Ballin'

Rick "Dutch" Cousin / 5:07

National Basketball Association (NBA) compilation (canceled): 1998 / **Musicians: Ice Cube, Shaquille O'Neal, and Michael Jackson:** lead vocals / **Recording: A&M Studio, Hollywood:** 1998 / **Technical team:** unknown

Genesis and production

Initially, *We Be Clubbin'* (1997), which became *We Be Ballin'*, was included in the original soundtrack to *The Players Club*, produced and performed by Ice Cube.

In 1998, Rick "Dutch" Cousin, Ice Cube's composer, remixed the song and renamed it *We Be Ballin'* before including new lyrics sung by Shaquille O'Neal and Michael Jackson. The remixing project was originally supposed to include a series of NBA songs and become part of an ad campaign for the basketball league. Many problems would taint the basketball season that year, including a strike by the players. The project fell through, and the song was set aside.

Ten years later, in 2008, the internet made two versions of the song available to fans: *We Be Ballin' (master mix),* 5'07, and *We Be Ballin' (street mix*), 5'14. Michael's voice rang out in both songs' refrains as Ice Cube and Shaquille O'Neal sang the intervening rap sections. In a confident, energizing, and almost sardonic tone, the King of Pop sang, "Nothing you can say, nothing you can do / We be ballin' you, we be ballin' you / No one to defeat, you'll see what we can do / We be ballin' you, we be ballin' you."

In 2009, a third version appeared, *We Be Ballin'—Work in Progress* (5'33), which was closer to Ice Cube's initial version and which included a few supplementary vocal elements that had been lost in the first two.

This song is likely to be officially released someday, given how unusual it is. It will allow the wider public to hear Michael Jackson sing in a genre he was not known for: gansta rap.

Ice Cube and Shaquille O'Neal at the American Music Awards, held in the Shrine Auditorium, Los Angeles, 26 January 1998.

1. UNBREAKABLE
2. HEARTBREAKER
3 INVINCIBLE
4. BREAK OF DAWN
5. HEAVEN CAN WAIT
6. YOU ROCK MY WORLD
7. BUTTERFLIES
8. SPEECHLESS
9. 2000 WATTS
10. YOU ARE MY LIFE
11. PRIVACY
12. DON'T WALK AWAY
13. CRY
14. THE LOST CHILDREN
15. WHATEVER HAPPENS
16. THREATENED

Invincible **ALBUM**

Released by Epic Records: USA (ref. 69400) and Europe (ref. EPC 495174), 30 October 2001
Chart position: USA R&B No. 1, Pop No. 1 / UK No. 1
RIAA: certified Platininum 3 December 2001 / certified double Platininum 25 January 2002

Michael Jackson performs *Black or White* during the concert *A Night at The Apollo*, a charity gala organized by the Democratic Party (New York, 24 April 2002).

2001

INVINCIBLE, THE END OF AN ERA

Invincible was Michael Jackson's sixth solo album at Epic. The design and launch of the record revealed underlying tensions between the artist and Sony Music. It was in this difficult climate that the singer delivered his last album in an attempt to renew his image as the new millennium dawned.

After finishing the *HIStory* tour in South Africa on 15 October 1997, Michael Jackson returned to Neverland to rest and enjoy family life with his young son Prince Michael. The King of Pop kept his distance from the music scene throughout 1998. Nevertheless, he announced to Sony Music that he was working on a new album. This decision was taken mainly for financial reasons: despite Michael Jackson's recent successful tour, his income had fallen in the US where his records no longer sold as well as they once did. This drop in profitability led to suggestions that the record label was relegating the artist's projects to the back burner.

As a result, Michael Jackson was feeling less and less appreciated by the new team at the label with which he had collaborated since 1975, and was not overly motivated to return to the recording studio. Despite having announced to the label that he was working on a new opus, he spent most of 1998 traveling. In March, he was in Germany, then in May it was Namibia: the King of Pop had caught the travel bug. He went on numerous trips mainly with the aim of developing theme parks, a business project that seemed to interest him more than music. Between two business trips, he discreetly celebrated his 40th birthday. Radio stations and the media marked the occasion by broadcasting his music and videos. *Billboard* published a classification that ranked him as male artist with the greatest number of hits since the US charts were created in 1936.

His charity work continued to take up a lot of his time. On 15 May 1998, at a press conference in the Beverly Hills Hotel in Los Angeles, he announced that he was organizing a series of benefit concerts with Luciano Pavarotti and Elizabeth Taylor for the World Peace Foundation for Children. The project was due to be launched at the Jamsil Baseball Stadium in South Korea. It gradually took shape and the following year emerged as MJ and Friends.

On 9 November 1998, Michael Jackson won a court case against the *Daily Mirror*, which in 1992 had published a retouched and unflattering photo of him. The tabloid was ordered to publish a right of reply in the form of an interview with the journalist Piers Morgan.

Following the birth of his daughter Paris in Los Angeles on 3 April 1998, the King of Pop's priorities definitively changed: he had already achieved many of his professional objectives and increasingly began to concentrate on his family life and personal projects.

He was looking to abandon pure music production, and envisaged producing movie soundtracks rather than classic albums.

MJ and Friends

Michael Jackson spent 1999 working on the MJ and Friends project. The idea for these charity concerts came about after meeting the tenor Luciano Pavarotti and President Nelson Mandela. The aim was to raise money for the South African

Michael Jackson visits sick children before the first MJ and Friends concert in Seoul in June 1999.

president's foundation, the Red Cross, and UNESCO.

The two concerts in Seoul and Munich on 25 and 27 June 1999, organized by the star's long-standing promoter Marcel Avram, with whom he had worked on the *Bad*, *Dangerous*, and *HIStory* tours, raised the tidy sum of $3.3 million. The King of Pop invited many other artists, such as Ringo Starr and Luther Vandross, to perform in this outdoor music festival-style concert. Luciano Pavarotti was also invited but the tenor declined. Possibly because he had been displeased by Michael Jackson's last-minute decision not to appear at the Pavarotti and Friends concert in Montana, Italy, on 1 June 1999.

The King of Pop's appearance at his MJ and Friends concert was limited to a 40-minute set at the end of the show. It featured the *Greatest Hits* medley that he had previously performed at the MTV Video Music Awards in 1995. To this he added a brand-new rendition of *Dangerous*, initially planned for the canceled concert on HBO in December 1995. The highlight of the performance was a dramatic version of *Earth Song*. In the middle of the number, the singer climbed onto a bridge across the stage, called the Bridge of No Return, which symbolized the border between North and South Korea. When he reached the upper level, the bridge was lifted across the stage, giving the impression that it was breaking into pieces. The show went according to plan in Seoul, but two days later in Munich, a mechanical failure caused the platform on which the singer was standing to collapse. Shaken by the fall but unperturbed, Michael Jackson limped back on stage to finish his performance. At the end of the show, he was rushed to hospital before going to Paris for several days to rest. As a result of this accident, he suffered back pain that affected him for the rest of his life.

A new image

Alongside the MJ and Friends project, Michael Jackson was working on a new, innovative image for the millennium. By chance, he came across a photograph on the front page of *The Sunday Times* fashion supplement taken by a young French photographer, Arno Bani. The star had the young artist come to New York where the two men discussed ideas. Bani returned to France and began working with his team, designing sets and backdrops. The photoshoot took place in the utmost secrecy in studios in Issy-les-Moulineaux, close to Paris. The make-up artist Topolino created different looks for the King of Pop to match the backdrops for the photos. The French team sensed the tensions and power struggles in the Jackson camp. Surrounded by a crowd of yes-men, the star was isolated and struggled to establish simple, objective relationships.

After the session, Arno Bani finalized the visuals and produced a series of smooth and uncluttered futuristic photos. The main image that came out of the sessions, called *The Gold Cape*, was a reproduction of the original cover image from *The Sunday Times*. Michael Jackson strikes a pose as if he were the king of a new world. Along with the others, this photo would go directly to the Sony Music vaults. Arno Bani signed a contract relinquishing the image rights to Sony for ten years. The rights reverted to him in 2009, several weeks after the star's death.

The King of Pop, forced by his label to come up with another concept, contacted the American photographer Albert Watson, with whom he had been due to work on the sleeve for the remix album *Blood on the Dance Floor*. The photoshoot had been canceled at the last minute because the singer was sick. Michael Jackson wanted visuals inspired by two famous images by the photographer: *Golden Boy*, the photo of a young boy also based on the idea of a king of a new world, and a panoramic shot of the actor Jack Nicholson in movement. In the end, the *Golden Boy*-inspired visual was scaled down to an overexposed illustration of the star's face on a white background in five colours, Andy Warhol-style.

In July 1999 the French photographer Arno Bani reinvented Michael Jackson's image. In this shot, entitled *The Blue Eye*, Michael Jackson wears an Yves Saint Laurent jacket.

Choosing the producer

The *Invincible* album took months to put together. The singer would record a few tracks, then leave the studios for a while to do other activities. In the meantime, new and successful producers were appearing on the music scene. Along with Rodney Jerkins, the man who ended up orchestrating the project, the King of Pop approached The Neptunes, a production duo composed of Pharrell Williams and Chad Hugo. They had been discovered by Teddy Riley in the early 1990s and had since notched up many successes, pushing R&B into new territory (see page 374). They suggested several songs to Michael Jackson, including *Rock Your Body* and *Señorita*, but the star found that their compositions lacked a hook in the chorus. The producers made up for the disappointment of not working with Michael Jackson by giving the tracks to the young Justin Timberlake, who recorded them for his first solo album, *Justified*.

The King of Pop turned to Teddy Riley, a man he trusted. At the time, the inventor of new jack swing was attempting to follow up on the global success of BLACKstreet's second album in 1996. But a run of ill-advised choices and bad luck meant that his career was beginning to flounder: *Invincible* would be the biggest project that he undertook in the 2000s. Thanks to Riley's contribution, Michael Jackson broadened his scope with ballads like *Heaven Can Wait* that added a new sound to his musical portfolio.

Jackson versus the suits

While struggling laboriously through the initial drafts of *Invincible*, Michael Jackson took stock of his career. He was aware that he was no longer a priority artist for Sony Music, so he started trawling through the many pages and amendments of the contract that he had signed with the label in 1991. It seems he was under the impression that the masters of his songs would be returned to him in the year 2000. He would then be able to market them how he saw fit, either with another record company or with a label that he set up himself to avoid having to split the profits. However, it turned out that the terms were in fact somewhat different. His frustration at discovering that, in his opinion, the contract was to his disadvantage made his relationship with the label even more difficult. His label had also granted him a number of advance payments to enable him to maintain his standard of living, which notably included the running costs of Neverland. Things got worse when the King of Pop announced that he intended to quit the label once *Invincible* was completed and his last commitments fulfilled.

Sony Music did not want to include tracks like *The Lost Children*, which were felt to be too mawkish and infantile. The singer won out with this particular number, but others like *What More Can I Give*, the new humanitarian anthem that he had recorded with a glittering array of stars, never saw the light of day. Ditto for the duet *This Is Our Time*, recorded with the singer Lauren Hill. Under the circumstances, Michael Jackson did his best to finish *Invincible*, but with little enthusiasm. For the first time in his career, his decisions were being systematically challenged and subjected to endless debate. *Invincible* seemed to become more a settling of scores through various lawyers and assistants than an artistic project. Especially so because, following the death of Sony's founder, Akio Morita, Michael Jackson had lost not only a friend but his staunchest supporter in the company. Using the delivery of the *Invincible* masters tapes as a bargaining chip, the King of Pop is believed to have demanded to be given a part in the movie *Men in Black II* with Will Smith and Tommy Lee Jones. Although the singer won that particular battle, his appearance in the movie lasted a mere few seconds.

Sony's Tommy Mottola had already had run-ins with other key artists such as George Michael and Mariah Carey, as well as the promising young singer Terence Trent D'Arby. All had become embroiled in battles and costly court cases.

Sony enforces promotion strategy

At this point some were claiming that, if the album did not sell, Michael Jackson would go even deeper into debt. The advances paid to the artist over the years plus the cost of producing the album, estimated at a record $30 million, and the $25 million budgeted for the launch would leave Jackson heavily indebted to the label, forcing him to dispose of his ATV shares.

It's believed that Sony refused to accept *Unbreakable* as the initial single. Instead *You Rock My World,* a revamped version of *Remember the Time*, was preferred to open the proceedings. A mediocre-quality version of the song was leaked to KTU radio, perhaps deliberately, but no culprit was ever found. Faced with a *fait accompli*, Michael Jackson was forced to accept the situation and start preparing a short film for this R&B track coproduced with Rodney Jerkins.

A record industry in flux

As if one piece of bad news were not enough, Michael Jackson was forced to stand by and watch powerless as the music industry changed beyond recognition. The emergence of the internet, MP3, and the then-illegal file-sharing service Napster completely transformed people's music-listening habits. Consumers were getting their own back on a record industry that had sold and resold the same albums in different formats. Napster, as well as other networks and software like e-Mule, were free, instantaneous, and enabled people to bypass the major labels. Initially, the record companies underestimated the devastation that would be wreaked by this new consumer tool known as the Internet. They thought that people who listened to music were too attached to CDs and other physical media. This error of judgment threw the major labels into crisis with mergers, buyouts, bankruptcies, and redundancies coming thick and fast in the 2000s.

In 2001, Michael Jackson, the man who had broken all sales records, found himself in an industry that had lost its sheen: CDs were on their way out and streaming was still far from being a legal and profitable enterprise. Notwithstanding all these factors, *Invincible* managed to sell six million copies in three months, making it one of the best album launches of the star's career, despite a much-reduced promotional campaign compared to his previous albums.

New York, September 2001

The recording of *Invincible* seemed to go on forever: Michael Jackson missed several delivery deadlines for the tapes, and

Michael Jackson and Dave Navarro in the charity concert *A Night at the Apollo,* organized by the Democratic Party in New York, 24 April 2002.

the album was postponed several times. Not content with dragging his feet about delivering the record, the artist refused to commit to another tour. The *Invincible* tour would be a huge global endeavor that he was unwilling to undertake. Weary of endless touring, he did not want to have to cope with the insomnia, which he kept at bay with a cocktail of drugs. However, he did acquiesce to his friend David Gest's idea of holding two special concerts in New York to celebrate the 30th anniversary of his solo career, which had begun in 1971 with *Got to Be There*. For the occasion, he performed onstage with his brothers for the first time since the famous *Victory* tour in 1984. Over the two evenings they played some of their greatest hits.

The concerts were held on 7 and 10 September 2001 in the legendary Madison Square Garden. They were produced by David Gest and filmed for broadcast on CBS in the US. Putting the show together was a real headache. As well as having to manage the artists who had been invited to pay tribute to Michael Jackson on stage, including Destiny's Child, Liza Minnelli, Marc Anthony, Usher, and Whitney Houston, the organizers had to use all their powers of diplomacy to bring the brothers together. Jermaine tried to impose his own ideas on the design of the show and went his own way on certain issues, refusing, for example, to wear the same costumes as the other group members. He was the only one to show up with his own wardrobe.

The first concert was instantly forgettable: the King of Pop was not on good form and his performance was under par. At a crisis meeting, David Gest told him in no uncertain terms to get his act together. The following evening, the star put on a dazzling show. Most of the sequences aired on television were filmed that evening. Michael Jackson was back onstage and the future looked bright. But the following morning, 11 September, the attacks on the World Trade Center, a few blocks away from Madison Square Garden, plunged the world into what was just the start of a long terror campaign. Michael Jackson had an appointment in one of the twin towers on the morning of the attacks. Luckily for him he overslept, but the tragedy, of course, left its mark on him.

September and October were taken up with preparations for the launch of the new album. On 15 October, Epic rereleased Michael Jackson's first four solo albums: *Off the Wall*, *Thriller*, *Bad*, and *Dangerous*. They all contained bonus tracks, as well as interviews with Quincy Jones and Rod Templeton. *Dangerous* was too long for additional tracks so a bonus CD was planned, but it never saw the light of day. Many bonus songs planned for the rereleases stayed in the vaults. These included *Sunset Driver*, *Got the Hots*, and *Monkey Business*.

On 31 October, *Invincible* finally hit stores. It got off to an excellent start, helped by a promotional campaign in which Michael Jackson had reluctantly agreed to be involved. On 7 November, he attended the first-ever record signing of his career at the Virgin Megastore in New York. Given the context, massive security measures were implemented, but the King of Pop managed to meet those lucky fans who made it to the head of the long queue, one by one. *You Rock My World* was released as a single, and a short film directed by Paul Hunter inundated the TV channels. The track was enormously successful, especially in nightclubs where people went crazy for this R&B gem. But the promotional campaign rapidly floundered. Sony backed *Cry* for the second single, but the public preferred *Butterflies*, which reached the Top 20 in the US R&B charts. Sony agreed to distribute the track on the promotional circuit only and commissioned a remix from the Track Masters team, who brought in the popular rapper Eve to give the song a hip-hop feel. Michael Jackson made the cover of two prestigious magazines: *TV Guide* on 12 November 2001, the day before the TV broadcast of the 30th anniversary celebration concert in New York, and *Vibe*, Quincy Jones's magazine, in February 2002.

The final battles

2002 got off to a downbeat start. In the US, the promotion of *Invincible* ground to a halt. Sony began to cease marketing activities for the album and move on to something else. In the UK and France a very small number of promotional records were pressed with the idea of getting airplay on the major radio stations. This did not produce the hoped-for results, and the album vanished from view.

Frustrated and angry, Michael Jackson opted for direct confrontation: with the support of some of his fan clubs, he attempted to organize demonstrations against Sony's chairman. He was spotted on a London bus brandishing banners and protesting outside the offices of Sony Music in England. The same evening, he attended an event organized by his fans at the Equinox nightclub, where he took the mike to announce that he had only one more box set and a few new songs to produce for the label before he would quit. There were similar scenes in New York on 6 July. This time, the King of Pop, accompanied by Reverend Al Sharpton, a controversial American Civil Rights activist, accused the record company of exploiting black artists. The duo were back together again in Harlem on 9 July where Michael Jackson gave a speech explaining his version of the recent issues with Sony Music and the record industry: "Once I started breaking sales records, I broke Elvis Presley's record, I broke The Beatles' record—once I started doing that, overnight they called me a freak, a homosexual, a child molester...They said I bleached my skin. They did everything they could to turn the public against me. It's a conspiracy."[135]

A few stalwart supporters

During this troubled period, the King of Pop could only count on a handful of supporters, including, for example, his long-standing friend Dick Clark, who twice invited him on television during primetime viewing hours. On 9 January 2002, the entertainer organized the 29th American Music Awards at Shrine Auditorium in Los Angeles. Michael Jackson received an award especially created for him, the artist of the century, which was presented to him on stage by Chris Tucker. On 20 April, the singer recorded a number for the 50th anniversary edition of *American Bandstand*, the top variety show hosted by Dick Clark.

On 24 April 2002, Michael Jackson gave the last public performance of his career when former President Bill Clinton invited him to a charity evening organized by the Democratic Party, called *A Night at the Apollo* after the famous Harlem, New York venue. The star only performed songs from his *Dangerous* album: the title track, *Black or White*, and *Heal the World*. Diana Ross, his professional godmother, joined him onstage for the finale, and it was as if everything had come full circle.

The *Invincible* album was a victim of personal and financial struggles: it was misunderstood at the time of its release and given very little opportunity with the public, due to the lack of decent promotion. This financial and artistic blow convinced the singer that his future no longer lay in the music world. More than ever he felt drawn toward film.

In the late 1990s, Rodney Jerkins had become the must-have producer on the US R&B scene.

PORTRAIT

RODNEY JERKINS
THE DARKCHILD SOUND

Rodney Jerkins was born in Pleasantville, New Jersey, on 29 July 1977 to a minister father and choir director mother. From the age of five, he became immersed in music, learning to play the piano. Along with his brother Fred, he soon began to write his own songs, a combination of gospel and rap. The formula was reminiscent of new jack swing, invented by Teddy Riley in the mid-1980s. In 1991, after Jerkins had pursued Riley through a parking lot begging to be given a chance, the highly talented writer, producer, and musician took Jerkins under his wing and introduced him to record production. The young Rodney thus became acquainted with the complex procedures of a recording studio. Teddy Riley offered him a contract, but the young musician preferred to go it alone and build his own empire.

First contracts

The Jerkins brothers published an album together in 1992, called *On the Move*. Two years later, Rodney signed off his first record as sole producer for the singer Casserine and her label Warner Brothers Records. But the first hits came in 1997 when he produced the tracks *I Don't Wanna Be a Player* and *I Can Love You* by Joe (Joseph Lewis Thomas) and Mary J. Blige.

The same year, he entered the Jackson orbit for the first time when he worked with the group No Authority, who had just landed a contract with the King of Pop's label, MJJ Music. The track in question, *Don't Stop*, sank into oblivion, but Rodney Jerkins was already on the up and his work was set to redefine the foundations of modern R&B in the late 1990s.

The young producer was responsible for the sound of Destiny's Child, producing the smash hit *Say My Name*. He also worked with Whitney Houston, for whom he oversaw production of the album *My Love Is Your Love* (1998). Borrowing the idea of a lovers' tiff from Michael Jackson's *The Girl Is Mine*, he produced a mid-tempo number for singers Brandy and Monica called *The Boy Is Mine*. Brandy continued to work with Jerkins, publishing the album *Full Moon* in early 2002 and setting the tone for R&B production, which was undergoing a radical transformation.

Over the years, Rodney Jerkins became known for his signature style, based on highly syncopated rhythms that continued the work begun by Timbaland in the early 1990s. To this, he added a soul feel and a love of melody, as seen in his productions for the gospel duo Mary Mary. The word Darkchild, the name of his company, identifies his productions and often appears in the intros of artists with whom he works.

MJ and RJ

In 1999, Rodney Jerkins joined Epic Records to launch the careers of the singer Rhona and the group So Plush. Neither of the two projects really took off, but in the meantime the producer was introduced to Michael Jackson by the singer-songwriter Carole Bayer Seger. The King of Pop, who was planning to add new talent to his team and make a comeback with an innovative album, had found just the man he needed.

The two men worked for many months on *Invincible,* but the recording sessions went on longer than anticipated, and the producer had to start working on Brandy's album *Full Moon* before *Invincible* was finished.

The mixed reviews for Michael Jackson's last solo album released in his lifetime did not curb Rodney Jerkins' ambitions. He went on to work with many other artists, including Beyoncé, for whom he produced *Déjà Vu* in 2006. The second half of the 2000s brought its own set of changes, including new producers who connected well with the public such as will.i.am of the Black Eyed Peas and Pharrell Williams.

Rodney Jerkins began the 2010s with a few productions for popular artists like Britney Spears and Nelly Furtado, but his glory days were behind him. When Michael Jackson decided to create some new songs in 2007 and 2008, he did not call on Jerkins. The producer nevertheless played a role in the King of Pop's posthumous career, reworking the song *Xscape* that he had developed with the singer in the early 2000s.

Like Teddy Riley, Jerkins had tried to stamp his style on Michael Jackson. Their collaboration may have led to the hit *You Rock My World*, but other songs, which were either not released as singles, attached to a short film, or performed onstage, are only remembered by the creator of *Billie Jean*'s most dedicated fans.

FOR JACKSON ADDICTS

A promotional maxi vinyl with the album version of *Unbreakable* was released in the United Kingdom. Only France released an edit version (4'48); the pressed CD-Rs were sent to radio stations.

UNBREAKABLE

2001

Michael Jackson, Rodney Jerkins, Fred Jerkins III, LaShawn Daniels, Nora Payne, Robert Smith, Carl McIntosh, Jane Eugene, Steve Nichol / 6'25

Musicians

Michael Jackson: lead and backing vocals, keyboards, and synthesizers
Brandy: backing vocals
The Notorious B.I.G.: rap (excerpt from the track *You Can't Stop the Reign*)
Rodney Jerkins: keyboards and synthesizers

Recording

The Hit Factory, New York / Criteria Studios, Miami: 2000 to 2001

Technical team

Producers: Michael Jackson and Rodney Jerkins
Recording engineer: Stuart Brawley
Assistant recording engineer: Paul Foley
Mixing: Bruce Swedien, Rodney Jerkins, Stuart Brawley

Michael Jackson greets fans at the Virgin Megastore in New York, 7 November 2001.

Genesis

For the song that opens his sixth solo album for Epic, Michael Jackson delivered a text in which he once again sought to settle the score with all those who were harassing him. Somewhat prophetically, he appears to predict the problems that were to arise with his label. "No matter what you do / I'm still gonna be here." This sets the tone; the King of Pop is not going to be told what to do. The paranoia that was subtly evoked in *Wanna Be Startin' Somethin'*, the lead-off track in *Thriller* in 1982, now became the promise of a full-blown fight, whatever the cost, with whoever stood in his way.

To give flesh to these vindictive lyrics, effectively a battle cry, Jackson and Rodney Jerkins' team composed an insistent bass line overlaid with a wild and pounding melody.

Production

Rodney Jerkins, creator of the Darkchild sound, rolls out the big guns on this track that has the onerous task of opening *Invincible*. The bass line, overdubbed by the same notes on a digital piano, sits on a solid heavy beat. Each bass note is reinforced by a bass drum programmed by Jerkins.

The singer Brandy, who was working with Jerkins at the time on her album *Full Moon*, performed backing vocals, but her voice is virtually inaudible in the final mix due to an excessively rich production that ends up burying the subtle nuances of certain arrangements. *Unbreakable* features a second guest appearance: the rapper Notorious B.I.G., aka Biggie Smalls, performing a posthumous rap. He was murdered in Los Angeles on 9 March 1997, but had previously recorded a track with Shaquille O'Neal in 1996 entitled *You Can't Stop the Reign*. Rodney Jerkins had been present for the Shaq and Biggie Smalls' sessions, and suggested to Michael Jackson that they use part of the rap. It was the second time, after *This Time Around* in 1995, that Jackson had recorded with the iconic rapper from the Bad Boy Records label.

Heartbreaker

Michael Jackson, Rodney Jerkins, Fred Jerkins III, LaShawn Daniels / 5'10

Musicians
Michael Jackson: lead and backing vocals, keyboards, and synthesizers
Mischke, LaShawn Daniels, Nora Payne: backing vocals
Fats: rap
Rodney Jerkins: keyboards and synthesizers
Recording
Marvin's Room Studio and Darkchild Studios, Los Angeles (rap) / The Hit Factory, New York and Criteria Studios, Miami (mixing): 2000 to 2001
Technical team
Producers: Michael Jackson, Rodney Jerkins
Recording engineers: Bruce Swedien, Stuart Brawley
Assistant recording engineers: Alex Greggs, Fabian Marasciullo
Rap recording: Bob Brown
Mixing: Bruce Swedien

Michael Jackson makes a surprise appearance in the song *Pop*, at the end of a performance by the group *NSYNC at the MTV Video Music Awards in New York, 6 September 2001.

Genesis

Michael Jackson's favorite theme, the femme fatale, creeps insidiously into the lyrics of *Heartbreaker*. The singer describes being emotionally tortured by a gorgeous creature whom he wishes he had never met. Written in collaboration with the Darkchild team, *Heartbreaker* is another variation on the songs typical of Michael Jackson's repertoire in the 1990s: syncopated, almost phrased verses following on from melodious choruses. The song breaks away from this predictable style at the bridge where the King of Pop writes in a melody and arrangements that bring welcome depth to the composition.

Production

The rhythm of *Heartbreaker* is directly inspired by Timbaland's productions. The rapper, who made his production debut with young artists like Jodeci at the Uptown label, redefined the basics of modern R&B. He notably produced singer Ginuwine's first album, *The Bachelor*, in 1996 as well as his chart-topping hit *Pony*, which stands out for the robotic frog sound alongside the bass drum at the start of each measure. Jackson took this idea and used it on *Heartbreaker*, which gave it a somewhat outdated sound pattern for a record released in late 2001.

Rodney Jerkins asked the young rapper Fats, who just signed with Sony, to perform on the track. Michael Jackson's vocals that come in at the bridge add phrasing, conferring a vintage Jackson melody. *Heartbreaker* stands out for the many sound effects toward the end, as well as its breaks and false endings. These sophisticated arrangements, programmed by Rodney Jerkins, were noticed by members of the band *NSYNC, who heard the song before it was released. At the time, they were working on their new album on which the track *Pop*, released on 15 May 2001, was inspired by the digital and electro arrangements on *Heartbreaker*. The group of youngsters, therefore, somewhat rudely jumped the gun, releasing their work before the King of Pop's came out on 31 October the same year.

INVINCIBLE

2001

Michael Jackson, Rodney Jerkins, Fred Jerkins III, LaShawn Daniels, Norman Gregg / 4'45

Musicians
Michael Jackson: lead and backing vocals, keyboards, and synthesizers
Fats: rap
Rodney Jerkins: keyboards and synthesizers
Recording
Record Plant Studios and Darkchild Studios, Los Angeles (rap) / The Hit Factory, New York, and Criteria Studios, Miami (mixing): 2000 to 2001
Technical team
Producers: Michael Jackson and Rodney Jerkins
Recording engineer: Bruce Swedien and Stuart Brawley
Rap recording: Bob Brown
Mixing: Bruce Swedien

Rodney Jerkins and the rapper Fats, who features in the songs *Heartbreaker* and *Invincible*.

Genesis

The album's title song was another collaboration between the Darkchild team and Michael Jackson. Rodney Jerkins's style clearly dominates the score. Some lines in the verses recall lyrics from songs by other artists that he produced, such as Jennifer Lopez.

The King of Pop sings of his love for an unattainable woman, whom he describes as invincible. Like *Heartbreaker*, he contributed to the bridge, which brought phrasing to the song as a whole. He ends some sentences with expressions like "My baby," which had already been used with specific intonation in *Dangerous*.

Production

For *Invincible*, Rodney Jerkins programmed a lighter but still clearly urban rhythmic base. Far from the terse, hammered-out beat of *Unbreakable*, this track is a continuation of the electro-inspired *Heartbreaker*, but the programming effects are more subtle. In a sense, this song is a more distinct sign of things to come on the US R&B scene.

The rapper Fats once again produces a workable rap, although his performance is nowhere near the league of other hip-hop artists such as Heavy D and the group Wreckx-N-Effect who had recorded for the King of Pop in the past.

Break of Dawn

Dr. Freeze, Michael Jackson / 5'32

Musicians
Michael Jackson: lead and backing vocals, all instruments
Dr. Freeze: backing vocals and all instruments
Rodney Jerkins and Teddy Riley: all instruments
Recording
Hit Factory, New York / Ocean Way Recording, Record One studios and John McClain Studio, Los Angeles / Neverland Valley Ranch Recording Studio, Los Olivos: 1999 to 2000
Technical team
Producers: Michael Jackson and Dr. Freeze
Recording engineers: Mike Ging, Brad Gilderman, Humberto Gatica, Dexter Simmons, and George Mayers
Drum programming: Michael Jackson and Brad Buxer
Mixing: Humberto Gatica, Teddy Riley, and George Mayers

Michael Jackson receives his award from the group *NSYNC on the occasion of his induction into the Roll Hall of Fame as a solo artist (New York, Waldorf Astoria Hotel, 19 March 2001).

Genesis

Many years after the song was recorded, the singer, composer, and producer Elliot Straite, alias Dr. Freeze (who was behind tracks such as *Poison* by Bell Biv DeVoe in 1990 and *I Wanna Sex You Up* by Color Me Badd in 1991), was interviewed by members of the MJFrance forum. John McClain, Michael Jackson's manager, contacted the musician, who then presented 30 songs to the King of Pop, of which only five or perhaps six, as he recalls, were developed with three ultimately released. *Break of Dawn* completed the tracklist of the *Invincible* album in 2001, while *A Place with No Name* and *Blue Gangsta* were relegated to the vaults before being resuscitated in 2014 for the *Xscape* project. *Rise above It All* remains unpublished to date and may not have been completely finalized.

Break of Dawn is a sensual and sentimental number. The singer makes love all night until dawn. The lyrics are an ecstatic declaration of love: "I don't want the sun to shine, I wanna make love / Just this magic in your eyes and in my heart."

Production

Michael Jackson left Dr. Freeze's composition for *Break of Dawn* untouched, and did not even make any changes to the backing vocals sung by the songwriter. "He loved the song!" recalls the composer. "He wanted to leave it just as it was! Everything I'd done to the piece, no one was allowed to change anything." [136] According to Dr. Freeze, it was Michael Jackson's voice that made the track truly magical. He still recalls how deeply moved he was by Jackson's rendition: "Sometimes, he recorded the lead vocals, sometimes just the backing vocals or the ad-libs...He would listen to the different mixes and change a few details here and there. He was in full creative control. We wanted the song to be perfect...He was a bit like a director who wanted to improve his film by developing the script...He used this type of process to create the song and the rest of the *Invincible* album." [136]

2001

HEAVEN CAN WAIT

Michael Jackson, Teddy Riley, Andreao Heard, Nate Smith, Teron Beal, Eritza Laues, Kenny Quiller / 4'49

Musicians
Michael Jackson: lead and backing vocals
Dr. Freeze: additional backing vocals
Recording
Future Recording Studios, Virginia Beach, Virginia / The Hit Factory, New York / Criteria Studios, Miami: 2001
Technical team
Producers: Michael Jackson and Teddy Riley
Coproducers: Andreao "Fanatic" Heard and Nate Smith
Conducting and orchestral arrangements: Jeremy Lubbock
Recording engineers: Teddy Riley, Bruce Swedien, and George Mayers
Mixing: Bruce Swedien, Teddy Riley, and George Mayers

Michael Jackson accepts the artist of the century award at the 29th American Music Awards ceremony at the Shrine Auditorium in Los Angeles (9 January 2002).

Genesis

The track *Heaven Can Wait* is a collaboration between Teddy Riley and Michael Jackson. The song could have appeared on a BLACKstreet album if the King of Pop had not insisted on using it for *Invincible*. Although death is the underlying theme in the song, the lyrics are mostly about love and a determination not to leave the loved one behind. Heaven, exclaims the singer, cannot compare to his love: "No, if the angels took me from this Earth / I would tell them bring me back to her." The angelic backing vocals reinforce the star's persistent pleas to be allowed to stay with his beloved. The song opens with a few synthesizer notes and the chorus, as if the supposedly dying man in the song wants the angels to understand from the outset that his time has not yet come.

Production

In an interview in July 2009, Teddy Riley spoke of how the great artists with whom he worked took time to patiently polish their productions. Referring to *Heaven Can Wait*, he said: "What I did with Michael doing strings on *Heaven Can Wait*, was like, we did the track first, that all took one day, and then the string section, and then we did the guitar session and that's about three days."[137] Dr. Freeze puts in an appearance on the backing vocals, consolidating the distinctive texture of the ballads on the *Invincible* album. Michael Jackson's voice glides easily through the grooves on the song, resulting in one of the best vocal performances of the album. He voices some magnificent declarations of love that authoritatively ricochet off the harmonies.

Sony Music included *Heaven Can Wait* on a promotional compilation of love songs entitled *An Epic Valentine* (US ref. ESK 56726) before sending the track to radio stations as they did with *Butterflies*. The song reached No. 70 in the *Billboard* R&B/Hip-Hop Airplay, and surprisingly made it to No. 72 in the Hot R&B/Hip-Hop Songs, although no single or supporting video was released. If the *Invincible* album had been promoted as it should have been, *Heaven Can Wait* had the potential to be what could have been the last major hit of the King of Pop's career.

You Rock My World

Michael Jackson, Rodney Jerkins, Fred Jerkins III, LaShawn Daniels, Nora Payne / 5'39

Musicians
Michael Jackson: lead and backing vocals, spoken intro, keyboards, and synthesizers
Chris Tucker: spoken intro
Rodney Jerkins: keyboards and synthesizers
Recording
Sony Studios, New York / Ocean Way Recording, Record One studios, Los Angeles / The Hit Factory, New York and Criteria Studios, Miami (mixing): 1999
Technical team
Producers: Michael Jackson and Rodney Jerkins
Recording engineers: Brad Gilderman, Rodney Jerkins, Jean-Marie Horvat, Dexter Simmons, Stuart Brawley
Assistant recording engineers: Harvey Mason
Mixing: Bruce Swedien and Rodney Jerkins

FOR LISTENERS

Jackson's vocal performance is the result of various takes juxtaposed in the final mix. The cuts and changes of takes are fairly audible in the a cappella version pressed on singles.

Single

USA
A- and B-sides: *You Rock My World* / 5'39
UK
A-side: *Intro*: 0'32 - *You Rock My World (album version)* / 5'07
B-side: *You Rock My World (radio edit)* / 4'25
Released by Epic Records: USA (ref. 34 79656) and UK (ref. 671765), 5 October 2001
Chart position: USA R&B No. 13, Pop No. 10 / UK No. 2

THE SONG

Genesis

When Michael Jackson, Teddy Riley, and Bernard Belle composed *Remember the Time*, they created a template that Rodney Jerkins replicated on several occasions, including on *You Rock My World*. The song is structured around well-ordered variations and groove progression. The continuity of the verses and choruses blending into one another evokes the narrative thread of a love story. Jerkins used the same pattern in 1998 for *The Boy Is Mine*, an R&B track by Brandy and Monica, two popular female singers at the time. A few months later, he used the same building bricks for *If I Told You That*, which sounds like a modern version of *Remember the Time*. *If I Told You That* was ultimately performed by Whitney Houston, but it had been planned as a duet with Michael Jackson. The King of Pop was excited by the idea, but after the news was leaked and the fans of both singers found out about it, he changed his mind and decided not to go ahead with it. George Michael replaced him on the radio edit version.

Rodney Jerkins did not give up on the idea of having Michael Jackson record a classic R&B track in the same vein as *Remember the Time*. This was how *You Rock My World* came into being in 1999. The song is a collaboration between the singer and the producer's team and is not hugely original, but it brings the kind of funk-soul feel to *Invincible* that had been absent on *HIStory*.

The lyrics are a classic declaration of love, with a rather excessive use of the clichés that appeared on popular R&B songs at the time. They nevertheless add spark to this positive love song that is filled with hope in a way that had not been seen in a Michael Jackson song since *Liberian Girl* and *I Just Can't Stop Loving You* on *Bad* in 1987.

Production

You Rock My World was recorded in 1999 in New York and Los Angeles. The spoken intro featuring the star and Chris Tucker joking around was recorded in 2001 after the song was finalized. Rodney Jerkins did all the programming for the track, on which a full groovy rhythm gradually takes shape. The decrescendo bass line is reminiscent of *Get on the Floor*, a funk number cowritten by Michael Jackson and Louis

Chris Tucker shares the stage with Michael Jackson during the *30th Anniversary Celebration* show in September 2001 at Madison Square Garden, New York.

> *You Rock My World* sealed a long friendship between Michael Jackson and Marlon Brando. In his twilight years, the actor said: "Michael is my best friend...at least the only loyal one. The other ones betrayed me." [138]

Johnson for *Off the Wall*. Piano chords follow the bass line, giving the song a richer, groovier feel. The measures before the first verse and in the choruses leave room for an arrangement written for strings, although played on a synthesizer it deprives *You Rock My World* of the kind of texture that comes from acoustic instruments. The piece unashamedly uses the kind of sonic gimmicks that feature in Jackson's short films or stage performances. The sound of steps can be heard in the first beats of each measure in the choruses, as if a group of dancers were tapping out the beat.

THE SHORT FILM

Director: Paul Hunter
Producer: Rubin Mendoza
Leading actors: Michael Jackson, Chris Tucker, Marlon Brando, Kishaya Dudley
Extras: Michael Madsen, Billy Drago, Miko Brando
Shoot dates: 13 to 21 August 2001
Shooting location: Los Angeles
Duration: 13'43

Genesis

You Rock My World was released as the lead-off single. The King of Pop had started working on an ambitious project for *Unbreakable*, and was forced to put it on ice. Under time pressure in mid-summer 2001 he designed a concept for *You Rock My World*: a short film that would encompass the whole of his visual universe. He hired Paul Hunter, a young movie director who had been producing successful music videos since the mid-1990s. Videos that he had directed for artists such as Notorious B.I.G. Christina Aguilera, and D'Angelo had won numerous MTV awards.

As well as looking back on the high points in his own career, Michael Jackson wanted to pay homage to his friend Marlon Brando. This would be the legendary actor's last significant on-screen appearance. The backdrops chosen for the short film for *You Rock My World* were inspired by two of Brando's films: *On the Waterfront* and *Guys and Dolls*.

Production

Michael Jackson was unhappy with the budget and support provided for *You Rock My World*. He had very little financial control over his short films, and here, even less than usual. In these difficult circumstances, he did not attend initial rehearsals, so for several days the dancers worked without him.

Paul Hunter got on with filming the sequences that alluded to the King of Pop's previous work. *You Rock My World* featured dialogue from previous short films (for example, the famous "You ain't nothing" from *Bad*, here spoken by Billy Drago) and some of the iconic images on which the Jackson legend was built (the silhouette behind a screen from the concert version of *Smooth Criminal*). It was an intentionally subjective summary by the man who had virtually invented the music video. It was as if he were consciously or unconsciously bringing the curtain down on his own body of work.

Michael Jackson's face is seen at the start of the video but from then on it is hidden in the shadow of his hat, using an effect that owes much to the miracles of postproduction. He physically appears on the screen, but is embodied only by his famous gestures, symbols he had created over the years that were all brought together in the editing of the video, which he supervised with Paul Hunter. The production of the *You Rock My World* short film is a perfect example of technical mastery, but it is not the best film the King of Pop ever made.

As for the ever-captivating Brando, attentive viewers will notice that Michael is dressed in black with a white tie, as Brando was in *Guys and Dolls*. The flower in his buttonhole is similar to the one Brando wore in the film so that the clandes-

Two long-time friends, Michael Jackson and Marlon Brando, came together on screen in the short film *You Rock My World* (2001).

tine gamblers could recognize him.

Chris Tucker makes a notable appearance. Having come to public attention when he starred alongside Jackie Chan in the film *Rush Hour* in 1998, he teamed up here with Michael Jackson for more exciting adventures.

The King of Pop asked Nicolas Pike, who had composed the music for the short feature film *Ghosts*, to create a few numbers for the soundtrack and background music. The composer knew Paul Hunter well, as the two men had already worked together on the Will Smith video *Wild Wild West*. Very quickly, and without requiring a full orchestra, he created the music that accompanies the action in *You Rock My World*.

On 21 September 2001, the 13'50 short film was broadcast in Europe. The US had to wait five more days. A second version, reworked and corrected by Jackson, was sent to TV channels a few weeks later. The opening sequence is significantly different, with contrasting camera angles: Michael Jackson and Chris Tucker chat in a Chinese restaurant as they observe the arrival of the young woman (actress Kishaya Dudley), whom Michael Jackson pursues throughout the film. A 6'0 and a 10'0 edit were also created to fit into the music channels' program scheduling.

On 23 February 2002, the National Association of the Advancement of Colored People (NAACP), the US Civil Rights group, presented *You Rock My World* with an award for best video.

FOR JACKSON ADDICTS

Michael Jackson asked the rapper Jay-Z to lay his vocals down on a version remixed by Track Masters to give *You Rock My World* a more hip-hop ambiance. Simply entitled *Track Masters remix*, this version is only available on promotional maxi vinyls and CDs released by Sony Music.

FOR JACKSON ADDICTS

The remix and instrumental versions, and two bonus tracks, *Michael—A Cappella* and *Eve—A Cappella*, are on a 12-inch US promo (Epic EAS 56719). The demo version by Floetry was pressed in 2002 on the *Floetic* album (DreamWorks Records 0044-50313-2).

2001

BUTTERFLIES

Andre Harris, Marsha Ambrosius / 4'40

Musicians
Michael Jackson: lead and backing vocals
Masha Ambrosius: backing vocals
Norman Jeff Bradshaw and Matt Cappy: horns
Andre Harris: all instruments
Recording
Jazz Studios, Philadelphia / Hit Factory, New York: March 2001
Technical team
Producers: Michael Jackson and Andre Harris
Recording engineers: Andre Harris and Bruce Swedien
Assistant recording engineer: Vidal Davis
Mixing: Bruce Swedien

The producer John McClain brought in the duo Floetry and their song *Butterflies* for the album *Invincible*.

Genesis

The British singer Marsha Ambrosius, one half of the group Floetry, alongside Natalie Stewart, composed the demo of the song *Butterflies* that John McClain took to Michael Jackson. The singer invited the two young women to the Hit Factory in New York to provide musical advice and guidance during the recording of the piece. The neo-soul vocal inflexions were new to the singer's repertoire: *Butterflies* showcased an entirely new artistic sensibility with very deep vibes. The hip-hop musicality indisputably makes this piece one of the gems on the *Invincible* album. Butterflies, as symbols of the artist in love, represent his fluttering heart. Here Michael Jackson passionately expresses his dream of winning over his beloved.

Production

Marsha Ambrosius has spoken about her memories of Michael Jackson in many interviews, emphasizing how humble and incredibly charismatic he was during the recording sessions, a prankster with an infectious laugh.

The final version of *Butterflies* does not differ greatly from the demo recorded by Floetry. The drum machine balance has been slightly altered to give it a more homogenous and percussive sound. Sony Music elected to broadcast *Butterflies* only on the US airwaves from early March 2001. It featured heavily on Michael Jackson's official website with a Flash mini-animation showing a butterfly flying above a megacity. No commercial single was ever released. A remix by the Track Masters team includes a delightful rap flow by the female rapper Eve. A big name in the rap world at the time, Eve often made guest appearances on work by great artists including The Roots, Missy Elliott, and Faith Evans. Her appearance on *Butterflies* (Track Masters remix), brought the song into the US hip-hop sphere. The remix was pressed on a very rare Canadian factory promo CD (Sony Music Radio Sampler SMPD 122). There are many, sometimes quite different edit versions loved by fans of this particular artistic period. Thanks to extensive airplay on US radio, the song charted at No. 2 on the *Billboard* R&B/Hip-Hop Airplay with no music video or commercial single.

Speechless

Michael Jackson / 3'18

Musicians

Michael Jackson: lead vocals

Andraé Crouch and Andraé Crouch Singers: Alfie Silas Durio, Valerie Doby, Maxi Anderson, Kristie Murden, Patrice Morris, Yvonne Williams, Vonciele Faggett, Tenika Johns, Angel Johnson, Linda McCrary, Sue Merriett, Deborah Sharp-Taylor, Marja Dozier, Zaneta M. Johnson, Gloria Augustus, Alice Jean McRath, Sandra Crouch, Zandra Williams, Judy Gossett, Geary Lanier Faggett, Johnnie Walker, Ron Taylor, Daniel Johnson, Harold Green, Laquentan Jordan, Tim Brown, Howard McCrary, Sam McCrary, Kevin Dorsey, and Andraé Crouch: backing vocals

Brad Buxer: keyboards

Novi Novoq and Thomas Tally: violas

Peter Kent, Gina Kronstadt, Robin Lorentz, Kirstin Fife, and John Wittenberg: violins

Recording

(unknown)

Technical team

Producer: Michael Jackson

Arrangements: Michael Jackson

Conducting and orchestral arrangements: Michael Jackson and Jeremy Lubbock

Recording engineers: Bruce Swedien, Brad Buxer, and Stuart Brawley

Mixing: Bruce Swedien

FOR JACKSON ADDICTS

The only indication that *Speechless* may have been considered for a single release is the promotional CDs for Taiwan and Korea. A few promo CDs and other Sony compilations also include it in their tracklists, which implies that they may have intended to release it, but fans waited in vain.

Genesis

Speechless is a very personal ballad composed by Michael Jackson himself. The singer twice spoke about this song, which was inspired by happy moments that he spent with children. In 2001, he explained the origins of the song during a live online chat with his fans: "I spend a lot of time in the forest...My favorite thing is to climb trees, go all the way up to the top of a tree and I look down on the branches. Whenever I do that it inspires me for music. There are these two sweet little kids, a girl and a boy, and they're so innocent; they're the quintessential form of innocence, and just being in their presence I felt completely speechless, 'cause I felt I was looking in the face of God whenever I saw them. They inspired me to write *Speechless*."[139]

He then discussed the piece with *Vibe* magazine a year later: "I was with these kids in Germany and we had a big water balloon fight —I'm serious—and I was so happy after the fight that I ran upstairs in their house and wrote *Speechless*. Fun inspires me. I hate to say that, because it's such a romantic song. But it was the fight that did it. I was happy, and I wrote it in its entirety right there. I felt it would be good enough for the album. Out of the bliss comes magic, wonderment, and creativity."[140]

The song is incredibly romantic with Michael Jackson delivering pure, dreamy, and extremely melodious lyrics. Like a poem, love appears on every line of the piece, as rarely before. The star expresses his feelings: "There's no mountain high I cannot climb / I'm humbled in your grace."

Production

Michael Jackson's masterpieces would not have taken shape without Bruce Swedien's contribution. Swedien was in a class of his own when it came to the King of Pop's most beautiful ballads. He has fond memories of working on this piece: "Everything with Michael is a stand-out moment but an absolutely gorgeous piece of music called *Speechless* was really an event," he recalled in 2001. "Michael sings the first eight bars a cappella. At the end, he closes it off a cappella—it was Michael's idea to add the a cappella parts."[141]

To capture the ever loyal and magical Andraé Crouch Singers, Bruce Swedien used the Neumann U 47 microphone that he had bought in 1956, which delivers an absolutely spectacular sound. He worked nonstop for two or three days on Michael Jackson's vocal parts to satisfy the singer's perfectionism.

2001

2000 Watts

Michael Jackson, Teddy Riley, Tyrese Gibson, JaRon Henson / 4'24

Musicians
Michael Jackson: lead and backing vocals
Teddy Riley: additional backing vocals, keyboards, and synthesizers
Recording
Future Recording Studios, Virginia Beach / Hit Factory Studios, New York / Criteria Studios, Miami : 2000-2001
Technical team
Producers: Michael Jackson and Teddy Riley
Recording engineers: Teddy Riley and George Mayers
Synthesizer programmers: Michael Jackson and Brad Buxer
Mixing: Bruce Swedien, Teddy Riley, and George Mayers

The model and singer Tyrese was originally meant to record the song *2000 Watts* for his own album.

Genesis

When former model Tyrese Gibson decided to pursue a career in music, he enlisted Teddy Riley's help in writing *2000 Watts* for his second album. The song was a nod to his birthplace of Watts, known as one of the most dangerous neighborhoods in Los Angeles. Michael Jackson fell in love with the piece as soon as he heard it and begged the two men to let him adopt it for inclusion in *Invincible*.

The young musician was grateful to be placing one of his songs in a Michael Jackson album. This did not stop him, however, from giving the song's name to his own album, *2000 Watts*, when it came out on 22 May 2000, even though the song did not appear on it.

The turn of the century and the threat of the famous Y2K—which turned out to be a dud—excited imaginations at the time. It was the dawn of digital revolutions and virtual reality and the feeling was that the future was now propelled by technological innovations that would affect every man and woman on earth. This was the mind-set that gave rise to *2000 Watts*. Throughout the song, the lyrics evoke the intense emotions of carnal relations by relating them to fuses blown and power overloads.

Production

Ahead of *Invincible*'s release, *2000 Watts* was marketed as a musical maelstrom ready to take over dance floors everywhere. But when listening to it, it's clear that the song leans heavily on the same sound kits and programmed effects that Teddy Riley had used on the Hall brothers' album *Guy III*, which came out the year before. The inspiration for *2000 Watts* is most palpable in songs like *Tellin' Me No* and *Spend Time*.

Except for the song reserved for the King of Pop, Teddy Riley's characteristic funk and groove disappear and are replaced by a colder, more industrial feel. The inventor of new jack swing intervenes throughout the song by issuing instructions or by echoing the singer's lyrics at the end of each verse.

Prior to this song, Jackson-Riley collaborations had been sound concoctions in which Michael's originality would prevail through his melodic ideas and arrangements. In *2000 Watts*, he ceded more control to the producer, who modeled this futuristic and ambitious song after his usual productions.

You Are My Life took on a whole new meaning when Michael paired it with a clip dedicated to his children. It appeared in the special program *Michael Jackson's Private Home Videos*, which he produced for Fox in 2003. The song became a declaration of paternal love.

You Are My Life

Michael Jackson, Babyface, Carole Bayer Sager, John McClain / 4'33

Musicians
Michael Jackson: lead and backing vocals
Babyface: additional backing vocals
Jason Edmonds, Nathan "N8" Walton, Tabia Ivery, Lynne Fiddmont-Lindsey: backing vocals
Babyface: acoustic guitar, keyboard, bass
Recording
Capitol Studios (strings) and Brandon's Way Recording, Los Angeles: August 2001
Technical team
Producers: Michael Jackson and Babyface
Recording engineer: Paul Boutin
Assistant recording engineers: Kb and EQ
String recording engineer: Tommy Vicari
Assistant string recording engineer: Steve Genewick
String session coordinator: Ivy Skoff
String arrangements: Bill Meyers
Mixing: Jon Gass

You Are My Life is a passionate declaration of Michael Jackson's love for his children.

Genesis

John McClain came up with the idea for *You Are My Life*. He was modifying a guitar exercise and created a gentle melody in the keys of E and G. Babyface and Carole Bayer Sager teamed up with him to finish the piece, which was initially called *You Are My World*. Michael Jackson fell in love with this simple song, but he decided to replace the word "world" with "life." This is how he became one of the song's cowriters.

The lyrics carry on the theme of unconditional love present in *Joy*, a song the King of Pop had cowritten with Tammy Lucas during the *Dangerous* sessions. It is an ode to an everlasting love for someone who supported him during the most difficult moments of his life. The melody, round and melancholy, allows him to loudly declare his feelings, as if he were baring his soul to this person who stood by him and helped him regain his will to live.

Production

Five weeks before the release of *Invicible*'s master tapes, Michael was still recording and writing songs for his new album. *You Are My Life* was among the very last songs to be finalized and recorded under the record company's increasingly tight deadlines. It replaced *Shout* in the final tracklist.

The short recording time frame led Michael and his team to act more spontaneously, which brought a touch of authenticity to the album. While the programmed drums ran like a well-oiled machine, or even clockwork, the rest of the production preserved a warmth befitting of the song. Jason Edmonds, Babyface's brother and the founder of vocal group After 7, was among the backing vocalists singing alongside the King of Pop during the refrains. The strings were recorded at Capitol Studios in Los Angeles under the supervision of Ivy Skoff. Babyface had already worked with her in 1994, when they made *I'll Make Love to You* by Boyz II Men.

Although it received poor reviews upon its release, *You Are My Life* came out exactly as intended and it allowed Michael to deliver a rich and varied vocal performance.

2001

Privacy

Michael Jackson, Rodney Jerkins, Fred Jerkins III, Bernard Belle / 5'05

Musicians
Michael Jackson: lead and backing vocals
LaShawn Daniels: backing vocals
Rodney Jerkins: keyboard and synthesizers
Michael Thompson: guitar
Nathan East: bass
Gerald Hayward, Emanuel "Bucket" Baker: drums
Recording
Sony Music Studios, New York / Hit Factory, New York and Criteria Studios, Miami (mixing): 2000 to 2001
Technical team
Producers: Michael Jackson, Rodney Jerkins
Recording engineers: Rodney Jerkins, Jean-Marie Horvat, Brad Gilderman
Assistant recording engineers: Harvey Mason, Jr., Paul Cruz
Mixing: Rodney Jerkins, Jean-Marie Horvat

At 2'55 in, Michael Jackson yells "Slash!" to invite the Guns N' Roses guitarist to perform a solo in the middle of the song. Due to a scheduling conflict, the famous musician couldn't attend this recording session. Michael Thompson replaced him at the last minute. But in the final version, the King of Pop still calls out Slash's name.

Genesis

As with *Dangerous* and *HIStory*, *Invincible* contains its own antimedia song. Strongly shaken by the tragic death of Princess Diana, the King of Pop wrote a song in which he lashed out at the paparazzi and scandal-driven press, both of which had long ago crossed the line in toying with the lives of their targets. "Some of you still wonder why, one of my friends had to die." The reference is clear: the lyrics denounce the hellish car chases and deadly traps of fame. The media often mocked Michael for writing lyrics that were full of spite for a system that, in some ways, he had fueled. However, Michael was not only animated by a long-standing anger but also by exasperation.

He wrote the basis for the song and presented it to Rodney Jerkins' team, which included Bernard Belle. Belle and Teddy Riley had already cowritten a song in the same vein for *Dangerous* (*Why You Wanna Trip on Me*).

Production

Michael supervised production for *Privacy*, placing it squarely within a tradition that began in the 1980s with the cover of The Beatles' *Come Together*. This was another play on the same structure: Michael superimposed phrased verses on a dry and binary rhythm before letting his voice soar during the refrains, which acted as respirations.

To ensure the successful outcome of this ambitious song, Michael asked Rodney Jerkins to create a rich and complex rhythmic track and align camera shutter sounds to a specific beat.

To highlight the dramatic intensity of the song, the orchestra—under the direction of Canadian composer and arranger David Campbell—based the bleak lamentations of the violins in the foreground. Campbell, who was as comfortable with Hollywood movie soundtracks (*Boogie Nights*, *Armageddon*, *Pearl Harbor*) as he was with albums for pop artists like Céline Dion, Aerosmith, or Art Garfunkel, had already worked with Michael in 1996, when he supervised the string arrangements for *Why* and *Anything*, by Michael's nephews in 3T.

Nathan East's incomparable bass punctuates the song's rhythm with staccato notes, while Michael Thomson's guitar arrangements give greater depth to the refrains.

Unfortunately, these first-class ingredients went to waste in the mix: in the final album version it was difficult to appreciate each carefully crafted track and component.

Don't Walk Away

Michael Jackson, Teddy Riley, Richard Carlton Stites, Reed Philip Vertelney / 4'17

Musicians
Michael Jackson: lead and backing vocals
Richard Stites: backing vocals
Teddy Riley: keyboard and synthesizers
Jeremy Lubbock: orchestra conductor
Recording
Future Recording Studios, Norfolk, Virginia / The Hit Factory and Criteria, Miami: (dates unknown)
Technical team
Producers: Michael Jackson, Teddy Riley
Coproducer: Richard Stites
Recording engineers: Teddy Riley, George Mayers
String arrangements: Jeremy Lubbock
Mixing: Teddy Riley, Bruce Swedien, George Mayers

On 9 February 2002, Michael Jackson attended the Art for AIDS event at the Laguna Art Museum (California).

Genesis

If Michael Jackson had continued to record albums like *Forever, Michael* (1975), his last album with Motown, he probably would have lent his voice more frequently to songs like *Don't Walk Away*. Against a backdrop of depression, neglect, and resignation, the lyrics express the hopeless agony of a lover's powerlessness in the face of an unattainable romance. The feeling of melancholy slowly grows with each refrain, reaching the same conclusion each time: "When there's nothing left to do but walk away."

Michael wrote the song with Teddy Riley, who brought two additional contributors on board. Richard Carlton Stites—whom Riley had already recruited in 1997 to write the lyrics to *It's True*, by Queen Pen—joined the team as coauthor and backing vocalist alongside the King of Pop. Reed Philip Vertelney—who regularly worked with Luther Vandross and lent his talents to creating original soundtracks for successful movies like *White Men Can't Jump*, by Ron Shelton—contributed his expertise, giving *Don't Walk Away* an even stronger soul feeling.

Production

Don't Walk Away contains all the elements of a 1990s R&B song. A far cry from the neo-soul productions that started to take over the airwaves and playlists in 1997, the song comes off as an epic saga in which Teddy Riley applies his usual but effective methods: its arrangements and production resemble those of *Let's Chill*, a song he'd recorded with Guy in 1990. At the time, this slow song had allowed the group to make a name for itself with a more mature sound. When the same musical grid was applied the King of Pop in 2001, it made the song timeless, perhaps too timeless. Before Bruce Swedien made the final mix, Teddy Riley used digital multitracks to enhance Jeremy Luddock's arrangements, which were performed by a string orchestra. Two acoustic guitars joined the fray. The first simply played scales as Michael sang his verses. The second, plaintive, brought a touch of originality to the piece by weaving a delicate link between Michael's style and country music.

The King of Pop's performance remains quite visionary. Although it doesn't have the same highly emotional feel as *She's out of My Life*, its serious, sad tonality drops a curtain of melancholy over the song.

2001

Cry

R. Kelly / 5'01

Musicians
Michael Jackson: lead vocals
Andraé Crouch Singers: backing vocals
John Robinson: drums
Paulinho Da Costa: percussion
Michael Landau: guitar
Recording
Hit Factory, New York: 2000 to 2001
Technical team
Producers: Michael Jackson, R. Kelly
Recording engineers: Mike Ging, Brad Gilberman, Humberto Gatica
Choral arrangement: R. Kelly
Synthesizer programming: Michael Jackson, Brad Buxer
Drum programming: Michael Jackson, Brad Buxer
Mixing: Michael Jackson, Mick Guzauski

Single

USA
A- and B-sides: *Cry (album version)* / 5'01
UK
A-side: *Cry (album version)* / 5'01
B-side: *Shout* (unreleased) / 4'17
Released by Epic Records: USA (ref. 79660) and UK (ref. 672138), 5 December 2001
Chart position: UK No. 25

THE SONG

Genesis

When Michael Jackson reenlisted R. Kelly's help to write some new songs for his next album, this prodigy of sensual R&B took the lessons he learned while recording *HIStory* and came up with *Cry*, a cleverly written, risk-free blend of Michael's best songs. *Cry* contains the same themes of solidarity and hope as *Man in the Mirror* and *Keep the Faith,* as well as the sadness of songs like *Stranger in Moscow*, without, however, pretending to be in the same league as these.

The song's slow melody crescendos throughout the piece and culminates in a final eruption of choral singing. Michael appears more solemn than usual, looking a little lost in a world he struggles to understand: "You can change the world, I can't do it by myself," he sings in the first lines of the refrain. The shock wave of humanitarian and heroic sentiments created by *We Are the World* had evaporated and was being replaced by a quiet realism, which, unfortunately, was in line with the prevailing mind-set of the early 2000s.

Production

Brad Buxer and Michael Jackson created a calmer and lighter version of the beatboxing rhythm from *Stranger in Moscow*. They then superimposed the synthesizers like layers, creating conventional arrangements that evoked Michael's humanitarian songs, or more charming songs like *Elizabeth, I Love You* and *You're the One*.

At 3'17 in, there is a rupture and the piece takes off: from his seat at the drums, John Robinson takes control and uses his instrument to keep a soothing beat.

The Andraé Crouch choir falls into step behind Michael and accompanies his vocal crescendo, whose culmination highlights the sad harmonies present in the song. After a few ad-libs, the choir brings the song to its conclusion as it holds one final note. Rather predictably, almost artificially, Michael hits this note with the words "Change the world," as if he were trying to repeat the effect of "Make that change" from *Man in the Mirror.*

Michael Jackson during the charity concert What More Can I Give: United We Stand at the RFK Stadium, Washington, DC, 21 October 2001, which paid tribute to the victims of the 9/11 attacks.

THE SHORT FILM

Director: Nick Brandt
Producer: (unknown)
Extras: (unknown)
Shoot date: October 2001
Shooting location: state parks and outdoor settings in California and Nevada
Duration: 4'58

Genesis

On 11 September 2001, the attack on New York's Twin Towers plunged the world into a state of terror. Artists were suddenly recording songs or organizing tribute concerts in support of the victims. The instinct for survival and the will to defend freedom quickly spread throughout the globe. Michael's arsenal contained an appropriate song for this context: *Cry*. In early October 2001, when *You Rock My World* came out as a single, Sony Music published a double-sided 7-inch (with the same song on both sides) of *Cry* for the US market, allowing Michael to put out a ready-made tribute right after the tragedy. The song's commercial potential was weak and it didn't make it far in the charts. Radio stations preferred *Butterflies*, the neo soul song from *Invincible*. The US promo for *Cry* was over before it even began, but continued in Europe and Japan, where the single came out in December 2001. The company also commissioned a video with a modest budget from photographer and director Nick Brandt.

Production

Filmed in October 2001 in outdoor settings in California and Nevada, a human chain spanning the country was used to illustrate *Cry*'s message of solidarity. The script required Michael to appear at the end of the piece, as if he were the only person who could unite the world and lead his people to change.

However, the King of Pop was avoiding travel after 9/11. He was supposed to have been in the famous towers on the day of the event, but was saved after he slept through his alarm. His trauma remained intense in the following weeks and he did not want to participate in the filming of *Cry*. He also took issue with the modest budget allowed for the video.

Instead, he chose to dedicate himself to the *United We Stand: What More Can I Give* benefit concert held on 21 October in Washington, DC, alongside 25 other international artists. Nick Brandt, who had agreed to leave his adopted land of Africa to shoot this video, understood his friend's state of mind. He told Michael he no longer had to appear in the video, assuring him that this would give greater meaning to the song and draw even more attention to its lyrics. Michael agreed, but continued to help the director with the editing. *Cry*, the second and last video from *Invincible*, soon wrapped up.

THE LOST CHILDREN

Michael Jackson / 4'00

Musicians
Michael Jackson: lead vocals
Baby Rubba and Prince Jackson: narration
Scotty Haskell, Andrew Snyder, Melissa Mackay, Monique Donally, Rose Beatty, James Lively, Aley Martinez, Ricky Lucchse, Brandon Lucas, Jonathon Hall, Justin Hall, Brett Tattersol, and Micha Haupman: children's choir
Recording
Unknown: 2001
Technical team
Producer: Michael Jackson
Arrangements: Michael Jackson
Keyboard programming: Michael Jackson and Brad Buxer
Choir director: Tom Bähler
Recording engineers: Bruce Swedien, Brad Buxer, and Stuart Brawley
Mixing: Bruce Swedien

Moonrise, a painting Michael Jackson commissioned from the artist David Nordahl, to hang in Neverland.

Genesis

Michael Jackson will forever be known for his concern for the fate of the "voiceless," as he stated in June 1992 at the launch for his foundation, Heal the World. He wrote *The Lost Children* as a prayer for children who had disappeared, been kidnapped, or whose parents and loved ones continued to hope, sometimes in vain, that they would someday return.

Production

The Lost Children is the second song in the album that was entirely written and produced by Michael Jackson. Home at last, and with no other producers around, he took over the direction of the song, which qualifies as one of his last masterpieces.

His voice takes on an innocent tone and vibrates with impressive precision across a series of pure musical lines. With each note, he brings unique charisma to a theme that other singers would struggle to perform in a credible way.

At 4' in, the children's choir, directed by Tom Bähler, unleashes the song's strong message of hope. Prince Jackson, Michael's eldest son, makes a quick appearance in his father's song, even though he is only four years old. The piece ends when a group of children, lost in a forest and caught offguard by nightfall, think it's time to return home. At the risk of breaking with the avant-garde style of *Invincible*, Michael made use of the purity of this piece to appeal once again to the public's conscience.

At the end of the piece, Michael Jackson and Carlos Santana surreptitiously say goodbye and thank each other. This polite exchange was recorded on tape from afar, since their respective schedules did not allow them the pleasure of meeting in person to make this song.

Whatever Happens

Michael Jackson, Teddy Riley, Gil Gang, Jasmine Quay, Geoffrey Williams / 4'56

Musicians
Michael Jackson: lead and backing vocals
Mario Vasquez and Mary Brown: additional backing vocals
Rick Williams: guitar
Carlos Santana: guitar and whistling
Stuart Brawley: whistling
Recording
Future Recording Studios, Virginia Beach, Virginia / Hit Factory, New York / Criteria Studios, Miami: 2001
Technical team
Producers: Michael Jackson and Teddy Riley
Orchestra director and arranger: Jeremy Lubbock
Recording engineers: Teddy Riley, George Mayers, and Bruce Swedien
Mixing: Bruce Swedien, Teddy Riley, and George Mayers

For *Whatever Happens*, Carlos Santana played his guitar line at home, and Teddy Riley made the trip to go and collect it.

Genesis

As of June 2001, Michael Jackson was still recording *Invincible*. He wanted a concise album made up of 10 to 12 tracks at the most. But weeks went by and his desire to add more of his favorite songs got the upper hand. We can thank Mario Vasquez for *Whatever Happens*, which came about after Vasquez brought the talents of Gil Gang and Geoffrey Williams to Teddy Riley's attention.

Written in 1997, the song starts off with an urban tonality before adding a bass line to the end of the mix. In the mid-2000s, a few years after they recorded the song, the writers posted their demo versions on MySpace. The entire basis for the song had clearly been there from the start. Michael Jackson, Teddy Riley, and Jasmine Quay shared the writing credits even though their contributions were mostly limited to fine-tuning the arrangements for the *Invincible* version.

Production

The song starts off with someone whistling over a musical motif worthy of a Western film, plunging the listener into a four-dimensional musical structure unlike anything Michael had done before. Next comes a rhythm with Latin pop inflections that accompanies the narration. Michael sings about a young couple's struggles after the birth of an unplanned child. He excels in his brilliant vocal variations, performing crescendos with ease and musicality.

Teddy Riley was able to convince Sony Music to spare no effort in enhancing the dramatic intensity of the song: "I told the label that I wanted a 40-piece orchestra to do strings on this record. And I told Michael that it would be great to have Carlos Santana on the song because of the guitars on there. Michael was like, 'Okay, we will make that happen.'"[142]

Santana accepted the role, but objected to leaving his home to go to the studio. So Teddy Riley went to the celebrated guitarist's home studio and recorded his parts there.

2001

Threatened

Michael Jackson, Rodney Jerkins, Fred Jerkins III et LaShawn Daniels / 4'19

Musicians
Michael Jackson: lead vocals and various instruments
Rod Serling: audio extracts
Rodney Jerkins: various instruments
Recording
Hit Factory, New York / Criteria Studios, Miami: 2001
Technical team
Producers: Michael Jackson and Rodney Jerkins
Recording engineer: Stuart Brawley
Mixing: Bruce Swedien, Rodney Jerkins, and Stuart Brawley

A brief musical section from *Threatened* was meant to be on-screen during *Thriller* in the *This Is It* tour; it can be seen in the rehearsal video.

In *Threatened*, Michael Jackson pays tribute to Rod Serling, creator of the legendary series *The Twilight Zone*.

Genesis and production

Michael Jackson and Rodney Jerkins wanted *Threatened* to embody the spooky "ghoul and ghost" theme popular at the time. A far cry from the melodic vocalizations and musical inspirations of *Heartbreak Hotel* or *Thriller*, *Threatened* was characterized by a fierce digital frenzy where Michael's voice was the only thing tethering the listener to reality. Recordings of Rod Serling, the creator of the successful television series *The Twilight Zone*, were used in the introduction and conclusion of the song. While Vince Price's words in *Thriller* had been written and performed specifically for that piece, Rod Serling's lines in *Threatened* were excerpted from the openings of *The Twilight Zone* episodes, mixed, and repurposed as bookends: "Tonight's story is somewhat unique and calls for a different kind of introduction / A monster had arrived in the village / The major ingredient of any recipe for fear is the unknown / And this person or thing is soon to be met / He knows every thought, he can feel every emotion / Oh yes, I did forget something didn't I? I forgot to introduce you to the monster." The innovative aspect of this resurrection of Rod Sterling, who died in 1975, lies in the structure of a rather well placed rap in the middle of the piece. Michael played the monster in the song, allowing him to directly denounce his staunchest detractors: "You're fearing me, 'cause you know I'm a beast" or "You should be watching me, you should feel threatened."

The album lacked a promotional budget, so the song did not get a dedicated video. Michel was greatly disappointed by this, as he particularly liked this kind of theme. In a similar way to *Thriller*, the musical frenzy ends with a final audio montage of Rod Serling's voice, though with less charisma: "What you have just witnessed could be the end of a particularly terrifying nightmare / It isn't. It's the beginning..."

FOR JACKSON ADDICTS

Slated as a replacement for *You Are My Life* on the vinyl version of *Invincible*, *Shout* was sidelined, though it appeared on the B-side of *Cry*, released in Europe and Japan.

[BONUS TRACK]

SHOUT

Michael Jackson, Teddy Riley, Claude "Quo" Forbes, Samuel "Cyph" Hoskins, Carmen Lampson, Roy Hamilton / 4'17

Musicians
Michael Jackson: lead and backing vocals
Carmen Lampson: backing vocals
Teddy Riley: keyboards and synthesizers
Recording
Future Recording Studios, Norfolk, Virginia / Hit Factory, New York and Criteria Studios, Miami (mixing): 2000 to 2001
Technical team
Producers: Michael Jackson, Teddy Riley
Recording engineers: Teddy Riley, George Mayers
Mixing: Teddy Riley, Bruce Swedien

From the mid-1990s, Michael Jackson relied on his faithful fans to denounce the sensationalist press.

Genesis

Shout was loosely inspired by the Isley Brothers' 1959 song of the same name. In this rage-filled piece, Michael Jackson launches into a tirade against the evils that are dragging down the world around him. Education, money, society: he exposes the absurdity of modern life. His lines sound like a fast-paced rap on a roller-coaster, interrupted by a brief and melodious bridge that emerges like a thin ray of hope: "We all must unite, to turn darkness to light / And the love in our hearts will shine."

Production

From a musical standpoint, *Shout* is a combination of a few good ideas that Teddy Riley had developed in the studio in previous years. In 1997, his group, BLACKstreet, released the single *Fix*. While the album version of *Fix* sampled the classic *The Message*, by Grandmaster Flash, the radio remix version adopted an energetic rock beat peppered with savage cries and Slash's guitar. Teddy Riley then created a sound that walked the line between R&B and rock, ending up with a logical sequel to Michael Jackson's *Beat It* and to Run DMC's *Walk This Way*. A few years later, in 2000, he got Guy back together with the release of an album simply called *Guy III*. The album's seventh track, *Do It*, had a modern funk sound bookended by a hypnotic beat, in line with the greatest new jack swing tradition. An excerpt was included in the video for the *Dancin'* single, which came out soon after. The musician and his peers took the opportunity to complement it with a short dance routine.

These two Teddy Riley songs, *Fix* and *Do It*, were the precursors to *Shout*: rock ambiance joined up with a powerful funky beat to yield a dark and captivating track that deliberately lacked melody and depth. The result was an oversaturated, stifling sound tunnel that Michael found particularly attractive. "He really was feeling that record, but, unfortunately, the record got railroaded by politics within the album and the dispute between MJ and Tommy [Mottola]."[143]

COMPILATIONS

Like all artists accustomed to popular success, the career of Michael Jackson was punctuated by compilations, released in parallel with his main albums. Starting in 1975—the year The Jackson Five left Motown Records for CBS/Epic—Motown released a series of compilations using material from their Jackson archives. This opportunistic and brazen approach produced several albums that Michael Jackson had not approved but was obliged to accept because he did not own the rights to those songs.

At Epic, the King of Pop went along with several "Best of" and retrospective projects. As well as the first record of the double album *HIStory* (1995), which gathered together 15 of his hits, he released the CD *Number Ones* in 2003 and the box set *The Ultimate Collection* in 2004.

Michael Jackson's posthumous career has been punctuated by the release of projects that were taken to be posthumous albums but which turned out to be compilations of previously unreleased material. As well as the original soundtrack of the documentary *This Is It*, which contains the title song, the star's beneficiaries made two records that brought together songs from different periods: *Michael*, in 2010, which caused a great deal of ink to be spilt because the authenticity of Michael Jackson's voice was widely questioned in three of its songs, and *Xscape*, a collection that met with success and that was curated by the CEO of Epic Records, L. A. Reid (2014).

The rich, intriguing body of work evident in the compilation albums reveals inspirations that never found a place on Michael's original albums, for various reasons.

1984

FAREWELL MY SUMMER LOVE

1. DON'T LET IT GET YOU DOWN
2. YOU'VE REALLY GOT A HOLD ON ME
3. MELODIE
4. TOUCH THE ONE YOU LOVE
5. GIRL YOU'RE SO TOGETHER
6. FAREWELL MY SUMMER LOVE
7. CALL ON ME
8. HERE I AM (COME AND TAKE ME)
9. TO MAKE MY FATHER PROUD

Farewell My Summer Love 1984 **COMPILATION**

Released by Motown Records: USA, May 1984 (ref. 6101ML) / UK, June 1984 (ref. ZL72227) / **Chart position:** USA R&B No. 31, Pop No. 46 / UK No. 9 / **Musicians: Michael Jackson:** lead and backing vocals / **Musicians on the new instrumental overdubs: Michael Lovesmith:** keyboards / **Mike Baird:** drums / **Tony Peluso:** guitar / **Steve Barri:** percussion / **Recording: Motown Recording Studios, Los Angeles / Sound Factory Studio, Hollywood:** January to October 1973 / **Recording of the new instrumental overdubs: A&M Recording Studios, Hollywood:** 22 March to 16 April 1984 / **Technical team: Producers of the original songs:** Freddie Perren, Fonce Mizell, Hal Davis, and Bob Crewe / **Producers of the new instrumental overdubs and mixes:** Tony Peluso, Michael Lovesmith, and Steve Barri / **Recording engineer:** Tony Peluso / **Assistant recording engineers:** Magic Moreno and Sabrina Buchanek / **Mixing:** Larrabee Studios, Hollywood

FAREWELL MY SUMMER LOVE 1984, THE FIRST MAJOR SOLO COMPILATION

In 1976, when the group was promoting the album *The Jacksons*, Motown was already compiling a few titles, among the last the brothers had recorded, and collected the most danceable of them on a CD entitled *Joyful Jukebox Music*. In 1979, before the release of *Off the Wall*, the *Boogie* project went down the same route, releasing a fine selection of up-tempo numbers. When *Thriller* burst onto the scene, establishing Michael Jackson as the world leader of the record industry, Motown was keen to follow in the wake of the star who was smashing all records. Alongside the album *Victory* and its tour, which were to showcase all the big hits from *Thriller*, Motown tried to position itself through marketing so as to make a few dollars at the same game.

On 17 May 1984, just under two months before the launch of the *Victory* tour, a record entitled *Farewell My Summer Love 1984* was sent to US radio stations before it was due to go on sale in the shops. The album's sleeve was cryptic: it bore a photograph of an electrified audience, their arms raised in the direction of a stage. The image, shot by Todd Gray, was well known to fans at the time (it had appeared on the inner sleeve of The Jacksons' album *Live*, in 1981). At first sight, it seemed as if a completely new recording of a Michael Jackson concert had gone on sale to the public. However, the information on the back of the record revealed that the content was totally unreleased, straight out of Motown's archives. Each song had been overdubbed and updated to suit the taste of the time. The misleading image, with its ambiguous message, was very quickly condemned, and later pressings suddenly lost the "1984" date from the title, retaining only the name of the compilation: *Farewell My Summer Love*.

To ride the wave created by the *Victory* tour, Motown needed to present its compilation as an exceptional event. Don Waller, author of the book *The Motown Story* (1985), took on the task of raising the temperature, in order to persuade the most reluctant buyers. In a few lines on the back of the sleeve, he related a nice story that took on the character of a veritable sales pitch. After a brief but eulogistic reminder of the greatest hits of The Jackson Five's career, the author explained how the public very nearly never got to hear the songs at Motown's disposal. As a result of a Motown office move, boxes containing unreleased tapes had (supposedly) mysteriously disappeared and had only been recovered following a long investigation; so it was that more than 40 sensational songs by Michael Jackson could finally be heard by everyone. Recorded in late 1972 and early 1973, the songs had been recorded during sessions for the albums *Skywriter*, *Get It Together*, *Dancing Machine*, and *Music and Me*. The record label's product positioning, which aimed to play the card of the exceptional and the rare, was rather clumsy. Happily, Motown's claims of authenticity were more sophisticated, hinging on the much more credible idea of the musical heritage of its child star, famous for being the timeless cornerstone of the Motown sound. *Farewell My Summer Love* sold barely three million, and struggled to make it onto the US charts. Its best placing was in the UK, where it got to No. 9 in the UK album chart.

Don't Let It Get You Down

Jerry Marcellino, Mel Larson, Deke Richards / 3'01

Musicians: (unknown) / **Michael Jackson:** lead and backing vocals / **Recording: Motown Recording Studios, Los Angeles:** during the sessions for the albums *Get It Together* and *Dancing Machine*, 27 July, 23 and 31 August, 14 September, and 5 and 9 October 1973 / **Technical team: Producers:** Mel Larson and Jerry Marcellino / **Arrangements:** James Anthony Carmichael / **Recording engineer:** Russ Terrana

The compilation begins positively with Jackson urging a young girl not to let herself be overwhelmed by sadness, offering to bring the sunshine back into her life. Mischievous and flirtatious, his voice pulsates with pleasure in rock tones reinforced by big doses of synthesizer and new musical effects created by Tony Peluso, Michael Lovesmith, and Steve Barri. The original mix, dating from 1 November 1973, was released in 1995 on *Anthology Series: The Best of Michael Jackson* (Motown 530 480-2) and 2009 on *Michael Jackson—Hello World: The Motown Solo Collection* (Hip-O Select/Motown B0012421-02).

You've Really Got a Hold on Me

William Robinson, Ronald White, Robert Rogers / 3'30

Musicians: (unknown) / **Michael Jackson:** lead and backing vocals / **Recording: Motown Recording Studios, Los Angeles:** during the sessions for the albums *Get It Together* and *Dancing Machine*, 13 and 22 June, 29 August, and 11 October 1973 / **Technical team: Producers:** Mel Larson and Jerry Marcellino / **Arrangements:** James Anthony Carmichael / **Recording engineer:** Russ Terrana

This hit by The Miracles, composed by Smokey Robinson, was first recorded by The Jackson Five in Detroit, a week after *Who's Lovin' You*, between 31 July and 2 August 1969. Produced by Bobby Taylor, the group's version was released in 1998 on *The Ultimate Rarities Collection 1: Motown Sings Motown Treasures* (Motown 314 530 960-2). In *Farewell My Summer Love*, Michael Jackson offers, as a solo, a completely new version of the song. The original 1973 mix was released in 2009.

Melodie

Mel Larson, Jerry Marcellino, Deke Richards / 3'21

Musicians: (unknown) / **Michael Jackson:** lead and backing vocals / **Recording: Motown Recording Studios, Los Angeles:** during the sessions for the album *Music and Me*, 5 and 15 January 1973 / **Technical team: Producers:** Mel Larson and Jerry Marcellino / **Arrangements:** James Anthony Carmichael / **Recording engineer:** Russ Terrana / **Deleted single: A-side:** *Melodie* / (unknown) / **B-side:** *Up on the House Top* / (unknown) / **Release originally planned by Motown Records:** USA, 1984 (ref. Motown 1914)

A veritable bonus on this compilation, *Melodie* is a little gem that would have deserved to be released as a single, so rich and captivating is its musical drive. Michael Jackson gives off an abundantly happy vibe in a song that is rather simple musically.

Although there is a certain sadness to it, very quickly the young singer's vigorous voice lights up every word. Another mix, with new overdubs by Tony Peluso, Michael Lovesmith, and Steve Barri, can be heard on *The Original Soul of Michael Jackson* (Motown 6250 ML / 1987). The song's original mix dates from 1 November 1973, and was released in 1995 on the compilation *Anthology Series: The Best of Michael Jackson* (Motown 530 480-2) and in 2009 on *Michael Jackson—Hello World: The Motown Solo Collection* (Hip-O Select/Motown B0012421-02).

Touch the One You Love

Artie Wayne, George S. Clinton / 2'47

Musicians: (unknown) / **Michael Jackson:** lead and backing vocals / **Recording: Motown Recording Studios, Los Angeles:** during the sessions for the albums *Get It Together* and *Dancing Machine*, 14 June 1973 / **Technical team: Producers:** Mel Larson and Jerry Marcellino / **Arrangements:** James Anthony Carmichael / **Recording engineer:** Russ Terrana

The choice of songs for the compilation *Farewell My Summer Love* again showed Michael Jackson to be a true crooner. And that is exactly what this version of *Touch the One You Love* sets out to do. Written by Artie Wayne and George Clinton (composers with Warner Brothers Music), who had already contributed *Little Christmas Tree* to the young star's career, the song makes the most of all the aspects of Michael Jackson's voice. The rhythmic structure is hard-hitting and very emphatic. Thanks to its rich musical inflections, the song admirably complements the selection of unreleased tracks. Its original mix, made in 1973, was released on the compilation *Michael Jackson—Hello World: The Motown Solo Collection* (Hip-O Select/Motown B0012421-02).

Girl You're So Together

Keni St. Lewis / 3'09

Musicians: (unknown) / **Michael Jackson:** lead and backing vocals / **Recording: Motown Recording Studios, Los Angeles:** during the sessions for the album *Get It Together*, 31 August, 10, 19, and 26 September, and 8 October 1973 / **Technical team: Producers:** Freddie Perren and Fonce Mizell / **Arrangements:** Freddie Perren and Fonce Mizell / **Recording engineer:** Russ Terrana / **Single: A-side:** *Girl You're So Together (album version)* / 3'09 / **B-side:** *Touch the One You Love (album version)* / 2'47 / **Released by Motown Records:** USA and UK, July 1984 (US ref. 1757 MF and UK ref. TMG 1355) / **Chart position:** UK No. 33 / Ireland No. 29

In 1973, Freddie Perren suggested to the composer Keni St. Lewis that he work on a few songs for the young Michael Jackson. *Girl You're So Together* and *Farewell My Summer Love* were recorded very quickly, but only released more than ten years later on this compilation. The two songs, which display a more pop-like influence, have a slow, sometimes funky or jazzy, progression. *Girl You're So Together* lends itself to the singer's unending optimism in the song. The electric guitars and the sonorous steelpan sounds blend seamlessly and reveal a new musical universe for the young artist. Summer love affairs and romantic assignations on the beach seemed to set the mood that *Farewell My Summer Love* wanted to portray in 1984. The original mix, made during a session at which the songwriter was present in 1973, was released in 2009 on the compilation *Michael Jackson—Hello World: The Motown Solo Collection* (Hip-O Select/Motown B0012421-02).

Released as a single in July 1984, the song went unnoticed, whereas *State of Shock* by The Jacksons was constantly heard on the airwaves the world over.

1984

FOR JACKSON ADDICTS

When *Farewell My Summer Love* went on sale, Motown released in the USA a 12-inch promotional single (PR-153). On the B-side was an exclusive medley, *The Jackson 5 Motown Medley*. Lasting 6'49, featuring *I Want You Back*, *The Love You Save*, *Dancing Machine*, *ABC*, and *I'll Be There*. These were boosted by sound effects exaggerating and imitating shouts from an audience, in an attempt to ride the wave of the *Victory* tour.

FAREWELL MY SUMMER LOVE

Keni St. Lewis / 4'21

Musicians: (unknown) / **Michael Jackson:** lead and backing vocals / **Recording: Motown Recording Studios, Los Angeles:** during the sessions for the album *Get It Together*, 4, 10, and 11 September 1973 / **Technical team:** Freddie Perren and Fonce Mizell / **Arrangements:** Freddie Perren and Fonce Mizell / **Recording engineer:** Russ Terrana / **Single: A-side:** *Farewell My Summer Love (single version)* / 3'41 / **B-side:** *Call on Me (album version)* / 3'38 / **Released by Motown Records:** USA and UK, May 1984 (US ref. 1739 MF and UK ref. TMG 1342) / **Chart position:** USA R&B No. 37, Pop No. 38 / UK No. 7

In the studio this bore the initial working title *Let Me Count the Ways*. In 2016, the writer, Keni St. Lewis, recalled creating the song that gave the compilation its title:

> Freddie [Perren] and I were talking and he asked me, "Hey, do you have any young love-sounding songs that we could use for Michael [Jackson]?" Well, I wasn't going to say "No," but the truth was that I didn't have any at that time…So when I got home, I just ran with pen in hand and began to write down lyrics as quickly as I could. That's why *Farewell My Summer Love* was written in the first place. It was written specifically for Michael…I was focused on creating a storyline for young people in love, and I remember thinking to myself, "What would it feel like to be young and in love when the girl is about to go away at the end of the summer?" So after getting all of the lyrics written, I recorded my little demo version and I remember thinking, "This has a really good sound to it." …I was there in the session with him and so was Freddie. Since Michael was only 14 at the time, he could only record for so many hours a day.[144]

Michael Jackson on stage with The Jackson Five at the Inglewood Forum, Los Angeles, 26 August 1973.

The original mix of *Farewell My Summer Love* was released in 2009 on *Michael Jackson—Hello World: The Motown Solo Collection* (Hip-O Select/Motown B0012421-02).

Call on Me

Fonce Mizell, Larry Mizell / 3'38

Musicians: (unknown) / **Michael Jackson:** lead and backing vocals / **Recording: Motown Recording Studios, Los Angeles:** during the sessions for the album *Get It Together*, 4, 5, 13, and 25 September 1973 / **Technical team: Producers:** Freddie Perren and Fonce Mizell / **Arrangements:** Gene Page and Fonce Mizell / **Recording engineer:** Russ Terrana

Call on Me, of which the working title in the studio was *Fussin' and Fightin'*, returned to the theme of amorous lament so often dealt with by the Motown prodigy. Michael Jackson calmly dispatched each sequence of the song, letting his finest vocal tones shine. The original mix of the song dates from 4 October 1973, and was released in 1995 on the compilation *Anthology Series: The Best of Michael Jackson* (Motown 530 480-2) and in 2009 on *Michael Jackson—Hello World: The Motown Solo Collection* (Hip-O Select/Motown B0012421-02).

Here I Am (Come and Take Me)

Al Green, Mabon Hodges / 2'53

Musicians: (unknown) / **Michael Jackson:** lead and backing vocals / **Recording: Motown Recording Studios, Los Angeles:** 6 June 1973 / **Technical team: Producer:** Hal Davis / **Arrangements:** David Blumberg / **Recording engineer:** Russ Terrana

Al Green's hit *Here I Am (Come and Take Me)* reached No. 10 in the US *Billboard* Hot 100 in June 1973. Michael Jackson recorded it immediately afterward, but his version lay forgotten until it reappeared on *Farewell My Summer Love*. Sensual and bewitching, the singer relentlessly presents us with the image of a young crooner. The original mix dates from 1973 and was released in 2009 on *Michael Jackson—Hello World: The Motown Solo Collection* (Hip-O Select/Motown B0012421-02).

To Make My Father Proud

Bob Crewe, Laurence Weiss / 4'04

Musicians: (unknown) / **Michael Jackson:** lead and backing vocals / **Recording: Sound Factory Studio, Hollywood:** 11 and 16 April, and 16 May 1973 / **Technical team: Producer:** Bob Crewe / **Arrangements:** Michael Melvoin / **Recording engineer:** David Hassinger

This song had a special resonance in the singer's career. Gentle and sad, it is disturbingly autobiographical. In order to earn his parents' pride, the singer declares: "If I don't come up, number one / I'll stand not well apart." Even more troubling are these words from the song, as if the young Michael already foresaw his fate: "In my eleventh hour / I'll be a man the way / To face whatever falls my way / Prepared that are a shame." The song's original mix dates from 26 May 1973; it was released in 2009 on the compilation *Michael Jackson—Hello World: The Motown Solo Collection* (Hip-O Select/Motown B0012421-02).

LOOKIN' BACK TO YESTERDAY

1. WHEN I COME OF AGE*
2. TEENAGE SYMPHONY (FEATURING THE JACKSON FIVE)
3. I HEAR A SYMPHONY (FEATURING THE JACKSON FIVE)
4. GIVE ME HALF A CHANCE (FEATURING THE JACKSON FIVE)
5. LOVE'S GONE BAD*
6. LONELY TEARDROPS*
7. YOU'RE GOOD FOR ME (FEATURING THE JACKSON FIVE)
8. THAT'S WHAT LOVE IS MADE OF*
9. I LIKE YOU THE WAY YOU ARE (DON'T CHANGE YOUR LOVE ON ME) (FEATURING THE JACKSON FIVE)
10. WHO'S LOOKIN' FOR A LOVER*
11. I WAS MADE TO LOVE HER (FEATURING THE JACKSON FIVE)
12. IF'N I WAS GOD*

* Only these songs, with Michael Jackson performing solo, will be featured here.

Lookin' Back To Yesterday **COMPILATION**

Released by Motown Records: USA and Europe, 11 February 1986 (US ref. 5384ML and EU ref. WL72424) / **Musicians:** (unknown) / **Michael Jackson:** lead and backing vocals / **Recording: Motown Recording Studios, Los Angeles:** 1969 to 1973 / **Recording of the new instrumental overdubs: Motown Recording Studios, Los Angeles:** 1985 / **Technical team: Producers of the original songs:** Hal Davis, Mel Larson, Jerry Marcellino, Bob Crewe / **Recording engineer on the new instrumental overdubs:** Bob Robitaille / **Mastering:** John Matousek / **Mixing:** Bob Robitaille

LOOKIN' BACK TO YESTERDAY, MOTOWN CELEBRATES THE CHILD STAR

When Michael Jackson and Lionel Richie went to collect the four Grammy Awards that rewarded the global success of *We Are the World*, and a few months before the first showing of *Captain Eo* at the Epcot Center, Disney World, Motown took advantage of the calm before the storm of *Bad* to release three compilations that were a landmark in the reassessment of the unreleased songs from Michael Jackson's first period. At the start of 1986, the first compilation to be released was entitled *Lookin' Back to Yesterday* and revealed a selection of never-before-released songs by the singer of the Jackson Five. After the lukewarm reception of *Farewell My Summer Love* two years earlier, it was no longer a matter of the label attempting to emulate the star's hits, but fair and square to highlight the musical heritage of its child prodigy. The sub-heading *Never-Before-Released Masters* sent out a very clear message this time, and there was no mistaking what was being communicated. Neither was there any question of adding ill-judged overdubs: the traditional instruments were allowed to breathe, strings sang out, and the harpsichord tones so dear to Hal Davis were reassuring. The cream of the outtakes from the star's solo albums made up the selection of 12 unreleased songs. During the summer of 1986, Motown completed its marketing plan with the release of two further compilations, available only in CD format: *Anthology – Michael Jackson* (MCD06195MD2) and *Anthology – Jackson 5* (MCD06194MD2). For the very first time in its history, the label digitized the master tracks of Michael Jackson and the Jackson Five. This switch to digital technology allowed myriad alternative versions, exclusive to these two CDs, to be unveiled. The selection delighted fans, and allowed some of the rarer songs, such as *Sugar Daddy*, to be rediscovered.

When I Come of Age

Dean Parks / 2'37

Musicians: (unknown) / **Michael Jackson:** lead/backing vocals / **The Jackson Five:** backing vocals / **Recording: Motown Recording Studios, Los Angeles:** (unknown) / **Technical team: Producer:** Hal Davis / **Arrangements:** (unknown) / **Recording:** Russ Terrana (?)

When I Come of Age appeared for the first time in 1986, on *Looking Back to Yesterday* and on *Michael Jackson – Anthology*. Musically, the song is reminiscent of *Music & Me*, in every sense: the languorousness of the lyrics gives way to a literally explosive vocal fervor in the choruses. As a child, Michael wonders about his future, and projects his dreams and wishes into it. Written specially for the young singer, this cute, touching song projects on its own all the energy, vocal ability, and talent Michael Jackson displayed at Motown. Later, an alternative version with slightly different lyrics appeared on the internet.

Love's Gone Bad

Brian Holland, Lamont Dozier, Edward Holland, Jr. / 3'08

Musicians: (unknown) / **Michael Jackson:** lead and backing vocals / **Recording: Motown Recording Studios, Los Angeles:** during the sessions for the album *Get It Together*, in 1972–1973 / **Technical team: Producer:** Hal Davis / **Arrangements:** David Blumberg / **Recording:** Russ Terrana (?)

Popularized in July 1966 by Chris Clark under the title *Love's Gone Mad*, this danceable song by Brian Holland and Lamont Dozier was initially distributed by the VIP label before being added to the Motown catalog. It appeared on the compilation *Boogie* in 1979, with backing vocals supported by the Jackson Five. The version on *Looking Back to Yesterday* is sparer in backing vocals, but retains its funky drive and soaring vocals. Never before had young Michael produced such a breathless rhythm, which foreshadowed his future style. "Love turns out badly when the heart feels sad," is the song's frenzied message. The original solo mix, dating from 22 November 1972, is exclusive to the 1995 *Anthology Series: The Best of Michael Jackson*.

Lonely Teardrops

Berry Gordy, Gwen Gordy, Tyrone Carlo / 2'40

Musicians: (unknown) / **Michael Jackson:** lead/backing vocals / **Recording: Motown Recording Studios, Los Angeles:** July 1972 / **Technical team: Producers:** Mel Larson and Jerry Marcellino / **Arrangements:** (unknown) / **Recording:** Russ Terrana (?)

Lonely Teardrops is one of the very first songs Berry Gordy wrote, and was his first big hit with Jackie Wilson, who recorded it in 1958. It reached No. 1 on the *Billboard* Hot R&B. The Motown boss entrusted it to Michael Jackson, like an exclusive present for someone he considered to be a son. *Lonely Teardrops* deals with the hoped-for return of a beloved after a breakup. There are some gospel flourishes, rather unusual for Michael Jackson, that produce a fine effect.

That's What Love Is Made Of

William Robinson, Robert Rogers, Warren Moore / 3'24

Musicians: (unknown) / **Michael Jackson:** lead and backing vocals / **Recording: Motown Recording Studios, Los Angeles:** during the sessions for the albums *Diana Ross Presents the Jackson 5* and *ABC*, 1969–1970 / **Technical team: Producer:** Hal Davis / **Arrangements:** (unknown) / **Recording engineer:** Russ Terrana (?)

This 1965 Miracles song was recorded by Michael Jackson when he was first with Motown, before it was considered for inclusion in the selection of tracks for the album *Got to Be There*, and was finally added to the selection of unreleased songs on *Looking Back to Yesterday*. The old-fashioned, bluesy piano playing gives the piece a certain maturity. Tambourines and drums quickly join in to accompany the tessitura of the young singer's voice. In the finest Motown tradition, Michael sings again of the eternal vagaries of love.

Who's Lookin' for a Lover

Leon Ware, Jacqueline D. Hilliard / 2'50

Musicians: (unknown) / **Michael Jackson:** lead and backing vocals / **Recording: Motown Recording Studios, Los Angeles:** (unknown) / **Technical team: Producer:** Hal Davis / **Arrangements:** (unknown) / **Recording engineer:** Russ Terrana (?)

With Leon Ware at the controls of this song, percussion and strings take off and explode. *Who's Lookin' for a Lover* is a veritable playground for the young singing prodigy: he alternates with ease between strong, powerful moments and calmer, more bluesy ones. This real vocal challenge was made to measure for the young Michael Jackson, who pushes his voice to extremes without ever failing. A distillation of his talent!

If'n I Was God

Richard Sherman, Robert Sherman / 3'02

Musicians: (unknown) / **Michael Jackson:** lead and backing vocals / **Recording: Sound Factory Studio, Hollywood:** April to May 1973 / **Technical team: Producer:** Bob Crewe / **Arrangements:** (unknown) / **Recording engineer:** David Hassinger

If'n I Was God was written in 1973 by Richard and Robert Sherman for the movie that adapted the story of Tom Sawyer in the form of a musical. The lyrics underline the young rebel's dreams of truth and freedom. The song is a hymn to the musical form, in the same way as *Morning Glow*. The singer's voice is in the process of breaking, which may explain why the song was not used at the time it was recorded. An original mix dating from 26 May 1973 was released in 1995 on the compilation *Anthology Series: The Best of Michael Jackson* (Motown 530 480-2).

THE ORIGINAL SOUL OF MICHAEL JACKSON

1. TWENTY-FIVE MILES*
2. DANCING MACHINE (FEATURING THE JACKSON FIVE)
3. IT'S TOO LATE TO CHANGE THE TIME (FEATURING THE JACKSON FIVE)
4. MELODIE
5. AIN'T NO SUNSHINE
6. GOT TO BE THERE
7. DOGGIN' AROUND
8. ROCKIN' ROBIN
9. IF I DON'T LOVE YOU THIS WAY (FEATURING THE JACKSON FIVE)
10. YOU'VE GOT A FRIEND
11. FOREVER CAME TODAY (FEATURING THE JACKSON FIVE)

* Only the unreleased song will be featured here.

The Original Soul of Michael Jackson **COMPILATION**

Released by Motown: USA, October 1987 (ref. 6250 ML) / Europe, February 1988 (ref. ZL72622) / **Musicians: Michael Jackson:** lead and backing vocals / **Kerry Ashby and Michael Rochelle:** all instruments / **Dale Echnoz and John West:** Synclavier / **Recording: Motown Recording Studios, Los Angeles:** 1969 to 1970 / **Recording of the new instrumental overdubs: Hitsville Recording Studio, Detroit:** 1987 / **Technical team: Producers of the original songs:** Hal Davis, Mel Larson, Jerry Marcellino, The Corporation, and Brian Holland / **Recording engineers on the new instrumental overdubs:** Michael Rochelle and Gregory Weldon / **Arrangements:** Michael Rochelle, Nigel Martinez, Art Wright, James Anthony Carmichael, The Corporation, Eddy Manson, Dave Blumberg, and Gene Page / **Mastering:** John Matousek / **Mixing (and remix):** Michael Rochelle, Gregory Weldon, Nigel Martinez, Derek Marcel, Dean Burt, Tony Peluso, Michael Lovesmith, and Steve Barri

THE ORIGINAL SOUL OF MICHAEL JACKSON, A LEGACY REMIXED

As the promotion of the album *Bad* was getting under way, and the title single was ruling the airwaves, Motown capitalized on the success by releasing a new project entitled *The Original Soul of Michael Jackson*. This compilation contained a selection of big hits from the singer's youth, as well as a few classics, remixed and boosted with Synclavier effects in order to bring the songs up to date.

This project was mostly driven by Dean Burt, who was keen to breathe new life into *It's Too Late to Change the Time*, *Ain't No Sunshine*, *If I Don't Love You This Way*, and *You've Got a Friend*. *Ain't No Sunshine* appealed to the singer's most ardent admirers because of its new vocal take, never before released, and laid down over remixed instrumental material. The pure original version, stripped of all remixed instrumental additions, has never been released to date. *Dancing Machine* also used a vocal take that differed markedly from the original, and had been given a makeover by the duo Nigel Martinez and Derek Marcil. Finally, *Melodie* was reworked from top to bottom, by Tony Peluso—who had already worked on the songs on the compilation *Farewell My Summer Love*—assisted by Michael Lovesmith and Steve Barri. Only *Twenty-Five Miles*, the sole unreleased song in the selection, was accorded the privilege of being released as a single in a few countries and benefited from being broadcast on radio stations in the US. Interest in this compilation was largely confined to the most passionate enthusiasts.

The Remix Suite

In the following years, Motown, always anxious to recycle the singer's legacy and to keep it abreast of musical fashion and sensibilities, exploited a new marketing tool: remixes. Thus the famous British remixer Phil Harding produced a modern, dynamic version of The Jackson Five hit *I Want You Back '88*, which went straight to No. 8 in the UK charts, just a few weeks after *Man in the Mirror*.

In 1992, *Dancing Machine* was released as a series of different mixed versions in parallel with the release of the compilation *The Jacksons: An American Dream*, which was the soundtrack to the TV miniseries of the same name. In 1995, *It's Your Thing* underwent several remixes that were timed for release with the compilation album *The Very Best of Michael Jackson with The Jackson Five*, after which Puff Daddy in turn reworked *I Want You Back* to create a 1998 version, which became best known in the United States. Since the 2000s, Motown has reissued and promoted songs by regularly making karaoke versions or stripped mixes (which are simple, spare, or even pared down) and has embarked on projects completely devoted to remixing songs by Michael Jackson and The Jackson Five. Thus *Michael Jackson: The Remix Suite* (2009) contains the work of big names on the current scene at the time, such as The Neptunes, Stargate, and Frankie Knuckles.

Michael Jackson at home in Encino during a photo session for *Right On!* magazine on 18 December 1972.

TWENTY-FIVE MILES

Johnny Bristol, Harvey Fuqua, Edwin Starr / 3'27

Musicians: (unknown) / **Michael Jackson:** lead and backing vocals / **Recording: Motown Recording Studios, Los Angeles:** during the sessions for the albums *Diana Ross Presents the Jackson 5* and *ABC*, 1969-1970 / **Technical team: Producers:** Hal Davis, Kerry Ashby, and Michael Rochelle / **Arrangements:** Michael Rochelle / **Recording engineer:** Michael Rochelle / **Single: A-side:** *Twenty-Five Miles* (*album version*) / 3'27 / **B-side USA:** *Up on the House Top* (*album version*) / 3'11 / **B-side France:** *Never Can Say Goodbye* (*album version*) / 2'56 / **Released by Motown Records:** USA (ref. 1914MF) and UK (ref. ZB 41685), October 1987

Twenty-Five Miles is a classic by Edwin Starr. In early 1969 it made the Top 10 of the Hot 100 and Top R&B on *Billboard*. The young Michael Jackson recorded it the same year, soon after his arrival at Motown. The song was for a time considered for the tracklist of the album *Got to Be There*, but was dropped. Almost 20 years after it was recorded, *Twenty-Five Miles* opened Motown's new compilation project; at the same time, it was released as a single in the United States and a few European countries. The remixed version and its Christmas song *sic* – unclear on the B-side, *Up on the House Top*, did not appeal to the public, and the song was not very well known by the fan base. The song's original version ended up being released in 2009 on the compilation *Michael Jackson – Hello World: The Motown Solo Collection* (Hip-O Select/Motown – B0012421-02).

FOR JACKSON ADDICTS

Many unreleased, alternative versions can be found on a multitude of compilations. Among the most noteworthy are: *Anthology Series: The Best of Michael Jackson* (1995), *Michael Jackson with The Jackson 5 – Soulsation!* (1995), *Michael Jackson – Love Songs* (2002), *Michael Jackson – Hello World: The Complete Motown Solo Albums* (2009), *Jackson 5 – I Want You Back! Unreleased Masters* (2009), *Jackson 5 – Come and Get It: The Rare Pearls* (2012).

HONDA
350

NUMBER ONES

USA version

1. DON'T STOP 'TIL YOU GET ENOUGH
2. ROCK WITH YOU
3. BILLIE JEAN
4. BEAT IT
5. THRILLER
6. I JUST CAN'T STOP LOVING YOU
7. BAD
8. SMOOTH CRIMINAL
9. THE WAY YOU MAKE ME FEEL
10. MAN IN THE MIRROR
11. DIRTY DIANA
12. BLACK OR WHITE
13. YOU ARE NOT ALONE
14. YOU ROCK MY WORLD
15. BREAK OF DAWN
16. ONE MORE CHANCE*
17. BEN (LIVE)

European, Japanese, and Australian versions

1. DON'T STOP 'TIL YOU GET ENOUGH
2. ROCK WITH YOU
3. BILLIE JEAN
4. BEAT IT
5. THRILLER
6. HUMAN NATURE
7. I JUST CAN'T STOP LOVING YOU
8. BAD
9. THE WAY YOU MAKE ME FEEL
10. DIRTY DIANA
11. SMOOTH CRIMINAL
12. BLACK OR WHITE
13. YOU ARE NOT ALONE
14. EARTH SONG
15. BLOOD ON THE DANCE FLOOR
16. YOU ROCK MY WORLD
17. BREAK OF DAWN
18. ONE MORE CHANCE*

2003

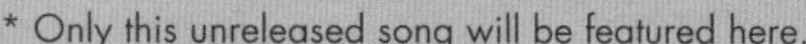

* Only this unreleased song will be featured here.

Number Ones **COMPILATION**

Released by Epic Records: USA (ref. 88998) and UK (ref. 513800), 18 November 2003 / **Chart position:** USA R&B No. 6, Pop No. 13 / UK No. 1 / **RIAA:** certified Gold 16 December 2003 / certified Platinum 18 November 2005 / certified three-time Multiplatinum 18 November 2009 / certified four-time Multiplatinum 16 May 2013

NUMBER ONES, THE KING CAUGHT UP IN A STORM

The King of Pop's supporters felt that Sony Music had managed to bury the album *Invincible* and the plans Michael Jackson had for this record. All the planned singles were canceled. Nevertheless, even though the King of Pop was not selling as many records in the United States, he remained a top artist on other continents. The number of times *Invincible* got to No. 1 in the charts during the very short time it was on sale confirmed this.

However, on 9 January 2003, the media reported that the CEO Tommy Mottola had resigned. Although relations between the record label and Michael Jackson remained complicated, a tentative dialogue slowly began to be established.

A good idea that backfired

The British TV journalist Martin Bashir contacted Michael Jackson during the summer of 2002 with the aim of making a documentary on his life. The King of Pop had appreciated the portrait Bashir had painted of Princess Diana, and opened the doors of his ranch over a period of several months, allowing Bashir almost total access to his private life. The result was a documentary entitled *Living with Michael Jackson*, which was aired exclusively on the British network ITV on 3 February 2003.

Michael Jackson was not asked to approve the editing, and did not see the film until it was broadcast on TV. The journalist had focused his documentary on the singer's friendship with a young boy with cancer named Gavin Arvizo. It showed sequences in which the star was seated next to the teenager, in such a way as to reawaken the ghosts of the 1993 Chandler affair and cast suspicion on the star once again.

In an effort to repair his image, Michael Jackson produced a program by way of right of reply, *Michael Jackson—The Footage You Were Never Meant to See*, which was broadcast in the US on Fox on 20 February. The footage shot by the star's cameras, in parallel with Bashir's footage, showed how the director encouraged the King of Pop to drop his guard, so as to be able to film sequences that ultimately suited Bashir's purpose. According to a poll, Fox viewers condemned the attitude of the British journalist.

On 24 April, Michael Jackson sent a new program to Fox, *Michael Jackson's Private Home Movies*, in which he described various important moments of his life to camera, with many rare, never-before-seen images drawn from his private archives. In this way he tried to set the record straight and cause the regrettable episode with Martin Bashir to be forgotten.

A new entourage

During the *Invincible* years, the star's entourage looked like a court, in which advisers crowded around his door, seeking favors. John McClain was the right-hand man in charge of the logistics of the King of Pop's musical projects. For several months, Charles Koppelman, an influential businessman with whom Michael had come into conflict in 1985 over the purchase of The Beatles catalog, was hired as manager. After firing Koppelman, in 2006 Michael surrounded himself with a

Fans turn out to see Michael Jackson on 19 November 2003 in front of the CMX Studios in Las Vegas, where the star was shooting the short film *One More Chance*.

new team, led by the spokesman Stuart Backerman, who took on the task of establishing more direct communication between the star, his fans, and the media.

This long process of repositioning Jackson's image took up the first part of the year 2003. The singer decided to relaunch the charity single project, *What More Can I Give*. He completed work on the video and re-signed each of the artists who had recorded the song with him. On 25 October 2003 he was in Las Vegas to officially launch the song at the Radio Music Awards. Two days later, the song was available to download legally from a dedicated website. Part of the profits was paid to his charitable causes.

With *What More Can I Give*, Michael Jackson brought to fruition a project begun in the late 1990s. In releasing this song independently, he was moving toward a different way of managing his work. He seemed determined to leave Sony and take off on his own. Nevertheless, he agreed to work with his record label to put together a compilation, as specified in his contract. He thus gave the green light to the *Number Ones* project, a collection of his greatest hits, spiced up with an unreleased song—a number coproduced with R. Kelly, *One More Chance*, from the sessions for *Invincible*. A documentary that described his solo career, with the unassuming title *The One*, accompanied the release of this compilation. CBS obtained exclusive TV broadcast rights and aired the documentary on 2 January 2004, before the release of a DVD version on 9 March the same year.

Under the media spotlight

The compilation *Number Ones* went on sale on 18 November 2003. The same day, more than 50 police officers raided his ranch, Neverland. The Santa Barbara County prosecutor, Tom Sneddon, had a warrant to search the property. It was he who had already pursued the King of Pop in 1993, in the Chandler affair. Now he was returning to the fray, based on accusations made by the Arvizo family, specifically the young Gavin, who, under the direction of the Chandler lawyer, Larry Feldman, accused the star of having touched him sexually.

Michael Jackson was in Las Vegas, shooting the short film of *One More Chance*, when the police visited his home. On 20 November a warrant was issued for his arrest. He then left the gambling capital to hand himself in to the Californian authorities. His arrival at Santa Barbara prison, in handcuffs, made the front pages of all the newspapers the next day. Despite this difficult situation, Sony Music did not abandon its artist, and saw the promotion of *Number Ones* through to its successful completion. Admittedly, it could not have been otherwise, because the financial interests binding the singer and the record label together were too significant. Like an elderly couple who have been through all the stages of a marriage, Michael Jackson and Sony remained together, not so much "for better" as "for worse."

One More Chance

R. Kelly / 3'50

Musicians: Michael Jackson: lead and backing vocals / **R. Kelly:** keyboards and synthesizers / **Donnie Lyle:** guitar / **Recording: Hit Factory Studios, New York:** 2001 to 2003 / **Technical team: Producers:** R. Kelly and Michael Jackson / **Voice recording engineers:** Brad Buxer and Jon Nettlesbey / **Recording engineer:** Jon Nettlesbey / **Assistant recording engineer:** Tim Roberts / **String arrangements:** Michael Jackson / **Pro Tools:** John Hanes / **Mixing:** Serban Ghenea / **Single (CD) USA: Track 1:** *One More Chance (album version)* / 3'50 / **Track 2:** *One More Chance* (*Paul Oakenfold mix*) / 3'50 / **UK: Track 1:** *One More Chance (album version)* / 3'50 / **Track 2:** *One More Chance* (*Paul Oakenfold urban mix*) / 3'37 / **Released by Epic Records:** USA, 22 November 2003 (ref. 76802) / UK, 2 November 2003 (ref. EPC 674 420) / **Chart position:** USA R&B No. 40, Pop No. 83 / UK No. 5

THE SONG

Genesis

While he was working on *Invincible*, Michael Jackson asked R. Kelly to write him some songs. Besides *Cry*, which found a place on the album, the composer created *One More Chance*, a melodious mid-tempo number reminiscent of the simple, cheerful songs Michael Jackson sang in the late 1970s. In this song, which has a very simple structure, the King of Pop sings of a love that is slipping through his fingers and which he wants to get back at all costs.

Production

The making of *One More Chance* had something of the caricature about it. Entirely programmed by R. Kelly on synthesizers and using a computer, the song owes its few traditional sounds to the guitar of Donnie Lyle, with whom the producer worked regularly.

The voice of Michael Jackson sounds similar to the way it does in some other songs, such as *You Rock My World*; however, the star's vocal quirks are more numerous than ever, with an avalanche of "dah" sounds that on occasion spoil the tune. The finishing touches are courtesy of the digital audio workstation Pro Tools—far removed from the handmade techniques of Bruce Swedien.

THE SHORT FILM

Director: Nick Brandt
Producer: (unknown)
Leading actor: Michael Jackson
Shoot date: November 2003
Shooting location: CMX Studios, Las Vegas
Duration: 4'24

Genesis

To support the launch of *Number Ones*, Michael Jackson agreed to shoot a short film for the song *One More Chance*. He managed to persuade Nick Brandt to leave his beloved Africa to make the video. Thus the King of Pop renewed contact with a work partner in whom he put all his trust. The staging was a simple one in that the auditorium was reversed: the audience gathers onstage, while in the space normally occupied by the audience Michael Jackson dances and puts on a performance.

Production

For *One More Chance*, Michael Jackson and his team set up in CMX Studios in Las Vegas. A set that was a recreation of the inside of a mini-auditorium awaited them. The shooting schedule was prearranged. Nick Brandt began by filming wide shots, before concentrating on closer shots in which Michael Jackson danced. However, on 18 November 2003, the Gavin Arvizo affair erupted. Two days later, the singer was obliged to leave the set in order to hand himself in to the authorities.

Thus this final short film remained unfinished. Originally planned as the ending of the documentary *The One* that CBS broadcast in January 2004, it was replaced by an edited sequence of archive footage of the singer. A version made from the rushes shot in Las Vegas was released posthumously, in 2010, on the anthology *DVD Michael Jackson's Vision*.

THE ULTIMATE COLLECTION

CD 1

1. I WANT YOU BACK
2. ABC
3. I'LL BE THERE
4. GOT TO BE THERE
5. I WANNA BE WHERE YOU ARE
6. BEN
7. DANCING MACHINE (SINGLE VERSION)
8. ENJOY YOURSELF
9. EASE ON DOWN THE ROAD (FEATURING DIANA ROSS)
10. YOU CAN'T WIN (FROM THE WIZ)
11. SHAKE YOUR BODY (EARLY DEMO)**
12. SHAKE YOUR BODY (DOWN TO THE GROUND)
13. DON'T STOP 'TIL YOU GET ENOUGH
14. ROCK WITH YOU
15. OFF THE WALL
16. SHE'S OUT OF MY LIFE
17. SUNSET DRIVER (DEMO)**
18. LOVELY ONE
19. THIS PLACE HOTEL

2004

CD 2

1. WANNA BE STARTIN' SOMETHIN'
2. THE GIRL IS MINE (FEATURING PAUL MCCARTNEY)
3. THRILLER
4. BEAT IT
5. BILLIE JEAN
6. P.Y.T. (PRETTY YOUNG THING) (DEMO)
7. SOMEONE IN THE DARK**
8. STATE OF SHOCK (FEATURING MICK JAGGER)
9. SCARED OF THE MOON (DEMO)*
10. WE ARE THE WORLD (DEMO)**
11. WE ARE HERE TO CHANGE THE WORLD (FROM CAPTAIN EO)**

CD 3

1. BAD
2. THE WAY YOU MAKE ME FEEL
3. MAN IN THE MIRROR
4. I JUST CAN'T STOP LOVING YOU
5. DIRTY DIANA
6. SMOOTH CRIMINAL
7. CHEATER (DEMO)**
8. DANGEROUS (EARLY VERSION)
9. MONKEY BUSINESS**
10. JAM
11. REMEMBER THE TIME
12. BLACK OR WHITE
13. WHO IS IT (IHS MIX)
14. SOMEONE PUT YOUR HAND OUT**

CD 4

1. YOU ARE NOT ALONE
2. STRANGER IN MOSCOW
3. CHILDHOOD (THEME FROM FREE WILLY 2)
4. ON THE LINE
5. BLOOD ON THE DANCE FLOOR
6. FALL AGAIN (DEMO)*
7. IN THE BACK**
8. UNBREAKABLE
9. YOU ROCK MY WORLD
10. BUTTERFLIES
11. BEAUTIFUL GIRL (DEMO)*
12. THE WAY YOU LOVE ME*
13. WE'VE HAD ENOUGH*

DVD

MICHAEL JACKSON'S DANGEROUS LIVE CONCERT TOUR IN BUCHAREST

Japanese edition bonus tracks:
CD1 / TRACK 11: THE JACKSONS—BLAME IT ON THE BOOGIE
CD2 / TRACK 6: MICHAEL JACKSON—HUMAN NATURE
CD3 / TRACK 3: MICHAEL JACKSON—ANOTHER PART OF ME
CD3 / TRACK 13: MICHAEL JACKSON—HEAL THE WORLD
CD4 / TRACK 12: MICHAEL JACKSON—ONE MORE CHANCE

* Unreleased songs covered in this chapter.
** Unreleased songs covered in previous chapters.

Michael Jackson: The Ultimate Collection **COMPILATION**

Released by Epic Records: USA (ref. E5K 92600) and Europe (ref. EPC 517743 3), 16 November 2004 / **Chart position:** USA R&B No. 48, Pop No. 154 / UK No. 75 / **RIAA:** certified Platinum 16 May 2013

THE ULTIMATE COLLECTION, AN INTIMATE CELEBRATION

From the late 1980s, Michael Jackson started toying with the idea of projects to celebrate his career to date. After planning a compilation album called *Decade—1980–1990* (which was replaced by the *Dangerous* album), then delivering his first greatest hits album as volume 1 of *HIStory*, he followed up in 2003 with a compilation album called *Number Ones*, a standard marketing ploy at the time. This CD was aimed at a broad audience and comprised shortened versions of his major hits, a concept that Jackson was not very keen on.

In mid-summer 2004, a few months before the Arcizo trial commenced, Michael Jackson and Sony collaborated on the final project stipulated on his 1991 contract: a box set looking back on his career. The record label had merged with BMG to become Sony BMG on 4 March 2004. Working with a new and motivated team, the box set comprised four CDs and a DVD and was simply entitled *The Ultimate Collection*.

The carefully selected tracks included 17 previously unreleased or rare songs. Some had already appeared in previous projects, such as the famous 2001 reeditions of the *Off the Wall*, *Thriller*, *Bad*, and *Dangerous* albums. Michael Jackson righted a few wrongs by retrieving certain gems such as *Sunset Driver* from the vault, and by officially issuing tracks like *Monkey Business* that had already been available for a number of years on the pirate circuit.

The embargo on *We Are Here to Change the World*, the song from the Disney theme parks' 3D *Captain EO* movie, was finally lifted. With demos of some of the major classics, like The Jacksons' *Shake Your Body* and *P.Y.T.*, and recently finalized tracks, like *We've Had Enough*, the King of Pop ensured that there was something for everyone.

He entrusted Matt Forger with the difficult job of supervising a team to create the best mix of each of the tracks. The tracklist structure followed a similar approach to the planned but never released *Decade* compilation 15 years earlier: the songs were ordered as they had been on the original albums, rather than according to single release dates. The DVD inside this substantial box set is the original HBO broadcast of the *Dangerous* tour concert in Bucharest on 1 October 1992.

The Ultimate Collection was released on 16 November 2004 and was mainly aimed at dedicated fans and music lovers. From a marketing point of view, a box set of this caliber can only be targeted at a niche market. The complex circumstances in which Michael Jackson found himself only served to reduce the potentially limited appeal of the work even more: it was released just a few weeks before the trial in which Jackson's reputation and freedom were at stake, and consequently the media had zero interest in his art.

Despite this, sales figures were reasonable, with 20,000 copies purchased in France, for example, an entirely respectable number for an item of this kind. A track called *Cheater*, an outtake from *Bad*, was sent to radio stations and also pressed on CDs and maxi-singles, which subsequently became highly valuable collectibles.

Michael Jackson takes a break in his hotel room in Orlando during the *Victory* tour in 1984.

FOR JACKSON ADDICTS

The credits on *The Ultimate Collection* indicate that the song is taken from a book by Michael Jackson called *Scared of the Moon*, about which nothing is known.

SCARED OF THE MOON (DEMO)

Michael Jackson, Buz Kohan / 4'41

Musicians: **Michael Jackson:** lead and backing vocals **Recording:** **Evergreen Recording Studios, Burbank, and Westlake Recording Studios, Los Angeles:** 1984 / **Technical team:** **Producer:** Michael Jackson / **Recording engineers:** Mike Riccio and Matt Forger / **Assistant recording engineers:** Ric Butz and Bruce Wildstein / **Vocal arrangements:** Michael Jackson / **Orchestral arrangements:** Marty Paich / **Mixing:** (unknown)

2004

Scared of the Moon emerged from a collaboration between Michael Jackson and Buz Kohan, and was one of the tracks initially developed for the *Bad* album. This gentle ballad cannot be considered an outtake from the album because the star always intended to resume work on the piece. According to Brad Sundberg, the recording engineer Matt Forger worked on the recording of the original demo in a single session at the Westlake studios in Los Angeles. This initial version comprised a piano track, a backing vocals track, and lead vocals. Matt Forger gave the original master of *Scared of the Moon* to Michael Jackson, although he was well aware that you should never entrust the original to the singer if you hoped to continue working on it someday. Two months later a second session, with the star present, took place at the Evergreen studio in Burbank near Los Angeles. The plan was to include an additional string line in the song. The recording engineer that day, probably Mike Riccio, requested the master tapes so he could add the new track. Matt Forger no longer had them in his possession but was able to supply a cassette on which he had copied the original recording. This was used to continue working on the song in the studio. The string track plus the three initial tracks were merged into one track on the cassette that was then used to create a new master, which this time the others were careful not to entrust to Michael Jackson.

In the early 2000s, the King of Pop worked briefly on *Scared of the Moon* with Steve Porcaro and Michael Prince during the *Invincible* sessions, but this added little to the song and, not yet finalized, it headed back to the vaults.

In 2004, Matt Forger finished the version that appears on *The Ultimate Collection* compilation. An additional guitar track can be heard, superimposed on the original piano/vocals/string version.

Scared of the Moon and *Beautiful Girl* were both on the list found in Jackson's bedroom in 2009. This list comprised songs that he intended to resume work on. Almost 25 years after it was first composed, the song was apparently still on the singer's mind, like a precious stone that he wanted to keep polishing. It is essentially a nursery rhyme about a child's nighttime fears: a little girl in her bedroom is unable to sleep because she is frightened of the moonlight shining through her window.

FALL AGAIN (DEMO)

Walter Afanasieff, Robin Thicke / 4'22

Musicians: Michael Jackson: lead and backing vocals / **Walter Afanasieff:** keyboards / **Recording: Wally World Studios and Blue Jay Studios, San Rafael, California / Hit Factory, New York:** 1999 / **Technical team: Producers:** Walter Afanasieff and Robin Thicke / **Coproducer**: Michael Jackson / **Synthesizer programming:** Walter Afanasieff / **Recording engineers:** David Gleeson, Robin Thicke, Pro-Jay, and Paul J. Falcone / **Assistant recording engineers:** Chris Ribando and Nick Thomas

In the late 1990s, Michael Jackson worked on some ideas for songs with Walter Afanasieff, the Russian composer known for his work with Mariah Carey. In 1994, Afanasieff and Carey wrote a song together called *All I Want for Christmas Is You*; it became the bestselling Christmas song of all time. The composer's distinctive style featured ballads with lavish string sections and spectacular arrangements. He composed *Fall Again* with the singer Robin Thicke in the hope that Michael Jackson would want to record it. On hearing the demo, the King of Pop instantly fell in love with the melody. However, the singer and composer's busy schedules left them with few opportunities to meet.

In 1999, Walter Afanasieff was finalizing an album called *Affirmation* with the Australian duo Savage Garden, and decided to organize a parallel recording session with the King of Pop. This enabled him to work on the two pieces at the same time. The session took place at the Hit Factory in New York, where Jackson recorded his vocals in a single take. However, he was unable to finalize the song that day because he had to leave the studio to look after his son Prince, who was sick. *Fall Again* was stopped at demo stage and failed to make the tracklist for *Invincible*. It was recorded in 2002 by the singer Glenn Lewis and appears on the soundtrack for the film *Maid in Manhattan*.

BEAUTIFUL GIRL (DEMO)

Michael Jackson / 4'03

Musicians: Michael Jackson: lead and backing vocals / **Brad Buxer and Steve Porcaro:** keyboards / **Steve Lukather:** guitar / **Recording: The Gallery, Ocean Way Recording, Record One, and Record Plant Recording Studios, Los Angeles / Hit Factory, New York:** 1998 and 2004 / **Technical team: Producer:** Michael Jackson / **Recording engineers:** Brad Buxer and Michael Prince / **Synthesizer programming:** Brad Buxer / **Drum programming:** Brad Buxer / **Percussion programming:** Eric Anest / **Pro Tools:** Michael Prince / **Mixing:** (unknown)

Michael Jackson worked on this song at various times between 1998 and 2004 before finally presenting his fans with the track, still at demo stage, on *The Ultimate Collection*. Accompanied by a simple melody and sublime harmonies, Jackson plays the frustrated lover who wishes he had a beautiful woman to hold. The candid lyrics and languorous vocals are laid down on musical tracks performed by Steve Porcaro and Steve Lukather, the two men who had long worked with Jackson on his ballads. Brad Buxer and Michael Prince fine-tuned the musical textures to perfect the warm, mellow atmosphere of the piece. In 2009, the King of Pop was planning to continue developing the song, which featured on a long list of numbers he wanted to finalize.

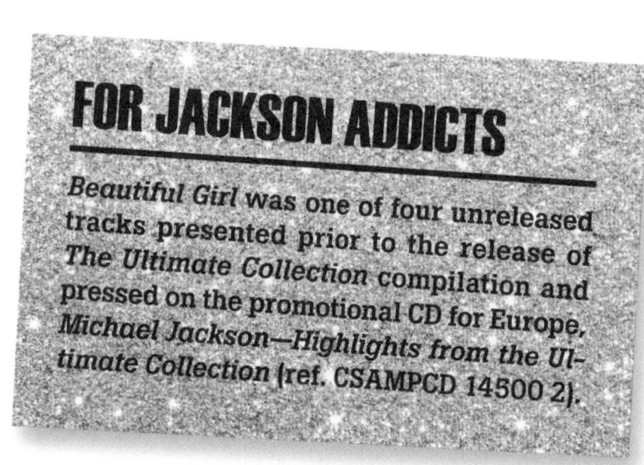

FOR JACKSON ADDICTS

Beautiful Girl was one of four unreleased tracks presented prior to the release of *The Ultimate Collection* compilation and pressed on the promotional CD for Europe, *Michael Jackson—Highlights from the Ultimate Collection* (ref. CSAMPCD 14500 2).

FOR JACKSON ADDICTS

In January 2011, this track was released as a digital single in South Korea.

On 20 March 1999, Michael Jackson appeared on the German TV show *Wetten, dass?* on the ZDF network, to announce the MJ and Friends concerts.

The Way You Love Me

Michael Jackson / 4'30

2004 version: *The Way You Love Me* / **Musicians: Michael Jackson:** lead and backing vocals / **Brad Buxer:** keyboards / **Paulinho Da Costa:** percussion / **Recording: Ocean Way Recording, Record One, Los Angeles / Hit Factory, New York:** 2000 to 2004 / **Technical team: Producer:** Michael Jackson / **Recording engineers:** Michael Durham Prince and Brad Buxer / **Synthesizer, keyboard, and drum programming:** Brad Buxer / **Percussion programming:** Eric Anest / **Pro Tools:** Michael Prince / **Mixing:** (unknown) / **2010 version:** *(I Like) The Way You Love Me* / **Musicians: Michael Jackson:** lead and backing vocals / **William C. Champlin:** piano / **Erick Donell Walls:** guitar / **Thomas Drayton:** bass guitar / **Paulinho Da Costa:** percussion / **Recording: Ocean Way Recording, Record One, Los Angeles / Hit Factory, New York:** 2000 to 2010 for the new musical tracks (studios unknown) / **Technical team: Producers:** Theron "Neff-U" Feemster and Michael Jackson / **Recording engineer vocals:** Michael Durham Prince / **Recording engineer mixing:** John Hanes / **Recording engineer:** James Murray / **Keyboard and percussion programming:** Theron "Neff-U" Feemster / **Mixing:** Serban Ghenea

The Way You Love Me was recorded during the *Invincible* sessions. The song was inserted as a bonus track on *The Ultimate Collection* compilation in 2004 and reappeared on the *Michael* compilation in 2010 as a new production by Theron "Neff-U" Feemster, featuring an intro in which Michael Jackson is heard giving Brad Buxer instructions for the song over the telephone. Rhythmically, the newer version is slightly different with the addition of digital cymbals and handclaps as well as a new piano line and a few additional words. The lyrics portray the singer completely surrendering himself to his new lover: "I was alone, there was no love in my life / I was afraid of life and you came in time."

We've Had Enough

Michael Jackson, Rodney Jerkins, LaShawn Daniels, Carole Bayer Sager / 5'45

Musicians: Michael Jackson: lead vocals / **Gerald Hayward:** drums / **Recording: Sony Studios, New York / Darkchild Studios, Pleasantville, New Jersey:** 1999 to 2000 / **Technical team: Producers:** Michael Jackson and Rodney Jerkins / **Recording engineers:** Jean-Marie Horvat, Brad Gilderman, Harvey Mason Jr., Dexter Simmons, and Bruce Swedien / **Assistant recording engineers:** Tim Roberts, Tom Sweeney, Jeff Burns, Dave Ashton, and Craig Durrance / **Digital edition:** Stuart Brawley / **String arrangements:** Jeremy Lubbock / **Backing vocals arrangements:** Betty Wright / **Pro Tools:** John Hanes / **Mixing:** Serban Ghenea

We've Had Enough is an anthem that Michael Jackson, Rodney Jerkins, and Jackson's friend Carole Bayer Sager started developing during the *Invincible* sessions. It is a visceral condemnation of war: "We're innocently standing by / Watching people losing lives / It seems as if we have no voice." The rhythm is stiff and metronomic at first, increasing in musicality as some cleverly layered digital and electric resonances gradually come in, enhancing rather than concealing the singer's timbre. Michael Jackson's vocals rise alongside a delightful crescendo that is not dissimilar to *Earth Song* on the *HIStory* album. This humanist number, which was ultimately not included on *Invincible*, became one of the standout pieces among the previously unreleased tracks on *The Ultimate Collection* compilation.

LAST LITTLE-KNOWN COLLABORATIONS

Michael Jackson's last collaborative creations were mostly minor affairs. Throughout the 2000s, Rodney Jerkins used a few unreleased Michael Jackson vocal tracks here and there in his own personal productions. Michael Jackson's only music-based project in 2003 was also the last charitable commitment of his career. *What More Can I Give* was a project he fought hard for, before ultimately making it available as an internet download. In 2011, in honor of Michael Jackson's admirers, Barry Gibb delivered a finalized version of a number called *All in Your Name* that he had started working on with the star.

SIDNEY FINE
SEEING VOICES

Sidney Fine / 3'17

Musician: Michael Jackson: lead and backing vocals / **Recording: (unknown):** 1999 / **Technical team: Producer:** Michael Jackson / **Recording engineer:** Matt Forger

Sidney Fine was the husband of Rose Fine, The Jackson Five's tutor in the early 1970s when they first came to Los Angeles. This resolute woman was responsible for educating the five young boys. Michael Jackson would stay in close contact with her up until her death on 5 June 2000. Sidney Fine composed music for movies and television, and he was part of the team on the Walt Disney movie *Lady and the Tramp* in 1955. In the 1990s, he composed *Seeing Voices*, which was inspired by Dr. Oliver Sacks' book of the same name. It recounts how students at Gallaudet University in Washington, DC, which specializes in the deaf and hard of hearing, protested in 1988, because they wanted a president with the same disability as them. The newly appointed president, Elisabeth Zinser, was forced to stand down in favor of Irving King Jordan, the university's first deaf president. Michael Jackson decided to record an homage to the event in the style of a song from a musical comedy.

The first version recorded by Sidney Fine featured two pianos and an acoustic bass guitar. The King of Pop felt that the arrangements lacked depth and asked the composer to give the piece more substance. The conductor Ray Charles (no relation to the famous singer) inserted some symphonic arrangements into this timeless waltz, while Matt Forger supervised the production.

Seeing Voices, produced by Michael Jackson and finalized in early 1999, was intended for inclusion on the *Invincible* album, but it was rejected. The song was performed only once in public, at a private ceremony organized by the Fines on 28 May 1999 at the Ventura Club in Los Angeles. Michael Jackson did not attend the event, despite it partly being held in his honor.

In the mid-1990s the young Brandy was the embodiment of the new generation of US R&B artists.

Brandy

It's Not Worth It

Rodney Jerkins, Fred Jerkins III, LaShawn Daniels / 4'23

From the album: *Full Moon* / **Released by Atlantic Records:** USA (ref. 83493) and Europe (ref. 7567-93110-2), 5 March 2002 / **Chart position:** USA R&B No. 1, Pop No. 2 / UK No. 9 / **Musicians: Brandy:** lead vocals / **Michael Jackson:** additional vocals / **Recording: Darkchild Studios, Pleasantville, New Jersey** / **Hit Factory, New York:** 2001

For Brandy's third album, Rodney Jerkins sampled Michael Jackson's vocals from one of their sessions in the early 2000s. Michael Jackson's voice echoes in the background, bringing added texture to the many drum machine layers on the piece.

Monica

All Eyez on Me

Monica Arnold, LaShawn Daniels, Quincy Jones, James Ingram / 4'00

From the album: *All Eyez on Me* / **Released by J Records:** Japan, October 2002 (ref. BVCP-21260) / **Single : released by J Records:** USA (ref. 80813-21181-1) and Europe (ref. 74321 96188 2), August 2002 / **Chart position:** USA R&B No. 32, Pop No. 69 / **Michael Jackson:** previously unreleased ad-libs from *P.Y.T. (Pretty Young Thing)* / **Recording: Patchwerk Studios, Atlanta:** 2001 to 2002

Michael Jackson gave the master tapes of *P.Y.T. (Pretty Young Thing)* to Rodney Jerkins, who sampled the track and extracted a few ad-libs for Monica's *All Eyez on Me.* The R&B production was released worldwide along with a whole host of remixes and a music video.

On 24 April 2002, Michael Jackson and Diana Ross were reunited on stage for *A Night at the Apollo*, the New York gala held by the Democratic Party.

AOL, Time Warner, and Tonos Competition
I Have This Dream

Michael Jackson, David Foster, Carole Bayer Sager, Ric Kipp / 4'03

Instrumental: 2001 to 2002 (no physical media)

In April 2002, AOL, Time Warner, and Tonos ran a competition for internet users in which the prize was to create the lyrics for a musical theme composed by Michael Jackson, David Foster, and Carole Bayer Sager. The instrumental version of the piece was broadcast on Tonos.com. The lyricist Ric Kipp won first prize in July 2002, but the finished result was never delivered. In 2015, Ric Kipp confirmed that a complete version of the song was never recorded. He partnered up with the singer Michael Ricks to use the lyrics on a new composition that had little in common with the original theme.

Barry Gibb and Michael Jackson
All in Your Name

Barry Gibb, Michael Jackson / 5'37

Work session and partial recording: Middle Ear Studios, Miami: December 2002

In 2011, Barry Gibb broadcast two video excerpts in which he is seen working with Michael Jackson composing and recording the song *All in Your Name*. According to an article in *Billboard* in 2002, the song was prompted by the US government's decision to invade Iraq. On 25 June 2011, two years to the day after the singer's death, Barry Gibb offered fans a version of the song that he had finalized himself as a legal download from his official website. (www.Barrygibb.com)

FOR JACKSON ADDICTS

The final mix of the song and the instrumental version, both of which should have been released as singles, are languishing in vaults. Due to the number of singers involved, it is unlikely it will ever be published.

UNITED WE STAND

WHAT MORE CAN I GIVE

Michael Jackson / 3'36
*Spanish version cowritten by Rubén Blade (*Todo Para Ti*)*

Internet single and a few very rare promo CDs: Released by MusicForGiving.com: 27 October 2003 / **Musicians: 3LW, Aaron Carter, Alejandro Sanz, Anastacia, Beyoncé, Billy Gilman, Brian McKnight, Bryton James, Carlos Santana, Céline Dion, Cristian Castro, Gloria Estefan, Hanson, Jon Secada, Joy Enriquez, Juan Gabriel, Julio Iglesias, Justin Timberlake, Laura Pausini, Luis Miguel, Luther Vandross, Mariah Carey, Michael McCary, Michael Jackson, Mýa, NSYNC, Nick Carter, Olga Tañón, Reba McEntire, Ricky Martin, Rubén Blades, Shakira, Shawn Stockman, Thalía, Tom Petty, Usher, and Ziggy Marley:** lead vocals / **Recording: (unknown):** 1999 to 2003

The initial creative work on the composition was done in 1998 and was apparently intended to be performed as a duet with Luciano Pavarotti. *What More Can I Give*, the title of which was said to have arisen from a discussion between Michael Jackson and Nelson Mandela, first appeared as a humanitarian slogan used to promote the two Michael Jackson and Friends concerts in Munich and Seoul in June 1999.

Following the September 11 attacks in 2001 and the example of *We Are the World*, the star reworked the song, recording it with a group of famous artists. There were two versions, one in Spanish and one in English. Just after completing the recording, the song was performed by 20 stars at the Robert F. Kennedy Memorial Stadium in Washington, DC, on 21 October 2001.

To Michael Jackson's disappointment, Sony Music decided not to market the CD. Only a few promotional copies were distributed to the participating artists and a few key media organizations. The King of Pop was determined to publish the song, and with the support of Clear Channel and MusicForGiving.com, he managed to get it released on the internet two years later, on 27 October 2003. Prior to the digital launch, a music video was broadcast at the Radio Music Awards in Las Vegas, prominently featuring all the stars who had agreed to forego their royalties in aid of the victims of September 11. Michael Jackson's last humanitarian and musical battle was marked by his perseverance and tenacity.

RODNEY JERKINS

RIDE WITH ME

Rodney Jerkins / 4'24

From the album: *Versatility* / **Released by Darkchild Independent Records:** USA (ref 02097 00972), July 2006 / **Musicians: Rodney Jerkins** (lead vocals) / **Michael Jackson:** additional vocals/ **Recording: Hector Diaz and Jeff Villanueva, Orlando, Florida:** 2005

For *Ride with Me*, Rodney Jerkins repeatedly looped Jackson's vocal segment from Brandy's *It's Not Worth It* on a mellow instrumental track.

FOR JACKSON ADDICTS

For the launch of his new group, So Plush, Rodney Jerkins had Michael Jackson record a promotional message that appears on a track called *Phone Messages* on the very rare promo CD *So Plush—Advance*.

THRILLER 25

1. WANNA BE STARTIN' SOMETHIN'
2. BABY BE MINE
3. THE GIRL IS MINE (FEATURING PAUL MCCARTNEY)
4. THRILLER
5. BEAT IT
6. BILLIE JEAN
7. HUMAN NATURE
8. P.Y.T. (PRETTY YOUNG THING)
9. THE LADY IN MY LIFE
10. VINCENT PRICE EXCERPT FROM THRILLER VOICE-OVER SESSION
11. THE GIRL IS MINE 2008 (FEATURING WILL.I.AM)
12. P.Y.T. (PRETTY YOUNG THING) 2008 (FEATURING WILL.I.AM)
13. WANNA BE STARTIN' SOMETHIN' 2008 (FEATURING AKON)*
14. BEAT IT 2008 (FEATURING FERGIE)
15. BILLIE JEAN 2008 (KANYE WEST MIX)
16. FOR ALL TIME (UNRELEASED TRACK FROM ORIGINAL "THRILLER" SESSIONS)

Japanese edition bonus track:
GOT THE HOTS

*Only the song on which Michael Jackson recorded a new vocal track is covered here.

Thriller 25 **ANNIVERSARY EDITION REISSUE**

Released by Epic Records: USA and Europe, February 2008 (ref. 88697220962) / **Chart position:** US Top Catalog Albums No. 1 / UK No. 3 / France No. 1 / **RIAA:** certified Gold and Platinum 31 January 1983 / certified 33-time Multiplatinum 16 February 2017

In late 2005, there were signs that a new single was under production. Entitled *From the Bottom of My Heart*, it was another charity record, this time in aid of victims of Hurricane Katrina. Many big names including Stevie Wonder, James Brown, Celine Dion, and Mariah Carey were mentioned for the single, which never got beyond the developmental stage.

THRILLER 25, FULL CIRCLE

As the 2000s drew to a close, Michael Jackson celebrated the 25th anniversary of his masterpiece, *Thriller*, by looking back on what now seemed like another era.

On 13 June 2005, he was found not guilty of the ten charges that had hung over him throughout the Arvizo case. During this long drawn-out legal process he had effectively been standing trial for both the Chandler and Arvizo cases. However, very few media commentators understood that this was in effect a double acquittal. In the United States, certain journalists realized that the legal actions against the singer were really thinly disguised attempts at extortion.

Michael Jackson left the Santa Maria court looking drawn and completely drained. The terrible ordeal had wiped him out. More than ever, he was aware of the damage that this had caused to his personal and professional life. Many people were left wondering how he would go forward from here. But the singer simply shut himself away from the world and, a few days after the verdict, left California for Bahrain.

A king in Bahrain

In Bahrain, the King of Pop and his children stayed with the royal family. Fairly soon after their arrival, Michael Jackson and Prince Abdullah discussed the idea of setting up a record company, and the 2 Seas Records label began to take shape. The artist agreed to record a humanitarian anthem called *From the Bottom of My Heart*, which never saw the light of day. He began discussing new ideas with Bill Bottrell, his long-standing friend and partner. But just as various song concepts began to crystallize, Michael left Bahrain for Europe. Bill Bottrell would never see him again.

In the meantime, *The Essential Michael Jackson* compilation, a project initiated by the French Sony Music team, was released on 19 July 2005 to great public acclaim, proving the King of Pop had not lost his audience. The star had left Bahrain in spring 2006 without honoring his commitments, so Prince Abdullah attempted to file a lawsuit against him, more out of principle than for financial reasons, it seems. The two men eventually came to an arrangement. Michael Jackson then began a long odyssey that took him to many countries, including Ireland, where he lived for a time. By then he had a new manager, Raymone Bain, who organized a number of exclusive and extremely pricey galas in Japan for his most devoted (and well-off) fans.

The years 2005 and 2006 saw a series of legal disputes with some of his former collaborators. In October 2006, the artist appeared to experience a spark of creativity, working with will.i.am in Ireland on a few song ideas. The journalist Billy Bush flew over to conduct a short interview with him, which was broadcast on NBC's *Access Hollywood* on 15 October 2006. It was filmed in the recording studio in the country house that the singer was renting in Ireland. During their discussion, the journalist mooted the idea of the King of Pop celebrating the 25th anniversary of *Thriller* with a deluxe version of the album, which would include some previously unreleased tracks. A few weeks later, the organizers of the World Music Awards persuaded the star to take part in the cer-

On 15 November 2006, Michael Jackson took part in the World Music Awards, the last ceremony of his career, at the Earls Court Arena, London.

emony in London on 15 November. They presented him with a special *Guinness Book of Records*-approved award for the historic and unequalled success of *Thriller*. Apart from this tentative return to the spotlight, the only news about Jackson revolved around his financial setbacks and the renegotiation of the huge loans that he had taken out in the 1990s.

Back to the United States

In late December 2006, Michael Jackson was convinced by the businessman Jack Wishna to return to the US for a meeting to discuss some potential show projects in Las Vegas. No sooner had the star set foot in the States than he had to attend the funeral of his friend and mentor James Brown, who had died on Christmas Day. The first few months of 2007 were taken up by society events organized by Raymone Bain as well as preparations with his new lawyer and right-hand man, Peter Lopez, for a low-key comeback.

The relationship between his manager and his lawyer was not without its ups and downs: in the 2000s too many people were competing to manage the career of a megastar who had been absent from the music scene for several years. Lopez planned the *Thriller 25* project with Sony Music, intending to celebrate the 25th anniversary of the album with a special edition.

Thriller 25

Michael Jackson traveled to New York to meet with the teams at Legacy Recordings, the label that dealt with reissues of the biggest albums in Sony's catalog. The initial plan was to include previously unreleased songs from the *Thriller* sessions, such as *Hot Street*, *Nite Line*, and *Trouble*. But the King of Pop was not keen on publishing them. During the discussions, he talked about wanting to produce new versions of his masterpieces. He asked Kanye West to remix *Billie Jean*, and he recorded a cover version of *Wanna Be Startin' Somethin'* with Akon. The only previously unreleased track on physical media—which had already leaked onto the pirate circuit—was *For All Time*, a ballad composed during the *Dangerous* years. It appears on the last track of *Thriller 25* to convey the message that *Thriller* was the bestselling album of all time. Some tracks from that period, like the demo versions of *The Girl Is Mine* and *Got the Hots*, were respectively pressed as bonus tracks on the single *The Girl Is Mine 2008* and the Japanese edition of *Thriller 25*.

Michael Jackson agreed to pose for the magazines *L'Uomo Vogue* and *Ebony* to support the launch of the album. This was his last-ever official shoot. The photographer was Matthew Rolston, with whom he had worked during the *Thriller* era.

When Michael Jackson signed up to the *Thriller 25* concept, he received a welcome advance payment that helped him meet his day-to-day costs. He was strapped for cash and had been forced to refinance various loans, including the one for Neverland Ranch. The investment company Colony Capital took on the complex dossier and turned the estate into a limited liability company called Sycamore Ranch, its original name. The star had no intention of returning to live in the property, which he felt had been violated by the Arvizo case and the police searches in November 2003.

The album reissue was due out on December 2007, but ended up being launched on 11 February 2008, because Jackson wanted to finalize a few remixes and new versions that included *Beat It* with Fergie of the Black Eyed Peas. The main single was the cover version with Akon, which reached out to a new generation of fans. *Thriller 25* sold over three million copies worldwide, a very respectable achievement for such an old album in a market severely damaged by the financial crisis.

Akon, a successful singer and songwriter in the 2000s, helped Michael Jackson on his nervous return to the stage with *Thriller 25*.

Wanna Be Startin' Somethin' 2008

Alioune "Akon" Thiam, Giorgio Tuinfort, Michael Jackson / 3'51

Musicians: **Michael Jackson:** lead and backing vocals / **Alioune "Akon" Thiam:** lead and backing vocals, keyboards, and synthesizers / **Giorgio Tuinfort:** keyboards and synthesizers / **Recording:** **Konkast Studios, Atlanta / Canada / France:** rhythmic tracks / **Wisseloord Studios, Amsterdam / Maze Studios, Atlanta / Paper V.U. Studios, North Hollywood / Ethanet Studios (unknown):** mixing / November 2007 / **Technical team:** **Producers:** Alioune "Akon" Thiam and Michael Jackson / **Coproducer:** Giorgio Tuinfort / **Recording engineer:** Mark "Exit" Goodchild / **Synthesizer programming:** Alioune "Akon" Thiam and Giorgio Tuinfort / **Backing vocals recording:** Angelikson Productions / **Mixing:** Mark "Exit" Goodchild and Dylan "3-D" Dresdow / **Single (CD):** **Track 1:** *Wanna Be Startin' Somethin' 2008* / 3'51 / **Track 2:** *Wanna Be Startin' Somethin' 2008 (Johnny Vicious Club, radio edit)* / 3'36 / **Released by Epic Records:** USA and UK, 7 March 2008 (US ref. 869729099 and UK ref. 869729099) / **Chart position:** USA R&B No. 5, Pop No. 81 / UK No. 69

Genesis

Michael Jackson preferred to keep unreleased material from the *Thriller* sessions in the vaults and simply commission remixes of the hits from popular contemporary producers such as will.i.am and Kanye West. However, he also made a tentative return to the studio to record a cover version of *Wanna Be Startin' Somethin'* with Akon. His lawyer Peter Lopez had introduced the two men in the belief that a joint collaboration between artists from two different generations could prove a successful marketing ploy. For the previous few years, Akon had been producing chart hit after chart hit, both as a performer and for other artists, such as Gwen Stefani.

Invited by Michael Jackson to take part in the *Thriller 25* project, the producer initially thought about doing a remix of *Billie Jean*, but he ended up plumping for his favorite song from the album: *Wanna Be Startin' Somethin'*. He added a few melodic lines to the intro and the bridge. The lyrics that he wrote diverged significantly from the song's original theme. Rather than a continuation of Michael Jackson's story, he produced a text about meeting and spending the night with a femme fatale.

Production

This cover version was produced by a scaled-down team. Akon and Michael Jackson discussed their ideas over the telephone, with each recording their vocals separately. The King of Pop's sessions took place in the Angelikson Productions studio that belonged to the Cascio brothers, the sons of his friend Dominic Cascio, a hotel employee whom he had met in the 1980s.

The drum machines and layers of computer-programmed synthesizers replaced the entirely organic approach on which the sonic identity of the track had been constructed 25 years before. Much of the song's appeal lay in the chorus "Ma ma se / Ma ma sa, ma ma coo sa," and this was retained, prompting Manu Dibango to once again sue for damages in the French courts (see page 208). But on 17 February 2009, a judge in Paris dismissed his claim and closed the case.

THIS IS IT

2009

1. WANNA BE STARTIN' SOMETHIN'
2. JAM
3. THEY DON'T CARE ABOUT US
4. HUMAN NATURE
5. SMOOTH CRIMINAL
6. THE WAY YOU MAKE ME FEEL
7. SHAKE YOUR BODY (DOWN TO THE GROUND)
8. I JUST CAN'T STOP LOVING YOU
9. THRILLER
10. BEAT IT
11. BLACK OR WHITE
12. EARTH SONG
13. BILLIE JEAN
14. MAN IN THE MIRROR
15. THIS IS IT*
16. THIS IS IT (ORCHESTRA VERSION)

*Only the previously unreleased song is covered here

CD Bonus (deluxe edition only):

SHE'S OUT OF MY LIFE (DEMO)
WANNA BE STARTIN' SOMETHIN' (DEMO)
BEAT IT (DEMO)
PLANET EARTH

This Is It **POSTHUMOUS COMPILATION**

Released by Epic Records: USA and Europe, 26 October 2009 (ref. 88697606742) / **Chart position:** USA R&B No. 1, Pop No. 91, UK No. 3, France No. 1 / **RIAA:** certified two-time Multiplatinum 4 December 2009

THIS IS IT, THE DEATH OF A KING

On 25 June 2009, Michael Jackson died of an overdose of propofol. This powerful anesthetic, administered by his personal physician Conrad Murray and normally used in operating rooms, was regularly purchased by the singer to help him cope with bouts of insomnia. In the last few months of his life, the King of Pop was preparing a project, albeit with no real motivation, that would have seen him back on stage for 50 concerts at the O2 Arena in London. Tickets sold out within a few hours. In 2009, with a heavy heart, he signed a contract agreeing to this concert residency in London. He was experiencing financial difficulties and was under pressure from Colony Capital, which had purchased his debts, as well as from the promoter AEG that had been wanting to work with him for years.

The star was not yet in his grave when AEG released a documentary simply entitled *This Is It,* featuring a collection of highlights from rehearsals for the show at the Staples Center in Los Angeles. This show, which Michael Jackson had never wanted to do, was woefully incomplete. The film was distributed by Sony Pictures and proved to be a hasty and uninspired montage of Michael Jackson's final moments in front of the camera. The singer's absence from many of the rehearsals forced Kenny Ortega, the tour's artistic director and director of the film, to use a combination of high- and standard-definition camera shots. This resulted in a clumsily assembled production aimed at a general audience. Its only merit was to show Michael Jackson's complete mastery of his art, notably in the scenes when he is giving the musicians and dancers detailed instructions.

The soundtrack

Sony Music acquired distribution rights to *This Is It* and marketed the soundtrack. As the label was unable to use the versions performed by the King of Pop during rehearsals because they were owned by AEG, it had to be content with publishing an album comprising the studio versions of the songs planned for the show.

John Branca and John McClain were named as coexecutors in Jackson's will, dated 7 July 2000, and after a court ruling validated their appointment, the two men found a song in the singer's vaults that was used as the film's theme tune. Cowritten with Paul Anka, this piece called *I Never Heard* was clumsily marketed under the title *This Is It*, which are the first words Michael Jackson sings at the start of the song. This cheaply produced soundtrack, which was essentially yet another greatest hits compilation with the addition of a previously unreleased number, ended up selling four million copies and became the Jackson keepsake in many homes prior to the later release of the famous documentary on DVD and Blu-ray.

Rehearsing *This Is It* at the Staples Center, Los Angeles, 23 June 2009.

This Is It (aka I Never Heard)

Michael Jackson, Paul Anka (not credited) / 3'36

Musicians: **Michael Jackson:** lead vocals / **The Jacksons:** backing vocals / **Alvin Chea:** bass guitar / **Greg Phillinganes:** piano / **Paul Jackson Jr.:** guitar / **Rafael Padilla:** percussion / **Recording:** **Paul Anka's studio:** 1983 / **Marvin's Room Recording Studios and Ocean Way Recording (mixing), Los Angeles:** 2010 / **Technical team:** **Producers:** Michael Jackson, John McClain, and Mervyn Warren / **Recording engineer:** Jon Nettlesbey / **Assistant recording engineer:** Wesley Seidman / **Vocal arrangements:** Mervyn Warren / **Mixing:** Allen Sides / **Single promo (CD):** **Track 1:** *This Is It (album version)* / 3'36 / **Track 2:** *This Is It (orchestra single version)* / 3'41 / **Track 3:** *This Is It (edited orchestra single version)* / 4'38 / **Released by Epic Records:** USA and Europe, 26 October 2009 / **Chart position:** USA R&B No. 18

2009

Genesis

In 1983, Michael Jackson and Paul Anka worked together for two weeks in the Canadian singer's studio. The two pieces to emerge, to date, from this collaboration are *I Never Heard* (re-named *This Is It)* and *Love Never Felt So Good*. Michael Jackson had recorded demos for the two numbers but ultimately relegated them to his vaults where they stayed for the remainder of his career. *I Never Heard* is a love song, whose joyful, laconic lyrics took on new meaning when the song became the singer's first posthumous single: "This is it... Here I stand / I'm the light of the World, I feel grand / Got this love I can feel / And I know, yes for sure, it is real."

Production

"This is it" are the first words heard at the start of the song. These three words are also the name of the series of concerts that Michael Jackson was due to perform in London, starting in the summer of 2009. This proved more than enough for John McClain to decide to rename the song *This Is It* and use it as the foundation stone for the first profitable posthumous marketing project. The Michael Jackson Estate and Sony Music stoked the rising excitement around the launch of the first previously unpublished song since the singer's death. However, the spark soon fizzled out when eagle-eyed fans spotted that the song had already been performed by the singer Safire. Paul Anka, the Canadian singer and cowriter of the song, was missed off the credits when the compilation was released. He spoke out publicly through the media, demanding an urgent meeting with the Michael Jackson Estate. The two parties rapidly agreed on a financial settlement, and stickers mentioning his name appeared on the sleeve of the *This Is It* compilation in guise of an apology.

For the King of Pop's first posthumous single, his brothers, The Jacksons, contributed a few backing vocals. Musicians such as Greg Philliganes and Paul Jackson, who had worked with the singer in the studio for many years, also made notable contributions to the song.

The digital single was available as a promotional copy only, with no commercial release. *This Is It* was mostly distributed along with a selection of the King of Pop's greatest hits and marketed as the setlist that Jackson would have performed for the London concerts. The compilation mainly served to support Kenny Ortega's film.

For Jackson Addicts

The *This Is It* compilation includes an orchestral version of the song. The collectors' version includes a bonus CD with three demos: *She's out of My Life, Wanna Be Startin' Somethin'*, and *Beat It*. The final track enables fans to hear Jackson's spoken voice, reciting his poem *Planet Earth*.

The song was previously recorded in 1991 as *I Never Heard* by Puerto Rican singer Safire, and it appeared on her album *I Wasn't Born Yesterday* (Mercury Records). It was the only known version of the song for almost 20 years.

MICHAEL

2010

1. HOLD MY HAND (FEATURING AKON)*
2. HOLLYWOOD TONIGHT*
3. KEEP YOUR HEAD UP
4. (I LIKE) THE WAY YOU LOVE ME*
5. MONSTER
6. BEST OF JOY*
7. BREAKING NEWS
8. (I CAN'T MAKE IT) ANOTHER DAY (FEATURING LENNY KRAVITZ)*
9. BEHIND THE MASK*
10. MUCH TOO SOON**

* Only the songs performed by Michael Jackson will be featured here.
** Unreleased songs covered in previous chapters.

Michael **POSTHUMOUS COMPILATION**

Released by Epic Records: USA (ref. 88697 66773) and Europe (ref. 88697 82867 2), 10 December 2010 / **Chart position:** USA R&B No. 1, Pop No. 3 / **RIAA:** certified Platinum 19 January 2011

MICHAEL, THE CONTROVERSIAL COMPILATION

When, on 16 March 2010, Michael Jackson's beneficiaries signed a contract with Sony Music for ten projects to be released over seven years, expectations were high. The first record, which got the ball rolling, was a compilation entitled simply *Michael*, but it was to make headlines.

Since the death of the King of Pop on 25 June 2009, speculation had been rife about songs kept under wraps and targeted for future release. In addition to songs that Michael had recorded by himself, and to which he had exclusive rights, there were songs made with other producers. These joint projects could not be released without a contract between the star's beneficiaries and the musicians concerned. And so the speculative market in Michael Jackson's creations came into being—a market in which prices were constantly rising.

The Cascio brothers, long-standing friends of Michael Jackson, suggested songs to the star's executors. Three of these were earmarked for the *Michael* project, and entrusted to Teddy Riley, who was given the job of completing them.

When one of the songs, *Breaking News*, appeared on the star's official website on 8 November 2010, his fans did not recognize their idol's voice. Controversy raged, to the point that boycotts were launched in several countries. These three songs, which tainted the compilation, eclipsed the others which, although they were not versions approved by the artist, nevertheless offered a glimpse of his work.

The compilation *Michael* missed the mark and opened an ever-widening rift between the star's fans and his beneficiaries. In June 2014 a young woman, Vera Serova, decided to file a class action lawsuit in the United States, claiming that she had been tricked into buying the record, and accusing Michael's lawyers and record label. In the view of some Michael Jackson admirers, the reputation of the producer Teddy Riley, who had been taken on to mastermind the project, was damaged.

For this reason, only songs over which there lingers no doubt as to the involvement and participation of Michael Jackson are featured on the following pages.

Hold My Hand

Alioune "Akon" Thiam, Giorgo Tuinfort, Claude Kelly / 3'31

Musicians: Michael Jackson: lead and backing vocals / **Alioune "Akon" Thiam and Giorgo Tuinfort:** all instruments / **Recording: Palms Studio, Las Vegas / Solitaire Studio, Atlanta / Metropolis Studios, London / Wisseloord Studio, Hilversum, and FC Walvisch Studio, Amsterdam, Netherlands:** 2008 / **Technical team: Producers:** Michael Jackson, Alioune "Akon" Thiam, and Giorgo Tuinfort / **Recording engineer:** Mark "Exit" Goodchild / **Assistant recording engineers:** Mack Woodward, Justin Pintar, Matt Paul, Miguel Scott, Kory Aaron, Eelco Bakker, and Ryan Wiese / **Orchestral** recording: Wessel Oltheten / **Assistant on orchest**ral recording: Dennis Krijnen / **String arrangements:** Franck van der Heijden / **General programming:** Alioune "Akon" Thiam and Giorgo Tuinfort / **Mixing:** Serban Ghenea / **Single (CD): Track 1:** *Hold My Hand (album version)* / 3'32 / **Track 2:** *Hold My Hand (vocals and orchestra version)* / 3'45 / **Track 3:** *Hold My Hand (alternate mix)* / 3'49 / **Track 4:** *Hold My Hand (instrumental version)* / 3'31 / **Released by Epic Records:** Europe and South Korea, 15 November 2010 (EU ref. 88697 83403 2 and South Korea ref. S10989C) / **Chart position:** USA R&B No. 33, Pop No. 39

2010

Genesis and Production

Akon and Michael Jackson met in 2007 on *Thriller 25*: they had a fine collaboration on *Wanna Be Startin' Somethin' 2008*. The young artist took advantage of this to suggest *Hold My Hand*, which quickly became their new project as a duo. The song exudes altruism and humanity, with a flood of lyrics that charmed Michael Jackson.

According to Akon, the voice of the King of Pop was recorded in barely an hour. About three months later, a first, unfinished version of the song was leaked online. Akon recalled: "Originally we meant to include this song on my new album, but yet again, it was the internet that took the decision for us! Very quickly there were leaks on to the web, and everyone downloaded it. It was quite massive, because more than 15 million downloads were supposedly recorded. So it was pointless including it on my record, because everyone had it on their iPod already!"[145] The two singers, very disappointed to see their anthem leaked so widely, reluctantly decided to shelve it.

Akon returned to the song and finished it in 2010 with Giorgo Tuinfort, producing a richer mix that retained all the power of the original message. In November that year, the song became the first single from the compilation *Michael*, accompanied by an emotional video tribute. *Hold My Hand* is one of the last projects in which Michael Jackson had a concrete creative input.

Hollywood Tonight

Michael Jackson, Brad Buxer, Teddy Riley / 3'35

Musicians: Michael Jackson: lead vocals / **Mischke:** additional backing vocals / **Taryll Jackson:** spoken bridge / **Danny Ray McDonald Jr. and Michael Durham Prince:** whistling / **Theron "Neff-U" Feemster and Edward Brown:** keyboards / **Erick Donell Walls and Eric Jackson:** guitars / **The Regiment:** horns / **Recording: (unknown):** 2001 / **Technical team: Producers:** Teddy Riley and Michael Jackson / **Coproducer:** Theron "Neff-U" Feemster / **Recording engineers (vocals):** Michael Durham Prince and Mischke / **Recording engineers:** Scott Elgin, James Murray, Michael Durham Prince, and Jon Nettlesbey / **Assistant recording engineer:** Quentin Gilkey / **Programming and finisher:** Teddy Riley / **Mixing:** Jean-Marie Horvat, Teddy Riley, and Scott Elgin

Genesis

Hollywood Tonight is one of the songs Teddy Riley and Brad Buxer worked on during the *Invincible* sessions. The lyrics deal with the hopes of a young girl seeking fame as an artist. Some of them sound like a warning, against a background of a complex and corrupted world. The protagonist seems at times highly motivated by her profession as a dancer, at other times mistreated as her career progresses, and left to her own devices.

Production

Hollywood Tonight opens with an intro whose instrumental textures are reminiscent of those in *Who Is It*. Michael Jackson pushes a beatbox that functions as the main bass line, solid and unchanging. Combined with the snare drum, this gives the song an unstoppable energy. "I was looking at just doing the next level of *Billie Jean* meets *Dangerous* or *Doggin' Me Around*," says the producer in 2010. "It's like one of those driving bass lines that you will remember."[146]

The producer wrote a bridge, which was performed by the rapper Taryll, son of Tito Jackson. Taryll creates a welcome break after the impressive energy given off by Michael Jackson throughout the first part. Guitars, keyboards, and horns sound like real added values in the song, which electrifies the listener throughout, and the return to these instruments brings an old-style musical warmth of the kind that they don't make any more—a real treat for the ears. Michael Durham Prince, in his capacity as recording engineer, took care of the texture and general effect of the whole production. He even allowed himself the passage marked by whistling at the end of the song.

A video clip was made by Wayne Isham (*You Are Not Alone*). Shot in front of the Pantages Theatre in Hollywood, it illustrates the song's subject matter rather well, from the arrival of a young dancer in Hollywood to her daily routine of castings and rehearsals, her nights out in the big city, and her need to work as a pole-dancer for day-to-day survival. The beautiful Franco-Algerian dancer Sofia Boutella moves through the many scenes in the clip, all punctuated by wonderful dance steps in the Jackson style!

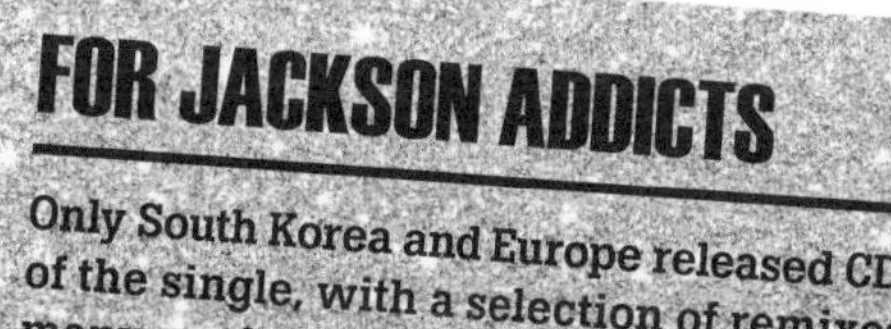

FOR JACKSON ADDICTS

Only South Korea and Europe released CDs of the single, with a selection of remixes, many made of this song. It wasreleased by Epic Records, 11 February 2011 (EU ref. 88697902982 and South Korea as a four-track CD, ref. S10988C).

Best of Joy

Michael Jackson / 3'02

Musicians: Michael Jackson: lead and backing vocals / **Mischke:** backing vocals / **Erick Donell Walls:** guitar / **Theron "Neff-U" Feemster:** synthesizers and keyboards / **Recording: Bel-Air Hotel:** 2008 / **(unknown):** 2010 / **Technical team: Producer:** Michael Jackson and Theron "Neff-U" Feemster / **Coproducer:** Brad Buxer / **Recording engineer:** James Murray / **Voice recording:** Michael Durham Prince and Mischke / **Mixing:** Serban Ghenea/ **Mixing engineer:** John Hanes, assisted by Tim Roberts

Best of Joy is among the last songs written by Michael Jackson. It is a gentle, romantic ballad imbued with nostalgia, in the same vein as *The Way You Love Me* and *Beautiful Girl*, both released on the box set *The Ultimate Collection*. Love is the central element in this tune that allows the singer to exploit different registers, having written a chorus and backing vocals especially for his head voice. At times the vocal harmonies are reminiscent of those the Bee Gees sang in the late 1970s, such as *How Deep Is Your Love*, a ballad of which Michael Jackson was fond. *Best of Joy* is the comfortable nest of unconditional love that a father or mother can promise to their children, perhaps the love without limits that the King of Pop sought all his life.

At the end of 2008 the singer recorded a version of *Best of Joy* in Bel Air Hotel, Los Angeles. He included it on a list of songs he was considering for future projects, and after his death a few notes written by him were leaked on the internet, revealing part of process of putting this song together.

From the mid-2000s onward, Neff-U worked with Michael Jackson and his long-standing partners, such as Brad Buxer and Michael Durham Prince. *Best of Joy* is one of the songs the singer entrusted to the young man. After the star's death, Neff-U completed it and handed it over to Michael's beneficiaries, who released it on the compilation *Michael* in 2010.

Michael Jackson and Lenny Kravitz backstage at the concert celebrating the star's 30-year solo career at Madison Square Garden, New York, in September 2001.

2010

(I Can't Make It) Another Day

Lenny Kravitz / 3'55

Musicians: Michael Jackson: lead and backing vocals / **Lenny Kravitz:** lead and backing vocals, Minimoog, electric guitar, 12-string electric guitar, timbals, gong / **Recording: Marvin's Room, Los Angeles** (Michael Jackson's voice) / **(unknown):** 1999, 2010 / **Technical team: Producer:** Lenny Kravitz / **Coproducer:** Michael Jackson / **Drums programming:** Dave Barron and Lenny Kravitz / **Synthesizer programming:** Dave Barron / **Recording engineer:** James Murray / **Assistant recording engineer:** Alex Alvarez / **Recording Michael Jackson's voice:** Henry Hirsch / **Mixing:** Lenny Kravitz

In 1999, Michael Jackson and Lenny Kravitz met to record a song written by the composer of *Mama Said*. The rock number was written with a structure the King of Pop was fond of: in the verses, his voice glides over a fairly slow, contemplative, dreamy tune, before hardening in the refrains to launch declarations of love at a person without whom he cannot spend another day.

This duet by two of the big names of the pop scene was dropped from the final tracklist for *Invincible*. A few weeks after the death of the King of Pop an extract from the song was leaked on the internet. Lenny Kravitz posted a short video on YouTube to condemn the unauthorized move. The declaration, made in a fairly nonchalant tone, created an expectation among the public, who wanted to hear *Another Day* in its entirety and put welcome pressure on Michael Jackson's beneficiaries, who eventually reached an agreement with Lenny Kravitz. After several months of negotiations, the song, was released in 2010 under the title *(I Can't Make It) Another Day*, thus becoming part of the first posthumous compilation. The rocker completed a pared-down version of the song, with vocal parts that were repeated by way of ad-libbing, which was of fairly short duration, close to that of a single.

The credits for the 2010 version show Dave Grohl as the drummer. However, in November 2011 the leader of the Foo Fighters revealed to *New Musical Express* that, although Lenny Kravitz had indeed invited him to play on this number, his tracks were not retained for the final mix.

For Jackson Addicts

Lenny Kravitz reworked *Another Day* to create the song *Storm*, featuring Jay-Z, for his album *Baptism* (2004).

> **FOR JACKSON ADDICTS**
>
> Greg Phillinganes' single release produced fine instrumental variations in 7-inch, 12-inch, and instrumental versions, with varied and percussive arrangements: single/edited version of 12-inch remix (4'07); extended version (6'27); instrumental (5'13).

Behind the Mask

Michael Jackson, Chris Mosdell, Ryuichi Sakamoto / 5'02

Musicians: Michael Jackson: lead and backing vocals / **Shanice Wilson and Alphonso Jones:** additional backing vocals / **Mike Phillips:** saxophone / **Greg Phillinganes and Jon Nettlesbey:** additional keyboards / **Alex Al:** bass guitar / **Paulinho Da Costa:** percussion / **Recording: (unknown):** early 1980s / **Technical team: Producers:** Michael Jackson and John McClain / **Recording engineers:** Jon Nettlesbey, Allen Sides, and Khaliq Glover / **Backing vocals arrangements:** Leon F. Sylvers III / **Keyboard and drums programming:** Big Jim Wright / **Drums programming, sequencing, and digital editing:** Jon Nettlesbey / **Mixing:** Jon Nettlesbey and Khaliq Glover / **Single: A-side:** *Behind the Mask* (*edit*) / 3'46 / **B-side:** *Hollywood Tonight* (*throwback mix*) / 3'39 / **Released by Epic Records:** USA and Europe, April 2011 (ref. 34-788083)

Genesis

In 1980, as the single *Off the Wall* was ruling the airwaves the world over, the new Japanese group Yellow Magic Orchestra (YMO), with Yukihiro Takahashi, Ryuichi Sakamoto, and Haruomi Hosono, was preparing to release a single entitled *Behind the Mask*. The number, which featured avant-garde electro-pop sounds, did not fail to delight the world of music-making. Chris Mosdell, an English poet living in Tokyo, wrote the original version of the song. He said: "The original *Behind the Mask* was based on the image of the classical Japanese masked drama, Noh, and also on a poem by W. B. Yeats entitled *The Mask*. These were the seeds of the lyrics—a bare-boned, unemotional mask behind which lies a hidden personality. The Michael Jackson version has no relevance to the inert, expressionless 'mask' I had in mind. Of course, this was decades ago, but it seems Quincy Jones visited Tokyo and discovered the song."[147]

Chris Mosdell learned that Michael Jackson was going to record *Behind the Mask*. He explained: "I actually wrote another complete lyric, upbeat in the Michael dance-vein and had it sent...I was told that Michael had added a new melody line and additional lyrics...You can still hear pieces of my original lyrics in Michael's chorus where he kept a complete line."[147]

Production

The song was not included on *Thriller*, and finally fell into the lap of Greg Phillinganes, who recorded it, retained the arrangements worked on with Michael Jackson, and boosted his version with frenetic new synthetic sonorities. Chris Mosdell added: "All other versions are based on Michael's rearrangement of the original song. I once met Greg Phillinganes when I was working in a recording studio...But basically it was Michael's baby and Greg had adopted it. Of course it's far removed from the concept and starkness of the original, but it's a wonderful song that Michael sings at the peak of his powers."[149]

To support the single by Greg Phillinganes in 1985, a video was shot in which he flaunts a magnificent red guitar/synthesizer, much in vogue at the time. In 1986 he joined Eric Clapton's band who, in turn, took up the song and gave it a more rock quality (*August*, 1986). For the occasion, *Behind the Mask* was once again released as a single. The following year, like a boomerang, the song returned to its country of origin and reappeared on Ryuichi Sakamoto's EP. To top it all, the new version from the former member of the YMO now mentioned Michael Jackson in the credits (*Behind the Mask* EP, 1987).

The version by the King of Pop was released posthumously in 2010 with new arrangements by Greg Phillinganes and additional backing vocals by Shanice Wilson. Its sound quality—warm, energetic, and fiery, direct from the *Thriller* era— brought some comfort to Michael's inconsolable fans.

> **FOR JACKSON ADDICTS**
>
> Two music videos were made for *Behind the Mask* in 2010. The Aggressive agency was commissioned to do the first, which featured all the masks worn by the singer during his career. This video was replaced by a second collaborative video called the *Behind the Mask Project*, for which fans submiited their own videos. Selected submissions were put together, and the final video went online in July 2013.

XSCAPE

2014

1. LOVE NEVER FELT SO GOOD*
2. CHICAGO*
3. LOVING YOU*
4. A PLACE WITH NO NAME*
5. SLAVE TO THE RHYTHM
6. DO YOU KNOW WHERE YOUR CHILDREN ARE
7. BLUE GANGSTA*
8. XSCAPE*

*Only these songs will be featured here, as the others have been covered in the Outtakes chapters (see pages 422–429).

Xscape **POSTHUMOUS COMPILATION**

Released by Epic Records: USA and Europe, 9 May 2014 (ref. 88843066762) / **Chart position:** USA R&B No. 1, Pop No. 2/ **RIAA:** certified Gold 18 September 2014

XSCAPE, THE MAKING OF A HIT

L A Reid and Justin Timberlake brought Michael Jackson's music to a new generation with *Xscape*, a compilation that pays tribute to the King of Pop and his body of work.

When plans for *Xscape* were announced, wounds were still fresh from the fallout of *Michael*, the album released in 2010. After publishing the 25th anniversary box set for *Bad* in 2012 and producing two shows with Cirque du Soleil—*The Immortal* and *One*—Michael's beneficiaries decided to release a second compilation comprised of new songs.

Xscape came about after the executors of Michael's estate met with L A Reid, then CEO of Epic Records, who wanted to participate in the new venture. Reid asked John Branca, the lawyer in charge of Michael's estate, to sort through any songs that locked away in the vault. There was one rule: to choose only songs Michael had sung from start to finish, a true sign that he was seriously thinking of finalizing and releasing them to the public. This is how the former producer came to discover new songs that had been written over the course of many years. Some of them had almost made it onto Michael's albums.

The plan was to find eight songs that various producers—including Timbaland, Stargate, and Rodney Jerkins—could remix and update. In addition, Michael's beneficiaries and L A Reid decided that the deluxe version of *Xscape* would include the original version of each song. This approach pacified most of their intended audience and partially repaired the damage caused by *Michael* in 2010.

L A Reid's stroke of genius was to combine Michael and Justin Timberlake's music. The former NSYNC singer had always openly admired the King of Pop, and this virtual collaboration on *Love Never Felt So Good* became his perfect tribute. The wider public welcomed it with open arms.

Xscape was launched on 13 May 2014. Of the eight songs on the album, six were already known to Michael's biggest fans. Since the pirated music market had taken over the internet, songs like *Love Never Felt So Good*, *Xscape*, and *Blue Gangsta* had been regularly leaked from the early 2000s onward. During his lifetime, Michael had never condemned this illegal distribution, nor did he ever sue anyone over the issue.

While *Xscape* failed to maintain consistency between songs, it did succeed in refocusing the debate about what constituted authentic Michael Jackson music.

LOVE NEVER FELT SO GOOD

(DEMO)

Michael Jackson, Paul Anka / 3'19

Musicians: Michael Jackson: lead vocals / **Paul Anka:** piano / **Recording: Paul Anka's studio:** 1983 / **Technical team: Producers:** Michael Jackson and Paul Anka / **Single (CD): Track 1:** *Love Never Felt So Good (album version 2014)* / 3'56 / **Track 2:** *Love Never Felt So Good (featuring Justin Timberlake, album version 2014)* / 4'06 / **Released by Epic/Sony Music Records:** USA and Europe, 2 May 2014 (ref. 88843087052) / **Chart position:** USA R&B No. 5, Pop No. 9 / UK No. 8 / France No. 2 / Germany No. 1

Genesis

In 1984 Paul Anka gave Johnny Mathis permission to record the song he'd written with Michael Jackson the year before, after he and Kathleen Wakefield slightly retouched the lyrics. The well-known Canadian–American crooner appropriated the piece and organized it around a mid-tempo "coconutty" sound. *Love Never Felt So Good* stood out among the many soft songs from the Mathis album, *A Special Part of Me*. David Williams, John Robinson, and Jerry Hey, known for their arrangements in *Off the Wall* and *Thriller*, brought style and substance to the whole production.

Not long before being officially released on *Xscape* in 2014, Michael's demo was leaked online in December 2006 and again in 2010, but with better quality. The piano/voice accompanies Michael's vocals so well that one wishes all the songs from *Off the Wall* had been recorded along this same model.

In the song, Michael is in love with a young woman and jumps for joy as he declares his happiness. Fresh, positive, and energetic, the song had incredible potential and quickly became the summer hit of 2014, more than 30 years after it was first recorded.

Production

Each note in this song is touched by greatness. Michael's voice resounds over the magnificent piano performance generously delivered by Paul Anka. The demo's particular strength is its simple and pure depth. Without sounding disingenuous, Michael opens his heart and succeeds in the rare task of imparting emotions that are unique, infectious, and touching.

The *Xscape* album begins with the 2014 version of *Love Never Felt So Good*. Giorgio Tuinfort (*Hold My Hand*, *Wanna Be Startin' Somethin' 2008*) added the right amount of funky flavoring to this tasty emotional cocktail. Handclapping and playful chords come together in the original track to build an incredible musical rainbow. *Love Never Felt So Good* is packed with fresh energy but gets a little lost toward the end, where the new digital handclaps do not add much to the piece.

The deluxe edition included a second 2014 version with J-Roc and Timbaland at the console. Justin Timberlake contributed vocals, masterfully performing a virtual duet with the King of Pop. Timberlake's modesty was as strong as the depth of his contribution. His rich tone and sophisticated, expressive vocal variations were in perfect harmony with Michael's youthful and passionate voice. The tribute was monumental: generations of fans gathered to listen to the intro, which sampled *Working Day and Night*. The song became an instant worldwide hit and the video created to accompany this single, respectable in and of itself, went viral, becoming an internet sensation. In the heat of July 2014, the world was paying tribute to King Michael once again and his fans were unanimously falling in love with *Love Never Felt So Good*.

FOR JACKSON ADDICTS

***A Special Part of Me*, the Johnny Mathis album that included a version of *Love Never Felt So Good*, was hard to find in CD format until it was rereleased in 2012 (Funky Town Grooves – FTG 310). In 2014, for the release of the *Love Never Felt So Good* single, a plethora of remixes were distributed promotionally.**

Chicago (aka She Was Loving Me)

Cory Rooney / 4'43

Musicians: Michael Jackson: lead and backing vocals / **Recording: Hit Factory, New York/Record Plant Studios, Los Angeles** (mixing): **1999** / **Technical team: Producers:** Michael Jackson, Cory Rooney / **Arrangements:** Brad Buxer / **Recording engineer:** Robb Williams / **Assistant recording engineer:** David Swope / **Mixing:** (unknown)

In early 1999, Tommy Mottola, his bodyguards, and Cory Rooney, the vice president of Sony Music Entertainment, went to see Michael at the Marvin's Room recording studio in Los Angeles. Michael played *Break of Dawn* as an example of what he was working on. On the way back, the CEO of Sony Music convinced Cory Rooney, who was working with some of the label's most prestigious artists, to write a song for the King of Pop. A composer and a musician, Rooney rose to the challenge and wrote *She Was Loving Me*, which talks about a doomed love, and recorded a first draft. He made a point to write the verses in a low key to give the chorus greater impact.

Mottola sent the recording to Michael, who instantly fell in love with it. He asked the composer to meet him at the Hit Factory in New York to fine-tune the song, and the two men subsequently spent several weeks working on it. The King of Pop's vocal coach, Seth Riggs, helped him warm up his voice before each take in which he had to scream the refrain as if he were in a rage. The song was almost finished when Michael and Rooney split up. At the same time, Michael's collaboration with Rodney Jerkins began in earnest. Rooney returned to his executive role at Sony Music and worked on the logistics for *Invincible*. *She Was Loving Me* was set aside.

In 2000, Rooney was assigned other jobs within the record label. Many songs with great potential, including *She Was Loving Me,* ended up paying the cost of this move.

The song popped up again in 2014 at the bequest of L A Reid, when he was working on *Xscape*. It was among the eight songs to appear on the album, retitled *Chicago*.

Loving You

Michael Jackson / 3'55

Musicians: Michael Jackson: lead and backing vocals / **Recording: Red Wing Studio, Encino:** (unknown dates) / **Technical team: Producer:** Michael Jackson / **Recording engineers:** Chris Desmond and Matt Forger / **Mixing:** Matt Forger

Created during the *Bad* sessions, *Loving You* was one of those happy-go-lucky songs Michael used to write at his family home in Encino. He recorded the first tracks at the Red Wing Studio, which he'd been using to create some of his first drafts, including *We Are the World*. The song couldn't help but reveal its lineage to the Motown school of thought: *Loving You* overflows with love and dreams of romance. The chords and some of the melody's passages recall the work of Motown master Stevie Wonder. The King of Pop recorded a complete first draft in order to see whether the song worked and deserved to be taken to the next level, which was the production of a more elaborate version at the Westlake studios. But for reasons beyond Michael's control, the song was left by the wayside. The singer considered other similar songs, including *Groove of Midnight*—a mid-tempo with Rod Temperton's name written all over it—but ended up rejecting that one as well, though Siedah Garrett picked it up in 1988 for her first album, *Kiss of Life*. L A Reid asked Matt Forger to revisit the *Loving You* draft in 2014 and fine-tune the mix for *Xscape*.

2014

A Place with No Name

Dewey Bunnell, Michael Jackson, Dr. Freeze / 4'55

Musicians: Michael Jackson: lead and backing vocals / **Dr. Freeze:** backing vocals, keyboards, and synthesizers / **C J DeVillar:** bass / **Recording: Ocean Way Recording, Record One** (production and mixing) **and Record Plant Studios** (vocals), **Los Angeles:** 1998 to 1999 / **Technical team: Producers:** Michael Jackson and Dr. Freeze / **Arrangements:** Brad Buxer / **Recording engineers:** Mike Ging, Humberto Gatica, and Eddie De Lena / **Assistant recording engineers:** Jeff Burns, Greg Burns, and Don Johnson / **Mixing:** Mike Ging and Humberto Gatica

John McClain acted as liaison between Dr. Freeze and Michael Jackson. Elliot Straite, aka Dr. Freeze, was one of those 1990s producers who had been able to rack up back-to-back commercial successes. He had signed Color Me Badd's hit, *I Wanna Sex You Up,* in 1991.

He suggested several songs to Michael, including *A Place with No Name*, a remake of *A Horse with No Name*, by America, which came out in 1972. In the new lyrics, the King of Pop sings about his car breaking down, forcing him to leave it on the side of the road. It is a troubling rendition of a day in 1992 when the star found himself on the side of the road with a flat tire: this incident caused him to run into Jordan Chandler's family in a car rental office belonging the boy's stepfather.

From July 1998 to February 1999, before starting his collaboration with Rodney Jerkins, Michael worked with Dr. Freeze to write *A Place with No Name*. Paul J Falcone prepared a mix in May 1999, but the King of Pop decided not to use the song. He revisited it in 2004, at home in his studio in Neverland, and again in 2008, with Neff-U in his rented place at Palomino Lane, near Las Vegas. At that time, Dr. Freeze briefly met with Michael in the gambling capital to discuss a few new song projects. However they would never see each other again. In 2014, L A Reid seized the moment to commission a remix of *A Place with No Name* from the two Stargate producers, Erik Hermansen and Mikkel Storleer Eriksen, which was included in *Xscape* and released as a single with a short video.

Blue Gangsta

Michael Jackson, Dr. Freeze / 4'16

Musicians: Michael Jackson: lead and backing vocals / **Dr. Freeze:** backing vocals, synthesized horns, and sound effects / **Eric:** drums and percussion / **Greg Phillinganes:** Minimoog / **Brad Buxer:** keyboards / **Jerry Hey:** horns / **Recording: (unknown):** 1999 / **Technical team: Producers:** Michael Jackson (vocals) and Dr. Freeze (rhythmic section) / **Recording engineers:** Mike Ging, Humberto Gatica, and C.J. DeVillar / **Assistant recording engineers:** Jeff Burns, Tom Sweeney, Rafa Sardina, and Adam Olmsted / **Mixing:** (unknown)

Genesis

Blue Gangsta was one of three songs Michael Jackson created with Dr. Freeze during the first sessions of *Invincible*. Following in the footsteps of *Smooth Criminal*, the King of Pop used this song to develop the mafia imagery he loved so much. In *Blue Gangsta*, he sings about romantic disappointment to the woman who broke his heart: "Look at what you've put me through," he exclaims throughout the song. Ironically, Michael's voice sounds piercing in this world of gangsters. Brass and accordion passages project the listener into a film-like atmosphere. Once again, the idea of a cursed, devastating love acts as the setting for Michael's superb vocal variations.

Production

Part of the song reached fans in December 2006, long before appearing on *Xscape*. After meeting Michael during his exile in Bahrain, rapper Tempamental posted a piece called *No Friend of Mine* to his Myspace page while promoting his mixtape, *Watevaz Fair.* The piece follows the general plotline of *Blue Gangsta* and is supplemented by a rap segment sung by Pras, of The Fugees. Michael didn't seem to object to the illegal distribution of this alternative version of the song he had written a few years earlier with Dr. Freeze. However Dr. Freeze recalled, in a 2011 interview with French fans: "It's not the real name of the song [*No Friend of Mine*], it's the chorus that contains these few words. The real title is *Blue Gangsta*. When I heard this remix, I couldn't believe it. A lot of people started calling me about it and I didn't understand what had happened. The problem is that I don't even know who released the song! It's a real mystery. Why did they do it? Where did that rap in the song come from? How did they go about it? We don't actually know anything about this, not me, not Michael. We really don't get where this leak came from."[136]

Blue Gangsta was officially released in 2014 on *Xscape*. Timbaland and J-Roc produced the special edition remix, making Michael's voice soar with a magnificent percapella in the first part of the song before adding metallic sounds similar to those in *Heartbreaker*, for example. Timbaland accentuates the dark tension of the song with snare drum percussion and fast beats, over which Michael alternates aggressive verses and plaintive cries.

XSCAPE

Michael Jackson, Rodney Jerkins, Fred Jerkins III, LaShawn Daniels / 5'44

Musicians: Michael Jackson: lead and backing vocals / **LaShawn Daniels:** backing vocals / **Rodney Jerkins:** backing vocals and beatboxing / **Harvey:** percussion / **Recording: Sony Studio and Hit Factory, New York / Marvin's Room, Larrabee Studios, Ocean Way Recording, Record One, Record Plant Studios, Los Angeles:** 1999 / **Technical team: Producers:** Michael Jackson, Rodney Jerkins, Freddie Jerkins,and LaShawn Daniels / **Recording engineers:** Bruce Swedien, Stuart Brawley, Jean-Marie Horvat, and Brad Gilderman / **Assistant recording engineers:** Greg Burns, Jeff Burns, Franny Graham, Larry Phillabaum, Steve Macauley, Craig Durrance, and Anthony Kilhoffer / **Mixing:** (unknown)

Genesis

Known to fans since 2002, the song hit the internet amid rumors that it was targeting Tommy Mottola, the CEO of Sony Music, especially in the lyrics: "The pressure that I face from relationships that's gone away." In *Scream*, Michael Jackson raged and rebelled against the media; in *Xscape*, which had been slated for inclusion in *Invincible*, he makes a sad and definitive statement, ultimately preferring to address his escape from the media: "I got to get away so I can free my mind / Xscape is what I need."

The song is organized around a host of ambiguities whose function can be read—in this complex year of 2002—as an attempt either to assail the press or the Sony executive: "The man with the pen that writes the lies that hassle this man." The same version was released in 2014 on the compilation that bears the name of the song.

With *Xscape*, Michael was looking for ways to feel newly empowered in his career. He wanted to leave what he considered a wholly corrupt and vile world behind: "This problem world won't bother me no more." The song emanates his resignation and more or less implies—through plays on words—that Michael wanted to break completely free of his public and artistic persona. In fact, Michael soon made himself increasingly scarce in the media and did not produce another album.

Production

From a musical standpoint, *Xscape* can be interpreted as a collection of Michael's best work. All the ingredients are there: the maniacal rhythms, the variations arranged in multiple layers to create incredible backing vocals, breathless performances that alternate gimmicks and beatboxing, and funky accelerations after mind-blowing bridges of electrifying and mechanical brilliance. The musical setting for such a piece could only come from the digital arsenal of producer Rodney Jerkins, who no doubt took a particular interest in this production.

Rodney Jerkins realized his vision on the 2014 version, as with *Scream Louder*, by Jimmy Jam and Terry Lewis. A defined bass line, a guiding guitar, and a bright brass section heighten the message and carry it all the way to Michael Jackson, as if to reassure him that he has definitively escaped this sad and oppressive world.

INDEX

The songs and albums analyzed in this book are shown in bold, along with the portraits.

*NSYNC : 531, 579, 595
2000 Watts : 521, **540**
2300 Jackson Street : **358-359**, 374
2300 Jackson Street: 358, 368, 370
2Bad : 437, 449, **481**, 493, 506-508
3LW : 579
3T : 368, 490, 491, 512, 542
A Brand New Day : 132
A Motown Christmas: 88, 89

A Place with No Name : 533, 594, **598**
Aaron, Kory : 590
ABC : 12, 24, **38**, 40, 44, 49, 61, 142, 423, 556, 561, 564, 570
ABC: 36, 46, 56, 92, 93, 180, 181, 204, 295, 360, 441, 480, 494, 497
Abdul, Paula : 316
Abel, Robert : 146, 180, 181
Access Hollywood: 581
Adams, Ace : 73
Adams, Brandon Quintin : 339, 345, 346
Adams, Regina : 73
Adler, Murray : 267, 270, 516
Afanasieff, Walter : 573
Agree, Lena : 85
Ahlert, David : 358
Ain't No Sunshine : 55, 56, **58**, 60, 65, 562, 563
Akimoto, Yasushi : 518
Akon (Alioune Thiam) : 580, 582, 583, 588, 590
Al Capone : 336, **355**
Al, Alex : 593
Al-Walid, prince : 496, 497
Alberle, Doug : 312
Alejandrino, Alberto : 302
All Eyez on Me : 235, **577**
All I Do : 50, **194**
All in Your Name : 576, **578**
All Night Dancin' : 14, 124, 186
All the Things You Are : 79, 80, **83**
Allen, Debbie : 210
Alper, Herb : 329
Alright Now : **361**
Alvarez, Alex : 592
Ambrosius, Marsha : 538
American Bandstand: 37, 71, 97, 181, 186, 276
American Bandstand 50th Anniversary: 37, 417, 528
Anastacia : 579
Anderson, Jon : 248
Anderson, Maxi : 322, 539
Anest, Eric : 489, 573, 574
Anka, Paul : 585, 586, 596
Another Part of Me : 286, 288, 291, **320-321**, 337, 350, 508, 570
Anthology – Jackson 5: 559
Anthology – Michael Jackson: 559, 560
Anthology Series: The Best of Michael Jackson: 554, 555, 557, 560, 561, 564
Anthony, Beth : 500
Anthony, Chuck : 491
Anthony, Marc : 527
Arata, Peter : 361
Armand, Renee : 100
Armatrading, Joan : 230
Arnold, Larkin : 202, 264
Arnold, Ryan : 510
Arquette, Rosanna : 316
Arvizo, Gavin : 567, 569, 571, 581, 582
Ashton, Dave : 574
Ask the Lonely : 179
Astaire, Fred : 92, 205, 245, 284, 298, 308, 337, 339, 340
Atkinson, Mike : 122, 124, 126
Aubrey, Lita : 178
Augustus, Gloria : 539
Austin, Dallas : 441, 464, 465, 481
Austin, Patti : 155, 170, 171, 195, 236, 248
Avant, Clarence : 243
Averill, Brent : 220, 221, 268, 269, 272, 352
Avram, Marcel : 443, 524
Aykroyd, Dan : 280, 316
Azur, Sybil : 500

Baby Be Mine : 155, 199, 202, **210**, 212, 232, 240, 326, 580
Babyface (Kevin Edmonds) : 51, 358, 361, 369, 370, 428, 448, 464, 490, 494, 512, 513, 541
Bacharach, Burt : 145, 170, 197
Backerman, Stuart : 568
Bad : 51, 296, **300-303**, 306, 308, 337, 354, 366, 382, 403, 468, 481, 536, 566, 570
***Bad* [album]** : 51, 135-137, 215, 237, 239-241, 286, **290-356**, 358, 366, 369-372, 380, 386, 391, 392, 396, 402, 407, 410, 416, 420, 429, 430, 431, 442, 444, 467, 470, 496, 524, 528, 535, 559, 563, 571, 572, 595, 597
Bad 25 : 51, 311, 321, 326, 330, 336
Bad 25: 328, 350, 352-354
Bad Girl: 23
Bähler, John : 64, 72-76, 161, 392, 393
Bähler, Thomas : 64, 70, 130-133, 145, **161**, 164, 165-167, 170, 220, 222, 236, 280, 393, 430, 518, 546
Bailey, Horace : 302
Bain, Raymone : 581, 582
Baio, Scott : 241
Baker, Emanuel *Bucket*: 542
Baker, Rick : 216-218, 507
Baker, Roy Thomas : 123
Bakker, Eelco : 590
Ballard, Florence : 20, 22, 30, 32
Ballard, Glen : 240, 322, 324, 410
Bani, Arno : 524, 525
Banks, Brian : 210, 214
Banks, Rose : 322
Banks, Tyra : 398, 399
Bano, Al : 407
Barclay, Eddie : 134, 135
Barnes, John : 264, 274-278, 280, 288, 300, 306, 310, 314, 315, 320, 326, 328, **329**, 330, 336, 341, 348, 352, 361, 396, 429
Barri, Steve : 552, 554, 555, 562, 563
Barron, Dave : 592
Barron, Siobhan : 230
Barron, Steve : 36, 203, 204, 230, 231
Basemore, Vicki : 82
Bashir, Martin : 567, 568
Bates, Steve : 220, 232, 234
Batten, Jennifer : 209, 346, 372
Battle, Hinton : 130
Baughman, Steve : 502, 510
Baum, Lyman Frank : 128, 130
Bautista, Roland : 122
Bayer Sager, Carole : 145, 170, 190, 197, 529, 541, 574, 578
Be a Pepper : 123
Be Not Always : 259, **267**, 314, 402
Beal, Teron : 534
Beastie Boys : 295
Beat It : 199, 202-204, 217, **220-225**, 230, 234, 238, 247, 263, 268, 278, 296, 300, 303, 308, 330-334, 366, 376, 430, 463, 549, 566, 570, 580, 582, 584, 586
Beattie, Rose : 518, 546
Beautiful Girl : 354, 570, 572, **573**, 591
Beck, Dan : 438
Becker, Robert : 489, 502
Bee Gees : 125, 206, 279
Behind the Mask : 588, **593**
Behind the Mask Project : 593
Belafonte, Harry : 93, 280, 281
Bell, Thom : 72, 108
Belle, Bernard : 380, 388, 535, 542
Ben : 58, 67-69, **70-71**, 80, 86, 88, 89, 100, 115, 150, 566, 570
***Ben* [album]** : 49, 61, **66-77**, 80, 161
Ben Ammar, Tarak : 496, 497
Benatar, Pat : 295
Bender, Tom : 426, 508, 516, 518
Benford, Vassal : 361
Benitez, John *Jellybean*: 254
Benjamin, William *Benny*: 34, 36
Bennett, Michael : 278
Benson, George : 135, 138, 155, 158, 173, 192, 195, 217, 248, 432
Bergman, Alan : 245
Bergman, Marilyn : 245
Bernard, Dara : 248
Bernstein, Elmer : 218
Best of Joy : 588, **591**
Bettis, John : 232, 233
Betts, Graham : 45, 62
Beyoncé : 60, 443, 529, 579
Bialik, Mayim : 316
Big Boy : 10, 14, **16-19**
Billie Jean : 25, 42, 133, 160, 199, 202-205, 214, 217, 223, 224, **226-231**, 232, 233, 238, 247, 252, 260, 267, 280, 306, 314, 336, 354, 366, 369, 370, 402, 403, 412, 449, 473, 508, 529, 566, 570, 580-584, 591
Billy Ward & The Dominoes : 22
Bird, Brad : 363
Birdsong, Cindy : 30
Bisharat, Charlie : 488
Black Eyed Peas : 234, 283, 582
Black or White : 224, 334, 345, 362, 365, 366, 369-372, 388, **396-401**, 444, 470, 497, 528, 566, 570, 584
Black, Chauncey : 435
Black, Don (Gerald Blackstone) : 70
Black, Tony : 508
BLACKstreet: 375, 435
BLACKstreet : 374, 375, 435, 525, 534, 549
Blades, Rubén : 328, 579
Blair, Seth : 324
Blake-Wilson, Bridget : 462, 469, 478
Blame It on the Boogie : 118, **122-123**, 570
Blashfield, Jim : 342
Blasingaine, Larry : 16
Bless His Soul : 164, 182
Bligh, Michelle : 489
Blood on the Dance Floor : 241, 334, 378, 425, 481, 493, 494, **498-501**, 566, 570
***Blood on the Dance Floor – HIStory in the Mix* [album]** : 462, 483, **492-511**, 518, 524
Blue Gangsta : 533, 594, 595, **598**
Blue Notes, The : 108
Blues Away : 13, 112, 113, **114-115**, 116, 354
Blumberg, Dave : 62, 86, 101, 557, 560, 562
Bob Hope Special: 90, 91
Bobbit, Charles : 496
Bobby Taylor & The Vancouvers : 20, 21, 43
Boddicker, Michael : 124, 152, 162, 168, 182, 208, 210, 214, 226, 232-236, 248, 264, 280, 300, 306-318, 330, 336, 376, 392-402, 406, 410, 414, 476, 477, 489
Body : 259, 288
Boekholt, Albert : 508
Bolas, Niko : 266
Bon Jovi, Jon : 475, 516
Boogie: 50, 553, 560
Bottrell, Bill : 241, 264, 265, 270, 274, 277, 299, 310, 329, 336, 337, 344, 345, 350-355, 369, 370, 396-404, 416-418, 422, 424, 429, 441, 449, 467, **470**, 489, 498, 502, 503, 581
Boulanger, Nadia : 134
Boutella, Sofia : 591
Boutin, Paul : 541
Bova, Jeff : 456
Bowie, David : 108, 115, 390
Boyette, Don : 346
Boylan, John : 362
Boyle, Tim : 502
Boyz II Men : 155, 442, 448, 464, 474, 482, 483, 541
Bradshaw, Norman Jeff : 538
Branca, John : 219, 251, 294, 496, 585, 595
Brancowitz, Laurent : 138
Brand New Heavies : 65
Brando, Marlon : 536, 537
Brando, Miko : 216, 263, 310, 312, 536
Brandt, Nick : 462, **466**, 469, 478, 545, 569
Brandy : 529, 530, 535, 577, 579
Brawley, Stuart : 530-532, 535, 539, 546-548, 574, 599
Bray, Bill : 312
Break of Dawn : 521, **533**, 566, 597
Breaking News : 375, 588, 589
Brecker, Michael : 130
Brett Garsed : 516
Breuer, Alex : 508
Bridgeman, Delroy : 16, 18
Bridges, Ben : 356
Bristol, Johnny : 564
Britt, Jim : 57, 63, 71, 77, 87
Britten, Terry : 241, 318
Broadnax, Morris : 194
Brock, Craig : 404
Brooks, Bobby : 489, 508, 516, 518
Brooks, Greg : 260
Brooks, Mel : 93
Brotherhood: 490, 491
Brothers Johnson, The : 145, 150, 155, 158, 160, 191, 195, 248, 432
Broughton, Bruce : 312
Brown III, Sam : 96, 100, 104
Brown, Austin : 358, 359
Brown, Ben : 19
Brown, Bob : 361, 370, 374, 389, 428, 531, 532
Brown, Clancy : 312
Brown, Edward : 590
Brown, James : 11, 24, 31, 56, 92, 292, 303, 387, 391, 496, 581, 582
Brown, Laurence : 64
Brown, Mary : 547
Brown, Ollie : 178-188, 306, 310, 318, 322, 324
Brown, Paulette : 178
Brown, Richard : 16, 18
Brown, Stacee : 358, 359
Brown, Tim : 539
Brown, William F. : 128
Brown, Yashi : 358, 359
Brownstone : 368
Bryant, Charlie : 489
Bubbles : 316, 342, 422
Buchanek, Sabrina : 552
Buckingham, Lindsey : 280
Buffalo Bill : 267
Bunch, Sekou : 489
Bunnell, Dewey : 598
Burge, Gregg : 302, 303
Burn This Disco Out : 104, 141, 145, 152, 155, 162, **172-173**
Burns, Greg : 502, 598, 599
Burns, Jeff : 574, 598, 599
Bush, Brigette : 178
Bush, Michael : 346
Butter Cup : 49, 168
Butterflies : 521, 528, 534, **538**, 545, 570
Butz, Ric : 288, 572
Buxer, Brad : 376, 392-402, 406, 407, 416, 420, 456-461, 471, 473, 476, 477, 484, 485, 488, 489, 498-503, 508, 516-518, 533, 539, 540, 544, 546, 569, 573, 574, 590, 591, 597, 598

Caillat, Ken : 310
Calderon, Paul : 302
Call on Me : 552, 556, **557**
Calnan, Ann : 270
Campbell, David : 488, 542
Campbell, Naomi : 370, 383, 384
Campbell, Tevin : 136
Can You Feel It : 37, 146, 175, 176, **178-181**, 203, 247, 264, 320
Can You Remember : 36, 56
Can't Get Outta the Rain : 133, 212, 214, 226, 239, 241
Can't Let Her Get Away : 365, **391**, 424
Canby, Vincent : 69
Canidate, Geron *Casper*: 303
Cannon, Bruce : 214, 215, 242
Cannon, Dyan : 248
Cannon, Mike : 87
Cappy, Matt : 538
Capra, Francis : 478
Captain EO : **284-289**, 294, 295, 302, 304, 320, 397, 559, 570
Carey, Mariah : 375, 446, 526, 573, 579, 581
Carlo, Tyrone : 560
Carmen, Eric : 491
Carmichael, James Anthony : 60, 64, 65, 72, 74, 76, 83, 87, 90, 93, 98, 99, 101, 102, 104, 554, 555, 562
Carnes, Kim : 280
Carney, Art : 254
Carney, Reeve : 476
Carousel : 232, **238**
Carpenter, Matt : 489, 498, 502, 508
Carpenters : 100
Carrasco, Joe *King*: 246
Carrington, Debbie Lee : 287
Carter, Aaron : 579
Carter, Nick : 579
Cartier, Crystal : 416
Castro-Neves, Oscar : 420
Castro, Cristian : 579
Castro, Lenny : 266, 422, 489
CBS Special – Michael Jackson: The Magic Returns: 303, 324

Centipede : **276**
Chaffin, Ceán : 454
Chamberlin, John : 420, 422
Champlin, William C. : 574
Chancler, Ndugu : 210, 214, 215, 226, 228, 234, 245, 326
Chandler, Evan : 372
Chandler, Jordan : 373, 434, 438, 442, 446, 450, 496, 502, 506, 568, 581, 598
Chaplin, Charlie : 139, 233, 240, 486, 487
Charles, Ray : 134, 136, 145, 245, 280, 282, 576
Chausow, Robert : 502
Chea, Alvin : 586
Cheater : **351**, 570, 571
Cheesman, Sean : 454
Cher : 32
Chic : 32, 52, 147, 412, 473
Chicago (aka She Was Loving Me) : 594, **597**
Chicago 1945 : 355
Chicago Nights : 298, 338, 339
Chiffons, The : 135
Childhood : 139, 437, 444, 450, 453, 466, **476-479**, 486, 503, 570
Children's Holiday : **516-517**, 518
Chilvers, Colin : 339, 340, 346
Chong, Tommy : 20, 21
Christensen, Erika : 478
Christmas Album: 88, 89
Cinderella Stay Awhile : 95, **101**
Cipollina, Mario : 280
Circus Girl : 238
Cirque du Soleil : 474, 595
Clan, The : 26
Clark, Chris : 560
Clark, Dick : **37**, 56, 92, 97, 105, 147, 181, 206, 212, 528
Cleveland Orchestra, The : 406, 407
Clinton, Bill : 33, 204, 372, 373, 414, 528
Clinton, George S. : 88, 464, 555
Clio, Uno : 465
Cocker, Jarvis : 444
Cody, Iron Eyes : 181
Cohen, Keith : 358, 502
Cole, Nat King : 80, 84, 486
Coleman, David : 440
Coleman, Gary : 178, 188
Coleman, Thelma : 23
Colla, Johnny : 280
Collins, Greg : 508
Collins, Jackie : 316
Colomby, Bobby : 14, 122-126
Color Me Badd : 533, 598
Coltrane, John : 210, 245
Come to Me: 23
Come Together : 160, 250, 298, **344-347**, 366, 369, 388, 414, 437, 442, 470, 471, 502, 542
Como, Perry : 61, 412
Complete Motown Singles | Vol. 9: 1969, The: 35
Consumer Rapport : 130
Contours, The : 24
Cooper, Alice : 215
Copperfield, David : 316
Coppola, Francis Ford : 180, 284, 285, 287
Corbett, Larry : 402
Cornelius, Don : 91, **92**
Corner of the Sky : 86
Corporation, The : 26-29, 35, 36, 38, 40, 44, 46, 56-61, 64, 65, 70, 72, 76, 82, 83, 90, 562
Corso, Gene : 184, 185
Cosby, Henry : 76, 82
Cotton, Ollie : 268
Cottrell, Richard : 362, 430, 504
Cousin, Rick *Dutch*: 519
Cox, Tony : 287
Crawford, Cindy : 384
Crawford, Randy : 240
Creed, Linda : 72
Crewe, Bob : 552, 557, 558, 561
Cronenweth, Jordan : 403
Crosby, Bing : 61, 65, 412
Cross, Christopher : 248
Crouch, Andraé : 28, 322, 324, 393, 406, 407, 410, 467, 468, 482, 539, 544
Crouch, Sandra : 26, 28, 322, 406, 410, 467, 468, 482, 539
Crow, Sheryl : 328, 470
Crusaders, The : 28
Cruz, Paul : 542
Cry : 466, 521, 528, **544-545**, 549, 569
Culkin, Macauley : 370, 398, 399, 400
Currell, Christopher : 296, 300, 301, 306-320, 326, 330, 331, 336, **338-349**, 345, 348, 349, 397, 472

D.S. : 345, 437, **471-472**
Da Costa, Paulinho : 124, 145, 148, 150, 156-159, 162, 168, 172, 182-188, 208, 232, 248, 268, 269, 280, 300, 306-318, 326, 406, 420, 489, 516, 518, 544, 574, 593
Daddy, Puff : 28, 464, 563
Daft Punk : 51, 494
Dancing Machine : 12, 14, **90-91**, 92, 96, 104, 116-119, 556, 562, 563, 570
Dancing Machine: 64, 96, 118, 178, 553-555
Dangerous : 37, 305, 350, 353, **416-419**, 443-445, 448, 449, 456, 460, 470, 473, 498, 508, 524, 532, 591
***Dangerous* [album]** : 33, 37, 139, 209, 239-241, 305, 351, 358, 362, 363, **364-429**, 432, 433, 435, 438, 441, 442, 467, 470, 494, 498, 502-506, 514, 528, 541, 542, 570, 571, 582
Dangerous: The Short Films : 381, 400, 403, 408
Daniel, Jeffrey : 92, 204, 302, 303, 340
Daniels, LaShawn : 530-532, 535, 542, 548, 574, 577, 599
Daniels, Soloman : 178
Dapper-Dan : 95, **104**
Darkchild Studios : 235, 529-532, 574, 577, 579
David, Mack : 101
Davidson, Aqil : 386
Davis Jr., Sammy : 142, 360, 412, 433
Davis, Clifton : 56
Davis, Clive : 13, 260, 274, 466, 469
Davis, Hal : 12, 44-46, 56, 60, 62-65, 69, 72, 76, 77, 80, 84, 85, 90, 91, 96, 101, 104, 552, 557-564
Davis, Miles : 232, 301, 366
Davis, Patricia : 91
Davis, Vidal : 538
Day, Bobby : 64
De Fina, Barbara : 302
De Lena, Eddie : 456, 457, 489, 498, 502, 508, 598
Deacon, John : 272
Deadrick, Tyrell *Rock* : 178
Dean, Burt : 502, 503
Dean, Lisa : 332
Dear Michael : 95, 102, **104**, 142
Decade – 1980-1990 : 366, 438
Decroix, Christine : 328
Dee, Sylvia : 84
Def Jam : 296
Del Barrio, Jorge : 402, 422, 489, 502, 503, 516-518
Delfonics, The : 36
Demorris, Jeff : 489
Dennis, Carolyn : 178
DePew, Gary : 287
Derouin, Joel : 489, 516
Desmond, Chris : 355
Destiny : **126**, 260
Destiny : 14, 37, 109, 120-127, 142, 145, 146, 148, 150, 156, 176, 178, 182, 183, 186, 221, 260
Destiny's Child : 446, 527, 529
DeVante Swing : 474
DeVillar, C.J. : 598
Diamond, Neil : 245
Diana : 32, 33, 46, 52, 131, 147, 192, 249
Diana Ross & The Supremes : 24, 25, 30, 56
Diana Ross Presents The Jackson 5 : 26-34, 36, 38, 561, 564
Diana, Lady : 332, 497, 542, 567
Diana! : 46
Dibango, Manu : 208, 583
Dicato, Paul : 489, 502, 504, 508
DiCicco, Bill : 415
Diener, Paul : 342
Different Kind of Lady : **118-119**, 120, 121, 184
DiLeo, Frank : 203, 262, 294-299, 302, 303, 305, 308, 312, 321, 332, 337, 339, 341, 342, 346, 369, 386
Dimitri from Paris : 28
Dimitrijević, Slobodan : 469
Dion, Céline : 145, 446, 542, 579, 581
Dirty Diana : 291, 296, 305, **330-333**, 346, 366, 388, 402, 404, 566, 570
Dixon, Eugène : 361
DJ Spinna : 98
Do the Bartman : **362-363**, 430, 504
Do What You Wanna : 118, **120-121**, 122
Do You Know Where Your Children Are : **429**, 594
Doby, Valerie : 539
Does Your Mama Know about Me? : 20
Doggin' Around : 79, **85**, 562
Don't Be Messin' 'Round : **352**
Don't Let a Woman (Make a Fool Out of You) : **246**
Don't Let It Get You Down : 552, **554**
Don't Stand Another Chance : **277**, 345, 470
Don't Stop 'Til You Get Enough : 141, 145-147, **148-151**, 152, 156, 157, 162, 164, 169, 366, 566, 570
Don't Walk Away : 521, **543**
Donally, Monique : 546
Donell Walls, Erick : 574, 590, 591
Doobie Brothers, The : 165, 170, 190
Dorsey, Kevin : 518, 539
Dougherty, Jim : 118, 120
Downward Spiral, The : 502
Dozier, Lamont : 24, 26, 30, 56, 65, 96, 99, 560
Dozier, Marja : 539
Dr. Freeze (Elliot Straite) : 533, 534, 598, 599
Drago, Billy : 536
Drayton, Clay : 188
Drayton, Thomas : 574
Dreamgirls : 224, 278
Dreams : 305, 381, 403
Dresdow, Dylan « 3-D » : 583
Dreyfuss, Emily : 316
Dreyfuss, Richard : 316
Drifters, The : 30
Dub, Shari : 268
Dudley, Kishaya : 536, 537
Duino Black, Tony : 489, 502
Duke, George : 162-165, 283, 304, 406
Dukov, Bruce : 489
Durham Prince, Michael : 574, 590, 591
Durio, Alfie Silas : 539
Durkee, Steve : 610
Durrance, Craig : 574, 599
Dylan, Bob : 280, 282, 305, 366, 502

E., Sheila : 280
E.T. : The Extra-Terrestrial Storybook : 155, 206, 215, 222, **242-245**, 252, 304, 397
E.T. (film) : 202, 215, 242-245, 283
Earth Song : 345, 437, 442-445, 466, **467-469**, 470, 488, 493, 524, 566, 574, 584
Earth, Wind & Fire : 125, 145, 183, 516
Ease On down the Road : 123, **130-131**, 132, 133, 144, 171, 570
East, Marcel : 280
East, Nathan : 274, 326, 328, 542
Eaten Alive : 33, 276, **279**, 288, 329
Echnoz, Dale : 562
Ed Sullivan TV Show, The : 35, 42, 43, 44, 46, 142
Edmonds, Jason : 541
Edmonds, Kevin *Babyface* (voir Babyface)
Edwards, Bernard : 32
Eisner, Michael : 284, 285
Electric Boogaloos : 92, 224
Eley, Paris : 125
Elgin, Scott : 590
Elisabeth, I Love You : 488, **514-515**, 544
Ellington, Duke : 138
Emerick, Geoffrey : 213, 252-256
Emmanuel, Tommy : 488
Emotions, The : 276
Encino Studios : 429
Enjoy Yourself : 13, **110-111**, 113, 123, 570
Enriquez, Joy : 579
Erickson, Paul : 264, 270
Ensigh, Mary M. : 223
Ervin, David : 264
Espinoza, Bino : 264, 270, 277
Estefan, Gloria : 579
Esters, Royce : 104
Ethanet Studios : 583
Eugene, Jane : 530
Euphoria : 79, 80, **85**
Evans, Keith : 433
Evans, Mary Lee : 356
Eve : 528, 538
Evergreen Studios : 267, 572
Everybody's Somebody's Fool : 67, 69, **73**, 76, 161

Fagen, Donald (Steely Dan) : 14
Faggett, Geary Lanier : 322, 539
Faggett, Vonciele : 322, 539
Fairlight : 222, 264, 301
Falcone, Paul J. : 573, 598
Falcons, The : 8
Fall Again : 570, **573**
Family Thing : 508
Faragher, Davey : 240
Farewell My Summer Love : 355, 552, 555, **556**
***Farewell My Summer Love* [album]** : **552-557**, 559, 563
Farrow, Larry : 193
Fats : 531, 532
Fearing, Charles : 361, 516
Feelin' Alright : 46, 192
Feemster, Theron *Neff-U* : 574, 590, 591, 598
Felder, Wilton : 26, 28, 38, 40
Feldman, Corey : 316
Fenceton, Don : 87
Forgie : 566, 568
Ferguson, Stacy : 283
Fergusson, Larry : 280, 358
Ferrigno, Lou : 316
Ferrone, Steve : 467
Fiddmont-Lindsey, Lynne : 541
Fields, Simon : 230
Fields, Venetta : 178
Fienberg, Gregg : 403
Fife, Kirstin : 502, 539
Fincher, David : 370, 399, 403
Find Me a Girl : 109, 118
Fine Is the Feeling : 193
Fine, Sidney : 576
Fire Island : 473, 493, 500
Fischbacher, Siegfried : 430
Fischer, Clara : 432
Fitzgerald, Ella : 80, 83
Flack, Roberta : 93, 192, 302
Flattery, Paul : 316
Floetry : 538
Floyd, Frank : 130
Fly Away : **351**
Foley, Paul : 530
Folsey Jr., George : 216-219, 405
For All Time : **426**, 580, 582
Forbes, Claude « Quo » : 549
***Forever, Michael* [album]** : **94-105**, 142, 543
Forger, Matt : 220, 221, 232, 234, 267, 268, 276, 278, 288, 289, 300, **304**, 306-320, 324, 329, 330, 336, 341, 350-355, 392-397, 406, 422, 429, 438, 456, 457, 483, 489, 508, 571, 572, 576, 597
Foster, David : 145, 164, 165, 170, 202, 212, 441, 467, 476, 477, 486, 487, 578
Foster, Marvin : 302
Foster, Ronnie : 178
Four Dukes : 16
Four Niggers and a Chink : 20
Four Pharaohs, The : 20
Four Tops, The : 24, 36, 46, 52, 329
Frager, Arne : 257
Frankfurt, Scott : 396
Frankie Valli & The Four Seasons : 138
Franklin, Aretha : 155, 158, 188
Frazier, Leah : 482, 483
Fredriksson, Kris : 272
Free : **354**
Free to Be… You and Me : 93
Freeman, Don : 238
Freeman, Morgan : 442
Freestone, Peter : 268, 272
From the Bottom of My Heart : 581
Fugees, The : 500, 599
Funes, Matthew : 489, 518
Funk Brothers, The : 34, 36, 108
Fuqua, Harvey : 564
Furusho, Stuart : 266
Fussin' and Fightin' : 557

Gable, Jim : 483
Gabriel, Juan : 579
Gadd, Steve : 130
Gadson, James : 90, 91
Gale, Eric : 130, 306
Gallen, Joel : 408
Gallin, Sandy : 369, 442, 496
Galloway, Roy : 178
Galuten, Albhy : 279
Gamble, Kenneth : 13, **108-109**, 110-121, 126, 236, 267
Gang, Gil : 547
Garabedian, Berj : 489
Garrett, Gerry : 178
Garrett, Siedah : 235, 322, 323, 326-328, 370, 410, 597
Garris, Mick : 506, 507
Gass, Jon : 433, 541
Gatica, Humberto : 279, 280, 281, 318, 533, 544, 598
Gaudio, Bob : 86
Gaye, Marvin : 10, 24, 31, 36, 52, 60, 92, 102, 124, 144, 279, 329
Geffen Records : 248, 278, 362
Geffen, David : 284
Geldof, Bob : 280, 281, 444
Genewick, Steve : 541
Gentry, Rhonda : 178
Gest, David : 43, 527
Get It : 51, **356**
Get It Together : 12, 90-92, 96, 101, 119, 553-557, 560
Get on the Bus : 494, 512
Get on the Floor : 104, 141, 145, 148, 152, **158-159**, 160, 162, 166, 176, 220, 535
Getschal, Douglas : 300, 301, 306, 310, 314, 330
Ghosts : 244, 449, 457, 481, 482, 493-497, **506-511**, 513, 537
Gibb, Barry : 279, 576, 578, 591
Gibb, Maurice : 279, 591
Gibson, Bill : 280
Gibson, Debbie : 316
Gibson, Michael : 180, 181
Gibson, Tyrese : 540
Gilbert, Kevin : 396, 397, 422
Gilderman, Brad : 533, 535, 542, 574, 599
Gilkey, Quentin : 590
Gillespie, Dizzy : 134
Gilman, Billy : 579
Gilstrap, Jim : 148, 158, 178, 195, 518
Ging, Mike : 518, 533, 544, 598
Giraldi, Bob : 203, 223, 224, 254, 255, 263, 305, 332
Girl Don't Take Your Love Away from Me : **61**
Girl You're So Together : 552, **555**
Girlfriend : 141, 145, 162, **164-165**, 202, 212, 220, 250, 314, 406
Give in to Me : 270, 345, 365, 371, 402, 403, **404-405**, 470
Give It Up : 175, 176, **188**
Gleeson, David : 573
Glover, Danny : 316

Glover, Khaliq : 280, 593
Glover, Linda : 64
Gluck, John : 135
Goin' Back to Alabama : 196
Goin' Places : 13, 109, 118-120, 126
Gold, Greg : 359
Gold, Jack : 100
Gold, Wally : 135
Goldberg, Whoopi : 316
Gone Too Soon : 365, 413, **414-415**, 426
Goodchild, Mark *Exit* : 583, 590
Gordy, Berry : 10-13, 18, 20, 21, **22-25**, 26-35, 38-49, 52-69, 74, 77, 84, 88-91, 96, 97, 128, 131, 135, 144, 204, 257, 260, 418, 446, 483, 497, 551, 560
Gordy, George *Horgay* : 64
Gordy, Gwen : 560
Gordy, Kennedy William (Rockwell) : 257
Gore, Lesley : 135
Gossett, Judy : 539
Got the Hots : 232, **239**, 528, 580, 582
Got to Be There : 25, 55, 56, **62-63**, 100, 101, 527, 562, 570
***Got to Be There* [album]** : 37, **54-65**, 69, 76, 105, 561, 564
Gotta Put Your Heart on the Line : 494, 497, 512
Gouché, Andrew : 322
Gowers, Bruce : 146, 154, 167
Grace, Geoff : 484, 516-518
Graham, Franny : 599
Graham, Larry : 160
Granat, Endre : 402, 489, 502, 516
Grandmaster Flash : 220, 549
Granet, Peter : 122, 124, 126
Grant, Gary : 148-158, 162, 164, 168-172, 208, 210, 214, 252, 254, 300, 306, 310, 318, 320, 336
Gray, Todd : 49, 553
Great Cola Commercials 2 : 228
Greatest Show on Earth : 67, 69, **72**
Green, Al : 557
Green, Harold : 539
Green, Linda : 322
Greene, Ed : 124, 126, 182
Greene, Susaye : 145, 168, 169
Gregg, Norman : 532
Greggs, Alex : 531
Griffin, Gene : 358, 370, 374
Griffin, Rayford : 489
Grigsby, Doug : 508, 516, 518
Grimes, Ray : 16, 18
Groening, Matt : 362, 363
Groove of Midnight : 597
Grossman, Larry : 414
Grower, John : 180, 181
Gruberth, Gerry : 178
Grundman, Bernie : 202, 341
Gruska, Jay : 274
Guess, John : 280
Guns N' Roses : 371, 396, 405, 471, 542
Guttenberg, Steve : 316
Guy, Jasmine : 316
Guzauski, Mick : 426, 489, 498, 499, 502, 516-518, 544

Haffner, Juliet : 502
Haifley, Chuck : 324
Hall, Aaron : 358, 374, 540
Hall, Conrad : 500, 540
Hall, Damion : 374, 432, 540
Hall, Daryl : 280, 540
Hall, Dave *Jam* : 452, 540
Hall, Justin : 518, 546
Hallelujah Day : 80, 82
Hamilton, Roy : 549
Hammerstein II, Oscar : 83
Hampton, Gladys : 73
Hampton, Lionel : 134
Hancock, Herbie : 155
Hanes, John : 420, 569, 574, 591
Hansen, Randy : 268
Hanson : 579
Happy : 70, 79, 80, **84**
Happy Birthday Lisa : 363
Harding, Phil : 563
Harmon, Linda : 402, 489
Harris, Andre : 538
Harris, James III : 480, 481, 510
Harris, Natalia : 476
Harrison, George : 50, 250, 344
Hart, Bruce : 93
Harthon : 43
Haskell, Scotty : 546
Hassinger, David : 557, 561
Hatcher, Mike : 267
Haupman, Micha : 546
Hayes, Chris : 280
Hayes, Nelson : 208, 209, 249, 260-270
Hayes, Otis : 16
Haynes, Tiger : 130
Heal the World : 33, 221, 365, 366, **392-395**, 415, 442, 467, 528, 570
Heard, Andreao : 534
Heartbreak Hotel : 176, 184, 185, 422, 508, 510, 548
Heartbreaker : 521, **531**, 532, 599
Heath, Richard : 148
Heatwave : 144, 152, 155, 162, 173, 504
Heaven Can Wait : 521, 525, **534**
Heavy D : 376-379, 398, 532
Heffington, Ryan : 255
Heijden, Franck van der : 590
Hemion, Dwight : 147
Hemsley, Sherman : 316
Henderson, Marlo : 148, 152, 162, 164, 170, 172
Henderson, Wes : 20, 21
Henning, Doug : 149
Henson, JaRon : 540
Herbig, Gary : 252, 254
Here I Am (Come and Take Me) : 552, **557**
Herman, Pee-Wee : 312
Heston, Charlton : 71
Hewett, Howard : 234
Hey, Jerry : 122, 144, 148-159, 162, 164, 168-173, 182-185, 208-214, 226, 228, 248, 252, 254, 264, 265, 267, 300, 301, 306, 310-322, 330, 336, 410, 481, 596, 598
Hill, Lauryn : 526
Hilliard, Jacqueline D. : 85, 561
Hirsch, Henry : 592
HIStory : 160, 438, 442, 449, **482-483**, 493, 497, 508, 512, 516, 518, 544
***HIStory* [album]** : 19, 139, 160, 209, 344, 345, 351, 375, 387, 428, 429, **436-489**, 490, 494, 496, 497, 499, 500, 502, 506, 510, 512, 522, 535, 542, 551, 574
HIStory on Film : 440
HIStory Volume I : 392, 571
Hodge, Steve : 450, 452, 510
Hodges, Mabon : 557
Hoffman, Rob : 456, 473, 474, 481, 485-489, 502, 508
Hold My Hand : 588, **590**, 596
Holdridge, Lee : 132
Holiday, Billie : 32, 42, 68
Holland Jr., Edward : 23, 24, 26, 30, 56, 65, 96, 98, 99, 102, 560
Holland, Brian : 24, 26, 30, 56, 65, 96, 98, 99, 102, 560, 562
Holliday, Jennifer : 60, 278, 329
Hollister, Dave : 375, 435
Holloway, Brenda : 77
Hollywood Tonight : 588, **590-591**, 593
Holtz Sr, Greg : 302
Hooper, Kristen : 506
Hopper, Sean : 280
Horn, L.T. : 98-105
Horn, Roy : 422, 430
Hornaday, Jeffrey : 255, 286
Horner, James : 286, 289
Horvat, Jean-Marie : 416, 535, 542, 574, 590, 599
Hoskins, Samuel *Cyph* : 549
Hosono, Haruomi : 593
Hot Street : 155, 210, 232, 238, **240**, 582
Houston, Thelma : 60
Houston, Whitney : 145, 170, 274, 326, 361, 466, 469, 527, 529, 535
Howard, Brie : 240
Howard, Francine : 322
Howel, Steve : 267, 314
Huff, Dann : 322, 326
Huff, Leon : 13, **108-109**, 110-121, 126, 236, 267
Hugo, Chad : 374, 525
Hull, Bunny : 178, 208, 234
Human League : 230, 341
Human Nature : 71, 199, 202, 205, **232-233**, 238, 426, 566, 570, 580, 584
Humphrey, Pete : 110-120
Hungate, David : 270
Hunter, Paul : 528, 536, 537
Hussey, Olivia : 316
Huston, Anjelica : 286-288
Hutch, Willie : 44-46, 61, 62
Hutchcroft, Kim : 148-158, 162, 164, 168-172, 300, 306, 310, 318, 320, 336
Hyperprism : 472

I Am Love : 64, 178
I Can't Help It : 50, 51, 141, 145, 148, **168-169**, 194, 202, 220, 300, 435
(I Can't Make It) Another Day : 588, **592**
I Found That Girl : 40
I Have This Dream : **578**
I Just Can't Stop Loving You : 291, 296, **326-328**, 349, 352, 366, 535, 566, 570, 584
I Like the Way You Love Me : 558, 574, 588
I Need You : 432, **491**
I Wanna Be Where You Are : 37, 55, 57, 58, **60**, 61, 72, 570
I Want You Back : 12, 24, 25, **26-29**, 34, 36, 38, 40, 43, 44, 61, 142, 274, 556, 563, 570
I Want You Back! Unreleased Masters : 38, 49, 91, 168, 564
I Was Made to Love Her : 48, 50, 558
I'll Be Satisfied : 22
I'll Be There : 12, 24, **44-47**, 60, 61, 188, 265, 305, 366, 556, 570
I'll Come Home to You : 95, **105**
I'm in Love Again : 192
I'm So Blue : **352**
Ice Cube : 519
Ideka, Suzy : 46
Idol, Billy : 330, 331
If We Can Start All Over : 474
If You Don't Love Me : **424**
If'n I Was God : 558, 561
Iglesias, Julio : 579
Iman : 370, 390
In Our Small Way : 55, **61**, 67, 69, **76**
In the Back : **489**, 494, 570
In the Closet : 365, 366, 370, **382-385**, 387, 396
Inaba, Koshi : 516
Ingram, James : 155, 158, 195, 208, 234, 235, 248, 280, 282, 577
Ink Spots, The : 407
Intruders, The : 108
Invincible : 168, 249, 252, 375, 428, 430, 521, **532**
***Invincible* [album]** : 126, 161, 197, 238, **520-549**, 567-569, 572-576, 590, 592, 597-599
Irving, Amy : 316
Is It Scary : 449, 486, 493, 494, 507, **510**
Isham, Wayne : 434, 475, 591
Isley Brothers, The : 24, 60, 549
It's Not Worth It : **577**, 579
It's the Falling in Love : 141, 145, **170-171**, 197, 202, 226
It's True : 543
Ivery, Tabia : 541

J-Friends : 161, 516-518
J-Roc : 596, 599
Jackson 5 – Come and Get It: The Rare Pearls : 564
Jackson Five Live at the Forum : 58
Jackson Five, The : 8-52, 56, 57, 60-64, 68, 69, 71, 72, 74, 80, 82, 86-92, 96-98, 101-105, 119, 164, 168, 237, 276, 305, 344, 361, 560
Jackson Jr., Jermaine : 358, 359
Jackson Jr., Marlon : 358, 359
Jackson Jr., Paul : 14, 184, 185, 221, 234, 236, 320, 330, 331, 341, 358, 362, 380, 586
Jackson, Andre : 433
Jackson, Anthony : 130-133
Jackson, Autumn : 358, 359
Jackson, Brandi : 358, 359, 394, 398
Jackson, Brandon : 8
Jackson, Brittany : 358, 359
Jackson, Dave : 122
Jackson, Eric : 590
Jackson, Jackie : 8-16, 19, 25-29, 34, 38, 40, 44, 57, 74, 88, 90, 110-112, 116, 122, 125, 176, 178, 185, 186, 188, 264-266, 268, 270, 277, 280, 358, 359, 368
Jackson, Jaimy : 358, 359
Jackson, Janet : 8, 97, 148, 156, 157, 188, 234, 235, 267, 277, 321, 329, 345, 358, 359, 361, 368-370, 383, 392, 426, 428, 434, 441, 448-454, 465, 470, 473, 480, 493, 496
Jackson, Jeremy : 358, 359
Jackson, Jermaine : 8-19, 25-29, 34-46, 57, 74, 88, 90, 97, 109, 111, 114, 116, 168, 179, 188, 257, 260-266, 270, 274, 275, 329, 345, 358, 359, 369, 428, 470, 527
Jackson, Jesse : 42, 72, 92
Jackson, Johnny : 16, 18, 19
Jackson, Joseph : 8-18, 25, 39, 43, 56, 62, 69, 96, 109, 114, 146, 193, 260, 359
Jackson, Jourdyn : 358, 359
Jackson, Katherine : 8, 12, 29, 31, 39, 71, 149, 178, 212, 260, 306, 359
Jackson, La Toya : 8, 128, 184, 193, 212, 224, 234, 235, 254, 255, 267, 280, 308, 358
Jackson, Marlon : 8-16, 19, 26-29, 34, 38, 40, 44, 74, 88, 90, 110, 112, 116, 122, 126, 157, 176, 184, 185, 188, 260-270, 277, 280, 358, 359, 368, 370, 432
Jackson, Mick : 122, 123
Jackson, Pee Wee : 358
Jackson, Prince : 394, 497, 514, 522, 546, 573
Jackson, Randy : 8, 12-14, 110, 112, 116-126, 148, 156, 157, 176-183, 186, 188, 260, 264-266, 270, 280, 358, 359, 368, 370, 432
Jackson, Rebbie : 8, 276, 351, 358, 359, 432
Jackson, Siggy : 358, 359
Jackson, Taj : 358, 359, 490
Jackson, Taryll : 358, 359, 490, 590, 591
Jackson, Terry : 396, 397
Jackson, Tito : 8-19, 27-29, 34-40, 43, 44, 74, 88, 90, 110-113, 116-126, 176-188, 260, 263-266, 270, 277, 280, 358, 359, 368, 490, 491, 591
Jackson, Tito (T.J.) : 358, 359, 490
Jackson, Valencia : 358, 359
Jacksons, The : 13, 14, 25, 106-127, 166, 174-189, 208, 214, 234, 270, 358, 570, 586
Jacobs, Jon : 252, 254, 256
Jaeger, Denny : 330, 336
Jagger, Mick : 268, 269, 570
Jam : 365, 370, **376-379**, 380, 452, 500, 570, 584
Jam, Jimmy : 361, 369, 375, 428, 441, **448-449**, 450-453, 480, 482, 483, 494, 507, 510, 599
Jamerson, James : 34, 36
James, Bryton : 579
James, Josie : 178
James, Kim : 433
Jarreau, Al : 280
Jason, Neil : 489
Jay-Z : 537, 592
Jazzy Jeff & The Fresh Prince : 136
Jean, Wyclef : 481, 500
Jenkins, Bob : 402
Jenkins, Ken : 507
Jenkins, Mortonette : 148, 158
Jennings, Waylon : 280
Jerkins III, Fred : 530-532, 535, 542, 548, 577, 599
Jerkins, Rodney : 150, 235, 375, 525, 526, **529**, 530-533, 535, 542, 548, 574-577, 579, 595, 597, 598, 599
Joel, Billy : 280
John Luongo Mix, The : 123
John, Elton : 49, 50, 288, 498, 502, 516
John, Mabel : 30
Johnny Raven : 79, 80, **85**, 87
Johns, Tenika : 539
Johnson, Angel : 539
Johnson, Augie : 148, 158
Johnson, Beverly : 316
Johnson, Daniel : 539
Johnson, Don : 598
Johnson, Jean : 322
Johnson, Louis : 145, 148, 150, 153, 156-159, **160**, 162-172, 190, 191, 208, 212, 226, 228, 234, 236, 248, 280, 281, 310, 402, 536
Johnson, Zaneta M. : 539
Joliet, Vincent : 394
Jones Boys, The : 135
Jones, Alphonso : 593
Jones, Brian : 312, 476
Jones, Caryn : 476
Jones, Dennis E. : 346
Jones, Quincy Delight : 32, 33, 50, 60, 70, 84, 128, 130-133, **134-137**, 138-176, 183, 185, 187, 190- 192, 195, 200- 203, 208-245, 248, 250, 252, 264, 280-283, 296, 299-304, 306-328, 330, 331, 336-350, 352, 356, 366, 369, 370, 374, 375, 384, 402, 406, 410, 415, 418, 422, 429, 430-432, 449, 470, 471, 528, 577, 593
Jones, Tom : 310
Jordan, Laquentan : 539
Jordan, Michael : 305, 370, 377-379, 481
Joshua, Maurice : 465
Joy : **435**, 541
Joyful Jukebox Music : 111, 553
Jump for Joy : 120
Just a Little Bit of You : 95, 96, **102**
Just Friends : **197**
Just Good Friends : 51, 291, **318**, 356
Justman, Paul : 249

Karlson, Phil : 68, 69
Katayama, Suzie : 488, 489, 514, 515
Kaye, Jerry : 276
Kb et EQ : 541
Keep the Faith : 139, 240, 365, **410-411**, 544
Keith, Gordon : 16, 18
Kellogg, David : 378, 379
Kelly, Claude : 590
Kelly, Jon : 252
Kelly, Patrick : 321, 324
Kelly, R. : 351, 441, 474, 544, 568, 569
Keltner, Jim : 422
Kenerly II, Roger : 178
Kenerly-Saint, Roger : 178
Kenerly, Yolanda : 178
Kenly, Pat : 180
Kent, Peter : 539
Kerber, Randy : 322, 324
Kern, Jerome : 83
Kerry, Ashby : 562, 564
Keys, Gary : 91
Kilhoffer, Anthony : 599
Kimball, Bobby : 270
King, B. B. : 138, 404
King, Carol : 56, 65
King, Don : 263, 316
King, Gary : 122
King, Lamont : 16, 18
King, Robbie : 20
King, Stephen : 496, 506, 507
KinKi Kids : 516, 518
Kipp, Ric : 578
Kleiser, Jeff : 440
Knack, The : 220
Knight, Gladys : 10, 20, 24, 26, 27, 90, 97, 196
Knox, Tom : 266, 270
Knuckles, Frankie : 563
Kohan, Buz : 204, 278, 360, **412-413**, 414, 415, 514, 572

Kool & The Gang : 125, 276
Koppelman, Charles : 295, 568
Kovács, László : 181
Kragen, Ken : 280, 281
Kramer, Jerry : 312, 344, 346
Kravitz, Lenny : 454, 588, 592
Kreeton's Overture : 304
Krenz, Gerd : 508
Krijnen, Dennis : 590
Kris Kross : 378, 379
Krohn, Elmar : 122
Kronstadt, Gina : 539
Krueger, Jim : 192

LaBelle, Patti : 414
Laboriel, Abraham : 414, 415
Ladanyl, Greg : 266
Lady Sings the Blues : 32, 42, 68-71, 80, 84, 86
Lampson, Carmen : 549
Landau, Michael : 274, 318, 544
Landis, John : 203, 206, 216-219, 398-400, 405
Landon, Tina : 454
Langford Scoble, Tom : 489
Larson, Christa : 392, 393
Larson, Mel : 64, 69, 72-74, 83, 87-89, 554, 555, 558, 560, 562
Last, Julie : 362, 422
Laues, Eritza : 534
Lauper, Cyndi : 200, 280, 281
Lawrence, Rhett : 318, 320, 358, 376, 406, 407, 410, 416
Lawrence, Stephen J. : 93
Lawson, Ricky : 252, 253
Leaner, George et Ernie : 16, 17
Leave Me Alone : 291, 295, 296, 298, **341-343**, 380, 450, 481, 514
Lee, Spike : 321, 336, 457, 458, 494, 512
Legend, John : 51
Legrand, Michel : 80, 84
Lemorande, Rusty : 284-287
Lennon, John : 250, 294, 344, 345, 414, 456
Lennon, Sean : 339, 346
Leonhardt, Ute : 408
Let Me Count the Ways : 556
Let's Get Serious : 168, 274
Levant, Gayle : 267, 489
Levert, Eddie : 194
Levinsky, Allen : 76
Lewis, Glenn : 573
Lewis, Huey : 280
Lewis, Terry : 361, 369, 375, 428, 441, **448-449**, 450-452, 480-482, 494, 507, 510, 599
Liberian Girl : 267, 291, 311, **314-317**, 346, 535
Life of The Party : 188
Lil' John Roberts : 516
Linn, Roger : 209
Lippman, Sidney : 84
Lipton Jones, Peggy : 214, 234, 248
Little Christmas Tree : **88-89**, 555
Little Daddy and the Bachelors : 20
Little Susie : 437, **484-485**, 517
Little, Levi : 375, 435
Live in Japan : 49
Lively, James : 546
Living Colour : 405
Living with Michael Jackson : 567
Livsey, Billy : 241
Loggins, Kenny : 190, 248, 280
Lonely Teardrops : 22, 558, **560**
Longsdale, Shep : 266, 270
***Lookin' Back to Yesterday* [album]** : **558-561**
Lopez, Becky : 208, 234
Lopez, Peter : 304, 582, 583
Loren, Bryan : 362, 369, 370, 396, 397, 402, 423-426, 430, 432, 494, 502-504
Lorentz, Robin : 539
Lorenzen, Jeff : 358
Love Is Here and Now You're Gone : 55, 56
Love Never Felt So Good : 255, 586, 594, 595, **596**
Love's Alright : 51, 433, 434
Love's Gone Bad : 558, **560**
Lovely One : 175, 176, **182-183**, 570
Lovesmith, Michael : 552, 554, 555, 562, 563
Loving You : **355**, 594, **597**
Lubbock, Jeremy : 226, 245, 476, 486, 490, 534, 539, 543, 547, 574
Lucas, Brandon : 546
Lucas, George : 284-287, 302, 400
Lucas, Tammy : 375, 435, 541
Lucchse, Ricky : 546
Lukather, Steve : 212, 220, 221, 232, 233, 248, 266, 270, 426, 429, 460, 573
Lumet, Sidney : 123, 128, 132, 135, 219
Luongo, John : 123, 187
Luther King, Martin : 50, 92, 194, 325, 483, 512
Lyle, Donnie : 569
Lyle, Graham : 241, 318
Lymon, Frankie : 27
Lynch, David : 370, 399, 441, 503

Macauley, Steve : 599
Mack, Bob : 178, 272
Mackay, Melissa : 546
Macrae, Joshua J. : 272
Madonna : 294, 334, 382, 396, 398, 448, 480
Madsen, Michael : 536
Madsen, Virginia : 316
Magic Johnson : 370, 390, 481
Making Michael Jackson's Thriller : 216, 217
Malone, Jena : 478
Maloney, Kevin : 280, 336
Malouf, Brian : 270, 353
Mama's Pearl : 40
Man in the Mirror : 240, 291, 298, **322-325**, 326, 366, 392, 394, 407, 410, 411, 458, 544, 563, 566, 570, 584
Man of War : 109, 118, 126, 267
Mandel, Johnny : 166, 167, 168, 406
Mandela, Nelson : 524, 579
Manilow, Barry : 274
Mann, Daniel : 68
Manson, Eddy : 58, 61, 76, 105, 562
Marasciullo, Fabian : 531
Marceau, Marcel : 233, 444, 477
Marcellino, Jerry : 64, 69, 72-74, 83, 87-89, 554, 555, 558, 560, 562
Marcil, Derek : 562, 563
Maria (You Were the Only One) : 55, 62, 64
Marinelli, Anthony : 210, 214
Marks, Jay : 110-120
Marley, Bob : 102, 246
Marley, Ziggy : 579
Marotta, Rick : 122
Martha & The Vandellas : 24
Martin, Bobby : 110, 112
Martin, George : 139, 213, 252-256
Martin, Ricky : 579
Martinez, Aley : 546
Martinez, Nigel : 562, 563
Martz, Jason : 350, 396
Marvelettes, The : 24
Mason Jr., Harvey : 542, 574
Mason, Dave : 192
Massenburgs, George : 229
Mathis, Johnny : 100, 596
Matousek, John : 558, 562
Mattacks, Dave : 256
Maxus : 274
Maxwell, Duris : 20
May, Brian : 272
Maybe Tomorrow : 57
Maybe Tomorrow : 12, 62, 105
Mayers, George : 420, 533, 534, 540, 543, 547, 549
Mbulu, Letta : 314, 315, 316
McCartney, Linda : 213, 250-256
McCartney, Paul : 37, 50, 138, 145, 162, 164, 165, 202, 203, 212, 213, 247, 249, **250-251**, 252-256, 269, 294, 295, 344, 355, 396, 570, 580
McCary, Michael : 579
McClain, John : 251, 448, 488, 496, 533, 538, 541, 568, 585, 586, 593, 598
McCrary, Howard : 539
McCrary, Linda : 539
McCrary, Sam : 539
McCuller, Arnold : 178
McDaniel, Hattie : 68
McDonald Jr., Danny Ray : 590
McDonald, Clarence : 26
McDonald, Michael : 158, 165, 170, 248
McDougal III, Weldon Arthur : 20, 35, **43**
McEntire, Reba : 579
McFadden, Gene : 109, 114-116
McGlown, Betty : 30
McGregor, Billy : 16
McIntosh, Carl : 530
McKenna, Paul : 428
McKenzie, Andres : 397
McKinney, Mike : 253
McKnight, Brian : 267, 579
McLean, Mike : 52
McQueen, Steve : 305
McRath, Alice Jean : 539
McWilliams, Paulette : 148, 158, 178
Meitzenheimer, Rand : 104
Melendrez, Sonny : 283
Melodie : 552, **554**, 562, 563
Melton, Tommie : 20
Melvoin, Michael : 557
Men in Black : **426**
Men in Black II : 526
Men of Vizion : 113
Mendoza, Rubin : 536
Mercury, Freddie : 260, 268, 269, 272, 273
Merriett, Sue : 539
Merry-Go-Round : 23
Messina, Joe : 34, 36
Meyers, Bill : 541
Meyers, Dana : 76
MFSB (Mother Father Sister and Brother) : 108-116
***Michael* [album]** : 375, 428, 429, 488, 551, 574, **588-593**, 595
Michael Jackson – Ghosts (Deluxe Collector Box Set) : 512
Michael Jackson – Hello World: The Motown Solo Collection : 80, 82, 85, 555-557, 564
Michael Jackson – Highlights from the Ultimate Collection : 573
Michael Jackson – King of the Pop (The French Fans' Selection) : 153
Michael Jackson – Love Songs : 35, 46, 564
Michael Jackson – Moscow Case 1993: When the King of Pop Met the Soviets : 463
Michael Jackson – Motown Legends : 80
Michael Jackson – The Footage You Were Never Meant To See : 567
Michael Jackson – The Stripped Mixes : 46
***Michael Jackson – The Ultimate Collection* [album]** : 124, 133, 197, 234, 241, 286, 288, 289, 304, 351, 420, 422, 474, 489, 512, 513, 551, **570-575**, 591
Michael Jackson – Tour Souvenir CD single : 346
Michael Jackson – Tour Souvenir Pack : 346
Michael Jackson – Visionary: The Video Singles : 388
Michael Jackson Plus The Jackson 5 – 18 Greatest Hits : 84
Michael Jackson Scrapbook, The : 43, 564
Michael Jackson with The Jackson 5 – Soulsation! : 46
Michael Jackson: Around the World : 321
Michael Jackson: The Life of an Icon : 43
Michael Jackson: The Remix Suite : 563
Michael Jackson's Journey from Motown to Off the Wall : 150, 168
Michael Jackson's Private Home Movies : 339, 379, 514, 541, 567
Michael Jackson's This Is It : 220
Michael Jackson's Vision : 483, 569
Michael White : 60
Michael, George : 200, 294, 407, 446, 526, 535
Mick Jackson : 122, 123
Middle Ear Studios : 279, 578
Midler, Bette : 280
Miguel, Luis : 579
Miles, Jason : 456
Miller, Shelley : 93
Mills, Stephanie : 130
Mims, Cornelius : 318, 359
Mind Is the Magic : 161, 370, **430-431**
Minnelli, Liza : 71, 527
Miracles, The : 23, 24, 30, 34, 48, 52, 63, 74, 329, 554, 561
Mironov, Jeffrey : 488
Mischke : 531, 590, 591
Mitchell, Dennis : 358
Mitchell, Jim : 404
Mizell, Fonce : 26, 27, 58, 82, 83, 105, 552, 555-557
Mizell, Larry : 557
MJ & Friends : 418, 468, 522, 524, 574, 579
Moby : 371
Moé, Bambi : 232
Moffett, Jonathan : 253, 277, 444
Mokran, Peter : 474
Money : 437, **473**, 493
Monica : 235, 529, 535, 577
Monkey Business : 345, **422**, 528, 570, 571
Monkeys, The : 426
Mooney, Jon : 489, 502
Moonwalker : 298, 299, 311, 312, 324, 338-346, 351, 369, 506
Moore, Chanté : 432
Moore, Rene : 277, 376, 464, 481
Moore, Warren : 561
Morahan, Andy : 405
Morales, David : 452, 465
Moran, Tony : 483
Moreno, Magic : 552
Morey, Jim : 442
Morgan, Perry : 322
Morgan, Tommy : 488
Morita, Akio : 368, 442, 446, 526
Morning Glow : 79, 80, 82, **86**
Moroder, Giorgio : 304
Morphine : 493, 494, **502-503**
Morris, Patrice : 539
Morrison, Ralph : 489
Mosdell, Chris : 593
Mötley Crüe : 397
Motown 25 : Yesterday, Today, Forever : 42
Motown at Hollywood Palace : 35, 36
Motown Sings Motown Treasures Volumes 1+2 : 554
Mottola, Tommy : 239, 241, 422, 442, 446, 447, 507, 522, 524, 526, 528, 530, 536, 545, 546, 549, 567, 568, 576, 592, 597, 599
Mourino, Edgard : 302
Moving Violation : 12, 111
Moxie, Jonathan : 420
Moy, Sylvia : 76, 82
MTV's 10th Anniversary Special : 397, 407, 408
Much Too Soon : **488**, 588
Mundo, Jerry : 18
Murden, Kristie : 539
Murphy, Eddie : 51, 370, 390, 433, 434, 475
Murray, Conrad : 585
Murray, Don : 122, 124, 126
Murray, James : 574, 590-592
Muscles : 33, 247, **249**, 276, 279
Music and Me : 79, 80, **87**
***Music and Me* [album]** : 63, **78-87**
Music Video Clip Dance 4 : 434
Musical Youth : 241
Musto, Tommy : 371
My Cherie Amour : 36, 48
My Girl : 67, 69, **74**, 86, 161
Mýa, : 579
Myrick, Don : 358
Mystery Girl : 382

Nathan, Adam : 302
Natural Ressources : 111
Naughton, David : 216, 217
Naughty by Nature : 378, 429, 452
Navarro, Dave : 527
Nelson, Willie : 280
Neptunes, The : 563
Nero : 311
Nesmith, Michael : 308
Nettlesbey, Jon : 569, 586, 590, 593
Never Can Say Goodbye : 56, 61, 366, 564
New Edited Version : 213
New York City's Children's Choir : 476
Newman, Mona : 489
Newton-John, Olivia : 278
Nichol, Steve : 530
Nicksay, David : 506
Nielsen, Brigitte : 316
Night Time Lover : **193**, 267
Nightline : 232, 238, **240**, 582
Nine Inch Nails : 502
Nite Line (voir ***Nightline***)
Nolen, Curtis Anthony : 257
Nordahl, David : 546
Northern Songs : 294, 295
Not My Lover : 226
Notarille, Crescenzo : 312
Notorious B.I.G., The : 464, 465, 530
Novoq, Novi : 539
***Number Ones* [album]** : 551, **566-569**, 571

O, Gary : 353
O'Jays, The : 13, 108, 109
O'Neal, Shaquille : 481, 519, 530
O'Neal, Tatum : 165
Oates, John : 280
Off the Wall : 145, 150, 152, 155, **162-163**, 165, 184, 190, 288, 366, 426, 473, 570, 603
***Off the Wall* [album]** : 33, 50, 100, 133, 135, 137, 138, 139, **140-173**, 176-179, 184, 186, 190, 191, 194, 195, 197, 200-203, 206, 208, 209, 212, 214, 220, 239, 241, 242, 248, 250, 254, 260, 262, 267, 296, 301, 371, 374, 415, 423, 499, 528, 536, 553, 571, 596
Ohio Players : 100
Olazabal, Gary : 356
Oliveira, Laudir de : 122
Olmsted, Adam : 598
Olodum : 458
Oltheten, Wessel : 590
Omartian, Michael : 274, 280, 358
On the Line : 494, 497, **512-513**, 570
One : 595
One Day In Your Life : 95, 96, **100**, 115
One More Chance : 44, 259, 351, 466, 566, 568, **569**, 570
Ono, Yoko : 295
Orbit, William : 272, 273
Orchard, Steve : 254
Ormandy, Eugene : 482
Ortega, Kenny : 372, 431, 444, 585
Osborne, Jeffrey : 280
Osmond, Donny : 56, 62, 63, 68, 70, 80, 84
Osmonds, The : 56, 62, 68, 70

P.Y.T. (Pretty Young Thing) : **234-235**, 366, 570, 577, 580
Padilla, Rafael : 586
Page, Billy : 85
Page, Gene : 61, 64, 65, 72, 73, 76, 77, 84, 85, 100, 557, 562
Paich, David : 210-213, 232, 233, 236, 248, 266, 270, 280, 314, 315, 326, 328, 392, 393, 402, 414, 426, 460, 462, 467
Paich, Marty : 392, 414, 415, 572
Paley, William S. : 366
Palms Studio : 590
Pan, Hermes : 340
Papa Was a Rollin' Stone : 91, **247**
Parker, Kellie : 339, 346
Parker, Ray Jr. : 274

Parks, Weldon Dean : 90, 91, 212, 226, 488, 560
Parsons, Geoffrey : 446
Passe, Suzanne de :11, 24, 25, **42**, 68, 132, 204
Paterson, Vincent : 217, 218, 223, 224, 298, 305, 308, 312, **334**, 337-340, 372, 378, 399, 407, 408, 500, 501
Patterson, Eddie : 20
Paul, Billy : 13, 108
Paul, Clarence : 48, 194
Paul, Matt : 590
Pausini, Laura : 579
Pavarotti, Luciano : 522, 524, 579
Payne, Antony : 223, 254
Payne, Nora : 530, 531, 535
Payne, Scherrie : 169
Payne, Travis : 454
Peake, Don : 26, 38, 40
Pearson, Rob : 378
Pello, Gene : 26, 38, 40, 44
Peluso, Tony : 552, 554, 555, 562, 563
Pendergrass, Teddy : 108, 109, 115, 124, 236
People Make the World Go 'Round : 67, 69, **72**, 161
People of the World : 161, 516, 517, **518**
Perez, Johnny : 246
Perren, Freddie : 26-28, 38, 40, 58, 82, 83, 105, 552, 555-557
Perry, Jaime : 302
Perry, Richard : 246
Perry, Steve : 280
Perry, Tom : 178-188
Persing, Eric : 310
Peters, Michael : 217, 218, 223, 224, 278, 286
Petersen, Paul : 36
Petty, Tom : 579
Pharcyde, The : 390
Phillabaum, Larry : 599
Phillinganes, Elaine : 280
Phillinganes, Greg : 14, 122-126, 148-152, 156-158, 162-172, 178-188, 195, 208, 212, 220-222, 226, 228, 233-236, 248, 274, 280, 300, 301, 306, 310, 318, 321-328, 341, 346, 349, 351, 406, 407, 422, 586, 593, 598
Phillinganes, Karla : 280
Phillips, Lou Diamond : 316
Phillips, Mike : 593
Phoenix : 138
Pierce, Tim : 396, 397
Pike, Nicholas : 507, 537
Pintar, Justin : 590
Pippin : 80, 86
Pips, The : 20, 24, 26, 90, 97
Pittman, Bob : 204
Plewa, Joey : 475
Pointer Sisters, The : 240, 280
Poitier, Sidney : 68
Pop, Denniz : 491
Popin' Pete : 224, 507
Poppy Girls : 130
Porcaro, Jeff : 212, 220, 221, 232, 233, 236, 264, 266, 270, 392, 426
Porcaro, Steve : 164, 165, 170, 171, 210, 212, 220, 221, 232, 233, 236, 237, 248, 266, 270, 280, 314, 315, 326, 392, 402, 414, 426, 460, 462, 467, 474, 484, 485, 516-518, 572, 573
Porée, Greg : 267, 518
Pratt, Guy : 467
Pre-History – The Lost Steeltown Recordings : 19
Prescott, Karie : 189
Prescott, Markita : 484
Presley, Elvis : 22, 64, 115, 138, 176, 185, 286, 414, 422, 447
Presley, Lisa Marie : 446, 447, 475
Pressner, Bud : 18
Preston, Billy : 489
Price of Fame : **354**
Price, Dennis : 302
Price, Lewis : 178
Price, Richard : 302
Price, Vincent : 202, 214-218, 548, 580
Primettes, The : 30
Prince : 51, 282, 292, 294, 300, 382, 386, 394, 425, 448, 512
Privacy : 521, **542**
Pro-Jay : 573
Promo Lights Clip! Back To... Dance 2 : 434
Puff Daddy : 28, 464, 563
Push Me Away : 37, 166
Putnam, Bill : 138
Pytka, Joe : **305**, 308, 309, 332, 346, 381, 394, 403

Quay, Jasmine : 547
Queen : 123, 260, 268, 272, 273
Quiller, Kenny : 534

Rabin, Trevor : 456, 457
Ragsdale, Russ : 315
Raheem : 194
Ramone, Phil : 152
Ramsey Lewis Trio, The : 72
Ray Nelson, Johnny : 268
Ray, Ola : 216-219
Ray, Steven : 208, 209, 234, 280
Reach Out : 46
Reardon, Jane : 383
Redding, Otis : 74, 414
Reed, Teri : 252
Reet Petite : 22
Regiment, The : 590
Reichenbach, William : 148, 152, 156-158, 162, 164, 168-172, 208, 210, 214
Reid, Antonio *L.A.* : 358, 361, 369, 370, 428, 448, 464, 551, 595, 597
Remember the Time : 344, 346, 365, 370, 374, 375, **388-390**, 433, 435, 452, 526, 535, 570
Reynolds, Debbie : 218
Rhett, Lawrence : 318, 320, 358, 376, 406, 407, 410, 416
Ribando, Chris : 573
Ricci, Christina : 506
Riccio, Mike : 572
Richard, Little : 295
Richards Deke : 26-28, 38, 40, 58, 554
Richards, Michele : 489
Richardson, Karl : 279
Richie, Lionel : 33, 37, 160, 196, 212, 248, 280, 559
Richter, Jason James : 478
Ride with Me : **579**
Riggs, Seth : 269, 597
Riley, Markell : 386
Riley, Teddy : 113, 232, 241, 358, 362, 370, **374-375**, 376-391, 416-423, 425, 426, 429, 435, 441, 448, 449, 452, 498, 499, 506, 508, 510, 525, 529, 533-535, 540, 542, 543, 547, 549, 589-591
Riperton, Minnie : 192, 329, 414
Rise above It All : 533
Ritts, Herb : 383, 384
Roberson, Kevin *Kayo* : 428
Roberts, Lisa : 178
Roberts, Tim : 420, 569, 574, 59
Robinson, Butch : 458
Robinson, Fatima : 390
Robinson, John : 145, 148-159, 162-165, 168-172, 209, 274, 280, 281, 300, 301, 306, 310, 314, 324, 330, 336, 337, 349, 544, 596
Robinson, William *Smokey* : 23-25, 30, 34, 36, 63, 74, 80, 84, 237, 280, 446, 554, 561
Robitaille, Bob : 558
Rochelle, Michael : 562, 564
Rock With You : 141, 146, 147, 149, **152-154**, 155, 163, 167, 208, 210, 366, 376, 402, 456, 566, 570
Rockin' Robin : 37, 55, 57, 64, 161, 562
Rockwell (Kennedy William Gordy) : 257
Rodd, John : 502
Rodgers, Nile : 32, 51, 473
Rogers, Kenny : 196, 280, 281
Rogers, Robert : 554, 561
Rogers, Susan : 282
Rogut, Rail : 420, 422
Rolling Stone : 63, 257
Rolling Stones, The : 74, 172, 262, 269, 489
Rolston, Matthew : 582
Romanek, Mark : 454
Rooney, Cory : 597
Rosa, Phil : 359, 378, 379
Ross, Arthur : 60
Ross, Bill : 467
Ross, Diana : 10, 21-25, **30-33**, 37, 42, 46, 52, 56, 63, 65, 68, 71, 93, 123, 128-133, 144, 147, 171, 188, 192, 204, 223, 224, 247, 249, 276, 279, 280, 282, 288, 329-331, 334, 373, 412, 444, 474, 486, 497, 528, 561, 564, 570, 578
Ross, Mark : 280
Ross, Robin Renee : 267, 502, 518
Ross, Ted : 128, 130, 131
Rouben, Jack : 361
Rouster, Keith : 464
Rowe, Debbie : 447, 497
Rubba, Baby : 546
Rubini, Michael : 336
Rudolph, Richard : 192
Ruffin, David : 36
Ruffin, Jimmy : 52
Rufus & Chaka Khan : 153, 155, 195
Run-DMC : 296, 481, 549
Russell, Brenda : 248
Russell, Nipsey : 128, 130, 131
Russo, Thom : 416, 420, 428
Ryden, Mark : 305, 371
Ryles, Marcus : 280

Sade : 200
Safire : 586
Sakamoto, Ryuichi : 593
Salisbury, Mike : 145, 159
Sample, Joe : 26, 44
Sanchez, Pedro : 302
Sander, Annette : 456
Sandin, Vanessa : 403
Sanford, Fred : 212
Santana, Carlos : 547, 579
Sanz, Alejandro : 579
Sardina, Rafa : 598
Sauvez Willy : 368, 408, 450, 476, 478, 490
Save Me : **192**
Save the Children : 72, 92
Saxton, Nick : 146, 150
Say, Say, Say : **252-255**, 286, 369
Scared of the Moon : 570, **572**
Scharf, Walter : 70
Scheps, Andrew : 457, 460, 474, 484, 485, 498, 503, 508, 510
Schneider, Rob : 316
Schroeder, Rick : 316
Schwartz, Stephen : 86
Scorsese, Martin : 302, 303
Scotell, Mike : 508
Scott, Miguel : 590
Scream : 442, 449, **450-455**, 476, 480
Scream Louder : 452, 474, 493, 599
Seawind Horns, The : 148, 152, 156-159, 162-165, 168-173
Secada, Jon : 579
Seeing Voices : **576**
Seidman, Wesley : 586
Sembello, Michael : 14, 122, 126, 182-188, 238
Semenya, Caiphus : 314
Seneca, Joe : 308
Seppanen, Keith : 241
Serban : 420
Serban, Ghenea : 569, 574, 590, 591
Serious Effect : **424**
Serling, Rod : 548
Serova, Vera : 589
Shake Your Body : 14, 37, 122, **124-125**, 142, 146, 176, 182, 183, 262, 570, 571, 584
Shalamar : 92, 204, 329
Shane, Reid : 390, 398, 403
Shapiro, Helene : 135
Sharp-Taylor, Deborah : 539
Shaw, Robert : 406, 484
Shawn, Dick : 287
She Drives Me Wild : 365, **386-387**, 392, 423
She Got It : **425**
She's a Rhythm Child : 188
She's Out of My Life : 70, 141, 145, 146, 161, **166-167**, 236, 266, 366, 518, 543, 570, 584, 586
She's Trouble : 232, 238, **241**
Sheinberg, Sid : 243
Shelton, Louie : 26, 28, 38, 40, 44
Sherman, Richard : 561
Sherman, Robert : 561
Sherwood, Michael : 426
Shifrin, Sue : 241
Shirley Smith, Justin : 272
Shoo-Be-Doo-Be-Doo-Da-Day : 49, 67, 69, **76**
Shout : 541, 545, **549**
Show You the Way to Go : 109, **112-113**, 126
Sides, Allen : 586, 593
Siegfried & Roy : 161, 370, 430, 431
Siegfried & Roy – Dreams & Illusions : 430, 431
Signature Series : 393
Silas Records : 432
Silas, Alfie : 322, 539
Silas, Louis : 361
Silk Electric : 33, 249
Silvers, Eddie : 16, 17
Simmons, Daryl : 428
Simmons, Dexter : 533, 535, 574
Simon, Paul : 280, 438
Simpson, Bart : 362, 363
Simpsons, The : 362
Sinatra, Frank : 135, 145, 161, 166, 245
Singleton, John : 371, 390
Singleton, Raymona : 23
Skoff, Ivy : 266, 270, 541
Skylark : 170
Skywriter : 80, 90, 553
Slash : 370, 371, 396, 397, 404, 405, 456, 457, 468, 471, 502, 503, 542, 549
Slave to the Rhythm : **428**, 594
Slon, Claudio : 122
Sly and The Family Stone : 35, 36, 452, 481
Smalls, Charlie : 128-132, 144
Smile : 139, 437, 477, **486-487**, 510
Smith, Chris : 252, 253
Smith, Greg : 220, 226
Smith, Jimmy : 300, 301
Smith, John Jay : 363
Smith, LaVelle : 308, 309, 418, 442, 454, 507
Smith, Nate : 534
Smith, Robert : 530
Smith, Will : 136, 157, 526, 537
Smith, Xavier : 510
Smooth Criminal : 224, 291, 298, 309, 334, **336-340**, 349, 350, 355, 366, 374, 386, 416, 418, 498, 506, 536, 566, 570, 584, 598
Sneddon, Tom : 471, 568
Sneed, Bernie : 20
Sneed, Floyd : 20
Snipes, Wesley : 302, 303
Snyder, Andrew : 546
So Shy : **247**
Some Girls Want Me for Their Lover : 18
Somebody's Watching Me : **257**
Someone in the Dark : 155, 244, **245**, 366, 570
Someone Put Your Hand Out : 234, **420**, 570
Somers, Suzanne : 316
Song Groove (aka Abortion Papers) : **353**
Sonnenfeld, Barry : 506
Sonny and Cher Comedy Hour, The : 71
Sonny and Cher Show, The : 111
Sorenson, Cindy : 287
Soul Source Jackson 5 Remixes 2 : 98
Soul Train : 91, 92, 108, 186, 204, 224, 303
Soul Unlimited : 92
Soulsation! : 46, 564
Spector, Phil : 139
Speechless : 521, **539**
Speed Demon : 292, 298, **310-313**, 316, 336, 349, 386, 397
Spielberg, Steven : 136, 202, 215, 242-245, 252, 284, 296, 302, 316, 426, 456
Spindler, Tracy : 476
Spinna : 98
Sprecher, Eve : 489
Springfield, Dusty : 61, 65, 100
Springsteen, Bruce : 280, 282, 366, 438, 481
Spruill, Stephanie : 184
St. James, Phyllis : 178
St. Lewis, Keni : 555, 556
Stallone, Sylvester : 312
Stanton, Harry Dean : 254
Staples, Mavis : 301
Stargate : 563, 595
Stark, Eric : 433
Starlight : 214, 288
Starr, Edwin : 329, 564
Starr, Maurice : 361
Starr, Ringo : 250, 524
State of Independence : 50, 160, 195, **248**
State of Shock : 259, 262, **268-269**, 272, 273, 366, 396, 471, 555, 570
Statik : 502
Stea, Kevin : 500
Stein, Jeff : 264
Stent, Mark *Spike* : 254
Stessel, Larry : 303, 324, 332, 369
Stevens, Bart : 362, 422
Stevens, Steve : 330-332
Stewart, Brandi : 476
Stewart, Jeff : 110-116
Stewart, Rod : 172
Stewart, Terry : 266
Stilwell, Brian : 178
Stites, Richard Carlton : 543
Stockman, Shawn : 579
Stokes, Arthur : 76
Stoller, Mike : 447
Story, Allen : 64
Straite, Elliot (Dr. Freeze) : 533, 598
Strange, Andy : 508
Stranger in Moscow : 437, 458, **460-463**, 466, 493, 544, 570
Streetwalker : 320, **350**, 351, 416, 417, 470
Streisand, Barbra : 32, 138, 188, 245, 252, 279, 326, 366
Stringer, Howard : 567
Strong, Barret : 247, 300
Style of Life : 13, 110, 113, **116**
Stylistics : 69, 72
Sudano, Bruce : 274
Sugar Daddy : 40, 90, 559
Summer, Donna : 50, 138, 155, 160, 193, 195, 248, 304, 414
Sundberg, Brad : 315, 326, 327, 404, 420, 422, 477, 572
Sunset Driver : **241**, 499, 528, 570, 571
Superfly Sister : 493, 494, **504**
Supremes, The : 20-26, 30-32, 52, 56, 65, 147, 160, 168, 169, 278, 330
Surrat, Paul : 414, 415
Sutton, Michael : 101
Sweat, Keith : 370, 374
Swedien, Bruce : 130-134, **138-139**, 144, 148-158, 162-173, 200-203, 208-241, 245, 267-269, 278, 296, 300-327, 330, 331, 336-341, 348, 349, 352, 370, 376-392, 406-411, 414-420, 426-429, 438, 442, 450-464, 467, 471-490, 499, 530-532, 534-540, 543, 546-549, 569, 574, 599
Sweeney, Tom : 574, 598
Swope, David : 597
SWV : 232
Sylvers III, Leon F. : 593
Szell, George : 406

Tabloid Junkie : 438, 449, **480**
Takahashi, Yukihiro : 593
Take Me Back : 95, 96, 98, **99**, 100
Tally, Thomas : 539
Tamla : 23, 24, 108, 194
Tañón, Olga : 579
Tarsia, Joe : 108-120
Tattersol, Brett : 546
Taylor, Bobby : 11, **20-21**, 24, 29, 34-36, 43, 69, 73, 74, 554
Taylor, Elizabeth : 33, 342, 390, 412, 446, 514, 515, 522
Taylor, Jeff : 510
Taylor, Roger : 272

Taylor, Ron : 539
Taylor, Skip : 130
Tee, Richard : 130, 131
Tell Me I'm Not Dreamin' (Too Good to Be True) : **274-275**, 345
Tempamental : 598
Temperton, Rod : 144, 145, 152, 153, **155**, 162, 163, 165, 172, 173, 191, 195, 210, 214-216, 229, 233, 236-240, 244, 245, 248, 288, 597
Temptations, The : 24, 36, 52, 69, 74, 90, 247
Terrana, Russ : 32, **52-53**, 61, 64, 65, 70-73, 76, 77, 82-87, 99-105, 554-557, 560, 561
Terry, Clark : 315
Thalia : 579
That's What Love Is Made Of : 558, **561**
That's What You Get (For Being Polite) : 14, 124, 126, 188
That's Why (I Love You So) : 22
The Boss : 32
The Chase : 305
The Dude : 160, 171, **195**, 236, 245, 264
The Essential Michael : 581
The Gallery : 516, 518, 573
The Girl Is Mine : 50, 65, 133, 160, 199, 202, 203, **212-213**, 232, 247, 250, 252, 254, 268, 318, 328, 355, 366, 396, 529, 570, 580, 582
The Hurt : 259, 266, **270**, 345, 470
The Immortal : 474, 595
The Jackson 5 Motown Medley : 556
The Jackson Family Honors : 446
The Jacksons : 109-118, 126, 553, 563
The Jacksons: an American Dream : 36, 42, 490, 563
The Lady in My Life : 155, 160, 199, 202, 203, 232, 234, **236-237**, 238, 580
The Legend continues : 82, 298
The Lost Children : 161, 521, 526, **546**
The Love You Save : 12, 24, 38, **40**, 44, 274, 556
The Man : 250, **256**
The Music from the New World : 432
The Music Thing : 105
The One : 568, 569
***The Original Soul of Michael Jackson* [album]** : **562-565**
The Triumph (aka *Can You Feel It*) : 37, 146, 176, 180, 181
The Ultimate Rarities Collection 1: Motown Sings Motown Treasures : 554
The Way You Love Me : **574**, 591
The Way You Make Me Feel : 224, 298, 305, **306-309**, 334, 341, 366, 445
The Wiz : 32, 111, 123, **128-133**, 135, 137, 138, 142, 144, 158, 166, 171, 217, 284, 506
There Must Be More to Life Than This : 268, **272-273**
They Don't Care about Us : 244, 387, **456-459**, 473, 488
Thicke, Robin : 573
Things I Do for You : 37, 124, 156, 182, 184, 214
(Think About The) Good Times : 109
Third Album : 44
This Had to Be : 160, **191**
***This Is It* [album]** : 167, **584-587**
This Is It (aka I Never Heard) : **586**
This Is It : 220, 418, 431, 467, 548, 551, 585, 586
This Is Our Time : 526
This Place Hotel (aka Heartbreak Hotel) : **184-185**
This Time Around : **464-465**, 510, 530
Thomas, Jimmie (Leon René) : 64
Thomas, Marlo : 93
Thomas, Nick : 573
Thompson, Marshall : 20
Thompson, Michael : 464, 467, 542
Threatened : **548**
Three Degrees, The : 108
Thriller **:** 133, 155, 202, 203, 206, **214-219**, 230, 232, 235, **238-241**, 257, 269, 288, 334, 366, 387, 399, 418, 430, 434, 454, 473, 481, 506, 507, 508, 548
***Thriller* [album]** : 33, 37, 71, 125, 135, 137, 138, 155, 160, 184, 190, 195, **198-241**, 242-244, 247, 248, 250, 252, 254, 256, 260-263, 266-268, 275, 286, 292, 294-298, 301, 304, 320, 326, 328, 331, 334, 344, 348, 352, 354, 369, 371, 373, 396, 414, 426, 528, 530, 553, 571, 581-583, 593, 596
***Thriller 25* [album]** : 426, **580-583**, 590
Thriller 25, Limited Japanese Single Collection : 133
Thriller Ringle CD Single : 133
Thumbtzen, Tatiana : 307-309
Tillman Waters, Julia : 184
Tillman, Audra : 171
Timbaland : 529, 531, 595, 596, 599
Timberlake, Justin : 443, 525, 579, 595, 596
Time Waits for No One : 176, 267
Tindall, T.J. : 110
To Be Loved : 22
To Make My Father Proud : 552, **557**
To Satisfy You : **432**
Tobacco Road : 16
Tokio : 516, 518
Tom Tom 84 : 124-126, 178, 182-186
Tompkins, Dennis : 346
Too Young : 80, **84**
Tornado :130
Torture : 259, 262, **264-265**, 276, 345, 470, 531
Toto : 171, 210, 213, 221, 232, 233, 266, 270, 392, 415, 467
Touch the One You Love : 552, **555**
Townes, Jeff : 136
Townshend, Pete : 222
Track Masters : 528, 537, 538
Travolta, John : 316
Trenten Gumbs : 433
Tresvant, Ralph : 361
***Triumph* [album] :** 145, 146, **174-189**, 214, 270, 320
Trouble : 241, 582
TSOP (The Sound of Philadelphia) : 108, 118, 120
Tucker, Chris : 535-537
Tuinfort, Giorgio : 583, 590, 596
Turner, John : 486
Turner, Tina : 17, 60, 241, 269, 280, 312, 318, 444
Twain, Shania : 65
Twenty-Five Miles : 562, 563, **564**
Twillie, Carmen : 178

Ufland, Harry : 302
Ulenberg, Patrick : 508
Unbreakable : 521, 526, **530**, 532, 536, 570
Underwood, Blair : 316
Underwood, Ian : 280
Ungar, Jonathon : 476
United We Stand : 545, 579
Unlimited Touch : 156
Uno Clio : 465
Up Again : 79, **83**, 85
Up on the House Top : 554, 564
Upchurch, Phil : 156
USA for Africa : 33, 50, 195, 280-283, 442
Usher : 527, 579

Vail Blum, Michael : 490, 491
Van De Pitte, David : 34
Van Dyke, Earl : 34, 36
Van Halen, Eddie : 202, 220, 222, 330, 331, 404
Van Nest, John : 464, 465
Van Passel, Danny : 474
Van Passel, Eddy : 474
Vandross, Luther : 524, 543, 579
Vangelis : 248
Vann, Ronald : 178
Vasquez, Mario : 547
Verdi, Beatrice : 61, 76
Vertelney, Reed : 543
Vicari, Tommy : 541
***Victory* [album]** : **258-271**, 272- 274, 277, 288, 314, 329, 345, 358, 369, 553
Vinton, Will : 311, 312
Volker, Armand : 508

Wade, Peter : 178
Wagner, Suellen : 394
Wainwright, Rupert : 441
Wait : 259, **266**
Wakefield, Kathy : 264, 596
Walczak, Diana : 440
Waldman, Randy : 330
Walk Right Now : 175, 176, **186-187**
Walker, David T. : 26, 38, 40, 44
Walker, Johnnie : 539
Waller, Don : 553
Walton, Nathan *N8* : 541
Wanna Be Startin' Somethin' : 160, 199, 202, 205, **208-209**, 210, 212, 214, 215, 232, 238, 247, 260, 288, 366, 402, 464, 530, 570, 582, 584, 586
Wanna Be Startin' Somethin' 2008 : 580, **583**, 590, 596
Wansel, Dexter : 109, 114-120
Ware, Leon : 60, 85, 561
Wargo, Jack : 264
Warner, Malcolm-Jamal : 316
Warren, Diane : 516
Warren, Mervyn : 586
Warwick, Dionne : 50, 248, 280, 414, 415
Washburn, Lalomie : 195
Washington, Dinah : 73, 138
Washington, Keith : 16
Washington, Ludie : 16, 18
Waters Willard, Maxine : 184, 208, 247
Waters, Julia : 184, 208, 247
Waters, Oren : 208, 247
Waters, The : 247
Watson, Bobby : 152, 153, 277
Watson, Wah Wah : 158, 159, 164, 170
Watts, Ernie : 252, 254
Watts, Nathan : 14, 122, 126, 178, 182-186, 253, 457
Way, Dave : 504, 508
Wayne, Artie : 88, 89, 555
We Are Here to Change the World : 286, 288, 289, 320, 570, 571
We Are the World : 33, 50, 160, 161, 190, 194-196, 221, 248, **280-283**, 294, 329, 392, 442, 516, 544, 559, 570, 579, 597
We Be Ballin' : **519**
We Can Change the World : 259
We Have Love : 22
We're Almost There : 95, 96, **98**, 99
We're Gonna Change Our Style : 188
We've Got a Good Thing Going : 60, 67, **72**, 98
We've Got Forever : 95, **101**
We've Had Enough : 197, 570, 571, **574**
Weather Girl : 276
Weathers, Carl : 316
Weatherspoon, Floyd : 76
Weaver, Jason : 36
Weiner, Herb : 135
Weisner, Ron : 260
Weiss, Laurence : 557
Weldon, Gregory : 562
Wells, Mary : 24
Wendt, George : 398, 399
West, Bob : 44
West, John : 562
West, Kanye : 580, 582, 583
Wharton, Alex : 254
What Goes Around Comes Around : 67, **76**, 161
What More Can I Give : 526, 545, 568, 576, **579**
Whatever Happens : 521, **547**
Whatzupwitu : **433-434**, 475
Whelan, Michael : 262
When I Come of Age : 558, **560**
When We Grow Up : **93**
When You Wish Upon a Star : 147
Where Are You Now : 168
White, Maurice : 125, 516
White, Ronald : 48, 74, 554
White, Ryan : 413- 415
Whitehead, John : 109, 114, 115, 116
Whitfield, Norman : 24, 90, 247
Whitten, Bill : 154
Who Is It : 160, 354, 365, 366, 370, 377, 383, **402-403**, 468, 470, 508, 570, 591
Who, The : 222
Who's Lookin' for a Lover : 558, **561**
Who's Lovin' You : 24, 26, **34-36**, 44-46, 56, 74, 237, 554
Who's Right, Who's Wrong : **190**
Why : **490**, 512, 542
Why You Wanna Trip on Me : 365, **380-381**, 429, 542
Wiese, Ryan : 590
Wild, Chuck : 456, 457, 471, 472
Wildstein, Bruce : 572
Will You Be There : 334, 365, **406-409**
Will.i.am : 234, 580, 581, 583
Willard : 68, 69
Willensky, Elliot : 62
Williams, Billy Dee : 316
Williams, David : 148-152, 156, 162, 172, 173, 178-188, 208-210, 214, 252, 253, 268, 269, 276, 300, 306, 310, 320, 330, 331, 336, 351, 410, 429, 596
Williams, Geoffrey : 547
Williams, John : 245
Williams, Larry : 148, 152, 156, 158, 162, 164, 168, 170, 172, 208, 210, 214, 300, 306-320, 336, 341
Williams, Pharrell : 51, 374, 375, 525
Williams, Rick : 547
Williams, Robb : 597
Williams, Walter : 194
Williams, Yvonne : 539
Williams, Zandra : 539
Williams, Zedric : 148, 158
Wilson, Crystal : 276
Wilson, Don : 324, 325
Wilson, Jackie : 22, 31, 56, 85, 560
Wilson, Mary : 20, 30, 169
Wilson, Shanice : 410, 432, 593
Winans, Carvin : 322
Winans, Marvin : 322
Winans, Michael : 322
Winans, Ronald : 322
Winding, Jai : 402, 410
Window Shopping : 188
Winfrey, Oprah : 372, 403, 426, 428, 476
Wings of My Love : 55, 60, 64
Winston, Stan : 217, 506, 507
Wishna, Jack : 582
With a Child's Heart : 79, 80, **82**, 83, 87, 100
Withers, Bill : 56, 58, 65, 158, 160, 329
Wittenberg, John : 539
Wolfe, Colin : 464
Wolfer, Bill : 178, 179, 208, 220, 221, 226, 228, 247, 249, 252, 253, 320, 348
Wolinski, David *Hawk* : 152
Womack, Bobby : 160
Wonder, Stevie : 10, 11, 14, 24, 28, 31, 36, **48-51**, 52, 69, 74, 76, 82, 92, 110, 115, 144, 145, 158, 168, 169, 176, 182, 190, 192, 194, 195, 202, 203, 221, 247, 248, 274, 280-282, 318, 352, 354, 356, 373, 406, 438, 581, 597
Wondering Who : 175-178
Woodward, Mack : 590
Work That Body : **423**
Working Day and Night : 141, 145, 152, **156-157**, 162, 234, 262, 430, 596
Workman, Jimmy : 506
Worthington, Cathy : 280
Wreckx-N-Effect : 374, 386, 398, 426, 532
Wright, Arthur : 44, 90, 91, 104, 562
Wright, Benjamin : 148, 149, 152, 158, 416
Wright, Betty : 194, 276, 574
Wright, Big Jim : 593
Wright, Gregory : 178
Wright, Syreeta : 195

Xscape : 529, **599**
***Xscape* [album]** : 350, 355, 428, 429, 533, 551, **594-599**

Yankovic, Weird Al : 316
Yarian, Christine : 61, 76, 83, 104, 105
Yeager, Denny : 348
Yeah : 51, 76, 118, 434
Yerke, Kenneth : 489
Yetnikoff, Walter : 13, 14, 144, 202-204, 206, 216, 243, 286, 296, 446
Yost, Brad : 510
You Are My Life : 197, 521, **541**, 549
You Are Not Alone : 437, 443, 445, **474-475**, 493, 566, 570, 591
You Are There : 95, **104**
You Can Cry on My Soulder : 67, 69, 70, **77**
You Can't Win : **132-133**, 144, 161, 422
You Don't Have to Be Over 21 (To Fall in Love) : 18
You Rock My World : 521, 526, 528, 529, **535-537**, 545, 566, 569, 570
You Were There : **360**, 412, 567
You're Supposed to Keep Your Love for Me : 168
You're the One : **278**, 544
You've Changed : 16, 18, 19, 36
You've Got a Friend : 55, 56, **65**, 105, 562, 563
You've Really Got a Hold on Me : 552, **554**
Young, Casey : 300, 341
Young, Freddie : 16, 18
Your Ways : 175, 176, 186, 268
Yukich, Jim : 316

Zadora, Pia : 275
Ziman, Ralph : 490
Zimmerman, Dick : 200, 203
Zuccarelli, Hugo : 326, 336

BIBLIOGRAPHY

1 Austen, Jake. *Chicago Reader*, 10 September 2009.

2 Jackson, Michael. *Moonwalk*. Translated by Michel Lafon, Paris, Doubleday, 1988 and 2009.

3 Mazzoleni, Florent and Gilles Pétard. *Motown Soul & Glamour*, Paris, Serpent à plumes, 2009.

4 Gordy, Berry. Interview on *Oprah's Masterclass*, 16 June 2013.

5 *The Complete Motown Singles, Vol. 9: 1969*. Motown / Universal Music, 2007.

6 Jisi, Chris. "Men in the Mirror, the Bassists of Michael Jackson," *www.bassplayer.com*, 1 February 2010.

7 Shelton, Louie. Interview by Alan Bryson, *www.allaboutjazz.com*, 27 January 2010.

8 Taraborrelli, J. Randy. *Michael Jackson: The Magic and the Madness*, New York, Birch Lane Press, 1991.

9 Jackson, Katherine. *The Jacksons, My Family*, New York, St. Martin's Press, p. 69, 1990.

10 Betts, Graham. *The Motown Encyclopedia*, New York, Smashwords Editions, 2014.

11 Jackson, Michael. Interview by Jesse Jackson, *www.keephopealiveradio.com*, 27 March 2005.

12 Worthy, Adam. "The Scoop on Weldon McDougal III," *www.j5collector.blogspot.fr*, 4 August 2010.

13 *Michael Jackson: The Life of an Icon*. Directed by David Guest, Universal Pictures, 2011.

14 *Soulsation!*, Motown, 1995.

15 Wonder, Stevie. "Remembering Michael," *Time Magazine*, 2009.

16 Jackson, Michael. Radio interview for Stevie Wonder's 33rd birthday, www.youtube.com/watch?v=6xWRXfQkBsc, 1983.

17 Terrana, Russ. Interview by Rob Bisel, *www.tapeop.com*, 2015.

18 Aletti, Vince. "Michael Jackson: Got to Be There," *Rolling Stone*, 7 December 1972.

19 Canby, Vincent. "Film: In *Ben*, a Boy Befriends a Rat," *The New York Times*, 24 June 1972.

20 Osmond, Donny. Interview by Pat Gallagher, *The Huffington Post*, 13 January 2015.

21 Gamble and Huff. Interview by The Quiet Storm, *WBLS Radio*, 2014 (official YouTube channel).

22 Jackson, John A. *A House on Fire: The Rise and Fall of Philadelphia Soul*, New York, Oxford University Press, 2004.

23 Cadman, Chris. *Michael Jackson, The Maestro*, UK, independently published, 2014.

24 *Michael Jackson's Journey from Motown to Off the Wall*. Directed by Spike Lee, Sony Music Video, 2016.

25 *Vibrations*, No. 130, December 2010 to January 2011.

26 Jones, Quincy. Interview by Gail Mitchell, *Billboard*, 14 March 2013.

27 *The One*. Directed by Jim Gable, Sony Music Video, 2004.

28 "Reaction to Michael Jackson's Death," *The Irish Times*, 26 June 2009.

29 *The Legend Continues*. Directed by Patrick T. Kelly, Polygram Music Video, 1988.

30 Radio Show Unistar, 1980.

31 Wright, Benjamin, Jr. Interview by Jeff "Chairman" MAO. *The Red Bull Music Academy*, 15 July 2014.

32 Jackson, Michael. *Off the Wall—Special Edition*, Rod Temperton voice-over, Sony Music, 2001.

33 "Michael Jackson's 20 Greatest Videos: The Stories Behind the Vision," *Rolling Stone*, 24 June 2014.

34 *The Invisible Man: The Rod Temperton Story*. Directed by Paul Gambaccini, BBC Radio 2, 23 August 2008.

35 Johnson, Louis. Interview by Adam Curry, MTV, 1989.

36 Johnson, Louis. Interview by Funk-U, *Funku*, 22 May 2015.

37 Bradman, E.E. "The Hard-Hitting Legacy of Louis 'Thunder Thumbs' Johnson," *www.bassplayer.com*, 15 September 2015.

38 Bahler, Tom. Interview by François Allard and Richard Lecocq. *Invincible Magazine*, No. 6, October 2015.

39 Greene, Susaye. Interview by Richard Lecocq. *Invincible Magazine*, No. 5, July 2015.

40 www.DavidFoster.com.

41 Austin, Patti. Interview by Joy Behar, *The Joy Behar Show*, 26 October 2011.

42 Wolfer, Bill. Interview by François Allard, *Invincible Magazine*, No. 3, January 2015.

43 Jackson, Paul, Jr. Interview, *www.woodshedjazz.com*, unknown date.

44 Luongo, John. "The Jacksons—Walk Right Now," *www.johnluongomusic.com*, 13 September 2016.

45 Drayton, Clay. Interview by MooiMuziek, *http://mooimuziek.blogspot.fr*, 13 May 2009.

46 Giles, Jeff. "35 Years Ago: Kenny Loggins Keeps the Fire Burning Bright," *www.ultimateclassicrock.com*, 29 October 2014.

47 "Richard Rudolph Tells Why Love Lives Forever," *Right On!*, September 1980.

48 Jackson, La Toya. Interview by Chris Yandek, *www.cyinterview.com*, 26 March 2011.

49 Jackson, Michael. Interview by Bryan Monroe, *Ebony*, December 2007.

50 Bayer Sager, Carole. *They're Playing Our Song: A Memoir*, New York, Simon & Schuster, 2016.

51 Lecocq, Richard. "World Music Awards 2006," *www.MJdatabank.com*, 2006.

52 "Michael Jackson Remembered: The Tributes," *Rolling Stone*, 25 June 2014.

53 "Michael Jackson Didn't Steal Song, Court Rules", *Jet Magazine*, Vol. 67, No. 17, 31 December 1984 to 7 January 1985.

54 Paich, David. Interview by Greg Prato, *ww.songfacts.com*, 18 March 2015.

55 Jackson, Michael. *Thriller 25th Anniversary: The Book, Celebrating the Biggest Selling Album of All Time*, London, ML Publishing, 2008.

56 Dineen, Catherine. *Michael Jackson in His Own Words*, London, Omnibus Press, 1992.

57 Forger, Matt. Interview by Richard Lecocq, *www.MJdatabank.com*, 2007.

58 Quan, Denise. "Eddie Van Halen Deconstructs His Collaboration on *Beat It*," CNN, 30 November 2012.

59 Michael Jackson. Interview, *MTV*, November 1999.

60 Paterson, Vincent. Interview by Richard Lecocq, Pierre-Bénite, November 2016.

61 Jackson, Michael. *Thriller—Special Edition*, Quincy Jones voice-over, Sony Music, 2001.

62 Swedien, Bruce. "Recording and Mixing *Billie Jean*," *www.gearslutz.com*, 7 September 2006.

63 Boddicker, Michael. "The Vintage Keys of *Thriller*," *www.keyboardmag.com*, 2009.

64 Ingram, James. Interview by Tavis Smiley, *Tavis Smiley*, PBS, 8 April 2009.

65 Jones, Quincy. *The Autobiography of Quincy Jones*, New York, Doubleday, p. 234, 2001.

66 Chancler, Ndugu. Interview by Richard Lecocq, *Invincible Magazine*, No. 10, October 2016.

67 Carrasco, Joe King. Interview by François Allard, *Invincible Magazine*, No. 5, July 2015.

68 Jackson, Michael. Interview by Bob Colacello, *Interview Magazine*, October 1982.

69 Interview with Paul McCartney by James Dean Bradfield, YouTube (Paul McCartney's official channel), 14 October 2015.

70 McCartney, Paul. Interview on the "Late Show with David Letterman," CBS, 15 July 2009.

71 Nightingale, Annie. *Pipes of Peace—Deluxe Edition*, Concord Music Group, 2015.

72 Newman, Jason. "How *Somebody's Watching Me* Singer Rockwell Created a Paranoid Pop Classic," *Rolling Stone*, 7 December 2016.

73 Freestone, Peter. "When Michael Jackson Met Freddie Mercury," *www.FanPop.com*, 2017.

74 Freestone, Peter. *www.montreuxmusic.com*, 2011.

75 Jackson, Jermaine. Intervie, "Friday Night Videos," NBC, 1984.

76 Allard, François. "Jermaine Jackson: Tell Me I'm Not Dreamin'," *Invincible Magazine*, No. 2, October 2014.

77 Wise, Scott. "Why Prince Was Not Part of *We Are the World*," *www.wtvr.com*, 22 April 2016.

78 Garratt, Rob. "Quincy Jones Explains How Prince Walked Away from a Duet with Michael Jackson," *The National*, 4 January 2017.

79 Giles, Jeff. "The Prince and Michael Jackson Collaboration That Never Happened: 365 Prince Songs in a Year," *www.Diffuser.fm*, 11 August 2017.

80 Price, Richard. "*Lush Life*, Martin Scorsese, and Michael Jackson," *Vulture*, 4 March 2008.

81 Currell, Christopher. "The Event Horizon: Synclavier, Music, and Michael Jackson," *www.headphone.guru*, 2015.

82 *Moonwalker—Limited Edition 10th Anniversary Commemorative Program*, Paris, Captain EO Productions, 1998.

83 Jackson, Michael. Interview by Darryl Dennard, *Ebony / Jet*, 26 September 1987.

84 Mbulu, Letta. Interview by Clyde Macfarlane, *www.TheQuietus.com*, 2 July 2015.

85 Swedien, Bruce. *In the Studio with Michael Jackson*, New York, Hal Leonard Corp., July 2009.

86 *Bad 25*. Directed by Spike Lee, Sony Music Video, 2012.

87 Jones, Quincy. Interview with *Rolling Stone*, 30 August 2017.

88 Jackson, Michael. *Bad—Special Edition*, Quincy Jones voiceover, Sony Music, 2001.

89 Siedah, Garret. Interview by Luka Neskovic, *HuffPost Canada*, 20 September 2013.

90 Siedah, Garret. Interview by Richard Lecocq, *Invincible Magazine*, No. 2, September 2014.

91 Forger, Matt. Interview by Lily Rothman, *Time*, 29 August 2012.

92 Wilson, Don. "The American Popular Culture Magazine—Man in the Mirror: On Michael Jackson," *Americana*, June 2009.

93 Lamarre, Carl, et al. "The Stories of the Album's Five No. 1 Singles," *Billboard*, 31 August 2017.

94 Stevens, Steve. Interview by Daniel Langlois, *www.MJJLegacy.com*, 2012.

95 Eugene, Michelle. *Michael Jackson, the Golden Book of Condolence*, RoseDogs Books, Pittsburgh, 2011.

96 "Matt Forger Speaks: The Secrets of *Bad 25*," *www.michaeljackson.com*, 2012.

97 *Xscape*, Epic / Sony Music, 2014.

98 "Teddy Riley on the Recording of *Dangerous*," *www.michaeljackson.com*, 25 January 2017.

99 Bruce, Swedien. Interview, *www.inthestudiowithbruceswedien.com*, 2013.

100 Riley, Teddy. Interview with *Keyboard Magazine*, May 1992.

101 Riley, Teddy. Interview by Future Music, *www.musicradar.com*, 3 July 2009.

102 Zwerling, Jared. "Oral History: MJ Meets MJ for *Jam* Video," ESPN, 14 March 2013.

103 Jackson, Michael. *Dangerous, the Short Films* (video compilation), Sony Music Video, 1993.

104 Riley, Teddy. Interview by Billy Bush, *www.accessonline.com*, 12 November 2009.

105 "Michael Jackson Remembered: John Singleton on Challenging His Hero," *Rolling Stone*, 9 July 2009.

106 Robinson, Fatima. Interview by Mathieu Schreyer, *www.kcrw.com*, 19 May 2010.

107 Lamrock, Bonnie. "Slash Speaks on Michael Jackson and More," *The Independent*, 29 September 2014.

108 Lee Curtis Taete, Jamie. "Meet the Mystery Man Who Rapped on Michael Jackson's *Black or White*," *Vice*, 5 May 2015.

109 Landis, John. Interview, *www.GoldenAgeofMusicVideo.com*, 1 December 2011.

110 Buskin, Richard. "Classic Tracks: Michael Jackson *Black or White*," *www.SoundonSound.com*, August 2004.

111 Jackson, Michael. Interview by Robert E. Johnson, *Ebony / Jet*, Vol. 47, No. 7, May 1992.

112 Kohan, Buz. Interview by Richard Lecocq, 2010.

113 *1994 Court Trial (Dangerous Case Deposition)*, audio track, 1994.

114 "Post Here if You Worked on Michael Jackson's *Dangerous* Album," *www.gearslutz.com*, June 2009.

115 Morinen, "Meeting Steve Porcaro and Hearing *Chicago 1945*," *www.MichaelJackson.ru*, 4 July 2014.

116 Sherwood, Michael. Interview by Preston Frazier, *www.SomethingElseReviews.com*, 9 April 2015.

117 Shields, Damien. *Xscape Origins*, Canton, Modegy Publishing, 2015.

118 Murphy, Eddie. Interview on *MTV News*, 1993.

119 Mokoena, Tshepo. "30 Minutes with...Eddie Murphy," *The Guardian*, 29 February 2015.

120 Jam, Jimmy. Interview by Michael Smallcombe, *www.makingmichael.co.uk*, 16 June 2016.

121 Appleford, Steve. "Jimmy Jam and Terry Lewis: Our Life in 15 Songs," *Rolling Stone*, 9 October 2015.

122 Romanek, Mark. "Michael Jackson Remembered: Mark Romanek on Experiencing *Scream*," *Rolling Stone*, 9 July 2009.

123 "Michael Jackson Changes *HIStory*," *VH1*, 10 November 1996.

124 Brandt, Nick and Brad Buxer. Interviews with *Black & White Magazine*, November 2009.

125 Hoffman, Rob. *www.gearslutz.com* (forum running from June 2009 to October 2011).

126 "Michael Jackson Talks to Oprah Winfrey," ABC, 10 February 1993.

127 Swedien, Bruce. Interview by Nick Batzdorf, *Recording Magazine*, www.ascstudio-acoustics.com, October 2015.

128 Sweeney, Daniel. "An Incredible New Sound for Engineers—Bruce Swedien Comments on the Recording Techniques and Production *HIStory* of Michael Jackson's Latest Album," *www.asc-studio-acoustics.com*, November 1997.

129 Hoffman, Rob. *www.gearslutz.com* (forum running from June 2009 to October 2011).

130 Dovido, Quagmire and Tristan. "Much Too Soon: Investigation into the Development of a Michael Jackson Posthumous Title," *www.mjfranceforum.com*, 2011.

131 Grant, Adrian. *Making HIStory*, London, Omnibus Press, 1997.

132 Riley, Teddy. Interview by Joseph Vogel, *The Atlantic*, 21 March 2012.

133 Interview with Teddy Riley, MTV, 5 July 1997.

134 Lecocq, Richard. *Michael Jackson—King*, Paris, Publibook, 2011.

135 Grant, Adrian. *The Visual Documentary*, London, Omnibus Press, 2009.

136 Dr. Freeze. Interview by Quagmire, *www.mjfranceforum.com*, January 2011.

137 Teddy, Riley. Interview, *www.HipHopWired.com*, 8 July 2009.

138 Porter, Darwin. *Brando Unzipped*, New York, Blood Moon Productions, p. 614, 2006.

139 Jackson, Michael. Interview by Anthony De Curtis, Yahoo Chat, www.GetMusic.com, 26 October 2001.

140 Jackson, Michael. Interview by Regina Jones, *Vibe*, March 2002.

141 Swedien, Bruce. Interview with *Monster Cable Company*, October 2001.

142 Riley, Teddy. Interview with *Vibe*, 14 March 2012.

143 Heldman, Breanne L. "A Lost Michael Jackson Tune...and His Final Concert?," *www.EOnline.com*, 29 June 2009.

144 St. Lewis, Keni. Interview by Christina Chaffin, *www.michaeljacksonreel.weebly.com*, 2016.

145 Akon. Interview, *www.chartsinfrance.net*, 7 November 2008.

146 Mitchell, Gail. "Michael Jackson's *Michael* Track-by-Track," *Billboard*, December 2010.

147 Mosdell, Chris. Interview by François Allard, *Invincible Magazine*, No. 4, April 2015.

****

In addition to the sources listed in the bibliography, here are some references we relied on throughout our research. If any materials were left out, it was unintentional.

ADDITIONAL SOURCES

Barron, Steve. *Egg n Chips & Billie Jean: A Trip Through the Eighties*, independently published, 2014.

Bush, Michael. *The King of Style, Dressing Michael Jackson*, New York, Pocket Books, 2012.

Cadman, Chris. *Michael Jackson—Off the Wall—For the Record*, London, independently published, 2016.

Gordy, Berry. *To Be Loved: The Music, the Magic, the Memories of Motown: An Autobiography*, New York, Warner Books, 1994.

Guesdon, Jean-Michel and Philippe Margotin. *The Beatles: In Total*, Paris, EPA Editions, 2013.

Knopper, Steve. *MJ: The Genius of Michael Jackson*, New York, Paperback, 2016.

Manœuvre, Philippe. *Michael Jackson*, Paris, Filipacchi, 1988.

Perrot, Christian. *Michael Jackson*, Paris, Albin Michel, 1984.

Pirenne, Christophe. *A Rock Music History*, Paris, Fayard, 2011.

Plassat, François. *Paul McCartney: The Footprint of a Giant*, Paris, JBZ & Co., 2010.

Taraborrelli, J. Randy. *Call Her Miss Ross*, New York, Ballantine Books, 1989.

Terry, Carol D. *Sequins and Shades: The Michael Jackson Reference Guide*, Ann Arbor, Popular Culture Ink, 1987.

Whitburn, Joel. *Billboard Book of Top 40 Hits*, New York, Watson Guptill, 2002.

WEB SOURCES

Artists

billbottrell.com, Brad Sundberg's Facebook page, carolebayer-sager.com, darkchild.com, davidfoster.com, donpeake.com, gamble-huffmusic.com, inthestudiowithbruceswedien.com, joeking.com, louieshelton.com, michaeljackson.com, pattiaustin.com, paulinho.com, steviewonder.org, thejacksons.com, thomasbahler.com

Labels

classic.motown.com
legacyrecordings.com
motownrecords.com

Organizations

disneyproject.com
freetobefoundation.com
stanwinstonschool.com
www.soultrain.com

Sites dedicated to Michael Jackson

damienshields.com, j5collector.blogspot.fr, jackson5abc.com, makingmichael.co.uk, michaeljackson.ru, mjackson.fr, mjda-tabank.com, mjfranceforum.com, mjjcommunity.com, mjlegend.com, mjofficialversions.blogspot.fr, mjstrangersite.com, mjstrout.fr, mj-upbeat.com, teammichaeljackson.com, onmjfootsteps.com

General sites

accesson-line.com, allmusic.com, discogs.com, funku.fr, gearslutz.com, musique.rfi.fr, nme.com, vibe.com, waxpoetics.com

Certificates and charts

bpi.co.uk officialcharts.com, riaa.com

Interviews

Bryan Loren's talk, Music First, 24 September 2016.

Interview with Sybil Azur, 28 April 2016.

Interviews with Matt Forger, 2007, 2010, and 2013.

Vincent Paterson's talk in Pierre-Bénite, 26 November 2016.

Booklets

Ritz, David. *Soulsation!*, Motown / Universal Music, 1995.

The Wiz Original Soundtrack, MCA Records, 1997.

Chin, Brian. *Diana Ross Presents The Jackson 5 and ABC* and other rereleases of the 2 in 1 CD, Motown / Universal Music, 2001.

Jackson, Michael. *Off the Wall—Special Edition*, Epic / Sony Music, 2001.

Weinger, Harry, et al. "*The Complete Motown Singles, Vol. 9: 1969*," Motown / Universal Music, 2007.

Michael Jackson: The Ultimate Collection, Epic / Sony Music, 2004.

Jackson, Michael. "Hello World: The Motown Solo Collection," Hip-O Select / Motown, 2009.

Bolton, Chris. *Gideon* and *Share Your Love*, Edsel Records, 2009.

Ralph Tee. *Philadelphia International Records—The 40th Box Anniversary*, Harmless, 2012.

Wikane, Christian John. *Donna Summer Re-Mastered and Expanded*, Driven by the Music, 2014.

PICTURE CREDITS

© AFP PHOTO : Kim Jae-Hwan 524 **© ALAMY STOCK PHOTO :** MediaPunch Inc 323 • Pictorial Press Ltd 279 • Ronald Grant Archive 408 • Trinity Mirror/Mirrorpix 125 • **© ARNO BANI :** 525 • **© BERNARD MOUILLON :** 309 • **© COLL. BILL BOTTRELL :** photo Evgenie Nesterov 471 • **© COLL. BILL WOLFER :** Rights reserved 247 • **© COLL. CHRISTOPHER CURRELL :** photo Sam Emerson 349 • **© COLLECTION CHRISTOPHEL :** 509, 511 • **© COLL JOHN BARNES :** Rights reserved 329 • **© COLL. MATT FORGER :** Rights reserved 304 • **© COLL. THOMAS BÄHLER :** photo Faith Hahn 161 • **© COLL. WELDON MCDOUGAL :** 43 • **© DICK ZIMMERMAN :** 201, 243 • **© DILIP MEHTA/CONTACT PRESS IMAGES :** 423, 425, 429 • **© DR :** 16, 17, 18, 42, 68, 74, 202, 235right • Maurício Almeida via Flickr 458 • **© FASTIMAGE :** Christian Rose 473 • Neil Zlozower 154, 167 • **© GETTY IMAGES :** ABC Photo Archives/ABC 97, 276, 360, 495 • Afro American Newspapers/Gado 12, 155, 160, 181, 233, 253, 265, 327 • Alain BENAINOUS/Gamma-Rapho 547 • Allan Olley/Mirrorpix 113top • Andy Freeberg 550 • Astrid Stawiarz/AFP 228 • Barbara Alper 375 • Barry King/Sygma/Sygma 278 • Becker & Bredel/Ullstein Bild 575 • Bertrand Rindoff Petroff 135 • Bettman 31, 50, 133, 204, 249 • BMI/Michael Ochs Archives 108 • Bob Chamberlin/Los Angeles Times 28 • Bob Riha Jr. 137 • Bobby Holland/Michael Ochs Archives 195 • Brad Elterman/FilmMagic 165 • Brian Rasic/Getty Images 194, 440 • CBS Photo Archive 35, 73, 140, 147, 548 • Chris Polk/FilmMagic 531 • Chris Walter/WireImage 59, 174, 211, 224, 225 • Clarence Davis/NY Daily News Archive 465d • Courtesy of Siegfried & Roy/The Mirage 431 • Daily Mirror/Mirrorpix 15, 215 • Dave Benett 442 • Dave Hogan 256, 472, 475, 497 • David Corio/Redferns 85, 113bottom• David McGough/DMI/The LIFE Picture Collection 258 • David Nordhal/Barcroft USA 546 • DMI/The LIFE Picture Collection 290 • Donaldson Collection/Michael Ochs Archives 86 • Douglas Kirkland/Corbis 363 • Ebet Roberts/Redferns 153, 180, 183, 189, 221 • Echoes/Redferns 76, 169 • Edwine Seymour 532 • Evan Agostini/ImageDirect 530 • Fin Costello/Redferns 101, 103 • Frank Edwards 145 • Frank Edwards/Fotos International 84 • Frank Micelotta/ImageDirect 533, 534 • Frank Trapper/Corbis 394 • Frazer Harrison/AFP 538 • GAB Archive/Redferns 170 • Gems/Redferns 54 • George Stroud/Express 344 • Gijsbert Hanekroot/Redferns 51, 121 • Gilles Petard/Redferns 11, 14, 22, 23 • Gregg Cobarr/WireImage 14 • Gregg DeGuire/WireImage 543 • Gus Stewart/Redferns 127 • Harry Langdon 577 • Hulton Archive 37, 197, 283bottom • Hulton-Deutsch/Hulton-Deutsch Collection/Corbis 273 • Images Press/IMAGES 33 • James Kriegsmann/Michael Ochs Archives 20, 21 • Janette Beckman 115, 191, 193 • Jason LaVeris/FilmMagic 529 • Jazz Archiv Hamburg/Ullstein Bild 123 • Jean-Pierre REY/Gamma-Rapho 383 • Jeff Kravitz/FilmMagic, Inc 443 • Jeffrey Mayer/WireImage 235left • Jim McCrary/Redferns 159 • Jim Shea/Michael Ochs Archives 270 • Jim Steinfeldt/Michael Ochs Archives 449 • Joe Traver/Liaison 372 • John D. Kisch/Separate Cinema Archive 111 • John Olson/The LIFE Picture Collection 9, 39 • John Springer Collection/CORBIS/Corbis 216 • Jonathan Exley/Contour by Getty Images 421, 451, 468, 537, 540 • Jonathan Leibson/FilmMagic 513 • Justin Sullivan/AFP 568 • Ken Hively/Los Angeles Times 207 • Kevin Mazur Archive 1/WireImage 527 • Kevin Mazur/AEG/WireImage 584, 587 • Kevin Mazur/Getty Images for Clear Channel 594 • Kevin Mazur/WireImage 239, 307, 523, 536, 545, 592 • Kevin Winter/AFP 566 • Keystone-France/Gamma-Rapho 484 • L. Cohen/WireImage 397 • Larry Busacca/Contour 447, 457 • Larry Busacca/WireImage 316, 477 • Lynn Goldsmith/Corbis/VCG 7, 149, 163, 179, 187, 222, 271 • M. Caulfield/WireImage 417, 520 • Mark Reinstein/Corbis 373 • Michael Marks/Michael Ochs Archives 223 • Michael Ochs Archives 13,19, 24, 25, 36, 45, 46, 47, 57, 65, 66, 69, 71, 78, 83, 87, 88, 89, 91, 92, 94, 105, 119, 131, 134, 144, 171, 196, 552, 556, 558, 562, 565 • Michael Putland 75, 109, 150, 155 • Michel Dufour/WireImage 588 • Nathaniel S. Butler/NBAE 378 • Nicholas Hunt/Patrick McMullan 583 • Olaf Selchow 549 • Paul Natkin 172, 380, 410 • Paul Warner/WireImage 359 • Paul Whitsitt/Contour 453 • Peter Power/Toronto Star 367 • Peter Still/Redferns 328, 483 • Phil Dent/Redferns 436, 445, 469, 499, 505, 580 • Popperfoto 391 • Princess Diana Archive 332 • Ray Tamarra 465left • Raymond Boyd 435 • Raymond Boyd/Michael Ochs Archives 361, 491 • RB/Redferns 27, 29, 41 • Richard Corkery/NY Daily News Archive 129, 578 • Richard E. Aaron 117 • Rick Diamond 157, 173, 185 • Robert Abbott Sengstacke 61 • Robert Gauthier/Los Angeles Times 136 • Ron Galella/WireImage 49, 198, 213, 251, 269, 360, 366, 390, 519 • Russell Einhorn/Liaison 515 • Sam Levi/WireImage 540 • Silver Screen Collection 93 • Stanley Bielecki Movie Collection 503 • Stephane Cardinale/Sygma 444 • Stephen Kim/WireImage 369 • Steven Paul Whitsitt/Contour 455, 466, 479, 487 • Taro Yamasaki/The LIFE Images Collection 415 • The Asahi Shimbun 517 • Thierry Orban/Sygma 492 • Tom Sheehan/Sony Music Archive 106-107 • Tony Barson/WireImage 583 • Victor Skrebneski/Michael Ochs Archives 32 • Wally McNamee/CORBIS/Corbis 263 • Walter Sanders/The LIFE Picture Collection 10 • Will & Deni Media Inc./Corbis 481 • Wilson Lindsay/Michael Ochs Archives 25 • **© GOTTFRIED HELNWEIN :** 485 • **© HARRISON FUNK :** 317 • **© JIM BRITT :** 53, 63, 77, 81, 99 • **© KRIS CUMMING :** 246 • **© MPTV :** 2009 Bobby Holland 139, 143 • 1980 Michael Jones 177 • **© RUE DES ARCHIVES :** Universal/courtesy Everett Collection 128, 244, 284, 298, 295 • Picture Alliance/ photo Fryderyk Gabowicz 439, 459 • **© SIPA PRESS :** AP Photo/Arne Dedert 405 • AP Photo/Chris Carlson 413 • Daily Mail/REX/Shutterstock 255 • Sipa Press 347 • Vaughan Stephen 218, 219 • **© STARFACE/POLARIS :** Sam Emerson 203, 205, 206, 209, 217, 226, 229, 230, 231, 237, 248, 257, 261, 262, 267, 275, 277, 281, 282, 283top, 285, 286, 287, 288, 289, 293, 294, 297, 299, 301, 302, 303, 305, 308, 311, 312, 313, 315, 319, 321, 325, 331, 333, 335, 337, 338, 339, 340, 342, 343, 345, 346, 350, 353, 355, 357, 364, 371, 376, 379, 381, 384, 385, 387, 389, 393, 395, 398, 399, 401, 403, 407, 409, 411, 418, 419, 427, 433, 434, 446, 461, 462, 463, 478, 514, 572 • Nancy Pastor 507 • **© STEPHEN HARVEY :** 151 • **© VINCENT PATERSON :** 501

ACKNOWLEDGEMENTS

We give our heartfelt thanks to the Michael Jackson authors, researchers, and investigators who provided extensive documentation for the writing of this book: onmjfootsteps.com, Chris Cadman, Damien Shields, mjofficialversions.blogspot.com, jackson5abc.com, Keith Hughes (dftmc.info), Laura Panunzio (mjjcollectors.com), Korg Nex, Jamie McCormick, Jeff Beasley, Lidwine Ducrocq (MJJ Top News), Daniel Langlois (MJJ Legacy), Keen Zhang (mjjcn.com), mjbeats.com.br, mjhideout.com, michaeljackson.ru, mjlegend.com, mjfrance.com, mjjcommunity.com.

Weldon McDougal Jr., Susaye Greene, Christine Snider–Decroix, Bill Wolfer, Jim Britt, Arno Bani, Gottfried and Cyril Helnwein, Mike Salisbury, Sam Emerson, Bernard Mouillon, Dick Zimmerman, Teddy Riley, Bryan Loren, Buz Kohan, Vincent Paterson, Matt Forger, John Barnes, Christopher Currell, Tom Bahler, Ndugu Chancler, Bruce Broughton, Nicholas Pike, Tammy Lucas, Siedah Garrett, Joe King Carrasco, Jonathan Moffett, Chris Mosdell, Jay Gruska, John Grower, Yuko Sumida, LaVelle Smith, Larry Stessel, Trent Jackson, Katherine Jackson, Tim Simon.

Our friends Julien Ombredane, Arnaud Da Costa, Marc Mercey, Sébastien Martin, Benjamin Wilputte, "Becane," Bruno Beltrano, Saykou Diallo, Rachel Houdas, and Jean DiLorio who made the MJStreet forum possible in 2004, as well as members of the MJStreet association and the team at *JAM*.

Thank you to EPA Editions: Jérôme Layrolles, Flavie Gaidon, Laurence Basset, Myriam Blanc, Béatrice Weité, and Charles Émeline: thank you for believing in us from the start. Thank you for sharing in this often crazy adventure and for understanding the parallel universe that is the music of Michael Jackson.

Thank you to Maxime Prieux for all her page layouts and ideas, which allowed us to illustrate and showcase our work and to pay tribute to the artist.

RICHARD LECOCQ:

I want to thank: my mother, Martine Arambol Lecocq; Julien for the precious advice he gave me when I started this project; Max Mazlo; Steve and Johan Larade; Aurélia Tadrist; Yannick and Annabelle Bono; Moonju Kim; Da-Eun Han; Alison Jeong; Camille Jamet; Christophe Langris; Romain Pizon; Jean-Baptiste Arreto; Johanna Alam; Nancy and Nelly Lessert; Stéphanie Bleuze; Cristiane Montenegro; Georges Célestin; Lionel Théraud; Franck and Chris Lucide; Eva Bénichou; Sly; Marguerite Lenoble; Magali Dubié; Jacques and Grégori Ferret. Thank you to my father, Richard Lecocq, Sr.

FRANÇOIS ALLARD:

I want to thank: Nelly Othelet and Michel Allard. The whole team from the Plume et Bulle, the bookstore café at 17, rue Irénée-Carré, 08000 Charleville-Mézières (plumeetbulle.fr); Willy Ippolito; Melvin Berek; Tsuyoshi Mizuno; Justin Carl; Mathéo and Jade Grébent; Nazim and Catherine Belgacem; Simon Pouyet; Aurore Dubus; Samuel Gondouin; Mickael Rocle; Sébastien Caron; Princesse Micha; Vincent Absou.